ROMAN RULE
IN ASIA MINOR

ROMAN RULE IN ASIA MINOR

TO THE END OF THE THIRD CENTURY AFTER CHRIST

BY DAVID MAGIE

VOLUME I: TEXT

PRINCETON, NEW JERSEY

PRINCETON UNIVERSITY PRESS

1950

PRINTED IN THE UNITED STATES OF AMERICA
BY PRINCETON UNIVERSITY PRESS AT PRINCETON, NEW JERSEY

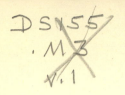

TO
THE MEMORY OF MY PARENTS
IN GRATITUDE

PREFACE

THIS book, planned in my youth, begun in middle life and finally completed in my old age, has been my constant companion for nearly a quarter of a century, alternately my hope and my despair. Its composition has been a long and arduous task, far longer and more difficult than was expected when the work was begun; for the literary sources are meagre and unreliable, and the inscriptions, which furnish more accurate information, still remain, pending the completion of the collection of the *Tituli Asiae Minoris*, inconveniently scattered through hundreds of volumes. At best, it has proved possible to piece together only a few fragments of a great mosaic.

The purpose of the book is to present what is known of the expansion of Rome's Empire in Asia Minor and the lands adjacent on the east and of her rule over the Asianic provinces in a study continued to the end of the third century after Christ. Mere surmises, based on insufficient evidence, and conclusions obvious to any reader have, in general, been avoided. Much of what is included is common knowledge; for in order to combine isolated statements into a connected narrative, it has been necessary to incorporate certain familiar facts of general history.

Such a work should, in strictness, begin with Rome's acquisition of the province of Asia in 133 B.C., or perhaps with the Romans' first appearance in the East when the Scipios expelled Antiochus the Great from his western dominions. In order, however, to show what the Romans found in Asia Minor when they crossed the Aegean, it has seemed necessary to include an account of the political and economic conditions which had their rise in the death of Alexander the Great and the consequent dissolution of his empire.

The early history of the six provinces ultimately comprised in Rome's Asianic dominions has been related in the order of their acquisition. The first five chapters are intended to serve as an introduction to the account of the formation of the province of Asia, the western portion of Anatolia. Other chapters, notably the eighth, the eleventh, the thirteenth, the nineteenth and the twenty-second, also contain introductory material presented in connexion with the acquisition of the provinces in question. In the earlier chapters, especially, to avoid overloading the text, much has been relegated to the notes, which, in consequence, have become unduly long. For the same reason, many details and all controversial questions have also been presented in the notes. These are intended for the use of professional scholars only.

Many readers will doubtless think that the book contains too much geography. It is, however, my firm conviction that a study of geography must go hand in hand with the presentation of history, for the latter without the former is often unintelligible. Strabo also, it will be remembered, in combining both, warned his readers that in dealing with famous places they must endure the difficulties of geography. Others, again, will miss an account of the cults of the deities or a presentation of the literary and artistic productivity of the Asianic provinces. But even without these interesting and profitable subjects the book has grown too large, and they must be left to other writers, since, with Vergil, *non omnia possumus omnes*.

No attempt has been made to include a systematic bibliography. A complete collection of the titles of the books and articles dealing with ancient Asia Minor would be a work in itself. The notes, however, mention those studies which have been consulted and found to be useful. They are cited for the twofold purpose of enabling a reader to pursue further any subject in which he may be interested and of recording my own obligation to their authors.

Like all students of Classical Antiquity, I am greatly indebted to the *Real-Encyclopädie* of Pauly-Wissowa-Kroll and, in particular, to the admirable geographical articles by Dr. Walter Ruge. I owe much also to the books and articles by Professor Louis Robert which deal with the history and the inscriptions of Asia Minor, as well as to Professor T. R. S. Broughton's valuable work on Roman Asia Minor in Frank's *Economic Survey of Ancient Rome*, which has proved an inexhaustible store of information. Much of my book was written before the appearance of Professor A. H. M. Jones's excellent works on *The Cities of the Eastern Roman Provinces* and *The Greek City*, of Professor Rostovtzeff's great *Social and Economic History of the Hellenistic World*, and of Professor Esther V. Hansen's careful study of *The Attalids of Pergamon*, but, fortunately, it was not too late to avail myself of the learning presented by these notable scholars, from whose conclusions I have, at times, felt constrained to differ, but always with reluctance. On the other hand, it has proved impossible to consult many of the books that have been published on the Continent of Europe during the late war; for much that appeared in those calamitous years has not yet found its way across the Atlantic.

The map at the end of Vol. II is reproduced from R. Kiepert *Formae Orbis Antiqui* VII. For the correct spelling of the modern Turkish place-names which occur in the notes I have relied partly on the census report (*Türkiye Nüfusu*) for 1935 and partly on the new official map (1:1,000,000) of Turkey, but chiefly on the expert knowledge of Professor W. L. Wright, Professor of the Turkish Language and History in Princeton University, for whose friendly assistance and expenditure of time I am particularly grateful.

I wish also to record my warm appreciation of the courtesy shown to me at the Archaeological Institute of Vienna, where, during a summer some twenty years ago, I was permitted to use the library and granted every possible facility for study. It is an especial pleasure to express my gratitude to the various friends who have given me aid and encouragement: to Dr. W. H. Buckler of Oxford, who kindly put at my disposal his card-catalogue of the inscriptions of Asia Minor; to Dr. L. C. West and Professor A. C. Johnson of Princeton, of whom the former courteously permitted me to use a similar catalogue of coins and both have answered many questions concerning numismatics and provincial administration; to my former colleagues, Dr. J. W. Basore, whose fine taste has saved me from many an infelicitous expression, and Professor W. K. Prentice, whose critical acumen has corrected many an obscure statement; and especially to my friends, the late Edward Elliott, Esq. and Dr. Samuel Shellabarger of Princeton, both of whom have read the entire manuscript of the text and have given me kindly criticism and frequent suggestions as to form and content that have been of inestimable value. For preparing my book for the press I am grateful to Mr. E. M. Ridolfi and especially to Mrs. Margaret Mott, who by intelligence in deciphering my handwriting and skill in typewriting my manuscript has done much to further the publication of the work. My warm thanks are due also to the authorities of the Princeton University Press and in particular to Professor Robert K. Root, one of its Trustees, and to Mr. Datus C. Smith, Jr., its Director, for the generous interest they have shown in this book. To all these, for their patience and assistance, I would fain offer a *charisterion*.

Princeton, 1 March, 1948.   D. M.

CONTENTS

xi

CONTENTS

A MAP OF ASIA MINOR WILL BE FOUND AT THE END OF VOL. II

LIST OF ABBREVIATIONS

A.E.M.=Archaeologisch-epigraphische Mittheilungn aus Oesterreich-Ungarn

A.J.A.=American Journal of Archaeology

A.J.P.=American Journal of Philology

A.M.=Mitteilungen des Deutschen Arch. Inst., Athenische Abteiling

Abh. Bayer. Akad.=Abhandlungen d. Bayerischen Akademie der Wissenschaften, philos.-philol. Klasse

Abh. Berl. Akad.=Abhandlungen d. Preussischen Akademie der Wissenschaften, philos.-hist. Klasse

Ainsworth *Travels*=W. F. Ainsworth *Travels and Researches in Asia Minor, Mesopotamia, etc.* (London 1842)

Alt. v. Hierap.=Humann, etc. Die Altertümer von Hierapolis=Arch. Jahrb., Erg.-heft IV (1898)

Alt. v. Perg.=Die Altertümer von Pergamon

Anat. Stud. Buckler=Anatolian Studies presented to W. H. Buckler (Manchester 1939)

Anat. Stud. Ramsay=Anatolian Studies presented to Sir W. M. Ramsay (Manchester 1923)

Ann. Arch. Anthr.=Univ. of Liverpool: Annals of Archaeology and Anthropology

Ann. d. Inst.=Annali dell' Instituto di Corrispondenza Archeologica

Ann. Ép.=L'Année Épigraphique

Ann. Scuol. Atene=Annuario della R. Scuola Archeologica di Atene

Anz. Wien. Akad.=Anzeiger d. Akademie der Wissenschaften in Wien, philos.-hist. Klasse

Arch. Anz.=Archäologischer Anzeiger

Arch. d. Miss. Scient.=Archives des Missions scientifiques et littéraires

Ἀρχ. Δελτ.=Ἀρχαιολογικὸν Δελτίον τῆς δημοσίας Ἐκπαιδεύσεως

Ἀρχ. Ἐφημ.=Ἀρχαιολογικὴ Ἐφημερίς

Arch. f. Pap.-Forsch.=Archiv für Papyrusforschung

Arch. Jahrb.=Jahrbuch des Deutschen Archäologischen Instituts

Arch. Ztg.=Archäologische Zeitung

Arundell *Discoveries*=F.V.J. Arundell *Discoveries in Asia Minor* (London 1834)

Atti Accad. Torino=Atti della R. Accademia delle Scienze di Torino, Classe di Scienze Morali, etc.

B.C.H.=Bulletin de Correspondance Hellénique

B.G.U.=Aegyptische Urkunden aus d. Königlichen Museen zu Berlin

B.M.Cat. = *Catalogue of the Coins in the British Museum*

B.S.A. = *Annual of the British School at Athens*

Beloch *G.G.*[2] = J. Beloch *Griechische Geschichte*, Ed. II (Strassburg and Berlin 1912-1927)

Ber. Sächs. Ges. Wiss. = *Berichte ueber die Verhandlungen der Sächsischen Akad. d. Wissenschaften*

Berl. phil. Woch. = *Berliner philologische Wochenschrift*

Bosch *Kl. M.* = C. Bosch *Die Kleinasiatischen Münzen der Römischen Kaiserzeit* II 1, 1 (Stuttgart 1935)

Bruns *Fontes*[7] = C. G. Bruns *Fontes Iuris Romani Antiqui*, Ed. VII (1909)

Bull. Acad. Belg. = *Bulletins de l'Académie Royale de Belgique, Classe des Lettres*

Bull. Comm. Arch. Com. = *Bulletino d. Commissione Archeologica Comunale di Roma*

Bull. Soc. Antiq. de France = *Bulletin de la Société Nationale des Antiquaires de France*

Buresch *Aus Lydien* = K. Buresch *Aus Lydien: Epigraphisch-geographische Reisefrüchte* (Leipzig 1898)

Byz. Ztschr. = *Byzantinische Zeitschrift*

C.A.H. = *The Cambridge Ancient History*

C.G.L. = *Corpus Glossariorum Latinorum*

C.I.G. = *Corpus Inscriptionum Graecarum*

C.I.L. = *Corpus Inscriptionum Latinarum*

C.O. = *Chroniques d'Orient* Vols. I-II (Paris 1891-1896)

C.P. = *Classical Philology*

C.R.A.I. = *Comptes rendus de l'Académie des Inscriptions et Belles-Lettres*

Cardinali *R.P.* = G. Cardinali *Il Regno di Pergamo* (Rome 1906)

Chapot *Prov. Procons.* = V. Chapot *La Province Romaine Proconsulaire d'Asie* (Paris 1904)

Cl. Rev. = *Classical Review*

Cohen *Descr. hist.*[2] = H. Cohen *Description historique des Monnaies frappées sous l'Empire Romain*, Ed. II (Paris 1880-1892)

Coll. Wadd. = E. Babelon *Inventaire sommaire de la Collection Waddington* (Paris 1898)

Cuinet *Turquie* = V. Cuinet *La Turquie d'Asie* (Paris 1890-1894)

De Sanctis *Stor. d. Rom.* = G. De Sanctis *Storia dei Romani* I-IV (Turin 1907-1923)

Denkmäler aus Lykaonien, etc. = Swoboda-Keil-Knoll *Denkmäler aus Lykaonien, Pamphylien und Isaurien* (Prague 1935)

Denkschr. Wien. Akad. = *Denkschriften d. Akademie der Wissenschaften in Wien*

Dessau = H. Dessau *Inscriptiones Latinae Selectae*

Dessau *G.R.K.* = H. Dessau *Geschichte d. Römischen Kaiserzeit* I-II (Berlin 1924-1930)

Diz. Epigr. = E. Ruggiero *Dizionario Epigrafico di Antichità Romane*

Droysen *Hellenismus*² = J. G. Droysen *Geschichte des Hellenismus* I-III, Ed. II (Gotha 1877-1878)

Drumann-Groebe *G.R.* = W. Drumann *Geschichte Roms, 2ᵗᵉ Aufl. herausg. von P. Groebe* I-V (Berlin 1899-1929)

Durrbach *Choix* = F. Durrbach *Choix d'Inscriptions de Délos* (Paris 1921)

Eckhel *D.N.* = J. Eckhel *Doctrina Numorum Veterum* (Vienna 1792-1828)

Econ. Surv. = T. Frank *An Economic Survey of Ancient Rome* I-V (Baltimore 1933-1940)

Eph. Ep. = *Ephemeris Epigraphica*

Ephesos = *Forschungen in Ephesos veröffentlicht vom Österreichischen Archaeologischen Institute* I-V (Vienna 1906-1944)

F. Gr. Hist. = F. Jacoby *Fragmente der Griechischen Historiker*

F.H.G. = C. Müller *Fragmenta Historicorum Graecorum*

Fellows *Travels and Researches* = C. Fellows *Travels and Researches in Asia Minor* (London 1852)

G.G.A. = *Göttingische Gelehrte Anzeigen*

G.G.M. = *Geographi Graeci Minores* ed. by C. Müller (Paris 1855-1861)

G.G.N. = *Nachrichten von der Gesellschaft der Wissenschaften zu Göttingen, philol.-hist. Klasse*

Geogr. Journ. = *The Geographical Journal*

Geogr. Rev. = *Geographical Review*

Hamilton *Researches* = W. J. Hamilton *Researches in Asia Minor, Pontus and Armenia* I and II (London 1842)

Hansen *Attalids* = E. V. Hansen *The Attalids of Pergamon* = *Cornell Stud. in Class. Philol.* XXIX (1947)

Harv. Stud. = *Harvard Studies in Classical Philology*

Haussoullier *Études* = B. Haussoullier *Études sur l'Histoire de Milet et du Didymeion* (Paris 1902)

Head *H.N.*² = B. V. Head *Historia Numorum*, Ed. II (Oxford 1911)

Herm. = *Hermes: Zeitschrift f. Klassische Philologie*

Herzog K.F. = R. Herzog *Koische Forschungen und Kunde* (Leipzig 1899)

Hicks-Hill² = E. L. Hicks and G. F. Hill *A Manual of Greek Historical Inscriptions*, Ed. II (Oxford 1901)

Hirschfeld V.B. = O. Hirschfeld *Die Kaiserlichen Verwaltungsbeamten bis auf Diocletian* (Berlin 1905)

Hist. Ztschr. = *Historische Zeitschrift*

Holleaux *Études* = M. Holleaux *Études d'Épigraphie et d'Histoire Grecques* (ed. by L. Robert) I-III (Paris 1938-1942)

Hunter. Coll. = G. Macdonald *Catalogue of Greek Coins in the Hunterian Collection* (Glasgow 1899-1905)

I.B.M. = *Ancient Greek Inscriptions in the British Museum*

I.G. = *Inscriptiones Graecae*

I.G.R. = *Inscriptiones Graecae ad Res Romanas pertinentes*

Imhoof-Blumer *Gr. Münzen* = Imhoof-Blumer *Griechische Münzen* in *Abhandlungen d. Bayerischen Akademie* 1890

Imhoof-Blumer *Kl.M.* = Imhoof-Blumer *Kleinasiatische Münzen* (Vienna 1901-1902)

Imhoof-Blumer *Lyd. Stadtmünzen* = Imhoof-Blumer *Lydische Stadtmünzen* (*Revue Suisse de Numismatique* V-VII [Geneva 1897])

Imhoof-Blumer *Monn. Gr.* = Imhoof-Blumer *Monnaies Grecques* in *Verhandelingen d. Koninklijke Akademie v. Wetenschappen* 1883

Ins. Creticae = *Inscriptiones Creticae* ed. by M. Guarducci I-II (Rome 1935-1937)

Ins. Delos = Durrbach-Roussel-Launey *Inscriptions de Délos* (Paris 1926-1937)

Ins. Magn. = *Die Inschriften von Magnesia am Maeander*

Ins. Perg. = *Die Inschriften von Pergamon* (*Die Altertümer von Pergamon* VIII)

Ins. Priene = *Inschriften von Priene*

Ins. Sardis = *Sardis: Publications of the American Society for the Excavation of Sardis* VII

Inschr. v. Olymp. = *Olympia: Die Ergebnisse der vom Deutschen Reich veranstalteten Ausgrabung* V

J.H.S. = *Journal of Hellenic Studies*

J.O.A.I. = *Jahreshefte des Österreichischen Archäologischen Instituts*

J.R.S. = *Journal of Roman Studies*

Jahresber. = *Jahresbericht über die Fortschritte der Klassischen Altertumswissenschaft*

A.H.M. Jones *Cities* = A.H.M. Jones *The Cities of the Eastern Roman Provinces* (Oxford 1937)

A.H.M. Jones *Greek City* = A.H.M. Jones *The Greek City from Alexander to Justinian* (Oxford 1940)

Keil-Premerstein I-III = J. Keil and A. von Premerstein in *Denkschriften d. Kais. Akademie d. Wissenschaften in Wien* LIII 2 (1910), LIV 2 (1911) and LVII 1 (1914)

Kiepert *F.O.A.* = H. and R. Kiepert *Formae Orbis Antiqui*

Kontoleon Μικρ. Ἐπιγρ. = A. E. Kontoleon Ἀνέκδοτοι Μικρασιαναὶ Ἐπιγραφαί (Athens 1890)

L.W. = Le Bas and Waddington *Inscriptions Grecques et Latines* Vol. III

Lanckoronski = Karl Graf Lanckoroński *Städte Pamphyliens und Pisidiens* I-II (Vienna 1890-1892)

Laum *Stiftungen* = B. Laum *Stiftungen in der Griechischen und Römischen Antike* (Leipzig 1914)

Le Bas *Voyage Arch.* = Ph. Le Bas *Voyage en Grèce et en Asie Mineure* (Paris 1888)

Leake *Journal* = W. M. Leake *Journal of a Tour in Asia Minor* (London 1824)

Liebenam *Städteverwaltung* = W. Liebenam *Städteverwaltung im Römischen Kaiserreiche* (Leipzig 1900)

M.A.M.A. = *Monumenta Asiae Minoris Antiqua*

M. B. Berl. Akad. = *Monatsberichte d. Königlich Preussischen Akademie der Wissenschaften*

Μ.κ.Β. = Μουσεῖον καὶ Βιβλιοθηκὴ τῆς Εὐαγγελικῆς Σχολῆς (Smyrna)

Maiuri *N.S.* = A. Maiuri *Nuova Silloge Epigrafica di Rodi e Cos* (Florence 1925)

Mattingly-Sydenham = H. Mattingly and E. A. Sydenham *The Roman Imperial Coinage* I-V

Marquardt *R.St.V.²* = J. Marquardt *Römische Staatsverwaltung*, Ed. II (Leipzig 1881-1885)

McClean Coll. = *Fitzwilliam Museum: Catalogue of the McClean Collection of Greek Coins* by S. W. Grose (Cambridge 1923-1929)

Mél. Beyrouth = *Mélanges de la Faculté Orientale de l'Univ. St. Josèphe* (Beyrouth)

Mél. d'Arch. et d'Hist. = *Mélanges d'Archéologie et d'Histoire de l'École Française de Rome*

Mél. G. Glotz = *Mélanges Gustave Glotz* I-II (Paris 1932)

Mém. Acad. Inscrs. = *Mémoires de l'Académie des Inscriptions et Belles-Lettres*

Mem. Accad. Torino = *Memorie della R. Accademia delle Scienze di Torino, Classe di Scienze Morali, etc.*

Mém. Soc. d. Antiq. de France = *Mémoires de la Société Nationale des Antiquaires de France*

Ed. Meyer *G.d.A.* = Ed. Meyer *Geschichte des Altertums*

Ernst Meyer *Grenzen* = Ernst Meyer *Die Grenzen der Hellenistischen Staaten in Kleinasien* (Zurich 1925)

Michel = C. Michel *Receuil d'Inscriptions Grecques*

Milet = *Milet: Ergebnisse der Ausgrabungen u. Untersuchungen* I, II 1-3, III 1, 2, 4, 5 (Berlin 1906-1936)

K. Miller *Itin. Rom.* = K. Miller *Itineraria Romana* (Stuttgart 1916)

Mionnet = T. E. Mionnet *Description de Médailles antiques, Grecques et Romaines* I-VII and *Suppl.* I-IX (Paris 1805-1837)

Mnem. = *Mnemosyne*

Mommsen *R.G.* = Th. Mommsen *Römische Geschichte*

Mommsen *R.St.R.* = Th. Mommsen *Römisches Staatsrecht* I-II (Ed. III) and III (1887-1888)

Mon. Ant. = *Monumenti Antichi pubblicati per cura della R. Accademia dei Lincei*

Mordtmann *Marm. Anc.* = J. Mordtmann *Marmora Ancyrana* (Berlin 1874)

Mus. Belge = *Musée Belge*

Newton *Hist. of Disc.* = C. T. Newton *A History of Discoveries at Halicarnassus, Cnidus and Branchidae* (London 1862)

Newton *Travels* = C. T. Newton *Travels and Discoveries in the Levant* (London 1865)

Niese *G.M.S.* = B. Niese *Gesch. der Griechischen und Makedonischen Staaten* I-III (Gotha 1893-1903)

Num. Chron. = *Numismatic Chronicle and Journal of the Numismatic Society*

Num. Notes and Mon. = American Numismatic Society, *Numismatic Notes and Monographs*

Num. Ztschr. = *Numismatische Zeitschrift*

O.G.I. = W. Dittenberger *Orientis Graeci Inscriptiones Selectae*

P.A.S. = *Papers of the American School of Classical Studies at Athens*

P.I.R. = *Prosopographia Imperii Romani*

Pap. Cairo Zenon = C. C. Edgar *Zenon Papyri* (*Catalogue générale des Antiquités Egypt. du Musée du Caire* I-IV [1925-1931])

Pap. Grenfell II = B. P. Grenfell and A. S. Hunt *New Class. Fragments and Other Greek and Latin Papyri* (Oxford 1897)

Pap. Oxy. = *The Oxyrhyncus Papyri*

Pap. Petrie = J. P. Mahaffy *The Flinders Petrie Papyri* I-III (Dublin 1891-1905)

Pap. Soc. Ital. = *Pubblicazioni della Società Italiana per la Ricerca dei Papiri Greci e Latini in Egitto: Papiri Greci e Latini*

Paton-Hicks = W. R. Paton and E. L. Hicks *The Inscriptions of Cos* (Oxford 1891)

Perrot *Exploration* = Perrot and Guillaume *Exploration Archéologique de la Galatie et de la Bithynie* (Paris 1862)

Pet. Mitt. = *Petermanns Geographische Mitteilungen*

Phil. Woch. = *Philologische Wochenschrift*

Philippson I-V = A. Philippson in *Petermanns Mitteilungen, Erg.-hefte* CLXVII (1910); CLXXII (1911); CLXXVII (1913); CLXXX (1914); CLXXXIII (1915)

Philol. = *Philologus: Zeitschrift f. das Klassische Altertum*

R.A. = *Revue Archéologique*

R.E. = Pauly-Wissowa-Kroll *Real-Encyclopädie d. Class. Altertumswissenschaft*

R.E.A. = *Revue des Études Anciennes*

R.E.G. = *Revue des Études Grecques*

R. Phil. = *Revue de Philologie, d'Histoire et de Littérature Anciennes*

Ramsay *C.B.* 1 = Sir Wm. M. Ramsay *The Cities and Bishoprics of Phrygia* I, 1 and 2 (Oxford 1895-1897)

Ramsay *H.G.* = Sir Wm. M. Ramsay *The Historical Geography of Asia Minor* (London 1890)

Ramsay *Stud. East. Rom. Prov.* = Sir Wm. M. Ramsay *Studies in the History and Art of the Eastern Roman Provinces of the Roman Empire* (London 1906)

Receuil = Waddington-Babelon-Reinach *Receuil général des Monnaies Grecques d'Asie Mineure*

Reinach *Mith. Eup.* = Th. Reinach *Mithridate Eupator* (Paris 1890)

Reinach *Trois Royaumes* = Th. Reinach *Numismatique Ancienne: Trois Royaumes de l'Asie Mineure, etc.* (Paris 1888)

Reisen I and II = Benndorf-Niemann and Petersen-von Luschan *Reisen im Südwestlichen Kleinasien* I and II (Vienna 1884-1889)

Rev. Belge = *Revue Belge de Philologie et d'Histoire*

Rev. Épigr. = *Revue Épigraphique*

Rev. Hist. = *Revue Historique*

Rev. Num.=*Revue Numismatique*

Rh. Mus.=*Rheinisches Museum für Philologie*

Riv. Fil.=*Rivista di Filologia e d'Istruzione Classica*

Robert *Coll. Froehner* 1=L. Robert *Collection Froehner* 1: *Inscriptions Grecques* (Paris 1936)

Robert *Ét. Anat.*=L. Robert *Études Anatoliennes* (Paris 1937)

Robert *Études épigr. et philol.*=L. Robert *Études épigraphiques et philologiques* (Paris 1938)

Robert *Villes*=L. Robert *Villes d'Asie Mineure* (Paris 1935)

Röm. Mitt.=*Mitteilungen d. Deutschen Archaeologischen Instituts, Römische Abteilung*

Rostovtzeff *Kolonat*=M. Rostowzew *Studien zur Geschichte d. Römischen Kolonats*=*Archiv für Papyrusforschung, Beiheft* 1 (1910)

Rostovtzeff *Hellenist. World*=M. Rostovtzeff *The Social and Economic History of the Hellenistic World* (Oxford 1941)

Rostovtzeff *S.E.H.R.E.*=M. Rostovtzeff *The Social and Economic History of the Roman Empire* (Oxford 1926; Italian Ed., Florence 1932)

Rostovtzeff *Staatspacht*=M. Rostowzew *Geschichte der Staatspacht in der Römischen Kaiserzeit*=*Philologus, Erg.-band* IX (1902)

Rott *Kleinas. Denkmäler*=H. Rott *Kleinasiatische Denkmäler aus Pisidien, Pamphylien, Kappadokien und Lykien* (Leipzig 1908)

S. B. Bayer. Akad.=*Sitzungsberichte d. Bayerischen Akademie der Wissenschaften, philos.-hist. Klasse*

S. B. Berl. Akad.=*Sitzungsberichte d. Preussischen Akademie der Wissenschaften* (*philos.-hist. Klasse* since 1922)

S. B. Wien. Akad.=*Sitzungsberichte d. Akademie der Wissenschaften in Wien, philos.-hist. Klasse*

S.E.G.=*Supplementum Epigraphicum Graecum*

S.G.D.I.=*Sammlung der Griechischen Dialekt-Inschriften*

Spratt and Forbes *Travels in Lycia*=T. A. B. Spratt and E. Forbes *Travels in Lycia, Milyas and the Cibyratis* (London 1847)

Stud. Pont.=J. G. C. Anderson and F. Cumont *Studia Pontica* I-III (1903-1910)

Syll.=W. Dittenberger *Sylloge Inscriptionum Graecarum*, Ed. II (1898-1901) and III (1915-1924)

T.A.M.=*Tituli Asiae Minoris*

T.A.P.A.=*Transactions and Proceedings of the American Philological Association*

Täubler *Imp. Rom.* 1 = E. Täubler *Imperium Romanum* 1 (Leipzig 1913)

Viereck = P. Viereck *Sermo Graecus quo Senatus Populusque Romanus . . . usi sunt* (Göttingen 1888)

Waddington *Fastes* = W. H. Waddington *Fastes des Provinces Asiatiques de l'Empire Romain* (Paris 1872, unfinished)

Welles = C. B. Welles *Royal Correspondence in the Hellenistic Period* (New Haven 1934)

Wien. Stud. = *Wiener Studien: Zeitschrift f. Klassische Philologie*

Wilhelm *Beiträge* = Ad. Wilhelm *Beiträge zur Griechischen Inschriftenkunde* (Vienna 1909)

Woch. Kl. Phil. = *Wochenschrift für Klassische Philologie*

Wood *Ephesus* = J. T. Wood *Discoveries at Ephesus* (London 1877)

Ztschr. f. Num. = *Zeitschrift für Numismatik*

ROMAN RULE
IN ASIA MINOR

CHAPTER I

THE BEQUEST OF ATTALUS

HIGH above the northern side of the broad fertile valley of the river Caïcus, sixteen miles from the Aegean Sea, rises the great rock on which stood the fortress of Pergamum.[1] Enclosed on the east and on the west by the deeply precipitous ravines of the river's tributaries, which flow down from the mountains on the north, and severed from those mountains by a depression scarcely less deep, the stronghold was impregnable save from the south. On this side a city grew up, standing on the terraces of the rock and gradually descending to the plain below. Here, during the third and second centuries before Christ, a succession of able rulers built up a kingdom which developed into one of the great powers of western Asia Minor. This kingdom, by the bequest of Attalus III, the last of his dynasty, fell into the possession of Rome in 133 B.C. and became the cornerstone of Roman rule in Asia Minor.

The history of Pergamum goes back to the early fifth century, when King Darius of Persia and his son Xerxes granted land in the plain of the lower Caïcus to immigrant exiles from Greece.[2] In 400 B.C. the city ruled by their descendants was visited by Xenophon and the soldiers whom he had led back to the Aegean after the defeat and death of the adventurous Cyrus. The Hellenic tradition which was established by these early settlers and later stimulated by a close association with the neighbouring Greek cities on the coast of the Aegean gave Pergamum a claim to a connexion with Greece, and this claim was afterwards strengthened by the development of a myth which represented Telephus, a son of the hero Heracles, as an early ruler of the country.[3]

It was not until several years after the conquest of Asia Minor by Alexander the Great that Pergamum attained to a position of real importance. During the strife and confusion that followed the conqueror's death the city came under the power of Antigonus, surnamed the "One-eyed," who under Alexander had been "satrap" of Phrygia but by agreement among the generals in 321 became commander-in-chief of the eastern armies. Later, by defeating his rivals, he made himself overlord of Asia Minor and eventually assumed the title of King. His rule, the greater part of which was spent in warfare with his enemies, was brought to an end in 301 B.C., when he was defeated and killed at Ipsus in central Asia Minor by the allied forces of Lysimachus, another of Alexander's officers and now king of Thrace, and Seleucus, lord of Syria and the East.[4] As the result of this victory, Lysimachus became monarch of central and western Asia Minor, and among the strongholds which he seized was the fortress of Pergamum.

In the summer of 281, after a reign of twenty years, Lysimachus was attacked by Seleucus, who coveted the rich kingdom of his former ally. The armies of the two rivals, both of them now old men, met on the plain of Corupedium, near the northern bank of the river Hermus across the mountains from the Caïcus.[5] The battle brought disaster and death to Lysimachus, and Seleucus added Asia Minor and Thrace to his large and unwieldy empire, which now extended from the Aegean to the border of India. Seven months later, however, he was murdered in Thrace, where he had gone for the purpose of consolidating his newly-won power.[6] His son, Antiochus I, although forced to abandon what his father had hoped to conquer in Europe, succeeded to Seleucus's possessions in Asia and thus became the overlord of the ruler who had established himself in Pergamum.

This ruler, Philetaerus, a native of Tieium on the southern shore of the Euxine Sea, had been charged by Lysimachus with the command of the fortress of Pergamum and the guardianship of a great treasure of 9,000 talents placed there for safe-keeping.[7] An adventurer of humble origin but of great shrewdness, he was evidently regarded by his lord as a faithful watch-dog of the treasure entrusted to his care. This trust, however, was to prove ill-founded, for when Seleucus appeared in Asia Minor to dispute Lysimachus's possession of the country, Philetaerus abandoned the cause of his master and threw in his lot with the invader.[a]

This act of betrayal and Seleucus's victory at Corupedium secured the permanent possession of Pergamum to Philetaerus. He further obtained the favour of Antiochus I by presenting him with the ashes of his father's body, which he had bought from the murderer.[b] The new Seleucid monarch, beset by wars on every side,[c] was ready to leave the Caïcus valley and the possession of Lysimachus's treasure to a faithful subordinate, who would rule as his vassal.[8] The tie was drawn closer by the marriage of Philetaerus's nephew Attalus to the daughter of Achaeus, Antiochus's younger brother. In consequence of his friendly relations with his overlord, Philetaerus was able to extend his power over the country surrounding Pergamum and became in fact, if not

[a] Strabo XIII p. 623: Pausanias I 10, 4.   [b] Appian *Syr.* 63.
[c] See below p. 94.

in name, the ruler of a principality of considerable size. Thus, in the early third century, at the time when Rome was preparing to meet Pyrrhus, the King of Epirus who invaded Italy in 280 B.C., there was laid the foundation of the kingdom which, a century and a half after the battle of Corupedium, was to become Rome's first province in Asia.

Apart from the question of his relations with Antiochus, the chief problems of Philetaerus were two in number: the maintenance of friendship with his neighbours, the independent Greek cities, and the defence of his dominions against the ravages of the Celtic Galatians, who preyed upon all possessed of wealth enough to repay their attacks.

The Greek cities lined the Asianic coast of the Propontis, the Hellespont and the Aegean.[d] Their ancient independence had been restored to them by Alexander, and their wealth, obtained largely through commerce, made them valuable allies. Some of them even had navies of considerable size. The value of cordial relations with his neighbours among these small republics was apparent to the Pergamene ruler, and he was shrewd enough to win their friendship by gifts and concessions, as he also, by similar acts of generosity to highly revered sanctuaries, showed himself desirous of obtaining a position of honour in the Hellenic world. Among the city-states of Asia Minor, he sought especially the friendship of Cyzicus, the chief city on the southern shore of the Propontis, whose territory lay across the mountains north of the Caïcus valley and whose port was connected by road with Pergamum.[e] Among his gifts to Cyzicus was a quantity of grain which he sent after the city's territory had been ravaged by the Celtic enemy who had become the scourge of western Asia Minor.[9]

Not long before the battle of Corupedium a large band of Celts from the region of the upper Danube arrived in Thrace, plundering the country as they came. Within three years after the death of Seleucus, King Nicomedes I of Bithynia at the northwestern corner of Asia Minor, needing troops with which to oppose his rebellious brother, invited a force of these Galatians, as they were called, to cross the Bosporus.[10] About 20,000 of the tribesmen, half of them fighting men, are said to have arrived in Asia at this time, but their subsequent prowess in war suggests that in reality the number was greater. The immediate purpose of their coming was soon achieved by the defeat of the rebel. Then Nicomedes, not unwilling to use this opportunity of weakening Antiochus I, whom both he and the cities on the Bosporus

[d] See below p. 73f.   [e] See Chap. II note 20.

and the Euxine regarded as a dangerous enemy, turned them loose on the Seleucid possessions in western Asia Minor.

A general devastation of the territories of the cities on the western coast ensued. The Galatians, divided into three bands, captured those cities which were defenceless, and when opposed by formidable walls, they carried off booty from the surrounding territory.[11] Conditions grew intolerable, and Antiochus, as ruler of Asia Minor, was forced to take action. In a great battle fought against the marauders, his elephants defeated their cavalry, with the result that he was hailed as the "Saviour" of the land.[12] Unable, however, to exterminate so numerous a foe, he seems to have compromised by settling them in central Asia Minor in a district which was thenceforth called from their name, Galatia.[f] Here they established themselves, with the families they had brought with them, in their own tribal organizations, a military aristocracy holding the native population in subjection and always ready to provide mercenaries for the armies of the princes who wished to employ them.[13] But despite the possession of a land of their own, they did not desist from seeking further wealth by raiding the lands of their more civilized neighbours, and their presence in the country continued to be a menace both to the Greek cities and to the lord of Pergamum.

Philetaerus, apparently, faced this menace boldly; he seems to have met a band of the raiders in battle and to have won a victory over them.[14] But when he died after twenty years of rule, his nephew Eumenes, who succeeded to his power, preferred an easier way of protecting his dominions. It had been discovered that the depredations of the Celts—like those of their remote kinsfolk in the Highlands of Scotland—could be averted by the payment of "blackmail."[15] Eumenes, accordingly, adopted this method of preventing their raids, paying them what amounted to tribute. The compromise at least left him free to enlarge his dominions at Antiochus's expense.

Within a year of his accession to power, Eumenes, not content with the position he had inherited from his uncle, determined to free himself from the suzerainty of the Seleucids. Collecting an army of mercenaries, he advanced beyond his borders and defeated Antiochus in a great battle near Sardis, thereby establishing himself as an independent prince.[16] His principality, it is true, was of modest size, consisting of a territory which extended from Mt. Ida on the northwest to the mountains which separate the basin of the Caïcus from that of

[f] See below p. 454.

the Hermus but did not include much of the coast of the Aegean, which was largely in the possession of free Greek cities.[17] The land at the mouth of the Caïcus, however, was Pergamene. Here, the old Aeolian city of Elaea, immediately east of the mouth of the river, became the port of Pergamum and, later, the naval station of its rulers.[18] The colossal foundations of its moles and protecting towers still show the scale on which it was developed. Eumenes's territory, however, was wealthier than its size would indicate. In addition to the rich valley of the upper Caïcus and the plain in front of Pergamum itself, he owned the copper mines in the mountains north of the city and probably also the rich deposits of silver in the region east of Mt. Ida;[g] from these he and his successors obtained the metal needed for the coinage which they used in the development of their capital and the payment of their soldiers.

On the death of Eumenes in 241 B.C. the rule of Pergamum passed to his kinsman Attalus, son of his cousin who had married the Seleucid princess. In the course of a long and brilliant reign the prestige and power of Pergamum were to be greatly increased by this monarch's alliance with Rome.

Attalus was a strong and vigorous young man still under thirty years of age at the time of his accession to power.[19] One of his first actions was to defy the Galatians, refusing to continue the payments by means of which Eumenes had bought off their raiding.[20] When, in consequence of this refusal, they invaded his dominions in full force, he met them with an army in the plain of the upper Caïcus about thirty miles east of Pergamum, and here he won so decisive a victory that the invaders were compelled to withdraw. He celebrated his success by assuming the title of King, borne by neither of his predecessors, thus formally proclaiming himself an independent monarch. Like Antiochus I after his victory over the Celts, he was hailed as "Saviour." This title meant even more than the formal assumption of an independent sovereignty, for it signified that he had become the champion of Hellenism against barbarism and the protector of the Asianic Greeks from those who had preyed upon them. His position in the Hellenic world was now definitely established.

Despite his great prestige, the kingdom of Attalus was still very limited in extent. It could be enlarged only at the expense of the Seleucid monarchs, formerly his suzerains, to whom through his mother he was bound by ties of kinship. An opportunity soon pre-

[g] See below p. 44.

7

sented itself, however, for the strife which resulted from rebellion within the House of Seleucus brought Attalus into conflict with the successful rebel, whom he finally defeated, thereby greatly increasing (albeit only temporarily) his own dominions.

About five years before Attalus became ruler of Pergamum Antiochus II, son of Antiochus I, died in Ephesus, leaving two sons.[21] A few years previously he had divorced their mother Laodice in order to marry Berenice, sister of Ptolemy III, the new king of Egypt. Although Berenice had borne him a child, Laodice's elder son was proclaimed King under the name of Seleucus II. War at once ensued, for Ptolemy invaded the dominions of Seleucus in Syria with the intention of upholding the claim of his sister and her infant son. It was necessary, accordingly, for Seleucus to set out for the East to take the field against him.[22] Although finally successful in repelling the Egyptian invaders, Seleucus was compelled, about the time of Attalus's accession, to send to Asia Minor for reinforcements. The price demanded by Laodice, who was acting as regent, was the recognition of her younger son, Antiochus, later surnamed Hierax ("The Hawk"), as ruler of the Asianic portion of the Seleucid Empire. Seleucus had perforce to accept his brother as co-ruler, but after the conclusion of peace with the Egyptians he returned with an army to recover the dominions he had surrendered.[23] Although at first victorious, he was finally defeated at Ancyra in central Asia Minor by Hierax in alliance with the Galatians and Mithradates II, King of Pontus,[h] and after losing most of his army, he was forced to take refuge in Cilicia south of the range of Taurus. Hierax was thereupon acknowledged as lord of Asia Minor.

The position of the new ruler, however, was weakened by the increasing power of Attalus, whose assumption of sovereignty constituted a direct challenge. Accordingly, Seleucus once defeated, the fiery young Hierax opened war on the former vassal of his house.[24] Unable to command the resources of the Seleucid Empire, the eastern portion of which was still held by his brother, he turned again to the Galatians, who had aided him at Ancyra and were doubtless not unwilling to take arms against the Pergamene King.

In the war that followed, Hierax and his allies seem to have advanced as far as Pergamum itself, but they proved no match for Attalus, who won a victory over their combined armies. The Celts withdrew, but the Seleucid prince continued the struggle. Three times, at least, he met Attalus in the field. In one of these engagements, which took

[h] See below p. 190.

8

place in Caria, the Pergamene ruler had evidently taken the offensive, for the district lay far outside the boundaries of his kingdom. In each case Hierax suffered defeat. Finally, discouraged by his repeated failures, he abandoned the attempt to make himself supreme in Asia Minor and withdrew eastward to Mesopotamia, hoping to seize his brother's eastern dominions. Defeated in this attempt also, he fled across the whole of Asia Minor to Thrace, there to meet his death in an encounter with a band of Celtic marauders.

The defeat of Hierax and his withdrawal to the East greatly strengthened the position of Attalus. His victories over the Galatians had already caused the Greek cities of the neighbouring coast to regard him as their friend and protector. With Cyzicus, especially, he had close ties, for his wife Apollonis was the daughter of a prominent citizen of the place and was highly honoured there. Many of the other cities also, including Lampsacus, Ilium, and Alexandria in the Troad and Smyrna toward the south, seem to have entered into an alliance with him.[1] Attalus had now begun to replace the Seleucids as the chief ally of the cities and the guarantor of their independence. It was not long, in fact, before he wholly supplanted the former rulers of Asia, for the unfortunate Seleucus II, whose reign had been an almost continuous succession of wars, was unable to take any step to reassert his claim to the Asianic dominions of his house. After Seleucus's death in 226, the same year, probably, in which his brother was killed,[j] his son, the youthful Seleucus III, also failed in his attempt to win back his ancestral supremacy in Asia Minor. In at least two battles his generals were defeated by Attalus, and when the young King set forth in person, accompanied by his mother's brother, Achaeus, he was assassinated by two of his officers before he arrived at the scene of action.[25] As the result of these victories and of Seleucus's death, Attalus became the dominant power in Asia Minor.[26]

Attalus's pre-eminence, however, was of short duration. Achaeus, who assumed the command of Seleucus's army, proved an able leader and carried on the war with great success. Not only did he recover Asia Minor for his new master, Antiochus III, brother of the murdered Seleucus, but, forcing Attalus to fall back on Pergamum, he reconquered all that the King had taken from Hierax.[k] In 220, after many years of fighting, Attalus was restricted to practically the dominions

---

[i] See Chap. IV note 36.

[j] Justin XXVII 3, 12. See also note 24.

[k] Polybius IV 48, 1 and 10f.

he had inherited from his predecessor. His attempt to create a vast kingdom had achieved but little success.

Nevertheless, ephemeral thought his conquests were, Attalus had in fact raised Pergamum to the rank of a real power. He also gave it a new importance by making his capital a centre of art.[27] He adorned the city with magnificent buildings and transferred to it as many masterpieces as he was able to collect in Greece, founding an art gallery which seems to have been still in existence in the second century of the Christian Era. His victories over his enemies, moreover, particularly over the Galatians, were commemorated in a series of monuments, some of them, at least, by the Pergamene sculptor Epigonus; the likenesses of the barbarians especially, copies of which are preserved in many museums, show a grim realism previously unknown in Greek art.

Attalus was destined, however, again to profit by family dissensions among the Seleucids. Achaeus, having recovered Asia Minor for his nephew, was not content to hold the position of a subordinate but proclaimed himself an independent monarch.[28] Although his army refused to follow him to Syria against the rightful ruler, he made good his position in the western part of the Seleucid Empire and became, for a brief period, "the most powerful and the most formidable of the rulers of Asia Minor north of the Taurus." Not satisfied, however, with the dominions he had gained, he wished to increase his kingdom by the addition of the southern districts, where the Seleucid power had never been more than nominal. With this purpose in view, he embarked, in 218, on a campaign in Pisidia and Pamphylia. Here he succeeded in defeating the army of the powerful city of Selge and forcing its inhabitants to pay him a large sum for refraining from an attack on the city itself, and he also brought much of southern Asia Minor under his power. Soon, however, his gains were more than offset by the loss of the northern districts he had previously conquered.

Achaeus's absence gave Attalus his opportunity. The Greek cities, save for those in the far north which remained faithful to their association with Pergamum, had been compelled to submit to the usurper. But when Attalus, after collecting an army composed chiefly of Celtic mercenaries from Thrace—for the conqueror of the Galatians did not scorn to make use of their kinsmen when it suited his purpose to do so— set forth along the coast, he found these Hellenic communities ready to receive him.[29] Some, it is true, demurred, fearing retaliation on the part of Achaeus, but they ultimately submitted to a show of force.

Respecting their long-established independence, Attalus again entered into relations with them, by the terms of which they became his allies. By this policy he gained the support of the cities of the coast of Aeolis and northern Ionia as far south as Ephesus, which was probably held by a force of Egyptians.

The King's next step was to recover the interior, and, leading his mercenaries into eastern Mysia, he overran this district.[30] But after a long march, an eclipse of the moon so frightened his Celts that they refused to proceed, an action which forced him to abandon his attempt at further conquest and withdraw to the Troad, where he renewed his friendship with the faithful cities.

By this time Antiochus III was ready to proceed against the rebellious Achaeus. Unable, however, to enter into hostilities against him with Attalus as an enemy, he was willing to overlook the defeats administered to his brother's armies by the Pergamene King and in 216 he began a joint campaign with Attalus against their common foe.[1] As a result, Achaeus was defeated and shut up in the citadel of Sardis, where, after a siege of at least two years, he was taken by treachery and put to a cruel death.[31] Thus Antiochus re-established his supremacy over the Seleucid dominions in Asia Minor, but what advantage, save the overthrow of a dangerous enemy, Attalus gained from this alliance is unknown. At least during the remaining sixteen years of his life there seems to have been no active enmity between him and Antiochus —perhaps because both were busy elsewhere.

Attalus, in fact, was about to take a step which was destined to be fraught with great consequences, not merely to the Kingdom of Pergamum, but to Asia Minor in general, namely the entry into friendly relations with Rome. Suggested perhaps by his inability to cope with the Seleucids unaided, the new combination actually came about as the result of Attalus's participation in the tangle of politics in Greece. For some time, indeed, the Pergamene King had been establishing connexions with the Grecian states. Perhaps even before he was attacked by Achaeus, he had presented the League of the Aetolians with a sum of money for the fortification of a stronghold.[32] Later, he built a portico at Delphi and redeemed the sacred land of Apollo at Sicyon, which in gratitude voted him a statue of colossal size.

For some years trouble had been brewing on the western side of the Balkan Peninsula. In 228 the Romans, determined to stamp out piracy in the Adriatic Sea, established a protectorate over the coast of what is

[1] Polybius v 107, 4.

now Albania and made an adventurer named Demetrius ruler of territory farther to the north.[33] The move, which seemed to constitute a threat to Macedonia and may perhaps have been intended to weaken this powerful neighbour, was resented by the monarch of the country. Occupied elsewhere, however, King Antigonus III could do no more than enter into friendly relations with Demetrius, who, impatient of Roman control, made overtures to the Macedonian King and finally in 219 raided the Roman protectorate. This rash act cost him his kingdom, for a Roman expeditionary force crossed the Adriatic, and Demetrius was forced to take refuge with the youthful and energetic Philip V, who had recently ascended the Macedonian throne.

At first, however, Philip, engaged in an unnecessary and fruitless war with the Aetolian League, could make no move to combat the danger in the West. But the signing of a peace with the Aetolians in 217 left him free to take advantage of the hard circumstances in which Rome had been placed as the result of the invasion of Italy by Hannibal. Having come to an agreement with the Carthaginian general for mutual assistance against the Romans,[m] Philip by the year 212 had gained a portion of the Adriatic coast, and Hannibal's capture of Tarentum in the same year made immediate co-operation possible between himself and his Macedonian ally. In the face of this danger the Romans finally took action. Entering into an agreement with the Aetolians, by which the latter were to receive all the conquered territory, while Rome was to have the booty only, the praetor Laevinus persuaded the League to take up arms against Philip.[n] Various states in the Peloponnese joined the Aetolians as allies, while the Romans brought into the war the Illyrian chieftain Pleuratus. As a friend of the Aetolians, Attalus, not unwilling to have the power of Macedonia diminished, was persuaded to join the coalition.

Little, indeed, was accomplished by this war save that the Romans, having embroiled Philip in hostilities with his neighbours, were enabled to devote their whole attention to Hannibal. To Attalus, however, it brought a position of greatly increased importance and, finally, recognition as a friend of Rome. A year after entering the struggle, he was elected to the high office of *strategos*, or presiding-officer, of the Aetolian League, his duties, to be sure, being entirely honorary.[34] A year later, probably, he furnished his allies with six companies of soldiers sent over from Asia Minor, and in 208 his navy, in co-operation with the Roman fleet, performed useful, if not distinguished, service

m Polybius VII 9.   n Livy XXVI 24, 1f.

off the eastern coast of Greece. It is true that Attalus's participation in the conflict was soon cut short; for a sudden advance on the part of Philip, taking him by surprise while on a land-expedition, forced him to retreat precipitately, and immediately afterward a report that the Pergamene Kingdom was being threatened by his neighbour and enemy, King Prusias of Bithynia, seemed to necessitate his return to Asia.[o] The war, however, lasted but a short time longer. In 206 the Aetolians, finally perceiving that they were little more than tools of their Roman allies, made a separate peace, and a year later the Romans, having now rendered Hannibal powerless, also concluded a treaty with Philip.[35] Attalus, whose support of their cause had won him the favour of his allies, was included among the signatories, being assured thereby of Rome's protection in the future.

This entry of Attalus into international affairs soon involved him in another war, one of greater magnitude and even more important in its consequences. Like the previous struggle, it had no connexion, in its early stages at least, with the Kingdom of Pergamum, but the menace it brought to the liberty of the Greeks ultimately caused the monarch who had acted as their champion in Asia to take a leading part in their defence.

The aggressor was Philip of Macedonia. Thwarted by Rome in his designs of extending his rule over all Greece, he evolved the plan of building up an empire in the Aegean. The successful accomplishment of this purpose, however, meant the destruction of the power of the island-republic of Rhodes, which not only possessed part of the Carian coast but had assumed a protectorate over the Aegean Islands.[p] Officially, there was "friendship" between Philip and the Rhodians. The King, therefore, was forced to the expedient of weakening the Republic by underhand means. Beginning this process in 205 by sending an agent to raid the coasts and the islands of the Aegean, he proceeded a year later to instigate his allies among the pirates of Crete to make war on the Rhodians and despatched another emissary to fire their naval arsenal.[36] About the same time, he caused still another agent, apparently a local dynast, to invade the territory of the city of Iasus in Caria; this action led the citizens to appeal to Rhodes for protection, with the result that the Republic's envoys assured them that, while preserving the existing friendship with Philip, their government would take whatever steps were necessary for Iasus's safety.[37]

o Polybius XI 7, 1: Livy XXVIII 7, 5f. For Prusias's invasion see below p. 313.
p See Chap. III note 76.

The King soon showed his intentions more openly. In 202, after seizing the European shore of the Propontis, he occupied Chalcedon on the Asianic side of the Bosporus. Then, continuing southward, he captured and destroyed the Greek cities of Cius and Myrleia, presenting their sites to his brother-in-law, Prusias I of Bithynia.[38] This attack on the cities, with its general threat to Greek freedom and the consequent menace to their own supremacy in the Aegean, aroused the Rhodians to action, and, abandoning even the pretence of "friendship," they declared war on the aggressor.[q]

But Philip's energy and resources and the powerful navy which he had built up during the previous three years made him too formidable an enemy for the Rhodians to oppose unaided. The obvious source of assistance was Attalus, who had already helped the Aetolians against Philip and had gained prestige as an ally of Rome. His power also would be endangered by Macedonian supremacy in the Aegean. The Rhodians' relations with Pergamum, it is true, were none too cordial, for Attalus's considerable navy and the possibility that he might attempt to add the islands to his dominions had caused the Rhodians to look on him with suspicion.[r] But the present need was too great to permit those threatened by Philip to indulge in mutual mistrust, and Attalus was persuaded to enter the war. While his motive was evidently the wish to preserve his own power against the aggression of Philip, it could easily be represented as a determination to protect Hellenic freedom.

In the spring of 201 the Macedonian navy entered the Aegean.[39] After occupying Samos and taking possession of the Egyptian war-vessels stationed there, Philip met the combined fleets of Rhodes and Pergamum, aided by some Byzantine ships, off the island of Chios. The result was a victory for the Allies, but Attalus's navy fared none too well in the encounter. His kingdom, moreover, was soon invaded by Philip, who plundered it cruelly, thereby forcing Attalus to concentrate all his efforts for its defence. Consequently, the Rhodians, compelled to face Philip unaided, were defeated in a second battle, fought off the island of Lade. The King then entered the neighbouring city of Miletus and, advancing southward with his navy, made a landing on the coast of Caria and led his forces into the interior.[40]

Philip's Carian expedition, although apparently successful at first, nevertheless resulted in failure. The Pergamene and Rhodian navies, once more united, took up a position off the coast, and the King was

---

[q] Polybius xv 23, 2f.   [r] See C. G. Starr in *C.P.* xxxiii (1938), p. 65f.

compelled to spend the winter of 201-200 at Bargylia, hard pressed by a lack of supplies.[41] In the spring, abandoning his ambitious plan, he slipped out through the opposing fleets and withdrew with all speed to Macedonia, closely pursued by the ships of his enemies.

But before the probability of this failure became apparent, Attalus and the Rhodians had taken a step which was to prove of great importance for the future of Asia Minor. In the autumn of 201 they sent embassies to Rome to inform the Senate of Philip's designs.[42] In order to arouse the fears of the Romans, these envoys represented the situation as exceedingly grave, asserting—probably with more eloquence than truth—that Philip had entered into an agreement with Antiochus III to seize the foreign dominions of Egypt, weakened by the recent death of Ptolemy IV and the accession of his son, still a young child. In this nefarious plot, it was said, the Aegean Islands and the Asianic coast were to be Philip's share.

The envoys accomplished their purpose. Philip's ambition to make himself master of the Hellenic world and the possible menace of an enemy immediately across the Adriatic could be represented as a danger to Rome.[43] The report of his alliance with Antiochus could be used to make the peril seem greater and even to cause men to envisage the possibility of a joint invasion of Italy by the two kings. Thus, although there is no reason to suppose that either monarch ever dreamed of extending his power west of the Adriatic, the Romans were frightened into an active participation in the affairs of the East. There were plausible grounds for a protest to Philip, for he had invaded the kingdom of Attalus, a Roman ally, and Macedonian troops had participated in a raid on the territory of Athens, also, probably, an allied state.

The Senate, accordingly, sent envoys to the East, ordering Philip to refrain from "making war on any of the Hellenes" and to submit to an impartial tribunal the question of the reparations owed to Attalus.[44] The demands were completely ignored. Philip, intent on holding the Hellespont, had already seized the southern coast of Thrace, and now, crossing the Strait, he proceeded to lay siege to Abydus on the Asianic side. A second demand from the Senate, presented during the siege, was couched in the form of an ultimatum; it was, in reality, although not technically, a declaration of war. In reply, the King bade the Romans refrain from breaking their treaty with him but none the less continued his attack on Abydus. When the city was finally captured after a desperate defence, during which many of the citizens killed

15

themselves rather than surrender, a Roman army had already arrived on the eastern shore of the Adriatic to enforce the Senate's demands.

During three years of the war for the declaration of which he had been so largely responsible, Attalus, with all his forces, naval and military, steadfastly supported the armies of Rome.[45] Although sixty-nine years of age, he at once led his troops in person to Greece, and throughout the struggle he took an active part in the operations against the Macedonian monarch, at the same time continuing his friendly relations with the cities of Greece. But this active participation in the hardships of war proved too great an effort for the old monarch. In 197, the fourth year of the conflict, while addressing an assembly of the Boeotians in an attempt to persuade them to ally themselves with Rome, he was suddenly stricken with apoplexy. He was carried paralyzed to Pergamum, where he died a few months later, but not until after the Romans, during the period of his helplessness, had finally defeated their common enemy, who subsequently, by the terms of the treaty imposed upon him by the victors, was forced to comply with all of Attalus's previous demands for full reparation.[46]

The greatest of the rulers of Pergamum, Attalus had spent his life in making his kingdom one of the important powers of the East. The champion of Hellenism against the barbarians, he died, according to the eulogy written by the historian Polybius, "in the course of his noblest work, fighting for the liberty of the Greeks."[8] This cause had served the Romans also as a ground for declaring war against Philip. Five years after Attalus's death, they were to resume the struggle, and in the name of Greek freedom were ultimately to put an end to Seleucid rule in Asia Minor.

The new King of Pergamum, Eumenes II, eldest son of Attalus, was an able young man, possessed, as his portrait shows, of a high degree of intelligence and refinement.[47] Remaining true to his father's policy of alliance with the Romans, he began his reign by participating in their war against Nabis, the tyrant of Sparta. His allegiance to Rome, however, was soon to be put to a severe test, and his fidelity was to be rewarded by an increase of power and prestige far surpassing all that his father had attained.

About seven years before Attalus's death Antiochus III had begun to turn his attention to the recovery of his ancestral dominions in western Asia, largely lost to the Seleucid House by internal dissension

[8] Polybius XVIII 41, 9.

and the need of safeguarding the eastern portion of the Empire. He adopted the policy of attempting to conciliate some of the Asianic cities which were not in alliance with Attalus by granting them privileges and so securing their allegiance.[t] For the time, he was unable to take more aggressive measures, for from 202 onward he was engaged in a war with Egypt for the recovery of southern Syria.[48] But in the spring of 197, a few months before Attalus's death, having driven the Egyptians out of Syria, he set forth to regain his Asianic possessions. Sending an army overland with orders to meet him at Sardis, he himself with his navy sailed along the coast of Cilicia, compelling the towns and strongholds to receive him.[49] On reaching Coracesium, at the western end of the district, he was met by envoys from the Rhodians, who, believing—or pretending to believe—that he might render aid to Philip, protested against his advance beyond the Chelidonian Islands off the southeastern corner of Lycia. Antiochus, wishing to avoid any open enmity toward the Republic, assured the envoys of his friendship and, reminding them of his cordial relations with Rome, promised them that neither the Rhodians nor their allies should have any cause for fear. Meanwhile, the Romans' victory over Philip was announced, and, now that there was no longer any danger of a combination between the two monarchs, the Rhodians allowed the King to proceed. Rounding the Islands, he brought the coast of Lycia under his control, but his attempt to gain the Carian cities of Caunus, Myndus and Halicarnassus as well as the island of Samos was checked by the Rhodians, who showed themselves ready to protect the independence of these "allies" of Egypt. It was not possible, however, to prevent him from establishing himself at Ephesus, where he spent the following winter.

In the spring of 196 Antiochus showed his intentions by announcing the programme of a New Order—the restoration in the West of the empire of Seleucus I. All the cities of Asia were to return to their former status; in other words they were to be "allies" of the Seleucid monarch. If possible, this was to be achieved by peaceful measures, the offer of independence at the price of an alliance, but the King was ready, if necessary, to use force.[u] With a view to controlling the Hellespont, he seized Abydus, which was declared free in the treaty with Philip then in the course of formulation, and, crossing the Strait into Thrace, he occupied the peninsula of Gallipoli on the European side.[v] When

---

[t] See Chap. IV note 48.

[u] Livy xxxiii 38, 1f. See Chap. IV note 52.

[v] Livy xxxiii 38, 4f.: Appian *Syr.* 1.

the cities in alliance with Pergamum, notably Smyrna and Lampsacus, refused his offer of independence, he sent troops against them, threatening them with a similar seizure. In fear of capture and the loss of their cherished freedom, the two cities appealed to the Romans for protection—a step of great significance, for as yet no city of Asia Minor save Ilium had had dealings with Rome.[w]

Although the Senators believed that if Antiochus carried out his evident purpose of making himself master of the Aegean, he would next advance to Greece and thus become a dangerous neighbour, they were reluctant to engage in another war. Accordingly, although their motive was rather the fear of possible danger from the King than any real interest in the freedom of the Asianic Greeks, they assumed the position thrust upon them by the cities, but at the same time staved off a conflict by protracted negotiations.[50] Their envoys maintained throughout the principle that if Antiochus asserted a claim to any part of Europe, as he had recently done by his occupation of Thrace, the Romans had a right to protect the freedom of the cities of Asia, preserving Rome's existing alliances with those cities and, if desirable, forming alliances with others. The King, on his side, declared with equal firmness that Rome had no place in Asianic affairs, and that the cities, not only of western Asia Minor but of Thrace as well, were his by right of inheritance and must derive their freedom from himself alone.

In this situation Eumenes was faced with a serious dilemma. Although, for the present at least, he could not be overcome by force, the success of Antiochus's programme meant ultimately the diminution of the power of Pergamum.[51] Antiochus, on the other hand, had as yet made no move against Eumenes's kingdom and was even seeking to gain his support by means of an alliance. He offered him the hand of his daughter and perhaps promised him the overlordship of the Greek cities as well.[52] But in any alliance of this kind Eumenes would necessarily play a secondary part. Moreover, the long antagonism between his dynasty and the Seleucids, as well as his father's policy, impelled him to side with Rome in a struggle of which the inevitability must have been apparent. He himself had more to gain from Rome than from a victorious Antiochus. He therefore rejected the proffered alliance and even urged the Senate's envoys to declare war on the King.[x] When, in the autumn of 192, Antiochus led an army across the Aegean and thus forced the Romans into war, Eumenes supported them in

[w] See Chap. IV notes 51 and 53.　　　　[x] Livy xxxv 13, 7f. (193 B.C.)

Greece.[53] After the King, defeated at Thermopylae in the following spring, retreated to Asia, the Pergamene fleet co-operated with the Roman navy in a campaign off the western coast, inflicting great losses on the enemy. Even when Antiochus sent an army into Eumenes's kingdom and plundered it far and wide, the Pergamene King adhered stoutly to his alliance with Rome.

Finally, in the late autumn of 190, a Roman army under the command of the two Scipios crossed the Hellespont.[54] A few weeks later, it met Antiochus's forces, vastly superior in number, in the plain on the northern bank of the Hermus, a short distance north of the city of Magnesia-near-Sipylus. Antiochus's huge and motley array was completely routed and the King fled the field. Eumenes's troops took part in the battle, and he himself, by a brilliant cavalry-charge, did much to win the day for Rome.

The battle of Magnesia put an end forever to Seleucid rule in Asia Minor. By the treaty which was signed at Apameia in Phrygia, a year after the battle, Antiochus was compelled to resign all claim to the entire portion that lay north of the range of Taurus and west of the line of the middle course of the river Halys, beyond which was the kingdom of Cappadocia.[55] Thus a vast territory fell into the hands of the victors. Rome, however, took none of this for herself. Instructions had been given by the Senate to the peace-commissioners, headed by the Scipios' successor, Gnaeus Manlius Vulso, to divide the dominions surrendered by Antiochus among those who had aided Rome's cause. The commissioners met the Allies' representatives at Apameia in 188, and here the spoils of the war were distributed. Save for single grants of land to some of the Greek cities which had furnished aid against the King, the conquered territory was divided between Rome's principal allies, Eumenes and the Rhodian Republic.[56] In this division Eumenes received the lion's share. As increased by this gift, his kingdom extended from the border of Bithynia to the river Maeander; in central Asia Minor it included the districts of Phrygia and Lycaonia, together with large portions of the mountain-regions of Pisidia and Milyas and the city of Telmessus on the coast of Lycia. Thus enlarged, his dominions were many times the size of his ancestral realm; his kingdom now comprised an area about equal in extent to England and Wales. There was ground, indeed, for the complaint of the jealous Rhodians that the possessions of Pergamum were being increased much more than ten-fold and for the comment of the historian Polybius that the new kingdom was "inferior to none."[y]

It was not wholly out of gratitude to Eumenes that the Romans thus extended his kingdom. There was a practical reason for the gift. The Senators were unwilling to assume the rule of Asia Minor or to add further to the responsibilities incurred by the recent establishment of a protectorate in Greece. They therefore adopted a temporizing policy and resorted to the expedient of creating a powerful buffer-state between Rome and the Seleucid Empire, the rulers of which were to be their faithful allies and to embark on no foreign policy that did not meet with their approval. Thus western Asia Minor would be governed in the interest of Rome but the responsibility for its rule would not devolve on the Romans. On the other hand, in order that Eumenes might not be too powerful, a large expanse of territory was given to Rhodes. It is probable that the King laboured under no misapprehensions as to the Romans' real motive. If he did, he was in the course of time to be undeceived.

During the years which immediately followed this increase in his power, Eumenes by a series of wars and alliances—all undertaken, doubtless, with the approval of Rome—added greatly to his prestige. His army, under the command of his brother Attalus, defeated Prusias I, King of Bithynia, and gained a portion of northern Phrygia which had been in dispute between Prusias and himself.[z] In a war against Pharnaces, King of Pontus, Eumenes was similarly successful, forcing the monarch to pay an indemnity and to cede all the territory conquered or claimed.[a] His prestige extended even beyond the limits of Asia Minor. In 183 he concluded a treaty of "friendship and alliance" with the cities of Crete, in which the two contracting parties apparently promised mutual assistance in war, and a few years later he was called upon to send aid to another Cretan community which had quarrelled with one of these allies.[57] In Syria he helped the Seleucid prince Antiochus IV to gain his ancestral throne after the murder of his brother and so won the monarch's friendship for life. But his chief claim to fame, as also to the gratitude to the people of his kingdom, lay in his notable victories over the dreaded Galatians.

The problem of the Galatians had not been solved either by the victories of Attalus I or by the power of Rome. Antiochus had per-

[y] Polybius XXI 22, 15 = Livy XXXVII 54, 12: Polybius XXIII 11, 7.
[z] Phrygia Epictetus; see note 56 and below p. 314.
[a] See below p. 192. The date of this war was 182-179 B.C.

20

suaded or hired them to join his army, and Celts had served among his forces at Magnesia.[b] With this as a pretext, Manlius Vulso, before the conference held at Apameia, led a punitive expedition into Galatia.[58] He was accompanied by Eumenes's brothers, Attalus and Athenaeus. It was probably necessary to show the turbulent tribesmen that the Romans were now masters of Asia Minor, but Manlius's methods resembled those practised by the Galatians themselves too closely to be worthy of Rome. After defeating them in two battles, he plundered their country cruelly, and his army returned laden with booty. In the general settlement of Asianic affairs the Galatians were ordered to desist from their raiding and to remain at peace with the King of Pergamum.[c]

Even Manlius's ruthlessness, however, did not terrorize the Celts for long, and Eumenes was soon compelled to take arms against them.[59] Not more than four years after the conference of Apameia, while Eumenes was at war with Prusias of Bithynia, Ortiagon, one of their princes, described as generous, intelligent and courageous, organized a movement the purpose of which was to free the Galatians from Pergamene supremacy. He seems to have been acting in conjunction with Prusias and so was all the more formidable. Nevertheless, Eumenes defeated him in a great battle, thereby freeing western Asia Minor, for a time at least, from the Celtic peril. In consequence of this exploit, in which he followed in his father's footsteps, he assumed, as Attalus had done, the title of Saviour. He also celebrated his success by extending an invitation to the communities of both Asia Minor and Greece to participate in a great festival held in honour of the Pergamene goddess, Athena "the Victory-bringer," thereby taking his place as a power in the Hellenic world.

Brought to submission by Eumenes's victory, the Galatians were compelled to acknowledge the suzerainty of Pergamum, an arrangement which remained unchallenged for fifteen years.[60] Meanwhile, the increasing power and pretensions of King Perseus of Macedonia, Philip's son, began to alarm both Rome and Eumenes; the latter, as his father had done when threatened by the ambition of Philip, informed the Senate of the monarch's preparations, urging a declaration of war.[61] The Fathers, in recognition of his efforts, granted Eumenes unusual honours and soon resolved to take his advice. When hostilities were opened in 171, he again followed Attalus's example by

[b] Livy xxxvii 8, 4; 18, 7; 38, 3; 40, 5 and 10f.; xxxviii 18, 1: Appian *Syr.* 6 and 32.
[c] Livy xxxviii 40, 1f.

bringing troops to aid the Romans and by co-operating with them during the three years' struggle. His activities on Rome's behalf, however, gave the Galatians their opportunity, and in 168 they again broke out in revolt.[62] Invading the eastern portion of the Pergamene Kingdom, they ravaged the country, slaughtering all whom they captured. Eumenes sent his brother Attalus to Rome to ask for the Senate's intervention but meanwhile advanced against the invaders. Although at first compelled to retreat, he finally succeeded in forcing the enemy to withdraw to their own territory. In the following spring, however, they advanced again, apparently with even greater forces, but Eumenes also had mobilized a larger army at Sardis and was ready to meet them.

Meanwhile the commissioners sent by the Senate at Attalus's request arrived in Asia.[63] A conference with the Galatians was held at Synnada in Phrygia, but the Romans refused to allow Attalus to be present, on the ground that his participation would only arouse the enemy's anger. At its conclusion, the head of the commission reported that the protests had merely increased the Galatians' ferocity and that nothing could be accomplished. It was evident that the Romans were unwilling to make any effort to aid Eumenes and that they were even playing him false. Accordingly, he took matters into his own hands. After increasing his army by a large force of mercenaries, he and Attalus met the enemy in Phrygia, where his skill and courage won a great victory.

The indifference, if not actual hostility, which the Roman commissioners showed toward Eumenes at this time was indicative of a change of attitude toward him in Rome. Despite his assistance in the war against Perseus and the congratulations which he sent to the Senate after that monarch's final defeat,[d] there were those who maintained that he had not been wholly loyal to the Romans and that he had even offered his services—for a price—to the Macedonian King for negotiating a peace.[64] The accusation was probably false, for it is hard to believe that Eumenes, after urging the Romans to enter into the war, became ready to sacrifice what he would gain by a complete Roman victory. The charge was utilized, however, by the new influences now dominant in the Senate, where a strong party thought that Rome's allies in Asia had grown too great. Especially now that Macedonia was no longer to be feared, the usefulness of these allies as an offset to that power had ceased to exist.[e] Those who held this

d Livy XLV 13, 12.   e See Mommsen *R.G.* I[7] p. 771 = Eng. Trans. II p. 510.

view succeeded in enacting a decree by which Rhodes was deprived of the dominions she had received in Caria and Lycia.[f] In the same year, Attalus, at the time in Rome, was offered a part of his brother's kingdom—an offer which the loyal prince rejected.[g]

Eumenes was promptly informed both of the charge against him and of the desire to weaken his power. So serious, in fact, did the situation appear that he deemed it necessary to go to Rome in person. But on his arrival in Italy in the early winter of 167-166, he was met by an official bearing an ominous message from the Senate: The Fathers had decreed that no more kings were to be permitted to visit Rome and any communication he might wish to make to them he was to hand to the official who met him and then leave Italy at once.[h] Eumenes had no choice but to yield, and, accordingly, he returned immediately to Pergamum.

The news of this affront at once stimulated Eumenes's enemies in Asia to active opposition. The Galatians, despite their recent defeat, were encouraged to further resistance, and when, in the following year, they sent envoys to Rome to present their case, the opponents of Eumenes prevailed upon the Senate to grant them complete independence, with the sole condition that they should refrain from invading the lands of others.[i] Prusias II of Bithynia, moreover, who was Eumenes's bitterest enemy in Asia and had stirred up the Galatians against him, also seized the opportunity to present his complaints. Although he was Perseus's brother-in-law and had given little or no aid to the Romans during their recent war in Macedonia, his envoys were permitted by the Senate to charge Eumenes with the seizure of a part of Bithynia and the failure to evacuate Galatia in accordance with the Fathers' decree.[65] He is said also to have persuaded some of the cities of Asia to appear with complaints; their charge was that Eumenes was too friendly with the Seleucid monarch, Antiochus IV.

It is possible that the Senators, none too conversant with Asianic affairs, were bewildered by the multiplicity of these charges. In any case, they sent a commission to Asia to investigate the truth of the accusations. The commissioners, however, returned in a similar state of bewilderment. Meanwhile, Eumenes's brothers had appeared in Rome in an effort to answer the accusations brought against him, but

[f] See below p. 110.

[g] Polybius xxx 1-2 = Livy xlv 19; see also note 76.

[h] Polybius xxix 6, 4; xxx 19 (20): Livy Per. xlvi: Justin xxxviii 6, 3f. (a speech attributed to King Mithradates VI of Pontus).

[i] Polybius xxx 19 (20), 12; 28 (xxxi 2); 30 (xxxi 6), 6.

although they were received with all honour, the Senators were not wholly convinced. Once more they resorted to an investigation, sending as special commissioner, Gaius Sulpicius Galus, well known as Eumenes's inveterate enemy.[66] On his arrival in Asia, he placarded the cities with notices ordering all those who wished to prefer charges to meet him in Sardis, and here he sat for ten days in the gymnasium, listening to attacks on the King. The result of his action, however, was the opposite of what the monarch's enemies had hoped, for "the more harshly the Romans seemed to treat Eumenes, the greater was the friendliness of the Greeks." It was soon found that the charges could not be pressed further.

The Greek cities, indeed, held in great esteem the monarch who had succeeded to his father's position as the champion of Hellenism and had himself vanquished their barbarian enemies. Immediately after the affront he had suffered in Italy, the federated cities of Ionia lauded him as the common benefactor of the Greeks and their defender against the barbarians, one "who is exercising all zeal and forethought to the end that the dwellers in the Grecian cities may be forever at peace and in a most prosperous condition."[67] They also voted him a golden wreath and a golden statue to be erected in whatsoever Ionian community he might designate. Even before this action, Miletus had constructed a sanctuary in which he was to receive the honours of a god. The island-state of Cos, moreover, created a priest for his worship and instituted a sacred procession as a compliment to him, and at Teos priests were created for the worship of his mother and his wife.[68] In Greece, too, he had received honours. After his defeat of Ortiagon the League of the Aetolians erected a special monument "in acknowledgement of his excellence of character and his benefactions," as well as a group containing an equestrian statue of Eumenes and statues on foot of his three brothers, with an inscription lauding them all, together with the Queen-mother Apollonis and the Pergamene people.

Eumenes, on his side, made every effort to maintain these cordial relations. He requited the Ionians' courtesy by a donation of money to be used at the Federation's festival for celebrating a day named after himself and by promising to bear the expense of the golden statue they had voted him, specifying that it should be placed in Miletus. He presented Miletus, moreover, with a sum of money to be used as an endowment, the interest of which was to be expended for a yearly distribution of grain to the citizens on his birthday; in return, the Milesians decreed that a sacrifice should be offered in his honour on this day, together with a procession and a public banquet.[69] At Cyzicus, his mother's native city, to which he and his brothers had once escorted her on a formal visit, he built, after the Queen's death, a magnificent temple for her worship; it was decorated with a series of reliefs depicting scenes illustrative of the love of a son for his mother. To the Rhodians—whose envoys had once protested against the enlargement of his kingdom—he promised both a marble theatre and a great quantity of grain, stipulating that this should be sold and that the money thus realised should constitute an endowment for the payment of teachers.[70] In Greece he presented the city of Delphi with endowments both for a supply of grain and for the support of a yearly sacrifice, in Thebes he gave money for the purchase of land for Dionysus, and in Athens he built a magnificent colonnade. His many gifts bear out the comment of the historian Polybius that the benefits he conferred on the Greek cities outnumbered those of any monarch of his time.[j]

In addition to winning the friendship of the Greeks, Eumenes succeeded in establishing cordial relations with a neighbour of a very different kind, namely the Priest of the ancient Asianic goddess known as the "Great Mother." Her sanctuary at Pessinus in Phrygia, lying between the Pergamene Kingdom and the country of the Galatians, owned domains of considerable size, and the priest of the temple was, in fact, the ruler of a small independent principality.[71] For some time past, the holders of this sacred office had cultivated the friendship of the Pergamene kings, perhaps as a means of protection against Galatian aggression, and the monarchs had responded by presenting the sanctuary with buildings of marble. In 205 relations had become so friendly that when the Romans were ordered by their sacred Sibylline Books to bring the Great Mother to Rome, Attalus I obtained from the temple a black meteoric stone, the symbol of the Goddess, which a few years later was enshrined on the Palatine Hill. When Manlius, accompanied by the two Pergamene princes, invaded Galatia in 189, the priests of the Goddess met them in solemn procession announcing that the Great Mother promised them victory. This friendship with Pessinus was strengthened by Eumenes into what amounted to an alliance. A series of letters written during the last years of his life to the Priest Attis shows him promising aid for the capture of a "holy place" and encouraging the Priest to take steps against his own brother, who had robbed the Temple of some votive offerings; on another occasion, when Eumenes led forth his army, Attis sacrificed to the gods for his

[j] Polybius XXXII 8 (22), 5.

safety. This close association seems to have been adopted as a general policy and was continued by Eumenes's successor.

Among his brother-monarchs of Asia Minor, Eumenes's closest tie was with Ariarathes IV of Cappadocia, to whose daughter Stratonice he was betrothed immediately after the conclusion of the treaty of Apameia.[72] He obtained the Romans' forgiveness for the Cappadocian monarch, who had fought on Antiochus's side at Magnesia. The two kings had afterward combined to withstand Pharnaces of Pontus, and Ariarathes, even when an old man, resisted an attack by the Galatians, in this also apparently co-operating with his son-in-law. Pharnaces's successor, Mithradates IV, who became an ally of Rome, showed no enmity toward Pergamum and, a few years after Eumenes's death, even supported the latter's brother Attalus against Prusias II.[k] Prusias alone remained hostile, and to the close of Eumenes's reign he continued, in conjunction with the Galatians, to send representatives to the Senate bringing various charges of aggression, so that it was again necessary to despatch Attalus to Rome to reply to his accusations.[l]

In addition to maintaining his father's policy of acting as protector to the Greeks of Asia, Eumenes also followed his example as patron of the fine arts. Surrounding himself with scholars and poets, he furthered the cause of learning and literature by founding a great library at Pergamum.[73] He also brought to his capital architects and artists, who beautified the city with many new and magnificent buildings and impressive works of sculpture. Of these monuments the most famous is the great altar of Zeus, which stood high above the city on a terrace of the citadel-rock.[74] Its astounding frieze in high relief, depicting, on an heroic scale, the combats of the Gods against the Giants, the overthrow of the forces of Barbarism by the powers of Civilization, commemorated the King's victories over the Galatians and symbolized his defence of Hellenism against the barbarians. A second, smaller, frieze told the story of the city's mythical founder, Telephus, son of Heracles, who, it was said, came from Greece to Asia under the protection of the gods.[m] Thus Eumenes not only showed that Pergamum was an Hellenic city but also expressed the divine right of his kingship.

After a reign of thirty-eight years, which made Pergamum, as far as was possible at this time, a worthy successor to the Athens of the fifth century and which, despite Rome's hostility toward him, rivalled

k See below p. 194.   l Polybius XXXI 32 (XXXII 3), 1; XXXII 1 (5), 5.
m See note 3.

in glory the rule of his father, Eumenes died in 159, at the age of at least sixty-two years.[75] His wife, the Cappadocian princess Stratonice, seems to have borne him no children. A few years before his death, he had acknowledged, as his son and successor, a boy whose birth is a mystery but who was probably his own illegitimate child.[76] This boy, however, was less than eleven years old when Eumenes died, and the King's will appointed his brother Attalus as guardian of the young prince, ordering that he should act as regent during the lad's minority. Accordingly, Attalus, who, in fact, appears already to have received the royal title,[n] became at the advanced age of sixty-one the actual ruler of Pergamum. His ward—also named Attalus—was officially regarded as heir to the throne, and on the occasion of a visit to Rome he was presented to the Senators, who conferred on him "such honours as were suited to his youth."[o] But even when the prince became of age, his uncle, now firmly established as ruler, retained both the title and the power of king.

The new monarch, Attalus II, had for years been his brother's right-hand man.[77] Although once tempted by the Romans, as has already been noted, with the offer of a portion of the kingdom,[p] he had remained loyal to Eumenes and in acknowledgement of his loyalty he had received the surname of Philadelphus. He had remained, however, *persona grata* at Rome, and soon after his accession to power he showed his intention of retaining her favour. In a conference at Apameia with the Priest Attis of Pessinus, his brother's ally, the two rulers decided upon some project—probably a military campaign—on which they were to embark together.[78] After discussion with his advisers at Pergamum, however, the King resolved to heed the advice of one of them, who urged that no step should be taken without the Romans' approval. Attalus, accordingly, abandoned the project, writing to Attis that henceforth, before taking any action, he would send envoys to Rome to make a report concerning all matters which could lead to disputes, while, nevertheless, taking measures for his own defence, should the need arise. The adoption of this policy was a distinct step toward closer relations with the Senate. At the same time, it meant a greater subordination of Pergamum to the power of Rome.

His submissiveness to Rome, however, did not prevent Attalus from engaging in military activity in regions where Rome's interests were not concerned. In the division of Antiochus's Asianic dominions, Eumenes had attempted to obtain possession of Pamphylia, thus ex-

[n] See note 75.   [o] Polybius XXXIII 18, 1f. (153-2 B.C.)   [p] See above p. 23.

tending his kingdom to the southern coast.[q] His request had been refused by the Senators, who solved the question by declaring the Pamphylians free. But their future was of no real interest to Rome, and no objection, apparently, was raised when Attalus made an expedition into the region. He marched through Pisidia to Selge, against which his brother seems to have made some hostile move, and, occupying at least a part of Pamphylia, he founded the city of Attaleia, thus obtaining a port on the Mediterranean littoral.[79]

The protection afforded by Rome, nevertheless, was of real benefit when Attalus was attacked by his foes. When his kingdom was invaded in 157 by his brother's enemy, Prusias II, he at once appealed to the Senate.[80] At first, the Fathers suspected that Attalus was merely seeking a pretext for a move against Prusias, and even when they intervened, their feeble remonstrances seem to have made but little impression. In consequence, the war dragged on, and it was possible for Prusias again to invade Pergamene territory and even to besiege Attalus in Pergamum itself. But finally, after a delay of two years, the Senate adopted a vigorous tone, forcing Prusias to lay down his arms and even pay an indemnity to Attalus as well as to the Greek cities whose territory he had ravaged. About five years later, when Attalus, in a series of intrigues supported Prusias's son, Nicomedes, in an attempt to take the Bithynian throne from his father and even accompanied the young man into his kingdom, the Senate made no serious response to the old King's appeals for intervention.[r] Prusias was murdered in his capital and Nicomedes was recognized as king. By his accession to the throne the long-standing enmity between Pergamum and Bithynia was brought to an end.

However determined the Roman Senate might be to dominate the foreign policy of Eumenes II and Attalus II, even to the extent of curtailing their independence, there is no indication of any interference with their internal administration of their kingdom. In this respect they were as free as their father Attalus. These enlightened monarchs, in fact, greatly bettered the condition of the dominions under their rule. Most noteworthy, perhaps, was the stimulus which they gave to the development of urban life. Eumenes and, especially, Attalus founded cities in suitable situations, which, modelled on the Greek *polis*, became centres of Hellenic civilization.[s] These cities, like the older ones founded by Antiochus I, were directly subject to the monarch's rule, thus differing from the independent city-states of the

[q] See note 56 and Chap. XII note 5.   [r] See below p. 317.   [s] See below p. 120.

Aegean coast. But the policy of the Pergamene kings was more liberal than that of their predecessors, and gradually both the earlier communities and the new foundations acquired limited powers of self-administration. Some cities were even permitted to issue coins, primarily, of course, for local use.

Another important measure of the Pergamene kings was the institution of a coinage for general use. The predecessors of Eumenes had issued silver pieces of their own and both he and Attalus II continued to do so.[t] Money for wider circulation, however, was highly desirable. The wealthier cities, accordingly, were encouraged to issue large silver coins, which by general agreement became a common medium of exchange, especially for trade with the East.[u] In addition, however, to this widely-accepted city coinage, the Kings themselves issued a silver coin of uniform type which became current throughout Asia Minor and also in Greece. These pieces bear the device of a serpent creeping into a mystical chest or *cista*, from which they derived their name *cistophori*.[81] During the second century they were minted not only in Pergamum itself but, presumably with the authorization of Eumenes, in eleven or twelve other places which were either subjects of the Pergamene king or city-states in alliance with him. Thus a medium of exchange was established which later was maintained for a time under Roman rule and, after a revival, lasted in another form to the end of the first century.

During his reign of twenty-one years Attalus showed himself Rome's faithful ally in war, thus following closely in his brother's footsteps.[82] He likewise followed Eumenes's policy by maintaining friendship with the Hellenic cities of Asia and by making generous gifts to the communities of Greece. Moreover, by purchasing works of art he increased the collection founded by his father.[83] By his marriage with Eumenes's widow, Stratonice, he allied himself closely with her brother, Ariarathes V of Cappadocia, whom he restored to the throne after the successful revolt of a younger brother.[v] As has already been noted, he was also an ally of the King of Pontus and had gained the friendship of Nicomedes II of Bithynia.[w]

Finally, at the ripe age of eighty-two, Attalus II was gathered to his fathers.[84] Although Eumenes's son Attalus had long since attained his majority, the old ruler had continued to hold all the powers of king.

[t] See *Abh. Berl. Akad.* 1884, p. 3f. and 1910 *Anh.* p. 7f.: Hansen *Attalids*, pp. 202f. and 434f.
[u] See Chap. IV note 86.
[v] See Chap. IX note 9. For his joint action with Ariarathes against Priene see Chap. IV note 93.
[w] See above pp. 26 and 28.

The younger Attalus, indeed, seems to have enjoyed certain prerogatives, and there is no reason to believe that he was dissatisfied with his
position or disloyal to his uncle; for the Queen Stratonice he seems to
have cherished a special devotion.[x] Nevertheless, it is probable that
during his uncle's later years the prince exercised no actual authority,
for the old monarch seems to have been under the control of an all-
powerful favourite. This man, Philopoemen by name, had led the
troops sent by Attalus to aid the Romans at the siege of Corinth in
146, and after his return he was vested with the title of keeper of the
royal seal and appears to have become the dominating force in the
kingdom.[85]

The reign of the new monarch, Attalus III, who finally ascended
the throne on his uncle's death in 138, is described in the meagre and
unsatisfactory accounts which have been preserved to us as a carnival
of bloodshed and murder.[86] We are told that the King, after poisoning
his uncle, executed his relatives on the charge that they were plotting
against him and had caused the death both of Stratonice and of Berenice,
to whom he was betrothed; that, suspecting the loyalty of the most influential of his father's friends, he removed them from power and even
caused many of them, as well as many commanders of soldiers or cities,
to be slain by barbarian mercenaries whom he had concealed in the
palace, not sparing even their wives and children; that after these
deeds of violence he shut himself up in the palace, living in squalor
and refusing to attend banquets or "show other signs of sanity"; that,
neglecting the affairs of his kingdom, he devoted himself to modelling
and bronze-casting and to the care of his garden, especially to the
cultivation of poisonous plants, which he used to send to his friends
as gifts; and that, in consequence of his cruelty, his subjects hated him
and eagerly desired another ruler.

This lurid narrative, evidently taken by our extant historical sources
from the work of some sensation-loving and inimical writer, is obviously not wholly true. It is, indeed, not improbable that on his accession to the throne Attalus found it necessary to remove from power
those who, like Philopoemen, had exercised undue influence over his
aged predecessor, and even that some sort of palace-revolution occurred, which was accompanied by turmoil and perhaps by bloodshed.
The story of the massacre which he is said to have perpetrated may
well have originated in the violent overthrow of a powerful palace-
clique. It is difficult, moreover, to believe that he killed his relatives

[x] See note 76.

in punishment for the death of Stratonice, not only for the reason that the Queen seems to have died only a short time before Attalus himself, but also because his only kinsmen seem to have been distant cousins, the descendants of the brother of his grandmother, Apollonis of Cyzicus.[87] On the other hand, there is sufficient evidence to show that he was not generally hated by his subjects and that his interest in plants was not due to morbid misanthropy.

As it happens, we have a decree, passed, probably, by the Pergamenes themselves, which honours Attalus in extravagant terms.[88] He is lauded for his bravery in war and his victory over his opponents as well as for the blessings he had conferred on the citizens. He is to be honoured by a garland of gold, by a colossal statue which is to share in the sacrifices rendered to the god Asclepius, by a golden equestrian statue to be placed by the altar of Zeus, and by a daily offering of incense. His entry into the city, furthermore, is to be celebrated by offerings and prayers and by a procession in which the whole body of citizens, with the priests and magistrates at their head, is to go forth to meet him. With all due allowance for the flattery characteristic of the Asianic cities, it is hard to suppose that a hated recluse would be honoured in such terms.

It could not fail to be remarked, however, that Attalus's favourite pursuits presented a poor comparison with the interests of his grandfather and father. They had adorned Pergamum with works of art and founded a famous library, whereas he busied himself with the care of his garden! His devotion to natural science, however, deserves no such sneer as that which was accorded to it; for his labours found a recognition of which his detractors never dreamed, and his published works were held in high repute. His book on scientific agriculture is named among those which should be consulted on that subject,[y] and he was regarded as an authority on zoology, botany and medicine.[89] Even in the second century after Christ, his investigations in pharmacology and toxicology were still cited. The respect in which technical writers held his works affords ample evidence that his pursuits were serious and the result of no mere selfish whim.

Attalus, robbed by death of his betrothed, had remained unmarried and was therefore the last of his line. His only surviving relatives appear to have been distant cousins, not of royal blood,[z] and a certain Aristonicus, an illegitimate son of Eumenes, who, as later events

y Varro *de Re Rust.* I 1, 8: Pliny *N.H.* XVIII 22.
z See note 87.

showed,[a] was wholly unfitted to be king of Pergamum. Accordingly, the problem of the ultimate disposal of his kingdom must have seemed to Attalus a difficult one. A general proclamation of "freedom" might result in chaos. The lack of a strong central ruler would permit the rise of local tyrants, adventurers who made themselves masters of cities or districts and lorded it over the inhabitants with oppression and even cruelty. There had been many of these in the Hellenic world since the dismemberment of Alexander's empire, and even in Attalus's own time two had arisen in lands where there was no stronger power to hold them in check.[90] There were also the independent Greek cities to be considered. Since the overthrow of the Seleucids, they had been accustomed to look to Pergamum for leadership and even protection. In their case, also, there was possible danger from tyrants, but an even greater peril was the likelihood that, if a controlling power were removed, factional strife might arise among the citizens themselves, the quarrels between aristocrats and democrats which had raged so frequently in the Hellenic world. It was necessary for Attalus, therefore, not only to find an heir to his dominions but also to devise some means of saving western Asia Minor from strife and disorder. The experiences of his predecessors had shown where the dominant power lay and that the only sovereignty capable of controlling the situation was that of Rome.[91]

An obvious solution of the problem, therefore, was to bequeath the royal possessions of Pergamum and, together with these, the supremacy of western Asia Minor to the Roman people. There was a precedent for such a bequest, of which, however, Attalus may not have been aware. The later Ptolemy Euergetes II of Egypt, at the time King of Cyrene, who in 154 B.C. appeared before the Roman Senate to accuse his brother, Ptolemy Philometor, King of Egypt, of an attempt to assassinate him, had in the previous year made a will which provided that in the event of his death without an heir to the throne the Romans should inherit his kingdom.[92] The terms of the will, however, were never carried out, for the two brothers subsequently went through the form of a reconciliation and, Philometor dying before Euergetes, the latter succeeded to the throne of Egypt, long outliving Attalus.

When Attalus died in 133, it was found that he had named the Roman people heir to all his possessions.[93] These included not only his private fortune but also the royal domain-lands, as well as the cities which had been directly subject to the monarch and now became sub-

a See below p. 148f.

jects of Rome. The bequest did not include the lands belonging to those temples of the gods which lay within the bounds of the kingdom, or, obviously, the territories of the independent Greek cities of the coast. Nor did it include the city of Pergamum itself; for Attalus in his will "left the city free, attaching to it also the civic territory which he adjudged to it," but imposing the condition that this clause of the will should be ratified by the Romans.

The will was promptly brought to Rome and the inheritance was speedily accepted.[94] As might perhaps be expected, it at once became the plaything of ambitious politicians. Just at the time of its arrival, Tiberius Gracchus, the champion of the common people, was seeking the money necessary to stock the farms on which he was settling the superfluous population of Rome. The bequest of Attalus seemed to him to afford the means both of strengthening his own position and providing for his partisans. The Senate, on the other hand, was bitterly opposed to such an encroachment on its control of the public funds. Gracchus, however, brought a bill before the Assembly of the Plebs, proposing to expend the treasure of the Pergamene monarchs for the benefit of the new Italian farmers. He planned also to submit to the Plebs the question of the disposition of the cities included in Attalus's kingdom, but the execution of this plan, as perhaps also the actual passage of his previous proposal, was prevented by his early death. The arrangements for the future of the Pergamene dominions, accordingly, were taken over by the Senate, which entered on the difficult task of forming the new province of Asia.

Attalus had done the best that he could for his people. He had saved them by his will from turmoil and chaos, perhaps even from attack by one of the powers still left in Asia Minor. But his bequest resulted in reducing Pergamum from a royal capital and a centre of art to a provincial city, and—what was much more disastrous—in ultimately fastening on his subjects the yoke of the Roman tax-farmer.

CHAPTER II

THE LAND AND ITS RICHES

FOR over sixty years after the death of Attalus III the country that he bequeathed to the Romans was often oppressed by dishonest governors and rapacious tax-gatherers. Its economic condition, furthermore, suffered cruelly through a three years' occupation by the invading army of the Pontic King, Mithradates. Nevertheless, Cicero, in an oration to the Roman people, could still say that "in the richness of its soil, in the variety of its products, in the extent of its pastures and in the number of its exports it surpasses all other lands."[a] It was, indeed, a rich legacy that the Romans received; the development both of its natural wealth and of its important industries made it the most valuable province that had as yet been included in the Roman Empire.

The new province, consisting of the greater part of Attalus's kingdom as well as of the southern district of Caria,[b] which for a time had been a possession of Rhodes, extended along the western coast of the Anatolian Peninsula from the Propontis and the great range of Mt. Olympus on the north to the Strait of Marmaris on the south. In addition to the coast, it included those islands of the eastern Aegean which were connected, not only geographically and economically but also in culture, with the mainland. Toward the east it extended up on the broad series of table-lands which, varying in altitude from 2,000 feet in the northwest to over 4,500 feet in the east, occupies the centre of the Anatolian Peninsula, a high-lying area, interrupted by ranges and by single peaks as well as by narrow river-valleys.[1] This central plateau, rimmed about on the north and the south by high mountain-chains, is broken on the northwest and west into single groups; on their slopes rise the streams uniting to form the great rivers which, after flowing through gorges cut down deep into the limestone rock, continue their courses through ever-widening plains into the Propontis and the Aegean. Between the plains that touch the western coast rise mountain-ranges, which reach down, like the fingers of a giant's hand, from the mass of the plateau to the sea, to emerge again as the islands near the coast. These mountains with their mines and timber, the well-watered plains with a fertile soil which produced rich stores of grain and fruit, and the cities which developed into centres of industry and

[a] Cicero *de Imp. Cn. Pomp.* 14.   [b] See Chap. VI note 30.

34

commerce, alike contributed to the wealth that made this land a valuable possession.

The greater part of western Anatolia in ancient times was divided into three main districts, Mysia on the north, Lydia in the centre, and Caria on the south, all named from the predecessors of the Greeks, but the narrow strips of plain which stretched along the Aegean seaboard, Aeolis, Ionia and Doris, took their names from those of the three branches of the Greeks who, setting forth across the Aegean, established themselves first on the islands, presumably, and then on the adjacent mainland.[c] The configuration of these three great districts shows marked divergences. In northern Mysia the mountain-masses projecting from the central plateau are interrupted by rivers which flow toward the northwest or the north and discharge their waters into the Propontis.[2] Chief among them are the streams known in Antiquity as Rhyndacus and Macestus; the former, from sources on the northeastern border of Lydia, flows northwestward, the latter, rising some fifty miles farther west in the Lake of Simav, flows westward and north until it joins the Rhyndacus near the sea. West of the Macestus, a series of smaller streams, rising in Mysia itself, also empty into the Propontis. All these rivers cut the mountain-area into distinct highland groups, with a bewildering succession of peaks and ridges broken by small plains, many of extraordinary fertility. Of these groups the most westerly is Mt. Ida, whose projecting spurs separate the Propontis from the Aegean and jut forward to the Hellespont. Its southern and most mountainous portion, cut by the rich valley of the river Scamander, was the Troad, more famous in song and story than any other region in the Hellenic world.

South of the Troad the Mysian coast is indented by the Gulf of Adramyttium, the estuary of the Euenus, most northerly of the streams which enter the Aegean. Still farther south, the seaboard is broken by the bays into which flow the other four great rivers of the western littoral, the Caïcus, the Hermus, the Caÿster and the Maeander. Unlike the streams of northern Mysia, all these flow westward, and their basins are barred off from one another by well-marked ranges that in narrow, approximately parallel lines extend from the central plateau to the sea.

Of these mountain-barriers the most northerly, lying between the Caïcus and the Hermus, was in general regarded as the boundary between Mysia and Lydia.[3] South of the Hermus, the similar ranges of Tmolus and Messogis, projecting together as one mass from the central plateau, are divided at first by a narrow valley, but soon, diverging widely, they continue their separate parallel courses to the Aegean.[4] Between them lies the valley of the Caÿster. Messogis, forming the northern watershed of the Maeander, was by some considered the southern boundary of Lydia, but in Roman times, at least, this district was regarded as extending to the Maeander itself.[5] These great ranges, on reaching the coast, jut out far into the Aegean, for Tmolus, after forming the mountainous peninsula of Erythrae, which protects the Gulf of Smyrna on the south, appears again as the island of Chios, and Messogis also extends into the sea as the conspicuous headland of Mt. Mycale and beyond this as the island of Samos.[d]

The wealth of Lydia was centered in its two great river-basins. The Hermus, rising in the mountains of the borderland of Mysia between the sources of the Rhyndacus and the Macestus,[e] flows southwestward through the district, skirting the northern edge of an old volcanic region called the "Burned Country" (Catacecaumene).[6] For the first part of its course, the river winds through a narrow valley in the mountain-country to its junction with the Cogamis, an inconsiderable stream flowing from the southeast.[7] From here, the combined rivers are carried westward into the wide and extraordinarily fertile basin around Sardis, which the geographer Strabo, writing at the beginning of the Christian Era, adjudged "the best of all plains."[f] Farther west, the river-basin broadens out still more widely into the Hyrcanian Plain, where the river varyingly known as the Hyllus and the Phrygius enters the Hermus from the north.[8] This plain is abruptly terminated on the southwest by the isolated massif of Mt. Sipylus. The western extension of this mountain, closing in to meet a projecting spur of the northern watershed of the Hermus, forms a narrow gateway, through which the river forces its way to the alluvial plain at its entry into the Aegean.

Farther to the south is the basin of the Lydian Caÿster, which, rising in the narrow valley where the outspread fingers of Mts. Tmolus and Messogis diverge, flows westward between the two ranges, increased by tributaries which enter it from the mountain-walls on either side. Both its upper and its lower courses run through prosperous plains, the first, the region of the Cilbiani, described as "wide, thickly-settled and productive,"[9] the second, a broad valley, ranked by Strabo with the valley of the Hermus.[10] Near the sea the Caÿster breaks through a

---

d See Philippson II p. 94f. and *Milet* III 5, p. 21f.   e See above p. 35.
f Strabo XIII p. 626; see also p. 627.

line of coastal hills into a silted marshland, which was once the Bay of Ephesus.

South of the range of Messogis lies the broad valley of the winding Maeander. Rising in a lake on the side of the great range of Sultan Dağ, an extension of the southern rim of the central plateau, the main stream descends for about a mile to the plain in front of the city of Apameia,[g] where four other streams immediately join it.[11] After traversing a flat marshy basin, it winds its tortuous course in great gorges through the mountains of southeastern Phrygia to the Plain of Hierapolis, where it is joined by the Lycus. This stream, rising in a swamp south of the mountain-group whose northern side is broken by the gorges of the Maeander,[12] cuts its way in a deep ravine to its junction with the greater river.[h] From here their combined waters flow westward through a broad plain to the sea. In Antiquity the river emptied into an arm of the Gulf of Miletus, which formed a gateway between the headland of Mycale and the mountain-masses on the Carian side.[i]

These rivers were the chief factors in the development of the cultural and economic life of Asia Minor, for, as will presently be shown,[j] through their valleys led the highways over which the influence of Hellenism penetrated to the remote interior and the trade of the ports was carried to the East. But while they brought prosperity to these ports, they also ultimately wrought their destruction. In their upper courses these streams are swift and their rapid waters have constantly carried down a weight of soil. Even in Antiquity their alluvial deposits had begun to cut off the ports from the sea.[13] Today, one arm of the Gulf of Miletus has disappeared and the other has become an inland lake, and the once busy harbour of Ephesus is completely silted up. Smyrna alone has survived, and even it, although situated some distance from the mouth of the Hermus, has been saved only by the diversion of the river's course.

South of the Maeander was the district of Caria, a rugged mountain-region, projecting westward from the central plateau.[k] Like those in Mysia, the Carian mountains are divided transversely into ranges by rivers running from southeast to northwest, the Morsynus, the Harpasus and the Marsyas, which cut their way to the Maeander through deep valleys, alternately narrowing to precipitous canyons

[g] See below p. 125.
[i] See Philippson v p. 2f. and *Milet* III 5, p. 7f.
[k] See Philippson v pp. 1 and 15f.

[h] See Philippson IV p. 85f.
[j] See below p. 39f.

and expanding into plains of considerable size.[14] In the east is the fertile table-land of Tabae,[l] bounded on the north by the wall of Mt. Salbacus[m] and its westward extension, and on the east by the high range which separates Caria from the plateau of Cibyratis. The streams of this region drain into the canyon of an affluent of the upper Harpasus.

On the west, the mountains of Caria descend steeply to the sea, leaving only a narrow fringe of land along the water's edge, bordered by a line of cities. The one river that empties into the Aegean, the Cybersus,[n] has a broad fertile basin, but its course is short. The Carian coast, however, is more deeply indented than any other part of the Aegean littoral. The greatest indentation of all, the Gulf of Cos, lies between the mountainous peninsulas of Halicarnassus and Cnidus, which, themselves cut by many smaller bays, run out far into the Aegean and enclose, at the ends of their finger-like projections, the island of Cos. From the southern side of the Peninsula of Cnidus, another long and jagged spur of land (the Peninsula of Loryma) extends toward the island of Rhodes, some fifteen miles away across the Strait of Marmaris. To the east, around the corner formed by this spur, the river Indus enters the Mediterranean in a wide plain which it reaches after cutting the mountains of the interior. The deep ravines, flanked by great terraces, through which this river flows in its upper course form a natural boundary between Caria and Lycia.[o] But on the coast, the river and the boundary did not correspond, for southeast of the mouth of the Indus the broad Gulf of Telmessus extends far inland, and its northern side, around the city of Daedala, belonged to the Rhodian Republic,[15] while Telmessus, on the southern shore, a possession of Pergamum in the second century, was finally attached to Lycia.

East of Mysia and Lydia was Phrygia, high up on the central plateau and separated from the western districts by the rough mountainous country through which the great rivers of the Aegean seaboard have to force their way to the coast.[16] The northern portion is a high-lying steppe broken by isolated mountain-peaks and occasional areas of great fertility.[p] Toward the east is a relatively depressed basin in which several minor streams unite to form the Sangarius. The main affluent of this river, however, is the Tembris, which, rising close to the sources of the Rhyndacus and the Hermus, flows to the east, joining the San-

---

[l] See Philippson IV p. 95 and v p. 107f.   [m] See Philippson IV p. 89f.
[n] For the name see a fragmentary inscription from Mylasa, *A.M.* xv (1890), p. 265f., no. 18.
[o] See Philippson v pp. 98 and 104 and (for the river) *Reisen* I p. 146f.
[p] See Philippson III p. 106.

garius near the ancient city of Gordium to round back with that tortuous stream to the west again and then north into the Euxine.[q] The watershed between these eastward and westward flowing rivers formed the northern boundary of Phrygia, and here, along the course of the upper Tembris, lay the region of Phrygia Epictetus, the "Newly-acquired," long a bone of contention between the monarchs of Pergamum and Bithynia.[r]

Along the eastern boundary of Phrygia, beyond the sources of the Sangarius, lay the temple-state of Pessinus and the bleak region which became the home of the Galatian tribesmen.[s] The southeastern corner of Phrygia is drained by the Caÿster,[t] which runs through a fertile plain, to lose itself in a lake near the border of Lycaonia. From here, along the southern side of the district stretches the high range of Sultan Dağ,[u] which separates Phrygia from the region of the great lakes in northern and eastern Pisidia and on the southwest breaks up into the mountainous country cut by the Lycus and the upper course of the Maeander.

Nowhere, perhaps, has Nature dictated more precisely than in western Anatolia the courses of the principal means of communication. Whether the seat of the government which dominated the Aegean coast was at Boğaz Köy in eastern Galatia, as in the Hittite period, or at Gordium, during the Phrygian supremacy, or even at Susa, under Persian rule, the great highways from the sea to the interior led along the same tracks. These courses were followed also by Romans, Byzantines and Turks, and, even now, when the camel has been displaced by the locomotive and the motor-car, the routes have undergone no essential change.

These time-honoured lines of communication between the Aegean and the East led up the Hermus and the Maeander and over the mountains at the rivers' sources to the central plateau, thence advancing to the Euphrates and beyond. That which followed the valley of the Hermus was the so-called "Royal Road" of the Persians, which long before their time had been used both for commerce and for the purposes of the government.[17] Up to the ancient city of Sardis led two branches, from Smyrna and Ephesus respectively, the first over a low pass south of Mt. Sipylus, the second over a saddle near the western

[q] See below p. 302. [r] See Chap. I note 56. [s] See above p. 6.
[t] The Akar Çay, to be distinguished from the Lydian Caÿster, the Küçük Menderes (see above p. 36).
[u] See below p. 454.

39

end of the range of Tmolus, where a Hittite monument still shows its course. East of Sardis, the united road followed the Hermus past the junction with the Cogamis; then, leaving the river, it traversed the "Burned Country," and so, not far from the modern railway, crossed the mountains into Phrygia. From here in the time of the Hittites the main route led eastward through central Anatolia; but in the Persian, as well as in the Graeco-Roman, period the great road probably diverged southward along the Phrygian Caÿster to the Lycaonian steppe. Over this road the Lydian monarch, Croesus, set forth from Sardis to fight his disastrous battle with the Persian Cyrus, and it also saw his return from that crushing defeat.

Less romantic, perhaps, than this ancient road, but of greater commercial importance was the Maeander route, which carried the bulk of the trade between the port of Ephesus and the interior.[18] Later in origin, probably, than the Royal Road, this Southern Highway was a more direct means of communication with the East and freer from natural obstacles. From Ephesus this road led through an easy pass in the western extension of Messogis to the Maeander and up that river to the Plain of Hierapolis. Here, where the Maeander comes down from the northeast through the gorges of the Phrygian highlands, the road turned southward along the Lycus, which it followed to its source, veering northward again to the ancient city of Celaenae, later renamed Apameia, above the plain where five streams meet to form the Maeander. After ascending rapidly over an abrupt rise to the central plateau, it proceeded northeastward through a great trough between the mountains and then southeastward along the course of the Phrygian Caÿster to Lycaonia and Cappadocia or Cilicia. From Celaenae to the Plain of Hierapolis this was the route of Xerxes, when he led his host against Greece, and over this section also, in the reverse direction, the younger Cyrus brought his troops in his ill-starred attempt to wrest the Persian throne from his brother. In the Hellenistic period this highway served as the principal thoroughfare for the Seleucid monarchs between Syria and the Aegean, as the names of the cities which they founded or refounded along its course clearly testify, and at the beginning of the Christian Era it was described as the "common road" used by all who travelled from Ephesus to the East.

The care of the highways leading through the Pergamene Kingdom was regarded by its rulers as a matter of prime importance. A "royal law," enacted, probably, by Eumenes II or Attalus II,[v] ordained that

[v] O.G.I. 483 (see Chap. V note 47).

these roads should have a width of at least thirty feet and that they should be kept in repair and free from encumbrances of any kind. It may be assumed without question that under these monarchs the government improved and developed not only the great highways from the West to the East but also the transverse routes which ran from north to south through the kingdom.

Of these transverse routes, the most westerly led along the coast itself from the Hellespont to Adramyttium, and thence along the Aegean to the mouth of the Caïcus, whence a branch ran eastward up the valley of this stream past Pergamum, while the main road continued southward to Smyrna and Ephesus, where it formed a junction with the Southern Highway.[19] Here, accordingly, it left the coast but continued in a southerly direction over the Maeander near Tralles and led up the valley of the Carian Marsyas to Stratoniceia, whence it crossed the mountains of southern Caria to Physcus on the Strait of Marmaris opposite Rhodes. Under the Romans this route, which connected the extreme north of the province of Asia with its southern limit, was destined to become a thoroughfare of great importance. Its usefulness was perceived by the organizer of the province, Manius Aquilius, who made it one of his first cares to repair, not only the Southern Highway, but also the section of this road that lay between Adramyttium and Ephesus, as well as the route from the mouth of the Caïcus to Pergamum.[w] He recorded his achievement in a series of milestones constituting the earliest official record of Roman rule in Asia.

A second transverse route, also of much importance, connecting the Propontis with the interior, led directly through the centre of the Pergamene Kingdom. Beginning at Cyzicus, this road at first followed in general the course of the lower Macestus as far as the deep gorge through which the river cleaves the mountains of eastern Mysia; from here, turning to the southwest, it traversed the rugged highland-country north of the upper Caïcus, finally descending into the broad valley near the springs which were usually regarded as the sources of the river, some thirty-five miles east of Pergamum.[20] From this plain the road, continuing southward, crossed without difficulty the low watershed which separates the basins of the Caïcus and the Hermus, and so reached Sardis and the Royal Road. Diverging from this at the entrance to the valley of the Cogamis, it led up this broad basin to the watershed at the river's source, where it crossed the mountains to

[w] See Chap. VI note 40.

the Plain of Hierapolis, here making a connexion with the Southern Highway.

This was an ancient route and had seen the passage of great armies. Xerxes led his soldiers over it from the Plain of Hierapolis at least as far as Sardis, and Alexander used it in the reverse direction when, after his victory on the Granicus, he advanced southward to the Lydian capital. It was regarded both by the Seleucids and the kings of Pergamum as the chief means of communication between north and south, as is shown by the sites of their cities, the Mysian Stratoniceia, situated at the point where the road enters the valley of the Caïcus, and Attaleia, a little further to the southeast.[x] Its continuation along the Cogamis, moreover, was dominated by the important city of Philadelpheia,[y] founded by Attalus II in the desire, evidently, of controlling this southerly section which led to the Maeander.

Farther to the north and east, routes connected the southeastern corner of the Propontis with Dorylaeum on the Tembris in northern Phrygia.[21] From this great centre many roads diverged, leading to the east, the southeast and the southwest. Of these, one led to Pessinus, the seat of the temple of the Great Mother, and onward into Lycaonia. Another traversed central Phrygia to Apameia, and still another, leading up the Tembris, continued toward the southwest, ultimately reaching Philadelpheia; the former of these, near the rock on which stands the fortress of Afyon Karahisar, crossed the road—probably a section of the Royal Road—which followed the valley of the Phrygian Caÿster to meet the Southern Highway near Ipsus, the "bottle-neck" through which passed the great routes leading to the East.

Thus a network of roads extended over the country that became the Roman province of Asia. The two great river-valleys carried the trade between the Aegean and the Euphrates, making possible the exchange of the manufactured goods of the West for the produce of the East. By the transverse routes the distant ports on the Propontis and the southeastern corner of the Aegean were brought into communication, not only with one another, but also with the thoroughfares leading to the Orient.

In keeping with the great variety of the physical characteristics of western Asia Minor, a land made up of rugged mountains and rich river-bottoms, was that variety of products which Cicero praised. The widely different character of the four districts which composed the

[x] See below p. 124.   [y] See Chap. V note 17.

country was reflected in the forms of wealth which they severally contained. But, taken together, the great fertility of the soil, the natural resources of minerals and timber, and the important industries, which even in remote Antiquity attained to a high degree of development and afforded a great stimulus to commerce, made western Anatolia a land coveted by the kings of Persia, by the successors of Alexander and, after them, by the Romans.[z]

In Mysia, where the interior was a great mountain-area cut by narrow valleys, where there were but few routes of importance and the ports along the Aegean were largely dependent on a carrying-trade, the chief wealth consisted of timber and minerals. These were exploited by the kings of Pergamum and formed the basis of the monarchs' great prosperity.[22] In the far northeast were the forests of Mt. Olympus on the border of Bithynia, which, extending toward the south, covered the adjacent portion of Mysia, and even in modern times have been described as impenetrable.[23] These forests, however, were remote and inaccessible, and, especially for the Pergamene kings, the principal supply of timber was furnished by the Troad. In the north, the hill-country near the entrance from the Propontis to the Hellespont took its name Pityua from the pine-tree. The main source of timber, however, was the region of Mt. Ida, which even in modern times is noted for its forests of fir and oak.[24] Although less extensive than those of the Euxine coast and the mountainous district of Cilicia on the southern slopes of the Taurus,[a] these forests afforded an abundant supply of material for the building of ships, and the wood was brought down to be sold at Aspaneus on the southern coast.[25] The pitch from these forests, moreover, was regarded as the best in Asia.[b] The region also produced a variety of ash-tree of such an excellent quality that when the bark was removed it could be palmed off as a cedar,[c] as well as the terebinth, valuable for its oil which was used for medicinal purposes.[d]

The Troad possessed also mineral-resourses. Gold was found near Lampsacus,[e] and in the mountains southeast of Abydus on the Helles-

---

[z] For the products of western Asia Minor see Broughton in *Econ. Surv.* IV pp. 607f., 685f. and 817f.: E. Gren *Kleinasien u. d. Ostbalkan i. d. wirtschaftlichen Entwicklung d. Röm. Kaiserzeit*, p. 62f.: Hansen *Attalids*, p. 192f.

[a] Theophrastus *Hist. Plant.* IV 5, 5.

[b] Pliny *N.H.* XIV 128. See also Vergil *Georg.* III 450 and IV 41: Theophrastus *Hist. Plant.* IX 2, 5f.

[c] Pliny *N.H.* XVI 62.

[d] Theophrastus *Hist. Plant.* III 15, 3: Pliny *N.H.* XIII 54; XXIV 34f.

[e] Pliny *N.H.* XXXVII 193.

pont were the mines which were regarded as the source of the wealth of Priam, the legendary King of Troy.[26] A more important region for minerals, however, was the northwestern part of Mysia, east of Mt. Ida. Here silver was mined at Argyria (which took its name from the metal), near the headwaters of the Aesepus,[27] and especially (along with lead) at Pericharaxis,[28] farther east in the upper valley of the river which has been identified varyingly as the Tarsius and the Enbeilus.[f]

Of the less precious metals, zinc seems to have been obtained in the Troad, at Andeira west of Mt. Ida.[29] According to Strabo, an ore (which was evidently zinc sulphide), when burned, became iron, and then, when heated with a certain kind of earth, distilled "mock-silver," which was alloyed with copper to make brass (*orichalcum*). There was a guild of coppersmiths at Sigeium, at the entrance to the Helles-pont,[g] and the metal itself was mined both in the central Troad and in the mountains north of Pergamum[30] near the short route which led from Adramyttium. From the Troad also came a variety of stone found at Assus, which, from its use for coffins, received the name *sarcophagus*,[31] and the island of Proconnesus in the Propontis yielded a white marble which was highly prized.[32]

In addition to forests and mines, the coast regions of Mysia were rich in products of the soil. The great plain along the southern shore of the Propontis, the commercial centre of which was the city of Cyzicus, was extremely fertile, producing grain and fruit of all kinds, especially grapes and olives.[33] In it was presumably grown the iris from which was made a famous perfume exported from Cyzicus. Farther west, the hilly region called Caresene, probably the basin of the upper Granicus, was described as "settled with many villages and beautifully cultivated."[34] In the Troad grapes grew in abundance on the hills above Parium and Lampsacus near the eastern end of the Hellespont[35] and also on the western slopes of Mt. Ida,[36] and the wheat of Assus was even exported to Persia.[37]

South of the Troad, the coast of Aeolis, a narrow strip between the mountains and the sea, and the adjacent part of Mysia were fertile regions, producing grain and fruit.[38] Especially rich were the alluvial plain of Thebe, through which flowed the Euenus, and the broad valley of the Caïcus, extending from the Aegean far into the interior. The former took its name from an ancient city which appears in the *Iliad* but in Strabo's time had long since disappeared;[39] the region,

---

[f] See note 2.   [g] *C.I.G.* 3639 and *Add.* p. 1130.

however, continued to be a rich farming country, and it also produced a kind of grape from which a perfume was manufactured, said to have been improved under the encouragement of Queen Stratonice. The valley of the Caïcus, described as "very rich and about the best land in Mysia,"[40] was the chief granary of the early Pergamene kings, whence, presumably, Philetaerus obtained the wheat and barley which he sent to Cyzicus and Attalus I the grain which he gave to Sicyon.[h]

A few miles off the coast of Aeolis lay the island of Lesbos. It had at one time a famous wood of pines, which was later burned to the ground,[i] and it also produced olives, which are still grown in great profusion.[41] The island yielded, moreover, a grayish marble and various semi-precious stones,[42] and it contained mines of iron and lead, especially in the hills at its northern end.[43] But its most famous products were its wines, which were highly esteemed in the ancient world and were exported to Egypt and to Italy.[44] One particular variety was rendered less sweet by the addition of a small amount of sea-water.

Of the districts which composed the Roman province of Asia, the richest by far was Lydia. The ranges of Tmolus and Messogis had forests, and even in the coast region, near the Ionian city of Colophon, there was a pine-forest, from which came a well-known resin.[45] Tmolus, moreover, contained gold, which was said to have been washed down by the river Pactolus and to have brought wealth to Croesus and his predecessors, but at the beginning of the Christian Era the supply had long since given out.[46] There were mines also in Mt. Sipylus, reputed to have been the source of the wealth of the legendary descendants of Pelops, but likewise exhausted in Strabo's time,[j] and the northern side of Mt. Messogis, toward the upper Caÿster, contained deposits of antimony,[47] which was used in a bronze alloy, as well as of cinnabar of a particularly excellent quality.[48] The mountains of Lydia also produced a saltpetre which was considered the best of all varieties.[k]

On the other hand, Lydia itself was largely lacking in quarries, although a bluish marble was found in the hilly country in the broad basin of the Hermus,[l] northwest of Sardis, and stone of various kinds seems to have been cut on the southern side of Messogis.[49] The Ionian coast, however, yielded stone of commercial value. The most famous was the variegated marble from the island of Chios, which was exported to Italy.[50] On the neighbouring coast a white variety was found

---

[h] See Chap. I notes 9 and 45.
[i] Theophrastus *Hist. Plant.* III 9, 5: Pliny *N.H.* XVI 46.
[j] Strabo XIV p. 680. [k] Pliny *N.H.* XXXI 113 (*aphronitrum*).
[l] At Marmara; see Keil-Premerstein I p. 61f.

near Ephesus, which was used for the Temple of Artemis,[m] and near Miletus, probably on the southern side of Mt. Latmus, there was a quarry which furnished marble for the Temple of Apollo at Didyma.[51] A grayish stone was quarried at Teos, which seems to have been exported in large quantities,[52] and there were quarries at Erythrae for milestones and farther north, at Phocaea, for a variety of stone used for pavements.[53] This coast also produced pigments, both a green chalk used for painting ships, found near Smyrna,[54] and a white variety, obtained from a mine on the island of Samos.[55]

Far more important than the mineral wealth of Lydia were the products of the land; for the broad valleys of the Hermus, the Caÿster and the Maeander were all famous for their fertility. The basin of the Hermus and its tributaries, in particular, was rich in fruit and grain,[56] and the plain of the lower Maeander also yielded quantities of fruit, especially olives and figs.[57] But, above all, Lydia was famous for its wines, grown in the interior on the lower slopes of Tmolus and Messogis and in the treeless volcanic region of Catacecaumene, the product of which was said to be "inferior in quality to none of the celebrated wines."[58] Well-known wines were also made in the coast region of Ionia, around Smyrna, Clazomenae, Erythrae and Ephesus,[59] and especially on the island of Chios, the sweetish wine of which was held in great favour throughout the ancient world.[60] Chios also exported figs, much esteemed in Italy,[61] as well as a white mastich-gum, which was famous in Antiquity—as it is today—and commanded a high price.[62] Samos also, although its wine was regarded as inferior and its grain was not always sufficient for the inhabitants' needs, exported olive-oil and was described as a rich and productive island.[63]

The great prosperity of Lydia and Ionia, however, was due in large measure to the development of trade and industry. Whereas the other districts of western Asia Minor were rich primarily in natural resources, these, together with the nearest part of Mysia and the adjacent southwestern corner of Phrygia, were important industrial regions. The cities both of the interior and of the Aegean littoral were not only markets but places of manufacture as well. Their activity, in existence even in the time of the Lydian kings, was continued for centuries, and the many inscriptions of the guilds of the Roman imperial period[n] afford ample evidence that it lasted until the economic structure of Asia Minor entirely collapsed.

[m] Vitruvius x 2, 11f.
[n] See J. Oehler in *Eranos Vindobonensis* (Vienna 1893), p. 276f.

By far the most important of these industries was the manufacture of textile fabrics.[64] This was carried on in the Ionian ports, above all at Miletus, and also in the cities lying in the basins of the Hermus and Maeander, notably Sardis and Thyateira in Lydia, and Colossae, Laodiceia and Hierapolis, which, although, strictly speaking, in Phrygia, were bound by close economic ties to the Aegean ports.

As early as the sixth century before Christ, the wool of Miletus had become so celebrated that Polycrates, the ruler of Samos, imported sheep from the city for the purpose of improving his own breed.[65] In the next century it was well known in Athens,° and it soon became famous throughout the ancient world for its softness and the fineness of its quality.[66] The textiles woven from it in the city itself—notably tapestries and garments—were regarded far and wide as objects of especial luxury,[67] and even in the third and fourth centuries after Christ, the purple fabrics of Miletus were still highly esteemed.[68]

The industry was an active one also in other cities of the coast. As early as the fourth century before Christ, a law was passed at Erythrae, prohibiting the sale of any inferior wool which might lower the standard of what was an important product,[69] and at the end of the century cloaks were manufactured in Teos of wool obtained from Miletus.[70] In the following century, at Aegae in Aeolis the weaving of fabrics was so important that it became a matter of especial interest to the city-government, which protected the industry by a treaty with another community, stipulating that the inhabitants of the latter should refrain from the weaving of wool and should not impose a duty on woollen cloaks woven at Aegae.[71] At Ephesus, during the Roman imperial period, the existence of prosperous guilds of "wool-workers," "wool-dealers" and "cloak-dealers" attests the importance of the industry in the city.[72] At Phocaea and Smyrna purple garments were manufactured,[73] and from the islands of Samos and Chios came tapestries which ranked with those of Miletus.[74]

In the interior, the most important and perhaps the most ancient centre of the textile industry was Sardis. The tradition that the process of dyeing was invented in the city, while certainly untrue, shows, nevertheless, that in early days Sardis was a leader in the industry.[75] The finely-wrought carpets made in the city were used in the palace of the kings of Persia, and the purple couch-covers were known in Athens as early as 400 B.C.,[76] and these continued to be regarded as

° Aristophanes *Lysistr.* 729.

47

specialties of the place.[77] In the fourth century after Christ, the "cloak-dealers" also formed a guild in the city.[p]

Other cities of Lydia in which this industry played an important part were Philadelpheia, which had a guild of "wool-workers,"[78] and Thyateira, where there was a similar organization of "wool-dealers."[79] Thyateira, in fact, seems to have been particularly important for its dyeing-processes, for its guild of dyers was evidently unusually prosperous;[80] one of the artisans, Lydia, "the seller of purple," even travelled to Macedonia, where she was converted at Philippi by St. Paul.[q]

As love of splendour and extravagance increased, Lydia seems also to have produced a fabric which was interwoven with threads of gold.[81] One particular variety, employed for both tapestries and clothing was called by the Romans "Attalic."[82] Late writers explained the name by the supposition that this fabric was used in the palace of the kings of Pergamum, but, in view of the general tendency to connect articles of great luxury with these monarchs, it is highly probable that the term originated as a trade-name in Rome.

The great rivals of the Ionian and Lydian cities in the textile industry were Colossae, Laodiceia and Hierapolis. Although they seem not to have begun their production until a later period, they nevertheless attained to great fame for their fabrics.[83] The glossy black wool of Laodiceia, in particular, was regarded as even finer than that of Miletus and was a source of wealth to the city. At Hierapolis there were guilds not only of "wool-workers" but also of "carpet-weavers" and "purple-dyers."[84] It was said that the water of the city, heavily charged with lime, was so well suited for dyeing that the purple wool, which was dyed with madder-root, rivalled that which was elsewhere treated with cochineal or the genuine purple mussel.[r]

Although the chief textile products of Ionia and Lydia were woollen fabrics, these regions were known also for their linen. While the principal centres of this industry in Antiquity were Egypt, Phoenicia and Colchis at the eastern end of the Euxine Sea,[85] the weaving of linen, during the Roman imperial period at least, was one of the industries of this part of Asia Minor. It is not improbable that flax was grown in Lydia in Antiquity, as it is in certain parts of the district in modern times.[86] There were prosperous guilds of linen-weavers at Miletus and Thyateira and also at Tralles in the valley of the

p *Ins. Sardis* 168. q *Acta Apost.* XVI 14.
r Strabo XIII p. 630. For the water see below p. 127.

Maeander.[87] Sardis was famous for its linen nets,[s] and even fish-nets of an especially durable character were made in the province of Asia from the broom-plant.[t]

Next in importance, perhaps, to textiles ranked the pottery, which was produced on a large scale and constituted one of the principal exports of the region. It was manufactured at Thyateira, where, during the early third century after Christ, the potters formed an important guild.[u] It was made also at Tralles and Pergamum,[88] but the principal centre of the industry was the Ionian coast. Even in the time of the poet Alcaeus, in the late seventh century before Christ, the drinking-cups made at Teos were famous,[v] and from this period onward the pottery of Miletus and Samos found a wide market. As excavations have shown, Milesian ware was not only sold on the coast of Asia Minor and the adjacent islands, but exported to the city's colonies on the northern shore of the Euxine Sea and even to Egypt,[w] and pottery made at Samos, so widely known that at the end of the third century the term "Samian ware" denoted clay vessels in general, was exported not only to Italy but also to Egypt and in the first century after Christ was used especially for table-services.[89]

Of importance also was the hide and leather industry. Parchment was made at Pergamum for the use of the great library founded by Eumenes II,[90] and there was a guild of leather-workers at Mitylene on the island of Lesbos.[91] Lydia, however, was the chief centre of production. At Thyateira and Philadelpheia and probably at Attaleia there were prosperous associations of tanners and workers in leather.[92] On the Ionian coast, Colophon was famous for its production of shoes.[93]

In addition to these useful products, there were also various articles of luxury, in keeping with the Lydians' reputation for the enjoyment of the amenities of life. The perfumes of Sardis were famous and were excelled only by those produced at Ephesus; various kinds were made also at Smyrna, Mitylene and Pergamum.[x] The art of metal-working also prospered; for two famous chasers of silver worked at Mitylene, there was a guild of goldsmiths and silversmiths at Smyrna, similar associations of coppersmiths existed at Thyateira and Hierapolis,[94] and so prominent were the silversmiths at Ephesus that St. Paul almost lost his life by provoking their enmity.[y] As a contribution to the

[s] Pollux v 26.
[t] Pliny *N.H.* xix 15.
[u] *C.I.G.* 3485=*I.G.R.* iv 1205.
[v] Athenaeus xi 61, p. 481 A.
[w] See H. Prinz *Funde aus Naukratis=Klio, Beih.* vii (1908), pp. 38f. and 42.
[x] Athenaeus xv 38f., pp. 689 A—691 D: Pliny *N.H.* xiii 10 and xx 177.
[y] *Acta Apost.* xix 24f.

gastronomic art, moreover, Clazomenae manufactured a much prized variety of *garum*, a preparation of the internal organs of fish steeped in brine which was highly esteemed and commanded an exorbitant price in Rome.[95]

The wealth of Phrygia, on the other hand, except for the textile industries of the cities in its extreme southwestern corner, consisted almost entirely of the products of the soil. The district had, indeed, an asset of great commercial importance, namely the quarries from which was taken the famous white, slightly translucent, marble with rich purple markings now called "pavonazetto."[96] This was quarried at Docimeium in the centre of the district, but as the administration, at least under the Romans, was carried on at the more important Synnada, somewhat to the southwest, the marble took its name from this city. It was used for sarcophagi in Asia,[z] but its principal market was Rome, to which, at the beginning of the Christian Era, monoliths and huge slabs were exported. Another and less famous marble came from the mountains near Thiunta on the upper Maeander, not far from Hierapolis, where it was extensively used for sarcophagi.[97]

Otherwise, the wealth of Phrygia lay in the forests with which its mountains were covered. Even in modern times they are clad with great growths of oaks and pines,[a] and in Antiquity they also produced cedars.[b] The lower slopes afforded a grazing-country where horses were reared, and the heights around the sources of the Maeander near Apameia produced grapes, the juice of which was especially suited for making a highly-esteemed honey-wine.[98]

In Caria there was a vast difference in wealth between the coast strip occupied by the Greek cities and the comparative poverty of the interior. This strip was, indeed, a narrow one, save for the broad basin of the Cybersus and its tributaries and, in the extreme south, the flat land surrounding the lake that lay back of Caunus.[99] These were areas of great fertility, in which fruit, especially olives and figs, grew in abundance. Carian olive-oil seems to have been known in Athens as early as the fourth century before Christ,[c] and later both oil and wine were exported from Pidasa and Euromus northwest of the Plain of Mandalya.[d] Dried figs also, especially those from Caunus, were shipped

[z] *Alt. v. Hierap.* nos. 56, 158, 209, 213, 323 and 335.
[a] See Cuinet *Turquie* IV p. 196.
[b] Theophrastus *Hist. Plant.* IV 5, 2: Pliny *N.H.* XIII 53; XVI 137.
[c] Ophelio, quoted in Athenaeus II 74, p. 67 A.
[d] *Milet* I 3, p. 350f., no. 149, ll. 19 and 41 (see Chap. IV note 78).

in large quantities to Egypt and Italy,[100] and the valley of the Cybersus produced an excellent variety of hemp.[e]

In general, however, the cultivable land between the mountains of Caria and the sea was so limited that it did not more than suffice for the needs of its inhabitants. At Iasus, on the Gulf of Bargylia, the soil was so poor that the people of the city were said to be dependent for their livelihood on fishing in the Aegean.[f] Halicarnassus and Myndus, having more fertile territories, produced wines, and the former is still surrounded by orchards which are rich in figs and other fruits.[101] Among the articles of export from this region was honey from the neighbouring town of Theangela, which in the third century before Christ was shipped to Egypt.[102] The long peninsula of Cnidus, although less fertile, also produced a well-known wine, recommended for its medicinal qualities, which was exported to Italy as well as to Greece and Egypt.[103] Cnidus also exported vegetables, in particular onions,[g] as well as reeds for making pens[104] and oils for various medicaments.[105]

The coast region of Caria had also mineral resources. In the north, Mt. Latmus, east of Miletus, contained iron, and traces of an ancient mine are still to be seen near its southeastern end.[106] There was an important silver mine in the hills behind Myndus at the end of the long promontory which took its name from the city.[107] At Iasus there was a quarry of mottled red and white marble,[108] and the mountain west of Mylasa yielded an excellent white limestone, which served for the construction of the public buildings of the city but seems to have been restricted to local use.[109]

Close to the Carian shore lay the rich island of Cos. Blessed with a fertile soil, it produced fruit of all kinds, but especially grapes.[110] These were dried as raisins but were used chiefly for the famous white wine of the island; as at Lesbos and other places, a certain amount of seawater was added to the juice.[111] This wine was exported in large quantities to Italy, and jars in which it was shipped, like those which contained Cnidian wine, have been found at Pompeii. The industries of the island included the manufacture of earthenware and copper vessels; as early as 300 B.C. the coppersmiths and potters were important enough to receive special portions of a sacrificial victim.[112] More famous products were articles of luxury, perfumes[h] and, above all, a silken

[e] Pliny *N.H.* xix 174.
[f] Strabo xiv p. 658: Athenaeus iii 66, p. 105 E. See also Pliny *N.H.* ix 33.
[g] Pliny *N.H.* xix 101.
[h] Pliny *N.H.* xiii 5: Athenaeus xv 38, p. 688 E.

fabric, which was made as early as the fourth century before Christ, from a species of silkworm bred on the island.[113] This fabric, which took its name from Cos, of especially fine, gauze-like, texture and usually dyed purple, was greatly affected by Roman women at the beginning of the Christian Era. But as it is never mentioned after the first century after Christ, it may have proved unable to compete with the better silks imported from the Orient and thus have fallen into disuse.

The interior of Caria, in contrast to the coast region, was of little economic importance, and its products, natural and industrial, were but few. The basin of the Marsyas around Alabanda, where it widens out into a broad plain to receive a tributary, was fertile,[i] and here a hemp was grown which was recommended as especially good for hunting-nets.[j] The mountains around the city also yielded a black marble,[k] and somewhere in Caria a variety of lime was found which was exported as a preservative for grain.[l] Otherwise, the wealth of the district consisted chiefly in the great fir forests which covered its mountains,[114] but, as in Mysia also, the very character of the country which produced them made the transportation of the timber a difficult and toilsome process.[m]

Great as was the natural wealth of western Asia Minor, the exploitation of its resources was dependent on the great routes which led from the interior to the sea. Along these were the manufacturing centres of the country, and the coast cities which lay at their termini were not merely themselves centres of industry but also the ports of shipment whence both natural and manufactured products were exported throughout the ancient world. The development of these cities and the busy trade to which largely they owed their great prosperity were due to the commercial shrewdness of the Greeks who had built up a series of settlements along the Aegean littoral. The importance and the history of these cities will form the subject of the following chapters.

[i] See Philippson v p. 39.　　[j] Pliny *N.H.* xix 174.　　[k] Pliny *N.H.* xxxvi 62.
[l] Pliny *N.H.* xviii 305.　　[m] See Cuinet *Turquie* iii p. 649.

CHAPTER III

THE GREEK STATES OF THE
WESTERN COAST

IT would seem as though Nature herself had ordained that the western seaboard of Asia Minor should become a land of rich and powerful cities. The excellent harbours, the highways which led up the river-valleys into the interior, and the abundant natural wealth of the country, all contributed to the development of great seaports. There was, furthermore, the advantage that along this coast led the sea-lanes which connected the Euxine Sea and the Propontis with Egypt and the ports of the eastern Mediterranean. It was to be expected that these opportunities would attract settlers from Greece, for among the outstanding characteristics of the early Hellenes were a love of adventure and an eager spirit of enterprise.

These emigrants from Greece, gradually moving eastward across the Aegean and taking possession of one island after another, arrived, presumably after a long course of time, on the mainland of Asia Minor.[1] According to current tradition, which is supported by various dialects later spoken in their cities, they established themselves in those districts which lay directly across the Aegean from their original homes.

Thus the coast of Mysia—the region which subsequently bore the name Aeolis—and the island of Lesbos were occupied by settlers from northern Greece, whose peculiar dialect, akin to that of the Thessalians and Boeotians, continued in use, although perhaps in an artificially revived form, as late as the early years of the Christian Era.[2] Farther south, emigrants from various parts of the coast of central Greece, Attica and Euboea, and perhaps from Boeotia also, took possession of a long stretch of seaboard, where they founded settlements extending from Phocaea, north of the Hermus, to Miletus on the southern side of the Maeander. These settlers gradually banded together in an organization for mutual protection, calling themselves Ionians and, in some cases, giving to their city-tribes names taken from those of their original homes.[3] Their dialect, though related to that of central Greece, differed somewhat from any spoken in the mother-country. Still farther south, near the southwestern corner of Asia Minor, was another group of settlements, founded by Dorians from the northern Peloponnese. They lay chiefly on the islands, the most notable of which were Rhodes and Cos, but they extended also to the mainland, where they included

both Halicarnassus and Cnidus at the entrance to the Gulf of Cos. Save
for Halicarnassus, which in the fifth century had adopted the Ionian
speech, these communities spoke the Dorian dialect which had been
brought from Argolis, and some of them retained the old Dorian
tribe-names.[4] They perpetuated the memory of their common origin
by a festival in honour of their patron-deity Apollo, celebrated originally by an "hexapolis" of six cities, later, by the expulsion of Halicarnassus, reduced to a "pentapolis."[5]

The Greek immigrants brought with them to Asia their religious
rites and their civic institutions, their love of independence and bold
adventure, above all, the intellectual and artistic habits of mind which
were especially characteristic of their race. Profiting by the greater
richness of Asia Minor in fertility of the soil and in natural resources,
as well as by the increased opportunities for trade, these newcomers
speedily attained to a high degree of prosperity. At the end of the
eighth century they had become leaders not only in commerce but
also in literature and learning. Their ships had begun to sail far and
wide, and their men of letters included the composers of the Homeric
epics and a brilliant galaxy of lyric poets, as well as the earliest
philosophers and the first writers of prose.

As in Greece itself, so also in the Hellenic communities of Asia, the
seventh century was a period of wide colonial expansion. The cities
which had been founded by settlers from across the Aegean proceeded,
in their turn, to send out colonists.[6] The reasons for this expansion
may be sought in a rapid growth of population and a correspondingly
rapid development of industries. It became necessary, especially in the
case of a city which had a limited territory, to obtain food for the inhabitants and to provide the landless with cultivable ground. Suitable
sites, accordingly, were chosen, and gradually groups of settlers, some
led by economic considerations, some impelled, perhaps, by political
conditions at home, moved to these places and became permanent
residents. Thus arose a great number of colonies, not only on the coasts
of the neighbouring Hellespont and Propontis, but also on the shore
of the Euxine, in Cilicia on the east and in Italy and Gaul on the west,
and emigrants from Asia Minor spread over a large part of the
Mediterranean basin, carrying with them the language and the civilization of their Grecian homes.

In some cases, perhaps, these settlements were originally trading-
stations, but, whatever their origin, they became commercial centres,
which provided raw materials, especially foodstuffs and timber, for

the older cities and served as markets for these cities' exports. In the course of time they became *poleis*—self-governing communities of citizens—each having a rural territory of its own. A relationship was nevertheless maintained with a "mother-city," for while the settlers did not necessarily all come from the same place, the tradition of a connexion with a particular city seems to have arisen from the predominance of some group among them, and this tie became officially recognized. Although the relationship between the mother-city and the daughter was only sentimental, save possibly in time of war, there was frequently an interchange of civic rights or even of such privileges as a reciprocal remission of tariffs.

During the sixth century, as the kings of Lydia extended their power, the neighbouring cities, especially those of Ionia, came under the sway of these monarchs. When the Persians succeeded the Lydians as rulers of western Asia Minor, the cities became subject to them. But in 479 B.C., the year which saw the collapse of Xerxes's ambitious attempt to conquer Greece, the Greeks of Asia defeated the Persians in a battle on the promontory of Mycale, destroying their army and burning their fleet.[7] Thus the cities of Ionia were freed from Persian rule.

After this notable success, Athens, taking the lead against the enemy of all the Greeks, organized the communities of the whole Aegean seaboard, together with its islands, into an "alliance" sometimes called by modern writers the Confederacy of Delos from the island where its treasury was originally placed.[8] Gradually, too, the cities of the Hellespont, the Propontis and even the Euxine, together with some on the coasts of Lycia, Pamphylia and Cilicia, were added to the organization. The purpose of this "alliance," which, at one time or another, included about 350 communities, at least 160 of them in Asia Minor or on the neighbouring islands, was to secure a common defence against Persian aggression. Under this arrangement, while the several cities had no obligation to one another, each was bound by an agreement with Athens as "leader," by the terms of which the "leader" had command of all military operations in time of war, and in time of peace a dominant influence over the foreign relations of the member-cities. These were under obligation to contribute ships or money for a joint defence, but in most cases they took the easier course of commuting the contribution of ships into a fixed payment of money on a yearly basis, and when in 454 B.C. the common treasury was removed to Athens, the "alliance" developed into an Athenian empire, which exacted from the cities what was, in reality, an annual tribute. But after the power of Athens was destroyed by Sparta, the Asianic cities were left to their fate, and by the shameful treaty of Antalcidas, concluded early in 386, all the Hellenic communities on the mainland of Asia Minor were declared subject to the Persian king.[9]

For just over a half-century the cities continued in this state of subjection. Then Alexander the Great, victorious over the Persians at the river Granicus, liberated the Greeks of Asia Minor. Sending his representatives to the various cities, he announced that they were henceforth free and independent.[10] The communities which had existed in the fifth century were now, to be sure, greatly reduced in number, as the result either of amalgamation or of natural decline, but those which were of sufficient size and importance were recognized as independent *poleis*. The condition, however, was imposed that the local tyrants and oligarchies which had been the instruments of Persian domination should be overthrown and that each should establish a democracy, which, it was assumed, was the normal form of government for a free Greek city.[11] Even the island communities, such as Chios, Mitylene and Cos, which the treaty of Antalcidas had not deprived of independence, were commanded to set up democratic governments and to restore to their civic rights all political exiles, *i.e.* those who in times past had been supporters of the "people's rule." By this regulation the principle was laid down that liberty and democracy were inseparable.

This restoration of the liberty of the ancient Greek communities of Asia Minor was based on the theory that those cities which had originally been free but for a time had been subject to an alien rule should again enjoy their primary status of independence.[12] Their deliverance from servitude to the Persians was, in fact, Alexander's professed purpose in beginning the war. The liberation of these cities, therefore, unlike the subsequent bestowal of the constitution of a Greek *polis* either on ancient native communities or on the cities founded by monarchs, was regarded as no mere act of grace, based on acquisition by conquest and revocable at the king's pleasure but as the restoration of an inherent right which had been lost by the treaty negotiated by Antalcidas. Whatever limitations the freedom of individual cities may have subsequently suffered from conquest or from the aggression of ambitious and unscrupulous kings, the ancient *poleis*, as re-established by Alexander, were, from the juristic point of view, independent self-governing states.

The rights of an independent Greek city-state, as fully enumerated, consisted of liberty, autonomy, exemption from any garrison and from the payment of a regular tribute.[13] They were usually stated more briefly as liberty and autonomy, signifying freedom from any master, whether local tyrant or outside ruler, and the right of the people to frame its own laws, conduct its own courts, and manage its own finances; the combination of the two terms denoted full sovereignty both in international relations and in internal administration.

The principle that a free state should be exempt from the payment of a fixed sum of money to any outside power was definitely recognized by Alexander.[14] On liberating the cities of Aeolis and Ionia, he expressly abolished the tribute which they had previously paid to the Persians, giving orders in the case of Ephesus, where a hostile oligarchy had been in power, that the amount hitherto paid to the Persian king should be paid henceforth to the Goddess Artemis.

The exemption thus recognized, however, did not free the city-state from all obligations to the king; for the relationship between them was in theory an alliance, under the terms of which each of the two contracting parties was bound to furnish assistance to the other in time of war.[15] Alexander, accordingly, expected the Greeks of Asia to support him in his campaign against the Persians. Thus he demanded ships from various states, as in the case of Chios, which was ordered to furnish twenty triremes, fully manned, to accompany the Hellenes' fleet.[16] On the other hand, as in the case of Priene, this assistance might be commuted into a money-payment, a "contribution" to be used for the purposes of the war but remissible by special order from the king. While such a contribution might be frequently demanded and, in the event of a protracted war, even be called for regularly over a number of years, there is every reason to suppose that under Alexander and most of his successors a distinction was observed between it and the tribute paid by a subject city to the monarch who was this city's ruler.

As thus constituted, the "free and autonomous" Greek states of Asia Minor maintained throughout the Hellenistic period the democratic form of government which was regarded as the special characteristic of an Hellenic *polis*. The ultimate authority was vested in the *Demos*, the body of formally enrolled adult male citizens, from whose numbers all other persons, even permanent residents, however numerous and influential, were rigorously excluded.[17] The *Demos* exercised its powers in a General Assembly, which in theory had legislative, elective, and even judicial functions. These, however, were usually limited in fact by the principle that the decrees of the Assembly must not contravene the established laws and by the transference of jurisdiction over all except political cases to the law-courts. But a greater limitation of the Assembly's activity was the lack of a power of initiation which resulted from the frequent restriction of action to proposals submitted after preliminary approval by a smaller deliberative body. This body by which legislative proposals were in most cases brought before the Assembly was the Council. The councillors, in most Asianic cities apparently elected by popular vote, held office for a limited term, usually a year but in certain places only six months.[18] In some cities these councillors, often a large body, were divided, as at Athens, into governing committees, each frequently corresponding to a city-tribe, which, acting in rotation, served for definite periods. Such committees were responsible for the transaction of the business which devolved upon the Council, and in many instances their chairmen presided over the meetings of the Assembly. In addition to the necessary action on proposals to be submitted to the Assembly—which were eventually enacted in the name of the "Council and People"— the Council exercised a general supervision over the conduct of the officials of the city and over its finances, as well as over the public buildings and the state-archives; it also granted citizenship or honours to deserving aliens and received the envoys sent by foreign states.

The actual administration of the affairs of a city-state and the enforcement of its laws devolved on a large body of officials.[19] These were usually elected by the Assembly from lists of nominees which were presented by the Council but might be increased by additions suggested by the voters. There was a growing tendency, however, toward the presentation of a complete list to which no additions were made, with the result that the recommendation of the Council became equivalent to election.

The highest of these office-holders in rank—although not in actual power—was the annually elected eponymous official, by whose name the year was designated and documents were dated. In many cases this office, which in the Hellenistic period had been shorn of most of its powers, was originally held by the head of the state. Consequently, these officials bore the imposing titles of "King," "Monarch," "Hipparch" and "Artificer" (Demiurge).[20] Another old title, more frequently found, was that of the "Ruler" (*Prytanis*), who held office at Ephesus and other places both in Ionia and in Aeolis.[21] In other cities the *eponymus* had a priestly character, as the Priest of the Sun at Rhodes or the "Overseer of Sacrifices" (*Hieropoios*) or the "Temple-Warden" (*Neopoies*).[22] Certain sacred functions may also have been performed by the "Wreath-bearer" (*Stephanephorus*), who held the eponymous office in a number of cities, first of all apparently in Miletus, where the presiding officer of a society vested with the privilege of wearing the sacred wreath of Apollo was made the *eponymus* of the city.[23]

The original powers held by this eponymous official had gradually so declined that, except for his presence at festivals and the offering of certain sacrifices, his duties seem to have been almost wholly nominal. The sacrifices, however, were often performed at his expense and he was also expected to give lavish entertainments; as a result, only wealthy citizens could accept the office, and when in a time of financial stringency no one could be found to assume the burden, the expenses had to be met from the revenues of a temple and the eponymous title was borne by the deity.[24]

The great diversity in the titles of the various eponymous officials in the cities during the Hellenistic period strongly suggests that the constitutions of the several communities dated from an earlier time when there was no attempt at a uniform system. This is equally true of the other officials who were charged with the conduct of the city's affairs. Most of them, in conformity with the democratic theory which prevented the exercise of too much power by any one man, were formed into boards, usually holding office for a year but in some cities for a term of six or even four months.[25] In our sources these boards bear different names in the various cities and all those known to us never existed in any one place. In the Rhodian Republic and in Miletus the chief civil powers were held by the "Rulers" (*Prytaneis*), usually five or six in number.[26] This title appears in many other cities also, applied either to the *eponymus* or to the governing committees of the Council, so that it is often impossible to determine whether the *prytaneis* who appear in the extant documents were members of such a committee or officials elected by the Assembly. In cities where no *prytaneis* are known, there were "Honour-holders" (*Timouchoi*)[27] or "Presidents" (*Prostatai*),[28] whose duties corresponded to those of the *prytaneis*, but in these cases also it is often uncertain whether they were a committee of the Council or a board of elected officials.

Unfortunately, the extant documents—principally decrees passed by the Assemblies—yield little information concerning the details of government and the actual administration of public affairs in the Asianic city-states during the Hellenistic period. It is, nevertheless, possible to obtain from our sources some knowledge of the manifold functions performed by their governing boards. It devolved upon these to initiate measures brought before the Council or the Assembly, to render judicial decisions in minor cases and impose small fines, to manage the revenues of the city and make appropriations for purposes approved by the Assembly, to take part in public ceremonies, to appoint envoys, and to represent the city in dealing with other states.

Besides these officials, most cities had also a board of "Generals" (*Strategoi*), originally charged, as is evident from their title, with the conduct of military affairs.[29] It was presumably their duty, when the city was compelled to raise an army, either for its own use or for the aid of an ally, to equip, and perhaps even to lead, these soldiers. But gradually—as was the case in Athens also—the *strategoi* were transformed into civil officials whose duties did not differ materially from those of the *prytaneis*.

Other boards were those of the "Auditors" (*Exetastai*),[30] who, properly examiners of the public accounts, as the name implies, recorded decrees and other state-documents and enrolled new citizens; and the "Temple-wardens" (*Neopoiai*),[31] who, responsible for the care of the temple-buildings and of the sacred funds, were also charged with the recording of public documents, since these were often inscribed on the walls of temples. Both boards, however, also acquired various functions not strictly connected with their special duties, sometimes joining the *prytaneis* and *strategoi* in proposing legislative measures and appropriating funds for various purposes; in the case of the temple-wardens, whose office was originally a sacred one, the fact that they might be ordered to supply money for purely secular purposes resulted in their becoming, in effect, officials of the city.

Besides these boards, whose functions were varied and not always clearly defined, there were other, usually single, officials, who performed specific duties. Thus most cities had a Clerk (*Grammateus*) of the Council (sometimes of the *Demos* also), who took the minutes of the public meetings and recorded and published decrees, treaties and other state-documents, and in some places enrolled new citizens.[32] This office, necessitating a specialized knowledge, was sometimes held for a long period, and the Clerk, as the result of his political experience, exercised great influence in city-affairs.

Lower in rank than the Clerk but charged with duties of real importance was the Controller of the Market (*Agoranomos*), who supervised the sale and purchase of commodities.[33] He had to keep the buildings of the market in repair and collect the rentals accruing to the city from the shops and stalls, to test the correctness of the weights and measures, to guarantee the quality of the merchandise offered for sale and to see that the market furnished commodities at fair prices. Perhaps the most onerous of the duties which might devolve upon him was that of solving the ever-difficult problem of the grain-supply by causing the merchants to sell at reasonable prices or by actually providing grain for sale. This task, however, certain cities assigned to a special commissioner appointed for the emergency and sometimes using public funds appropriated for the purpose.

While the control of a city's finances was properly one of the functions of the Council, there was in some cases a special official who seems to have had the public revenues under his care.[34] Almost everywhere, however, there were Treasurers (*Tamiai*), sometimes a single official, sometimes a board whose members might serve in rotation. As a rule, these treasurers had no authority of their own, their duties being to receive the income of the city and to make payments ordered by the Council or by a decree of the Assembly. Sometimes, as for example at Miletus, their functions were limited to depositing the public income in the bank which was owned by the city and managed by elected commissioners and to paying over the amounts allotted by these commissioners for definitely specified purposes.

In most cities there were certain public services—the so-called "liturgies"—which were not performed by elected officials but assumed by the wealthier citizens as a compulsory duty toward the community.[35] These liturgies naturally varied from city to city, but, in general, they included the defrayal of the cost of hiring and training choruses for festivals, holding musical and athletic contests, and maintaining the public gymnasia. Other obligations of this kind were the expenses incurred by the envoys of the city, both those who were despatched on political missions and those who represented the community at festivals, and, in time of war, the cost of equipping a warship. Originally and in theory, there was a distinction between such a service and a public office; but in time, when the liturgies demanded not only the expenditure of money but also a personal care and attention, and when some of them, especially the post of gymnasiarch, became elective, this distinction tended to disappear.

Of these services, that which probably affected most widely the communal life of a city was the maintenance of the gymnasium, one of the most characteristic institutions of an Hellenic *polis*, adopted also by cities whose public life and customs were modelled on those of the Greeks.[36] While serving a special purpose in providing a place for bodily exercise, especially for the *ephebi*—the youths engaged for a year or more in compulsory training, originally military and athletic but later also cultural—the gymnasium was in most cities a place not merely for the physical but also for the mental development of the citizens. The building was usually provided not only with places for exercise, both indoors and in the open, and with baths, hot and cold, but also with lecture-halls and sometimes even a library, and with rooms for general conversation. Thus, as supplying needs of various kinds, the gymnasium became the centre of the social life of the community.

The maintenance of this institution, so necessary to the general welfare, devolved upon the gymnasiarch. It was his duty to arrange for the training, both athletic and intellectual, which the gymnasium offered to the citizens. He had also to provide, often at his own expense, for the care of the building and its equipment, for the heating of the baths, and, at times, for the lighting of the rooms after dark. A duty of especially great importance—at least in the eyes of many citizens— was that of furnishing the oil used both as a cleanser and as a lubricant by those who exercised in the place; the cost, apparently a large item, was sometimes met by appropriations from the city-treasury, but usually it was supplied by some generous donor or, more often, by the gymnasiarch himself.

Among the responsibilities of the office was the organizing of contests and the giving of prizes. Sometimes, since the gymnasium served as the place of training for the athletes who took part in the games connected with the city-festivals, the gymnasiarch acted also as agonothete, or president of the contests, a post which also was a liturgy, entailing no small expense on the holder.

In many places the gymnasium attained to such importance that in the course of time several were established in a single city for the use of those of different ages, the boys, the ephebes, the young men, and the elders. These various gymnasia became the centres of organizations which played an important part in the communal life. The associations of the Young Men, composed of those who had completed their training as ephebes, were ordinarily definite groups, whose activities were carried on in their gymnasia.[37] Primarily athletic, these associations assumed also a social character, similar to that of a modern club. Of greater importance, however, were the corresponding organizations of the elders, which in the course of time became so general that in the Roman imperial period they existed in almost every city. An association of the Old Men (*gerousia*) is first heard of in Asia Minor at the end of the fourth century before Christ, when it seems to have taken part in the administration of the Temple of Artemis at Ephesus.[38] The reason for this participation and its extent are obscure, for neither in Ephesus itself nor in the other cities in which an organization of this kind existed is there any evidence indicating that the *gerousia* engaged in any administrative activity or that it was other than a purely social organization. Nevertheless, by reason of the age and the prestige of its members, the *gerousia* seems everywhere to have enjoyed great respect and even to have exercised a certain influence in public affairs, and in many cases it acted concurrently with the "Council and People" in conferring honours.

Both the Young Men's and the Elders' associations had funds of their own, derived from gifts or legacies invested as endowments and used for the maintenance of their gymnasia. As their organizations became more elaborate, they had their own officials, a president, a secretary and sometimes a treasurer. They also acquired a corporate character, with an officially recognized status and the right, in some cities at least, of instituting proceedings before a court of law.

As "free and autonomous," the city-states not only enacted their own laws and elected their officials but also managed their finances, possessing sources of income of their own.[39] Usually avoiding any direct taxation of the citizens save in time of an emergency, when personal taxes and property taxes might be imposed, the city, as a rule, obtained its income from indirect levies. A form of income-tax, it is true, was laid on income derived from slaves or animals on hire or engaged in profitable employments and perhaps from the rentals of houses. Sometimes, apparently, the actual possession of slaves and animals was taxed. Otherwise, the public revenues were derived from customs and transit duties, from harbour-dues, and from the taxes levied on agricultural produce brought into the city and on the sales not only of merchandise in the market but also of real estate and slaves. Further income was obtained from the license-fees imposed on certain occupations, from the sale of priesthoods (on which the purchaser also paid a tax), from the returns from state-owned monopolies and utilities, such as fisheries, salt-pans and ferries, which, like most of the other revenues, were leased out to contractors, and especially from the rentals of public property. This property consisted of houses and shops in the city and, in the country-districts, of farms and pasture-lands. The farms, usually, although not necessarily, in the rural territory governed by the city, were frequently held on hereditary leases and paid rentals either in cash or in produce, ordinarily collected by a contractor, while the pastures were used in common by the owners of live-stock, who paid fees to the city for the privilege.

In fact, the territory, or rural domain, which belonged to the city was in many cases its chief source of income. This territory might include the estates of individual landlords, who had obtained their holdings sometimes from the city itself, sometimes by gift or sale from a monarch; in the latter case, these proprietors might attach their lands to the territory of a city, thereby becoming subject to its laws and taxes while at the same time they had full title to their properties.[40] In general, however, the city owned the land comprised in its rural territory, often consisting of "village"-communities, some of which might be composed of people of native stock and consequently of an inferior status.[41] The territories, varying greatly in size according to the importance of the city, might be increased by purchase or gift from a king or by a union with another community.[42] They were jealously guarded and, although their boundaries were often carefully marked, territorial disputes were not uncommon and sometimes even led to war.[43]

The cities may also have derived a small amount of revenue from the coining of money.[44] Controlling their own finances, they ordinarily had coinages of their own, and when, as was the case in the third century, city-issues consisted of small silver and bronze pieces and the nominal value of the coins exceeded the bullion-value, a profit might be obtained from such coinage. Large silver pieces (tetradrachms), it is true, were issued in many places under Alexander and his immediate successors, Antigonus and Lysimachus; for the conqueror permitted at least some cities which had mints of their own to continue the issuing of coins, with the stipulation that these, bearing in addition to the king's head and name the symbol or monogram of the city, should have the same weight and denomination as the coins issued by the monarch. In the third century, however, the kings of the Seleucid dynasty maintained mints of their own in several of the cities, and, either because the right of coining large silver was a royal prerogative or because the local issues could not compete with those of the monarch, the city-coinages were confined to the small silver and bronze pieces. These were issued merely as a token-currency for local circulation. Only those cities which were "allies" of the kings of Egypt appear to have minted coins exceeding the drachm in value, a fact which suggests that these monarchs were more liberal than the Seleucids in permitting or encouraging the issue of silver in the cities under their control.

As an independent state, the free city might raise and maintain an army or a navy, wage war or serve as a mediator in disputes or in armed conflicts between other cities, conduct negotiations, conclude treaties and form alliances. The alliance, in theory an arrangement, not necessarily based on a formal treaty, binding either party to aid the other in the event of war, often became political in character, involving a closer relationship. An alliance might be formed between two or more cities of substantially equal power and like political status either for mutual defence against attack or, on more general terms, for the maintenance of friendly relations.[45] It might also, as has been previously observed, be made with a king. In such cases the usual provision that both parties should "have the same friends and foes" tended to bring the city's foreign policy under royal control and so factually to limit its freedom. Especially when the city's territory adjoined that of the king, the royal power tended to become dominant. It was with some justification that an ancient historian observed that although a "king at the beginning of his reign may perhaps hold out the name of liberty and address as friends and allies those who make common cause with him, nevertheless, being once established in power, he treats those who have trusted him not as an ally but as a master."[a]

There is no reason to suppose that during the reign of Alexander there was any change in the status of the free Greek cities.[46] Their relations with one another, moreover, became closer as the result of the King's policy of restoring or creating federations, which held them together in local organizations. Of these, we know of two, the resuscitated Federation of the Ionians and the newly-formed Federation of the cities of the Troad.

The Ionian Federation, the larger of the two, seems to have been formed before the end of the eighth century for the furtherance of the common interests of the member-cities and the maintenance of a common worship.[47] According to tradition, some of the cities, perhaps about 700 B.C., combined for the destruction of Melia, on the coast south of Ephesus, and in the partition of its territory among the neigh-

[a] Polybius xv 24, 4.

bouring communities the Temple of Poseidon Heliconius became the property of the Federation. This sanctuary, thenceforth called Panionium, was used as the place of worship for the Ionians in common, and in it the representatives of the cities held their meetings and celebrated their festival, the Panionia.

Before the beginning of the fifth century the number of cities in the Federation had risen to twelve, extending along the coast from Phocaea on the north to Miletus on the south.[48] The strength of the organization, however, was greatly impaired by the disastrous revolt of the Ionians against Persian rule in 499 B.C., and during the supremacy of Athens no steps were taken to improve its position or even to celebrate its festival.[49] In the fourth century its activities may have been resumed, but, if so, it was only to a limited extent.

With the restoration of freedom by Alexander the Federation obtained a semblance of its old importance. Its religious character, at least, was emphasized, and the twelve members (subsequently increased to thirteen by the addition of the rebuilt Smyrna[50]) established the festival of the Alexandreia, which they celebrated on the King's birthday as a mark of loyalty to their deliverer.[51] At first, this festival was held in the various member-cities, presumably in rotation, but later it was transferred to a grove consecrated to Alexander's memory on the isthmus of the Erythraean Peninsula. The new festival seems to have superseded to some extent the old Panionia, and the importance of the Temple of Poseidon diminished correspondingly. Nevertheless, at the end of the first century before Christ the Federation still held a festival here and offered a sacrifice to Poseidon.[52]

In contrast to the ancient Ionian Federation, the organization formed by the cities of the Troad has no history antedating Alexander, and it is probable that he was the founder.[53] These nine "cities sharing in the Sanctuary," as they are called in the earliest known decrees of the Federation, passed about 306 B.C., included not merely the old city of Ilium and six of its neighbours but also Lampsacus and Parium at the eastern end of the Hellespont. This Ilian Federation had as its common sanctuary the famous temple of Athena at Ilium, and here the representatives of the cities met to transact business and to celebrate their festival of the Panathenaea.

It has sometimes been supposed that Alexander, in restoring or creating these federations, intended to use them as administrative bodies, which might serve to facilitate the government of his kingdom.[54] It is indeed true that as federative bodies they had certain somewhat fictional powers and could take action on some minor matters. The measures which their delegates took, however, cannot be regarded as pertaining in any way to the administration of the monarch's empire. Without a federal army or judiciary or any organ except a council composed of delegates, these organizations never held any real powers or attained to positions of political significance. Their activities were practically confined to the celebration of their festivals and the enactment of decrees in praise of those whom they wished to honour. After the coming of the Romans the Ionians carried on their tradition of establishing honorific cults by instituting a sacrifice to the Goddess Roma, but during the first and second centuries of the Christian Era they did little but confer their high-sounding eulogies, while their officials, with the characteristic vanity of the Asianic Greeks, bore the grandiose titles of "King" and "Chief Priest."

In the chaos that accompanied the dismemberment of Alexander's empire during the years which followed his death in 323 B.C., it is probable that the cities feared for their independence. The efforts of the Ephesians to win the favour of the various claimants to power seem illustrative of the anxiety which prevailed. Sending an embassy to Craterus, who had been appointed governor of Macedonia by Alexander and was now practically prime minister of the empire, they nevertheless conferred honorary citizenship on Alcetas, the brother of Craterus's rival and enemy, Perdiccas, and on Clitus, the satrap of Lydia, who at the time was Alcetas's associate, as well as on Neoptolemus, who at first supported Perdiccas but afterward turned against him.[b] A little later, some of the cities seemed to be in danger of coming under the power of Egypt; for Asander, the satrap of Caria, associated himself with Ptolemy I and compelled the cities to join him as "allies."[55] The Ephesians appear to have tried to conciliate Ptolemy by sending envoys to him, and although the Milesians, some years afterward, were reminded by Ptolemy's son, then King of Egypt, of the "benefits" which they had received from his father, the fact that Asander became stephanephorus of Miletus suggests that he made himself master of the city.

The freedom of the Asianic Greeks, however, seemed assured when Antigonus "the One-eyed" after several years of warfare became ruler over Asia Minor, for he adopted the principle of the cities' independence as a fundamental part of his policy.[56] Even before he

[b] *J.O.A.I.* XVI (1913), p. 235f., nos. II i, II n and II p.

established himself in power, Antigonus in 319 had taken up the cause of the city of Cyzicus against the satrap of the Hellespontine district on the ground that Cyzicus was an Hellenic state and his ally, and soon afterward, perhaps as a result of this action, he obtained possession of Ephesus. Four years later he committed himself definitely to the maintenance of the freedom of the cities. Faced by a coalition of his rivals, Cassander of Macedonia, Lysimachus of Thrace and Ptolemy of Egypt, he sought to weaken these claimants to power by issuing a proclamation which declared that all Greek cities were to be "free, ungarrisoned and autonomous." His purpose was evidently to gain the support of the communities of Greece against Cassander, who had placed garrisons in the various cities of Macedonia. So obvious, in fact, was this purpose, that Ptolemy, an ally of Cassander's, in entire disregard of any incompatibility with his associate's practice, replied with a similar manifesto. Antigonus, however, maintained the policy which he had adopted. Attacking Asander, he forced him to free the Greek communities.[57] In 311, on concluding agreements with his rivals to assure the permanence of the *status quo*, he retained the independence of the Greeks as a principle and insisted on the insertion of clauses guaranteeing Hellenic freedom.[58] The further step was taken of inviting the Asianic cities to join in binding themselves by an oath to aid one another in protecting their independence, a measure designed to cause them to enter into a pact of their own. By thus swearing to uphold those clauses which affected themselves, they became parties to the agreements and obtained recognition as independent powers.

In adopting this policy Antigonus was undoubtedly moved, at least to a large extent, by expediency. The freedom of the Greeks was a watchword of which he made skilful use, and by acting as the champion of the cities' independence in these agreements he expected to obtain their support in the event of a new war on the ground that his rivals had violated the principle which they had formally accepted.

In actual practice, Antigonus seems to have acted on the theory that in confirming the cities' freedom as announced by Alexander he was recognizing an already existing right. Two years before entering into the agreements of 311, after compelling Asander to surrender Caria, he had "restored" the "democracy" in Miletus, and somewhat later he expressly recognized the liberty and autonomy of the Ionian cities, Erythrae and Colophon, both of which constructed new and more extensive city-walls.[59]

It is, nevertheless, true that when it seemed expedient Antigonus did not hesitate to interfere in the cities' affairs. This seems especially to have been his policy after his assumption in 306 of the title of King.[60] In certain cases, when the need arose, he appears to have placed his own ordinances on the same footing as the cities' laws.[61] Antigonus's greatest offence, however, against the cause of Greek freedom was his attempt to compel the Rhodian Republic to form an alliance and, when this was refused, his attack in 305 B.C. on the island, resulting in the famous siege of Rhodes by his son, Demetrius.[62] This lasted for the greater part of two years and was ended only by the Rhodians' promise to become Antigonus's ally in war (except against Egypt) but on condition that their complete independence should be preserved.

Another instance of the violation of the cities' rights by Antigonus might seem to be afforded by his policy of combining smaller cities into larger communities. The most important of these was the new city in the southern Troad, which, originally named Antigoneia after its founder, was afterwards called Alexandria Troas.[63] It was formed by moving to the new site the inhabitants of several smaller, neighbouring, places, some of them communities of great antiquity, including Scepsis, which in 311 had been formally recognized as Antigonus's ally. Another example of this policy appears in his project of combining the two Ionian cities of Teos and Lebedus, both of them in a bad financial condition, into a single, stronger, community.[64] The plan, the details of which are known from two manifestoes of Antigonus himself, provided that Lebedus should be razed to the ground and its inhabitants moved to Teos. The project, however, was never carried out, perhaps because its fulfilment was prevented by Antigonus's death.

Concerning the details of the founding of Alexandria Troas and the extent to which it was carried out with the consent of the component communities we have no knowledge. But whatever infraction of rights was involved, the plan may have seemed justifiable on the grounds of expediency; for a group of evidently decayed towns was replaced by a city which soon attained great commercial importance. In the case of the union of the two Ionian cities, those clauses in the project which provided that a royal order should be valid in judging lawsuits pending in either city and reserved to Antigonus the right of approving the laws to be framed for the united community and punishing those who proposed any legislation "not for the best" suggest that the King was acting rather as a ruler than as a mediator.[65] It must be taken into consideration, however, that the purpose of the second of these clauses may have been to ensure the adoption of a democratic constitution, on which Alexander had insisted in the case of those cities which he declared free. In regard to the project itself, it must also be remembered that it was formed, at least nominally, in response to a petition from the communities themselves and that the union was to be carried out with the consent of both. In any case, this plan also may be regarded as economically sound and conducive to the cities' future prosperity.

Another plan for creating a strong and prosperous city was that which led to the restoration of Smyrna. In this case, to be sure, there was no question of any infraction of already existing rights. After the capture and destruction of the city by the Lydians in the early sixth century, the inhabitants were dispersed among neighbouring village-communities, and although in the early fourth century one of these retained the ancient name with some sort of civic organization which enabled it to issue silver coins, it could not have had the status of a *polis*.[66] Now, however, it was restored to its long-lost position. Antigonus, collecting the folk from the various village-centres, established them in a new city situated in a favourable place on the long gulf which indents the coast. His action in so doing was consistent not only with his general policy of encouraging and strengthening the cities but also with his interest in establishing them on a sound economic basis. Smyrna promptly became a member of the Ionian Federation and developed rapidly into a city of great importance.

However arbitrary some of Antigonus's actions concerning the cities may appear to those who question his sincerity, it cannot be denied that he was consistent to the end in his policy of using the Greek communities as his allies. In 302 he caused his son Demetrius, who had declared war on Cassander for the professed purpose of freeing the cities of Greece, to convene at Corinth a congress of representatives of the "free and autonomous" communities.[67] At this meeting the assembled delegates, binding themselves by oaths both to one another and to their "leaders," Antigonus and Demetrius, for the common defence, concluded a general treaty of "friendship and alliance," an act which has been well described as the successful culmination of the old ruler's efforts to make the Hellenic city a political body. In the following year, the last of the fourth century, Antigonus, at the age of eighty, meeting the combined armies of Lysimachus and Seleucus at Ipsus in Phrygia, was defeated in a disastrous battle and left dead on the field.

In the course of the third century the cause of Hellenic freedom found its most consistent champion in the Republic of Rhodes, which during this period attained to the position of one of the great powers of the eastern Mediterranean. The Republic had been formed in 408 B.C. by the union of the three ancient communities of the island, Lindus, Ialysus and Camirus, which had been members of the old Dorian federation of the Hexapolis.[68] Upon their union they founded an administrative centre in a situation of great natural beauty at the northeastern point of the island near a sanctuary of the Sun-god Helius, who became the special patron of their state. This new city, situated on the narrow strait which separates Rhodes from the mainland, throve on the sea-traffic from the Aegean world to Syria and especially to Egypt, and rapidly developed into a commercial power of the greatest importance.[69] So widespread, in fact, was its trade that the standard which it adopted for its silver coins was accepted during the fourth century by the principal cities of western Asia Minor, as well as by many of the Aegean islands and even by communities in Thrace. In spite of the suffering and loss caused by Demetrius's siege of the city in 305/4[c] and the damage wrought by the disastrous earthquake which about 227 destroyed its walls and its dockyards as well as its famous "Colossus" erected in commemoration of Demetrius's repulse,[70] the power of the Rhodians, nevertheless, steadily progressed. The excellence of the Republic's laws and its wise administration of public affairs commanded wide respect, and the strength and efficiency of its navy made it so desirable an ally that various kings sought its support.[71] Their offers of friendship were accepted, but although, for reasons of trade, the Rhodians cultivated especially cordial relations with Egypt, they refrained from any military alliances and so were able to avoid embroiling themselves in the monarchs' numerous wars. By this policy of neutrality they succeeded in strengthening their city's position as the centre of a widespread commerce.

Unlike the other Greek communities of Asia Minor, Rhodes was no mere city-state, for its political power was not restricted to the island alone but included wide dominions on the mainland.[72] The extension of Rhodian power began before the middle of the fourth century, when, in addition to several of the neighbouring islands, the Republic owned all the nearest portions of the mainland, the so-called Peraea. This consisted originally of the southern side of the long Peninsula of Cnidus, together with the projecting spur of Loryma and the adjacent coast as far as Physcus on the Bay of Marmaris, but

[c] See note 62.

during the third century it appears to have been extended northward to include the southern shore of the Gulf of Cos. The Peraea was regarded, not as a dependency, but as an integral part of the Republic and its inhabitants possessed full Rhodian citizenship. On the other hand, when, at the opening of the second century, the Rhodians obtained Stratoniceia in the interior of Caria from Antiochus III and acquired Caunus, by purchase, as they afterwards asserted, from the generals of Ptolemy V, they treated these cities as subjects.[73]

During the latter half of the third century the ever-increasing wealth of the Rhodians made it possible for them to develop still further that navy which had already brought them fame. The weakening of Egypt's sea-power and the Macedonians' failure to maintain the strength of their fleet gave the Rhodian navy the leading place in the eastern Mediterranean.[74] This supremacy was fully recognized in 220, when, in answer to a general appeal from the merchants on the ground that they were "pre-eminent in all that concerned the sea," the Rhodians, by declaring war on the Byzantines, forced the abolition of the tolls which had been imposed on merchandise passing through the Bosporus.[d] Their mastery of the sea, moreover, made them for many years to come the main source of protection for the Hellenic world against the ravages of the pirates.[e]

Before the end of the third century, Rhodes, as one of the great powers, had become the promoter of harmony among the Greeks and the champion of their freedom. With the co-operation of Ptolemy IV and the Chians, and later with that of Mitylene and Byzantium also, the Rhodians tried repeatedly to intervene in the disastrous war waged by Philip V and his allies against the Aetolian League and so to put an end to the strife between Greeks.[75] As a result of the increasing decline of the power of Egypt and the dissolution, about the middle of the third century, of the "Federation of the Islanders," an organization which the earlier Ptolemies had used as a means of maintaining their supremacy, the Republic had already become the protector of the islands of the Aegean.[76]

The aggressive policy of Philip V of Macedonia, with the consequent threat to the power, if not the independence, of Rhodes, and the joint appeal of the Rhodians and King Attalus of Pergamum to Rome for assistance in the war against the ambitious monarch have already been described.[77] During the struggle which ensued, the Republic's warships, together with those of Attalus, rendered material assistance to

[d] Polybius IV 47f. See also Chap. XIII note 36.   [e] See Chap. XII note 9.

the Roman navy.[f] The collapse of Philip's plan for an Aegean empire resulted in the further increase of the Rhodians' influence and power, and their position was greatly strengthened when Rome by proclaiming the freedom of the Greeks established the principle for which they had contended.[g]

A few years later, however, when the Seleucid ruler Antiochus III attempted to make himself master of the Greek cities of Asia,[h] it became necessary for the Rhodians again to defend the cause of Hellenic freedom. Once more they associated themselves with Rome in a war against the aggressor, and their fleet contributed much to the ultimate success by winning a great victory over the King's navy commanded by the Carthaginian leader, Hannibal, and, later, by supporting the Romans in a decisive engagement off the coast near Teos.[78] For these services they were rewarded after the final defeat of Antiochus by a large addition to their mainland possessions.[i]

With the exception of the Rhodians, the Greeks of Asia Minor lived in the city-states which were reconstituted by Alexander and recognized as free by Antigonus. These, extending in a long line on the coast and the neighbouring islands from the Propontis to the Strait of Marmaris, were, in the third century, about forty in number. A presentation of their economic and political importance should include as a background a survey of their geographical situation, and therefore at the risk of some tedium a description will be given of those which attained during this century to a position of prominence.

Outstanding among these states were the cities which formed the Ionian Federation, the principal centres both of the commerce and of the artistic achievement of the Asianic Greeks. Of these, the foremost place was held by the three great ports, Miletus, Ephesus and Smyrna, situated at or near the mouths of the three chief rivers which flow downward from the central plateau into the Aegean Sea.

Miletus, which in early times, at least, surpassed the others in importance, lay, near the site of an older settlement, at the end of a narrow peninsula projecting northward into the broad gulf which was the estuary of the Maeander.[79] Its territory—the hilly country on the south —was restricted and unproductive, but the situation of the city gave it every advantage for commerce by sea. The four separate harbours, indenting both sides of the peninsula, not only afforded abundant

---

[f] Livy XXXII 16, 6f.; 19, 3f. (198 B.C.)
[g] See below p. 88.   [h] See below p. 104f.   [i] See Chap. IV note 61.

shelter for merchantmen of Miletus but made it an important centre for transshipment to vessels from other ports, especially from its numerous colonies.[80] On the other hand, the city's land-trade with the interior was greatly hampered by the deep indentation of the gulf, extending as far inland as the jagged mass of Mt. Latmus. The only connexion with the valley of the Maeander and the Southern Highway led around this arm of the gulf by a wide circuit, difficult and toilsome because of the mountain-spurs which reach down to the water's edge. These obstacles, it is true, did not prevent all commerce by land, nor were they an insuperable barrier against the invading army of Alexander. Nevertheless, the city's communications with the mainland must have been carried on chiefly by ship across the gulf. Here, near the mouth of the Maeander, lay Myus, which in the fifth and fourth centuries was an independent community but later came under the power of Miletus.[81] Its annexation gave the Milesians a foothold on the other side of the gulf and a direct connexion with the valley of the Maeander.[82]

The territory of Miletus included the famous temple of Apollo, situated at Didyma, some ten miles to the south, and connected with the city by a "Sacred Way," the route followed by the processions from Miletus to the Temple, of which the section nearest Didyma was flanked by a line of statues dating from the seventh and sixth centuries.[83] This sanctuary was the seat of an oracle believed to antedate the coming of the Greeks to Asia Minor. The early temple, founded, according to a legend officially accepted before the end of the third century, at the place where Leto conceived Apollo and Artemis, was destroyed by Darius when he captured Miletus. In the third century, after the oracle, long silent, had gained fame as the result of the belief that it had announced the divine origin of Alexander and prophesied his victory over the Persians, a new building was begun, intended to surpass in size and magnificence all other sanctuaries of Asia Minor. Its extant ruins are in keeping with the intention, but so ambitious was the plan that, although in the first century after Christ an effort seems to have been made to carry on the work of construction, the building was never completed.

The situation of Ephesus, more favourable than that of its great commercial rival, Miletus, possessed every opportunity for trade by land as well as by sea.[84] Lying on the south side of what was originally the long narrow estuary of the Caÿster, it was readily accessible from the Aegean. It also had the advantage of direct communications with the interior, for it was not only the terminus of the ancient "Royal Road," which led across Mt. Tmolus from Sardis, but it was also connected by an easy pass with the valley of the Maeander and the Southern Highway. Thus the city had a double means of communication with the interior.[j] In the Hellenistic period, at least, Ephesus owned a fertile territory in the valley of the Caÿster, whence it could obtain the food needed by its inhabitants. It seems not improbable that some of this land was in its possession in early times also, and that it was because of the ease with which both grain and raw materials could be obtained from its *hinterland* that Ephesus does not appear to have founded colonies overseas.

The Greek settlers seem to have established themselves chiefly on the plain that bordered the estuary and on the slopes of the hill rising behind it.[85] The situation was near the sanctuary of the great Asianic Mother-goddess, who was identified by the Greeks with Artemis and became one of the most widely honoured deities of the ancient world.[86] The temple which was erected to the Goddess in the sixth century received rich gifts from King Croesus of Lydia. At the same time this monarch seems to have forced the Ephesians to move from the bank of the Caÿster to a situation somewhat farther inland.[87]

In the fourth century the Ephesians began to construct a new temple of Artemis to replace the ancient building, which had been destroyed by fire.[88] This was still unfinished when Alexander in 334 took possession of the city. It is said that he offered to bear the cost of construction on the condition that his name might appear in the dedicatory inscription but that the offer was indignantly refused. Alexander did, however, enlarge the limits of the inviolable area and he greatly increased the revenues of the Goddess by ordering that the money which the Ephesians had hitherto paid to the Persians as tribute should thenceforth be paid to her. The new sanctuary was embellished with the works of famous artists, and such was its magnificence that it was accounted one of the Seven Wonders of the ancient world. The throngs of worshippers brought to Ephesus by its widespread fame contributed greatly to the prosperity of the city, and it was doubtless not merely fanaticism that in the middle of the first century after Christ caused St. Paul's supposed attack on the worship of the Goddess to be met with shouts of "Great is Artemis of the Ephesians."[k]

A new era began for Ephesus at the beginning of the third century, when Lysimachus made important changes both in its situation and

<hr>

[j] See Chap. II notes 17 and 18.   [k] *Acta Apost.* XIX 24f.

in its size. The former site was no longer accessible to the sea, for the silt carried down by the Caÿster had blocked up the estuary and cut off the harbour from the Aegean, thus greatly damaging the city's trade.[89] Lysimachus, therefore, wishing to restore its former commercial prosperity, moved the inhabitants to a new site on the hills near the river some distance below their original settlement, where a harbour could be constructed behind the end of a long ridge.[90] He increased the population by forcibly removing some of the inhabitants of the Ionian communities of Colophon and Lebedus to the new city, which he renamed Arsinoeia in honour of the Egyptian princess whom he had taken as his third wife. He also strengthened it by building a great wall, in part, at least, at the citizens' expense, which extended for more than five miles along the summits of the hills on the slopes of which the city stood.

During the third century Ephesus was in turn the residence of the Seleucid Kings and a vassal of Egypt.[l] Becoming subject to Eumenes II in 188, when the Roman commissioners distributed Antiochus's Asianic dominions,[m] it seems to have flourished under Pergamene rule, and Attalus II attempted to improve its harbour by constructing a mole intended to deepen the entrance.[n] The attempt was unsuccessful, but the city continued to grow in size and importance and at the beginning of the Christian Era it was said to be the "largest trading-centre in Asia this side of the Taurus."[o]

The third of the great Ionian ports, Smyrna, lay about forty-five miles north of Ephesus, at the end of the long gulf which takes its name from the city.[91] The original settlement, which was destroyed in the sixth century, seems to have stood on a low hill overlooking the northeastern corner of the gulf, but Antigonus, when he restored Smyrna, placed his new city on its present site at the southeastern corner, where the hill of Pagus served as an acropolis. This city was provided with a wall, apparently in the time of Lysimachus, who, as also in the case of Ephesus, gave it a new name, calling it Eurydiceia after his daughter.[92] In a situation of real loveliness, with its crescent-shaped harbour, its rectangular plan and its many two-storied colonnades, Smyrna was characterized at the beginning of the Christian Era as the "most beautiful of them all."[p] Its claim to fame as the birthplace of Homer was expressed not only by a coin struck in the poet's honour

[l] See Chap. IV notes 27 and 31.   [m] See Chap. IV notes 56, 60 and 75.
[n] See Chap. I note 82.   [o] Strabo XIV p. 641.   [p] Strabo XIV p. 646.

and bearing his name but also by a memorial, consisting of a quad-
rangular portico, which contained his statue and a shrine.[93]

Like Ephesus, Smyrna was connected with the interior, for a route
led over an easy pass south of Mt. Sipylus to the basin of the Hermus
and the Royal Road.[q] For trade by sea, however, it was less favourably
situated, for the long gulf, although it provided an excellent harbour,
made the city less accessible to the Aegean sea-lane.[94] Nevertheless,
during the third century Smyrna seems to have prospered greatly, and
it soon outstripped the communities at the mouth of the gulf. The
international status of the city was greatly improved about the middle
of this century by a general guarantee against attack, but Smyrna
probably derived more strength by entering into an agreement, concluded in consequence of an invasion of its territory, with the military
colonists domiciled in and around the stronghold of Magnesia-near-
Sipylus in the valley of the Hermus.[95] Under this arrangement not
only the rights of citizenship in Smyrna but also homes in the city
were granted both to the former soldiers and to the free "Greek" inhabitants of the place, with the stipulation that they should take an
oath of allegiance to the Seleucid king. At the beginning of the second
century the Smyrniots formally placed themselves under the protection
of the Romans,[r] and later they furnished aid both against the Pergamene claimant, Aristonicus, and against the Italians fighting to obtain
Roman citizenship.[s] In 43 B.C. they could still be called by Cicero the
oldest and the most faithful of Rome's allies.[t]

Among the Ionian communities comparable in importance to the
three great cities of the coast were the island-states of Chios and Samos,
the former separated from the Peninsula of Erythrae by a strait less
than five miles wide at its narrowest point, the latter less than a mile
distant from the projecting headland of Mt. Mycale.

The city of Chios itself lay in the midst of a rich and beautiful plain
on the eastern side of the island.[96] Situated on the strait through which
all traffic passed, and having a large harbour, well protected by moles,
it had long maintained a flourishing trade, and in the late fifth century
the Chians were accounted the most prosperous of all the Greeks save
for the Spartans alone. From early times they owned territory on the
mainland south of the Caïcus, and their navy was so powerful that it
was said that they ruled the sea. Resisting attempts by the Egyptian
kings and by Philip V of Macedonia to gain possession of their island,[u]

q See Chap. II note 17.　　　　　　　　　r See Chap. IV note 53.
s Tacitus *Ann.* IV 56: Aristides *Orat.* XIX 11 Keil.　　　　t Cicero *Phil.* XI 5.
u See Chap. IV notes 25 and 42.

the Chians nevertheless maintained friendly relations with the rulers of Pergamum, one of whom gave them a sum of money for the construction of their city-wall.[97]

The city of Samos, like Chios, lay on the eastern side of the island from which it took its name, facing the narrow strait which separated it from the coast.[98] Two hills rose behind the city, the more easterly of which served as the acropolis and by a projecting spur helped to enclose the excellent harbour. Less than four miles distant was the famous Temple of Hera, described by Herodotus as the greatest of all that he had ever seen. Samos owned an extensive territory on the mainland, which included the western end of Mycale and the rich plain of Anaea farther to the north. The southern boundary of this tract was the source of a long-standing dispute with the city of Priene, begun in the early seventh century and a continued cause of friction until, in the late second century, it was finally settled by the authority of Rome.[99]

Priene, the most picturesquely situated of all the Ionian cities, stood on a series of terraces on the southern side of Mt. Mycale above the estuary of the Maeander, with an acropolis on the mountain-side at its back.[100] Founded originally on a different, now unknown, site, it was rebuilt, about the middle of the fourth century, in its present situation and constructed on the rectangular principle with a market-place in the centre and near it the beautiful Temple of Athena, the whole arrangement affording an excellent example of Hellenistic town-planning. Priene's territory included the central part of Mycale and also the port of Naulochum, some three miles to the southwest, which Alexander gave to the city; many of the citizens settled in it as the silting-up of the estuary of the Maeander gradually cut off Priene from the sea. Another portion of the city's territory, lying farther inland in the direction of Magnesia-on-Maeander, was cultivated in the early third century by the dependent Pedieis, probably of native stock.[v] These lands appear to have been cruelly ravaged by a band of marauding Galatians.[w]

Magnesia, about seventeen miles northeast of Priene, was the only one of the Ionian cities without direct access to the Aegean and the only one which was not a member of their Federation.[101] Originally situated on the Maeander itself, the settlement was moved at the beginning of the fourth century to a place some three miles north of the river at the foot of Mt. Thorax, a spur projecting from the eastern end

---

[v] See note 41 and Chap. IV note 13.   [w] *Ins. Priene* 17 = *O.G.I.* 765.

of Mycale, and close to the ancient sanctuary of the goddess Artemis Leucophryene, who became the city's special patroness. The territory of Magnesia was a large one; for it included a portion of the Maeander valley with sacred lands belonging to Apollo, to which, it was maintained, exemption from taxation had been granted by the Persian kings.[102] It was further increased by Philip V, whose gift, made at the expense of Miletus, led, as will be shown, to war between the two cities.[x]

Of the less important cities of Ionia, the most northerly, Phocaea, was situated at the end of a small hilly peninsula on the eastern side of the entrance to the Gulf of Smyrna, and Clazomenae lay on an island in the gulf itself, a few hundred yards from the southern shore, with which it was connected by a causeway.[103] In the seventh century Phocaea, thanks to its excellent harbour and the trade-route which led down the Hermus valley, enjoyed great prosperity and established colonies far and wide, including even Massalia on the southern coast of Gaul.[104] Clazomenae, on the other hand, was far removed from the Aegean sea-lane and was without a *hinterland*. It had, moreover, a very restricted territory.[105] Both cities suffered greatly after Antigonus's re-establishment of Smyrna, for the former commerce of Phocaea was diverted to its docks, and Clazomenae was too near Smyrna to compete successfully for the trade of the ships that entered the gulf.

Almost due west of Clazomenae lay Erythrae, situated on the eastern side of the mountainous peninsula known by the name of the city.[106] Although the commerce of the Aegean naturally favoured the greater port of Chios, across the strait, the capacious harbour of Erythrae, lying between two projecting capes and well protected by islands, had a share in the carrying-trade of the coast, on which it depended for its prosperity, for the road which connected it with the interior was long and toilsome. At the end of the fourth century, perhaps, the city was much strengthened by the construction of a great wall, which, with a circuit of nearly three miles, protected it on the landward side.[107] About 275 its territory was plundered by a band of Galatians, who compelled the citizens to pay a ransom and to give hostages.[108]

On the southern side of the Peninsula of Erythrae were the two cities of Teos and Lebedus, the former on a neck of land connecting a hilly peninsula with the mainland, the latter about thirteen miles farther southeast on a fortified rocky foreland.[109] East of Lebedus lay Colophon, some distance back from the coast but with a port at Notium on a

[x] See Chap. IV notes 43 and 47.

79

promontory about nine miles to the south; between the two, at Clarus, there was a sanctuary of Apollo with an oracle of great fame.[110]

In early times these had all been places of wealth and Colophón and Teos were the homes of famous poets.[111] At the end of the fourth century, however, their prosperity had declined. Nevertheless, under Antigonus the citizens of Colophon were rich enough to build a new wall around their city. The plan of Antigonus to combine Teos and Lebedus into a single community was never carried out,[y] but the population of Colophon and Lebedus was diminished when Lysimachus transferred some of their inhabitants to his new Ephesus-Arsinoeia.[112] The two cities, however, continued in existence, and Teos during the later Hellenistic period seems to have been a place of considerable importance.

This continued importance of Teos was due in large measure to the worship of Dionysus, whom the Teans regarded as the founder of their city.[113] The cult, probably an early one, received a new significance when, at the end of the third century, there was a general recognition of the city and its territory as sacred to the God. Either at this time or a half-century later the Teans built a new temple for Dionysus, a particularly beautiful specimen of Ionic architecture, said to be the work of Hermogenes, to whom was attributed also the temple of Artemis at Magnesia.

Even before this time, however, the worship of the God had caused Teos to become a centre of the dramatic and musical arts; for it was the home of the Asianic "Artists of Dionysus," a society consisting not only of actors but also of poets, musicians and singers, who gave performances throughout western Asia Minor.[114] The Society seems to have enjoyed a certain degree of exterritoriality, which made it independent of the city. In the early second century the citizens were on good terms with the Artists and even bought them a piece of property. Soon, however, friction arose, chiefly over the management of the Society's festival, and so serious was the quarrel which developed that both sides sent delegates to Eumenes II of Pergamum asking him to act as mediator. The King made recommendations and ordered that an agreement should be drawn up by a commission composed of representatives of both sides, together with a royal appointee. This arrangement, however, failed in its purpose. Under Attalus II or his successor further trouble occurred, and the Artists were forced to take refuge in Ephesus. When the King's plan for giving them a new home on the promontory of Myonnesus near Teos was forbidden by the Romans at the Teans'

[y] See note 64.

request, the Artists established themselves at Lebedus, which gladly welcomed the addition to its population. They did little, however, to strengthen the city permanently, for a century later Mark Antony moved them away to Priene, and Lebedus was humorously referred to by Horace as a deserted village.

Far to the north, on the southern shore of the Propontis was Cyzicus, a Milesian colony founded during the first half of the seventh century.[115] One of the strongest and most beautiful of the cities of Asia Minor, it stood on the southernmost point of what was originally an island but, perhaps before the historic period, had become a peninsula, connected with the mainland by an isthmus formed by two parallel dykes and accumulations of sand. East and west of this isthmus were the harbours, sheltered by moles projecting from the peninsula, and in the centre was a lagoon connected with the harbours by canals. The southern side of the city facing the isthmus was protected by a great wall, which, built out upon the moles, also defended the harbours, and on the north rose the long range of Mt. Dindymus, which afforded shelter from the storm-laden northeasterly wind.

At the beginning of the route which led up the valley of the Macestus and carried the trade from the Propontis to Pergamum and the cities in the basin of the Hermus, and at the same time a great clearing-house for the trade of the Euxine, Cyzicus early attained to a high degree of prosperity.[116] In the Hellenistic period its territory was a large one, extending far inland along the river Aesepus and probably reaching as far as the boundary of the Kingdom of Pergamum. Part, at least, of this territory suffered, as has been observed, from the raids of the Galatians, but the loss of grain incurred thereby was made up by Philetaerus of Pergamum, who had already shown his friendship for the citizens by sending them gifts of money as well as troops for their protection.[117] These good relations, strengthened by the marriage of Attalus I to Apollonis, the daughter of a citizen of Cyzicus, were continued throughout the second century.

West of Cyzicus, on the northern coast of the Troad, lay Lampsacus and Parium, members of the Ilian Federation.[z] Lampsacus, near the eastern end of the Hellespont, settled in the second half of the seventh century by emigrants from Phocaea, developed rapidly and, thanks to its good harbour and its commanding position, soon became a place of great wealth.[118] Its coins, first of electrum, then of gold, were widely

[z] See note 53.

current from the late sixth century onward, and in the fifth century its annual "contribution" to Athens was sometimes as great as twelve talents, one of the largest amounts paid by any Asianic city. Although involved in the war between Lysimachus and Demetrius in 301 B.C.,[a] Lampsacus maintained its independence during the third century and was the first of the cities of Asia, except Ilium, to enter into negotiations with Rome.[b]

In the Troad itself the famous city which had given its name to the district survived as the town of Ilium built on the site of ancient Troy.[119] Little more than a mere village, apparently, during the fifth and fourth centuries, the place was of importance only as the seat of the worship of Athena Ilias. The Homer-loving Alexander, however, raised Ilium to the rank of *polis*, declaring it free and exempt from tribute, and he greatly enriched the temple of Athena. Later, probably under Lysimachus, a new wall was built around the city,[c] and toward the end of the third century, Ilium, as the home of Aeneas, was the first of the Asianic cities to establish relations with Rome.[d]

In the fifth century the Troad was a land of many cities, but at the beginning of the Hellenistic period many of them, as the result either of amalgamation with the larger communities or of actual extinction, had ceased to exist.[120] Of those which survived, the most strategically situated was Abydus, which, facing the narrowest part of the Hellespont and provided with an excellent harbour, was the easiest point of crossing between Europe and Asia. For this reason its possession was greatly desired by the monarchs who wished to control the Strait, by Lysimachus, whose attempt to seize it in 302 was temporarily frustrated,[e] by Demetrius, by Philip V of Macedonia, who captured it after a long and famous siege terminated only by the self-inflicted death of many of the citizens,[f] and finally by Antiochus III, who in 196 occupied it in preparation for his projected invasion of Thrace.[g]

Farther south, on the coast beyond Cape Sigeium at the entrance to the Hellespont, was the new city of Alexandria Troas.[121] Founded, as has been described, by Antigonus and extended by Lysimachus, it occupied a position so favourable for securing the trade of the northern Aegean that, gradually outstripping Lampsacus in commercial importance, it became one of the great cities of the Graeco-Roman world.

In the interior, some thirty miles from the coast at Alexandria Troas,

a See Chap. IV note 3.   b See Chap. IV note 51.   c See Chap. IV note 16.
d See Chap. I note 35.   e See below p. 89.   f See Chap. I note 44.
g Livy XXXIII 38, 4 and 8.

lay Scepsis, an old Aeolic community increased by settlers from Miletus.[122] On a height which dominated the valley of the upper Scamander, it controlled the route leading across the northern spurs of Mt. Ida to the Aesepus. It suffered a loss in population when Antigonus moved some of its citizens to Alexandria Troas, and while these were returned to their homes by Lysimachus, Scepsis, although a free city under the early Seleucids, having no real commercial advantages, remained a place of little consequence, finally becoming subject to the rulers of Pergamum.

On the southern coast of the Troad, opposite the northern end of the island of Lesbos and separated from it by a strait not over seven miles in width, stood Assus in an impressive situation on the terraces of a steep volcanic cone.[123] The city was probably in early times the landing-place for the transportation of cargoes overland to places north of the narrows of the Hellespont, a portage which enabled mariners to avoid the head winds and the strong current off the southwestern corner of the Troad. But when, with the development of navigation, the need for such transportation ceased, and especially when Alexandria Troas grew into a great commercial centre, Assus became primarily an agricultural community. It continued, nevertheless, to maintain a coastwise trade; for the ship which bore St. Paul and his companions to Samos and Miletus included Assus among its ports of call.[h]

East of Assus the coast is deeply indented by the Gulf of Adramyttium, and on a low hill at the southeastern corner stood the city from which the gulf took its name.[124] Originally a native settlement, Adramyttium was presented in 422 B.C. by the Persian governor to a group of exiles from the island of Delos, whom the Athenians had driven from their homes, and thereafter it was regarded as an "Hellenic city." Its territory included the plain of Thebe near the mouth of the Euenus, famed for its fertility. The situation of the city was a favourable one, for it had a good harbour, used as a naval-station, and it lay at the end of a route which led across the mountains into central Mysia and served to transport the silver from the mines of the district.[i] Despite its distance from the line of traffic in the Aegean, Adramyttium seems to have maintained an extensive trade, and in the first century after Christ one of its merchantmen was plying between the ports of Asia and the coast of Syria.[j]

The entrance to the Gulf of Adramyttium is protected by the island

[h] *Acta Apost.* XX 13f.   [i] See Chap. II note 20.   [j] *Acta Apost.* XXVII 2.

of Lesbos, the largest of the islands which line the western seaboard of Asia Minor.[125] Its principal cities were Mitylene on the eastern side of the island, Eresus near the southwestern point, and Methymna at the northern end, long a rival of Mitylene but finally superseded by it. The situation of Mitylene on a long promontory with an islet at its end was not merely convenient for commerce, for the islet furnished two harbours, but was also one of extraordinary beauty. In addition to an extensive territory on Lesbos, the city owned a large tract of land on the coast south of Adramyttium; part of this, seized by Seleucus I and sold to Pitane by his son Antiochus, became the cause of a long-standing dispute between the two cities, which was finally settled in the later second century by a commission of referees from Pergamum. For part of the third century the Lesbian cities were more or less dominated by Egypt, but as Egyptian rule in the Aegean grew weaker, they turned to the Rhodians, with whom, probably in view of the ambitions of Philip V, they seem to have formed some kind of treaty-relations. In the second century they appear to have joined in establishing a federation of their own, with reciprocity of civic rights.

On the coast southeast of Lesbos and north of Ionia was the district of Aeolis, a fertile strip of territory and well suited to agriculture.[k] In consequence, commerce and industry had not progressed far, and urban life was less highly developed than in Ionia. Its cities included Cyme, on a small bay north of the peninsula of Phocaea, Myrina, on two low hills some seven miles north of Cape Hydra near the mouth of the small river Pythicus, Aegae, on the upper Pythicus in the heart of the mountain-mass which separates the basin of the Caïcus from that of the lower Hermus, and Pitane, on a long tongue of land west of the mouth of the Caïcus.[126] Myrina possessed a large territory, including an enclave in the mountains some twenty miles to the southeast and perhaps also the temple of Apollo at the neighbouring Gryneium. Cyme, however, seems always to have been the most prominent of these cities, perhaps because its harbour was more favourably situated for coastwise trade. This trade the citizens attempted, apparently, to stimulate by the device of refraining from the exaction of harbour-dues, a policy for which they were later ridiculed. Nevertheless, Cyme prospered, and at the beginning of the Christian Era it was described as the largest and best of the Aeolian communities and "almost their metropolis."

[k] See Chap. II note 38.

South of the Ionian cities, beyond Miletus, the coast of Caria is broken by the gulf through which the river Cybersus enters the Aegean. On its northern side, on a small rocky island close to the shore, lay the city of Iasus.[127] According to tradition, it was originally settled by Argives but later occupied by emigrants from Miletus. On the southern side of the gulf but nearer the entrance was Bargylia, on a peninsula projecting from the shore and forming a bay on its eastern side, which was the city's harbour.[128] The territory of Iasus was rocky and unproductive, and its people depended largely on the fishing in the gulf and in a lake in the neighbourhood, the rights to which were guaranteed to them by Alexander. The patron-deity of the Iasians was probably Apollo, who held the office of stephanephorus when it became necessary for the expenses of this office to be borne by the temple-treasury, but apparently the chief temple of the city was that of Artemis Astias. Of great importance was the cult of Dionysus, to whom the theatre was dedicated and whose festival made Iasus, especially in the second century, a musical and dramatic centre. Apollo was worshipped also at Bargylia, but the most highly venerated deity of the city seems to have been Artemis, with a sanctuary in the neighbouring village of Cindya, of whose statue, standing in the open air, it was said that it was never wet either by rain or by snow.

Of the cities of inland Caria which had a Greek tradition and in the fifth century paid tribute to Athens—Alinda, Pidasa, Euromus, Olymus, Chalcetor and Mylasa—by far the greatest was Mylasa.[129] It lay some ten miles from its port of Passala, near the mouth of the Cybersus, in a plain of extraordinary fertility on the eastern side of an isolated mountain-group which bars the course of the river and forces it into a wide detour. The city owned a large territory, and, on a route from northern Caria to the sea, it was evidently a commercial centre of considerable wealth.

Mylasa, although it was a member of the "Confederacy of Delos" and in the fourth century had a civic organization of the Hellenic type, was originally a Carian city, and the ancient temple of the native god, renamed Zeus, which was within its territory had been from early times the common sanctuary of "all the Carians." The city's territory also included the village of Labraunda with a large sacred precinct of Zeus, in the mountains some eight miles from Mylasa and connected with it by a paved "Sacred Way."

At the close of the third century, as will be noted later,[1] Mylasa

---

[1] See Chap. IV note 35.

arranged with Miletus for an interchange of civic rights. In the next century a "sympolity" was formed with Euromus, by which the two cities entered into a political union with each other,[130] and afterward a similar combination was effected with Olymus;[131] both arrangements were in keeping with the general tendency toward union which seems to have been gradually carried out by the communities of inland Caria.[132]

On the shores of the Gulf of Cos, which deeply indents the coast of Caria south of the Gulf of Bargylia, as well as on the neighbouring islands, were the cities which, together with the communities of Rhodes, formed the association originally known as the Dorian Hexapolis.[m] Of these the most prominent—although in its early history it was expelled from the association—was Halicarnassus.[133] Situated on the northern side of the gulf, on a bay extending into the coast and divided into two portions by a projecting spur, the city had an excellent harbour, well suited for the development of commerce. On the landward side it could be easily defended, for the road which led from the interior of Caria and brought the trade of the district to its docks approached the city through a narrow pass in the mountain-ridge at its back.

During the greater part of the fourth century Halicarnassus was ruled by a family of tyrants, the second of whom, Maussolus, raised the city to the height of its splendour and power. He extended its territory by incorporating neighbouring communities and even brought more distant regions under his rule.[134] Although nominally a Persian vassal, he became, in fact, an independent sovereign, contracting alliances and concluding treaties in his own name. The magnificent tomb, built in his honour by his sister-wife Artemisia, was regarded as one of the Seven Wonders of the ancient world and gave its name to all later buildings of a similar kind.

Alexander, on his arrival in Caria in 334, found Halicarnassus in the possession of the Persians, to whom it had been delivered by Pixodarus, a younger brother of Maussolus.[135] Having captured the city after a long and famous siege, at the close of which many of the buildings were levelled to the ground, the conqueror gave what remained of Halicarnassus to the only surviving member of Maussolus's family, his younger sister Ada, who was also made ruler of the surrounding part of Caria. In 309 an attempt to seize the city was made by Ptolemy I

---

[m] See note 5.

but without success.[n] Early in the third century, however, Halicarnassus came under the power of Egypt, and throughout this century it continued to be an "ally" of the Egyptian kings.[o]

At the end of the long peninsula of Halicarnassus, about twelve miles west of the city, was Myndus, which, although it was under the protection of Apollo, was never a member of the Dorian Hexapolis.[136] As the result of its remoteness and the mountains at its back, the city was less favourably situated than Halicarnassus for trade by land. It had, however, an excellent harbour, which was formed by a projecting headland and thus, hook-shaped, was sheltered on three sides. The city was protected by a strong wall of excellent workmanship and so was able in 334 to resist Alexander's army.[p] In the following year, however, the Persian commander was forced to yield it to the King's general, Ptolemy, later king of Egypt.[q] In 308 the city was still in Ptolemy's hands and during the following century, it remained, like Halicarnassus, under Egyptian domination.[r]

Across the Gulf of Cos from Halicarnassus, at the end of the long peninsula which forms its southern side was Cnidus.[137] Its situation, on terraces rising from the water's edge to the acropolis above, was one of great beauty. The projecting headland of Triopium, extending in a long line in front of the coast and connected with it by a narrow isthmus, gave the city a double harbour, the moles of which are still to be seen. On the summit of the cape stood the temple of Apollo, the patron-god of the Hexapolis, whose festival was celebrated jointly by the member-cities. Cnidus itself seems to have been under the protection of Artemis Hyacinthotrophus, to commemorate whose appearance in some time of danger the citizens founded a festival.

In its island-like position and cut off from the interior by the Rhodians' possessions on the long peninsula, Cnidus had a very restricted territory. The length of this peninsula rendered land-commerce difficult and the city must have depended for its prosperity on the carrying-trade of the Aegean. This trade, however, was evidently an extensive one, for the wine of Cnidus was widely used throughout the Hellenic world.[s]

At the entrance to the Gulf of Cos is the beautiful and fertile island which has given the gulf its name.[138] The ancient town of Astypalaea, situated, perhaps, near the southwestern end of the island, may have been the community which originally was a member of the Dorian

[n] Plutarch *Demetr.* 7, 3.   [o] See Chap. IV notes 21 and 25.
[p] Arrian *Anab.* 1 20, 5f.   [q] Arrian *Anab.* 11 5, 7: Diodorus xx 37, 1.
[r] See Chap. IV note 21.   [s] See Chap. II note 103.

Hexapolis; but as early as the fifth century there was a settlement of considerable political importance on the site of the city of Cos, which, after the union of several smaller places in 366, became the centre of government. In a favourable situation at the eastern end of the island and enjoying the advantage of a good harbour, Cos obtained a share of the trade that passed from the Aegean to Rhodes, and its merchantmen carried its products as far as the ports of the Propontis and the Euxine. The wealth and fame of the city were increased by the Temple of Asclepius, built on terraces on the mountain-side two miles distant.[139] The renown of the temple was largely due to its school of medicine, which, maintaining the tradition of the illustrious Hippocrates, was known far and wide in the Hellenic world and became a much-frequented centre for medical treatment.

Before the end of the fourth century Cos came under the power of Egypt. It received Ptolemy I in 309 and seems to have become for the time a royal residence, for in the following year Ptolemy's son and successor was born on the island.[140] For nearly a hundred years thereafter, the Coans, taking no part in the vicissitudes which successively established and overthrew the rulers of Asia Minor, remained "friends and allies" of Egypt, receiving various favours from its kings. In the later third century Cos increased its possessions by annexing some of the neighbouring islands, especially Calymnos, which became a subdivision of the state. Toward the close of this century, when the power of Egypt was on the wane, the Coans became closely associated with the Rhodians, whom they joined both in fighting against the Cretans and in the war which Rhodes, in conjunction with the Romans, waged against Philip V in the name of Hellenic freedom.[141] After this struggle had been brought to a successful conclusion, Cos erected a statue of Quinctius Flamininus, the victorious Roman general, who a little more than a century after the death of Antigonus caused the herald to proclaim before an assembly at Corinth that "All the Greeks, those who dwell both in Asia and in Europe, are free, ungarrisoned, exempt from tribute and governed by their own laws."

CHAPTER IV

THE GREEK STATES DURING THE THIRD
AND SECOND CENTURIES

THE championship of the cities' freedom which had been the policy of Antigonus and was consistently maintained in the treaty concluded in 302 by his son Demetrius with Cassander, guaranteeing this freedom, had won for these rulers gratitude and support both in the mother-land and in Asia.[1] Consequently, when Lysimachus crossed the Hellespont for the campaign which was to result in Antigonus's defeat, he found little disposition on the part of the Asianic cities to accept his rule. Lampsacus and Parium, to be sure, received him, and he, as a reward, recognized the freedom of both cities. Sigeium in the southern Troad, however, offered opposition, which was quelled by the capture of the place. At Abydus the resistance was more successful; the invader was forced to abandon the siege of the city by the arrival of a relieving-force which Demetrius sent by sea.

After this initial failure, Lysimachus himself advanced into the interior, leaving the task of conquering the Greeks of the coast to his general, Prepelaus, who was despatched with a small army against the cities of Aeolis and Ionia.[2] After taking Adramyttium by force, Prepelaus marched rapidly southward, where Ephesus capitulated, apparently without resistance. The ships in the harbour were burned, but the citizens were spared, and the victor, in response to a plea of the Elders charged with the supervision of the affairs of the Temple of Artemis, granted the Goddess exemption from all taxation. Teos and Colophon also submitted, but both Clazomenae, strengthened by reinforcements sent by sea, and Erythrae offered resistance, and Prepelaus, failing to capture them, was compelled to be content with devastating their territories. Unable to accomplish more, he withdrew into Lydia, where the city of Sardis, although not its citadel, was surrendered to him by Antigonus's generals.

Meanwhile Demetrius arrived with his fleet in Ephesus, where the small garrison left by Prepelaus surrendered.[3] Stationing soldiers of his own to hold the place, Demetrius sailed northward through the Hellespont. Lampsacus and Parium were forced to submit, and before advancing in the spring of 301 to join his father in Phrygia, he left a small force to hold the Asianic side of the Bosporus. Thus the little that Lysimachus and Prepelaus had accomplished was quickly nullified.

Although by the victory won at Ipsus Lysimachus gained the mastery of western Asia Minor, his rule did not remain undisputed;[4] for the indomitable Demetrius, having escaped from that disastrous battle, did not cease to oppose his father's enemy. Ephesus, remaining in his power, served as his headquarters; when, during a temporary absence, the commandant entered into negotiations with Lysimachus, who offered him fifty talents for surrendering the city, Demetrius, returning in haste, put the traitor to death.[5] Even the marriage of his daughter Stratonice to his father's enemy Seleucus was used as a means of strengthening his position with the cities, for the envoy who announced the event both to the Ephesians and to "all the Hellenes" also assured them of the "good will" of both monarchs.

Evidence of this "good will" was at once apparent in the case of Miletus, which the new allies—short-lived though their alliance was—wished to bind firmly to their cause. At the outset of his career Seleucus—or so it was later maintained—had received a prophecy from Apollo at Didyma declaring that he would become king, and afterward he and his dynasty claimed descent from the God.[6] In any case, he sought, probably at this time, to win the favour of both Apollo and the Milesians by returning the bronze statue of the God which King Darius, after capturing Miletus, had carried away to Persia. His son Antiochus, in furtherance of the King's policy, likewise presented Miletus with a colonnade with shops, serving the purpose of a modern bazaar, the income to be used for the Temple at Didyma.[7] The citizens, in acknowledgement of the gift, erected statues of Seleucus and his first wife, Apame, recalling with gratitude the Queen's interest in the Milesians who had served in her husband's army. Demetrius also established a hold on Miletus, where in 295 he was elected to the office of stephanephorus.

During this time, however, other cities enjoyed neither peace nor prosperity. Priene fell into the hands of a tyrant named Hiero, a native of the place, who, seizing supreme power, ruled for three years.[8] Ephesus, during Demetrius's absence, was in charge of the commandant Aenetus, who showed himself ready to co-operate with the city-authorities when, in response to an appeal from some exiles from Priene, now acting as the garrison of a border-stronghold, they promised arms and assistance. But no money was available for the purpose, and the expense could be met only by selling the rights of citizenship in Ephesus to a specified number of duly qualified applicants.[9] During this period also it was necessary for the Ephesians to adopt drastic measures for the relief of those citizens who had mortgaged their property and were unable to discharge their indebtedness; accordingly, a law was enacted which provided that instead of a general foreclosure public officials should estimate the value of the land in question and divide it between creditor and debtor in proportion to the amount that was owed.[10]

Demetrius, in fact, occupied with his desire for conquest, first in the East at the expense of Seleucus, and then in Greece, gave no protection to the cities of Asia. They were therefore soon overpowered by the armies of Lysimachus.[11] Ephesus, commanded by Aenetus, was captured by a ruse; the resistance offered by Smyrna and Colophon proved to be vain; and there is no reason to suppose that any of the other cities which had supported Demetrius was able to make a successful stand.

As the result of this victory, Ionia was now conquered territory. The cities were no longer in possession of the independence which Alexander had recognized as theirs. The victor, although permitting them to retain their Federation, nevertheless placed them under a prefect appointed by himself.[12] If we may suppose that the Federation's resolution in praise of one of these prefects—a citizen of Miletus, who bore the official title of "friend of the King"—was actuated by genuine gratitude rather than by expediency, this particular appointee, at least, was wisely selected.

There can be little doubt that, high-handed though certain of Lysimachus's acts may have seemed, some cities benefited materially under his rule.[13] The removal of Ephesus to a new—and henceforth permanent—site nearer the sea could not fail to stimulate its trade, and the wall which the King caused to be built, perhaps for the purpose of resisting an attack by Demetrius, served to protect the city against all enemies. Its population, moreover, was increased by the addition of some of the inhabitants of Colophon and Lebedus, whom Lysimachus compelled to move to Ephesus, and although the two cities must have suffered as the result of this action, both, nevertheless, survived. In the case of Smyrna, Lysimachus, although the city had resisted his army, furthered Antigonus's efforts for its rehabilitation, and here also he seems to have been responsible for the construction of a new wall.

Priene, too, had reason to be grateful; for, freed from its tyrant, it was aided by the ruler to repel the Magnesians, who, in conjunction with the native inhabitants of the neighbourhood, were plundering its territory. The citizens, in return, sent envoys to Lysimachus to congratulate him on the success of his administration, and, as the King himself expressed it, they "obeyed with enthusiasm" the commands of a royal officer. They even presented Lysimachus with a golden wreath and erected an altar for his worship. Somewhat later their gratitude was increased by the favourable decision of the ruler when he acted as arbitrator in their long-standing territorial dispute with Samos.

Meanwhile, the peace of the cities was again endangered when Demetrius, in 287/6, made another attempt to gain possession of those places which had been his father's allies.[14] With his fleet and an army said to number 11,000 men, he arrived at Miletus, where he was received by the citizens. Other cities also submitted, some voluntarily, others under compulsion, and, advancing into the interior of Lydia, Demetrius captured Sardis. With this success, however, his power came to an end, for, unable to cope with an army led against him by Lysimachus's son, he was compelled to retreat with a part of his force to eastern Asia Minor. In the course of his flight, during which both he and his men suffered great privations, he was taken prisoner by Seleucus, and after three years of captivity his tempestuous career was ended by an illness said to have been caused by dissipation. Lysimachus, it may be supposed, had little difficulty in reasserting his power over the cities which had received his rival. Miletus was punished by an indemnity so heavy that the citizens could pay the second installment only by borrowing the sum of twelve talents from Cnidus.[15]

In the Troad there seems to have been little resistance to Lysimachus and there is no reason to suppose that the cities of this district were treated as conquered territory.[a] Lampsacus and Parium, it will be remembered, had received him on his first arrival in Asia Minor and their subsequent capture by Demetrius could hardly have afforded grounds for depriving them of the independence which Lysimachus had previously recognized. Ilium, we are told, was increased in size by the incorporation in it of some "ancient cities" in the neighbourhood and was fortified by the construction of a new wall.[16] Alexandria Troas, which Antigonus had founded and named after himself, was likewise improved and renamed after the conqueror of Asia, and here also a new wall seems to have been constructed.[17] The city of Scepsis was rehabilitated by granting permission to those of its inhabitants whom Antigonus had moved to Alexandria to return to their former home.

[a] See note 12.

In thus strengthening places of importance, particularly those having the possibility of development as centres of trade, Lysimachus carried out Antigonus's policy of reducing the number of small and impoverished cities by combining them into larger communities with a greater promise of future prosperity. It is easy to see, however, that these measures could not always have been carried out without compulsion, and that this policy must have been regarded as an infraction of the cities' rights.[18] Equally distasteful to the cities, perhaps, was Lysimachus's action in serving as arbitrator in territorial disputes, such as that between Priene and Samos; on the other hand, it must be taken into consideration that he may have done so at the request of the disputants. His action, moreover, in subjecting the conquered cities of Ionia to the rule of a prefect was undoubtedly a restriction of their liberty. At the same time, by their defection to his rival they had put themselves in the position of enemies. Nevertheless, they were allowed to retain their city-governments and to administer their own finances. The honours bestowed on Lysimachus at Priene were the result of action taken by the *demos*, which was formally addressed by him in his reply, and his letter to Samos was sent with like formality to the "Council and People." The Milesians had complete freedom in making their arrangements to raise the money needed for the payment of the indemnity, and the Ionian cities, which rewarded the consideration shown them by their prefect by granting him exemption from all charges imposed by them, were evidently able to levy their own taxes. In thus permitting the cities to retain their autonomy in internal affairs, while at the same time taking the position of a superior and often acting arbitrarily to accomplish what seemed conducive to their advantage, as well as in adopting certain measures to ensure their support, Lysimachus appears to have desired not so much to reduce them to the position of subjects as to weld them together into a empire.

Nevertheless, when Lysimachus, twenty years after his defeat of Antigonus, was in turn overthrown by his former ally, Seleucus,[b] the cities, hoping for greater freedom, welcomed the change of ruler.[c] Their status undoubtedly seemed precarious, for, having through necessity supported Lysimachus, they might now, with the rest of Asia Minor, be regarded as conquered territory. The victor, however, was disposed to respect their rights, and they, in turn, made every effort

b See Chap. I note 5.   c Memnon 8, 2.

to gain his favour and, with it, the recognition of their independence. Seleucus had already shown his friendship for Miletus both in the construction of his son's colonnade[d] and subsequently, about the time of Demetrius's last invasion of Caria, in a truly regal gift to the Temple at Didyma, consisting of gold and silver vessels, incense and sacrificial animals.[19] Now, to requite his kindness and at the same time to strengthen their own position, the Milesians elected Antiochus to the office of stephanephorus. At Ephesus the partisans of Seleucus hastened to seize the place by violence. Arsinoe, Lysimachus's widow, was forced to flee for her life, and the city resumed its ancient name. At Priene statues of Seleucus and Antiochus were erected in the Temple of Athena, and at Erythrae a festival called Seleuceia was established and a stanza added to a hymn to Asclepius, in which Seleucus was hailed as the son of Apollo. Both at Magnesia-on-Maeander and at Colophon one of the city-tribes was called Seleucis, and the people of Ilium decreed an altar to Seleucus with a sacrifice and a festival to be held in a month which received his name.

Seleucus, however, was unable to deal with the question of the cities' freedom; for only seven months after his victory over Lysimachus he met his death in Thrace at the hands of an assassin.[e] The determination of their status, therefore, devolved upon his son Antiochus. The new ruler had succeeded to a troubled inheritance, for he was faced by wars in various parts of his widespread empire, of which the districts of Asia Minor, connected with his ancestral kingdom of Syria by a long and dangerous route, constituted only a comparatively small part. He was forced at the same time both to suppress a rebellion in Syria and in the western part of his dominions to cope with two dangerous enemies, Demetrius's son, Antigonus Gonatas, now king of Macedonia, who had as allies in Asia the ruler of Bithynia and the cities of the Euxine coast, and, particularly, Ptolemy II of Egypt, who, as the owner of a formidable navy, was eager to build up an empire in the Aegean.[20] Antiochus had also to deal with the Celtic Galatians, whom Nicomedes, the new king of Bithynia, brought across the Strait in 278 and presently turned loose on Asia Minor.[f]

Antiochus, it is true, soon made peace with Antigonus and his allies and about five years after succeeding to the throne broke the strength of the Celts by defeating them in a great battle. But the powerful King of Egypt continued his attempts to wrest the Asianic coast from the Seleucid monarchs, and against him Antiochus and his son and suc-

[d] See note 7.   [e] See Chap. I note 6.   [f] See Chap. I note 10.

94

cessor, the second of the name, during the thirty-five years of their combined reigns, waged two—perhaps three—wars.

The aggressions of Ptolemy II began about the time of the death of Seleucus, when he extended his power to the coast of Caria by establishing a control over Halicarnassus and Myndus.[21] Advancing still farther, he increased the number of his dependencies by the addition of Samos, a place of great strategic importance for maintaining a hold over the neighbouring coast. He also obtained a hold on Miletus, which, despite the benefits previously received from both Seleucus and Antiochus, in the year following the latter's tenure of office as stephanephorus accepted a gift of territory from the Egyptian King. Somewhat later the citizens entered into closer relations with him by making a compact of "friendship and alliance."

Both Antiochus and his son after him, accordingly, needing the aid of the coast cities in the various wars with Egypt and especially the use of their ships and their harbours, were willing to make concessions and by recognizing their independence to gain their support.[22] The cities, on their side, also sought to win the royal favour. Ilium, having little to furnish in the way of practical assistance amid the wars which beset Antiochus at the outset of his reign, offered prayer and sacrifice in his behalf and apparently even created a priest for his worship.[g] Later, after he had "established peace for the cities," the Ilians celebrated a festival in his honour and voted to erect a golden equestrian statue of him as "Saviour of the People." The freedom of Ilium was recognized, as was also that of the neighbouring Scepsis, which had been restored by Lysimachus, and both cities, as well as, presumably, the other communities of the Troad, became Antiochus's allies.[h]

In Ionia Antiochus, likewise refraining from using whatever power the right of conquest gave him, recognized the cities as independent democracies. Erythrae, sending a special delegation—apparently to him rather than to his successor—cited the precedent established by Alexander and Antigonus, who had declared the city free and exempt from tribute.[23] In response, it received the assurance that the King would "join in maintaining its autonomy and grant it exemption from all charges as well as from contributions to the Galatian fund," presumably the city's share either of the cost of Antiochus's campaign against the Celts or of the "black-mail" paid them to refrain from raiding. Priene, if we may believe a story of doubtful credibility, was

g *O.G.I.* 219 (see note 22).
h *O.G.I.* 221 = Welles, nos. 12-13 (see Chap. III note 40).

declared free at the instance of a royal favourite.[i] Similar recognition was also accorded to the others, save for Miletus and Samos, allies of Egypt, and a few years before the end of Antiochus's reign the Ionian Federation sent envoys from the several cities to announce that they had established in his honour a festival modelled on the one which they celebrated in memory of Alexander and were proposing to build a sanctuary for his worship.[24] The envoys were charged also to exhort the King to "take all care for the Ionian cities, to the end that in the future, being free and under the people's rule, they may be governed in accordance with their ancestral laws." The implied comparison of Antiochus to Alexander seems to show that the monarch was regarded (and regarded himself) as carrying out the policy of their liberator and confirming the action taken by him and by Antigonus.

As a result, perhaps, of Antiochus's concessions to the cities, Ptolemy II made little progress in extending his sphere of influence along the Aegean coast.[25] The Carian cities of Caunus, Myndus and Halicarnassus, as well as smaller places like Calynda, were dominated by Egypt, and while they preserved their local autonomy, this domination, professedly an "alliance," actually amounted to an outright rule. These coast cities were subject to a military governor and a royal controller; at Halicarnassus there was a representative of the King's treasury and Calynda had an Egyptian garrison, the soldiers of which were billeted on the citizens. Miletus and Samos also continued their relations with Ptolemy, although in the case of the former the apparent lack of any Egyptian officials suggests that the alliance which existed in name really connoted a position of equality. But even in Caria, Bargylia maintained an alliance with Antiochus, and in Ionia, although about the time of his death Ephesus was held by Ptolemy's son, the occupation did not last long. Teos and the cities farther north remained allies of the Seleucid King. Only the Aeolic Methymna on Lesbos, where Ptolemy's wife Arsinoe had an estate, appears to have come under the power of Egypt.

Nevertheless, the possible extension of this power still constituted a threat to the supremacy of the Seleucids in western Asia Minor, weakened, as it was, by the victory of Eumenes I which cost Antiochus the suzerainty of Pergamum.[j] It was natural, therefore, that Antiochus II, who succeeded to the throne in 261, should continue his father's policy toward the cities. Their support was all the more necessary when, a

[i] Sextus Empiricus *adv. Math.* 1 293: Athenaeus 1 34, p. 19 D.
[j] See Chap. I note 16.

year or two after his accession, another war broke out with Egypt.[26] In this struggle Antigonus Gonatas of Macedonia also was involved, and with him Antiochus joined forces. Their combined fleets met Ptolemy's ships in a great battle off the island of Cos, in which the Egyptian navy was defeated and presumably seriously weakened. It was perhaps in consequence of this battle—the actual order of events is unknown—that an adventurer named Timarchus was able to seize Miletus and set himself up as tyrant of the city. He appears also to have captured Samos, and his cause was strengthened when Ptolemy's son, in possession of Ephesus, rebelled against his father and supported the new ruler of Miletus. Timarchus, however, was soon overthrown by Antiochus. Thereupon the grateful Milesians conferred high honours upon the King, especially the surname of "the God," and the city became his ally. At Ephesus the younger Ptolemy was killed by his own soldiers, and after a sea-battle near the entrance to the harbour resulted in the defeat of the commander of the Egyptian fleet by Antiochus's navy combined with that of Rhodes, Ephesus fell into the hands of the Seleucid King.

It has sometimes been held that Antiochus II issued a general proclamation recognizing the freedom of the cities of Ionia.[k] However this may be, it is evident that at least some cities were treated with great consideration. Continuing and extending his father's practice of establishing royal mints, Antiochus issued silver tetradrachms not only, as his father had done, in important commercial centres in Ionia, but in those of Aeolis and the Troad as well.[27] Ephesus, it is true, which seems to have become the royal residence, was placed under a governor, but Miletus, in addition to the recognition of its freedom, received from him "great benefactions." Samos, which, after the overthrow of Timarchus, presumably fell into Antiochus's hands, experienced similar treatment; for certain lands in the plain of Anaea, in the city's mainland territory, which the King assigned to some of his "friends," were restored to the Samians when their envoy presented a protest against the seizure. Antiochus also attempted to act as arbitrator for Samos and Priene in their ancient dispute. It was presumably in gratitude for favours received from him that Smyrna founded the festival called Antiocheia and not only conferred divine honours on both Antiochus and his mother Stratonice but gave the name of the Queen-mother to the Goddess Aphrodite, who had a temple in the city. The Smyrniots

k See note 22.

appear also to have named three months in their calendar after Antiochus, his mother and his wife, Laodice.

Thus when in 255 B.C. or soon afterward a general peace was concluded by Antigonus and Antiochus with Ptolemy, all Ionia was lost to Egypt.[28] This peace, however, contained the seeds of another war, for according to its terms, already described, Antiochus agreed to divorce Laodice and marry the sister of Ptolemy III, the new ruler of Egypt. As a result, when Antiochus died at Ephesus in 246, his son, Seleucus II, was forced to take up arms against the Egyptian King in defence of his eastern dominions, which Ptolemy, professing to support the rights of his sister's infant son, had promptly invaded.[1]

On setting out for Syria soon after his accession, Seleucus attempted to ensure the allegiance of the Aegean cities by reaffirming his father's policy toward them.[29] A letter to the Milesians, evidently written at this time, expressed his gratitude for a "holy wreath from the sanctuary," with which they had crowned him, as well as his desire to raise their city "to a more illustrious condition." This policy was apparent in a greater degree in his action with regard to Smyrna. It may be supposed that the city, re-established as a *polis* by Antigonus and so without the right to freedom which was the inheritance of the ancient cities, had never been formally recognized as free. This freedom, together with the exemption from all tribute which was properly its concomitant, was now specifically granted by Seleucus. Acting, according to his own statement, in obedience to the oracle of Apollo at Delphi, he greatly strengthened the position of Smyrna by declaring both the city and its territory sacred to Aphrodite and therefore inviolable. The importance of this declaration was much increased by the King's request to his fellow-rulers, as well as to the city-states in general, to take like action, thereby obtaining for Smyrna a guarantee against attack. This is the first known instance among the cities of Asia of such a guarantee, but as time went on, other communities also obtained similar assurances.

The prevailing lawlessness and the increasing tendency to disregard the ordinary sanctity of a temple and the right of protection for those who sought refuge in it led to the need of securing inviolability for individual sanctuaries. This was obtained, as in the case of the Temple of Aphrodite at Smyrna, by special promises assuring the safety of the building and its worshippers as well as of the participants in the festival of the deity. Such an assurance was given, probably soon after 240 B.C.,

[1] See above p. 8.

to the famous Temple of Asclepius at Cos by cities not only in the Balkan Peninsula but even in Sicily and Italy, and also by as many as four monarchs, including Ziaëlas, King of Bithynia, and probably Seleucus II, who showed himself not unwilling thus to conciliate an ally of his enemy, Ptolemy.[30]

But in spite of the precautions taken by Seleucus to retain his hold on the Greek cities, Ptolemy III, although his armies were defeated in the East, not only regained what his father had held in Asia Minor, but also succeeded in extending his power toward the north, where he seized islands as far as the Hellespont and even places on the coast of Thrace.[31] Samos was quickly recovered, and Priene and Ephesus fell into his hands. Lebedus, too, came under the power of Egypt and received the name of Ptolemais. Smyrna, which incurred "many great dangers" but was "undaunted by the enemy's approach," may have been the object of a fruitless attack on the part of an Egyptian landing-party, but there is nothing to show that any city on the mainland north of Lebedus came under Ptolemy's control.

During the war between Seleucus and Ptolemy, while the former's mother acted as regent of his western dominions, and especially during the subsequent disastrous struggle between Seleucus and his younger brother, Antiochus Hierax,[m] the waning power of the Seleucids and the lack of any strong central authority tended to increase the strength of those cities which had succeeded in holding out against Egyptian domination. The pretender Hierax seems for a time to have kept a hold over the cities of the Troad, where the royal mints issued his coins.[32] He did not, however, long maintain his position, and his defeat at the hands of Attalus I of Pergamum and consequent flight from Asia Minor left the country in a condition of chaos. This finally made it possible for Attalus, who by his victories over the Galatians could represent himself as the champion of the Greeks, to come forth in the role of the cities' protector.

Meanwhile, as the power and prestige of the Seleucids diminished, the ties of relationship between the Asiatic cities which had been their allies and the mother-country grew stronger. After the general recognition of the inviolability of Smyrna at the beginning of the reign of Seleucus II, the city was invited to participate in the festival of the Soteria, which had been founded to commemorate the deliverance of the Temple of Apollo at Delphi from the depredations of the Galatian invaders and was reorganized about this time on a more elaborate

[m] See above p. 8f.

scale by the powerful league of the Aetolians.[33] A similar invitation had been extended, apparently two or three years prior to that received by Smyrna, to Chios. About the same time Chios was also invited to become a member of the Amphictyonic Council, which, dominated by the Aetolians, included the representatives of other states also and exercised a weighty influence in Greek affairs. It was a distinction as yet held by no other Asianic city. The invitation was more than a compliment, for the decree conveying it contained the promise that the privateers of the members of the Aetolian League, which harried the islands of the Aegean, would refrain from any attack on the Chians or their merchantmen. Somewhat later, similar guarantees were given to Miletus and, toward the close of the third century, to Mitylene and to Magnesia-on-Maeander, which also received a seat in the Amphictyonic Council.

The danger from the Aetolians was not the only peril with which the sea-faring communities had to contend, for the pirates of Crete also were constantly preying on the islands and the coast cities. Although the powerful navy of the Rhodians had done much to hold these marauders in check,[n] it was not able wholly to suppress the evil. It was necessary, accordingly, for the cities to make their own arrangements for the protection of their commerce and their citizens. Thus we find the Milesians concluding agreements with some of the cities of Crete by which each party bound itself not to purchase citizens of the other if offered for sale as slaves.[34] This was an arrangement conducive to the interest of Miletus rather than to that of the Cretans, since it was evidently designed to protect the citizens against capture and sale into slavery by the pirates of the island. About the same time the Milesians, perhaps with a view to maintaining better relations with the Cretans and also protecting themselves against any aggression from outside, employed mercenaries from Crete, who on the expiration of their term of service received allotments of land and, together with their families, were enrolled as Milesian citizens.

About this time also the Milesians developed a policy of entering into closer relations with other cities. This policy they had adopted as early as the time of Alexander, when, perceiving the advantages to be gained by forming combinations of cities to better their economic position, they began to employ the principle of isopolity or the reciprocity of civic rights.[35] This relationship, first formed with the neighbouring city of Pygela on the coast near Ephesus, was soon extended to cities

[n] See Chap. XII note 9.

which, according to long-established and tenaciously held traditions, had been founded by Milesian settlers, namely Cyzicus, Olbia in south Russia and (somewhat later) Istrus near the mouths of the Danube. Now, about the time of the hiring of the Cretan mercenaries, these rights in Miletus were granted to citizens of Cius on the Propontis, and soon afterwards an interchange of citizenship was arranged with Tralles in the Maeander basin and Mylasa in Caria, although with these two cities Miletus had no racial or sentimental connexion.

During this period there was an increase in the tendency of the Asianic cities to play a more important role in the affairs of the Hellenic world. Thus in 219 a request was made to Cyzicus by the ministers of Ptolemy IV to join the Rhodians, Aetolians and Byzantines in sending ambassadors to Antiochus III, the new Seleucid king, for the purpose of deterring him from a projected invasion of Egypt.[o] About the same time and again in the following year, the Chians, perhaps as the result of their relations with the Aetolians, likewise joined the Rhodians in attempting to intervene in the war between the League and Philip V of Macedonia. Later, in 209 and 208, both Chios and Mitylene, acting with Rhodes and Byzantium, made a similar effort to mediate in the war of the allied Aetolians and Romans against Philip.[p]

Meanwhile, in consequence of the victory won by Attalus I of Pergamum over the generals of Seleucus III, who had succeeded his father in 226, and the assassination, three years later, of the young monarch, the prestige of the Seleucids in Asia Minor had sunk to a low ebb.[q] Attalus, accordingly, was able to consolidate his power by forming alliances with those cities which were neighbours of his kingdom. Cyzicus from the time of Philetaerus onward had been well disposed to the royal house of Pergamum.[r] At this time, however, Lampsacus, Ilium and Alexandria Troas and probably even Smyrna, for all its former devotion to Seleucus II, entered into relations with the Pergamene King.[36] For a short time, to be sure, Attalus's strength was seriously diminished by the success of the rebellious Seleucid general, Achaeus, to whom some cities, especially those in Aeolis, submitted out of fear. But the departure of Achaeus for southern Asia Minor in 218 enabled Attalus again to assert his power and to persuade or, when necessary, compel the cities to enter into an alliance. Thus, not only those which had previously accepted him, but also the Aeolian cities

[o] Polybius v 63, 5.
[q] See above p. 9.
[p] See Chap. III note 75.
[r] See above pp. 5, 9 and 81.

of Cyme, Aegae and Temnus, as well as the Ionian Phocaea and even the more distant Teos and Colophon, became allies of Pergamum. Ephesus and Samos and the cities of the Carian coast were still in the power of Egypt, but those in the Troad and in Aeolis and in the greater part of Ionia were lost to the Seleucid monarchs. Antiochus III, to be sure, was able with Attalus's help to defeat and kill Achaeus and thus reassert his supremacy in the interior of Asia Minor,[s] but for the Greeks of the coast the dominant power was Pergamum. There is every reason to suppose that Attalus's allies maintained their position as free and independent states, and even in Caria, as Egypt under the feeble Ptolemy IV gradually relaxed its hold, the cities probably recovered a certain amount of liberty.

During this period of freedom there is evidence of a growing tendency among the cities to play a further part among the communities of the Hellenic world by instituting festivals in which all Greeks were invited to participate. Such a step had already been taken by Cos, where the contests held in connexion with the Asclepieia had been made Pan-Hellenic.[t] This example was followed about 212 by Miletus, where the contest held periodically in honour of Apollo at Didyma, hitherto a purely local celebration, was transformed into a general "sacred" festival after the pattern of the great festivals of Greece. Since the contests were now open to all Greeks who were willing to take part, it was necessary to obtain a general recognition of the festival as worthy of this rank, and to this end envoys were sent to cities and kings to ask for their endorsement.[37] To encourage a general participation, a general assurance of safety for the contestants was also obtained, as well as a guarantee of the inviolability of the Temple. A little later, about 207, Magnesia-on-Maeander, in obedience to an oracle of Apollo issued in 220 after Artemis Leucophryene had "appeared" to her priestess, also founded a Pan-Hellenic festival with musical and athletic contests, to be held every four years in honour of the Goddess. Envoys were sent to the various city-states and monarchs, asking for their official recognition and a promise that the inviolability of Magnesia and its territory should be respected.[38] About two years later, the Teans, following the Magnesians' example, instituted a similar festival in honour of their patron-god, Dionysus. They also sent out envoys, who bore similar requests to the Aetolian League and various communities both in Greece and in Crete to declare Teos and its territory sacred to the God and inviolable.[39] In spite of the city's alliance with Attalus, the envoys

[s] See above p. 11.   [t] See above p. 98f.

who were sent to some of the Cretan cities were accompanied by a
representative of Antiochus III. The King evidently exercised great
influence in the city, for ten years later his ambassador in Rome presented a similar request from the Teans to the Senate. This was answered by a letter declaring the city and its territory sacred and inviolable and, as far as the Roman people was concerned, free from all
obligations.

The Romans had, indeed, begun to play a part in Asianic affairs.[40]
Toward the end of the third century a wide acceptance of the myth
which connected Rome with the Trojan Aeneas had aroused an interest in Ilium, and relations of some sort seem to have been established with the "kindred" city. While little credence can be placed
in the genuineness of an "ancient letter," on the basis of which the
claim was made in A.D. 53 that the Romans promised to make a treaty
of friendship and alliance with a "King Seleucus" on the condition
that he would declare their "kinsmen" the Ilians exempt from tribute,
Ilium became an ally of Attalus I, and like Attalus, was "included" in
the treaty of Phoenice, concluded in 205 by the Senate with Philip V
of Macedonia. Thereby Ilium obtained recognition as an independent
state under the Romans' protection, and when, in 190 B.C., their army
arrived in Asia, one of the first acts of the commander was to offer
a sacrifice to Athena Ilias commemorating the relationship between
the city and Rome.[u]

When, four years after the treaty of Phoenice, Philip's aggressions
and the fears aroused by Attalus and the Rhodians caused the Senate,
in the name of Greek freedom, to enter the war against him, Rome
became a protector of the city-states of the Hellenic world.[v] Philip's
seizure and destruction of the Greek cities of Myrleia and Cius on the
Propontis in 202 had caused the Rhodians to declare war against him,
and his occupation of Samos in the following year[41] and the attempt
which he seems to have made to capture Chios revealed him still more
clearly as the foe of Hellenism.[42] The coast cities, therefore, generally
supported Attalus and the Rhodians against the aggressor. After the
Allies' naval victory off Chios the Rhodians' fleet retired to the harbour
of the city, and Attalus found shelter in Erythrae.[w] Miletus, on the
other hand, proved unable to resist. The city was forced to receive
Philip, and the King requited its surrender and the honours which
the citizens paid him by seizing a portion of their territory and pre-

[u] Livy XXXVII 37, 2f. [v] See above p. 14. [w] Polybius XVI 6, 5 and 13; 8, 5.

senting it to the Magnesians in payment for supplies of food for his troops.[43] Although his ensuing expedition into Caria, at first successful, soon collapsed, his forces were nevertheless able to hold some places until the end of the war.[x] But when, after three years of fighting in Epirus and Macedonia, the Romans forced Philip to make peace, they ordered him at the Rhodians' demand to evacuate Bargylia and Iasus, together with Pidasa and Euromus in the interior of Caria, as well as Abydus on the Hellespont.[44] These cities were thereupon declared independent. This step was followed by the proclamation at Corinth in 196, in which the Senate's commissioners, in fulfilment of the obligation assumed on entering the war, announced the freedom of the Greeks, both in Europe and in Asia.[y]

Meanwhile a war of potentially serious consequences was being waged in Asia between Miletus and its neighbour, Magnesia-on-Maeander, the bone of contention being the territory which Philip had taken from the former and given to Magnesia. The public finances of Miletus seem previously to have been in a depleted condition, for in 205—four years before Philip's seizure of its territory—the city-authorities found it necessary to arrange a loan amounting to somewhat over twenty-three talents.[45] The prosperity of the individual Milesians, however, appears not to have suffered, for the full amount of the loan was subscribed, and in the year after Philip's act of aggression a public-spirited citizen presented the city with the sum of ten talents to be used as an endowment for the education of free-born boys.[46] In any case, the Milesians found themselves able to take advantage of the withdrawal of Philip's troops from Caria and embark on a war with Magnesia for the recovery of the territory of which they had been deprived.[47] The neighbours of the two combatants were also drawn into the conflict, for the Milesians obtained the aid of Heracleia and Magnesia that of Priene. So serious, in fact, did the struggle become that there was a general demand for its termination and finally, in 196, a peace between the warring cities was effected by the mediation of Rhodes and eight Asianic city-states, aided by Athens and the Achaean League. The outcome, however, was unfavourable for Miletus, for the disputed territory remained in the possession of Magnesia.

There can be little doubt that both Rome's declaration of the freedom of the Asianic cities and the efforts of the Rhodians and their associates to end the war between Miletus and Magnesia were due to a general anxiety over the pretensions of Antiochus III; for in 197 this monarch

[x] See Chap. I note 40.   [y] See Chap. III note 141.

had begun to carry out a plan for the restoration of the Seleucid power in western Asia Minor by bringing the free cities into his empire.[z] For some years past, Antiochus had been strengthening his influence over the cities by using every opportunity to show his good will.[48] Thus in 205, while in Persia, he and his son had written courteously to the Magnesians "approving" the honours paid to Artemis, and a year or two later his representative aided the Teans in their mission in Crete. Privileges were also conferred on the ancient city of Amyzon in Caria and on the native community of Alabanda, as well as on Tralles and Nysa on the northern bank of the Maeander.

The arrival of Antiochus on the Aegean coast with his army and navy and his occupation of Ephesus in the autumn of 197 have already been described.[a] The significance of the King's aggressive policy and his evident intention of bringing western Asia Minor, including the city-states, under his sovereignty were clearly apparent to the Greeks of the coast. The Rhodians, by declaring themselves ready to defend Caunus, Myndus, Halicarnassus and Samos, still nominally allies of Egypt, forestalled any plan that Antiochus may have had for seizing these places.[49] He seems actually to have made overtures to Cos, but with what success is unknown. Iasus, which had previously looked to Rhodes for assistance against an accomplice of Philip V, received from Antiochus the assurance that its independence would be "preserved," a promise which the King afterward fulfilled by stationing a garrison in the city and driving out all those who had opposed him.

In the far north, Cyzicus appears to have been unmolested by Antiochus, in consequence probably of its strength and its remoteness from his field of operations rather than because of the inviolability which it had recently received by the declaration of the oracle at Delphi that the city was sacred.[50] The people of Lampsacus, aware of the danger even before Antiochus's seizure of Ephesus and feeling the need of an ally stronger than Attalus, appealed directly to Rome for protection and the recognition of their city's independence.[51] Their envoys, approaching the Roman naval commander who was still in the Aegean, obtained a promise to maintain the "democracy, autonomy and peace" of their city; but, wishing a further guarantee, they travelled on to Massalia in Gaul, like Lampsacus a colony of Phocaea, and after obtaining spokesmen from the Council of the city they appeared with these before the Roman Senate. Their petition that Lampsacus might be included among the signatories of the treaty about to be made with Philip and so taken under the protection of Rome was courteously heard, and the Senators seem to have given them to understand that their plea would be granted. At the same time, however, evading responsibility for any possibly inexpedient decision, they referred this and the envoys' other requests to the Roman commissioners then in Greece.

The action thus taken by the Lampsacenes was without precedent among the Asianic cities. It was a step of great importance, for it showed that Lampsacus was ready to accept the position which Rome had taken on entering the war against Philip and was about to take in the treaty concluded with him, namely that of protector of the Greeks of Asia as well as of the mother-land. For the present, little was accomplished by the Lampsacenes' request, for they did not become a party to the treaty. Antiochus, moreover, seizing Abydus in order to control the crossing of the Hellespont, not only disregarded Rome's previous declaration that the place was free, but also made use of his troops stationed there to threaten Lampsacus. At the same time he offered to recognize the city's independence on condition that it would become his ally. The offer was so evidently a ruse for reducing Lampsacus to the position of a subject that it was firmly rejected. A similar offer made, now or later, to Alexandria Troas was likewise refused.[52] Ilium, however, was unable to hold out, and four years later, Antiochus, on his way to invade Greece, stopped in the city to offer sacrifice to Athena.

Like the Hellespontine cities, Smyrna also resisted the attempts of the Seleucid King to obtain control of the city by either persuasion or force.[53] At the invitation of the Roman commissioners who held a conference with Antiochus in Thrace in 196, a representative from Smyrna, as well as two from Lampsacus, took part in the discussion and angered the monarch by the freedom with which they presented their case. In the following year Smyrna formally placed itself under Rome's protection by consecrating a temple to the deified *Urbs Roma*, a new cult, hitherto unknown either in Italy or in Greece. As created at this time by the Smyrniots, it was destined to be founded in many other cities also as the symbol of their allegiance to Rome.

It is not improbable that Antiochus's hope that those cities which were ill-protected by walls or armed forces would submit to his threats or his offers was at least partially fulfilled.[54] The readiness, however, with which the great majority of them, as will presently be shown, supported the Romans when they at last entered the war is an indication that although for a time some were compelled to accept the King's terms, they were willing enough to abandon him as soon as the opportunity arose.

During the four years which elapsed between Antiochus's arrival in Asia and the actual outbreak of the war the Romans in the course of their negotiations with the King maintained the position taken by their commissioners in Corinth in 196, namely, that Antiochus must refrain from making war on any of the autonomous cities of Asia.[55] It may indeed be true that this policy was used as a ground for opposing the King's pretensions, and that had he consented in 193, when his envoys asked for an alliance, to refrain from entering Europe, the Romans would have been willing to sacrifice the cause of the cities. But, as it was, the Romans' insistence on holding fast to this principle constituted a promise to recognize the cities' sovereignty. Neither Rome nor the cities admitted the validity of Antiochus's claim that those communities which had an inherent right to liberty might receive this only as an act of the King's grace or regarded his demand that they yield to his will as anything but an act of aggression.

When finally in 192 war broke out between Antiochus and the Romans in alliance with Rhodes and Pergamum, the cities with but few exceptions supported the cause of the Allies.[56] Ephesus became the King's headquarters, and Magnesia-on-Maeander and Iasus were held by his troops. Teos had already been brought under his control; during the war Phocaea, which had at first declared for Rome, was betrayed to him by his partisans in the city; and Cyme and other places in Aeolis were compelled to surrender. But, on the other hand, Chios and Samos served as the headquarters of the commissaries of the Roman army and navy, Cos, Mitylene, Erythrae and Smyrna furnished ships, and Miletus, Cnidus, Halicarnassus and Myndus carried out orders given by the Roman naval commander, presumably for the requisition of supplies.

The aid thus furnished doubtless contributed to the success of the Allies in the naval campaign of 190, which was followed by the advance into Asia Minor of the Roman army under the command of Lucius Scipio assisted by his elder and abler brother, Publius. On its arrival on the Asianic side of the Hellespont, Antiochus, thoroughly alarmed, offered to abandon all claim not only to those cities which the Romans had undertaken to defend but to the others which had sided with them.[57] But the Scipios, refusing all compromise, demanded the evacuation of the whole of Asia Minor north of the Taurus. This was followed by a promise of complete independence to any city which would place itself under their protection, thus carrying out Rome's professed purpose in entering the war.[58]

After the overwhelming victory of the Romans, aided by the Pergamenes, at Magnesia-near-Sipylus, Ephesus and the other cities which had been held by the King hastened to surrender.[b] During the following year most of the city-states, like the Rhodians and Eumenes of Pergamum, sent delegations to Rome to present their various pleas.[59] The ancient historians relate that the question of the cities' future status was debated in the Senate and, according to the common practice of the writers of history in Antiquity, they included in their narratives speeches purporting to present the arguments for and against the case; one, attributed to Eumenes, maintained that a general liberation of the cities would merely result in increasing Rhodes's power at his expense, while the other, attributed to the Rhodian ambassador, urged the Senators to preserve the cities' freedom. It is possible that the arguments represent two points of view actually held by the Pergamenes and by the Rhodians at one time or another, but the speeches are evidently apocryphal, and it is difficult to believe that the abandonment of the principle of the freedom of the Greeks was ever seriously considered by Rome.

In any case, the Roman commissioners at the conference held at Apameia in 188, acting on general instructions received from the Senate, made the arrangements necessary for the future of the Greek states of Asia.[60] The Rhodians, in return for their loyalty to the cause of the Allies, received a portion which, although smaller by far than the large area assigned to Eumenes, greatly enlarged their possessions on the mainland of Asia Minor. With regard to the free cities, the principle was adopted that those which had supported Rome during the war should retain their status of independence, but those which had aided Antiochus should lose their freedom and be made subject to Eumenes. To some cities which had furnished substantial aid against the King, including Miletus, Smyrna, Chios, Erythrae and Clazomenae, an increase of territory was given. Even Ilium, although it had contributed nothing and had even received Antiochus, seems to have been awarded some of the neighbouring settlements, and Notium, which had resisted the King but appears to have taken no active part in the war, was declared independent. Samos was presumably permitted to retain its recently acquired freedom, as were also the cities of the Carian coast,

b Livy xxxvii 45, 1f.

Halicarnassus, Myndus and Cnidus, while Mylasa, a short distance inland, was expressly declared independent of Rhodes. On the other hand, Ephesus, which had received Antiochus and had been his head-quarters during the war, lost thereby all claim to freedom and became subject to Eumenes. Other cities, however, which had submitted to the enemy received lenient treatment. Thus Magnesia-on-Maeander, which did not surrender to the Romans until after the final defeat of the King, seems to have been permitted to retain at least the right of the inviolability of its temple; freedom was granted to Phocaea, al-though it had deserted to Antiochus, and to Cyme, although it had been forced to surrender to his army. With regard to the subject cities, the principle was adopted that Eumenes should retain those which his father had possessed and should receive in addition those which had supported Antiochus and were now treated as conquered territory, but those which had once been subject to the King but had deserted him for Rome should thenceforth be free.

By the distribution of the Asianic dominions of Antiochus the Rhodians profited far more than the city-states.[61] The territory which they acquired included nearly all of inland Caria, extending on the north to the Maeander and on the east to the mountains which formed the boundary of the district, as well as at least the coast of Lycia, at the southwestern corner of Asia Minor. These new possessions the Rhodians formed into an empire, placing them under the rule of governors with subordinate officials of various ranks.[62]

This gift, to be sure, was not made without protest on the part of some of those who were thus handed over as conquered territory to the Republic, nor was this empire held without opposition.[63] The Lycians, at the outset, refused to accept their new rulers, and after a rebellion a few years later, in the suppression of which the Rhodians were aided by Eumenes of Pergamum, they appealed to Rome. Their appeal was not in vain, for in 177 the Senate, reversing the terms of the commissioners' grant, declared that Lycia had not been an outright "gift," but its people had been placed under Rhodes's supremacy only as "friends and allies."[64] Ten years later, Caunus rebelled, and Mylasa, aided by Alabanda, took advantage of the situation to overrun northern and western Caria.[65] Although these outbreaks were quickly repressed by a Rhodian force, the very fact that they took place affords evidence of the diminution of the Republic's prestige on the mainland.

A much greater loss, however, both of prestige and of power was

soon to follow. In the year in which Caunus rebelled, the Romans defeated Perseus of Macedonia, and although at the beginning of the
war the Rhodians had offered them some warships, the King's overtures to the Republic and an attempt on its part to negotiate a peace
furnished a pretext to those in Rome who wished to weaken the powerful state.[66] Accordingly, in 167 B.C., soon after the conclusion of the
treaty with Perseus, the Senate arbitrarily revoked the grant of 188
and, commanding the Rhodians to remove their garrisons from Caria
and Lycia, declared the two districts free and independent; by this
action both were taken under the protection of Rome.[67] As though this
were not enough, a second demand was made which ordered the evacuation of Stratoniceia and Caunus, cities which the Rhodians had acquired without Rome's assistance.[68] Thus their once extensive mainland
possessions were reduced to the original Peraea, a narrow strip along
the coast. About the same time a blow was struck at the Republic's
commercial prosperity, for a decree of the Senate declared the island
of Delos a free port.[69] By this action not only did the consequent
decrease in customs-dues greatly reduce the public revenues, but
Rhodes's position as the leading trading-centre for the merchantmen
of the Aegean was seriously impaired. It was but a poor compensation
for all these losses that in 164 the Rhodians, after several unsuccessful
attempts, finally obtained from the Senate a formal recognition as
"friends and allies" and therewith the assurance that in the event of
a defensive war they would receive aid from Rome.[70]

Although no longer a first-class power, Rhodes still commanded
respect in Asia Minor. When the Caunians, now independent, tried to
reduce to subjection the neighbouring town of Calynda, the citizens
appealed to the Rhodians for aid, offering to place themselves and
their city under the power of the Republic.[71] The aid was given, but
it was not until the Senate granted its approval that Calynda's offer
was accepted. About the same time, perhaps, Ceramus on the northern
shore of the Gulf of Cos entered into an alliance with Rhodes, receiving a guarantee of safety for both the city and its territory. With the
monarchs also the Republic preserved friendly relations. Demetrius I,
the new King of Syria, presented a quantity of grain to the citizens,[c]
and Eumenes II, also a victim of Roman jealousy, forgave the charges
that the Rhodians had brought against him and not only made them
a gift of grain but promised to build them a marble theatre.[d]

The prestige of the Rhodians, however, was destined to suffer an-

[c] Diodorus XXXI 36.   [d] See Chap. I note 70.

other blow. About 155 a war broke out with the Cretans, caused, presumably, by an attempt to quell their inveterate piracy.[72] The Rhodian navy, now much inferior to that which had once been the pride of the Republic, found it hard to cope with the fleet of small but swift boats which the Cretans, united against a common foe, sent out to battle. The enemy seems to have come off victorious in at least one encounter, and the Rhodian island of Siphnos with its treasure was forced to surrender. An appeal to Rome resulted at first in only the appointment of the usual investigating commission, but while we have no knowledge of the final outcome of the struggle, it is not improbable that Roman intervention played some part in it. Nevertheless, the war effectively limited Rhodes's power to police the seas, with the result that piracy greatly increased in the eastern Mediterranean, so that for nearly a century these robbers were a general scourge.[73]

With the weakening of Rhodes, Roman ill-will toward the Republic gradually declined. When, in 100 B.C., the Senators appealed to the princes of the East to unite in suppressing piracy, they asked the Rhodians to assume the task of conveying their requests,[e] and during the following century the island became a favoured resort for those Romans, who, whether banished from Italy or attracted by the charm of the place and the advantages that it offered for study, chose it as a congenial place of residence.[74]

During the fifty-five years which elapsed between the conference at Apameia and Rome's acquisition of the province of Asia the position of the free cities differed little from their status during the third century. As the result both of the readiness with which most of them had aided Rome during the war against Antiochus and of the leniency shown to those which had been compelled to surrender to the King, the commissioners confirmed the freedom of practically all save Ephesus, which, as has been already observed, was made subject to the King of Pergamum.[75] The Romans, it is true, had as yet adopted no definite policy of imperialism in the East and had taken for themselves no part of Antiochus's dominions. Nevertheless, it was inevitable that they should become the dominant power in Asia Minor, holding a position not very different from that of the earlier Seleucid monarchs. The assumption, however involuntary and unforeseen, of this position made Rome the protector of the cities and the "preserver" of their independence.

e See Chap. XII note 13.

The relationship thus established was essentially the same as that which bound Rhodes and Pergamum to the Romans.[76] The cities' independence, recognized by Rome as an existing right and duly proclaimed by order of the Senate, could not lawfully be affected by any measure taken by the Roman government save in the event of some hostile action. Their position with regard to Rome was one of "friendship," formally established by act of the Senate, by which the name of the "friend" was entered in an official register. This connexion ensured the maintenance of cordial relations and the enjoyment by the cities of full diplomatic rights. They might send their envoys to the Senate and receive a patient and courteous hearing; Rome, in turn, was careful to observe the forms of politeness customary between powers nominally equal. In the event of war the "friend" was under obligation to observe a strict neutrality. Did the friendly city so desire, it might furnish armed or other assistance, but by action of the Senate commanders were forbidden to exact any supplies which the Senators had not duly authorized. Neither in peace nor in war, moreover, was any fixed payment of money exacted. The "golden wreaths" which embassies from cities presented from time to time to Jupiter Capitolinus were voluntary offerings, and even if such gifts took the form of money theoretically used for this purpose, or if the aid furnished in war was commuted into actual cash, such payments were not regarded as recurrent or compulsory.

It is true that in addition to the observance of neutrality which precluded any association with an enemy of Rome, the "friend" might not enter into an offensive war with any other friend of Rome. To this extent the cities' freedom in international affairs was limited. Save for this restriction, however, they might enter into diplomatic relations with other states.[77] Thus they conferred honours on the kings of Pergamum and in turn received gifts from these rulers, on whose friendship, in fact, their prosperity was in a large measure dependent. They were free also to carry on negotiations with other cities, form alliances with them and conclude treaties as independent powers.

This freedom is especially apparent in the political combinations effected by the cities. Thus it was possible, as has already been observed, for the Lesbian cities to form a federation of their own and for Mylasa to bring the neighbouring communities into a union.[f] More conspicuous instances of such combinations are to be found in the agreement made by Miletus with Pidasa,[78] in the mountains toward the

[f] See Chap. III notes 125, 130 and 131.

southeast, and the treaty with Heracleia-near-Latmus.[79] By the terms of the former the Pidasans were admitted to Milesian citizenship and 390 families were allowed to become domiciled in the city. The treaty with Heracleia, in addition to the provision that the citizens of either of the two contracting cities might, after the fulfilment of certain formalities, be enrolled among those of the other, included agreements for mutual defence and a reciprocal exemption from transit and customs duties. An interchange of civic rights was effected also between Priene and Bargylia, and there was perhaps a similar arrangement between Miletus and Apollonia-on-Rhyndacus in northern Mysia.[80] This city, about the middle of the second century, sent envoys to Miletus to renew the tie of "kinship" based on the ascertainment by a Milesian commission that Apollonia was one of its colonies, and as a result it doubtless received some privileges from the mother-city.

The maintenance of relations among the cities appears also in the continuance of the custom by which one city requested another to send one or more men to render judgements in law-suits between its citizens —perhaps even between the community and a citizen—or persuade the disputants to arrive at an agreement with each other.[81] By this custom, which had been in existence in Asia Minor since the late fourth century, litigants might be assured of a verdict unaffected by partiality or corruption. The extent to which it was practiced during the second and first centuries is shown by the fact that among the free cities there are in existence at least forty instances of such a request.

Somewhat similar was the method, already mentioned, of terminating disputes between cities, usually over territory, by submitting the question at issue to a third city, and this procedure also was freely used during the second century.[82] It had, in fact, been endorsed by the Roman commissioners at Apameia, who may have had in view the recent war between Miletus and Magnesia. In cases actually pending, these commissioners appear to have appointed neutral cities, acceptable to both parties, to render judgements on the questions at issue. It was natural, therefore, that subsequently, when a similar controversy arose, the disputants should ask the Senate to name a referee. This happened some twenty years after the conference at Apameia in a dispute between Priene and Magnesia over territory near the mouth of the Maeander. The two claimants sent representatives to the Senate, which bade the praetor appoint as adjudicator some free city agreed upon by both, but with the provision that if no such agreement could be reached he himself should make the appointment. The question was then referred to Mylasa, whose commissioners rendered a decision in favour of Magnesia.

Other disputes of this nature seem also to have been brought to the Senate, as one between Mylasa and Stratoniceia and another perhaps between Priene and Miletus.[83] It may not be supposed, however, that the cities were under any compulsion to submit their quarrels to Rome for adjudication. In the controversy between Priene and Magnesia the disputants took the initiative in presenting their case to the Senate. Moreover, in the respective claims of Priene and Samos to the land long in dispute between them, although the Senate, after an appeal by the two claimants, approved a verdict formerly rendered by the Rhodians but invalidated by the Roman commander Manlius Vulso, the final decision was rendered by a neutral city, which established a definite boundary.[84] Similar disputes were also settled without reference to Rome, such as the long-standing controversy between Mitylene and Pitane arising from the latter's purchase of territory from Antiochus I, which was adjudicated by the Pergamenes, and the question of the boundary between the possessions of Rhodes and Stratoniceia, which, after the case had been presented to the Senate, was submitted by the disputants to Bargylia. Another controversy—apparently not over land but concerning the conduct of law-suits—between the citizens of Eresus and Methymna was decided by referees furnished by Aegae, Samos and Miletus. Even in the early first century, when western Asia Minor was a Roman province, a protest made by Priene to the Roman governor against the seizure by the tax-farmers of the salt-pans claimed by the Temple of Athena seems to have been referred by the Senate to Erythrae for a decision.

However dependent in substance the free cities may have been on the favour of their protector and however much their position with regard to Rome restricted their external relations, in the administration of their internal affairs they were completely independent. A free city continued to have its Council and Assembly empowered to enact legislation and elect magistrates.[85] It retained its power of exercising full jurisdiction over its citizens and managing its own finances, and it paid no tribute or tax to Rome. Its rights also included full ownership by the community or the individual citizens of all property in the city or its territory and the enjoyment of the revenues therefrom, as well as a guarantee that no garrison or other military force should be stationed on its lands. The city-government, therefore, was still conducted according to the democratic principle. It is true that under the influence of the Romans, whose general policy it was to ensure a greater stability by entrusting government to the wealthier and more responsible citizens, there was a growing tendency to lessen the power of the Assembly in favour of the Council. It may not, however, be maintained that by this change a serious limitation was imposed on a city's right of sovereignty.

The position of the free cities during the second century is, in fact, well illustrated by their right of coinage. Under the Seleucids, it will be remembered, these cities issued only small silver pieces—drachms and fractions of drachms—for the minting of the large silver tetradrachms was a royal prerogative.[86] During the second century, however, these coins were issued freely. In fact, about forty of the free cities in western and southwestern Asia Minor are known to have struck tetradrachms bearing either the head and superscription of Alexander or the device of the city itself; in most cases they were based on a uniform standard which facilitated their general circulation. In inland Caria, moreover, the liberation from Rhodian rule was celebrated during the second and first centuries by issues of bronze and even fractional silver coins in many small communities, some of which appear in history for the first time.

In the course of the second century, apparently in connexion with the war against Perseus of Macedonia, the relation of "friendship" maintained with the cities of Asia Minor became one of "friendship and alliance."[87] This status was granted by action of the Senate in 170 B.C. to Lampsacus, in 164 to the Rhodians, before 160 to Priene and Magnesia, and before 135 to Samos. Under such an arrangement a city-state, while retaining its national existence and even the right to adopt an independent policy unless other "friends and allies" were thereby affected, was bound to furnish aid to Rome in a defensive war and, in return, might in case of attack call upon Rome for assistance.

At first, an alliance of this kind depended on a decree of the Senate. This was a unilateral act, which, like all legislative measures, might be rescinded did the Roman Government so decide.[88] In the course of time, however, the friendship and alliance formed with the various free cities of Asia was in many cases placed on a securer basis, that of a formal treaty.[89] By such a treaty, providing both for the neutrality of each of the contracting parties in the event of war and for the rendering of aid in case of an attack, each party bound itself not only to deny passage through its territory to the enemies of the other and to refuse to supply those enemies with arms, money or ships, but also to

come to the help of the other in a defensive war. A final clause authorized either party, with the consent of the other, to add or remove any
provision and ordered copies of the document to be placed both in
the Temple of Jupiter Capitolinus at Rome and in an important sanctuary belonging to the other party to the treaty. In a covenant of this
kind both members were legally on an equal footing. While it was
inevitable that the difference in strength should cause Rome to seem
by far the more important of the contracting parties, there is nothing
in the terms of any of the extant treaties which suggests any difference
in status. Such a treaty, to whose observance representatives of each
party pledged themselves by an oath, was a bilateral action. As a solemn
obligation binding both sides, it might not be revoked save by common
consent, and only a breach of faith could justify the injured party in
denouncing the compact.

The value to the Romans of their relations with the cities of Asia
became apparent when the Senate, in 171 B.C., declared war on Perseus
of Macedonia, who, partly as the result of charges brought by Eumenes
of Pergamum, was suspected of harbouring ambitions and designs
inimical to Rome's interests. On the outbreak of this war not only
Rhodes but Samos also, as well as the northern cities, Chalcedon on
the Bosporus and Heracleia Pontica, offered contingents of ships for
the Roman navy.[90] In the following year, many others also offered to
contribute vessels and, when these were refused, responded to a request
for grain, and the Milesians promised to furnish whatever assistance
the Senate might desire.

During the period that followed the defeat of Perseus in 167, these
relations between Rome and the cities grew closer, and the beginning
of the conclusion of the treaties of alliance may probably be placed in
these years. It is possible that the Senate, which just at this time adopted
the policy of reducing the prestige both of Eumenes II and of the
Rhodians, saw in the small states a means of offsetting the strength of
the greater powers. It is perhaps more probable that the strengthening
of friendly ties was due to the realization of the cities' usefulness in the
event of a war. In any case, when Prusias II of Bithynia had invaded
the kingdom of his neighbour Attalus II, and the Romans, after a
delay of two years, finally decided, in 155 B.C., to renounce their friendship and alliance with the Bithynian King and thus make it possible for
Attalus to attack him, the Senate's envoys called upon the allied cities
to follow the same course and to support Attalus.[91] Rhodes and Cyzicus

thereupon sent ships to join the Pergamene fleet, and other cities also responded to the call. Similarly, when, a few years later, Rome was engaged in her last war with Carthage, the commander, Publius Scipio the younger, was empowered to ask for the assistance of the allied states, and Rhodes, at least, seems again to have sent part of her navy to take part in the struggle.[92]

While friendship with Rome was not without its responsibilities, it had advantages that might be considered, at least in some measure, compensatory. Thus when Prusias was defeated, the Senate's demands included an indemnity for Cyme, Aegae and Methymna, whose territories had been ravaged during the King's invasion of Pergamum.[g] About the same time, moreover, Priene also received benefit from its connexion with Rome.[93] The city's territory had been plundered and the place itself besieged by Attalus II and his brother-in-law, Ariarathes V of Cappadocia, because of its refusal to surrender to the latter a treasure of 400 talents deposited in Priene by his rebellious half-brother Orophernes. The citizens, unable to resist the attack of the two kings, appealed to Rome. The situation was a difficult one, for both monarchs were also Roman allies. Nevertheless, the Senate, responding to the appeal, remonstrated with the kings for their act of aggression and thus prevented all further violence.

There is no indication that during the second century any of the free cities of Asia Minor was deprived of its status of independence. On the contrary, there is some reason for supposing that before Rome acquired the province of Asia Ephesus obtained its freedom from Pergamum by the Romans' aid; certainly before the end of the century both it and Sardis, previously a subject city, were recognized as independent.[94] The freedom of Pergamum, provided for by the testament of Attalus III, was also confirmed. Moreover, if we may judge from the case of Miletus, where, during this period, additions were made to the public markets, the prosperity of the cities was in no way diminished. It is even possible that the influx of Italian business-men, some of whom appear to have settled in Asia before Rome made the country a province, stimulated trade and brought wealth to the cities where they became domiciled.

It may well be true that Rome's protectorate over the cities of Asia resulted in a certain degree of paternalism and weakened that spirit of independence which was characteristic of the Greeks. Yet, as far as our knowledge extends, during the period that elapsed between the

[g] Polybius XXXIII 13, 8. See also Chap. XIII note 43.

battle of Magnesia and the formation of the province, Rome was not guilty of any act of aggression toward the cities nor, with the exception of her harsh treatment of Rhodes, did she make any misuse of her power. On the other hand, there is every reason to believe that a general peace was established in Asia and the welfare of the individual communities promoted. They themselves, moreover, seem to have acquiesced in whatever loss of liberty was involved. When, after Attalus III bequeathed his kingdom to the Roman people, his half-brother Aristonicus raised the standard of revolt to dispute the bequest, the Greek cities, perceiving where their advantage lay, held fast to their alliances with Rome, and none of them, with Phocaea as the only known exception, willingly supported the pretender.[h]

[h] See below p. 148f.

CHAPTER V

THE SUBJECT COMMUNITIES
OF THE INTERIOR

WHEN Alexander came to Asia Minor, the interior of the country, in contrast to the Aegean littoral with its line of Greek cities, had been but little affected by the advance of Hellenism. The Persian kings, indeed, had encouraged Greek immigrants to settle in the basin of the Caïcus,[a] but there is no reason to suppose that the influence of these new-comers had spread beyond their own communities. The monarchs had also encouraged the development of certain towns, necessary alike as administrative and economic centres, but in none of them, although many of their inhabitants might be Greeks, was there a genuine Greek tradition or a real connexion with Greece. These places, accordingly, had no claim to the independence recognized by Alexander as the right of those cities which traced their Hellenic origin to the period antedating the rule of the Persians. They remained, therefore, directly subject to the Hellenistic monarchs, of whose kingdoms they formed an integral part, and they were presumably under the authority of the royal governors charged with the rule of the districts in which they were situated.[1] This was still the status of all save a few especially favoured communities when the Romans assumed a dominant position in Asia Minor.

Fundamental though the difference was between the position of these communities and that of the old city-states, there was subsequently in many of the larger places a definite trend toward Hellenization. Coming into contact with the cities of the coast and including among their inhabitants many men of Greek origin, these places, especially the chief commercial centres, gradually assumed a definitely Hellenic character. This change, resulting originally perhaps from the desire of the wealthier citizens to imitate the Greek way of life, showed itself in the acceptance of the language and the customs of their neighbours but particularly in the adoption of the form of government which was characteristic of the Greek *polis*. As the rule of the monarchs grew more liberal and these cities obtained the privilege of self-government, their civic institutions resembled more and more closely those of the city-states on which they were modelled. Only the remoter regions and especially those parts of the country which retained an early tribal

[a] See Chap. I note 2.

119

organization or were made up, according to the old Asianic custom, of rural village-centres were not subjected to this influence; for the veneer of Hellenism tended to grow thinner in proportion to the distance from the Aegean seaboard or from the great routes which led into the interior.

The cities thus Hellenized included ancient communities which, as centres of administration or commerce, had long possessed an urban character. Many, however, were royal foundations, established by the monarchs, probably sometimes on the sites of earlier settlements, in positions which had a strategic value or because either the prospect of commercial activity or the fertility of the soil gave promise of future prosperity.

The example of creating such cities had been set by Alexander, whose foundations included not only Alexandria in Egypt but also many places of this name throughout his eastern dominions as far as India.[2] This practice was followed both by Antigonus and by Lysimachus, of whom the former seems to have established not only the community which later became the free city of Alexandria Troas, but at least three other places in Asia Minor called by his name. The chief founders, however, were the Seleucid monarchs Antiochus I and Antiochus II, who not only allowed a considerable degree of local autonomy to existing communities but established a large number of cities in their Asianic dominions, many of them bearing names taken from those of members of the royal dynasty. The same policy was adopted by the rulers of Pergamum. Eumenes II and Attalus II, especially, not only encouraged the development of local autonomy but carried on the work of urbanization to an extent which compared with that of the early Seleucids. Among the foundations of the Seleucid and perhaps of the Pergamene kings also were colonies of former soldiers, who may perhaps have been liable to a recall to service, but whose primary function was to ensure by their presence the rulers' hold on the country.[3] In the course of time, these military colonies were either amalgamated with neighbouring settlements or developed into communities with civic organizations of their own.

In this process of urbanization the geographical configuration of the western portion of the Anatolian Peninsula was the all-important factor in determining the position of the cities subject to the Hellenistic monarchs. Thus the urban centres of Lydia and the adjacent portions of Mysia and Caria, through which ran the chief rivers and the great highways, far exceeded in number those of the less accessible regions to the north and the south. This preponderance will appear more clearly in the description of the several cities, the most important of which, as in the case of the Greek city-states, will now be passed in review. This review will include first the chief cities of the great river-basins of the Hermus (with the upper Caïcus) and the Maeander, and then those of the more outlying districts, the valley of the Carian Marsyas, the Lydo-Phrygian borderland, and the hill-country of central and eastern Caria.

The region of the Hermus and its tributaries, the broadest and most fertile of all the river-basins of Asia Minor, was dominated by the famous city of Sardis, the ancient capital of the monarchs of Lydia and, after their rule had been overthrown, the centre of the Persian power in Asia Minor. Its situation on the Royal Road, near the junction of routes leading from Ephesus and Smyrna,[b] made it a commercial centre even in remote Antiquity.[4] The acropolis of the city stood on a projecting spur connected by a narrow ridge with the northern foot-hills of the range of Tmolus and rising about 1,000 feet above the level of the Hermus, nearly five miles distant. So strong was its position that the difficulty of capturing it became proverbial. Sardis itself lay to the west of the acropolis, on the lower slopes which descend gradually to the Pactolus, the "gold-bearing" stream famed as the source of the wealth of the Lydian kings.[c] The city was built around a temple of Artemis, originally, like Artemis at Ephesus and at Magnesia, the Asiatic Mother-goddess who had been assimilated to the Grecian deity. In the course of time the city extended northward into the broad valley of the Hermus, where lay its fertile territory.

On the arrival of Alexander in Lydia the foremost citizens of Sardis and the Persian commandant surrendered to him.[5] According to an ancient historian, he permitted the city "to use the old laws of the Lydians." This evidently means that he granted the citizens a certain measure of self-government, and, in fact, about this time Sardis had some kind of civic organization which enabled it to offer "friendship" to Miletus and place the Milesians residing in the city under the care of certain officials. Nevertheless, Alexander continued to exact tribute and left a garrison in the acropolis. Whatever rights the city may have received, therefore, its status was not equal to that of the free and autonomous city-states of the coast.

During the campaign of Seleucus against Lysimachus, which was

[b] See Chap. II note 17.   [c] See Chap. II note 46.

121

ended by the former's victory at Corupedium near Sardis, the acropolis of the city and its treasure were surrendered by the official whom Lysimachus had left in command of the place, and under the Seleucid dynasty Sardis was the administrative centre of Asia Minor.[6] It was presumably the official residence of the monarchs, as well as the seat of one of their most active mints. Occupied in 216 B.C. by the usurper Achaeus, the city held out for more than a year against Antiochus III; when at last captured by a trick, it was looted and burned. The citadel, nevertheless, resisted for another year, and it was not until after Achaeus was taken prisoner by treachery and the members of his garrison began to quarrel among themselves that the stronghold finally surrendered.[d]

During the war between Rome and Antiochus III Sardis shared with Ephesus the distinction of serving as the King's headquarters, and after his defeat at Magnesia he took refuge in the city.[7] It surrendered to the Scipios, however, without a struggle and, together with the other communities which had been subject to Antiochus, the city was given by the Roman commissioners to Eumenes II of Pergamum. The citizens maintained cordial relations with the King and under his rule and that of Attalus II Sardis seems to have had the rights of an autonomous community. At the beginning of the first century before Christ it had become an independent city-state.

West of Sardis, the plain of the lower Hermus was dominated by the strong fortress of Magnesia on a high spur of Mt. Sipylus, a position which gave the name of Magnesia-near-Sipylus to the city in the plain below.[8] The situation of the place was of importance both strategically and commercially. Only a few miles east of the defile through which the Hermus forces its way to the sea, Magnesia commanded this entrance to the interior; moreover, its proximity to the junction of the Royal Road with a route leading to the northeast gave easy communication not only with central Asia Minor but also with the valley of the Caïcus and, by the road to Cyzicus, even with the Propontis.[e]

The early history of Magnesia and the origin of its name are alike unknown. It seems to have been used as a stronghold by the Seleucid kings and in the middle of the third century it was held by the soldiers whom the monarchs established as permanent residents.[9] Under Seleucus II these men and their families were admitted by formal agreement to citizenship in Smyrna. Thus Magnesia was connected in a close relationship with its greater neighbour. Antiochus III, during

d See Chap. I note 31.   e See Chap. II note 20.

his war with Rome, took possession of the place, doubtless because of its commanding position; the great battle which cost the king his dominions north of the Taurus was fought only a few miles distant in the plain on the northern side of the Hermus. After this battle Magnesia surrendered to the Romans and in the ensuing settlement of Asianic affairs was given to Eumenes II. Nevertheless, like Sardis, it possessed a certain amount of autonomy under the Pergamene kings. Its valiant resistance to Mithradates of Pontus was rewarded by the Romans with a grant of freedom, and under their rule it owned an extensive territory.

Across the Hermus from Magnesia, the river-basin widens out far to the north in a plain of great fertility, through which flow the Phrygius and its tributaries.[f] Near one of the latter, the Lycus, the city of Thyateira stood on the end of a spur which projects into the plain from the hills farther east.[10] Its name indicates that Thyateira was an ancient settlement, but the place gained greatly in size and importance after it was selected by one of the early Seleucid kings for a colony of former soldiers. The choice was presumably due to its strategic position at the junction of the roads leading northwest to Pergamum, southeast to Sardis, and southwest to Magnesia and Smyrna.

Together with the surrounding country, Thyateira in the later third century seems to have come under the power of Attalus I, and coins intended for local use were perhaps issued during this period.[11] The territory of the city suffered during the invasion of Philip V in 201, but Thyateira itself was not captured; it evidently remained under Pergamene rule, for in 196/5 silver cistophori were minted in the city. During the war between Rome and Antiochus, the King seems to have taken possession of both Thyateira and its territory, with the result that the latter was ravaged by Eumenes II and some Roman troops. After the battle of Magnesia the city surrendered to the Scipios and became subject to Eumenes, under whom, however, it possessed its own civic organization.

In addition to Thyateira, there were other towns in the basins both of the Phrygius and of the upper Caïcus which were foundations either of the Seleucid or of the Pergamene monarchs. Some of them, like Thyateira, were colonies of soldiers to whom the kings had granted holdings taken from the royal lands. The sites of these settlements were chosen partly, doubtless, because of the fertility of the soil, but especially because of the strategic position of the region; for the great

[f] See Chap. II note 8.

route from Pergamum to Sardis led over the low watershed which separates the two river-basins.[g]

North of this watershed, Stratoniceia was built on a height overlooking the wide plain in which several streams unite to form the Caïcus and at the entrance to the valley of a tributary flowing from the north.[12] Through this valley a route led to the basin of the Macestus and thence to Cyzicus and the Propontis.[h] The town was in all probability a foundation of Antiochus I, placed here before the rise of Pergamum in order to maintain a hold on this rich plain as well as on the route leading northward.[13]

The watershed itself was guarded by the colonies of veterans established at Nacrasa and probably at Acrasus, both on the northern side.[14] On the southern side were the Pergamene foundations Attaleia and Apollonis, placed, not like the Seleucid colonies, in sites important strategically, but in regions where there was fertile land for the settlers to till. Attaleia, about ten miles north of Thyateira, stood on a hill overlooking the plain along the upper Lycus.[15] Apollonis, about the same distance west of Thyateira, was on the western side of a group of hills above the narrow valley of a tributary of the Phrygius.[16] Named after the wife of Attalus I, it was probably founded on the site of an earlier settlement and under Eumenes II it appears to have been enlarged by the incorporation of two neighbouring colonies of veterans. In the first century before Christ it had adopted the institutions of a Greek *polis*.

The most important of the Pergamene foundations was Philadelpheia, which Attalus II Philadelphus named after himself.[17] It was situated on the southwestern side of the broad valley of the Cogamis, some twenty-five miles southeast of the junction of this river with the Hermus. The acropolis stood on a projecting spur of the range of Tmolus rising above the level of the river; the town lay partly on the slopes and partly on the flat land below.

The situation of Philadelpheia was in most respects advantageous. Not only was the region fertile, but the city commanded the road which, leading up the Cogamis, crossed the mountains to the basin of the Maeander, joining the Southern Highway at Laodiceia. This was the shortest route from Pergamum to southern Asia Minor. On the other hand, because of the proximity of the volcanic region of Catacecaumene, the city was in constant danger from the numerous earthquakes. Its houses, we are told, were frequently demolished, and so

---

[g] See Chap. II note 20.   [h] See Chap. II note 20.

great was the peril that many of the inhabitants preferred to live in the open country round about. Nevertheless, Philadelpheia prospered greatly. Like Apollonis, it seems to have annexed a neighbouring settlement of veterans, and in course of time it acquired a large territory containing many villages. Soon after its foundation by Attalus it had a civic organization which issued coins of its own, and under the Romans it was a place of great wealth. In the fifth century after Christ its temples and religious festivals had given it such distinction that it was referred to as a minor Athens.

The principal Seleucid cities were in the basin of the Maeander and its chief tributary, the Lycus. Here the monarchs founded or refounded at least five communities, which, together with other, more ancient, settlements, lined the course of the Southern Highway and throve upon its trade. The greatest, probably, was Apameia, named by Antiochus I for his mother, Apame.[18] The city was built on the foothills of the mountain-rim rising above the eastern side of the rich plain in which the still tiny Maeander unites with four other streams. It was close to the site of an older settlement, Celaenae, whose acropolis stood on a high hill at the back of the later city. The position of Apameia, "in the midst of plains and the noblest of mountains" and "with the most abundant springs and a territory of great fertility, bearing countless products," was also one of great strategic importance; for it commanded the cut in the mountain-range through which the Southern Highway climbed from the plain to the high plateau of central Anatolia. This was the gateway to the East through which passed the main stream of traffic enriching the city. It was not, however, the only avenue of commerce, for roads led also toward the northwest into western Phrygia and to the southeast into Pisidia.

The advantages of the place, as well as its great natural beauty, were appreciated by the Persian monarchs. Xerxes is said to have fortified the citadel of Celaenae and to have built a palace below it, and the younger Cyrus also had a residence and a hunting-park in the neighbouring hills. Even then, Celaenae was "large and prosperous." On the arrival of Alexander, the inhabitants fled, leaving the place deserted, and the garrison of the citadel, although, trusting in its strength, it at first defied the Macedonian army, finally agreed to capitulate. The conqueror designated Celaenae as the capital of the satrapy of Phrygia, and Antigonus used it as his chief residence.

The new Seleucid city succeeded to the position held by its predecessor. Here Antiochus III met the last of the Roman embassies which carried on negotiations prior to the outbreak of the war, and here he found a refuge on retreating from Sardis after his defeat at Magnesia.[1] Here also he was forced to sign the treaty by which he gave up all claim to his possessions north of the Taurus, and the conquering Romans, in the presence of Eumenes II and the representatives of the Greek city-states, distributed the spoils of the war.[j] Apameia itself became subject to the kings of Pergamum, but under their liberal rule it had the city-council and the gymnasium which were characteristic of the Greek *polis*.[19] In the early first century the city was largely destroyed by one of the earthquakes to which the region was subject, but it was soon rebuilt by the aid of Mithradates of Pontus, who, in return for its surrender, presented the large sum of a hundred talents to remedy the disaster.[20] The commerce which passed through the city, however, was probably a more potent factor in its recovery. At the beginning of the Christian Era it ranked second to Ephesus as a market and a distributing-centre for the merchandise of both Greece and Italy.

At the northernmost point of the plain of the upper Maeander, some twenty-five miles northwest of Apameia, Attalus II founded the city of Eumeneia, named after his brother Eumenes.[21] It lay at the edge of the plain, where the Glaucus breaks forth from the mountains behind; up the valley of this river ran the route which connected the region with western Phrygia. The settlers appear to have included a number of Achaeans from Greece, who had perhaps been soldiers in the royal service. It would seem, however, that they were placed here as civilian settlers and not as a garrison, for the undefended situation of the city, in the plain and without an acropolis, shows that it was founded during a time of general peace. It was evidently intended, like Philadelpheia, to strengthen the influence and power of Pergamum in the territory acquired by the defeat of Antiochus III, and in order to promote its growth, city-rights were at once conferred upon it. Under the Roman emperors, Eumeneia seems to have had a garrison and to have been a place of residence for veterans.

After leaving the plain around Apameia, the Southern Highway followed the valley of the Lycus to its junction with the Maeander. In this valley were the ancient town of Colossae and, eleven miles below it, the Seleucid city of Laodiceia. Colossae, in a romantic situation at the beginning of a precipitous gorge, into which the Lycus plunges in a rapid descent from its upper to its lower valley, was a "great city" in

[1] Livy XXXV 15, 1f.; XXXVII 44, 6; XXXVIII 15, 12f.
[j] See Chap. I note 55 and Chap. IV note 60.

the fifth century, "populous and prosperous."[22] Its acropolis, on a completely isolated hill on the south side of the Lycus, was a fortress of great strength. The importance of the city was due partly to its position on the Highway and partly to its woollen industries. The foundation of Laodiceia and the commercial prominence which it attained may have had an unfavourable effect on Colossae's prosperity, but nevertheless it continued under the Romans to enjoy the rights of a city.

Laodiceia, the successful rival of Colossae in commerce, was founded by Antiochus II and named in honour of the wife whom he later divorced.[23] It was situated on the southern bank of the Lycus at the junction of the Southern Highway with a route which led over a pass in the range of Mt. Salbacus, southeast of the city, to Cibyratis and Pisidia and so to the Pamphylian coast. Behind the city was its acropolis, on a flat-topped isolated hill protected by two streams which flow down from the mountains on the south, and, although not more than three hundred feet above the Lycus, a well-fortified stronghold. Laodiceia's first appearance in history was in 220, when Achaeus, on rebelling against Antiochus III, assumed the crown there, proclaiming himself king. Under either Attalus I or one of his sons it received some favour from Pergamum which caused it to name two of the city-tribes after Attalus and his wife. For part of the second century, at least, Laodiceia seems to have belonged to the Pergamene Kingdom, and the Romans, perhaps before they acquired the province of Asia, appear to have granted it some privilege, in gratitude for which the citizens erected a monument at Rome to their "saviour and benefactor." Although the city frequently suffered from the earthquakes to which the whole region was subject, its position on the Southern Highway and the development of its textile industries brought it great wealth, and in the first century before Christ it was a rich and prosperous place and so thoroughly Romanized that the citizens enjoyed gladiatorial combats.

About seven miles north of Laodiceia, on the other side of the Lycus, was the "sacred city" of Hierapolis.[24] It stood picturesquely on a terrace projecting from the mountain-side and over three hundred feet above the plain in which the Lycus and the Maeander meet. The situation was all the more striking for the reason that the hot mineral springs which burst forth behind the place have covered the rocks below with gleaming white deposits of lime, the stalactite formation of which has been likened to a "frozen cascade." To this spring Hierapolis owed both its name and its existence, for the cave whence it issued in Antiquity was regarded as an entrance to the Lower World and so held peculiarly sacred. It was presumably consecrated to the Mother-goddess, for her eunuch-priests, it was said, were alone able to endure the exhalation arising from the water.

As a city, Hierapolis is first known under Eumenes II, who perhaps transformed the settlement around the sanctuary into an imitation of a Greek *polis* similar to others founded by himself and his brother throughout their kingdom.[25] In any case, during his reign it had a municipal administration. Situated on the route which diverged from the Southern Highway at Laodiceia and led across the mountains to Philadelpheia and the basin of the Hermus, Hierapolis flourished under Roman rule. Its prosperity was due partly to the excellence of its dyeing processes and partly to the number of visitors who were attracted by the baths in the hot water from its spring.

On opposite sides of the lower Maeander, below its junction with the Lycus, were the two Seleucid cities Antiocheia and Nysa, foundations, probably, of Antiochus I, who may have combined older communities into cities. The situation of Antiocheia, on a height on the south bank of the Maeander near the mouth of the Morsynus, gave it a position of considerable importance.[26] Not only was the city at the end of the bridge which carried the Southern Highway across the Maeander, but it was also at the junction of a route which led up the valley of the Morsynus to the cities of eastern Caria.

On the other side of the Maeander, some miles farther down stream, Nysa stood in a situation of romantic beauty, on both sides of a precipitous gorge, through which a stream pours down through the foothills of Mt. Messogis to join the great river.[27] The gorge was spanned both by bridges and by a vaulting, which extended perhaps for a distance of 300 yards and connected the two portions of the city. Less than two miles toward the west was the village of Acharaca, famous for a grotto containing a sulphur spring sacred to Pluto and Persephone, the deities of the Lower World, whose temple stood close at hand. It was believed that the exhalation from the waters was fatal to all save those initiated into the holy mysteries, but the priests were reported to have wrought marvellous cures for persons bidden by the gods to visit the sacred place. Such was its sanctity that a special grant from Seleucus I conferred on it the privilege of receiving suppliants, as well as inviolability and exemption from taxation, and these rights were recognized also by later rulers as well as by a Roman proconsul. In the first century Nysa seems to have been a place of wealth and importance;

but, cut off by its elevated position from the traffic of the Southern Highway, it was not so much a commercial city as a centre of culture and education and the resort of those who came to worship in its Plutonium and especially to undergo the medical treatment furnished there.

Between Nysa and Magnesia-on-Maeander, about eighteen miles from each, was the city of Tralles.[28] It occupied a strong position on a flat-topped spur of Mt. Messogis which projects into the plain of the Maeander, descending more or less steeply on both its eastern and its western sides. At the northeastern corner of this spur rose the acropolis, built on two terraces and defended by a precipitous descent toward the east and also toward the north, where only a narrow saddle connected it with the range of Messogis. The situation was favourable, not only for defence, but also for commerce, for it was at the junction of the Southern Highway with the route which led across the Maeander and up the valley of the Marsyas through the heart of Caria. Tralles was also famous as the seat of the cult of Zeus Larasius, which, known to have been in existence in the third century before Christ, was undoubtedly much older and under Roman rule was still maintained in the third century of the Christian Era.

According to legend, Tralles was founded by emigrants from Argos and by members of a Thracian tribe named Tralles, from whom its name was supposed to be derived.[29] The Argive tradition, however, was doubtless fictitious and the connexion with Thrace wholly fanciful and based only on the coincidence that Thracian troops called Tralles served in the armies of the Hellenistic kings. The origin of the city is unknown, but it was evidently a place of some consequence in the fifth century, for in 400 B.C. it was able to resist an attack by a Spartan army, and in the middle of the fourth century it may have had some kind of civic organization. On the arrival of Alexander in 334, the citizens surrendered voluntarily, but when they resisted Antigonus during his conquest of Caria in 313, even the natural strength of the place could not save it from capture by siege. Under the Seleucids Tralles was renamed Seleuceia and during this period it was able to issue its own (bronze) coins. At the end of the third century Antiochus III granted the city certain privileges, perhaps even a nominal independence. It naturally, therefore, supported Antiochus against Rome, with the result that after surrendering to the Scipios in 189, it was given to Eumenes II as a subject city. Resuming its former name of Tralles, the place flourished under the Pergamene kings, who built a royal residence in it, and under their rule the city had a government of its own. In the first century the place was a centre of wealth and culture and well known for its teachers of oratory and rhetoric.

On the road which led southward from Tralles through central Caria lay the two principal cities of the interior of this district, Alabanda and Stratoniceia. Alabanda, some sixteen miles from the Maeander, had a highly favourable situation on the western edge of the broad plain in which the Marsyas is joined by a tributary flowing from the southwest.[30] The city rested on two low hills separated by a stream and picturesquely likened to the two panniers borne by an ass. Not only was the plain rich and fertile but it throve on the trade of the highway along the Marsyas as well as on that of a branch-route, which, leading up the broad valley of the tributary river, crossed the mountains by way of Labraunda to Mylasa and the basin of the Cybersus. Its prosperity became proverbial and its inhabitants acquired a reputation for luxury and even debauchery.

Alabanda was an ancient Carian city, the tyrant of which in 480 B.C. was captured by the Greeks in the naval battle of Artemisium.[31] In the third century it was a member of the Carian League or "Nation" of the Chrysaoreis. At the close of this century the city took the name of Antiocheia out of gratitude to its "benefactor" Antiochus III, who, assuming the position of protector of its "democracy and peace," encouraged the citizens to send envoys to various states asking for a recognition of their city and territory as sacred and inviolable. These precautions against attack, however, proved of little avail, for within less than four years Philip of Macedonia, during his invasion of Caria, ravaged the city's territory in order to obtain food for his soldiers. Four years later, the force which he had left in the district was defeated and routed near Alabanda by a Rhodian army.

When the Romans divided the Asianic dominions of Antiochus and inland Caria fell to the share of Rhodes, it is probable that Alabanda for a time became subject to the Republic. In any case, the city was free at the beginning of the war with Perseus of Macedonia, when envoys were sent to the Roman Senate, bringing a gift to Jupiter Capitolinus.[32] These envoys announced that Alabanda had founded a temple to the Goddess Roma and instituted a festival in her honour, thereby placing the city under the protection of Rome. Shortly afterward, when Rhodes fell into disfavour with the Senate, with the result that the gift of Caria was revoked, Alabanda attempted, in conjunction with Mylasa, to conquer a portion of the district. The attempt, however, was promptly quelled by a Rhodian force, which defeated the troops sent by the two cities. Alabanda, nevertheless, seems to have retained its independence, for it was a free city early in the first century before Christ and also at the beginning of the Christian Era.

Stratoniceia, some twenty miles south of Alabanda, lay in the hill-country on an undulating plateau which slopes gradually eastward toward the upper Marsyas, in a situation more favourable for access than defence.[33] The river, somewhat over three miles distant, flows through a small but fertile plain formed by the union of the main stream with several minor affluents. Through this plain the highway led on southward to cross the hills to Idyma near the eastern end of the Gulf of Cos and, eventually, to Physcus on the Strait of Marmaris. Stratoniceia was founded by Antiochus I, who named it in honour of his wife, settling in it a group of "Macedonian" soldiers, presumably in order to bind the region more closely to himself. He assigned to his new foundation a large territory containing a number of ancient village-communities. These had previously been members of the ancient "Nation" or League of the Chrysaoreis, which held its meetings in the old temple of Zeus Chrysaoreus near the city. It was by virtue of its possession of these villages that Stratoniceia obtained a place in the organization. The city's territory included also the neighbouring villages of Lagina, in the hills six miles to the north, and Panamara, a little farther to the southeast, famous, respectively, for the sanctuaries of Hecate and of Zeus Panamaros.[34] The city, accordingly, was both an ancient Carian religious centre and a newly organized *polis* with an Hellenic system of government. In this double role, it developed into the most important place in interior Caria, for crowds flocked to the yearly festivals of its gods and the monarchs adorned it with costly buildings.

Like Alabanda, both Stratoniceia and Panamara were captured by Philip V and held by his troops until the end of the war. Later, Antiochus III, wishing to conciliate the Rhodians, presented the city to them, and when they received interior Caria from the Romans in 188, Stratoniceia remained in their possession.[35] But when, by act of the Senate, Caria was taken from Rhodes, Stratoniceia became independent. In recognition of its liberation it seems to have founded a festival in honour of the Goddess Roma. In 81 B.C., because of its valiant attempt to resist Mithradates, the Senate recognized Stratoniceia as free and independent and assigned to it a substantial increase of territory. At the same time the cities of Greece and Asia Minor guaranteed the inviolability of the temple at Lagina.

In addition to these, the principal cities of native origin during the Hellenistic period, there were others in western Asia Minor which, although of less note in the third century, gradually acquired civic rights under the later kings of Pergamum or during the early rule of the Romans. In the borderland between Lydia and northern Phrygia were Temenothyrae and Grimenothyrae, and in the western portion of the latter district was Acmonia, all on or near the line of the Royal Road.[36] Far to the north, in the region where Mysia, Lydia and Phrygia met, lay Aezani, with a temple of Zeus, the ruins of which are among the most beautiful of the Hellenic world. Toward the south, on the border between Lydia and southern Phrygia, was Blaundus, where a colony of "Macedonian" soldiers was established, probably by the Seleucid kings.[37] In central Phrygia, Synnada lay on a high plain surrounded by mountains, and about thirty miles to the northeast was Docimeium, with great quarries of marble, which was usually known as Synnadic because the stone was exported through Synnada over a road leading across the mountains to the Southern Highway. In the second and first centuries before Christ Synnada was a place of considerable importance, but it was, nevertheless, described as "not a large city."

Far from these places, in a remote corner of eastern Caria, were Aphrodisias and Tabae, connected with the greater centres by the road which left the Southern Highway at Antiocheia on the Maeander and led in a southeasterly direction up the valley of the Morsynus.[k] Aphrodisias, about fifteen miles from Antiocheia, was built around a low hill, which formed its acropolis, overlooking a broad plain into which several streams flow to join the Morsynus from the high range of Salbacus.[38] During the second century before Christ, probably, the city entered into a combination with the neighbouring community of Plarasa to form a common civic unit. The chief deity of the place was Aphrodite, whose sanctuary was recognized as inviolable by an edict of Julius Caesar as well as by a senatorial decree of 39 B.C., which also conferred freedom on the united communities.

Tabae, about twenty miles southeast of Aphrodisias, stood on a high spur projecting from the mountains on the east and flanked by two deep ravines, which, uniting in front of the city, surrounded it on all sides but one, thus giving the place a position of great natural strength.[39]

[k] See note 26.

Toward the north stretched a wide high-lying plain watered by the tributaries of the upper Harpasus, and it was only from this side that the city was accessible. Tabae seems to have been in existence in the early third century, when it may even have had the organization of a *polis*. In 189 the citizens attempted to resist the proconsul Manlius Vulso during his predatory raid through Caria and Pisidia, but they were finally compelled to buy him off by the payment of twenty-five talents and 10,000 measures of grain. Later, Tabae erected a monument at Rome on which it was called a "friend and ally," and after the defeat of Mithradates of Pontus in 85, a decree of the Senate rewarded the city's brave resistance to the King by recognizing its full independence.

The process by which both the ancient subject cities and the new royal foundations adopted constitutions of the democratic type characteristic of the Greek *polis* began in the early Hellenistic period. Even in the time of Alexander, Sardis, as has already been narrated, had a civic organization, although apparently of a very simple type which showed only a slight resemblance to that usually found in a *polis*.[1] In the course of the third century, however, as the result of the urbanizing policy of Antiochus I and his son and successor, more and more of the subject cities obtained governments of their own, with the right to make laws for themselves and the administrative machinery customarily employed by their Hellenic neighbours. In some cases, indeed, their autonomy in local matters was so complete that their position was not far from independence.

As in a Greek city-state, the citizens of the cities enjoying autonomy met as the *Demos* in an Assembly, and a selected body acted as the Council.[m] Thus, perhaps about the middle of the third century, the "people" of Sardis sent envoys to Delphi to renew the privileges which the Sardians had enjoyed "from ancient times."[40] During this century also the "Council and People" of Tralles conferred honours on two citizens for their services as envoys, and in 212/11 the city made arrangements with Miletus for an interchange of civic rights. In 206 B.C. Laodiceia-on-Lycus was organized as a *demos*, and about the same time it had a city-council, and in 201 Philip V, during his invasion of Asia Minor, received honours from a "Council and People," which were presumably those of Thyateira.

In certain cases the privilege of local self-government seems to have

[1] See note 5.   [m] See above p. 57.

been extended by Antiochus III into at least a semblance of "freedom and autonomy." This policy, it will be remembered, the King attempted to employ with regard to some of the Greek cities of the coast, whose independence he offered to recognize on the condition that they would become his "allies,"[n] and he may have considered it a means of securing the allegiance of some of the subject cities as well. Tralles appears to have received some favour from him which may have been the grant of this status.[41] In any case, a nominal independence was granted to Alabanda, which, sending envoys to several cities and to the Amphictyonic Council at Delphi, boasted that Antiochus, "according to the principle of his ancestors, was protecting the democracy and peace" of the city.[o]

The status of quasi-independence which subject cities obtained from the ruler differed essentially from that of the ancient city-states.[42] It was not a right to which they were entitled by virtue of a long-established position of freedom but a favour accorded by the king's grace. Consequently, it existed only as long as the monarch willed and it was revocable at his pleasure. The city-governments, while empowered to administer the community's affairs, were, therefore, under the practical necessity of complying with the royal demands.

Under the rulers of Pergamum the subject cities, although likewise only as a favour from the monarch, possessed a large measure of autonomy, including the right to make their own laws and manage their own finances. Even the city of Pergamum, although it was the royal capital, had an administration of its own. In the early third century—perhaps before the rulers had consolidated their power—the "Council and People" took formal action in decreeing an exchange of civic rights with Temnus.[43] Later in the same century, at the request of Eumenes I, the *demos* enacted a decree in honour of the "generals" (*strategoi*) who were the leading officials of the city. In this particular case, it is true, the generals were appointed by the King, who thus made sure that no measure could be brought before the people of which he did not approve and also maintained a hold on the administration of the city's affairs. There is no evidence, however, that this method of control was used by the rulers of the second century either in Pergamum itself or in the other cities of the kingdom.

During the second century, as a result of the Hellenizing policy of Eumenes II and Attalus II, the right of the subject cities to govern themselves seems to have been general. Measures were passed by the

[n] See above p. 17 and Chap. IV note 48.   [o] See note 31.

"Council and People" or the Council or People alone, not only in Pergamum but also in the old communities and the new royal foundations.[44] In the interior of Caria, likewise, the cities, after they were freed from subjection to Rhodes, adopted a similar form of government.

In these cities the civic affairs were administered by officials with titles and functions similar to those of the old city-states. There was, however, the notable difference that, while in the latter, which retained the individual constitutions of earlier times, there was great diversity in the magisterial titles,[p] the Hellenized communities and the new foundations adopted a more or less uniform pattern. Thus, while in the city-states the title of the eponymous official, whose powers were merely nominal, varied greatly, this office in Pergamum was held sometimes by "The Priest" (of what deity is unknown) but more often by the prytanis, but elsewhere by the stephanephorus.[45] The titles of the executive officials show a corresponding uniformity. These powers were vested in a board of *prytaneis* at Laodiceia and also at Stratoniceia in Caria, where they were probably imitated from the similar board at Rhodes.[46] Usually, however, the principal civil magistrates, as in Pergamum, were the "generals."[47] In Pergamum these presided over the Assembly, administered oaths to their minor colleagues, imposed fines, supervised the public finances, announced the bestowal of honours and arranged for the publication of decrees; both here and elsewhere measures passed by the Council or the Assembly were ordinarily proposed by them. Pergamum and other cities had also a secretary of the people, treasurers, who had the custody of the city's funds and disbursed them on order, and a controller of the market, all of them imitated from the constitutions of a genuinely Greek *polis*.

This imitation of the organization of an Hellenic state included also the formation of city-tribes. Some of the old Ionian and Dorian cities were originally divided into the traditional tribes of their respective homelands, while in others the tribes bore names derived from those of deities or heroes or taken from the provenience of some of the inhabitants.[q] In the new cities, which had no tradition connecting them with Greece, the tribe-names were wholly artificial, formed on a basis which varied not only from place to place, but even in a single city.[48] At Pergamum, while some tribes were named after places in Greece from which early settlers presumably migrated, others were called by the names of gods or local heroes or by those of the Attalid dynasty.

[p] See above p. 59.   [q] See Chap. III notes 3 and 4.

In the other cities names of deities prevailed, but in these also the tribes often bore dynastic and sometimes, apparently, local names.

Certain cities, indeed, appear to have been organized on different (and varying) principles.[49] Thus, in the Roman imperial period, at Philadelpheia the tribes seem to have corresponded to the trade-guilds, and at Apameia the fact that the cost of erecting statues decreed by the "Council and People" was borne by those who lived in certain "streets" may possibly indicate that the city was divided into sections resembling modern wards. At Stratoniceia in Caria the divisions of the people corresponded to the old village-communities of which, as has already been observed, the city was composed.

Like the city-states, the Hellenized cities had their own law-courts and they might send to other places for impartial men to act as referees in suits which could be settled by arbitration or as judges in cases which required legal procedure.[50] They had also the power of issuing coins of their own.[51] This was primarily a practical concession to convenience, for their coins, which were of bronze and of low denominations, were evidently intended only for local circulation.

On the other hand, the subject cities had, obviously, no military forces, and, unlike the free city-states, they could not engage in wars or disputes with one another. Nor, strictly speaking, did they have any international status. It is true that, as has been already narrated, Sardis "renewed" its ancient relations with Delphi, and Pergamum and Tralles formed agreements with Temnus and Miletus, respectively, for an interchange of civic rights.[52] These cases, however, may not be regarded as typical; for the action of Pergamum, as previously suggested, was perhaps taken before the establishment of royal rule in the city, while Sardis appears to have had special privileges, and Tralles in 212 may have possessed at least some of the rights of a free city. The position of the subject cities with regard to their international relations in the third century may be illustrated by the procedure employed in the case of the Magnesians' invitations, about 207 B.C., to participate in the festival of Artemis.[53] Those extended to the subject cities were not despatched directly, like the invitations to the city-states, to the intended recipients but referred to the ruler, in order that he might authorize their acceptance and the sending of replies. In the second century, on the other hand, under the rule of the Pergamene kings, the subject cities received visits from Magnesian envoys and accepted their invitations without permission or any other action on the part of the monarch.

Unlike the free cities also, the subject cities paid a money-tribute to the king.[54] This differed from the "contributions" of the city-states in that it was ordinarily a fixed amount paid each year to an agent of the royal treasury. It was presumably based on the city's capacity to pay, as determined by the normal revenues, but, were these diminished as the result of war or some other disaster, the usual payments might, at the ruler's pleasure, be reduced or even remitted.

In fact, specific cases are known in which the ruler showed consideration for a city in time of misfortune. The most conspicuous is that of a community which, although its name does not appear in the extant text of the inscription containing an account of its plight, was evidently situated near the Hellespont or the Propontis.[55] This city had formerly had its "ancestral government" and its own laws, but as the result of war it had fallen on evil days; there was a general lack of grain for food as well as of money to provide sacrificial victims; the citizens were impoverished; some had already lost their lands—presumably through indebtedness—while others were on the point of losing theirs. The city—whether as a result of the war is uncertain— had come under the power of a certain Corrhagus, a "Macedonian," governor of the Hellespontine region, an official, apparently, of Eumenes II. He, on "taking possession" of the place, brought its misfortunes to the notice of his royal master. The monarch, accordingly, was persuaded not only to restore to the city its former status of autonomy, the property of the gods, the funds needed both for sacrifices and for the civic administration, the oil used by the young men in their gymnasium "and all else that had appertained to the people from the beginning," but also to provide grain "for seed and sustenance," to enable those who had lands to retain them, to furnish land to the landless at the expense of the royal treasury, and to grant exemption from all money-payments to the monarch during the ensuing five years.

Similar action was taken in other cases also. A community, the name of which has likewise been lost, sent envoys to a royal official to inform him that the city had been burned "in the war" and that most of the citizens had perished after losing their possessions; the envoys presented a petition for remission of tribute and the settling of new inhabitants in the place.[56] Their request was granted by the official in question, obviously with the monarch's endorsement: for seven years they were to be released from all payments to the royal treasury and at the expiration of that time they might pay in three installments annually what was evidently a reduced amount; further concessions, too, were granted, among them freedom from a garrison and a release from the obligation to perform public services. In another community, Amlada in Pisidia, one of the most remote possessions of Pergamum, a yearly tribute of two talents had been imposed, and, in addition, the city was required to pay a special impost of 9,000 drachmae in some connexion—the exact nature is not clear—with the war waged by Eumenes II against the Galatians.[57] When the city, however, impoverished and unable to pay, presented a request to the King for relief from the burden, a letter written to the "*Polis* and Elders," probably by the later Attalus II during his brother's reign, granted a release from the impost and the reduction of a quarter of the amount heretofore paid as tribute.

It is probable—although far from certain—that the yearly payments made by the subject cities to the monarchs were regarded as rent; for in general the land, save for the territories of the free cities, the estates belonging, as will presently be shown, to the temples, and, probably, the holdings of some private landlords, was considered the property of the king. Under the Persians large portions of Asia Minor had been royal domain-land, belonging to the monarchs, and Alexander, as their successor, retained as his own what he did not "restore" to the free Greek cities.[58] Antigonus, acting on the same theory, regarded the domain as "tributary" to himself, and the Seleucids, by right of conquest from Lysimachus, held the "royal land" as crown-property.

From this "royal land" were taken the tracts assigned to the cities which were founded by the Seleucid monarchs. Portions of it also were sold by the kings to free cities or given or sold to royal favourites or assigned as "allotments" to veterans.[59] Other tracts were leased out to tenants on leases which were heritable and apparently of indefinite tenure, even permitting the property to be mortgaged. The land sold to a free city became, of course, the outright property of the purchaser. The "allotments" of the veterans appear in certain cases to have been granted in full ownership, but it may not be assumed that this practice was universal, for frequently such holdings were subject to taxes or tithes. On leasehold property the lessee paid a rental to the king. With regard to the lands acquired by private individuals by gift or sale by the monarch, the question arises whether they became the outright property of the grantee or purchaser, and the opinion has often been expressed that under the Seleucids no privately owned property might be held outside the free cities. This view is based on the provision in the gift of land by Antiochus I to his "friend" Aristodicides that the new owner might incorporate his holding in the territory of a free city and on the record of the sale of an estate by Antiochus II to his divorced wife, Laodice, who was likewise "empowered" to attach her new property to any city she might wish. In neither case, however, was the transfer obligatory, and the clause which permitted Laodice, before attaching her estate to a city, to sell or otherwise dispose of it seems to indicate that land in the Seleucid Empire might be held by a proprietor other than the monarch.

Under the Pergamene kings, while certain tracts were the personal property of the monarch, the land in general appears to have belonged to the crown.[60] It may be assumed that there were also some large private landlords, but neither their existence nor that of any hereditary leaseholders is attested by any evidence. Our knowledge is restricted to the small allotments of land held by military colonists, some of whom paid a rental in tithes, while others seem to have bought their holdings outright from an official representing the king.

The grants and sales made by the Seleucid monarchs must have resulted in a gradual diminution of the royal land, and this tendency was even more marked under the rulers of Pergamum.[61] Even before the great expansion of their kingdom in 188, settlements were established on land owned or seized by the kings, and the urbanization under Eumenes II and Attalus II, by which native communities were organized as cities, must also have led ultimately to a considerable shrinkage in the lands held by the crown. It may not be supposed, however, that there was a corresponding diminution in the royal revenues; for the amounts paid annually by the new urban communities doubtless exceeded the tithes derived from the rural settlers who had previously occupied these lands.

The kings and whatever great landlords there may have been, however, were not the only landed proprietors, for large estates were owned also by the gods.[62] This was especially the case in eastern Asia Minor; for in the kingdoms of Pontus and Cappadocia great tracts of land were still held in the first century by the principal temples, whose priests, as representatives of the deities, ruled over these vast domains, cultivated by temple-slaves. A somewhat similar condition existed, as has been already observed, at Pessinus, on the border of Phrygia and Galatia, where the lands of the Temple of the Great Mother formed virtually an independent principality, ruled by the Priest of the Goddess, and even in eastern Mysia, where at the close of the first century the

Priest of Zeus Abrettenus ruled the sacred domain with the power of a "dynast."

These instances of temple-ownership in regions little affected by the influence of Hellenism have given rise to the view that in western Asia Minor also a large part of the land originally consisted of sacred domains, and that these were gradually seized by the rulers, especially the Hellenistic kings, who assigned some portions to their new foundations and incorporated others in the land belonging to the crown.[63] It is indeed possible that with the growth of the city-states the holdings of the several deities worshipped in these places may have been curtailed as the need of land increased with the size of the community. There is, however, no evidence of any extensive seizure on the part of the monarchs, for the only recorded instance of any such aggression is to be found in the appropriation by "the Kings" of the revenues (probably from fisheries) from a lake near Ephesus belonging to Artemis. On the other hand, Alexander seems to have shown all respect for the property of the gods, as at Ephesus, where he extended the boundaries of the inviolable land of Artemis and ordered the citizens to pay to her the tribute which they had formerly paid to the Persian king.[r] The privileges, moreover, granted by Seleucus I to the Temple of Pluto at Nysa[s] and by Antiochus III to that of Apollo at Amyzon[t] suggest that the Seleucid monarchs also were more ready to conciliate than to offend the gods. Under the Pergamene kings certain new cities, as, for example, Hierapolis, received names which suggest that they may have been founded on what was once sacred domain, but it is perhaps more probable that they were originally temple-villages, which, as will presently be shown, developed spontaneously into cities of the Hellenic type.[u] The actual policy of the kings of this dynasty toward the temples is perhaps reflected in a gift of land (as well as of cows and herdsmen) by Attalus II to Athena at Ilium,[v] as well as in a letter, probably of Attalus III, referring to the grants made both by earlier rulers and by his own ancestors to the sanctuary of the "Persian Goddess" in the "Sacred Village," Hiera Come, in Lydia.[w]

Many of the temples of western Asia Minor, in fact, continued to hold domains of their own. Although, for the purpose, perhaps, of promoting the cultivation of the country, the land assigned by Attalus I and Prusias I to the Temple of Zeus at Aezani was divided into in-

r See Chap. III note 88.

t Welles, nos. 39-40; see Chap. IV note 48.

v Welles, no. 62; see Chap. I note 82.

s Welles, no. 9; see note 27.

u See note 65.

w Welles, no. 68; see note 65.

dividual allotments, these seem to have remained temple-property and the holders were under obligation to pay an annual rental to the God.[64] At Smyrna, Aphrodite Stratonicis, whose cult was founded by Antiochus II, owned land from which an income accrued "to the sacred revenues." In the second century before Christ, Artemis of Magnesia-on-Maeander had "sacred land," from which she drew revenue. Hera of Samos had an estate on the mainland in the Plain of Anaea, the tithes from which were paid to her, and Athena of Priene seems to have claimed the ownership of salt-pans near the city. In the following century, Athena of Ilium possessed sacred territory, the revenues from which the *publicani* attempted to seize, and the temples at Mylasa and Olymus in Caria owned farms which were leased out to tenants both for cash-rentals and for payments in kind. Even in the time of Augustus, Artemis of Ephesus possessed tracts of land in the Caÿster valley, and as late as the second or third century after Christ, Apollo Lairmenos in southwestern Phrygia had a village and apparently an estate of his own.

It may be assumed that most of the gods' estates contained villages which served as the centres of trade and even as the residences both of the temple-officials and of those who tilled the land. This was the case at Comana in Cappadocia and at the place of the same name in Pontus, in each of which the throngs of the worshippers of the goddess and of the visitors to the festivals gradually increased the size and importance of the settlement.[65] As a result, these places developed into large towns, and in the first century after Christ the Cappadocian Comana was an Hellenic city with the name Hierapolis. A similar development seems to have taken place in the case of the settlement attached to the sanctuary of the "Persian Goddess," assimilated to Artemis, on the Lydian river Phrygius (Hyllus), a tributary of the Hermus; the "Sacred Village," Hiera Come, attained to such importance in the first century before Christ that it issued coins of its own; under Augustus it had a city-government and a little later the new name Hierocaesareia. This process likewise occurred at Dios Hieron (Sanctuary of Zeus) in the valley of the upper Lydian Caÿster, which issued coins in the first century after Christ and in the third century ranked as a *polis*.

The transformation of these temple-villages into cities suggests that this may have been the origin also of those *poleis* whose names contain the word "sacred," as well as of those which were derived from the name of a god.[66] Of these, the best known is Hierapolis ("Sacred City"), near the junction of the Maeander and the Lycus, where there was a holy cave, sacred, apparently, to the Great Mother and perhaps a sanctuary of the Goddess. The early name of the place, Hieropolis ("City of the Sanctuary"), suggests that it was originally a village connected with this sanctuary, but the transformation into a city is probably to be dated under Eumenes II, when it had its own civic organization. A similar development perhaps took place at another Hieropolis in Phrygia north of Apameia, which was a *polis* in the Roman imperial period, and at Dionysopolis, near the upper Maeander, which in 59 B.C. was sufficiently organized to send a delegation to Rome.

The sacred domains and the villages attached to the temples ordinarily returned to their divine owners incomes which, save in times of natural catastrophe, were very well secured. The money thus received enabled richer temples to play an important part in the economic life of the period; for the large cash-reserves obtained from these sources, as well as from the money deposited for safe-keeping under the divine protection, became a frequent source for loans both to communities and to individuals.[67] The most important of these temple-banks, probably, was that of Apollo at Delos, but many of the sanctuaries of Asia Minor carried on similar operations. As early as the fifth century the Temple of Artemis at Ephesus received deposits on account, and at the close of the First Mithradatic War it had many loans still outstanding. At Sardis, during the third century, the Temple of Artemis lent the sum of 1,325 gold staters (the equivalent in value of nearly four and a half talents) to a certain Mnesimachus, who, when unable to repay the loan, gave the temple a mortgage on his land. About 77 B.C. the Temple of Athena at Ilium advanced the funds needed by seven cities of the Federation which had its common sanctuary in this temple, and during this century Asclepius at Cos had his own bank, which might invest his capital and also serve the needs of those who attended his festival.

The territories granted by the kings to the cities which they founded comprised only a comparatively small portion of the "royal land," for the greater part of western Asia Minor still consisted, as in pre-Persian times, of extensive districts held by rural tribes.[68] These persisted in regions more or less remote. Some of them, like the Cilbiani and the Caÿstriani in the basin of the Lydian Caÿster, the Mocadeni in eastern Lydia, the Hyrgaleis east of the great bend of the Maeander and the Moxeani in western Phrygia, were in fairly accessible places; others, like the Olympeni, Abretteni and Abbaïtae in eastern Mysia, lived in areas far removed from outside influences. Tribes such as these, known in later times, were evidently only the remnants of a larger number, whose principal village-centres had developed into *poleis* with their own territories or whose lands had become part of the territories of the royal foundations. Under the Romans, the development of these villages, especially those which were natural centres of trade, continued to progress. In the case of the Hyrgaleis in Phrygia and a number of places in Caria, various communities united to form a kind of federation or "commonalty."

The tribal districts were organized according to the old Asianic system which, long antedating the spread of Hellenism, persisted in the parts of the country as yet not urbanized. This system was one of villages which were rural centres, serving as market-towns and the seat of whatever political organization and economic life the community possessed and also as the place of worship for its god.[69] Some of these villages had in early times come into the possession of the free city-states and had been incorporated into their territories, and others were acquired by the subject cities as they developed civic organizations of their own. Others, on the estates of the great landlords or the temples, were owned by the proprietor or the god, but by far the greater number, situated on the royal domain-land, belonged to the king. Under the Romans they continued to exist as individual rural communities.

In the course of time these villages developed a rudimentary form of civic organization with a limited amount of local administration.[70] Our information concerning their organization, it is true, is derived almost entirely from what is known of them in Roman times, but even in the Hellenistic period they had officials of their own, who had the titles of "village-chief" and "arbiter." Under the Romans, other officials also appear, bearing the titles, and presumably performing the duties, of similar officials in the cities. While these functionaries were evidently charged with the conduct of the affairs of the community, the supreme power, as the influence of Hellenism grew stronger, was vested in the villagers themselves, assembled in a mass-meeting, which passed resolutions concerning the public business and presumably elected the officials, a form of self-government evidently imitated from that of a *polis*. Money-payments were made to the king as the owner of the land; but in the case of villages leased by him to a private landlord, the payment was made by the latter, who, in turn, exacted from the villagers both money and tithes as well as a certain amount of labour.[71]

The village-communities which in the Roman period had their own officials and managed their own affairs were evidently composed of free peasants. While this may have been the case to some extent in the Hellenistic period also, both the domains of the kings and the estates of individual landlords were at least in part cultivated by serfs, who paid rental in money or produce to the proprietor, whether royal or private.[72] They differed from slaves in that their persons were not owned by the proprietor, but they and their possessions were regarded as belonging to the land, and with a change of ownership they passed to the new owner. They might migrate to other places, but they were still considered members of the village-communities in which they were originally registered.

It is probable that during the third century this system of serfdom gradually declined. The increase in the number of cities and the consequent shrinkage of the royal domain-land must have resulted in a decrease in the number of the peasant-serfs. The liberal policy of the Pergamene kings naturally tended in the same direction. In fact, as early as the reign of Attalus I a step was taken for the improvement of the status of the royal peasants in his kingdom when the monarch appointed a judge for the district of Aeolis, to whom disputes might be brought for decision.[73] During the second century the population of the new cities and their territories must have been supplied in part at least from the peasants. A corresponding development seems to have taken place on the kings' domain-land with the gradual transformation of serfs into free peasants who paid tithes to the monarch's treasury, and although in 132 the rebel Aristonicus was still able to recruit an army on the royal estates,[x] it is highly probable that by this time the majority of those who tilled these estates had passed from serfdom into freedom.

More typical of the old Asianic system, however, than the villages of Lydia and Phrygia were the communities of inland Caria.[74] The Greeks who built their cities on the coast had not penetrated into the interior, and consequently the district in general, unaffected by the spread of Hellenism, long remained a land of villages. The Seleucids, although Antiochus I founded Stratoniceia, never succeeded in wholly establishing their power over this remote region, and Caria had never undergone any such process of urbanization as the other districts subject to their rule. Even Antiochus III, despite his efforts to strengthen himself in Caria, seems to have made no change in the prevailing order other than to declare Alabanda free and autonomous. While it may be

[x] See below p. 151f.

supposed that here also the land in theory belonged to the monarchs, their hold on it could not have been strong. In the second century, during the twenty years of Rhodian rule, the land was presumably owned by the Republic, but after the Senate in 167 declared that Caria was free, the communities themselves must have become the proprietors.

It was characteristic of the village-system as developed in Caria that the villages were organized in combinations, called federations or "commonalties."[75] These existed both in the interior of the district and along the shores of the Gulf of Cos. Their names were taken, presumably, from the communities most conspicuous in the regions in which they were respectively situated. The original purpose of such a group may have been the celebration of a common worship, but by the second century, at least, some of those in the interior had assumed a semi-political character. They held assemblies competent to take action, conferred the rights of citizenship and various honours, elected officials of different kinds, and in general exercised many of the administrative powers characteristic of a *polis*.

Apart from these village-federations, the Carians had, in the fifth century if not earlier, a national organization, which included, apparently, the natives of the entire district. Like all such organizations, the "Carians" had a common sanctuary, the temple of Zeus Carius at Mylasa.[76] In the fourth century they appear to have obtained some political recognition, for in 367/6, acting as a body, they sent an envoy to King Artaxerxes II, apparently to bring some charge against Maussolus, the ruler of Halicarnassus and most of the coast region. The fact, however, that the King condemned the envoy to death—although possibly because he had exceeded his instructions—suggests that, at least as compared with Maussolus, the "Carians" had little influence at the Persian court. The organization, however, continued to exist throughout the Hellenistic period. At the beginning of the first century it still held meetings, if only to confer honours, and among its officials was one with the high-sounding title of "priest and king." It is probable that at this time the activities of the Carian Federation, like those of the Ilians and the Ionians,[y] were restricted to sacrifices and the bestowal of compliments.

Another Carian organization was the "Nation of the Chrysaoreis," which met in the temple of Zeus Chrysaoreus near Stratoniceia for the purpose of offering sacrifice and deliberating on matters of common concern to the members.[77] Its relationship to the Carian Federation is

y See Chap. III notes 53 and 54.

145

unknown, but as the latter existed as late as the first century before Christ, the two organizations seem to have been maintained simultaneously. The "Nation" is known from a document of the late third century, but its origin was evidently earlier, for it was constituted according to the ancient village-system. At its meetings each village represented was entitled to cast one vote, and a village-federation or a city had as many votes as there were villages contained in its territory. Thus the city of Stratoniceia itself, which had been founded in the early third century, probably long after the "Nation" was originally formed, had no vote of its own but controlled the votes of its villages. How much of Caria was included in the Nation is unknown, but at least a large portion of the district was represented in it, for in addition to Stratoniceia, we know that Alabanda and Alinda in the north and Mylasa and Ceramus in the west were members, probably on the basis of their possession of villages, but possibly because, although *poleis*, they were the successors of ancient Carian village-centres.

The subject communities included civic organizations of many types and diverse origins: ancient Asianic cities which at the end of the third century had the municipal institutions of a *polis*; Seleucid foundations which in some cases replaced an older town; Pergamene settlements built for the purpose of controlling a region of strategic importance; and communities which were originally temple-villages but grew into cities. Alongside of these were the rural village-centres, sometimes on "royal" sometimes on "sacred" domain-land, which, obtaining more and more organization, developed with the increasing urbanization of the country from villages into communities that resembled, more or less closely, the Hellenic *polis*. As western Asia Minor was a land of great natural contrasts, with fertile river-basins traversed by highways terminating in busy ports and, on the other hand, inaccessible mountain-groups, to which neither trade nor Hellenism had penetrated, so its population also presented a marked diversity, which extended from the lively Greek, with his commerce and industries and his complicated political machinery, through the native city-dweller, more or less Hellenized and urbanized, to the toiling peasant of the rural districts, with no rights save what his overlord, royal or sacred, deigned to accord him and concerned chiefly with the question of how much of his produce would be left after making the necessary payments to the owner of the land which he tilled.

CHAPTER VI

REVOLT AND ANNEXATION

AT Rome, when the news of Attalus's bequest arrived, there seems to have been no hesitancy in accepting this new addition to the Empire. No excuse was made for embarking on the new course of imperialism which was to carry Roman rule across the Aegean. The ruling class, it may be assumed, was not averse to the acquisition of a rich province which its members could govern with financial advantage to themselves, and to the business-men the prospect of opportunities for investment with great profit was far from unwelcome. In fact, all who regarded the situation realistically must have considered it the natural outgrowth of the policy of the Scipios, who, on their entry into Asia in 190 B.C., had ordered Antiochus III to resign all claim to Asia Minor north of the Taurus Range and thus brought about the expansion of the Pergamene Kingdom.

The only question that arose was a not unfamiliar one, namely, which class should profit by the new acquisition. Over this question there was the equally familiar quarrel between politicians. As we have seen,[a] Tiberius Gracchus, to the great indignation of the Senate, introduced a bill appropriating Attalus's treasure to the use of the colonists who were to be established throughout Italy, and this proposal was followed by a project for legislation concerning the organization of the new province.[b] Both of these measures were without precedent, and, in the eyes of the senatorial party, revolutionary, since by long-established custom both the accceptance of the bequest and the formation of Attalus's kingdom into a province devolved, like all matters of international policy, upon the Senate.[c] It was probably fortunate for harmony at Rome that any further action on the part of Gracchus was prevented by his murder.

The removal of its turbulent antagonist enabled the Senate to resume its usual position as the directing power in foreign affairs. It proceeded at once upon its customary course, and five members were appointed commissioners to take over the inheritance and to make arrangements for the government of the newly acquired territory.[1] At their head was Scipio Nasica, the leader of the aristocrats against Gracchus in the armed attack which resulted in the death of the popular leader; it was

---

[a] See above p. 33.   [b] Plutarch *Ti. Gracch.* 14.
[c] See Mommsen *R.St.R.* III p. 1170f.

now found desirable to remove him from the city and from the hatred of Gracchus's followers, who were clamouring for revenge. But the Senators, preoccupied with a war in Spain and a slave-revolt in Sicily, as well as with the agitation in the city caused by the death of Gracchus, had not found it possible to act promptly. Accordingly, it was not until the spring of 132 that the commission arrived in Asia. When it did arrive, it found the country in the throes of civil war.

The only one of the blood of the Attalids now surviving was Aristonicus, an illegitimate son of Eumenes by the daughter of a lyre-player of Ephesus.[2] There is no reason to suppose that he had ever been recognized in any way by the royal family of Pergamum, or to believe that he had made any plan to secure the succession to the throne. But whatever hopes he might have cherished of succeeding either to the wealth or to the domains of Attalus were dashed to the ground by the bequest of the King. Aristonicus determined, therefore, to seize the throne by violence, and after Attalus's will was made known he gathered together a band of followers, hoping to forestall the Romans in any steps they might take to enter on their inheritance.[3] He was a man of boldness and ability, and he doubtless found little difficulty in gaining the support of those who were either jealous or fearful of Rome.

With his followers Aristonicus raised the standard of revolt at Leucae, a stronghold on the northern side of the entrance to the Gulf of Smyrna.[4] The neighbouring city of Phocaea joined him,[d] and he evidently found supporters among the subject population of his half-brother's kingdom, for we are told by one historian that he "easily won over those who had been wont to render obedience to the kings."[e] Even in Pergamum itself Aristonicus may have found adherents, for some persons left the city—either to join him or out of fear—and others were suppressed by force.[5] He also included among his troops some soldiers from Thrace, but whether these were serving as mercenaries in the Pergamene army or whether they were recruits who had left their native land because of the troubled conditions there cannot be determined.[6]

But assistance of greater importance was rendered by a fleet, possibly provided by Phocaea, but more probably composed of royal warships stationed at Leucae or perhaps Elaea. With this the rebel leader was able to harry the Aegean seaboard, taking by force cities which offered resistance, such as Colophon (or more probably Notium)[f] and Samos.[g]

d Justin xxxvii 1, 1.   e Florus 1 35, 4.   f See Chap. III note 110.
g Florus ibid. (Myndus, Samos, Colophon)

He seems even to have carried on naval operations as far as the coast of Caria, where he captured Myndus, which, at the end of the long peninsula of Halicarnassus, he could have approached only by sea.

Thus western Asia Minor was plunged into war. The alarm of the Greek cities must have been great indeed; yet none save Phocaea supported Aristonicus voluntarily, regarding him, apparently, as the foe both of Hellenic civilization and of commercial prosperity. They evidently preferred the hope of the freedom which they might enjoy under Rome's supremacy to the certainty of being ruled by a native prince, a potential tyrant like those in Thrace who had recently perpetrated horrible cruelties on the Greek inhabitants of the country[h]—and, in fact, the policy which Aristonicus subsequently adopted showed that he was not the kind of man to bestow favours on the more civilized elements in the Pergamene Kingdom. Accordingly, making every possible effort to defend themselves, the Greek and Hellenized communities in general remained steadfastly loyal to Rome—a fidelity of which, one hundred and fifty years later, eleven of them boasted to the Roman Senate.[7]

At Pergamum also, at the very beginning, elaborate preparations were made for self-defence.[8] Soon after Attalus's death and before the announcement was made that his will had been ratified by the Romans, the citizens, taking advantage of their newly gained freedom, adopted every means of strengthening their forces "for the sake of the common safety." In order to secure the loyalty and support of all the inhabitants, they conferred citizenship on the duly registered resident-aliens, on the soldiers of Attalus settled in the city and its territory, on the military colonists, Macedonians, Mysians, and "those registered in the garrison of the ancient city," soldiers "from Masdye," rural guardsmen and others, probably veterans, who were domiciled or landholders in the city or its territory, together with the wives and children of all. They raised to the status of aliens all freedmen and the slaves belonging both to the King and to the people; and all those persons who had left Pergamum or its territory since the death of the King or who might leave it now (*i.e.* perhaps to join Aristonicus) were proclaimed outlaws and their property declared confiscate to the city. These measures evidently obtained the approval of the Roman commissioners, for otherwise they would not have been recorded on stone. Moreover, they were wholly successful, for Pergamum did not fall into the hands of

[h] See Chap. I note 90.

Aristonicus; the commissioners on their arrival took up their quarters in the city, and Nasica, who died soon afterward, was buried there.[9]

While it is impossible to determine the time of the commissioners' arrival, it is evident that when they reached Asia the war was well on its way.[10] They were, of course, powerless to take action against the rebel. There were no Roman troops in Asia, and, except for the inadequate contingents that the cities were able to furnish, the only forces that could be obtained were those of the allied native kings. Accordingly, on receipt of the news of the revolt, which doubtless reached Rome soon after the commissioners' departure, the Senate had sent a call for assistance to Nicomedes II of Bithynia, Mithradates V of Pontus, Ariarathes V of Cappadocia and Pylaemenes of Paphlagonia, all of whom responded to the summons.[11] Their forces, however, proved insufficient and it became necessary to take active measures at Rome. Early in 131, therefore, an army was raised and sent to Asia under the command of Publius Licinius Crassus Mucianus, the Consul.

The addition of this force to the contingents led by the monarchs greatly strengthened the cause of Rome in Asia. The cities, moreover, encouraged by this increase in strength, but probably also under pressure from Rome, continued to send reinforcements. From the north, Byzantium contributed aid,[12] and Cyzicus sent envoys to the Roman general, of whom one, presumably with some troops furnished by the city, took part in the campaign.[13] In Caria, far to the south, Halicarnassus, doubtless alarmed by the capture of the neighbouring Myndus, sent a ship to Crassus, while Bargylia contributed troops.[14] Another city, possibly Mylasa, furnished munitions of war.

Nevertheless, little was done by Crassus to defeat the enemy.[15] It was said of him that on his arrival in Asia he showed greater interest in securing the treasure of Attalus than in prosecuting the war.[i] But, as he had been a partisan of Gracchus and, furthermore, had secured the command against Aristonicus only by using his power as Pontifex Maximus to estop his fellow-consul from attempting to obtain the appointment,[j] he must have had bitter political enemies, and perhaps this charge originated with them.[k] In his favour it was said that he had acquired such a command of Greek that he could use five different dialects and delighted the inhabitants of Asia by rendering decisions in the dialect of each petitioner.[l] Of the five characteristics, however, which were cited as his chief claim to merit—his wealth, his noble birth,

---

[i] Justin xxxvi 4, 7f.   [j] Cicero *Phil.* xi 18.   [k] So Münzer in *R.E.* xiii 336.
[l] Valerius Maximus viii 7, 6 = Quintilian xi 2, 50.

his eloquence, his knowledge of law, and his office as chief pontifex[m]—none seemed to qualify him for the command of this war. He did, nevertheless, engage in at least one conflict with the enemy, and this cost him his life.

It would appear that Leucae, the scene of the first outbreak, was still in the hands of a garrison of Aristonicus, and against it, when his command in Asia was drawing to a close, Crassus made an attack. He was caught off his guard, however, and forced to retreat northward, and he was finally captured by the Thracians who had been defending the place. It was said that in order to escape the disgrace of being taken to Aristonicus while alive, he used his riding-whip to thrust out an eye of one of his captors and was at once slain. Only his head was brought to the rebel general; his body was buried in Smyrna. About the same time, perhaps, King Ariarathes of Cappadocia met his death.[n]

In spite of the success that he had won by the defeat and death of Crassus, the tide soon turned against Aristonicus. For the victory, however, which was the beginning of the end of the revolt, it was not the Romans who were responsible, but Ephesus, for the city made a bold stand against him although it had been his mother's home. Evidently his capture of Colophon and Samos, near neighbours, brought the citizens to the determination to take some measures to check the growth of the revolt. The city manned a fleet and sent it forth against the enemy, meeting his ships somewhere off Cyme on the coast of Aeolis.[16] The naval battle that ensued resulted in a complete victory over the fleet of Aristonicus. This victory was an important one for the cities of Aeolis and Ionia, for it saved them from all immediate danger from their enemy, inasmuch as Aristonicus was forced thereby to abandon the coast and withdraw into the interior.

As the result of this withdrawal the character of the revolt changed completely, for Aristonicus now came forth in a new light, in which he appeared no longer as the claimant to a Hellenized kingdom but as the leader of an army of outlaws and a foe to Hellenic civilization. Taking possession of the hill-country of central Mysia, he made an appeal to all who were destitute and particularly to slaves who were dissatisfied with their lot and ready to turn against their owners.[17] Such an appeal would naturally find a response among the peasants on the royal domains, for they would be ready to follow a son of Eumenes against new and foreign masters. To the slaves he made the usual promise of freedom, and to the destitute he presumably held out the

[m] Gellius I 13, 10.   [n] Justin XXXVII I, 2.

equally usual promise of economic relief. Whether these elements of the population of Mysia had previously been in revolt is not clear, but in any case they responded to Aristonicus's call and flocked to his standard. Clever enough to see the advantage of giving a national character to the movement, he invented a name for his followers, calling them "Heliopolitae," "citizens of a Sun-state," a name perhaps borrowed from one of the Utopias of contemporary Stoicism,[18] but to the Asiatic peasant-population hardly meaning more than freedom from their present economic status. With the force thus gathered together, evidently a large body, he advanced against the cities of northern Lydia, where he succeeded in capturing first Thyateira and then Apollonis. One can imagine what these communities suffered at the hands of peasants and slaves provided with arms and roused to action by the hope of plunder and liberation. Not content with these successes, Aristonicus led his forces against other places also, and it is not surprising that to many he seemed a "regular king."[19]

Aristonicus's policy of appealing to the impoverished and the discontented and identifying their cause with his own was perhaps a shrewd move on his part in that it ensured to him a large number of followers. The pillaging of the urban communities, furthermore, brought to him and his supporters a great amount of booty. But, now more than ever, the owners of property, not merely in the cities, but throughout the rural districts, and especially the great landed-proprietors, must have regarded him as their bitter enemy. His promises to the slaves, in particular, seemed subversive of the whole economic structure of the country. By the ancient world there was little that was more dreaded than a slave-rebellion, and the leader of such a movement was regarded by all responsible persons with hatred and terror. The followers, moreover, whom Aristonicus's promises brought to his standard were of questionable value as soldiers. While doubtless brave individually and capable of plundering defenceless communities, they were undisciplined and not trained to fight in military formation. Consequently, they proved wholly unable to face a regularly organized army under a leader of skill and experience such as the Roman who now appeared to quell the revolt.

Through the death of Crassus the conduct of the war devolved upon his successor in the consulship, Marcus Perperna, who had been chosen Consul for the year 130 and, on hearing of Crassus's defeat and death, hastened to Asia to take over the command.[20] He soon showed himself a general of a very different stripe from Crassus, and, taking the offensive, he marched into the interior, where he caught Aristonicus unawares and defeated him overwhelmingly in the first engagement. All the forces of the rebels fled the field, and Aristonicus himself was forced to seek refuge in the city of Stratoniceia above the plain through which flows the upper Caïcus,[21] where he was besieged by the Roman general. The city was starved into surrender and Aristonicus himself was captured alive. He was thrown into chains, taken to the coast and thence conveyed to Rome, there to await the triumph which his captor hoped later to celebrate.

After his spectacular victory Perperna evidently supposed that the revolt, now without a head, had been finally quelled. He announced a festival, with sacrifices and contests, to be held at Pergamum in celebration of his success, and requested the cities to send their representatives to participate.[22] Meanwhile, he himself was busy with what was doubtless a more congenial task than the rounding up of fugitive rebels; returning to Pergamum, he took over the treasure of Attalus. After gathering it in, he shipped it to Rome, where the valuables of the royal house of Pergamum were sold at public auction.[23] But before he himself could embark on his homeward voyage he was stricken at Pergamum with an illness which proved fatal. He was the third Roman victim that Asia claimed in the space of three years.

Before Perperna's death, however, Manius Aquilius, the new Consul for the year 129, arrived on the scene.[24] He had hastened to Asia, hoping to forestall Perperna in laying hands on the treasure and to secure Aristonicus as his own prey. But, as we are told by an historian, "death put an end to the strife between the Consuls." As for Aristonicus, he was afterwards strangled in the prison at Rome by order of the Senate.[25]

It was believed in the Capital that the revolt in Asia had been completely stamped out, for along with Aquilius came ten commissioners, appointed for the purpose of organizing the new province. But before this could be done, it was found necessary to undertake still another campaign against the rebels. They were holding out in the district of Abbaïtis, the mountainous country lying between Mysia and Phrygia. Hither Aquilius proceeded, leaving a legate, Gnaeus Domitius Ahenobarbus, with some of the Roman forces and the native contingents, to guard the coast region. His success seems to have been complete, for he took by storm strongholds supposed to be impregnable. It was regarded, however, as an everlasting disgrace to Roman arms that he could capture some places only by poisoning the water-supply.° The

° Florus 1 35, 7.

revolt of the native population of Asia Minor had been put down with the strong hand, and Rome and the Greek cities had combined to save the country from a master who perhaps might not have differed greatly from the tyrant whom Attalus had hoped to ward off. But so far were Attalus's heirs from fulfilling his hope that when, forty-one years later, a native king entered into conflict with Rome,[p] these same Greek cities espoused the cause of the invader rather than that of the masters who had bled the land of its resources and were by this time regarded as tyrants indeed.

The last stages of the revolt were crushed, probably, before the end of 129, but Aquilius found it necessary to remain in Asia for two years longer in order to organize the province. It was no easy task that confronted him and the ten commissioners, and probably no country which the Romans had as yet taken over had presented so difficult a problem. For the kingdom of Attalus was heterogeneous in character and diversified in interests, containing different types of peoples and civilizations, cities modelled on the Greek *polis* and Asianic rural communities with their village-centres, as well as the royal estates and the temple-domains—various elements which the Pergamene kings had held together, not merely by the strong hand, but by tact and diplomacy, and, when the need arose, by lessening the burdens borne by their subjects.

The first question that presented itself was evidently the extent of the territory to be included in the province. The outlying districts on the east and southeast, especially, were not only remote and but little affected by the spread of Hellenism, but they were also, economically, the least valuable portions of the country. These districts, which would prove difficult to administer, were handed over to the native kings who had supported Rome during the war; for, as the heirs of Attalus, the Roman people, acting through the senatorial commissioners, had the right of bestowing the domains it had received on those whom it desired to reward. The greater part of Phrygia, accordingly, was granted to Mithradates of Pontus,[26] perhaps on the basis of a shadowy claim to the region which the King asserted, but possibly, as seems to have been alleged later, as the result of a bribe which he gave to Aquilius. It has sometimes been held that the grant was made in the face of violent opposition from Nicomedes of Bithynia, and that the two kings tried to outbid each other in bribing the electorate at Rome, but this appears to be without foundation.[27] The less

p See below p. 214f.

desirable district of Lycaonia was handed over to the sons of Ariarathes of Cappadocia, who had given his life to support the cause of Rome against Aristonicus.[28] The disposal of that portion of Pisidia which had belonged to Attalus is unknown, but it is not probable that at this time it was included in the province of Asia. The non-Asianic domains—the Thracian Chersonnesus and the island of Aegina—were incorporated in the province of Achaea-Macedonia.[29] Of the dominions of Attalus, therefore, only Mysia with the Troad, Lydia, the coast of Aeolis and Ionia, and the southwestern corner of Phrygia were taken into the province of Asia; but these, not only in civilization but also in natural resources and commercial importance, were the most valuable portions of the Pergamene Kingdom. Moreover, the large district of Caria south of the Maeander, granted to Rhodes by the Treaty of Apameia but withdrawn in 167 when the Senate wished to weaken the island-Republic, seems also to have been incorporated in the province.[30] The new "Asia," therefore, extended from the Propontis on the north to the Gulf of Cos on the south and included the islands along the coast, which must inevitably have been in close economic connexion with the mainland.

The extent of the new province determined, the next problem was that of the status of the various types of communities it contained. The "free and autonomous" cities, which did not form part of Attalus's kingdom, were not included in his bequest. Their independence had been recognized in 188 and for years they had been "friends and allies" of Rome, protected, when the need arose, against aggression even from the King of Pergamum.[q] During the recent war they, in their turn, had shown themselves loyal to Rome by sending troops and ships to her aid. It is true that Colophon, Samos and Myndus had been unsuccessful in their resistance to Aristonicus and had been compelled to surrender, but as far as we know, only one city, Phocaea, had voluntarily sided with him. While we have no knowledge of the status accorded to the three cities which had succumbed to force, it is hardly probable that they were punished for their surrender. In the case of Phocaea, guilty of an actual breach of faith, the Senate went so far as to order the destruction of the disloyal city.[31] The execution of the sentence, however, was averted by the intercession of the people of Massalia, a former colony of Phocaea and a valued ally of Rome. Phocaea was pardoned for its offence, but we do not know whether its former independence was restored.

q See Chap. IV note 93.

The cities which retained their freedom continued to be, in theory at least, independent states, enjoying a *de jure* sovereignty and possessing all the rights which they had previously enjoyed.[32] They were not subject to the orders of the governor of the Roman province, nor did Rome have any claim on them except that which was made necessary by the existing relationship. This relationship, as previously, was that of "friendship and alliance," under the terms of which the assistance rendered by the cities in time of war might take the form of a contribution of troops, ships or supplies, furnished at the request of the Senate. As heretofore, this contribution might be commuted into a money-payment, but there is no evidence that any such commutation was enforced or that fixed payments at regular intervals were made during this period into the Roman treasury by an allied city-state.

Those cities, on the other hand, which had not been recognized as independent states but, while enjoying a very limited autonomy, had been subject to the kings of Pergamum and paid tribute into the royal treasury constituted a part of Attalus's bequest. The opinion has, indeed, been expressed that Attalus had intended that those which had governments modelled on that of an Hellenic *polis* should be made independent, but this view is not supported by the available evidence.[33] The determination of their future status, therefore, devolved upon Aquilius and his fellow-commissioners. The clause in the King's will by which, subject to ratification by the Romans, Pergamum was declared free was carried out in full, and the city was recognized as independent.[34] Sardis, the ancient capital of Lydia, seems also to have received its freedom,[35] but we know of no others on whom the privilege was conferred at this time.

As a general rule, therefore, the subject cities were retained by the commissioners in a position similar to that which they had had under the Pergamene kings. They preserved their limited degree of local autonomy and their outward show of administrative trappings, but they were subject to the Roman governor and, as they had paid tribute to Pergamum, so they henceforth paid it to Rome.[36]

The question of the cities settled, there remained the rural districts, which also had been directly subject to Attalus and constituted by far the larger part of his kingdom. They included the royal domain-land with its village-centres, as well as any properties which were held by individual landlords either in full ownership or on unlimited leasehold and paid taxes or tithes to the monarchs. The landed possessions of Attalus became the domain of the Roman people and over it the Roman government had full property-rights.[37] The private holdings, on the other hand, remained in the possession of the proprietors, who, under such an arrangement, would continue to derive income from these estates but henceforth paid to Rome the tithes they had previously paid to the royal treasury. Thus the two types of communities of which the Pergamene Kingdom had been composed were retained by the Romans, and officially the new province consisted of organized "peoples" and unorganized "districts."[38]

An important part of the organization of the new province was the construction of roads, and this task likewise devolved upon Aquilius.[r] It has been shown that the Pergamene kings had not neglected the highways of their kingdom and that they had taken pains to connect their new foundations with the capital.[s] But concentrating, as they naturally did, on Pergamum and the northern part of their kingdom, they had done less for the southern portion, and to this region, accordingly, Aquilius devoted his chief attention. True to the policy by which the Romans had unified Italy by constructing roads throughout the peninsula, he now proceeded to bind the different parts of the province more closely together by roads designed, not only to facilitate travel and commerce, but also to connect distant places with what was to be its chief port and the residence of its governor—the rich and renowned city of Ephesus. To accomplish this end he sought to rebuild old roads rather than to construct new ones. From the Persian period onward, as has been already shown,[t] two main routes had connected the interior with Ephesus, the more northerly, which led down the valley of the Hermus to Sardis and thence over Mt. Tmolus, and the Southern Highway, which came down from the central plateau at Apameia and thence followed the valleys of the Lycus and the Maeander. Both of these great highways Aquilius rebuilt, thus uniting the remoter portions of the province with the sea and securing for Ephesus the commerce of the two great trade-routes leading from the Euphrates.[39] Of this proud achievement he left a simple record, the milestones which bore only his name and title—*M'. Aquilius M'. f. Consul*—written in both Greek and Latin. Besides these two routes, he rebuilt a third, leading northward from Smyrna and onward toward Adramyttium.[40] Thus not only was the chief port of the province connected with the *hinterland* and even with the Euphrates, but the

---

[r] For Aquilius's roads see Haussoullier in *R. Phil.* xxiii (1899), p. 293f.
[s] See above p. 40f.   [t] See above p. 39f.

great cities of the western seaboard were assured of communication and trade with one another.

Aquilius remained in Asia for three years, carrying on his work of conquest and subsequent organization and construction. This work was well received both by the Asianic Greeks and by the government at Rome. In recognition of his services the people of Pergamum created a priest to perform sacrifices to him,[u] and on his return to Rome he received the distinction of a triumph for his termination of the war and his work as an organizer.[v] It is true that his enemies presently brought him to trial for extortion,[41] practised, presumably, in his settlement of Asia, but of this charge he was acquitted, and he could proudly retain the claim of being the first to receive the highest honours that both the Greeks of the East and the Romans of the West could confer.

[u] *I.G.R.* IV 292, l. 39.
[v] On 11 Nov. 126 B.C.; see *Acta Triumphorum, C.I.L.* I² p. 176.

CHAPTER VII

THE CONSEQUENCES OF ANNEXATION

WHEN the rule of the Pergamene kings was replaced by that of Rome the change affected the various inhabitants of the new province in various ways. The small proprietors and the peasants who cultivated the land which was now the property of the Roman people[a] probably felt it least; they still toiled to pay their tithes, and it signified little to them whether the payments were made to the Roman tax-collector or to the representative of the king. To the city-folk the difference was greater, but not even they were all affected alike. The "free and autonomous" communities, as has already been observed,[b] continued to govern themselves according to their own laws and to administer their own finances. But during the war against Aristonicus their privileges had been somewhat curtailed by the demands made by the Romans, for they were obliged not only to furnish troops but also to provide winter-quarters for the Roman army.[1] In the case of Pergamum, the city-authorities had been ordered to submit the municipal accounts and even to make certain payments of money. The subject cities, on the other hand, realized the change more keenly. It is true that they were permitted to keep their limited local autonomy, and the tribute that they were forced to pay to their new rulers was probably no greater than that which had been exacted by their own monarchs.[c] But instead of a king who might in an emergency be ready to make reasonable concessions, they could expect little consideration from the stranger who now lorded it over them.

This, in fact, was the all-important difference between the old régime and the new, that instead of a ruler of their own race both the country-folk and the city-dwellers were subject to a governor sent to them annually from Rome who was alike unknown to them and ignorant of their circumstances.[2] He arrived each spring from across the sea, usually a former praetor but vested with the powers of a consul. With him came a quaestor, who was responsible for the management of the money appropriated by the Senate for the governor's use and received the income derived from the province, and also three assistants called *legates*, to whom were delegated such duties as the governor could not or would not perform in person. On his honesty or good

---

[a] See Chap. VI note 37.   [b] See above p. 156.   [c] See Chap. VI note 36.

159

nature all were dependent during his year of office, for his command was supreme. He administered the laws and presided over the courts, having both criminal and civil jurisdiction. He might levy troops and quarter them on the inhabitants. He might even pillage property, and redress was hard to obtain, for not only was an appeal to the court at Rome which dealt with extortion expensive, but the results were extremely uncertain.[3]

Besides these practical considerations, there was, sentimentally, a great change, of which all the inhabitants of the province must have been keenly aware. No one could think of the practical and business-like Roman official as surrounded by the semi-divine aura with which the former monarchs had been enveloped. Despite the divine honours which Pergamum had accorded to Aquilius,[d] it is difficult to imagine an annual governor received, like Attalus III,[e] with offerings and prayers to the gods, and a procession of priests, magistrates and victors in the sacred contests, the whole body of citizens bringing up the rear. No governor could succeed in presenting to a pageant-loving Greek the imposing figure of a Eumenes II, the saviour from the dangers of a Galatian invasion and the patron of art and literature, as well as of commerce and all that the Hellenic civilization held dear. Compared with the brilliant and often easy-going rule of Pergamum, that of Rome must have seemed drab and frequently tyrannical.

Apart from disadvantages which the change of government might in the future bring to the new province, its immediate condition was dreary indeed. The citizens of Pergamum itself, and, if we may generalize from this one known instance, probably other cities also, were deeply in debt. They were compelled to pay a ruinous rate of interest, with the result that some people lost their property altogether. Among the services for which a patriotic citizen of Pergamum named Diodorus Pasparus was honoured by his native city was his success—how effected we do not know—in reducing this interest and in the cancellation of the promissory notes which had been exacted by force and had become valueless.[f] The causes of this economic depression are to be found, presumably, partly in the requisitions made necessary by the three years' war, as well as in the damage which it wrought, and partly in the expenditures which the new government forced on the province.

At the beginning of the revolt of Aristonicus, the free cities, doubtless in response to a call for aid from Rome, had despatched contin-

[d] See above p. 158.   [e] See above p. 31.
[f] *I.G.R.* IV 292, ll. 4 and 12 as restored by Wilhelm (see note 1).

160

gents of ships and troops to fight against the rebel.[g] The Pergamene kings had had their own mercenary forces and, as a rule, did not call upon the cities for assistance in their wars. Consequently, the outlay of men and resources which the Romans demanded proved a burden all the greater because the cities were unaccustomed to it. Diodorus Pasparus had, indeed, persuaded the new rulers to grant Pergamum exemption from the obligation of furnishing troops as well as from the outlay of money entailed by the winter-quarters of the Roman army, but he was not able to obtain a remission of the war-contribution which had been imposed.[h] There had been a similar demand for men at Bargylia. Here also a public-spirited citizen prevailed upon a legate of Aquilius to grant a discharge to the soldiers whom the city had supplied for the suppression of the revolt, and thus obtained relief from the expense to which it had been subjected.[i]

Not only was the province in general suffering from the consequences of the civil war, but, as a result of the demand for troops and money, the ordinary business activities of the communities were interrupted by the cessation of their usual commerce and by the departure of men for active service against the enemy. The cost of these naval and military contingents could be met only by increased taxation levied by the local governments. Moreover, in the second phase of the war, when Aristonicus seized the interior and especially the plains of northern Lydia, the industries of that district, as, for example, the weaving and dyeing at Thyateira, doubtless suffered greatly. The rebels' occupation of this productive area could not but result in widespread damage to agriculture, especially when the men who tilled the land flocked to Aristonicus in the hope of bettering their condition. The consequent rise in the price of grain, an adequate supply of which always presented a problem to the cities on the coast, must have added to the hardships endured by the townsfolk.

In addition to these miseries, fresh expenditures were demanded. The treasure of Attalus had been sent intact to Rome to be used there for the benefit of the farmers planted throughout Italy,[j] and thus the costs of all the improvements carried out by Aquilius devolved on the provincials themselves; one cannot build a series of roads for nothing.[k] It is therefore not difficult to see that, between the effects of the war

[g] See above p. 149f.   [h] See note 1.
[i] Foucart in *Mém. Acad. Inscrs.* xxxvii (1904), p. 327f. = Holleaux *Études* ii p. 180f. (see Chap. VI note 14).
[j] See above pp. 33 and 153.   [k] See above p. 157.

and the exactions of the new administration, the business-men of the cities must have found themselves short of funds and have been forced into debt in order to meet their obligations. Nor is it hard to understand why those who had money should have demanded exorbitant rates of interest from those who wished to raise loans. The rates were naturally not decreased by the fact that many a promissory note had proved to be valueless.

There is another side to the picture. At the very time when the citizens of Pergamum were in debt and when the city had petitioned in vain for the abolition of the war-contribution demanded by the Romans, the Council and People voted to honour Diodorus by bestowing on him a golden wreath and by erecting no less than five statues of him, two of gold and two of bronze, one of each kind to be on horseback, and one of marble, the last to be set up in a temple which was likewise to be reared for his worship.[4] Such an outlay of public funds immediately after an economic crisis seems indeed to indicate a reckless management of the municipal finances and shows why the city, as well as its citizens, became involved in debt.

The loans which the citizens of Pergamum had contracted may have been advanced in part by the richer men of the city, but it is highly probable that in some cases, at least, they were made by Roman capitalists, who had come from Italy in the wake of the army. One of the decrees honouring Diodorus includes among other groups that of "the resident Romans,"[5] and it can hardly be supposed that these were residing in Pergamum for any other purpose than the exploitation of the country.

This is the earliest mention in Asia Minor of a type of organization which grew up in the provinces of Rome—a definitely constituted group of Italians permanently domiciled in a city and existing as a special association alongside of the citizens.[6] Technically, such a group was known as a *conventus Civium Romanorum*, but for practical purposes it was called more simply "the resident Romans" or "the Romans engaged in business." With the love of organizing that is characteristic of their kind, these business-men established associations, each having officials and a treasury of its own. They passed resolutions, sometimes acting conjointly with the Council and People of their city, and conferred honours on some important person, a Roman, a member of their own association, or a citizen of the community. As time went on, the groups of the entire province would sometimes combine for some joint action.[7] In the second or early first century before Christ, these groups existed in many cities, not only at Pergamum but also at Ephesus, Priene, Tralles, Adramyttium and Caunus and on the islands of Chios and Cos. During the first forty years of the province of Asia the influx of Italians must have been great indeed, for in 88 B.C. as many as 80,000 are said to have been massacred by order of King Mithradates.[1] But it was especially after the expulsion of the Pontic King that Italian settlers crowded into the province and the real heydey of exploitation began. In the first century and under the emperors there was an association of "resident Romans" in almost every city of importance.

These associations evidently regarded themselves as constituting a body apart from and independent of the community in which they lived.[8] They were also so regarded in cases where the law was concerned. In the free cities, at least during the Republican period, they were subject to the city's jurisdiction unless specifically exempted, but elsewhere they could not be tried by local magistrates but only by the Roman governor or his substitute.[9] From the more important groups were chosen members of the governor's *consilium*, or panel from which he drew referees or jurymen for the lawsuits of the provincials conducted by him.[10] Despite their independence of the community, these Italians shared in all the advantages which the communal life afforded. They were eligible for election to the local offices,[11] and, as at Pergamum they were included among those invited to the public banquet given by Diodorus,[m] so in other places also they shared in benefactions made to the people by dignitaries or public-spirited citizens.[12]

The groups included not only Romans but also all citizens of the Italian towns which were in alliance with Rome; with the extension of citizenship in 89 B.C. to all the Italian allies this differentiation, of course, ceased, and all those whose homes were south of the Po became "Romans" in the eyes of the law. Men of all classes were eligible to membership—exporters of the products of Asia, merchants great and small, agents of the tax-farming corporations, veterans domiciled in the province, bankers who made loans to bankrupt cities, and minor capitalists who lent money to individuals. No distinction among the Roman settlers was made, either economic or social.

The settlers appear to have bought up lands in the territories belonging to the cities, and on these they established permanent homes.[13] Some of them may have taken up holdings in the rural districts also, although it is not likely that there were many actual

[1] See below p. 216f. [m] See note 5.

farmers among the Italian immigrants, and these probably did not buy up much of the former royal domains. This land, now the property of the Roman People, as well as the land of the native private proprietors, fell into the hands of the Roman tax-farming corporations.

Six years after the formation of the province and before it could have recovered entirely from the financial depression which has been described, a fresh blow fell upon the inhabitants. They were now caught in the clutches of the Roman tax-farming syndicates, who exploited them for the next seventy-five years.[n] In 123 B.C. Gaius Gracchus, in his efforts to become a popular leader, sought to win the support of the great middle class of Rome, composed of share-holders in the companies which bid for the collection of the revenues accruing to the state. For some time these *publicani* had farmed the revenues from the state-owned properties in Italy, and after the annexation of Sicily they collected them from the city-territories and the domain-land acquired by the Roman People as the successors of the Syracusan monarchs.[14] Now, by virtue of a law enacted by Gracchus, companies were permitted to make similar contracts for the revenues from the province of Asia also.[15] Henceforth, their representatives in Rome, appearing before the censors, or, when these for any reason had not been elected, before the Consuls, presented bids for the revenues of the next four years, basing their offers, presumably, on what was supposed to be a fair yield during preceding periods. If an offer was accepted, the amount was guaranteed to the government by the company, which thus became underwriter for the payment of what was due. What remained over and above this amount constituted the profits of the share-holders.

The revenues thus farmed out to the companies consisted chiefly of tithes on produce, taxes on pasture and customs-duties—the last, at the rate of $2\frac{1}{2}$ per cent, levied, apparently, both on imports and on exports.[16] According to the method eventually employed, the agents did not deal directly with the individual tax-payers but, with the approval of the governor, made sub-contracts with the several communities, which thus became responsible for the payment of their respective quotas;[17] if these were not paid punctually, interest at a rate specified in the agreements was charged on all arrears. If tithes on the harvests were actually delivered in kind, they seem to have been sold and the proceeds credited to the company.[18]

The three sources of revenue were farmed by three separate or-

[n] See below p. 407.

ganizations,[19] but, obviously, there was no clash of interests among them. The same persons might be share-holders in all three, and when the need arose, as, for example, in making bids or asking for the cancellation of their contracts, the three companies seem to have combined together into a unit of a larger size.[20]

In the system as finally developed, the companies had their headquarters in Ephesus, from which their agents carried on their operations.[o] The actual head of the organization, the *magister*,[21] remained in Rome, but he was represented in the province by a deputy (*pro magistro*), whose duty it was to conduct all negotiations both with the governor and with the communities, to handle the funds of the company, and to turn over to the quaestor of the province the amount specified in the contract made with the government at Rome. He had under his supervision a host of clerks and agents, both free men—some of them members of the company—and slaves, who were actively engaged in the business of collecting the taxes.[22] The *publicani* had despatch-bearers of their own, who carried communications to and from the Capital and through whom letters could be sent by persons of influence even though they were not connected with the companies.[23] They had also their own banks at Laodiceia and Ephesus, in which were kept the proceeds of their exactions, and of these a Roman official might avail himself for the deposit of his ready money, as might also the government for the purpose of giving bills of exchange to its officers.[24]

In a speech supposed to have been delivered by Mark Antony eighty-one years after the passage of Gracchus's law, the statement was made that by this method of taxation a great benefit had been conferred upon the peoples of Asia; for, whereas they had previously paid a fixed sum to their kings, whether the yield was good or bad, the Romans demanded only a proportion of their annual harvests, thus sharing adverse circumstances with them.[p] This specious plea disregarded the fact that not only were the bids of the *publicani* made in Rome, where no one could estimate what the yield would be, but they were made for four years in advance; only an approximate average of previous years, therefore, could determine the probable amount of the future harvests, with no adequate allowance for possible years when the crops might fail. The argument also ignored one of the worst consequences of the system. For a failure on the part of the farmer to deliver his quota, either in grain or in money, constituted a lasting obligation en-

---

[o] Cicero *Epist. ad Fam.* v 20, 9; *ad Att.* v 13, 1.　　　[p] Appian *B.C.* v 4.

tailing payment of interest on all arrears,[q] and this interest the unhappy farmer was compelled to pay to the *publicani*. Usually, of course, it was necessary for him to borrow the funds, and the source of a loan would be a Roman banker engaged in business in the province. Thus the tax-gatherer and the money-lender together involved the provincial in continually increasing indebtedness.

The agents of the tax-farmers, with an eye to greater profits, naturally attempted to tax all land to which they could successfully assert any claim. Their aggressions are attested by the cases where decisions are known to have been rendered against them in their attempts to impose taxes on those categories of land not under their control—the territory of the free cities and the estates belonging to the temples. In the case of Pergamum, for example, a magistrate at Rome, in conjunction with a board of advisers, was ordered by the Senate to investigate a complaint that the *publicani* were taxing part of the city's territory and to determine the actual boundaries of the Pergamenes' lands.[25] The extant examples of aggression on temple-properties are more numerous. Thus the right to tax land belonging to the Temple of Athena Ilias at Troy, which was asserted by the tax-farmers, was denied by Lucius Caesar, censor in 89, in consequence of an appeal made by advocates of the Goddess.[26] A similar case arose in connexion with the revenues (probably fishing-rights) from the lakes near Ephesus, which had originally accrued to the Temple of Artemis, but had been taken over by "the kings."[r] The Romans had restored them to the Goddess, but nevertheless, about the end of the second century before Christ, the *publicani* laid violent hands on them; it was only after a special ambassador—the famous geographer Artemidorus—was sent to Rome by the temple-officials to present the case to the Senate that these revenues were given back. Another case arose at Priene, where not only lands formerly the property of Attalus III but also the salt-works belonging to the sanctuary of Athena Polias were claimed as taxable.[27] When the salt-works were seized by agents of the tax-farmers, a patriotic citizen appeared before the governor to protest against their action. Although the aggressors went so far as to use violence, he succeeded in having their proceedings halted until the Senate granted a favourable reply to the city's appeal. Evidently the *publicani* had no scruples in asserting claims to all possible sources of revenue, but it is to the credit of the government at Rome that in several instances, at least, their claims were disallowed.

[q] See note 17.   [r] Strabo XIV p. 642; see Chap. V note 63.

Nevertheless, in spite of the havoc wrought by the revolt of Aristonicus, the free cities appear during the late second century to have enjoyed a certain degree of prosperity. The drain of the war-contributions removed, these communities, not subject to the Roman tax-gatherers' greed, found it possible to make use of the natural resources of their territories as well as of their industries and their commerce to repair the ravages caused by the war. Thus at Magnesia-on-Maeander and at Teos the erection of the temples of Artemis and Dionysus, the work of the architect Hermogenes, if, as has been suggested, the buildings may be dated in this period,[s] testifies to the wealth of the communities. At Magnesia also the celebrations of the festival in honour of the Goddess Roma, with dramatic contests consisting of tragedies, comedies and the farces known as "satyr-dramas," are evidence of the generosity of those well-to-do citizens who, as "agonothetes," paid the expenses of the performances.[t]

At Miletus, although its commerce had suffered in consequence of the increased importance of its rival, Ephesus, the resources of the city still sufficed to found a cult of Roma with a sanctuary for the Goddess and a festival in her honour.[28] At the end of the century we hear also of a gymnasium for the Elders' Association with a festival in connexion with which a banquet was given and a sacrifice performed,[29] and at this time, too, Milesian youths were able to carry on their studies at Athens, where they were enrolled among the *ephebi* of the city.[30] One of the chief centres of the Milesians' wealth was the great temple of Apollo at Didyma, to which a prosperous citizen gave a sum of money and "sacred envoys" brought gifts from the cities of Asia Minor and Greece.[31]

The decline in the commercial importance of Miletus was due in part to the silting-up of the Gulf of Latmus already noted,[u] a process which had gone so far that the city could now be approached only by a narrow channel. At the beginning of the first century the use of this waterway became the object of a dispute with the city of Priene, whose communication with the Aegean the Milesians attempted in some way to hamper, presumably in order to obtain greater commercial advantages for themselves.[32] The dispute, after decisions had been rendered, apparently, by referees from Erythrae and Sardis, was later brought before the Roman governor, who submitted the case to the Senate with the result that the controversy was ultimately decided in favour of Priene. The increasing difficulty of obtaining access to

[s] See Chap. III note 101.   [t] *Ins. Magn.* 88 = *Syll.*[3] 1079.   [u] See Chap. III note 79.

the sea which is implied in this dispute must inevitably have been greatly to Priene's disadvantage, but nevertheless in the latter part of the second century the city seems to have enjoyed a considerable amount of prosperity. The western end of the temple of Athena was perhaps completed before the revolt of Aristonicus and, together with it, the great altar of the Goddess, modelled on that which Eumenes II had built at Pergamum; but the rebuilding of the colonnades surrounding the market-place and especially the construction of a new gymnasium and the adjoining stadium seem to belong to the period that followed the formation of the Roman province.[33] The prosperity of the city during this time is also apparent from various decrees in praise of public-spirited citizens for their "good-will," by which was meant their generosity to the community.[34] The benefactions of a certain Moschion, continued over a long succession of years, included, besides numerous gifts of both grain and money for supplying the needs of the city in times of shortage, contributions toward the construction of the gymnasium, the repair of the shrine of Alexander the Great, and the payment of Priene's share of a sum of money owed by the Ionian Federation. Further evidence of Moschion's generosity appears in the fact that when, on various occasions, he acted as the city's envoy, not merely to Asianic communities, such as Magnesia, Tralles and Cibyra, but to two of the kings of Syria, to the king of Egypt and even to the ruler of Petra in Arabia, he himself ordinarily bore the expense of the mission. The cost of such embassies, indeed, must have formed no small item in the city's budget, for their frequency and the distances covered called for a large outlay of money. Of a contemporary of Moschion we are told that in addition to his appearances before at least four Roman officials, he served as the envoy of Priene to Miletus, Magnesia, Samos, Tralles, Alexandria Troas, Ephesus, Mylasa, Erythrae, Sardis, Colophon, Alabanda, and a Syrian prince, the later Seleucus VI.[v] The multiplicity of these missions—especially in connexion with the great number of those performed by Moschion—casts an interesting light on the amount of negotiation carried on by a community of only moderate importance with other city-states and even with the great powers.

Thirteen years after Aquilius carried out his work of organization, the new province was greatly enlarged by the addition of the district of Phrygia. This district, it will be remembered, had been granted in

[v] *Ins. Priene* 121.

129 to Mithradates V of Pontus in return for the aid which he had rendered against Aristonicus.[w] The King's possession of Phrygia, however, was of but short duration; for about 120 B.C. he was murdered by some of his courtiers, leaving two young sons, the elder of whom was only eleven years of age.[x] To those in Rome who desired a greater province and new lands for exploitation the King's death and the minority of the new monarch, Mithradates VI, must have seemed most opportune. The pressure that they exerted on the Roman government finally had its effect, and the Senate declared that Phrygia was now part of the province of Asia. In an extant fragment of a senatorial decree dated in 116 the commissioners "who crossed over into Asia" were commanded to ratify all enactments, grants and remissions made by Mithradates "down to his last day"[35]—a command somewhat similar to that which had been given to the commissioners previously appointed to organize the province.[y] It seems evident that the decree of 116 was preceded by an earlier measure which ordered the seizure of Phrygia as well as its annexation.

An attempt was subsequently made to justify this act by the plea that Phrygia was not declared tributary to Rome but merely made free and autonomous.[36] This plea, contained in a speech which the Roman general, Sulla, is supposed to have made at his conference with Mithradates VI in 85,[z] has been taken seriously by certain modern historians.[37] An analogy for such a declaration of autonomy has even been sought in the grant of freedom which was made to certain cities after the death of Attalus III, and the somewhat abstruse theory has been advanced that both the annexation of Phrygia and the formation of Asia into a province could be effected only by annulling previously existing royal rights and substituting a protectorate. It is difficult, however, to regard as an historical fact a statement in a speech evidently composed for the purpose of justifying the seizure, and it seems very improbable that the Senate proceeded on any such elaborate theory or compromised by giving Phrygia this temporary status. The Roman People had a *de jure* claim to all the lands included in Attalus's bequest, and the government may well have considered itself within its legal rights in annulling the grant of Phrygia which had been made by its commissioners in 129 and in resuming the ownership of the district. There is no evidence to show that Phrygia was regarded thenceforth in any other light than as an integral part of the province of Asia.

[w] See above p. 154.   [x] See below p. 194.   [y] See Chap. VI note 1.
[z] See below p. 230.

By the incorporation of Phrygia the province was increased almost to the size which it later attained.[38] The only additional increment was the small district of Cibyratis, lying along the eastern boundary of Caria, which was annexed to it more than thirty years afterward.[a] As thus constituted, it covered an area slightly larger than that of England.[39]

This extension of the province to the eastern border of Phrygia brought Rome into contact with the Temple of the Great Mother at Pessinus. With the priests of this sanctuary—who to all intents and purposes were independent rulers—the kings of Pergamum and, through their agency, the Romans also had maintained friendly relations ever since the third century.[b] At least a sentimental interest in the Temple must have been felt at Rome because the symbol of the Goddess, which had been procured with the aid of Attalus I and established on the Palatine Hill, was regarded with great veneration. Now, relations must inevitably be closer. Unfortunately, however, they were strained by some outrage perpetrated by Romans. In 102 B.C. the priest Battaces himself came to Rome to protest.[40] Appearing before the Senate, he complained that the sanctuary of the Goddess had been defiled, and demanded that the process of ceremonial cleansing should be carried out officially by the Roman government. What indignity commensurate with the trouble and expense of so long a journey had been committed we do not know, but one suspects some aggression on the part of the *publicani*. The Senate seems to have granted the priest's request. He was entertained at the cost of the state and presented with the gifts usually accorded to foreigners of distinction. He also received permission to address the people from the Rostra. He, in his turn, pleased the Romans by announcing that the Goddess had revealed to him that they would be successful in the impending battle against the Teutones. The general satisfaction, however, was marred by an unpleasant incident. Battaces appeared before the people arrayed in his official robe embroidered with gold and wearing his golden diadem. The robe elicited—as was doubtless the wearer's intention—much interest and admiration. The diadem, however, was too much for Roman tradition. A tribune of the Plebs, doubtless wishing to use the gesture as political capital with his plebeian supporters against the Senate, forbad Battaces to wear this symbol of kingship. Thereupon the priest withdrew to his lodging and refused to reappear in public, declaring that not he alone but the Great Mother had been affronted;

[a] See below p. 241f.   [b] See above p. 25.

and when, a few days later, the tribune died from an affection of the throat, the more superstitious declared that the Goddess had avenged the affront. Battaces thereupon was not only permitted to wear all his insignia but also presented with further gifts of honour, and when he set out on his homeward way he was escorted as far as the gates by crowds of citizens. The Roman government was evidently disposed, not only to avoid the anger of the Goddess, but also to remain on good terms with its eastern neighbours.

Probably even before the annexation of Phrygia a new method of administration had been established in the province, and on the incorporation of this additional territory the innovation was introduced into it as well. The new system was characteristic of the legally-minded Romans. The province was divided into a number of judiciary districts, or "dioceses," to which, as also to the groups of resident Romans, the name *conventus* was given.[41] In each of these the governor would appear during his term of office to hold court and grant audiences to the inhabitants. If he so desired, he could designate one of his staff to take his place.[c] Each of these dioceses had a definite centre in which he ordinarily appeared and where both Romans and provincials gathered to meet him, but he might, if he so wished, order the people from several districts to appear in one of these centres.[d] On the occasion of his visit all the inhabitants of the diocese except the citizens of "free and autonomous cities" had to bring their law-suits to be judged by him, with the assistance of a jury composed of the Romans residing in the city where the trial was heard. The decisions thus rendered were final. At this time also complaints might be presented, and, in general, an opportunity was afforded the provincials of bringing in petitions of every kind.[e]

As far as is known, in the first century before Christ the judiciary dioceses of the province of Asia, including Phrygia, were twelve in number.[42] Mysia and Lydia were divided into four, which had as their centres Adramyttium, Pergamum, Sardis and Tralles. Ionia contained three: Smyrna, Ephesus and Miletus; Phrygia three: Laodiceia-on-Lycus, Apameia and Synnada; and Caria two: Alabanda and Mylasa. These dioceses varied greatly in size. In the more sparsely settled Phrygia and Caria they covered large areas, whereas the densely populated portions of Ionia and Lydia included four districts and a portion of a fifth. This new arrangement seems to have neglected, at least in

[c] Cicero *Epist. ad Att.* v 21, 6. [d] Cicero *Epist. ad Att.* v 21, 9; vi 2, 4.
[e] Cicero *Epist. ad Fam.* iii 8, 5; xv 4, 2; *ad Att.* v 21, 7.

part, the former division of the country into its four great units, for in the cases of the diocese of Smyrna, which contained a great part of Aeolis on the Mysian coast, and that of Pergamum, in which were included portions both of Mysia and Lydia, the old division was disregarded. The statement of the geographer Strabo,[f] therefore, that the Romans in their new organization did not observe the ancient "tribal" divisions but adopted a "new principle" is applicable to these dioceses. It is probable that their failure to do so was due not to the desire of breaking with the old traditional boundaries but to considerations of convenience and accessibility.

In the greater part of the province we find judiciary centres established in free cities. This was the status of Smyrna, Ephesus and Miletus when the Romans took over the kingdom of Attalus,[g] and by the King's will Pergamum received its freedom.[h] The Carian cities Mylasa and Alabanda appear also to have been free.[i] It seems indeed surprising that trials conducted by a Roman governor should have been held in cities which, strictly speaking, did not belong to his province but were independent states, over whose inhabitants he had no jurisdiction.[43] But it must be remembered that long before the coming of the Romans these cities had been the chief places of the regions which surrounded them, and that the people had been accustomed to regard them as natural centres. Indeed the very fact that they were free might seem an advantage, since suits between members of different communities would thus be settled on neutral territory. Moreover, it is not improbable that these cities themselves welcomed their selection as judiciary centres. Not only was the pride of the citizens gratified thereby, but from the more practical point of view it was advantageous. The influx of the crowds which the governor's presence and the holding of trials would naturally attract was undoubtedly a stimulus to the business-life of the city and a means of increasing its prosperity.[44]

While there were advantages to be derived from a formal visit on the part of the governor and his train of attendants, this might also prove a great burden to the citizens. Any city, however free, would not unnaturally desire to ingratiate itself with an influential Roman who would shortly be returning to the capital and might prove useful in obtaining some favour. The prospect of a visit from a certain type of governor and his staff may even have been viewed with alarm.[j]

[f] Strabo XIII p. 628. [g] See above p. 117. For Sardis, free in 94 B.C., see note 47.
[h] See Chap. VI note 34. [i] See Chap. IV note 75 and Chap. V note 32.
[j] See below p. 247f. (Verres in Lampsacus).

For although early in Rome's career of imperialism a law had been passed with a view to preventing acts of aggression, it had apparently accomplished little.[45] It is significant that when Scaevola, proconsul in 94, insisted on paying out of his own pocket all the cost entailed on a city by his presence or that of his staff, this exceptional conduct won him, as will be shown, the warm gratitude of the provincials, and did much, we are told, to reconcile them to the rule of Rome.[k]

Of the earlier governors of Asia we know nothing, but, if it is possible to form any estimate of their character from the behaviour of the *publicani*, they were none too careful of the interests of the natives. In the case of two, however, the province was more fortunate, for they represented the finest type of Roman. These were Quintus Mucius Scaevola, the Augur, and his nephew of the same name, who held the proud office of Pontifex Maximus. Of both we hear much in the pages of Cicero, their pupil and ardent admirer. The elder Scaevola, governor in 120/19, was the son-in-law of Gaius Laelius and so an inheritor of the traditions of the political and literary group that surrounded the younger Scipio Africanus.[46] A jurist of great note, he interested himself also in philosophy. Practically all that we know of his term of office in Asia is that during a stay in Rhodes he held a conversation—the like of which, perhaps, no Roman governor before him had ever held—with the rhetorician Apollonius of Alabanda. The subject was the philosophy of the Stoic Panaetius, himself a member, during his stay in Rome, of the cultured circle of Scipio. It is safe to say that, trained as Scaevola was in the best of all Roman traditions, his governorship was a good one, and it was the bitter irony of fate that, on his return to Rome, he should have been accused of maladministration in office. His accuser was a foolish imitator of all things Greek, one Titus Albucius, who had been ridiculed by Scaevola for his affectations and in revenge brought the returning governor to trial. Scaevola, however, was triumphantly acquitted and in 118 was elected to the consulship for the following year.

The nephew, who governed the province in 94/3, was the first to systematize into one great work the scattered formulae and decisions on which Roman private law was based.[47] The founder of a school of jurists, he enjoyed great fame also as a polished orator. In accord with his character as a jurist, Scaevola, on entering upon his office as governor, issued an *edict*, or statement of the principles which he proposed to follow during his governorship, and such was its excellence

---

[k] Diodorus XXXVII 5, 1 and 4.

that it became a model for future provincial governors in their proclamations on entering office. In it he seems to have been particularly considerate of the cherished claim of the Greek cities to conduct trials according to their own laws. As it happens, we have an actual illustration of his policy—a compact which he negotiated between the cities of Sardis and Ephesus. In this document the two communities agreed upon an arrangement by which suits for wrongs suffered by a citizen of either city should be tried in the city of the defendant; they also promised to refrain from making war on each other or aiding each other's enemies and to submit all differences arising out of a possible breach of the compact to the arbitrament of a neutral city. As the result of this policy, as well as of his generosity in assuming the burden of the expenses incurred by himself and his staff, and his principle of never appointing a member of this staff as a referee in a civil suit, he was regarded by the communities of Asia Minor with gratitude and admiration. Even in distant Olympia they erected a monument to him as "the saviour and benefactor" of the Asianic Greeks and as "preeminent in righteousness and integrity." The communities of various types, both the Hellenic "peoples" organized in *poleis* and the unorganized "nations," the rural tribal districts, as well as all persons who were "individually received in friendship with Rome," united in establishing a festival in his honour, to be called Mucia after his name.[48] It was celebrated every four years by the communities which founded it and which seem, accordingly, to have been formed into an organization for this purpose. It is possible to see in this organization the beginning of the "Commonalty" or "Federation" of Asia, which is known to have existed in the middle of the first century and which later, under Augustus, became an important agent in strengthening Rome's rule in the province.[1] The festival of the Mucia became so highly respected that even Mithradates of Pontus, desirous though he was of extirpating Roman rule and Roman influence in western Asia Minor, did not abolish it.

Scaevola remained in office for only nine months and then returned to Rome, leaving the province in the charge of his legate Publius Rutilius Rufus. Such was his record for ability and conscientiousness that on his return the Senate ordered all who henceforth became governors of Asia to take him as their model and exemplar.[m]

No small part of Scaevola's success as governor was due to his friend Rutilius Rufus, whom he had taken with him to Asia in the capacity

---

[1] See below pp. 407 and 447.　　　　　[m] Valerius Maximus VIII 15, 6.

of legate.[49] Rufus, a man about fifteen years older than Scaevola, had in his youth fought under Scipio in Spain and, like Scaevola the Augur, was imbued with the traditions of that great man. As Consul in 105 B.C., he had had to levy new troops after the slaughter of the Roman army by the Cimbri at Orange. Now, at the age of sixty, he accompanied his friend in a position that was nominally subordinate but in fact one of great influence; for all of Scaevola's official orders and decisions were issued only after consultation with him. During their year of office Scaevola and Rufus, true to their tradition, made it their policy to protect the provincials from the rapacity of the tax-farming corporations. To all who had been injured by oppressive exactions a hearing was promptly given, and when justice demanded it, punishment was inflicted. In cases of mere extortion the *publicani* were forced to disgorge, but when their agents' cruelty had resulted in death these agents paid with their own lives. One of them, who was a slave and had contracted with his owners for emancipation, was even crucified. This policy did much to improve, for the time being, the economic condition of the province, but it won for Scaevola and Rufus the bitter enmity of the great middle class at Rome, whose financial interests suffered damage thereby. The eminence and influence of Scaevola protected him from successful attack; accordingly, Rufus was selected as the victim. After his return to Rome he was accused of maladministration in office and brought to trial before a jury composed of members of the very class whose exactions he had tried to repress—for ever since the legislation of Gaius Gracchus they had controlled the courts. His accusers even sought to blacken his character by charges of debauchery and bribe-taking. All knew that he was innocent, but such was the determination of his foes, who were aided by his personal enemy, the still powerful Gaius Marius, that he was convicted and sentenced to pay a sum greater than he could realize even by the sale of all his property. He was therefore, to the great indignation of all right-thinking men, compelled to depart into exile. As the place of his banishment he chose, with a fine sense of irony, the very province with the maltreatment of which he had been charged, and betook himself to Mitylene on the island of Lesbos. Here he was received by deputations from many of the communities of the province and presented by the free cities and the kings with gifts. Later he went to Smyrna and there, respected by all, he lived for the rest of his life, spending his time in composing his memoirs, as well as a history of Rome, written in Greek, perhaps an enlargement of his autobiography.

The investing classes had had their revenge, but within five years Rufus was to be avenged of them. Their greed brought on their representatives in Asia, as well as on their more innocent fellow-countrymen, a cruel penalty in the bloodshed into which the province was soon to be plunged.

CHAPTER VIII

THE RISE OF THE POWER
OF PONTUS

MORE than ten years before the younger Scaevola governed his province, a storm began to brew in northeastern Asia Minor which in course of time was to burst upon both the Greeks and the Romans of the western part of the country and involve them all in a common ruin. Its originator was the young and ambitious king of Pontus, Mithradates VI, surnamed Eupator, who conceived the plan of making himself the ruler of a great Asianic empire and of driving out the foreigners who had come from Italy to tyrannize over Greeks and natives alike.

The kingdom of Pontus—or, as it was more correctly called, Cappadocia on the Pontus—lay in the northeastern corner of Asia Minor.[1] It is a land of mountain-ranges, running more or less parallel to the Euxine coast and separated by river-valleys, "like lines of gigantic entrenchments scored along a hillside."[a] In its rugged grandeur it is surpassed in Asia Minor by the region of the Taurus alone.

In the north the district is traversed by the long mountain-range (the "Pontic Alps") which extends throughout the breadth of Asia Minor from Trans-Caucasia to the Propontis. This range forms a great barrier between the narrow strip of flat land at the edge of the Euxine and the mountainous inland-region—the broken escarpment of the Anatolian Plateau. South of the Pontic section of this coast-range—which in ancient times bore the name Paryadres—the mountain-masses are broken by long river-basins.[2] These rivers have their sources on the eastern border of the Anatolian Peninsula and flow, in general, toward the west and north. Swollen by numerous affluents, which the heavy rainfall of the mountains supplies with an abundance of water, they wind their tortuous ways to the Euxine, breaking through the coast-range in precipitous gorges. Chief among them are the Lycus and the Iris, which rise not far from each other in the mountains of the western watershed of the upper Euphrates. The former flows directly northwestward; the latter describes a wide curve to the south before its junction with its chief tributary, the Scylax, whence it bends north again to unite with the Lycus in the Plain of Phanaroea. From here the combined streams force their way through the Paryadres

---

[a] So Munro in *J.H.S.* XXI (1901), p. 52.

to the sea. South of the Iris is the valley of the upper Halys, the longest river of Asia Minor. Rising, like the Lycus and the Iris, in the watershed of the Euphrates, where its sources are distant less than 200 miles from its mouth, it pursues an erratic course, as the mountains bar the way, flowing for some 700 miles, southwestward, then northward, then northeastward, until, after breaking through the coast-range in terrific gorges, it discharges its reddish waters into the Euxine.[3] Between its upper course and the Iris towers a high range, with summits of 10,000 feet in altitude, the northern wall of the mountainous area at the back of the central plateau. South of the upper Halys is a parallel range, through which the river breaks on its way toward the southwest.[4] This formed the southern boundary of Pontus, separating it from the kingdom of Cappadocia.[b] On the southwest the country was separated from Galatia by the watershed between the Scylax and the basin of the lower Halys.

It was largely in the valleys of the Lycus and the Iris that the economic life of interior Pontus was concentrated. The plains through which these rivers flow, rising "like terraces one above another,"[c] enjoy the advantages of a mild climate and a fertile soil and so produced rich harvests of grain and fruit; and through them led the highways that connected this remote portion of Asia Minor with the East and West. The most fertile of all was Phanaroea, a basin about 700 feet above sea-level, some forty miles long but nowhere over five miles in width.[5] This "Garden of Pontus" was rich in olives and vines and "possessed all other good qualities." Of almost equal importance were Dazimonitis, the plain of the upper Iris, and Chiliocomum (the "Thousand Villages"), the basin of one of its tributaries. The former may have been the property of the wealthy temple of the Great Mother at Comana. The latter belonged to the city of Amaseia; it was probably the scene of King Mithradates's mobilization of the great army with which he carried out his first invasion of western Asia Minor.[d] It is still very fertile, and the many remains of ancient buildings bear witness to a dense population in Antiquity. On the north, between the lower Iris and the Halys, lay the wealthy region of Phazimonitis, which was not only fertile but had other resources as well.[6] It contained Lake Stiphane, which was well stocked with fish and surrounded by excellent pasture-land. In it were also the hot springs which were much frequented in ancient times and still draw many visitors. Between the two was the city of Laodiceia, which was founded

[b] See below p. 200.   [c] So Munro in *J.H.S.* xxi p. 53.   [d] See below p. 211.

by one of the Pontic monarchs, perhaps on the model of an Hellenic community.

But it was in the mountains of Pontus that the chief wealth of the kingdom lay. The Paryadres was clothed with magnificent forests of oak and beech and, in the upper levels, of fir, which the comparatively heavy rainfall of the region supplied with sufficient moisture.[7] These furnished limitless supplies of timber for export to the forestless countries of the Mediterranean, as well as abundant material for local use in the construction of ships. The number of the merchantmen used by the cities of the coast for their extensive carrying-trade,[e] as well as the fleet with which Mithradates Eupator invaded the Propontis in 73,[f] afford striking evidence of the activity of these shipyards.

The greatest wealth of the mountains, however, lay in the minerals for which northeastern Asia Minor was famous. The richest deposits were found in the Paryadres, and from a remote period these had been carried to the West from the ports of the Euxine. As early as the fifth century, the Chalybes, who lived along the coast east of the Plain of Themiscyra, were commonly regarded as *par excellence* the forgers of iron and even as the inventors of the process, and from their name was derived the word *chalybs* as a designation for steel.[8] In the mountains south of their country and that of their neighbours farther east and even beyond the *hinterland* of Trebizond, were mines, not only of iron, but of copper and silver as well. The Paryadres also contained deposits of alum, which were known to the ancients and have been used in modern times.[9] Farther south, along the upper Halys east of Sivas, are salt-mines, which were operated in Antiquity and have recently been reopened. In the central and western portions of the kingdom also there are deposits of minerals which could scarcely have been unknown to the ancients. For the mountains around the Plain of Dazimonitis contain rich stores of iron and copper,[g] and there is silver in the hill-country south of Phazimonitis.[h]

It is not surprising that inland Pontus, remote and mountain-girt as it was, should have remained unaffected by Hellenism. In fact, save for the adjacent Cappadocia, no portion of Asia Minor was so untouched by the influence of the West. Down to the time of the Roman conquest there prevailed the old Asianic system of domain-land belonging to the king or to the nobles on whom he had probably bestowed it.[10] Both king and nobles owned fortified strongholds which

---

[e] See below pp. 183f. and 186.   [f] See below p. 324.   [g] See Cuinet *Turquie* 1 p. 716.
[h] See Cuinet 1 pp. 751 and 756f.: *Stud. Pont.* 1 p. 100: Ravndal *Turkey*, p. 150.

they used as residences, and around these were villages which served as economic centres. Altogether separate from these domains were the vast estates—almost minor principalities in themselves—that belonged to the great sanctuaries. The tillers of these lands, both royal and sacred, paid tithes directly to the monarch or the priest and were little better than serfs.

In such a system cities, in the Greek sense of the word, were entirely lacking. Some of the villages in the neighbourhood of the strongholds, however, which served the needs of the country-folk and were used as general markets, gradually developed into towns of some commercial importance. Among these was Cabeira, where Mithradates Eupator had a palace and a hunting-park and where there was a "water-mill," presumably for grinding the grain of the neighbourhood.[11] Situated on the southern foothills of the Paryadres, the place was protected by a citadel of great strength, which rose on a projecting spur of the mountain and commanded the valley of the Lycus. Farther south, on the Iris below Dazimonitis, was Gaziura, also a royal residence and an important place in the last years of Persian rule. It was built around an isolated rock, rising to a height of 600 feet above the plain and bearing on its summit a rigorously guarded fortress, which no stranger might enter without the express permission of the commandant. Both these centres developed into communities which gradually obtained certain rights, and under Mithradates Eupator coins were issued which bore their names.

The only real city in the interior of the kingdom had likewise grown up around one of the royal strongholds. This was Amaseia, on the Iris a few miles below the fertile plain where the river is joined by the Scylax.[12] In a situation famous for its romantic grandeur, the city lies in a defile formed by two massive cliffs, which tower above the course of the Iris. The higher of these, which rises precipitously above the western bank of the stream to a height of over 700 feet, is cut off from the mountains behind it by a deep ravine; thus it is impregnable on every side. Its two summits, connected by a narrow saddle, bear aloft the powerful fortress to which the city owed its existence and where a royal garrison was maintained to control the route leading through the defile. Cut into the face of the rock high above the river and approached only by terraces and stairways, are five magnificent tombs, the burial-places of princes, it may be, of the Persian period, and below these, on a terraced spur of the rock, stood the palace of the kings of Pontus. High up in the mountains toward the east was the sanctuary of their protector, Zeus Stratius, the "God of armies." In the third and at least a part of the second century Amaseia was the royal capital. During this period it seems to have taken on a semblance of Hellenic culture; for the tomb of a native Pontian bears an epitaph in Greek verse, and two officers evidently of high rank had Grecian names. Shortly before the middle of the first century before Christ, Strabo, the renowned geographer of the ancient world, was born in the city.

The land in this interior portion of Pontus that was not the domain of the king or of those to whom he assigned it, belonged to the gods. Of the powerful and wealthy temples of the kingdom the most important was that of the Mother-Goddess—Ma, as she was locally known—at Comana.[13] The cult carried on here was in every way similar to the worship of the same deity at the Cappadocian Comana, of which it was probably an offshoot. The temple of the Goddess stood on a low hill overlooking the Iris, a few miles above the Plain of Dazimonitis, its tetrastyle fronts formed by huge columns of grayish marble. Around it, as around the royal fortresses, grew up a town, in which lived, not only the many officials of the Temple as well as the "temple-slaves," but also the votaries of the Goddess, who had vowed themselves to her service. These included a large number of women whose sacrifice was the surrender of their chastity. The townsfolk attained to great wealth, not only because of the vineyards which they cultivated, but also on account of the throngs of the merchants and their customers who flocked to the place during the great festival, which occurred twice a year. On these occasions the statue of the Goddess—said to have been the image of Artemis brought by Orestes from the Taurians—was carried about in procession, escorted by priests and worshippers, often in a wild frenzy. According to a Roman poet's highly-coloured description, the more violent—like the dervishes of a later time—practised flagellation and slashed themselves with axes or thrust spears into their breasts. So numerous were the visitors at these times and so great the amount of money which they spent both in worship and in pleasure that Comana was referred to as a lesser Corinth.

The wide domains belonging to the Temple were tilled by the "temple-slaves," who at the beginning of the Christian Era were said to be six thousand in number. They were directly subject to the priest of the Goddess, who had not, indeed, power to sell them but was in all other respects their lord. Their tithes were paid to him, and he alone was empowered to spend the sacred revenues. In importance this priest ranked next to the king himself, and on the occasion of the great festivals his hair was bound with the royal diadem as a symbol of his position as prince-priest.

Similar, although smaller, domains were owned by the temples at Zela, in the southern part of the kingdom on a tributary of the Iris, and at Ameria, the site of which is unknown.[14] The former, the seat of the cult of Anaïtis and the "Persian Deities," stood on a low isolated hill, which, according to tradition, had been constructed either by the legendary Semiramis or by certain Persian generals, but, in fact, is a natural eminence. The latter, dedicated to Men, the "God of Pharnaces," was held in peculiar veneration by the Pontic kings. Around both these sanctuaries towns grew up, in which lived both the priest and the temple-slaves; as a Comana, the priest had sovereign power over the sacred domain, the revenues of which accrued to him.

Very striking is the contrast between the mountains of inland Pontus and the region that borders the Euxine and is walled in on the south by the forbidding range of the Paryadres. This riviera is a narrow strip, widening out only at the mouths of the Halys and the Iris into the alluvial plains of Gazelonitis and Themiscyra, the legendary home of the Amazons.[15] Throughout its length, however, it is fertile and well watered by the streams that pour down from the mountain-slopes at its back. In it were produced grain of many varieties and nuts and all manner of fruits, which were exported to foreign countries. The marshy portions afforded abundant pasture-land; Gazelonitis was famous for its sheep, the wool of which was carefully protected by covering the animals with hides, and Themiscyra fed large herds of horses and cattle. These plains also produced other articles of commercial value, such as honey and wax, especially from Themiscyra, perfumes and aromatic gums, wormwood, hellebore and other drugs, all of which were exported from this coast throughout the Mediterranean world.[16]

Equally marked was the difference between the primitive system of royal and sacred possessions that prevailed in inland Pontus and the municipal organizations and civic life of the coast. Here, from the seventh century onward, the influence of Hellenism had been dominant. The enterprising Greeks, in the pursuit of commerce, had penetrated into the farther parts of the "Inhospitable Sea"[17] and established themselves on this narrow plain, where they formed a world of their own, having little connexion with the life and conditions characteristic of the interior. Building ports where there were no natural harbours and developing the routes across the mountain-barrier, they founded trading-stations which served not only for exporting the products of the interior, but also as ports of call for the merchant-men of the Euxine and as bases of commerce with the mother-country. These trading-stations soon became cities, as Greek in spirit and customs as those of the Aegean coast and even of Hellas itself.

Of the Hellenic communities on this remote shore the most prominent were Sinope and Amisus, but east of the latter there stretched out a line of less noteworthy *poleis* as far as Sinope's colony of Trapezus (Trebizond). The great city of Sinope, famed for the beauty of its situation, lay on a promontory on the eastern side of the wide peninsula of Lepte, which reaches out into the Euxine west of the mouth of the Halys and forms the northernmost point of Asia Minor.[18] Established in the second half of the seventh century by settlers from Miletus, the city was prosperous enough in the sixth to issue its own coinage.[1] In the time of Pericles it was strengthened by the coming of a group of Athenians,[j] to whom houses and lands were assigned. Nevertheless, the Milesian tradition continued to be dominant, and chief among the city's gods were Poseidon Heliconius, the patron of the Ionian federation, and Apollo, the especial deity of Miletus.[19] Early in its history Sinope greatly increased both its power and its wealth by placing colonies on the coast farther east—at Cotyora, Cerasus and Trapezus—all of which paid tribute to the mother-city. Its remote position long enabled it to escape Persian domination, and until the early fourth century it retained its rights as a "free and autonomous" state. Although for a brief period after 375 B.C. it was occupied by Datames, the satrap of Cappadocia who rebelled against the Persian king, nevertheless, after his fall, it regained at least a semblance of autonomy, although nominally under Persian rule.

The prosperity of Sinope was largely due to its carrying-trade on the Euxine.[20] With the energy characteristic of Grecian settlers, its inhabitants constructed two harbours, one on each side of the isthmus on which the city lay, thus affording ample facilities for vessels even of the deepest draught. At the most northerly, and at the same time the central, point of the northern shore of Asia Minor, it became an emporium for the local coastwise trade as well as the chief port of call

[1] See *Receuil* I[2] p. 194*f.   [j] Plutarch *Per.* 20.

for the merchantmen trading with the northern and western shores of the Euxine and to a less extent with Greece and Egypt. It was not, however, without exports of its own. The high coast-range yielded an inexhaustible supply of timber, and the lower slopes nearer the city produced woods of finer grain, maple and walnut (or chestnut) used for the manufacture of furniture. The nuts from its forests were shipped far and wide, and the large territory of the city produced an abundance of olives. The fishing also was a great source of wealth. The mullets from Sinope were highly esteemed by connoisseurs, but much more important were the catches of tunny, which, in their return from their spawning-places, reached Sinope before they came to the Bosporus and were of a suitable size for salting; the salted fish were exported to Greece and later to Italy, where they commanded a high price. Local manufactures included steel,[k] made presumably from the iron brought from the colony of Cotyora, the port for the mines of the Chalybes, and used especially for carpenters' tools.

While Sinope's chief commercial importance consisted in its trade by sea, it was also the end of an ancient land-route from the interior, which led from the Euphrates to the Euxine.[21] In early days, especially before the development, in the fourth century, of her great rival Amisus,[l] the products of Pontus and Cappadocia, and even of the lands beyond, were carried to Sinope for shipment. By this route was brought the red ochre, which was mined in Cappadocia but, before the development of overland commerce by way of Ephesus, was exported through Sinope and took its trade-name *Sinopis* from the city.[22] It was used far and wide both for medicinal purposes and as a pigment.

During the third century Sinope maintained its independence, for the remoteness of the place secured it against aggression on the part of the Seleucid monarchs or even the rulers of Pontus.[23] At some time in this period the citizens entered into friendly relations with Rhodes, which stood them in good stead in 220, when threatened by Mithradates II of Pontus; for the Rhodians supplied their envoys with a credit for the purchase of armour and other materials for war. Mithradates, indeed, seems to have abandoned whatever plan he had made for the conquest of the city, but the ambition of his grandson, the warrior-king Pharnaces I, brought an end to Sinope's freedom. In 183, as a prelude to his war against Eumenes II of Pergamum, this mon-

k Stephanus Byzantus *s.v.* Λακεδαίμων = Eustathius *Commentary to Iliad* 11 581.
l See below p. 185.

arch advanced against the city and captured it by a surprise-attack.[m] When the Rhodians, still faithful, appealed to Rome for intervention in behalf of their stricken friends, the Senate did nothing more than promise to send envoys to make inquiries; and although the treaty imposed on Pharnaces four years later demanded the surrender of his conquests, including Paphlagonia, no provision was made for Sinope.[n] Thus both the city itself and its colonies Cotyora and Cerasus remained in the possession of the conqueror. Because of its commercial supremacy and its strategic position as a base for the new Pontic navy, Sinope was regarded by the kings as a place of great importance and it soon superseded Amaseia both as their capital and as their place of burial.[o] It was embellished with buildings and colonnades and became a magnificent city. The birthplace of Mithradates Eupator, it was also the scene of the mobilization of the great armada which he sent forth in 73 B.C. to conquer the western coast,[p] and it was to Sinope that the King returned, a shipwrecked fugitive, after the destruction of that mighty fleet;[q] here also his body was finally laid to rest by his victorious enemy, Pompey.[r]

Sinope's rival for commercial supremacy in the eastern Euxine was Amisus, a settlement of Ionians, probably from Miletus, who established themselves here about the middle of the sixth century.[24] About a hundred years later they were joined by a group of Athenians, through whose influence the place was renamed Piraeus after the port of Athens. It soon developed into a free city-state, and although perhaps for a time it was subject to Persian rule, it received from Alexander full recognition of its independence, and about the same time it seems to have resumed its former name.

Situated on a low plateau rising from the water's edge on the western side of a wide deep bay, Amisus had no such harbour as that afforded by the peninsula of Sinope, for it was protected only on the west and, except for moles, exposed to the north and east. Nevertheless, it surpassed its rival in facility of commerce by land. The trade-route from the interior, which connected Cappadocia and inland Pontus with the sea, descended from the coast-range into the plain on which the city lay, and so reached Amisus long before it came to Sinope.[25] As

[m] Strabo XII p. 545f.: Polybius XXIII 9, 2 = Livy XL 2, 6. For the war see above p. 20 and below p. 192.

[n] See below p. 192.

[o] Cicero de Imp. Cn. Pomp. 21: Strabo XII p. 545f.: Diodorus XIV 31, 2: Appian Mith. 113: Memnon 36, 3.

[p] See below p. 324.   [q] See below p. 331.   [r] See below p. 364.

transportation by sea was cheaper and easier than further carriage by the toilsome route along the hills rising steeply from the sea,[s] the merchandise from the interior was diverted from Sinope to the docks of Amisus. Thus, although the older city long maintained her supremacy in the carrying-trade of the Euxine, Amisus developed at Sinope's expense and in modern times has greatly outstripped her neighbour.[26] Her exports included timber from the coast-range, steel and iron from the neighbouring district of the Chalybes as well as semi-precious stones, and a characteristic variety of pottery seems to have been manufactured in the city. The pre-eminent position resulting from this trade was further advanced by the productiveness of the fertile land in the vicinity, the alluvial plains at the mouths of the Halys and the Iris, which were rich in grain and in fruit.[t] Such was the city's importance that she has been well characterized as "the commercial capital of Pontus."[u]

A city as wealthy as Amisus was naturally coveted by the monarchs of Pontus, and in the early years of their power it was brought under their sway.[27] It is not improbable that Mithradates II annexed it to his kingdom before his attempt to take Sinope; certainly his grandson Pharnaces I, who conquered the lands both on the east and on the west, had possession of Amisus also. Although she thus lost her freedom, the city suffered no other harm from her subjection to the kings of Pontus. Mithradates Eupator, in particular, adorned Amisus with temples and public buildings and added the new suburb of Eupatoria, designed to serve as a royal residence.[v] Both city and suburb, however, were destined to be destroyed by the brutality of a Roman army.[w]

On the west of Pontus across the lower Halys lay the district of Paphlagonia, extending as far westward as the high mountain-ranges which buttress up the great central plateau and separate Paphlagonia from the kingdom of Bithynia.[28] On the north was the Euxine, and on the south the district was, in general, bounded by the watershed from which streams flow into both the upper Sangarius and the central Halys and which formed the limit of the holdings of the Galatians. As in Pontus, the coast-range, rising to an average height of 3,500-4,000 feet, divides the district into two portions, a narrow strip of great

---

[s] See note 21.   [t] See above p. 182.   [u] So Munro in *J.H.S.* xxi (1901), p. 53.
[v] Cicero *de Imp. Cn. Pomp.* 21: Strabo xii p. 547: Appian *Mith.* 78: Pliny *N.H.* vi 7. For Eupatoria see Chap. XIV note 33.
[w] See below p. 337.

fertility and beauty, bordering the Euxine, and a large tract of inland mountainous country. As the result of this division, the name Paphlagonia in the Hellenistic period, at least, was rather a geographical than a political designation. Soon after 300 B.C. the mouth of the river Parthenius at the western end of the strip of coast was taken by Queen Amastris of Heracleia,[x] and within a century not only this region but the whole littoral, from the Parthenius eastward to Sinope, came under the power of the rulers of Pontus.[y]

Inland Paphlagonia is a land of rugged mountains separated by rivers, which flow now through fertile and productive plains and again between steeply-rising spurs thrust forward from the higher peaks.[29] The eastern portion of the district consists mainly of the river-basins of the Amnias and the Devrek Çay—both of them tributaries of the Halys. These basins are separated by the great mountain-mass of Olgassys, which rises to a height of over 7,500 feet. In their course from west to east they contained the principal settlements and the chief means of communication within the district. The Amnias has its sources in the watershed of the region which, in late Byzantine times at least, was known as Castamon. From the western slope of this up-land country the Araç Çay flows down to join the Billaeus. The latter river, rising in the great mountains in southwestern Paphlagonia, pursues a serpentine course, first toward the east and then toward the northwest, finally flowing northward through a great gorge in the coast-range into the Euxine west of the mouth of the Parthenius. This western portion of the district also included the high forest-clad plateau of Timonitis near the Bithynian border.

The chief wealth of this mountainous district lay, naturally, in its timber.[30] The great forests of beech, oak and fir with which the coast-range is still covered have deeply impressed travellers in modern times. But this range also forms a barrier between the interior and the sea, for between the Parthenius and the Halys there are no river-valleys to serve as means of communication. Consequently, there was no natural access to the Euxine, and the exportation of this timber was most difficult. The only other article of commerce of which we know was the realgar mined in a mountain overlooking the lower Amnias. It was used as a red or orange-coloured pigment and also in medicine. But because of the poisonous dust in the mines the process of extracting it was so dangerous that only slaves could be used for the purpose,

[x] See below p. 309.   [y] See below pp. 189 and 191.

and the mortality among these was so great that, on account of the expense involved, the operations had often to be suspended.

Between this rugged mountainous area and the Euxine lay a narrow strip of plain. Here were situated the few Greek settlements that arose in the district. At its eastern end was the great city of Sinope, and farther to the west was the poor port of Abonuteichus, which in the second century before Christ had a constitution modelled after that of a Greek *polis*, as well as Greek religious institutions.[31] Between it and the mouth of the Parthenius were the towns combined by Queen Amastris into the city to which she gave her name.[z]

The interior, on the other hand, like Pontus, was wholly Asianic in character. Its mountain-folk, largely small farmers, lived in the primitive village-organizations characteristic of a country which was unaffected by Hellenism.[a] The only city of which we know was Gangra, not, geographically speaking, in Paphlagonia at all, but in the fruitful valley of a river which flows southward from the watershed separating the district from Galatia.[32] Its acropolis became the seat of the local ruler who established himself here about 200 B.C. and made Gangra his capital.

The chief importance of Paphlagonia lay in its situation between the two kingdoms of Bithynia and Pontus, for through it passed the routes which led from the Propontis through Bithynia and the valleys of the Devrek and the Amnias across the Halys to Pontus and thence to the upper Euphrates and Armenia.[33] Unlike the great Southern Highway which led to Ephesus, however, these two roads were important not so much from the commercial as from the military standpoint. Ordinary trade, as we have seen, was carried by the merchantmen of the cities on the Euxine coast, chiefly Sinope and Amisus, but any army led across northern Asia Minor, whether by native monarch or Roman general, would naturally follow one or the other of these roads. Over the Amnias route in 88, the unfortunate King Nicomedes IV of Bithynia marched to invade the dominions of Mithradates Eupator, only to be driven back ingloriously, and the Paphlagonian portion of it, at least, was twice used by Mithradates when he led his mighty armies to conquer the province of Asia. There was therefore every reason why a district of such strategic value should be eagerly coveted by the monarchs of Pontus when they began to expand their dominions.

The expansion of the power of the Pontic kings from a small prin-

[z] See Chap. XIII note 29.   [a] See above p. 143.

188

cipality into a state which could claim equality with the kingdom of Pergamum and was even deemed worthy of an alliance with Rome was a process which lasted somewhat over a hundred years.[34] The foundation of this power was laid in the early third century by an adventurer named Mithradates, perhaps of Persian origin but the nephew of the last of the tyrants of the Greek city of Cius on the Propontis. In 302, when his uncle was put to death by Antigonus, then lord of Asia Minor, this young man, with a few attendants, made his escape to the mountains of Paphlagonia. Here he took possession of the stronghold of Cimiata, on the southern slopes of Mt. Olgassys, which he made his headquarters. With a band of followers, gathered from the independent mountaineers, he advanced eastward to the region beyond the Halys, where he seized the basin of the Iris and established himself in the fortress of Amaseia. In the course of time he assumed the title of King.[35]

By his assumption of the royal title Mithradates declared himself independent of Seleucus I, who by his victory over Lysimachus at Corupedium in the early summer of 281 became supreme in Asia Minor.[b] This act of defiance was either the cause or the consequence of an invasion of Pontus by a general who was sent by Seleucus to reconquer the land.[36] The repulse of this invader greatly increased the prestige of Mithradates, and when Seleucus sent a commissioner to take over the command of northwestern Asia Minor, the free cities of Heracleia, Chalcedon and Byzantium, members of the so-called "Northern League," fearing for their liberty, invited the new king of Pontus to join in an alliance against their common foe. So great, in fact, did his reputation become that a few years later the commandant of Amastris, formerly subject to Heracleia, surrendered the city to the King's son, Ariobarzanes, giving him thereby not only a rich territory but also a foothold on the Euxine coast.

After Mithradates "the Founder" died in 266 B.C., thirty-six years after his flight from Cius,[c] his successors continued his policy of expansion. This policy, it is true, was not always successful, for it involved his son Ariobarzanes in hostilities with the Galatian tribes, who invaded and sacked a portion of the kingdom.[37] Their action, to be sure, was not wholly a misfortune for Pontus, for it brought the ruler into closer relations with the city of Heracleia, which, mindful perhaps of its former alliance, presented a quantity of grain to the King's youthful

[b] See above p. 4.   [c] Diodorus XX III, 4.

son and successor.[d] This son, Mithradates II, by his marriage with the sister of Seleucus II gained recognition as a sovereign from the most important ruling house in western Asia.[38] Thereby his prestige and his position among his fellow-monarchs were greatly advanced. It was later claimed by his descendants that the princess brought him the district of Phrygia as her dowry. Although not unwilling to weaken the power of his brother-in-law by supporting the latter's rebellious brother, Antiochus Hierax, in his revolt against the lawful monarch, Mithradates nevertheless continued his policy of alliance with the dynasty by marrying his daughter Laodice to Seleucus's son, Antiochus III. In 224, when the city of Rhodes was devastated by the great earthquake, he took his place among his brother-monarchs by coming to its relief with gifts.[e]

Before the death of Mithradates II, Pontus was definitely established as a power in Asia Minor. Although the monarch's threat against Sinope seems to have been averted by the aid furnished by Rhodes,[f] a considerable part of the Euxine coast was incorporated in the kingdom, and it may be assumed that the rulers controlled much of the territory that lay between the upper Halys and the sea. The semblance of an Hellenic monarch was taken on by the kings, and the legends on the coins of Mithradates's successors show that their official language was Greek.[39]

Thus far, the rulers of Pontus had not come into collision with any great power. Their rise was due to a gradual absorption of neighbouring lands which were not under the direct control of another monarch. This policy, however, was reversed by the grandson of Mithradates II, Pharnaces I, who came to the throne about 185. He soon embarked on a career of violent aggression for the expansion of his kingdom, and in his plan for the seizure of lands lying outside Pontus he appears as the precursor of his successor in the third generation, the last and the greatest of the rulers of the kingdom.[g]

Although the portraits of Pharnaces seem to suggest weakness and even stupidity,[h] he was, in fact, a man of great ability and boundless ambition.[i] The recent victory of the Romans at Magnesia over his kinsman Antiochus had apparently failed to convey a warning against a policy of imperialism. This failure to grasp the fact that Rome was no longer indifferent to an attempt of one ruler to conquer the do-

---

[d] Memnon 24. See also Ed. Meyer *Gesch. d. Königreichs Pontos*, p. 46 and Stähelin *Gesch. d. Kleinasiat. Galater*[2], p. 17.

[e] Polybius v 90, 1. See Chap. III note 70. [f] See above p. 184.

[g] See below p. 195f. [h] See *Receuil* I[2] p. 11, no. 4f. [i] Polybius xxvII 17.

minions of another brought him into collision with the great power of the West.

Pharnaces's first step was taken in 183, when he captured Sinope and added it to his dominions.[j] The seizure of the city's colonies, Cotyora and Cerasus, soon followed. As the result of these conquests, the Euxine littoral from Amastris to the promontory of Zephyrium— a distance of some 400 miles—was brought under Pontic sway. This, however, was but the beginning of Pharnaces's plan for expansion. Having gained possession of the coast of Paphlagonia, he next turned to the inland portion of the district.

Up to this time the sturdy mountaineers who inhabited this region seem to have resisted successfully all attempts to bring them under a foreign domination and to have lived under the rule of their own native chieftains.[40] About the beginning of the second century, one of these, named Morzius, more powerful, perhaps, than the others, established himself in the stronghold of Gangra. Allying himself with the Galatians, he aided them in 189 against Manlius Vulso and shared their crushing defeat. But he escaped punishment at the hands of the Roman general, perhaps because of the remoteness of his capital, and continued to rule over his fellow-countrymen. He was, however, no match for Pharnaces. The Pontic monarch entered Paphlagonia, where he devastated the country and seized the treasure that Morzius had gathered together.[k] He also carried off a number of the inhabitants of the district, whom he established in his own kingdom.

This act of aggression, combined with his previous seizure of Sinope and her colonies, made it evident that Pharnaces was planning to enlarge his kingdom at the expense of his neighbours. The capture of the great city on the Euxine coast had aroused the sympathy of the Rhodians, and the King's advance into Paphlagonia and especially his apparent attempt to gain the support of the Galatians, whether by threats or the promise of pay, evoked the fears of Eumenes II of Pergamum, whose recent defeat of the Celts had made him their overlord.[l]

But the power of Rome now loomed large in Asia Minor. Both the Rhodians and Eumenes made protests to the Senate, and Pharnaces sent his representatives to answer their charges.[41] The Fathers' only action, however, was the usual appointment of a commission to investigate the complaints. The commissioners' report exonerated Eumenes and condemned the rapacity and arrogance of the King of Pontus, but, nevertheless, no further measures to restrain the latter

[j] See above p. 185.   [k] Polybius xxv 2, 5 and 9.   [l] See above p. 21.

were taken at Rome. The Senate was apparently unwilling to become involved in a war which lay outside the sphere of Roman influence and concerned only the Asiatic allies. Pharnaces, therefore, continued his policy of aggression. A raid into Cappadocia and the seizure of royal treasure caused King Ariarathes IV to join his son-in-law, Eumenes, in a second appeal to Rome. The capture of Tieium, on the Euxine coast,[m] where the Pontic general Leocritus, contrary to his pledge, slaughtered the mercenaries defending the place, forced Prusias II of Bithynia into the war.[n] Morzius also joined the allies, and thus a coalition was built up against the aggressor. Even distant rulers, the king of Greater Armenia and a Sarmatian prince, entered the struggle, although their participation was perhaps only nominal. Against this combination, Pharnaces was aided by Mithradates, the king of Armenia Minor, and by some Galatian chieftains,[o] who, however, showed themselves ready to desert in the face of danger. His cousin, Seleucus IV, did indeed make preparations to join him, but, reminded by the Romans of the obligations imposed by the Treaty of Apameia, he promptly abandoned the project.[42]

In the autumn of 181 a Pergamene army under Eumenes's brother Attalus, supported by the demands of a Roman commission, forced the proclamation of an armistice. It was evident, however, that Pharnaces had no desire for peace. In fact, before the winter was over, Leocritus led a raid into Galatia and in the early spring the King himself made ready to invade Cappadocia. The Allies then took the offensive, and an army under the joint command of Eumenes and Ariarathes crossed the Halys. A third Roman commission, which arrived at this juncture, found Pharnaces obdurate, and the delegates, whom, on the Romans' insistence, he consented to send to a conference at Pergamum, refused to make any concessions. On the failure of these many attempts at negotiation, the allied monarchs took matters into their own hands and invaded the enemy's country. Their efforts were wholly successful and Pharnaces was compelled to sue for peace.[43] By the terms of the treaty he gave up his conquests in Galatia and Paphlagonia, including Tieium, as well as the treasures taken from Ariarathes and Morzius, estimated at 900 talents; he also bound himself to pay Eumenes 300 talents to meet the cost of the war. Thus his ambitious plan for building up an empire in central Asia Minor came to nothing. Of all that he had taken, he retained only Sinope and her colonies.

m See Chap. XIII note 28.　　　　　　　n See below p. 315.
o For one of these, Gaezatorix, see note 40.

The war and the terms imposed by the treaty left Pharnaces impoverished.[44] Even after twenty years had passed he was still unable to meet his financial obligations. Among these was a promise, made apparently before the war, to give the city of Athens a large sum of money for some public purpose. In consideration for his lack of ready money, the Athenian Council and People consented to let him pay the promised amount in yearly installments. His energy, however, was not crushed by defeat. Turning his attention to the consolidation of his power in the region he had acquired in the northeast, he founded a new, fortified, city on the site of Cerasus, which, after the example of other Hellenistic rulers, he named Pharnaceia after himself.[p] In order to increase its population he moved to it the inhabitants of Cotyora also. He thus gained a firm hold on the iron-mines in the mountains on the south. His capture of Sinope, moreover, giving him, as it did, the best harbour on this coast, enabled him to enter into relations with the other side of the Euxine. Deprived by the allied kings of his hope of expansion in Asia Minor, he conceived the plan of extending his influence across the sea and creating an empire on its northern coast. To this end he made a treaty with the city of Chersonesus in the Crimea, though it had sided with his opponents during the war.[45] In this treaty of mutual friendship he swore to furnish aid to Chersonesus against any attack on the part of the surrounding "barbarians" and to respect the city's independence; he doubtless received some privileges in return. He also sought to strengthen his position by closer relations with the dynasty of the Seleucids, and late in life he married Nysa,[q] the niece, apparently, of Antiochus IV, brother and successor of the Seleucus who had failed him during the war. He expected, perhaps, in the event of another attempt at empire to obtain from the energetic Antiochus the assistance he had failed to receive from the latter's timorous brother. But whatever hopes he may have cherished, either of expansion in Russia or of aid from the Seleucid monarch, were cut short by his death a little over twenty years after the end of the war.[46]

The Senate's attempts at diplomacy during the struggle between Pharnaces and the allied monarchs had contributed nothing to the ultimate success of the latter; nevertheless, the arrival of three successive commissions in Asia Minor at least served as a reminder of the power of Rome. One after another, the kings of Pergamum, Bithynia and Cappadocia had entered into relations with her and in time be-

[p] Strabo XII p. 548: Arrian *Periplus* 16, 4 Roos.   [q] See note 44.

came her allies.[47] It is not surprising, therefore, that Pharnaces's brother and successor should have followed their example. Soon after his accession, this monarch, Mithradates IV Philopator Philadelphus, formed a relationship by virtue of which the Senate declared him a "Friend and Ally"; in return, he made a ceremonial offering at Rome.[48] By this act he renounced, at least implicitly, any extension of his dominions at the expense of his brother-monarchs. Soon after he began to reign, he gave proof of his good faith; for when war broke out between Attalus II of Pergamum and Prusias II of Bithynia, instead of taking advantage of the situation for his own aggrandizement, he supported Attalus against his enemy.[r]

The alliance with Rome was renewed and faithfully maintained by Mithradates's successor, Mithradates V Euergetes.[49] Not long after he ascended the throne, about 150, he sent some warships and a small force of soldiers to aid in the third war against Carthage,[s] and in 133 he responded promptly to the Senate's request for assistance against the Pergamene claimant Aristonicus.[t] This service was rewarded by the gift of the district of Phrygia, but the King later came into disrepute in Rome because of an alleged attempt to purchase support among the voters for some favour he wished to obtain.[u] He seems to have inherited Pharnaces's desire to make Pontus a power in Asia, and with this ambition in view he gradually built up a force of mercenaries, recruited by his general Dorylaus in Thrace and Greece and especially in Crete, whither desperadoes flocked to sell their services to the pirates.[v] He then attempted to gain control of Cappadocia by entering the country with an army,[w] but, soon abandoning violence for more subtle means of establishing a hold upon the country, he married his eldest daughter, Laodice, to the boy-king Ariarathes VI.[x] This alliance was destined to involve Laodice's brother, Mithradates Eupator, and her second husband, Nicomedes III of Bithynia, in a struggle which was to be a prelude to the former's invasion of the Roman province.

About 120 B.C. Mithradates Euergetes was assassinated in Sinope by a group of courtiers.[50] He bequeathed his kingdom to his wife and his two young sons, the elder of whom was about eleven years of age. The situation in Pontus afforded an opportunity to those at Rome who had opposed the gift of Phrygia to the late monarch, and, as has been already described, the measure was revoked and the district annexed

r Polybius XXXIII 12, 1 (156 B.C.). For this war see above p. 28 and below p. 316f.
s Appian *Mith.* 10.   t See above p. 150.   u See above p. 154 and Chap. VI, note 27.
v Strabo X p. 477.   w Appian *Mith.* 10 and 12.
x Justin XXXVIII 1, 1. For Laodice see Stähelin in *R.E.* XII 710f., no. 28.

to the province of Asia. It was a step which could not fail to arouse the resentment of the young king and imbue him in his childhood with hatred for Rome.

If we may believe the romance which has been woven about the career of Mithradates VI Eupator, the boy, after escaping various plots aimed at his life, fled to the mountains of Pontus, where for seven years he lived in the forests, building up his strength by conflicts with wild beasts.[51] The story was perhaps invented to account for his harsh and ruthless nature, a proof of which was soon forthcoming. For, when he was not more than twenty years old, he murdered both his mother and his younger brother, taking the royal power into his own hands.

Young though Mithradates was, he soon began to form his plan for building a mighty empire, which was to include the whole of Asia Minor.[52] It entailed patience and long preparation, for it meant the expulsion of the Romans from their province on the Aegean coast. His first need was an assured source of the supplies necessary for a difficult and protracted war.

About seventy years previously, it will be remembered, Mithradates's great-uncle, Pharnaces I, had promised protection to the Grecian inhabitants of the city of Chersonesus in the Crimea.[y] Now, hard pressed by their Scythian neighbours, the citizens called on Mithradates for aid. It was a request which must have appeared most opportune. Accordingly, assuming the role of champion of the Greeks against the barbarians, the King responded eagerly to the appeal.[53] Within a very few years his general Diophantus not only delivered the Greeks from their enemies but established the supremacy of Pontus on the northern shore of the Euxine and set up a viceroy at Panticapaeum at the entrance to the Sea of Azov. Thus the Crimea became a part of Mithradates's realm, and with it not only the neighbouring regions but apparently the Greek cities on the western shore of the Euxine also were brought under his power. The yearly tribute from his dominions in southern Russia was estimated at 200 talents and 270,000 bushels of grain.[z] The country was also a useful recruiting-ground for the army he was planning to construct.

During these years Mithradates also extended his power toward the east. By forcing the ruler of Lesser Armenia—the country west and

[y] See above p. 193.

[z] Strabo VII p. 311 (180,000 *medimni*). For the importance of the grain from southern Russia see E. C. Semple *Geography of the Medit. Region* (London 1932), p. 356f.

north of the upper Euphrates—to cede this district to him, he gained possession of the eastern Paryadres and also of the Euxine coast beyond Pharnaceia as far as Trapezus.[54] The rich iron and silver mines of this mountainous district supplied him both with material for arms and with the funds needed for his enterprises, and in its fastnesses he is said to have built as many as seventy-five strongholds for the storing of his treasure. Not content with these acquisitions, however, he pushed his conquests further and annexed to his dominions the country of Colchis, the basin of the Phasis. This district was of the greatest value for building a navy, for the mountains of the Caucasus yielded timber for the construction of ships as well as pitch and wax for caulking and painting the hulls, and the plain at the eastern end of the Euxine produced hemp and flax for the ropes and the sails. Moreover, Lesser Armenia furnished horsemen and archers for the army.

Before completing his plans for the invasion of western Asia Minor, Mithradates, it was reported, travelled incognito through the province of Asia and the neighbouring kingdom of Bithynia for the purpose of spying out the land.[55] If the report is true, it is not improbable that during his journey he saw for himself a widespread hatred for the Roman oppressor[a] and conceived the idea of using this to give his invasion the appearance of a national uprising against a foreign yoke. As he had appeared in southern Russia in the role of champion of the Greeks against the barbarians, so he would present himself as the deliverer of Hellenic Asia Minor from domination by a foreign power.

Before entering the Roman province, however, it was necessary for Mithradates to extend his present kingdom toward the west. By this step he might hope to control the route that led to the Roman border and at the same time deprive his opponents of possible allies. With this end in view he revived the plan of Pharnaces for the conquest of Paphlagonia.

By the terms of the treaty which Pharnaces had been forced to accept,[b] the ruler of inland Paphlagonia, Morzius, was established in the power which he had held prior to the Pontic invasion. He seems already to have called himself king,[c] and this title was assumed also by his successors. These rulers, with the purpose, apparently, of strengthening their position by a connexion with the past, as well as of emphasizing their national character, regularly took the name of Pylaemenes, the Paphlagonian hero who appears in the *Iliad* as bringing his forces to fight for Troy.[56] This royal house entered into treaty-

[a] So Geyer in *R.E.* xv 2166.   [b] See above p. 192.   [c] Polybius xxv 2, 9.

relations with Rome, and less than fifty years after the defeat of Pharnaces the Pylaemenes of the time, as the ally of the Romans, helped to suppress the revolt of Aristonicus.[d] At the death of this monarch or, more probably, of his successor, Mithradates determined to seize the territory which Pharnaces had failed to conquer.

For the accomplishment of his purpose he felt the need of an associate. He therefore invited Nicomedes Euergetes, King of Bithynia,[e] whose dominions adjoined Paphlagonia on the west, to collaborate in the enterprise. As in the case of partitions known to later history, a pretext was devised to lend a semblance of legitimacy to the plan, and Mithradates asserted that his father had received Paphlagonia by inheritance. Nicomedes readily agreed to the proposal. He also was a "friend and ally" of Rome, but he had grown lukewarm in his attachment since the Roman money-lenders had begun to hold his subjects in thralldom.[57] The two kings, accordingly, overran the district and divided it between them. Mithradates, however, seems to have taken the lion's share, for he acquired the valley of the Amnias and probably also that of the Devrek, while Nicomedes obtained the western and more mountainous portion, including the region of Timonitis.

This partition of a country whose kings had been faithful allies was not viewed with favour at Rome. But the Romans were now engaged in a struggle with the Germanic invaders, who between 109 and 105 inflicted no less than four defeats on their armies. Consequently, there were no available forces to deal with such a *fait accompli*. The only step, therefore, that the Senate could take was the appointment of a commission to remonstrate with its two "friends and allies," now turned robbers, and to order the evacuation of the territory they had seized. To this demand Mithradates haughtily replied that since the Romans made no protest when his father received Paphlagonia by inheritance, there was no reason why they should do so now. Later, however, he seems to have taken the precaution of sending emissaries to Rome to bribe his opponents into silence. Nicomedes, less bold and more crafty, fell back upon a ruse. Changing the name of one of his sons to Pylaemenes, he made him king of his portion of Paphlagonia and then announced to the Roman commissioners that the country had been restored to its former status of independence. The Romans, at the time, were unable or unwilling to press the matter further, and the two kings continued to hold the territory they had seized.

Having thus succeeded in maintaining his position in Paphlagonia,

Mithradates went on to establish his power in the district of the Galatians, which lay between his kingdom and Phrygia. Taking advantage of the lack of union which usually prevailed among the princes of the tribes, he occupied at least the eastern part of their country.[f] In order to hold it in subjection he built a fortress in the southwestern part of his kingdom, calling it after his own name, Mithradatium.[58] The control of Galatia gave him access to the province of Asia, but the Romans, still occupied with the war against their Germanic enemies, seem to have raised no protest.

Despite his control of Paphlagonia and Galatia, however, Mithradates made no move against the Roman province, and more than ten years passed before he was ready to strike his blow. During this interval he was occupied, by intrigue and violence, in strengthening his position in eastern Asia Minor and in protecting himself against possible attack from a Roman ally in his rear.

[f] Justin xxxvii 4, 6.

CHAPTER IX

THE COMING OF MITHRADATES

SELDOM has there appeared in the drama of history a character more powerful and picturesque than Mithradates Eupator, and seldom has one man shown such vigour of body and of mind or such a combination of great intelligence and complete unscrupulousness.[1] The qualities of energy and intelligence which appear in his portraits[a] were well exemplified in his life and character. So huge was the physical stature of this astonishing monarch that men marvelled at the size of his armour, and such his strength and endurance that he was reputed to be able to ride 120 miles in a single day and drive a chariot drawn by sixteen horses. In keeping with this physical prowess were the force and resoluteness of his character. Ambitious, indomitable and unrelenting, he yielded neither to fatigue nor to wounds nor to defeat. Farsighted beyond the wont of Hellenistic rulers, he laid his plans with skill and shrewdness and often with cunning. The descendant of a line of princes who ruled first in a Greek city and later in an Asianic kingdom and had adopted Greek as their official language, he was well versed in Hellenic culture. He has sometimes been pictured as a barbarian, without the nobler qualities that have been considered characteristic of the Greeks. This view, however, is founded on the belief that ruthlessness and cruelty were un-Hellenic traits and that a complete disregard for the lives and rights of others was confined to those tyrants who ruled over barbarous nations. The tastes of Mithradates were those of an educated Greek—his love for music and for works of art, his power as an orator, his study of the religious cults of the Hellenes and his interest in letters and philosophy which caused him to invite poets and scholars to his court.

It was said of Mithradates by an unfriendly Roman[b] that he resembled the snake, which, when its head has been crushed, threatens to strike with its tail. Although twice forced by defeat to withdraw from western Asia Minor, and twice driven in total rout from his kingdom of Pontus, nevertheless, in his ambition to establish a great empire he remained indomitable to the end.

But there is another side to the picture. The relentless energy of his character could take the form of a savage cruelty and his intelligence

[a] See *Receuil* I² p. 13f. and Pl. II-III.   [b] Florus I 40, 24.

descend to ignoble intrigues. The murderer of his mother and brother, he did not hesitate to use the most brutal measures when moved either by self-interest or by anger. Beneath his culture there lay the despot who knew no law but his own will, and great as his mental powers were, he knew no way to govern save through terror and violence. For this reason he failed both in his effort to win the support of those to whom he professed to offer deliverance from a foreign tyrant and in his attempt to inspire in his troops a loyalty which would impel them to face the smaller, though better disciplined, armies of Rome.

The perseverance and shrewdness that were among the foremost traits of Mithradates's character enabled him within the short space of ten years to expand his ancestral kingdom into a great state. In 100 B.C. this new exponent of imperialism—now scarcely more than thirty years of age—had become the most powerful of the monarchs of Asia Minor, and less than a hundred years after the overthrow of Antiochus III he seemed likely to restore the empire of the Seleucids. His power, if not his actual sovereignty, extended from the foot of the Caucasus on the northeast to the upper Sangarius on the southwest; he had, furthermore, built up an empire in southern Russia, and by his partition of Paphlagonia with Nicomedes Euergetes of Bithynia he seemed to have gained the support of this monarch.[c] The riches of northeastern Asia Minor, the grain of the Crimea, and the manpower of both regions assured him the means of creating and supporting both an army and a navy.[d] But before he could proceed with his programme for the expulsion of the foreigner from western Asia Minor, it was necessary to safeguard his position from attack by his neighbours. This necessitated the establishment of his power over the neighbouring kingdom of Cappadocia. In view of the part which this kingdom played in the events leading up to Mithradates's invasion of western Asia Minor, a brief account both of the country itself and of the dynasty which ruled it seems to be demanded.

Cappadocia, lying immediately south of Pontus, extended from the mountains along the upper Halys, which separated it from its neighbour, to the high range of the Taurus, which divided it from Cilicia.[2] On the east it reached to the Euphrates, and on the west to the great salt Lake Tatta—the largest of the lakes of Asia Minor—and the steppe of Lycaonia.

In this land, largely wild and mountainous, the same primitive conditions obtained that prevailed in Pontus.[e] It contained only two

[c] See above p. 197.   [d] See above p. 195f.   [e] See above p. 179f.

communities that could be regarded as cities, Mazaca, the residence of its monarchs, and Tyana, a prosperous centre of commerce. Mazaca stood on a height dominating the plain at the foot of the great volcano Argaeus, the highest peak in Asia Minor, which rises to an altitude of over 12,000 feet, and near the river Melas, which joins the Halys northeast of the great bend of the latter toward its northward course.[3] Although none too favourably situated by reason of the unproductive soil of the surrounding region and the widespread marshes, the city, lying at the junction of the Southern Highway leading from Melitene to the Aegean coast with routes which ran from Bithynia through Galatia and from the Euxine through Pontus to Cilicia and the Mediterranean, attained to great importance as one of the principal road-centres of Asia Minor. Tyana, on a fortified hill rising from a plain in the southwestern part of the kingdom, was a large and wealthy place as early as the fifth century, and in the latter part of the second it had taken on at least a semblance of Greek civilization.[4] Its prosperity was due to its position on the road which led from Mazaca to Cilicia, as well as to a branch-route which connected it directly with Iconium and so with the Southern Highway and the Aegean ports.

As in Pontus, so in Cappadocia the land belonged to the king or to the holders of large estates, both sacred and secular. The chief sanctuaries were those of the Mother-Goddess Ma at Comana in a deep gorge of the river Sarus among the mountains of central Cappadocia—the cult from which was probably derived that of the goddess worshipped at the Pontic Comana—and of Zeus at Venasa in the western part of the kingdom.[5] Both owned wide tracts of land which were tilled by slaves and yielded large revenues to the temples; their priests ranked second and third, respectively, to the king himself. The other principal landholders were the great nobles, who probably had their seats in some of the strongholds known to have existed in Cappadocia.[6] They appear to have enjoyed greater power here than in Pontus, and their position seems to have been comparable to the barons of Europe in the Middle Ages. When the royal house eventually became extinct, one of them was chosen king of the country.[f]

The princes of the royal dynasty of Cappadocia had ruled the land under the domination of the Persians, but it was not until the middle of the third century that the then head of the house, Ariarathes III, took the title of King.[7] His marriage with Stratonice, daughter of Antiochus II, was doubtless of advantage to him in assuming this

[f] See below p. 205.

rank. His son, Ariarathes IV, surnamed Eusebes, who ascended the throne in 220 B.C., also married a Seleucid princess, the daughter of his cousin, Antiochus III, and his soldiers fought in Antiochus's army at Magnesia. On the expulsion of the Seleucid monarch from western Asia Minor, Ariarathes turned to Pergamum and, by betrothing his daughter Stratonice to Eumenes II, secured the latter's help in obtaining the "friendship" of Rome.

Ariarathes's son, Ariarathes V Eusebes Philopator, who became king about 164, was an enlightened man, deeply imbued with Hellenic culture.[8] Together with his kinsman by marriage, the later Attalus II, he studied philosophy at Athens and even became an Athenian citizen. So great, in fact, was his devotion to the city that, after succeeding to the throne, he gave a generous gift to the society of actors and musicians, and he is said to have made Cappadocia known to the Hellenic world as the resort of men of learning.

One of the first actions of this monarch was to renew his father's treaty of alliance with Rome.[g] A commission appointed by the Senate to investigate a charge of aggression brought against him by the Galatian Trocmi exonerated Ariarathes and declared him a true friend of the Romans.[9] In consequence, the King sent envoys to the Senate bearing a golden wreath as an expression of his devotion and in return was presented by the Fathers with a sceptre and an ivory chair—the symbols of royalty. In spite of this recognition, however, the Romans failed Ariarathes in his time of need, for when his brother Orophernes revolted and seized Cappadocia and he himself journeyed to Rome to present a plea for aid, the Senate settled the dispute by dividing the kingdom between the two claimants. Later, when, with the help of Attalus II, Ariarathes had driven out the rebel and tried, also with Attalus's aid, to seize the treasure which Orophernes had left in Priene, the Romans rebuked the two kings for their action. Nevertheless, Ariarathes maintained the alliance loyally, and when the Senate issued a call for aid against Aristonicus he responded at once, with the result that his life was sacrificed in the cause of Rome.[h] His devotion was posthumously rewarded when Aquilius presented the district of Lycaonia to his son and heir.[i]

This youth, Ariarathes Epiphanes Philopator, was still a minor, and until he reached his majority his mother Nysa acted as regent.[10] In order to maintain her position she seems to have been ruthless in

g Polybius xxxi 3 (14), 1f.; 7 (17), 1: Livy Per. XLVI: Diodorus xxxi 19, 8.
h See above pp. 150 and 151.   i See Chap. VI note 28.

stamping out opposition to her rule. The resultant strife in the kingdom gave the ambitious king of Pontus, Mithradates V, an opportunity of increasing his own power by interfering in the affairs of his neighbour; by sending troops into Cappadocia and by subsequently marrying his daughter Laodice to the young monarch,[j] he contrived to make the influence of Pontus paramount in the kingdom.

The mere exercise of this influence, however, was not sufficient for the projects of his son, Mithradates Eupator, nor was the latter content to dominate Cappadocia through the agency of his royal brother-in-law, Ariarathes VI. About the time of his attempt to gain power in southern Russia[k] he conceived the plan of gaining more direct control of Cappadocia also.[11] To this end he instigated, or at least connived at, the assassination of Ariarathes by a Cappadocian noble named Gordius. Laodice became regent for her young son, Ariarathes VII Philometor, and her brother evidently expected that she would rule in his interest. This expectation, however, was thwarted by a like project formed by his recent associate in the partition of Paphlagonia,[l] for Nicomedes of Bithynia had also cast covetous eyes on the Cappadocian throne. When he went so far as to enter the kingdom with an army, Mithradates hastened to make preparation for the rescue of his sister and her endangered realm. But before this act of fraternal devotion could be carried out, Laodice, evidently preferring the invader to her brother, married Nicomedes.[m] This seemed tantamount to an annexation of Cappadocia to Bithynia. Mithradates was thus placed under the necessity of adopting a new plea, namely, that he was protecting his nephew. Forcing Nicomedes and his new wife to leave Cappadocia, he reinstated the young Ariarathes VII on his ancestral throne. All might have gone well had not the King of Pontus insisted on restoring to his native land the treacherous Gordius, who was commonly supposed to have been his agent in the assassination of the late king. This restoration the youthful monarch resented bitterly, and he prepared to resist with arms the encroachments of his uncle. Then the latter, now casting aside all his dutiful pretences, entered Cappadocia with a huge army. Preferring, however, to try craft rather than force, he persuaded Ariarathes to meet him for a conference, and at this meeting he stabbed the young man in full view of both their armies. Thereupon he proclaimed his own eight-

[j] See above p. 194.   [k] See above p. 195.   [l] See above p. 197.
[m] About 102 B.C.; see Reinach *L'Hist. par les Monnaies*, p. 172 and Daux in *B.C.H.* LVII (1933), p. 81f.

year-old son King of Cappadocia under the national name of Ariarathes and appointed as regent the hated Gordius.[12]

This act of violence and intrigue was at first successful, for during the next five years this child was titular King of Cappadocia. Then, however, the nobles of the country, unable to endure the tyranny of the Pontic officials, revolted and set up as monarch the second son of Ariarathes VI, who had meanwhile been reared in the Roman province of Asia.[n] He also was proclaimed king under the royal name of Ariarathes. But neither his rightful claim to the throne nor the support of the Cappadocians availed to protect him against his uncle. He, too, was overcome by Mithradates and driven from his kingdom, and he did not long survive his expulsion. At the end of 96 B.C. Mithradates seemed to have gained complete control of Cappadocia.

He had failed, however, to reckon with the Romans and with their possible interest in his imperialistic designs. He had failed, too, to remember that the sixth Ariarathes, whom he had caused to be assassinated by Gordius, had been under their protection. Nor had he heeded the advice which is said to have been given him by Gaius Marius in a personal interview soon after he had placed his son on the Cappadocian throne, namely, that he should either try to make himself stronger than the Romans or do their bidding in silence.[13] He had also reckoned without Nicomedes and Laodice and their claims to his new conquest. The Queen, it was known, had borne only two sons to Ariarathes VI, but now a handsome boy was trumped up as a third child, and he and Laodice were sent to Rome to present to the Senate a claim to the kingdom of Cappadocia.[o] Mithradates, not to be outdone and with equal self-assurance, also sent a representative, the notorious Gordius, to assure the Senate that the child whom he had set upon the throne was indeed a descendant of Ariarathes V, the faithful ally of Rome.[p]

The falsifications of both monarchs, however, failed to achieve their purposes. Often, indeed, had the Senators been taken in by the wiles of the Asiatics and by their flow of words, but this twofold attempt at deceit was too crass. Rejecting both claimants as palpable frauds, they ordered Mithradates and his son to depart from Cappadocia; also, in order to show their perfect impartiality, they bade Nicomedes evacuate Paphlagonia. Not knowing what else to do with the two countries, they declared them "free."[q] To their surprise, however, they

[n] Justin xxxviii 2, 1f.   [o] Justin xxxviii 2, 3f.

[p] Justin xxxviii 2, 5.   [q] Justin xxxviii 2, 7.

found that this supposedly great boon was unwelcome to those whom it was designed to benefit. The Paphlagonians seem to have used their freedom to retain their Bithynian monarch.[14] In Cappadocia the barons showed that they had none of the illusions about liberty which were cherished by the republics of Greece and Italy. These nobles had perhaps observed that often it had meant only freedom for aristocratic and popular factions to cut each others' throats, and they doubtless realized that in a country long used to monarchy the abolition of the kingship would result only in anarchy. Greatly to the surprise of the Romans, therefore, a deputation of Cappadocians asked to be excused from the blessings of a republican government and requested a king.[15] The Senators, though evidently failing to understand how such a request could be made, acceded to it and bade them choose a monarch from among their own countrymen. Their choice fell on a noble named Ariobarzanes, who was later to prove a staunch supporter of the Romans, to suffer as their ally and finally to be rewarded. In devotion to their cause he afterward assumed the title of "Friend of Rome."

Neither Mithradates nor Nicomedes dared gainsay this decision of the Senate; for the Romans, for the time being, were not engaged in any foreign war and so were able to enforce their demands. So the King of Pontus found that all the intrigues and the violence which for the past eighteen years he had carried out in Cappadocia had profited him nothing, and that after all he must follow the counsel of Marius. He must either seek an alliance which would make his strength superior to that of Rome or acquiesce in her will.

Such an ally did not exist in Asia Minor. Nicomedes had shown himself both untrustworthy and powerless, but soon even he was not available, for not long after the Senate's decision against him in 95, he was gathered to his fathers,[r] and his son Nicomedes, who succeeded to the throne as the fourth of the name, was little more than a Roman tool. Mithradates, therefore, turned toward the East. Here Tigranes, who had recently ascended the throne of Greater Armenia, the mountainous plateau beyond the Euphrates, was pursuing the same course of self-aggrandizement that Mithradates had adopted in Asia Minor, and was transforming the kingdom of his predecessors into a powerful state.[16] By his conquest of Sophene, on the eastern bank of the Euphrates, he had become a neighbour of Cappadocia. The possession of the much-used crossing of the river at Tomisa, which

r In 94 B.C. or soon afterwards; see Reinach *Mith. Eup.* p. 112, note 2. For Nicomedes IV see below p. 319.

had been sold by a predecessor of Ariobarzanes to the ruler of Sophene, made it easy for him to send troops over into eastern Cappadocia, whence his army could march without difficulty into the heart of the kingdom. What inducement was offered him besides a marriage with Mithradates's daughter Cleopatra we do not know, but an alliance was concluded, with the result that Tigranes's generals invaded Cappadocia and drove out Ariobarzanes. Mithradates's youthful son, the spurious "Ariarathes," was once more proclaimed king.

The Senate could not overlook this act of defiance. While the overt act was Tigranes's, the instigator was evidently the King of Pontus, for he it was who profited by this expulsion of the protégé of Rome. On the other hand, the Italians were clamouring for Roman citizenship, and it must have been apparent to many that a civil war was imminent. No elaborate or costly steps could be taken for the sake of so remote a "friend and ally." Nevertheless, it seemed necessary to the Senators to make a gesture of some kind, and the order was given that Lucius Cornelius Sulla, one of the praetors of 93, should restore Ariobarzanes to his kingdom. It was Sulla's first appearance in the East, where, seven years later, he was destined, after annihilating two Pontic armies, to impose a humiliating peace on the King himself and force him to give up all that he had gained by his war against Rome.[8]

Sulla's entry into Cappadocia in the summer of 92 B.C. was a notable event, for it was the first appearance of a Roman general with an army in eastern Asia Minor.[17] Neither Tigranes nor Mithradates had the courage to oppose him, and the Armenians hastily evacuated the country, taking with them Gordius and, presumably, the usurping son of the Pontic King. Ariobarzanes was once more placed upon the throne. In his royal capacity he advanced with Sulla as far eastward as the bank of the Euphrates, and here with every formality the Roman leader and the Cappadocian monarch met an envoy of the Parthian king and accepted his offer of friendship. This, the first meeting with a representative of the eastern ruler, impressed the Romans far more than the restoration to power of a vassal-prince.

The Senate had ordered Sulla to restore Ariobarzanes, and this order he carried out literally. No order had been given to keep the King on his throne and nothing to this end was done by the Roman general. As on a later occasion, after his defeat of the Pontic monarch, so now also he departed from the scene of action leaving his work only half-completed. Within a year of his departure Mithradates entered Cappa-

---

[8] See below p. 220f.

docia and once more installed the oft-enthroned "Ariarathes."[t] Now, however, the Senate was unable to take action, for by this time the war with the Italians had begun, and all the resources of Rome were being utilized to save the Republic.[18] Ariobarzanes took refuge in Italy.[u] There he and another royal victim of Mithradates joined in importuning the Senate to reinstate them on their thrones.

Nicomedes IV, the new king of Bithynia, was a depraved weakling.[v] Mithradates, who had already scorned him as an ally, soon saw that he could be easily ousted from his kingdom. He therefore decided to carry out in Bithynia the policy he had successfully prosecuted in Cappadocia and to place on the Bithynian throne a monarch who would be under his control. A ready instrument was at hand in Socrates, an illegitimate son of Nicomedes III.[19] This prince had received from his half-brother every mark of honour as well as the flattering surname of Chrestos ("the Good"). Nevertheless, with the encouragement of Mithradates he went to Rome and presented a petition to the Senate asking for the kingdom of Bithynia. He was probably as worthy a claimant as his half-brother, but early in 91 a decree was passed by which Nicomedes IV was recognized as king. His attempt having failed, Socrates could not return to his native land. He therefore appeared openly in Pontus and asked Mithradates to aid him in an attempt to gain the Bithynian throne. The King saw his opportunity; the Senate was fully occupied with the Italian war and would not be able to interfere. He therefore promised not only to help Socrates to seize his brother's kingdom but also, or so Nicomedes later maintained,[w] to assassinate the monarch himself. Supported by a Pontic army, Socrates conquered Bithynia without difficulty.[x] Nicomedes, however, succeeded in making good his escape; taking refuge in Rome, he joined Ariobarzanes in a plea for restoration.[20]

Mithradates had now achieved success in all his designs. With the establishment of his son in Cappadocia and his creature, Socrates, in Bithynia, he had gained control of all Asia Minor north of the Taurus save for the Roman province. He had a powerful ally in Armenia and he had greatly strengthened his armies by reinforcements from southern Russia.[y] It was even said that he had promised Rome's enemies in Italy that when he had established his power in Asia he would come to their aid.[21]

---

[t] Appian *Mith.* 15 and 57.　　[u] Justin xxxviii 3, 3.　　[v] See below p. 319.
[w] Appian *Mith.* 57 (a speech attributed to Sulla).
[x] Appian *Mith.* 10 and 13: Memnon 30, 3.　　　　[y] Justin xxxviii 3, 6f.

The King was ready to strike at Rome's Asianic dominions, but his necessary preparations had lasted too long; peace in Italy came too soon for his plans. In the early autumn of 90 a law was enacted bestowing citizenship on all Italians who had not taken up arms, and this concession dispelled the fear of a more widely spread war in Italy. The Senators, accordingly, now felt able once more to take a strong hand in foreign affairs, and an order was given that the two kings should be restored to their thrones. A special commission, headed by Manius Aquilius (probably the son of the organizer of the province of Asia), who had been Consul in 101 and in the following year had finally put down a slave-revolt in Sicily, was sent to the East to co-operate with Gaius Cassius, the governor of Asia, in effecting the restoration.[22] In the hope of ensuring the compliance of Mithradates, the King was officially informed of the mission. Perhaps even before the commissioners could take any action, a second law, passed early in 89, a few months after the first measure, granted citizenship to all Italians who would lay down their arms, and, save for a few last struggles with the die-hards, the civil war was over. Mithradates, disappointed in his expectation that Rome would be unable to make a move, offered no resistance to the demands presented by Aquilius. The small army of Cassius, strengthened by a larger force collected from Galatia and Phrygia, compelled the usurpers to withdraw, and the two monarchs, brought back from Rome, were restored to their kingdoms. The puppet Socrates was put to death by Mithradates himself.[z] Thus the situation was suddenly reversed; for the two dependent kingdoms on which Mithradates had been counting were given to their rightful rulers and he himself was reduced to the position in which he had been before he began his machinations.

Aquilius and his fellow-commissioners, however, were not willing that this *status quo ante* should remain in effect. Perhaps they realized that as soon as they departed, their restorations would prove as ineffectual as Sulla's. In any case, they resolved to take the offensive. They rendered Mithradates a bill for damages, and when he refused to pay, presenting them in turn with a statement of the expenditures he had incurred, they ordered the two reinstated kings to invade Pontus, promising them the assistance of Rome.[a] Both, unwilling to take the risk, demurred. But on Nicomedes IV, at least, Aquilius knew how to bring pressure. It was said that the King had agreed to pay a

z Justin xxxviii 5, 8 (a speech attributed to Mithradates).
a Appian *Mith.* 11f.: Cassius Dio frg. 99 Boiss.

large sum of money to the Roman commissioners in return for his restoration but was unable to fulfil his promise. What is more probable is that he had borrowed great amounts from Roman money-lenders and these, too, he could not repay. His debts served the purpose of a club, and in the summer of 89 the unhappy monarch was constrained by the commissioners to invade Mithradates's territory. Much to his surprise and doubtless to that of the Romans also, the Pontic King offered no resistance. Nicomedes marched into the western end of Paphlagonia as far as Amastris on the Euxine, plundering as he went and returning with much booty. He seems also to have closed the Bosporus against the ships of Pontus.[b] With the proceeds of the raid he was probably able to make good his debts to the commissioners and perhaps even to satisfy some of his Roman creditors as well.

It is difficult to believe that, in presenting Mithradates with their bill and in instigating the raid of Nicomedes, Aquilius and his fellow-commissioners were actuated solely by the motive of cupidity.[c] The similar order issued to Ariobarzanes shows that they were embarking on a definite policy of provoking Mithradates into a war. The King, however, was not to be drawn so easily. He held back his troops and sent an envoy, Pelopidas, to protest against the plundering of his territory and the closing of the Strait; he also demanded that either the Romans should themselves punish Nicomedes or permit him to do so.[23]

Mithradates's policy of forbearance has laid him open to the criticism of a lack of statesmanship and an inability either to prepare for a conflict or to submit gracefully. His slowness to act has been attributed to a supposition that the Romans had no desire to provoke a war and to the hope that by temporizing he might hold out until confronted with a general whom he could bribe into inactivity.[d] It is more probable, however, that in his forbearance he was showing great shrewdness. His demand was not unreasonable and it would involve the Romans in a difficult dilemma:[e] Should they endorse the hostile act of Nicomedes or disavow him and his invasion of Pontus? Since a disavowal could not but expose the Bithynian monarch to the vengeance of his enemy, they must inevitably endorse the raid and so put themselves in the position of taking the offensive. This would necessarily be regarded as a breach of the treaty between Rome and the Pontic King, and the responsibility for war would be the Romans'.

[b] Appian *Mith.* 12 (a speech attributed to Mithradates's envoy); 14; 19.
[c] As supposed by Geyer in *R.E.* xv 2168f.
[d] So Mommsen *R.G.*[7] ii p. 281 = Eng. Trans. iv p. 26.　　　[e] Appian *Mith.* 12.

Thus in the eyes of the Asiatics Mithradates would be the injured party and his cause would be greatly strengthened. As formerly in the Crimea he had appeared in the role of saviour of the Greeks, so now he would be able to come forth in western Asia Minor as the deliverer of the inhabitants of the province from the rule of Rome. He would also gain time for sending to southern Russia for reinforcements.

This dilemma the commissioners tried to evade. They replied that while it was not their wish that Mithradates should suffer at the hands of Nicomedes, they considered it contrary to the interests of Rome that he should make war on the Bithynian King. This answer Mithradates evidently considered tantamount to an endorsement of Nicomedes, and he resolved to strike a blow. Once more he invaded Cappadocia and again—for the third time—drove the unhappy Ariobarzanes from his throne.[f] In reply to this challenge the commissioners could only order him to refrain from attacking Rome's two royal allies and announce their intention of restoring Ariobarzanes. They commanded Pelopidas, who had again appeared before them, to leave their camp, and at the end of 89 war was inevitable.

The responsibility for the struggle which was to cost Rome dear was thus placed on the commissioners; by authorizing an invasion of Mithradates's territory and then refusing to allow him to avenge the raid they had played directly into his hand. They not only put themselves in the wrong from the standpoint of diplomacy but they involved their government in a war of the first magnitude and ultimately caused the massacre of large numbers of their fellow-citizens.

However inevitable the conflict might ultimately have proved, the moment was ill-chosen for Rome. Mithradates had been patiently building up a great army, recruited not only in Asia Minor but also in the lands north of the Euxine from the Danube to the Don.[g] His forces are said to have numbered 250,000 infantry and 40,000 cavalry and 130 scythed chariots, and he had a fleet of 400 vessels, large and small. In addition, he drew from Lesser Armenia a body of 10,000 horsemen.[24] However greatly these numbers may have been exaggerated in the narrative which has been preserved to us, there can be no doubt that his army was a vast one. Against this force the Romans could put into the field only the small body of troops permanently

[f] Appian *Mith.* 14f.: Livy *Per.* LXXVII: Cassius Dio frg. 99 Boiss.: Eutropius V 5, 1f: Orosius VI 2, 1.
[g] Justin XXXVIII 3, 6f.: Appian *Mith.* 15: Memnon 30, 3.

stationed in the province, new recruits hastily levied in Phrygia and Galatia,[h] and the army of Nicomedes. It may be that the commissioners regarded an army led by Roman generals as more than a match for any Asiatic force, however great, and that for this reason they were ready to begin the conflict at once.

Despite the unfavourable situation, the Romans took the offensive and in the spring of 88 Nicomedes was ordered to invade northern Paphlagonia.[25] His army is said to have numbered 50,000 foot and 6,000 horse, but it was evidently very much smaller. Setting out, probably from Bithynium near the eastern border of Bithynia, the King marched eastward through Paphlagonia to the Amnias and thence down the course of this stream as far as a "wide plain along the river." Here he was met by a Pontic force. The invasion had evidently proceeded more rapidly than Mithradates expected, for he was unable to send up his heavy infantry in time to meet the Bithynian King, and only his light foot-soldiers and his Armenian cavalry with a few scythed chariots were present. The Pontic generals, Archelaus and Neoptolemus, realizing their inferiority in numbers, endeavoured to strengthen their position by sending a small body of men to occupy a hill which commanded the plain. When these were dislodged by the Bithynians, Neoptolemus advanced to their aid, but the superior forces of the enemy soon compelled him to fall back. He and his men were in retreat, perhaps a pretended one, when Archelaus, hastening up from his position on the right wing, attacked the pursuers. When they turned on him he retreated slowly, thus giving his colleague an opportunity to rally his men and return to the charge. Then the Bithynians were caught between the two divisions of the Pontic army and attacked at the same time by the Armenian cavalry and the scythed chariots; the latter seem to have created especial havoc. Thus entrapped, Nicomedes could not make use of his superior numbers. Although his men fought long and bravely, he lost the greater part of his army and fled the field, leaving to the victors his camp and a vast amount of treasure. After this defeat, in which he had been completely out-generalled by Mithradates's commanders, Nicomedes made no further attempt at resistance but with the remnant of his army, chiefly cavalry, retreated by the road along which he had advanced and took refuge with Aquilius.

Meanwhile the King of Pontus himself came up from Amaseia, where he had mobilized his forces. He brought with him a great

[h] Appian *Mith*. 11.

army, said to have been 150,000 strong.[1] With this he swept westward through Paphlagonia, driving out the puppet-king Pylaemenes and advancing without opposition as far as Mt. Scorobas on the Bithynian border.[j] Here a small body of Nicomedes's cavalry had been left to hold the pass, but on the approach of the Pontic horsemen they at once surrendered. The way was now open for an advance against Aquilius, who had with him Nicomedes and what was left of his demoralized army.

As though the folly of the Roman generals in using Nicomedes as a catspaw to draw out Mithradates was not enough, they had committed a further act of imprudence by dividing their forces into three armies too widely separated to come to the aid of one another should the need arise.[26] Aquilius himself had taken a position in the eastern part of Bithynia; Cassius, the governor of Asia, was stationed farther south near the frontier of Galatia; and a third division, under Quintus Oppius, was on the border of Cappadocia or, more probably, Lycaonia. Each army, according to the evidently exaggerated estimate of our principal source, was composed of about 40,000 men. What plan underlay this tripartite arrangement the meagre narrative of the ancient historian does not enable us to determine. It is probable, however, that the three generals were attempting to hold the three important thoroughfares to the East, the northern route through Paphlagonia, over which Nicomedes had advanced and then retreated, the road which led through Galatia into Pontus, and the Southern Highway, which ran through Lycaonia and Cappadocia to the Euphrates. It may be that Aquilius expected to be able to hold the King in check while the others advanced into Pontic territory. But whatever the plan which their folly had devised, it was a total failure. Aquilius was the first to succumb. At the mere news of Mithradates's approach the wretched Nicomedes and his troops deserted, and Aquilius was soon dislodged from his position by the Pontic general Menophanes and forced to retreat southward.[27] On his retreat he was overtaken by Neoptolemus and the Armenian cavalry under Naimanes and lost a fourth of his army as well as his camp. In total rout, he succeeded in crossing the Sangarius and so made his escape to Pergamum. Bithynia was completely at Mithradates's mercy.

Cassius, on the other hand, did not even attempt a battle. Nicomedes, on leaving Aquilius, had fled to him and perhaps infected him with

[i] More probably his total strength (see *C.A.H.* IX p. 240, note 2).
[j] Unknown; see Chap. VIII note 33.

his own fears. Withdrawing his army from the position he had taken, Cassius sought the shelter of the stronghold of Leonton Cephale in central Phrygia.[28] He attempted to drill his army of recruits and to add to its numbers, but he soon grew discouraged (perhaps as Mithradates drew nearer) and retired to Apameia. Here he and his troops were received and victualled by Roman sympathizers, among whom Chaeremon, a wealthy citizen of the city of Nysa on the lower Maeander, brought him 60,000 modii (about 15,000 bushels) of grain for the support of his army. Nicomedes, however, did not feel safe even here but went on to Pergamum and from there made his way to Rome.[k]

The third general, Oppius, was no more valiant in meeting the enemy. He also withdrew from his post on the road to Cappadocia and retreated westward along the Southern Highway. Presumably his retreat took place while Cassius was still at Leonton Cephale, for he did not join him at Apameia but hastened on his way until he came to Laodiceia-on-Lycus.[1] Here he found shelter with the inhabitants and barricaded himself in the city, though the protection it afforded him proved later to be illusory.

Mithradates with both his army and his fleet now advanced without opposition. Perhaps before Cassius left the protection of Leonton Cephale, the King's forces overran Bithynia and took possession of its cities, apparently without any resistance.[m] Even the Romans in command of the ships which were guarding the Bosporus fled at the news of his advance. As a result, the ships surrendered,[n] and the way into the Aegean was opened to the royal fleet, said to have numbered 400 vessels large and small. The King himself, leaving the further subjugation of Bithynia to his generals, crossed the upper Sangarius with his large army and marched southward through Phrygia, thinking himself a second Alexander.[o] When he reached the Southern Highway, presumably at Ipsus, he turned westward. His advance must have seemed to him rather a triumphal progress than an armed invasion. On his approach Cassius fled from Apameia and found a refuge in Rhodes.[29] The city itself surrendered, and its submission was rewarded with a gift of one hundred talents to aid in repairing the damage caused by a recent earthquake.[p] Roman sympathizers, like Chaeremon and his sons, were declared outlaws and a price was set

[k] Strabo XII p. 562.   [1] Appian *Mith.* 20.

[m] Strabo XII p. 562: Appian *Mith.* 20: Memnon 31, 3.

[n] Appian *Mith.* 17 and 19.   [o] Livy *Per.* LXXVII: Appian *Mith.* 20.

[p] Strabo XII p. 579. See also above p. 126.

on their heads.[q] Chaeremon himself took refuge in the sanctuary of Artemis at Ephesus but succeeded in sending his sons to Rhodes along with the fugitive Romans.

The first resistance to the King's westward march was encountered at Laodiceia. He thereupon laid siege to the city, and when the towns-folk had been duly terrified by the resultant damage,[r] he announced that he would spare the place if Oppius were surrendered. The citizens were in no position to refuse his offer and with mock ceremony they delivered over the Roman commander together with his lictors. The King, evidently thinking that Oppius would be more useful alive than dead, took the unhappy man about with the army, displaying the Roman as his captive.[s] Meanwhile from Laodiceia he sent some of his generals southward to overrun Lycia and Pamphylia; but it is a question how far they were able to penetrate the Lycian mountains, and there is no evidence that the troops despatched to Pamphylia advanced farther than Termessus and the pass leading to the southern coast.[30]

In contrast to his treatment of the Romans, the native forces which had surrendered to Mithradates were allowed everywhere to go free and were even furnished with supplies.[t] An act of generosity such as this was an important part of his programme. He had come, not to subdue the inhabitants of the province, but to deliver both Greeks and Asiatics from a foreign yoke, which the greed of Rome's tax-gatherers and business-men had made intolerable. By his well-calculated for-bearance at the outset of the struggle he had represented himself as the aggrieved party; so he could now put forth a claim to the sympathies of the Asiatics as one who also had suffered from the over-bearing Romans.

As he marched down the Maeander from Laodiceia to the coast, Mithradates was received everywhere with enthusiasm, at least by the less responsible element among the citizens, and hailed as the pre-server of Asia and a new Dionysus.[31] Tralles opened its gates in re-sponse to his invitation[u] and, like Apameia, was liberally rewarded for so doing. Magnesia-on-Maeander followed the example set by its neighbour,[v] as did also Ephesus, where the mob, in their eagerness to win his favour, overthrew all the statues that had been erected in honour of Romans.[w] Here the King seems to have established himself

[q] See note 28.
[s] Livy *Per.* LXXVIII: Appian *Mith.* 20.
[u] Cicero *pro Flacco* 57f.
[w] Appian *Mith.* 21.

[r] Strabo XII p. 578.
[t] Diodorus XXXVII 26: Appian *Mith.* 18f.
[v] See note 32.

after his long march from Pontus to the Ionian seaboard. Meanwhile his generals overran Mysia on the north and Caria far to the south.[x]

Some resistance, indeed, there was, and some cities had to be taken by force.[y] In Lydia the citizens of Magnesia-near-Sipylus defied the royal general Archelaus and defended themselves successfully until the end of the war.[32] In Caria, especially, although coast cities, such as Caunus,[z] Cnidus and Cos[a] surrendered, there was stubborn opposition in the interior, as at Tabae[b] and Stratoniceia.[c] But in the case of the latter, at least, the defence was fruitless, for the city was ultimately captured, then fined and placed under a garrison. Such cases of resistance, however, were more than offset by the surrender of Pergamum, which capitulated in response to the King's demand.[d] But the surrender came too late to deliver into his hands Aquilius, for he had taken refuge in Mitylene. Even so, the ill-fated man did not escape. This island-city also capitulated and, along with the other Romans in the place, he was delivered over to the King of Pontus.[e] The Roman settlers on the island were slain, and only the beloved Rutilius Rufus, doubtless with the connivance of the Mitylenians, escaped in disguise and fled to Smyrna.[f] But a cruel revenge was exacted by the King from the enemy whom he held responsible for the war. During a victorious progress through the province he took Aquilius with him, bound to an ass and compelled to proclaim his name and rank.[33] Finally at Pergamum, the city which had once conferred divine honours on his father, the wretched man was put to a cruel death.

A large part of the province thus fell into Mithradates's hands, and he appointed "satraps" to command the various districts it contained.[34] In many cities there were evidently two opposing factions, which supported the King and the Romans respectively. The adherents of the latter included, presumably, members of the wealthier and more responsible classes, men like Chaeremon of Nysa and perhaps Diodorus, surnamed Zonas, a rhetorician from Sardis, whom Mithradates accused of encouraging resistance.[g] Adventurers, on the other hand, who

[x] Appian *Mith.* 20f.: Strabo XII p. 562.   [y] Memnon 31, 3.

[z] See below p. 217.

[a] Plutarch *Luc.* 3, 3. See also below p. 217.

[b] *O.G.I.* 442=*M.A.M.A.* VI 162, l. 1f. (*senatus consultum de Tabenis*, see Chap. X note 9).

[c] Appian *Mith.* 21: *O.G.I.* 441, ll. 6f., 39, 49f. and 82f. (*senatus consultum de Stratonicensibus*, see Chap. X note 9).

[d] Cicero *pro Flacco* 57.

[e] Diodorus XXXVII 27: Livy *Per.* LXXVIII: Velleius Paterculus II 18, 3.

[f] Cicero pro *Rab. Post.* 27. For Rutilius Rufus see above p. 174f.

[g] Strabo XIII p. 628.

had nothing to lose by a change of ruler, supported the King. Thus at Adramyttium another Diodorus, a self-styled philosopher who had succeeded in obtaining the office of *strategos*, caused the members of the city-council to be slaughtered and so brought the city over to Mithradates's side.[35] It may be supposed that in many another city the all too frequent factional strife now took the form of partisanship for or against the invader. To judge from the general surrender to the King, his adherents seem uniformly to have gained the upper hand. Meanwhile he himself used every means to retain their support. At Ephesus he used the somewhat spectacular device of shooting an arrow from the roof of the Temple of Artemis and then granting to the sanctuary the right of inviolability as far as the spot where the arrow fell, thus extending the limit slightly beyond that fixed by Alexander.[h] Thereby he secured the support of the priests, who saw in the King of Pontus, the land where the great sanctuary at Comana was still powerful,[i] a ruler who might show more favour than the Hellenic citizens to the interests of the ancient Asianic temple.[j]

The conquest of the province achieved, Mithradates proceeded to a step which has caused him ever afterwards to be branded with obloquy. Forty years' exploitation of Asia had brought into the country crowds of Romans and Italians—tax-gatherers, bankers, and merchants large and small—said to number about a hundred thousand in all, an estimate doubtless much too large. Some of them were hated for acts of greed and oppression, and some were envied for the profits they had made. They had no place in the nationalistic programme which the King offered the Asiatics, and their wealth would be useful for his plans. Obviously, they must be removed if the promise of deliverance from Roman oppression was to be fulfilled. Obviously, also, they could not be deported, for their numbers were too great. The only solution that presented itself to the ruthless invader was a general massacre. Accordingly, from his headquarters at Ephesus Mithradates issued an order to his officers in cities of the province, commanding that on a given day, thirty days later, all Romans and Italians, adults and children, free men and slaves, should be put to death.[36] Their bodies were to be cast out unburied, and their property divided between the slayers and the King. Those who buried the dead or concealed the living were to be punished, rewards were offered to all who revealed hiding-places or killed those in concealment, slaves who murdered their masters

[h] Strabo xiv p. 641; but see note 28. [i] See above p. 181.
[j] So Curtius in *Abh. Berl. Akad.* 1872, p. 26=*Ges. Abh.* 1 p. 258.

were to be freed and debtors who slew their creditors were to be absolved of half of their indebtedness. No means of securing the execution of the order was left unused.

In many a city the command was doubtless welcomed, most of all probably by the rabble, eager for the booty to be obtained. In any case, on the appointed day the intended victims were everywhere attacked and slaughtered, the innocent along with those guilty of oppression and cruelty. At Ephesus and Pergamum, the two chief centres of resident Romans, even those who had fled to the temples for sanctuary were slain. In Caunus, which, eighty years earlier, the Romans had freed from subjection to Rhodes,[k] a similar slaughter was carried out. In Adramyttium those who had taken refuge in the sea were killed in the water. In Tralles the citizens, unwilling to take the guilt upon themselves, hired a savage Paphlagonian to perpetrate the butchery for them. Only at Cos, or so the Coans afterward claimed, were the Romans saved by the sanctity of the Temple of Asclepius.[l] With such thoroughness was the massacre carried out everywhere that as many as eighty thousand are said to have perished.[37]

The massacre has been characterized as a "meaningless act of brutally blind revenge" without a rational object.[m] This characterization, however, seems to be over-stated. It is true enough that, shrewd as he had been in his dealings before the war, Mithradates had little political wisdom and that he was not the man to construct an empire. But it was not mere revenge that he sought. He had a programme, and to one of his nature violence seemed the easiest method of putting it into effect. From one point of view, his action was a political blunder, for any reconciliation with Rome was henceforth out of the question. But as yet he had had no reason to suppose that Rome's generals would win the war and that any reconciliation would be necessary. On the other hand, the cities of Asia were now irrevocably bound to his cause. They had broken their treaties of alliance with Rome and must support him or suffer the punishment that the Romans knew how to mete out to their foes. The King, furthermore, was enabled to strengthen his hold on the Asiatics by means of the wealth that he derived from the confiscation attendant upon the massacre. The funds thus obtained were increased by other robberies, such as that at Cos, where, when the citizens resisted his attempt to violate the Temple of Asclepius, he laid his hands on 800 talents deposited by Jewish bankers in vari-

[k] See above p. 110. [l] Tacitus *Ann.* IV 14, 3.
[m] So Mommsen *R.G.*[7] II p. 286 = Eng. Trans. IV p. 32.

ous sanctuaries on the island, together with other treasures and works of art left there by the Egyptian queen Cleopatra III, widow of Ptolemy VII.[38] So much money, in fact, did he accumulate that he was able to cancel the indebtedness of the cities which had submitted, as well as to promise them five years' exemption from taxes.[n]

Although the greater part of the mainland was now in the hands of Mithradates, the island-republic of Rhodes refused to submit. Here not only Cassius and the sons of Chaeremon but also other Italians who had escaped the massacre had found a refuge. The Rhodians had apparently received favours from Mithradates, but nevertheless, despite the ill-treatment they had suffered from the Romans in the previous century, they remained faithful to their alliance.[39] Their fidelity, to be sure, was based on self-interest, for they were shrewd enough to perceive that Mithradates's power would not be lasting, and they had no desire to incur Rome's enmity. Their defiance angered the King, and he determined to subdue them by force. After building additional ships for the purpose, he launched an attack on the island in the autumn of 88.[40] The Rhodians were aided by troops sent by Telmessus on the mainland and by some Lycian soldiers, but they had fewer ships than their opponents. Nevertheless, they had a long tradition of sea-warfare behind them and surpassed the King's forces both in knowledge of naval tactics and in the training of their crews. Their navy therefore ventured to put out boldly against the enemy. The Rhodian commander, however, afraid of being surrounded by superior numbers, refused to give battle and soon withdrew slowly to port, barring the entrance to the harbour. This withdrawal enabled the King to land his available troops on the island and begin a siege of the city. Needing a larger force, he sent to Caria for additional soldiers. But while these were on their way, the Rhodians, whose admiral meanwhile in a series of minor engagements had done no small damage to the Pontic navy, fell upon the transports, scattered by a sudden storm, and captured or sank a large number.

Nevertheless, the King planned a joint attack by both land and sea. The premature advance of his land-forces, however, enabled the Rhodians to man their walls and repel the assault. His fleet was equally unsuccessful, for a huge mechanism, a sort of drawbridge, by which he expected to land troops on the top of the ramparts, fell of its own weight, with the result that this attack also was a complete failure. Then Mithradates, discouraged by his double defeat and fearing the

[n] Justin xxxviii 3, 9.

approach of winter, abandoned his attempt to take Rhodes and withdrew to the mainland. Here he laid siege to the city of Patara on the southern coast of Lycia, but soon, abandoning this project also, he returned to the province of Asia.°

Despite his failure at Rhodes, Mithradates, in the course of one campaigning season, seemed to have accomplished an almost impossible feat. It must be taken into consideration, however, that his success was due in part to political conditions in Rome, which prevented the adoption of any serious measures against him. On receipt of the news of the invasion of Asia, his former adversary, Lucius Sulla, now Consul, was entrusted by the Senate with the command of the province and the task of repelling the invader. Sulla's political opponents, however, forced a bill through the Plebeian Assembly taking this post from him and conferring it on the old general, Gaius Marius, who coveted the further distinction of a victory over Rome's latest foe. With this arrangement Sulla refused to comply. Entering Rome with an army, he drove out his political enemies, abrogated their laws and assumed the command assigned him by the Senate. These violent measures and the legislation necessary for the re-establishment, although for a brief period, of the power of the aristocratic faction, occupied the remainder of the year. It was, therefore, not until early in 87 that Sulla, despite an attempt made by the new Consul, Lucius Cornelius Cinna, to prevent his departure, set sail across the Adriatic with five legions (25,000-30,000 men), a tiny force in comparison with that of the enemy. By this time a Pontic army was in Greece, and the war begun in Asia was to be ended in Europe.

Mithradates, like Antiochus III, not content with an Asianic empire and apparently carried away by a lust for conquest and power, had resolved to annex the Balkan Peninsula to his rule, and in the autumn of 88 he sent two armies across the Aegean.[41] One of these, under the joint command of one of his sons and his general Taxiles, invaded Thrace and Macedonia; the other, led by Archelaus, crossed over to Greece. Stopping on his way at the island of Delos, Archelaus caused the Italian settlers who had taken control of the island to be massacred and in the name of his master seized both Delos and the sacred treasure of Apollo. In order to ensure the support of the Athenians he presented them with the treasure, sending on also an adventurer named Aristion, formerly an Epicurean philosopher, who with the aid of a

° Appian *Mith.* 27.

Pontic force established himself as tyrant of the city, ruling in the interest of Mithradates.[42]

It was not long before most of Greece fell into the hands of Mithradates's leaders. Athens was completely controlled by his creature, Aristion. In the north, the Thessalian coast, Euboea and Boeotia were seized by his generals, and the larger part of the Peloponnese likewise submitted to the invaders. In vain did Quintus Braetius Sura,[p] the brave legate of the Roman governor of Macedonia, with the few troops at his command, attempt to oppose the Pontic forces advancing into Boeotia. Although he engaged Archelaus and Aristion and drove them back into Attica, when reinforcements arrived to help them, he was unable to hold out against superior numbers and so was compelled to retreat.

Thus Sulla, on landing in Epirus with his five legions in the spring of 87, found the larger part of Greece in the hands of Mithradates's generals. Not only was his army much smaller than that of the King but he had no fleet with which to dispute the enemy's control of the sea. Advancing boldly, however, he defeated Archelaus and Aristion and forced them back to Athens. The cities and states of northern Greece, believing that they had more to fear from the Romans than to hope for from the Pontic "deliverers," submitted, one after another, to Sulla.[43] The Roman general then laid siege to Athens as the centre of Mithradates's power in Greece. The King's fleet, however, was master of the sea and brought not only reinforcements but also supplies from Macedonia, and Archelaus, who held the Piraeus, was able to convey food to the beleaguered city. All through the autumn and winter the siege dragged on, but both the supplies and the courage of the Athenians waned, and on the first of March, 86, Sulla succeeded in capturing the city by storm. It was given over to the Roman soldiers to pillage, but its ancient liberty and its possessions were restored. Soon afterward, the Piraeus also was forced to surrender and was thereupon destroyed; Archelaus, however, succeeded in making his escape.

In the autumn of 86 the war in Greece was finished and the issue decided. The army which Mithradates had sent into Thrace was successful both there and in Macedonia, but its march southward was too leisurely to save Athens for the King. In the course of this march, Mithradates's son, its leader, fell ill and died, and Taxiles resigned the command to Archelaus, who had gone northward to meet him. The Pontic army is said to have numbered as many as 60,000 men, while

---

[p] For his name see *I.G.* IX 2, 613.

Sulla had a force of only 15,000 foot and 1,500 horse.[44] Archelaus, how-ever, though his military skill had sufficed to defeat Nicomedes, proved to be no match for the Roman leader. When, in the spring of 86, the two armies met near Chaeroneia in western Boeotia, although his superiority in strategy made it possible for him to force Sulla to meet him on ground chosen by himself, the story of Magnesia was repeated. Once more a vast and motley host of Asiatics was unable to cope with a Roman army that was smaller by far, and once more the superior discipline of the legions and their loyalty to their commander, com-bined with the tactical skill of the commander himself as well as of his subordinates, won the day for Rome. The huge Pontic force was dispersed in total rout. Only 10,000 men, it is said, survived to take refuge, along with Archelaus, on the island of Euboea.

Mithradates, however, resolved to make one more attempt, sent a second army across the Aegean. Under the command of the King's "foster-brother" Dorylaus, it landed on the coast of Euboea, where it was joined by Archelaus and the remnant of his defeated force.[45] This army, however, shared the fate of its predecessor. Meeting Sulla and his troops near Orchomenus in Boeotia, it suffered a crushing defeat. The Pontic loss was estimated at 15,000, besides a great number of prisoners; Archelaus himself once more made his escape to Euboea.[q] This was the end of Sulla's fighting; for in the following winter, Mithradates, discouraged both by his defeat at Orchomenus and by the growing opposition in Asia, sent orders to Archelaus to begin ne-gotiations for peace.[46]

Sulla's victories in Greece had won the war for the Romans, but even before they were gained, he himself had been placed in a pre-carious position. Not only was he legally no longer commander of the Roman army, but he was even an outlaw, and a Roman force was actually marching against him. After his departure, his bitter enemy, the demagogue Lucius Cinna, Consul in 87, had by means of the utmost violence made himself master of Rome and caused the aged Marius to be recalled from exile. The return of the old leader with an army of desperadoes was followed by a reign of terror accompanied by a general massacre of his aristocratic opponents. Sulla himself was deprived of his command and declared an enemy of the Roman People; his house in the city was destroyed and his country-estates were plundered.[r]

q Appian *Mith.* 49: Licinianus p. 26 Flemisch.
r Plutarch *Sulla* 22, 1: Appian *Mith.* 51; *B.C.* 1 73.

Marius and Cinna, apparently without even the formality of an election, proclaimed themselves Consuls for the following year.

The next step taken by Sulla's opponents was the appointment of a successor to his command of the army in the East. A fortnight after his inauguration as Consul for the year 86, Marius died as the result of his excesses.[s] His successor, Lucius Valerius Flaccus, was soon invested with the command of the war against Mithradates and sent to Greece with the wholly inadequate force of two legions. It was evidently expected that he would succeed in adding Sulla's army to his own. As he was without either military talent or experience in war, a former comrade of Marius and Cinna both in arms and in massacre, Gaius Flavius Fimbria, was sent with him as legate.[t] About the time of the battle of Chaeroneia Flaccus and his troops landed in Epirus and began a march eastward, plundering the province of Macedonia as they proceeded on their way.[u] The presence of Dorylaus and the newly-arrived Pontic army prevented Sulla from an immediate advance against his rival, and it was not until after defeating the enemy at Orchomenus that he was able to turn his march northward. He made no attempt, however, to save Macedonia from rapine, nor did he attack Flaccus, evidently content for the present with the loyalty shown by his soldiers, who refused to recognize the authority of his opponent. In fact, instead of the expected desertion of Sulla's army, Flaccus's men began to abandon him. He, therefore, afraid to come to blows with superior numbers and a loyal force and also fearing further desertions, did not dare face Sulla but marched on rapidly through Thrace to the Bosporus. His intention, apparently, was to cross over into Asia and with his tiny force prosecute the war that had been committed to his charge. Sulla, content to let him bear the brunt of the struggle and himself awaiting the development of his negotiations with Mithradates, in the late autumn of 86 took up quarters in Thessaly, where he remained during the winter.[47]

Meanwhile in Asia Minor, Mithradates, after his withdrawal from Patara, had begun to lay aside the role of "deliverer" and to show himself in his true character of Oriental despot. However great his ability in organizing a campaign and carrying out an invasion, he was lacking in the qualities necessary to the ruler of cities accustomed to a certain measure of freedom, and he soon began to lord it over the

[s] Livy *Per.* LXXX: Plutarch *Marius* 45f.

[t] Livy *Per.* LXXXII: Orosius VI 2, 9: Cassius Dio frg. 104, 1 Boiss. Strabo (XIII p. 594) incorrectly calls him quaestor.

[u] Diodorus XXXVIII 8.

Greeks of the coast districts as though they belonged to his kingdom of Pontus. Taking up his abode at Pergamum, he established himself as monarch, keeping the populace content with doles of food and distributing wealth and offices to his favourites.[48] Not satisfied with having appointed "satraps" to rule the country-districts, he established royal governors over many of the cities also. Thus Ephesus was placed under the command of Philopoemen of Stratoniceia,[v] the father of the King's newest wife, Monime; and "tyrants," that is, governors with unlimited powers, were established in Tralles and in Colophon.[w] The cities indeed sought to win Mithradates's favour by monuments and compliments. At Pergamum the community set up a statue of Victory in his honour,[x] and at Miletus he was appointed to the office of stephanephorus, the greatest mark of respect that the city could bestow.[49] Despite these attentions, however, there was undoubtedly an undercurrent of discontent, and it may be assumed that in many a city the Romans had their secret adherents. After a year's experience of the methods of their self-styled "deliverer" some of those who had welcomed him began to realize that they had gained nothing by preferring his rule to that of Rome. The King, in fact, had already begun to take repressive measures. His first victims were Galatians. Some time previously, he had summoned to Pergamum sixty of their nobles, including several "tetrarchs" of the nation, who, though they were brought in the guise of "friends," were probably hostages.[y] Believing—perhaps correctly—that a member of the group was planning to assassinate him, he caused them all save one to be slain. This act of violence was followed in Galatia itself by a massacre of those princes who had not submitted, together with their wives and children; only three of the princes succeeded in making their escape. He then confiscated the property of all who had been slain, and also took measures to ensure the submission of the nation by sending one of his generals, Eumachus, to act as its governor.

During the summer of 86, after the capture of Athens and especially after the news of Sulla's victory at Chaeroneia, the disaffection in Asia began to take on a more open form.[50] It became still more evident after the conscription of the new army which was sent to Greece under Dorylaus. The growing opposition aroused the anger of the King, and he resolved to take sterner measures toward those whose fidelity seemed doubtful.

---

[v] Appian *Mith.* 48.
[x] Plutarch *Sulla* 11, 1.

[w] Strabo xiv p. 649: Plutarch *Luc.* 3, 3.
[y] Plutarch *Mul. Virt.* 23: Appian *Mith.* 46.

Among the communities which Mithradates suspected was Chios. It had aided him in his attack on Rhodes,[z] but many of its inhabitants had favoured the cause of Rome. Although these had long since fled to Sulla, they had left possessions on the island, and Mithradates, not unwilling to enrich himself at their expense, confiscated the property of these refugees as well as of all the resident Romans.[51] He then ordered Zenobius, an officer who was on his way to Greece, to seize the fortifications of the city of Chios and, this done, to bid the townsfolk surrender their arms and deliver up the children of the foremost citizens as hostages. The Chians, seeing their town in the hands of the enemy's troops, complied perforce with the command. Then Zenobius appeared before the townsfolk once more. This time he demanded in the name of the King the sum of 2,000 talents as a fine for their alleged disloyalty. Again, they were obliged to submit, and the money was collected from all possible sources, even including the offerings in the temples. Zenobius, however, accused the citizens of giving him short weight, and thereupon ordered them all to be thrown on shipboard and deported under guards chosen from among their own slaves. It was his intention to send them to the King's possessions in Colchis and to replace them by colonists from Pontus. They proceeded on their melancholy voyage as far as the free city of Heracleia, which had not fallen under Mithradates's power. Here they were rescued by the city's navy and cared for by the friendly citizens until, after the end of the war, they were brought back again to their homes.

From Chios Zenobius and his soldiers went to Ephesus, where the magistrates, evidently alarmed by the fate of the Chians, bade him leave his troops outside the gates and enter with only a few attendants.[a] Trusting to the supposedly submissive spirit of the Ephesians, he complied, but after a conference with the royal governor Philopoemen, he summoned the citizens to an assembly. They, however, expecting some demand like that made at Chios, resolved to anticipate the measure. Accordingly, seizing Zenobius, they put him to death. Having thus committed themselves, once and for all, to a revolt against Mithradates, they began preparations for defence, arming the populace, manning the walls and in general making ready for a siege. Without great regard for the truth, they passed a formal decree, declaring that they, like neighbouring cities, had submitted to Mithradates only because they were terror-stricken by the size of the King's army and the suddenness of his invasion; now, however, desirous of maintaining their an-

---

[z] Appian *Mith*. 25 and 46.   [a] Appian *Mith*. 48.

cient friendship for Rome and finding an opportunity to aid the common cause, they were declaring war on Mithradates in behalf of Roman rule and the common freedom.[b] To the end that the city and the sanctuary of Artemis might be successfully defended, all those who by reason of indebtedness to the Goddess or to the city had been deprived of citizenship or imprisoned were now restored to their former status; likewise those against whom judgements had been rendered because of their debts were released from their obligations. The decree also promised full citizenship to all resident aliens, freedmen and strangers who took up arms, and freedom and the status of resident aliens to all the city's slaves who did likewise. The seriousness and energy of the measures thus adopted go far to atone for the mendacity of the preamble and show that even a submissive Asianic city could resist when driven to the wall.

Encouraged by the example of Ephesus, other communities also began to rid themselves of the liberator now turned tyrant.[52] During the autumn of 86 the neighbouring cities, Hypaepa, Metropolis and Colophon, and even the more distant Tralles, Smyrna and Sardis, as well as other places, also revolted against the King and expelled his garrisons. Mithradates, now thoroughly aroused, proceeded with an armed force against the rebellious communities. On those which he succeeded in capturing he inflicted terrible punishments. He then resorted to a desperate expedient. All the Greek cities which had not revolted he restored to their previous status of freedom and autonomy; he added, however, the provision that all debts should be cancelled and all slaves set free. This dubious step did, indeed, win him, as he had purposed, the support of a considerable element of the population, but it also won him the hatred of the richer citizens and the owners of slaves. Perhaps even before the revolt of the cities, plots were being made against him. Four prominent citizens of Smyrna and Mitylene, all of them on terms of intimacy with the King, formed a conspiracy for his assassination. It was only because one of them turned traitor that their plot was detected and they themselves arrested and punished. At Pergamum a wide-spread plot, formed by eighty conspirators, just failed of its purpose. His suspicious cruelty now thoroughly aroused, Mithradates sent out spies far and wide, and all who were accused of designs against him were put to death. A reign of terror began, and, if we may believe our sources, as many as 1,600 persons were slain.

The King had, indeed, cause for alarm. The province which he had

[b] Syll.³ 742 with corrections in A.J.P. LX (1939), p. 468f.

regarded as conquered was in a general ferment. In the West the army which he had sent to Greece under Dorylaus had been completely defeated, and in the East the Galatians under the leadership of the princes who had escaped the slaughter had risen in revolt and expelled their "satrap" and his garrison.[c] Moreover, there was now a Roman army in Asia.

Early in the winter of 86-85, as has been previously related, Flaccus and Fimbria, after marching through Thrace, arrived at the Bosporus.[d] Here the soldiers, whose hatred for their incompetent commander had been stimulated by his unscrupulous subordinate, broke out into open mutiny.[53] The ill-feeling between the two leaders had come to a head in a violent quarrel, with the result that Flaccus deprived Fimbria of his post. The sympathies of the soldiers, however, were wholly with the deposed legate. Aroused by a speech which he made while the general was absent at Chalcedon, on the Asiatic side of the Strait, they drove Flaccus's deputy out of the camp and placed Fimbria in command. Under the leadership of the traitorous legate they attacked Flaccus on his return and, forcing him back across the Bosporus, pursued him to Nicomedeia in Bithynia. Here he was found in hiding, but Fimbria was prepared to show no mercy. Throwing aside all decency and with a brutality equal to that which he had previously shown in the massacres at Rome, he fell upon his commander and put him to death. Flaccus's head was cast into the harbour and his body left unburied. Fimbria then began a campaign against Mithradates, disregarding completely the fact that the King, through Archelaus, had already begun negotiations with Sulla.

About the same time Mithradates was assailed by a new danger. During the siege of Athens the quaestor Lucius Licinius Lucullus had been sent out by Sulla to assemble a fleet, which was urgently needed to overcome the King's superiority on the sea.[e] After a long delay and many adventures, including an attack by pirates, Lucullus succeeded in obtaining some ships from the cities on the coasts of Syria and Pamphylia. Learning, however, that a hostile fleet was waiting to intercept him, he put into Cyprus, as though intending to winter there. Having by this manoeuvre eluded the enemy, he sailed on to Rhodes, where the friendly citizens gave him additional vessels. With these and others, which the cities of Cos and Cnidus, now ready to revolt against Mithradates, placed at his disposal, he set forth early in

[c] Appian *Mith.* 46.   [d] See above p. 222.
[e] Plutarch *Luc.* 2, 2f.; 3, 2f.: Appian *Mith.* 33 and 56.

85 to sail northward along the coast of Asia. He aided the people of Colophon to expel the "tyrant" whom Mithradates had placed in command, and, landing at Chios, he drove out the royal troops which had been stationed in the city. But for his refusal to co-operate with Fimbria, he might have succeeded in capturing Mithradates himself, who by this time had been forced to leave Pergamum and withdraw to the coast.

Fimbria, meanwhile, after declaring himself commander of the Roman army, had advanced through Bithynia after allowing his soldiers to plunder the city of Nicomedeia.[54] He terrorized the population and at the same time curried favour with his soldiers by encouraging them to pillage both the cities and the rural districts. The King, in an attempt to oppose him, sent his son, also named Mithradates, attended by Taxiles and other generals, to bar the invaders' way. The young man was at first successful, but in an ill-advised cavalry attack on the Romans while encamped near the river Rhyndacus, he was badly defeated and after losing 6,000 men was forced to fall back. He retired west of the Rhyndacus, but here he was overtaken by Fimbria, his camp stormed during the night, and his army annihilated. He himself barely escaped to join his father at Pergamum.

The destruction of this, his last, army left Mithradates completely crushed. Already shaken by plots against his life and by the defection or the capture of many of the cities he had conquered, he was now reduced to despair. When Fimbria, after entering Cyzicus as a friend and then showing his characteristic brutality to the citizens, began a rapid march southward through Mysia, the King was stricken with terror. Having now no army with which to defend himself, he decided to abandon Pergamum and take refuge at Pitane, on the coast near the mouth of the Caïcus, where his fleet at least could protect him. His spirit was at last broken and his only hope was to save himself and his ships.

Fimbria, meanwhile, advanced through Mysia, plundering the country as he came. He appears to have regarded himself as a conqueror and to have believed that he had won the war. When he arrived before Pergamum, the city, now undefended, opened its gates in surrender. Hurrying on to Pitane, he began to invest the place. Having no ships, however, he could conduct the siege from the landward side alone, so that it was still possible for Mithradates to escape by sea. In this emergency Fimbria called on Lucullus to act in conjunction with him and blockade the coast, hoping that by acting together they could capture the King. In this proposal, however, Lucullus refused to co-operate. It is possible, as was suggested by his biographer, Plutarch, that the reason for his refusal was a sense of loyalty to Sulla, but it seems more probable that he had received orders from his commander to refrain from action. Sulla, perhaps not unnaturally, wished to deal with the enemy himself and to prevent his rival from reaping the glory of capturing the King. Perhaps, too, the negotiations already opened with Mithradates made Sulla hesitate to make a hostile move. On the other hand, it is also possible that Lucullus did not dare to face the Pontic fleet, knowing that it would do its utmost to thwart any attack upon Mithradates himself. In any case, he took no steps to aid Fimbria in closing the net. Accordingly, Mithradates was able to make his escape and sailed over to the island of Lesbos. Here he found refuge in Mitylene, which, by its surrender of Aquilius, was irrevocably bound to his cause.

Thus forced to let the enemy slip through his fingers, Fimbria marched through the northwestern part of the province, punishing all who had supported Mithradates and plundering the territories of those cities which refused to open their gates. Among those which would not admit him was Ilium. When he began a siege, the citizens, unable to resist him unaided, sent envoys to Sulla, asking for assistance. This was promised, but before it arrived, Fimbria, after a mocking allusion to the long-claimed kinship of the city with Rome, persuaded the townsfolk to admit him. Once inside, he ordered a general slaughter, and those who had served as the envoys to Sulla were tortured in various ways. He then set fire, not only to Ilium itself, but also to the ancient temple of Athena Ilias, the inviolability of which Rome had long acknowledged. With this act of sacrilege Fimbria's name was ever afterward connected.

Lucullus, after his rejection of Fimbria's proposal, proceeded northward to join Sulla. He had received orders to meet the General at the Hellespont, for the negotiations for peace that had been carried on with Mithradates had at last reached a successful conclusion, and Sulla and his army were about to cross the Strait to receive the monarch's formal surrender.[f] Lucullus's voyage, however, was not accomplished without opposition. Near the promontory of Lectum, at the southwestern corner of the Troad, he was attacked by some royal ships.[g] After driving these away, he fell in with a stronger fleet off the island of Tenedos. This, too, he defeated, thanks in part to the skill of the same Rhodian

[f] Plutarch *Luc.* 4, 1: Appian *Mith.* 56. [g] Plutarch *Luc.* 3, 8f.

commander who had previously won distinction by destroying the Pontic transports while on their way to the island.[h]

When Lucullus arrived at his destination, all was prepared for the final act of the drama; for after long negotiation the terms had been at last formulated by Archelaus and Sulla. During the late autumn of 86 apparently, the two men had met on the coast of Boeotia, and here the opening discussion took place.[55] At first, Archelaus proposed that Sulla should abandon Asia and content himself with the ships, the troops and the money with which Mithradates was ready to provide him for a war against his enemies in Rome. Sulla, on his side, offered Archelaus the kingdom of Mithradates and an alliance with Rome if he would surrender the royal fleet. This proposal and counter-proposal were obviously only the preliminaries to a real discussion of terms. In any case, both were rejected with scorn. Then, perhaps during the winter in the course of his advance northward into Thessaly, Sulla named the actual conditions on which he would consent to make peace:[56] Mithradates must resign all his conquests, Asia, the Aegean Islands, Paphlagonia and Galatia, and restore Nicomedes and Ariobarzanes to their respective thrones; he must pay the Romans an indemnity of 2,000 talents and surrender seventy of his warships with their crews and equipment; he must deliver up all prisoners and deserters and restore to their homes all whom he had caused to be deported; in return, he was to be recognized as King of Pontus and ally of Rome and the cities which had submitted to him were not to be punished for their defection. To Archelaus himself Sulla promised the coveted title of Friend and Ally of Rome; he also gave him a large estate on the island of Euboea.

These terms offered to Mithradates, Sulla marched onward into the borderland of Macedonia and Thrace. From here, in the spring of 85, he sent part of his army under a legate to chastise the neighbouring tribes, which had taken advantage of the war to raid Roman territory; thus he passed the interval which elapsed before the messengers sent to Mithradates could return.[i] Meanwhile, with the approach of Fimbria on land and of Lucullus on the sea, the King's position had grown increasingly precarious. Nevertheless, in true Oriental fashion, he was disposed to haggle and replied that he would not relinquish Paphlagonia or surrender his fleet.[j] At this Sulla threatened to invade Asia

---

[h] See note 40.

[i] Appian *Mith.* 55: Licinianus p. 27 Flemisch: Livy *Per.* LXXXIII: Eutropius v 7, 1: *Liber de Vir. Ill.* 75, 7. See also note 57.

[j] Plutarch *Sulla* 23, 3: Appian *Mith.* 56.

with his army. Finally, however, he consented to allow Archelaus to go in person to the King, on a guarantee that he would persuade his master to accept the offered terms. Meanwhile, advancing in person into the territory of the Macedonian raiders, he received their formal submission.[57] Mithradates during the interval had fled from Pergamum to Pitane and was ready to accept almost any conditions. Archelaus, therefore, was able to return to Macedonia with the announcement that his master would consent to surrender. The King's only stipulation was that Sulla should meet him in person. Sulla, not unwilling to dictate his terms on the soil of the province which Mithradates had come to liberate, crossed the Hellespont, using Lucullus's fleet for the purpose. Then Mithradates, leaving his refuge in Mitylene, advanced to the city of Dardanus, not far from the ravaged Ilium.[58] Here, in the early autumn of 85, the Roman general and the King of Pontus met. As Sulla in his Memoirs described the interview, Mithradates, on the presentation of the terms, maintained a sullen silence. When rebuked for this by the victor, he attempted to justify himself, putting the blame for the war partly on Fate and partly on the Romans. Again Sulla rebuked him, this time for endeavouring, like a rhetorician, to use specious words as a cloak for deeds that were unlawful and evil. He then asked the King again whether he would accept the terms, and at last Mithradates, no longer able to counter Roman directness with Oriental evasion, was forced to reply that he would. The two opponents then went through the form of an embrace, and also Nicomedes and Ariobarzanes performed similar acts of histrionic reconciliation with their enemy. The royal fleet of seventy ships was handed over to the victor and Mithradates at once set sail for Pontus, forced to be content with the territory he held when he began his reign.

It must have been apparent to Sulla that, as in Cappadocia seven years previously, his work was only half accomplished; the snake to which the Roman historian compared Mithradates had been scotched, not killed. Even the soldiers murmured because the king who had massacred their fellow-countrymen had been allowed to depart unharmed. But Sulla's position was a difficult one, depending, as it did, solely on the personal loyalty of his troops. He himself was legally an outlaw, and a Roman force, as hostile to him as to the Pontic monarch, was still in Asia. Though the peace might prove to be of short duration, it was necessary to conclude it as soon as possible, in order that he might be free to return to Rome and overcome his enemies, and thus not merely legalize his position but even safeguard his life. So indifferent was he to the permanence of the treaty that he seems never to have taken the steps necessary to secure its ratification by the Senate and its formal acceptance by the Assembly of the People.[k] Even before he landed in Italy in the spring of 83, his successor in Asia attempted to justify an invasion of Pontus on the ground that no written treaty was in existence,[l] and four years later the formalities had not been carried out.[m]

Despite the superficial character of the victory, the last great anti-Roman and nationalistic movement in Asia Minor was a total failure. Never again, while the province was under Roman rule, was a serious attempt made by the inhabitants to oust the foreigner and conserve Asia for the Asiatics. The provincials had found that a native monarch might be more tyrannous even than the foreigner and that, moreover, he could not fulfil his promise of deliverance. Twelve years later, when Mithradates next entered the province of Asia, he met with a stubborn resistance from the first city he approached.

[k] For this procedure see Täubler *Imp. Rom.* 1 p. 99f.
[l] See below p. 243.   [m] See below p. 321.

CHAPTER X

RECONSTRUCTION AND EXPLOITATION

ALTHOUGH Mithradates had departed for his ancestral kingdom of Pontus, having lost all his recent conquests, there still remained an enemy for Sulla to face before he could begin the reconstruction of the prostrate province. Fimbria, having failed in his plan for entrapping the King in Pitane and having seen the glory of the victory taken from him by his rival, had withdrawn from the coast and established himself at Thyateira. He was evidently intending to retreat along the road that led northward and to make his way back to the Bosporus through the kingdom of Bithynia. Though his invasion of Mysia had contributed not a little to Sulla's victory, since it had made Mithradates more ready to agree to the terms proposed, he could expect no mercy from his victorious rival. In fact, after the conference at Dardanus, Sulla, with the troops he had brought with him, advancing to Thyateira, appeared before Fimbria's camp and called on him to surrender.[1]

The situation was unusual, for the status of neither leader was legal. The one was an outlaw and the other had secured his command by murdering his superior officer. Sulla, however, had the confidence and the loyalty of his troops, and Fimbria had not. On his refusal to surrender, his camp was closely invested by Sulla, and his men began to desert and even to help in the work of investment. His appeals to his soldiers to resist their fellow-Romans and to take an oath of allegiance to himself were rejected, and the desertions continued. In his despair he even made an attempt to assassinate Sulla, but the slave whom he sent for the purpose was seized and tortured into making a confession. Fimbria then asked for a personal interview with his opponent, but this Sulla naturally enough refused to grant; he did, however, send a representative, the aged Rutilius Rufus, who had come forth from his retreat at Smyrna when the Roman army arrived in Asia. Rufus offered Fimbria terms that were not ungenerous; namely, his life and a safe-conduct to the coast, but on condition that he would at once leave Asia, of which, Sulla asserted, he himself was lawfully in command. To these terms Fimbria agreed. Realizing, however, that he could expect no mercy from his own government, whose regularly appointed commander he had murdered, he proceeded on his way to the coast only as far as Pergamum. Here, in the Temple of Asclepius, he fell upon his sword. His soldiers, who had surrendered and received a pledge of safety, were added to Sulla's army. When the General left for Italy in the following spring he ordered them to remain in Asia.

Sulla's next step was to restore to their kingdoms the two monarchs whom Mithradates had expelled. This was done with every formality. His subordinate, Gaius Scribonius Curio, who had won distinction by forcing the surrender of the Athenian Acropolis, was charged with the task of escorting both Nicomedes and Ariobarzanes to their dominions and establishing them once more upon their thrones.[2] With a fine regard for the proprieties, Sulla described all these achievements in a formal report addressed to the Senate, ignoring the fact that he had been outlawed and deprived of his command.[a]

Sulla was then free to turn his attention to the much-needed reconstruction of the province. Its position was altogether different from that of 129, for it was now conquered territory. The status of the free cities, in particular, which had been allies of Rome had greatly changed, for they had forfeited their position of independence. By receiving the enemy in violation of their treaties they had *ipso facto* cancelled those treaties and, from Rome's point of view, were no longer in possession of any of their former rights.[b] They were, therefore, completely at the mercy of the victor, and whatever rights and privileges they might now receive were granted by his grace.

There was one free state, to be sure, whose position needed no formal confirmation, namely Rhodes. The island-Republic had resisted the common enemy and had loyally fulfilled all the terms of its treaty with Rome. Its status, therefore, remained unchanged, and it was rewarded by an extension of its dominions, a grant which was probably obtained by a special envoy sent to Sulla[c] and later confirmed by the Senate as the result of an oration delivered by the famous rhetorician, Apollonius Molo.[3] By this grant the Rhodians acquired not only some of the neighbouring islands, but also, on the mainland, the city of Caunus (which by the massacre of the resident Romans in 88 had forfeited all its rights) and perhaps further territory in Caria which had been given to them by Rome in 188 and taken away 22 years later.[d]

In the northern part of the province, which seems to have remained untouched by the invasion of Mithradates, the cities had not sur-

[a] Appian *Mith*. 60.
[b] See Mommsen *R.St.R.* III p. 1204f.
[c] *I.G.* XII 1, 48 = *Syll.*[3] 745 = Dessau 8772.
[d] See Chap. IV note 68.

rendered to the enemy; it may therefore be supposed that their previous status remained unaltered. Cyzicus, indeed, had suffered cruelly from the depredations of Fimbria,[e] but there was all the more reason why it should be permitted to retain its freedom—a privilege which it amply justified ten years later by its gallant resistance to the Pontic King.[4] In the Troad, Ilium had likewise experienced great cruelty at the hands of Fimbria,[f] who had set fire both to the city and to the Temple of Athena; in compensation Sulla confirmed all the city's privileges, and the sentimental "kinship" with Rome impelled him to restore much of what had been so wantonly destroyed.[g] Lampsacus, which seems to have escaped the invaders, both Pontic and Roman, evidently retained its freedom, as did likewise the other cities that shared in the common worship of Athena Ilias—Dardanus, Scepsis, Assus, Alexandria Troas and Abydus.[5]

In contrast to these cities, which, by reason of their situation, had not been compelled to submit to the King, those of Ionia and Lydia had borne the full brunt of his invasion. Chios, it will be remembered, had been forced by the treachery of Zenobius to surrender,[h] but so cruel was the fate that the citizens had suffered at this man's hands that Sulla was disposed to be merciful, and the city's full independence was restored by a decree of the Senate.[6] Smyrna also had submitted, but the citizens seem to have refrained from massacring the Romans and finally to have gathered sufficient courage to expel the King's garrison and bar the gates of their city.[7] They afterward boasted before the Senate that during the winter which Sulla spent in Asia they had even stripped off their own clothing in order to give it to the Roman soldiers. The neighbouring stronghold of Magnesia-near-Sipylus, on the other hand, which had stoutly resisted Mithradates's general, Archelaus,[i] though previously not a free city, was now rewarded by the recognition of its independence.[j]

In Caria, Cnidus and Cos had been forced to surrender, but the citizens of the latter had been successful in protecting the Romans against the general massacre ordered by Mithradates.[k] In the winter of 86-85 both cities had furnished Lucullus with ships for his naval campaign,[l] but only Cos seems to have been restored by Sulla to its status of independence.[8] In the interior, Tabae and Stratoniceia had remained

e See above p. 227.   f See above p. 228.

g Strabo XIII p. 594: Appian *Mith.* 61: Orosius VI 2, 11.

h See above p. 224.   i See above p. 215.

j Strabo XIII p. 621: Appian *Mith.* 61.   k See above pp. 215 and 217.

l See above p. 226.

faithful; the latter, it is true, had finally surrendered, but only after a protracted siege.[m] Both were now rewarded for their fidelity or their sufferings by the grant of "freedom and autonomy" and were declared friends and allies of Rome.[9] The status thus conferred on Tabae and Stratoniceia was duly confirmed by senatorial decrees passed in 82-80, when Sulla was dictator. That which ratified the grant to Stratoniceia was issued in response to the city's envoys who had come to Rome to bring a golden wreath and to make sacrifice for the success of the Roman People. The document confirmed the previously existing autonomy of the city and its alliance with Rome, together with the validity of the measures it had passed concerning the war against Mithradates; it confirmed also the possession of those places in Caria, including the port of Ceramus, together with the revenues accruing therefrom, which Sulla had promised to the city, as well as the restoration of all that had been lost as a result of the war; finally, it guaranteed the inviolability of the sanctuary of Hecate at Lagina in the territory of Stratoniceia. Not only were the city's rights and privileges confirmed but its territory and income were greatly increased.

While these, and probably other, cities thus recovered their freedom and autonomy or, as the senatorial decree for Stratoniceia expressed it, the right to "use their own laws and customs" and were recognized as "friends and allies" of Rome, their position was in fact not wholly that which it had been in the second century; for the grant of their present status came to be regarded not as the restoration of an inherent right but as an act of grace on the part of Rome. Like any other Roman commander, Sulla could bestow "freedom and autonomy" on any city, but this grant would last only for the duration of his command and was revocable by any successor of equal power. It was a promise which became valid permanently only if confirmed by a decree of the Senate, and such a confirmation was, in fact, the usual means of recognizing autonomy. The Senate's recognition of this status was valid as long as the decree remained in effect, but in the case of those cities whose freedom and autonomy were further guaranteed by a formal treaty of alliance accompanied by an oath in the name of the Roman People these rights were regarded as having an enduring validity, to be terminated only by a breach on the part of one of the contracting parties.[n] As time went on, however, the view that in many cases the freedom of a city was based merely on sufferance seemed

---

[m] See above p. 215. [n] See above p. 115f.

to make it possible arbitrarily to annul that freedom, and even, on occasion, a trifling pretext might be used to void a formal treaty.

In addition to the cities which were received into friendship and alliance with Rome, individuals also—apparently citizens of subject cities—to whom the Senate wished to show especial favour were honoured with the title of "Friend of Rome."[o] Thus at the beginning of the first century, together with the communities which erected statues of the younger Scaevola and various provincials of distinction, there appear "those who have individually been approved in friendship with the Romans."[p] The privileges enjoyed by these "Friends" are specified definitely in a senatorial decree of 78 B.C. enrolling in this category three ship-captains who had served with distinction in "the Italian War" (presumably in that against the Italian Allies), citizens, respectively, of Miletus and Clazomenae in Asia and Carystus on the island of Euboea.[10] By this decree the three men and their descendants were declared exempt not only from the taxes and other burdens imposed by their native cities, but also from contributions demanded by Rome and from all the taxes collected by the *publicani*. Law-suits, moreover, in which they and their descendants appeared either as plaintiffs or as defendants might be conducted at their option either in their native places according to their own laws, or before a Roman magistrate and "Italian" jurors, or, finally, in a free city "which remained in friendship with the Roman People." Thus a position was granted these men which was somewhat analogous to that of an allied state, and a class of highly-privileged provincials was established, whose existence, as their numbers grew, was evidently resented by their less fortunate fellow-citizens, on whom the municipal burdens fell more heavily.

As was to be expected, every effort was made by the cities to obtain forgiveness for siding with the enemy and reinstatement as friends and allies of Rome, and when the Senate, after Sulla's return, took up the question of their status, many sent representatives to present their pleas. Thus Xenocles of Adramyttium, one of the foremost orators of the day, defended "Asia" against the charge of "Mithradatism."[11] There is no reason, however, to suppose that the arrangements made by Sulla as commander in the field were not confirmed by the Senators. Those cities which had received the enemy and especially those which at his command had massacred the resident Italians[q] were deprived of their independence. No longer allies of Rome, they were henceforth

[o] See Chap. IV note 76.   [p] See Chap. VII note 48.   [q] See above p. 217.

236

subject and liable to the payment of the regular taxes collected by the *publicani*. Ephesus was not saved by its tardy defiance of Mithradates and its assertion that it was declaring war on him for the sake of the Romans.[12] Pergamum, guilty not only of the massacre but also of conferring honours on the King, and Adramyttium, where even those Italians who had fled into the sea were slain, were likewise punished; the fate of Tralles and of Colophon, which had been ruled by "tyrants" placed in command by Mithradates but, after his power began to wane, had expelled his garrisons and barred their gates,[13] is doubtful. Miletus, on the other hand, which had honoured the King, as well as Clazomenae and probably Phocaea, lost its status of freedom.[14]

The cities were, of course, wholly unable to resist in any way the decisions of Sulla, supported, as he was, by an army. The citizens of Mitylene alone, knowing that after their betrayal of Aquilius they could expect no mercy, refused to surrender.[r] The others opened their gates, and, if we may trust the highly-coloured narrative of an ancient historian, they were made to rue the day on which they had received the King of Pontus and obeyed his command to massacre the Italian settlers.[s] Many cities were plundered and the walls of some were razed to the ground. Citizens who had supported Mithradates were condemned to death or sold into slavery. In an attempt to restore the economic condition that prevailed in the pre-war period, Sulla issued a proclamation that all the slaves who had been set free by the general order of Mithradates[t] should at once return to their owners. This measure was also designed to win the support of the wealthier classes. Not unnaturally, it resulted in further disorders, since many of the slaves refused to obey, and rioting ensued, in which both free men and slaves in great numbers lost their lives.

The misery of the helpless cities was greatly increased by the billeting of the Roman army for the winter of 85-84; for not only was each householder compelled to furnish his unwelcome guest with meals for himself and as many of his friends as he desired to invite, but also to give him a sum of money in addition, sixteen drachmae per day for a soldier and fifty for a military tribune, besides two sets of clothing, one for use in the house and one for out-of-doors.[15] Meanwhile Sulla established himself at Ephesus, and here, after trying and executing the principal supporters of the rebellion,[u] the Roman general announced their fate to the representatives of the cities. As a penalty for

---

[r] Livy *Per.* LXXXIX.　　　　[s] Appian *Mith.* 61.　　　　[t] See above p. 225.
[u] Appian *Mith.* 61: Licinianus p. 28 Flemisch.

its disloyalty the province was to pay a fine of 20,000 talents, which may have covered the arrears of taxes for the preceding five years as well as the costs of the war.[16] In the spring of 84, as soon as navigation permitted, Sulla sailed away to Greece. Here he remained during the winter and in the following spring left for Italy, to take vengeance on his opponents at home.

Cities which Sulla had favoured may have erected statues in his honour, as did Halicarnassus,[v] but the great majority of the provincials must have regarded him with a bitter hatred. Never, since the days of the Persians, had Asia Minor been treated so harshly. The amount of the fine that had been imposed was apportioned among the several cities, and for the purpose of facilitating the collection the province was divided into a number of districts.[17] All alike, subject cities as well as those which had formerly been free but had lost their rights, were required to contribute their shares, and from all of them immediate payment was demanded.[18]

Sulla, on his departure for Athens, assigned the duty of collecting and re-coining the money to his quaestor, Lucullus,[19] while the command of Lucullus's fleet was apparently transferred to the legate Aulus Terentius Varro.[20] Lucullus, we are told, fulfilled this unpleasant task with justice and the greatest consideration possible, and, in fact, both at Synnada and at Thyateira statues were erected to him as protector and benefactor of the city, and at Delos Greeks and Italians combined to honour him. He seems to have been ready to receive deputations sent to him by the cities; for he gave audience to envoys from the Rhodians, who came to ask for some favour, possibly the remission of that portion of the fine which had been assigned to some city in the territory granted to them by Sulla.

But however considerate Lucullus may have been in collecting the fine, the fact remains that the cities, exhausted by the depredations of Mithradates, and put to further and unbearable expense by the billeting of the Roman troops, were in no position to pay the amount demanded. In this predicament, therefore, their only recourse was to borrow the necessary money at any rate of interest whatever. The result, as will be shown, was financial ruin.[w]

While it is not improbable that the ancient writers may have exaggerated the evil plight of the province after the war, there is nevertheless sufficient evidence to show the serious depletion of many a municipal treasury. For some years no city except Ephesus seems to have

v Dessau 8771.   w See below p. 251f.

been able to mint silver coins.[21] At Pergamum the festival of Heracles could not be held because no one was in a position to underwrite the expense it involved, and at Miletus two of the festivals regularly celebrated at the Temple of Apollo at Didyma were suspended for several years.[22] At Priene no one was able to hold the costly office of stephanephorus, and all public banquets had to be given up and the association of the Young Men was temporarily dissolved.[23]

Even in the Troad, a region which had not been forced to submit to Mithradates, there was similar poverty. Seven of the cities which composed the Federation of the Troad[x] lacked the money necessary to defray their shares of the cost of their common festival.[24] They therefore applied to the Temple of Athena in Ilium, the common sanctuary of the Federation, for a loan to meet the emergency. The application was not unnatural, for the incomes of the temples, largely derived from land, were usually secure and their cash-reserves had always been an important source for loans. On the present occasion the temple-treasurers granted them the necessary sum at an interest-charge of 6 2/3 per cent, a rate which for this time of financial stringency was so low that it is evident that the cities were receiving a favour. Even this moderate charge, however, they were unable to meet, and in 77 B.C. they were compelled to ask not only for the cancellation of all arrears but also for a reduction of the interest-rate to 1 2/3 per cent for the ensuing ten years, with the agreement that after that interval they would once more pay the charge originally named in the contract.

To the economic miseries resulting from the ruinous war were added the attacks made on the coast cities by the pirates. As will be described in a later chapter,[y] these sea-robbers, whose headquarters were on the rocky coast of western Cilicia, had become the terror of the eastern Mediterranean. Mithradates had seen the value of an alliance with them, and they had aided him by falling upon Lucullus during his attempt to collect a fleet for Sulla and capturing or sinking some of his vessels.[z] With an eye to further services, Mithradates had aided them in fitting out their ships, with the result that, at the end of the war, they were organized in what amounted to regular fleets, with which, after the signing of the Treaty of Dardanus, they ravaged the Aegean coast.[a] Before Sulla had left the East, they invaded the island of Samothrace, where he was staying at the time, and robbed the Temple of

[x] See Chap. III note 53.
[z] Plutarch *Luc.* 2, 5 (see above p. 226).
[y] See below p. 282f.
[a] Appian *Mith.* 63.

the Cabiri of votive-offerings valued at one thousand talents. But of more consequence to Asia was their capture of the island of Samos and the coast cities of Clazomenae, Iasus and Cnidus, and their pillage of the temples at Notium and Didyma. The whole Aegean littoral seemed to be at their mercy. At Ilium in the year 80/79, honours were conferred on a commander of militia from Poemanenum in northern Mysia, who, at the order of the governor, Gaius Claudius Nero, brought a company of soldiers to protect the favoured city—presumably from an attack by these pirates.[25]

Sulla, after he had returned to Rome and driven his enemies from power, celebrated a two days' triumph over Mithradates.[26] He boasted that by his victories he had taken 1,500 pounds of gold and 115,000 of silver; he was regarded as the great reorganizer of Asia; it was from the year of his reconquest of the province that dates were reckoned in most of its districts as long as the rule of the Romans lasted; he enacted a law designed to benefit the provincials, which, among other provisions, forbad the communities, in sending envoys to Rome to present laudatory resolutions on the conduct of a returning governor, to expend more than a definite sum, and he even regulated the details of the government of the subject cities. But he had put to death great numbers of Rome's Asianic subjects; contrary to the clause of the Treaty of Dardanus which guaranteed amnesty to the cities, he had deprived many of them of the freedom they had enjoyed since the coming of Alexander; he had imposed on the communities a fine which exhausted them financially for years to come; he had done nothing to protect the coast cities from the ravages of the pirates; and he left a vain and reckless legate as governor of the bleeding and bankrupt province.

Lucius Licinius Murena had been one of Sulla's legates during his campaign in Greece and had distinguished himself during the siege of the Piraeus and especially at the battle of Chaeroneia.[b] It was, therefore, natural enough that, when the victorious general departed for Rome, he should appoint his most conspicuous subordinate to the command of the two legions of Fimbria, which he was leaving in Asia, and assign to him the duty of administering the distracted province, over which he was later appointed governor by the Senate.[c]

Murena's first duty was to deliver the coast of Asia from the raids of the pirates, and at this he seems to have made at least an attempt.

[b] Appian *Mith.* 32 and 43: Plutarch *Sulla* 17f.
[c] Appian *Mith.* 64: Memnon 36, 1: Julius Exuperantius 3.

He collected a fleet by the expedient of ordering some of the cities to use for the construction of ships a portion of the payments which they were to make to Rome;[27] as Miletus alone furnished ten, it may be supposed that this fleet was a considerable one. Murena may have temporarily driven the pirates out of the Aegean, but he did nothing really to check the evil,[d] for in 78 they were active off the coast of Lycia.[e] In fact, the extension of the boundaries of the province was evidently a more congenial occupation.

On the east of Caria lay the state of Cibyratis. It included the four communities of Cibyra, Bubon, Balbura and Oenoanda, which formed a federation, known as the Tetrapolis, in the valley of the Horzum Çay and the mountainous region on the east and south.[28] Of these communities, Cibyra itself, situated on a ridge overlooking the broad plain of the river, was much the largest and most important. Its chief industry seems to have been the embossing of iron; but its importance commercially, and certainly strategically, was due to its position near a through trade-route. This road, leaving the Southern Highway at Laodiceia, led southward over a pass into the basin of the Horzum Çay, a few miles north of Cibyra, and then, turning to the southeast, ran over the western Taurus by way of Isinda and Termessus to the Pamphylian Plain; thus it afforded the chief means of communication between the province of Asia and the southern coast. It was probably as the result of its position near this route and the presence in it of a multiplicity of traders that the city possessed a polyglot population, speaking, we are told, no less than four different languages—Pisidian, Greek, Lydian, and the tongue of the Solymi, who lived in the mountains on the Pamphylian border.

Originally a settlement of Lydian emigrants, combined with the native Pisidians, in the second century after Christ Cibyra claimed to be a colony of Lacedaemonians.[29] When the Romans first came to Asia it was ruled by a "tyrant" named Moagetes, who was characterized as cruel and treacherous, and it seems to have been similarly governed by a single ruler, though perhaps unofficially, down to the time of Murena.[30] At some time early in the second century the city erected a statue of the Goddess Roma and concluded with Rome a formal treaty of friendship and alliance, by the terms of which each of the contracting parties bound itself by an oath to aid the other in the event of war.

The relationship established by this treaty, as well as the independ-

---

[d] Appian *Mith.* 93. See also note 25.   [e] See below p. 287.

ence of the state of Cibyra, Murena brought to an abrupt end. Entering the district with an army, he overthrew the reigning "tyrant," who, like his predecessor of the previous century, bore the name of Moagetes.[f] The southern half of the Tetrapolis, consisting of the mountain-communities of Bubon, Balbura and Oenoanda, he turned over to the Lycian Federation,[f] but Cibyra and its territory, with the broad and fertile valley of the Horzum Çay, covering in all an area of about 2,470 square miles,[h] he annexed to the province of Asia.

What provocation, if any, impelled Murena thus to disregard an ancient treaty of alliance and reduce an independent state to subjection we do not know. It has been suggested that the inhabitants of the district were in a state of unrest and had offered support to the brigands who had established themselves on the Lycian coast and that Murena's occupation was part of a plan for an extensive campaign against the pirates, which was to consist of simultaneous attacks from the northern side of the Taurus as well as from the sea.[31] In view, however, of Murena's later aggressions it seems hardly necessary to suppose that there was any reason for his action other than a desire for the glory to be obtained from the extension of Rome's dominions. It is possible that he found a pretext in Cibyra's reception of Mithradates's army; for it has been previously related that the King, at the time of his siege of Laodiceia-on-Lycus, sent some of his generals to subjugate Lycia and Pamphylia,[i] and although they may never have succeeded in conquering these southern districts, it is clear that they advanced beyond Cibyra. If, as may easily have happened, the city was forced to submit to them, Murena may have made use of its surrender, as Sulla had previously done in the case of the cities of Asia, to declare the alliance null and void and to rule that Cibyra had forfeited its status of independence, thereby reducing it to the condition of a subject city. The real reason for his action, however, was more probably his desire to control the road which connected the province of Asia with the southern coast, and, at the same time, to establish a common frontier with the new province of Pamphylia-Cilicia.[j]

The territory thus acquired was combined with Laodiceia-on-Lycus into the judiciary district which henceforth took its name from Cibyra, although the assizes seem usually to have been held at Laodiceia.[32] Roman exploiters promptly flocked to this important trading-centre and

[f] Strabo XIII p. 631.   [g] See Chap. XXII note 1.
[h] 6,400 sq. km. according to Beloch (Chap. VII note 39).
[i] Appian *Mith.* 20f.; see Chap. IX note 30.   [j] See below p. 285.

established themselves there with their customary local organization.[33]

Murena, however, was not the man to be content with the annexation of an insignificant state or with the pacification of the province. His ambition for greater glory led him to seek a more spectacular achievement—namely a victory over the King of Pontus himself.[34] In this design he received the encouragement of Mithradates's general, Archelaus, who, because of his negotiations with Sulla, had fallen into disfavour with his master and deemed it wise to flee from the court.[35] Taking refuge with Murena, Archelaus pointed out that the King was mobilizing an army and building a fleet, and that while the ostensible reason was a revolt in the Crimea,[k] the real purpose of this armament might well be another invasion of Roman territory. Murena also discovered, doubtless to his satisfaction, that a part of Cappadocia was being withheld from Ariobarzanes. This failure to comply with the terms of the Treaty of Dardanus served as a technical excuse for action. Without any authorization from the Roman government or any provocation from the King, he determined to invade Pontus.

In 83 B.C., about the time when Sulla was landing in Italy, Murena with his two legions and perhaps some native contingents entered Pontus, apparently by way of Cappadocia.[36] The long march thither must have consumed a considerable portion of the campaigning season; but since the King, maintaining the policy which he had used at the time of Nicomedes's raid in 89,[l] made no move against him, the Roman general succeeded in advancing for a considerable distance into the kingdom. A rich prize offered itself in the Temple at Comana, the most wealthy sanctuary in the royal dominions.[m] After killing a force of cavalry, perhaps the guard of the temple-domains, Murena seized the sacred treasure and pillaged the surrounding country. When Mithradates, with great restraint, contented himself with despatching envoys to remind the Roman general of the treaty made with Sulla, Murena merely replied that he had seen no treaty, for it had never been drawn up in written form and had never been submitted to the Roman People for ratification.[n] He then withdrew for the winter into Cappadocia, where, doubtless to the gratification of his vanity, a town near the frontier was given the name of Licineia in his honour.[37]

We are told that some of the envoys sent by Mithradates, who were "Greeks and philosophers," showed little loyalty to the King and even

[k] Cicero de Imp. Cn. Pomp. 9.   [l] See above p. 209.
[m] See above p. 181.   [n] See above p. 231.

ridiculed his claims. Whether encouraged by these traitors or not, Murena, in the spring of 82, again entered Pontus. This raid was both more extensive and more profitable than that of the preceding year. Crossing the Halys, perhaps in its upper course, he plundered the King's country far and wide, and no less than four hundred villages, it is said, fell a prey to his ravaging. Although this success was due only to the fact that Mithradates had refrained from using his large and well-organized army against the insignificant forces of his opponent, the Roman general magnified his paltry raids into a real victory. In his desire for military glory he assumed the title of Imperator, as though he had inflicted a great defeat on the foes of Rome.[38]

Mithradates, meanwhile, made no hostile move. During the previous winter, after his vain appeal to Murena, he had sent envoys to the Senate to complain of the unprovoked attack. It evidently seemed to him the wisest policy to avoid any possible offence and to place upon the Romans the entire responsibility for the raids. Murena was able, therefore, to withdraw with his booty into Phrygia. Here he met a commissioner named Calidius, who, in consequence of the complaint made by the Pontic envoys, had been despatched by the Senate with instructions to the general to desist from his attacks on a nominally friendly king. These instructions were given publicly and in the hearing of all, but it was noticed that Calidius also conversed with Murena in private, and the suspicion arose that the tenor of this conversation differed from that of the message previously delivered in public. In any case, Murena embarked upon a third raid. Some of his staff, we are told,[o] urged an advance on Sinope; but it is hardly credible that even the reckless commander seriously considered a course which would involve a march across the whole of the kingdom of Pontus to the coast of the Black Sea. But the failure of his embassy to the Senate and the third raid of the Roman general exhausted Mithradates's forbearance. Realizing that he must protect his kingdom and perhaps believing that the Roman government was really about to renew the war, he took the offensive. He sent an army into Cappadocia under Gordius, the murderer of King Ariarathes VI and later the regent for Mithradates's son,[p] to make a retaliatory raid, in which the country was devastated and men and beasts were carried off as prey. On his return, Gordius found Murena encamped on the bank of a river, but he made no move against the Romans until the King himself, with a stronger force, appeared on the scene.[39] In the ensuing battle

o Memnon 36, 3.   p See above p. 203f.

Murena was completely defeated. After retreating across the river, he attempted to take a stand on a hill which seemed to offer the possibility of resistance. But he was forced from this position also, and after losing many of his soldiers he was driven back in total rout to the border of Phrygia.

The report of this victory spread far and wide and won great prestige for Mithradates. Following up his success by an advance into Cappadocia, he attacked the garrisons left there by Murena and drove them out of the country. He celebrated his victory by a spectacular offering to Zeus Stratius, the "God of Armies," carried out on a large scale according to an ancient ritual.[q] To many this must have seemed the preliminary to a great campaign, and even in Rome men saw that steps must be taken to prevent another war.

The defeat of Murena, indeed, was not without effect on the Roman government and the now powerful Dictator. Sulla now realized that if the war was not to be renewed the treaty of peace must be strictly observed. Accordingly, in 81 he sent Aulus Gabinius, who, like Murena, had served with distinction at Chaeroneia, to convey a peremptory message forbidding all further fighting.[r] The additional task was assigned to Gabinius of patching up a peace between Mithradates and Ariobarzanes. Thus a treaty was concluded by which the King of Pontus solemnly betrothed his four-year-old daughter to the son of the Cappadocian monarch.[40] But in return for the favour he forced the latter to agree to his possession not only of that portion of Cappadocia which he then held but other territory besides, an arrangement which was later to result in further dispute.[s]

Murena was ordered back to Rome.[t] Nothing had been accomplished by his folly but disgrace to Rome's honour and defeat to her army. Yet such was the power of Sulla that his former legate, soon after his return, was accorded a triumph over the King of Pontus,[u] with the result that eighteen years later Cicero, in defending Murena's son, had the hardihood to refer to this outrageous war as a victory which brought glory and honour to Murena's house.[v]

Meanwhile Lucullus had been carrying out the task assigned him in the province, but he also was to have a taste of warfare. The citizens of Mitylene, fearing punishment for their betrayal of Aquilius, still held out, refusing to obey a summons to surrender.[w] Accordingly,

[q] See Chap VIII note 12 and below p. 324. [r] Appian *Mith*. 66: Plutarch *Sulla* 16f.
[s] See below p. 321. [t] Cicero *de Imp. Cn. Pomp*. 8.
[u] Cicero *de Imp. Cn. Pomp*. 8; *pro Mur*. 11 and 15: Licinianus p. 31 Flemisch.
[v] Cicero *pro Mur*. 12. [w] Plutarch *Luc*. 4, 2f.

Lucullus with some ships, including perhaps those collected for attacks on the pirates, sailed over to the island, and, after defeating the force which came forth to meet him, laid siege to the city. Unable, however, with the men at his disposal, to force the citizens to capitulate, he resorted to a trick. Putting out by daylight for Elaea on the mainland, he made the citizens believe that he had abandoned the siege; then, returning unobserved, he placed his men in ambush near Mitylene. When the townsfolk came out to plunder his deserted camp, he caught them unawares and succeeded in killing as many as four hundred of those who resisted and in capturing many besides. Mitylene was unable to resist much longer; when it fell, countless booty and six thousand slaves came into the possession of the Romans.[41] The city lost all its rights, to regain them eighteen years later at the request of a favourite of Pompey.[x] Among those who won distinction at its capture was the young Julius Caesar, then serving his first military campaign as a member of the governor's staff.

Nothing seems to have been done for the welfare of Asia either by Murena's successor in the governorship, Marcus Minucius Thermus, or by the latter's successor, Gaius Claudius Nero. Nero did, perhaps, show sufficient energy to arrange for the defence of Ilium,[y] but, in general, the province had little cause to be grateful to him. He showed no readiness to protect its inhabitants from the thefts or the vengeful cruelty of a Roman official, whose name has ever afterwards been a byword and a synonym for oppression—the notorious Gaius Verres, through whose prosecution Cicero was later to gain lasting fame.[z]

In 80 B.C. Verres went to the East as the legate of Gnaeus Dolabella, propraetor of Cilicia.[a] His coming was referred to by Cicero as a disaster, and such, indeed, it was. After various outrages perpetrated in Greece and an attempt to carry off some statues of great age and value from the Temple of Apollo in Delos, he arrived on the coast of Asia. Here his art-collector's passion—which, later, impelled him to countless thefts in Sicily—found opportunity for gratification. He visited various temples on the coast and the adjacent islands—Samos, Chios, Erythrae, Halicarnassus and Tenedos—and from all he carried away famous statues and paintings. In Samos, especially, his robbery of the Temple of Hera was so shameless that the angry citizens not only brought suit against the Chian ship-captain who, at Dolabella's command, was conveying Verres from the province, but also sent envoys

[x] See below p. 365.
[z] For Verres in Asia see Cicero II *Verr.* I 49f.; IV 71.
[y] See above p. 240.
[a] See below p. 285f.

to Nero, the governor of Asia, to complain of the outrage. But the only reply they received from the propraetor was that a complaint against a legate of the Roman People must be lodged at Rome and not brought to the governor. It is perhaps significant of the point of view in the Capital that ten years later Cicero, in his attempt to convince the jury of the heinousness of Verres's action, advanced the argument that, whereas many other Romans had robbed the provinces of works of art, they had always presented these to the Roman state, while Verres kept his plunder for his own enjoyment.

Verres found ways and means of enriching himself, however, as well as of adding to his art-collection. On the occasion of a voyage from Miletus to Myndus in Caria—a journey along the coast of not more than forty miles and involving no great peril—he ordered the Milesians to provide a ship to act as escort to his vessel. Although the legate of the governor of Cilicia had no official position in the province of Asia, the citizens dared not refuse. They therefore put at his disposal an armed vessel, one of the ten which a few years previously they had constructed at Murena's bidding to serve against the pirates. It was destined, however, to seizure by a pirate of a different kind. On his arrival at Myndus, Verres ordered the captain and crew to return home by land; he then sold the ship to two Romans, formerly officers of Fimbria but now residents of Myndus, who were later to act as Mithradates's agents in his dealings with the Roman rebel, Sertorius, and to use this very ship in their negotiations.[b] When the indignant Milesians entered a statement of this action in their public records they were ordered by Dolabella to remove the entry. They obeyed, but only for the period of Dolabella's stay in the East; on his departure they not only restored it to their records but also added the reason why it had not been inscribed in the proper place.

But what most of all aroused the indignation of the province was the outrage perpetrated in the free city of Lampsacus and the ensuing miscarriage of justice. In the course of an official mission from Dolabella to King Nicomedes IV of Bithynia, Verres stopped in the city. As was the custom, various prominent citizens entertained the legate himself as well as his suite, including a henchman named Rubrius, who was billeted upon a distinguished citizen named Philodamus. After a banquet given by Philodamus for his undesired guest the latter bade the host bring his daughter to the banqueting-room. When the astonished Philodamus refused, Rubrius summoned his slaves and

[b] See below p. 322.

seemed about to take violent measures. Thereupon the host called his own slaves as well as his son to aid in the defence of his daughter; a crowd of townspeople, aroused by the noise, also assembled at the house. In the fighting that ensued, Rubrius and some of his slaves were wounded, and Verres's lictor, who was present in attendance on Rubrius—a suspicious circumstance—met with a violent death.

In the morning a crowd of angry townsfolk, convinced that the legate was responsible for the incident, attacked the house where Verres was lodged. They were making ready to fire the building when some of the resident Romans implored them to refrain from violence to an official of the Roman government, promising that Verres would leave the city forthwith. Their efforts were successful and the legate and his following were allowed to depart.

A servant of the government, however, had been killed and his death could not be ignored. Philodamus and his son, therefore, were brought to trial before the governor. In the proceedings the desire manifested by Verres for their conviction and Nero's acquiescence in it became a public scandal. Dolabella himself was prevailed upon by his legate to leave his province of Cilicia and attend the trial. The court was convened at Laodiceia-on-Lycus, which had the advantage of being far removed from Lampsacus and also convenient for Dolabella because of the road leading thither from the southern coast through the newly-acquired district of Cibyra. It was arranged that the accusation should be made by a Roman citizen who had lent money to the city of Lampsacus; there was a strong suspicion that, if he were successful in presenting his case, he would receive the aid of Verres's lictors in collecting the amount of his debt. The jury included not only Dolabella—who by virtue of his rank would give his vote first—and Verres but also several of their military officers, as well as a number of Roman money-lenders, to whom, as to the accuser, the legate's influence might prove useful. Philodamus, on the other hand, could find no advocate. Despite the packing of the jury, the sentiment in favour of the accused was so strong that the complaisant Nero deemed it wise to adjourn the case. At a second session, however, the efforts of Dolabella were successful, and Philodamus and his son were convicted by a small majority of the votes cast by the jury. To the great indignation of the province, they were publicly beheaded in the market-place of Laodiceia. The trial had shown the Asiatics how great an influence in the administration of justice could be exercised by a powerful Roman.

Another case of official privilege was perhaps less scandalous in itself but in reality of greater importance because of the principle involved. The inviolability of the Temple of Artemis at Ephesus, like that of the other great sanctuaries in Asia, had been observed for many centuries. Not long after the farcical trial at Laodiceia, the slave of a Roman quaestor, Marcus Aurelius Scaurus, escaped from his master and sought sanctuary in the Temple.[c] When Scaurus, disregarding the sanctity of the place, attempted to lay hands on the fugitive, Pericles, a noble citizen of Ephesus, insisted on the right of the Goddess to protect her suppliant and barred the way. Scaurus, therefore, accused him of using force against him and the Ephesian was summoned to Rome to answer for his action.

Dolabella, as will be seen,[d] was later brought to book for his misdeeds in Cilicia. A similar indictment for extortion in Asia was brought against a Roman official, Terentius Varro.[42] His trial, held in 74, affords ample evidence of the difficulty of securing a verdict against a senator brought before a jury of his peers. Varro was defended by his cousin, Quintus Hortensius Hortalus, the foremost pleader of the time. In order to secure an acquittal, the jurors had been freely bribed; this was nothing new, but an innovation which caused great scandal was Hortensius's distribution of ballots of a special colour to those of the jury who were in his pay, in order that he might know whether they had earned their reward. As a result of this bribery Varro was acquitted.

It was not, indeed, through any lack of endeavour on the part of the provincials to conciliate their governors that oppression existed. Thus Marcus Junius Silanus, governor in 76/5, was persuaded by a prominent citizen of Mylasa to pay a formal visit to the city in order to see with his own eyes "the citizens' zeal both for him and for the Roman People" and to receive the honorary title of the city's patron.[43] He had some time previously been quaestor of Asia, and so, it was hoped, he might be well disposed toward its inhabitants; but even he did not leave the province without carrying off a valuable painting, which the Emperor Augustus later hung in the Senate-chamber.[e]

In contrast to the corruption of governors of this period and to the indifference which they showed toward the welfare of the province, it is refreshing to turn to an example of energy and courage set by a young man, still only a private citizen but destined to be one of the greatest figures of Roman history. Early in 74 it so happened that the young Julius Caesar went to study rhetoric at Rhodes.[44] On his journey thither he fell into the hands of pirates operating off the coast

[c] Cicero II *Verr.* 1 85.   [d] See below p. 286f.   [e] Pliny *N.H.* xxxv 27 and 131.

of Caria. No effort was made by the governor, Marcus Juncus, to rescue him, and he saved himself from the hands of the robbers only by despatching his attendants to the neighbouring Miletus to procure the fifty talents which he had promised as ransom. Thus freed, he revenged himself on his captors. After manning some ships at Miletus on his own responsibility, he attacked the pirates, routed their fleet and took not only booty but many prisoners as well. The booty he used to pay for the ransom, but the prisoners he conducted in person to Pergamum, where he presented the governor with a demand for their execution. Juncus, however, was engaged in a more congenial task than the suppression of piracy. It had chanced that Nicomedes IV, the King of Bithynia, had recently died, bequeathing his domains to the Romans,[f] and the governor of Asia, as the nearest Roman official, had gone to Bithynia to take over the inheritance. His indifference and his greed alike impelled him to refuse Caesar's plea. He declined to put the captives to death, but proposed to sell them as slaves, having an eye to the profit to be obtained through their capture. Caesar, however, refused any such compromise; returning to Pergamum, he proceeded without any official authority whatever to put the pirates to death by crucifixion.

When high officials flouted the authority of the government by making raids into a country with which Rome was officially at peace, when they perverted justice to satisfy a selfish desire for revenge, violated the long-established rights of ancient sanctuaries, neglected the safety of the seaboard, and practised extortion so manifestly that a jury must be bribed to secure an acquittal, it was not unnatural that the ordinary man often showed little regard for the welfare of the provincials or little hesitancy in the exploitation of the province.

Those most concerned in this exploitation were the tax-gatherers and the men who had money to lend. To the former the war against Mithradates brought increased opportunity. Whereas, previously, the free cities had been exempt from their demands, and attempts to impose taxes to which they were not entitled had been unsuccessful,[g] the fact that many of these cities had been deprived of independence greatly enlarged the field of their operations. In the general impoverishment which followed the imposition of the war-indemnity, it became doubly hard for these *publicani* to gather in the taxes that were due, and their methods, often ruthless, caused wide-spread misery. As has been suggested, the men who during the decade that followed Murena's

f See below p. 320.　　　　　　　g See above p. 166.

retirement were sent out to govern Asia were not the kind to show consideration to its inhabitants or to protect them from the greed of these oppressors. A law of Sulla's, to be sure, by which the control of the courts, and among them the tribunal for cases of extortion, was transferred from the Equestrian Order to the members of the Senate, made it impossible for the tax-farmers to take revenge on a governor who restrained them, as they had done in the case of Rutilius Rufus.[h] Otherwise, however, the new law did nothing to check their greed and oppression. Although the comparison is undoubtedly overdrawn, there was probably some truth in the description that likened the tax-farmers and money-lenders to "harpies which snatched at the people's food."[i]

While it is not improbable that the tax-farming corporations sometimes engaged in money-lending ventures,[j] this business, in general, was carried on by the banker, sometimes a native, but more often an immigrant from Italy. It has been shown that in the early years of the province, Italian business-men had come to Asia in considerable numbers and established themselves in many of the cities.[k] They and their descendants, to be sure, had largely perished in the massacres of 88, but after the defeat of Mithradates, when property in Asia was cheap and money was scarce, the opportunity for easy profit brought a new throng of investors across the Aegean. In 66 B.C. Cicero was able to speak of the "active and industrious" Roman business-men who had either established themselves in Asia or had invested large sums in the province.[l]

Of these business-men, the bankers were the most prominent, if not the most numerous, class. They made loans both to cities and to individuals. Thus the city of Lampsacus had borrowed money from the man who conducted the prosecution of Philodamus for the death of Verres's lictor, and the jury which condemned him included several Roman citizens to whom provincials were in debt.[m] The greatest opportunity for money-making, of course, lay in advancing to the cities the money needed for the arrears of the indemnity imposed by Sulla. In this they worked hand in hand with the *publicani*, for when the cities, impoverished by the indemnity, needed cash to meet the tax-gatherers' bills, they were compelled to turn to the money-lenders. As a result, the communities were forced to mortgage their public

[h] See above p. 175.
[j] See Broughton in *Econ. Surv.* IV p. 541.
[l] Cicero *de Imp. Cn. Pomp.* 18.

[i] Plutarch *Luc.* 7, 6.
[k] See above p. 162f.
[m] Cicero II *Verr.* 1 73f. (see above p. 248).

buildings and the revenues from their harbours, as well as to sell their works of art.[n] According to the highly-coloured account given by the biographer of Lucullus, individual citizens were actually forced both to sell their children into slavery and to become slaves themselves, and stories were even told of instances of actual torture.

It is true that money was scarce. Even in Rome, as the result of the losses caused by the recent war against the Italian Allies, followed by those incurred by the investors in Asia during the invasion of Mithradates,[o] there was a financial crisis of such magnitude that in 86 a law was enacted which compelled a creditor to accept, in full discharge, one fourth of the amount of his outstanding loans.[p] In Asia, where economic conditions were even worse, the security which the cities could offer was poor indeed. It is therefore not surprising that, in such a dearth of ready money and in investments involving so great a risk, the bankers demanded a high rate of interest.[45] But the rate was such that the debt became greater than the provincials could possibly discharge. We are told that in 71 B.C.—thirteen years after the indemnity had been imposed by Sulla—although twice the original amount of 20,000 talents had been paid to the money-lenders, the total indebtedness of the province, as the result, evidently, of the compounding of the arrears of interest, had risen to the almost incredible sum of 120,000 talents.[46]

This terrible burden of indebtedness Lucullus found when, nine years after the completion of his work as Sulla's proquaestor in Asia, he was made governor of the province.[47] The general impoverishment called for a drastic remedy, and this Lucullus proceeded to apply.[48] He declared illegal all usurious interest and established 12 per cent as the maximum lawful rate; he forbad the compounding of interest under penalty of forfeiture of the whole loan; he ordered that no creditor should receive arrears of interest in excess of the amount of the principal, or seize more than a fourth of the debtor's annual income; finally, in order to raise the amounts demanded from the cities he authorized the imposition of a levy of 25 per cent on the crops and a special tax on slaves and buildings. By these measures the total indebtedness of the province was reduced to 40,000 talents, and such were the recuperative powers of Asia that in four years' time, it is said, the entire debt was repaid and the mortgaged properties re-

[n] Plutarch *Luc.* 7, 6 and 20, 1f.: Appian *Mith.* 63.
[o] So Cicero *de Imp. Cn. Pomp.* 12.
[p] See Last in *C.A.H.* ix p. 265f. and Frank in *Econ. Surv.* 1 p. 270f.

stored to the owners. Lucullus won the admiration of those whom he governed[q] and the grateful cities instituted in his honour festivals named Lucullea;[r] but he incurred the hatred of the business-interests of Rome and in time he was to feel their revenge.

In the very year of Lucullus's reforms, in fact, the power of the business-interests in Rome was greatly increased. A new law, proposed in 70 B.C. under the Consuls Pompey and Crassus, restored the influence of the Equestrian Order in the courts by restricting the Senatorial members of juries to one third of those who composed the panels. Three years later, these interests punished Lucullus by supporting a bill which deprived him of what remained of his military command,[s] and in the following year they combined with the lower classes to elect Pompey to Lucullus's former post.[t] Cicero, in supporting this proposal, directed his appeal chiefly to the large number of those who were financially interested in the tax-farming corporations.[u]

The strength of these interests was presently put to a severe test. In 61, after the corporations which farmed the taxes of Asia had made a bid which proved to be so high that a loss was inevitable, they presented a petition to the Senate asking for the cancellation of their contract.[49] The request met with great opposition and months of discussion ensued. Finally, the Conservatives among the Senators won the day and the petition was rejected. The decision created a serious breach between the Senate and the financial interests, shattering Cicero's deeply-cherished hope of a coalition between the Senators and the Equestrian Order as a means of opposing those political leaders who were planning, with the support of the masses, to gain office and power. These leaders saw their opportunity. A year after the rejection of the corporations' petition, a law proposed by Julius Caesar granted them a reduction of one third of their bid.

Cicero, moved by expediency and not by the merits of the case, had supported the tax-farmers' petition. He was, in fact, fully aware of their power, and although he resented their arrogance,[v] at the same time he did not dare to oppose them. An instance illustrative of their influence occurred in the same year 59, when the company which farmed the customs-duties of Asia demanded the payment of duty on merchandise brought into a port but not sold there and consequently carried on to another harbour, where a second duty was im-

q Cicero pro Flacco 85; Acad. Pr. II 3.
s See below p. 348.
u Cicero de Imp. Cn. Pomp. 16.

r Plutarch Luc. 23, 1.
t See below p. 351f.
v Cicero ad Att. IV 7, 1 (56 B.C.).

posed.[50] The demand aroused the opposition alike of the merchants and the inhabitants of the province, and, acting together, they presented an appeal to Quintus Cicero, the governor. He, unwilling to antagonize the *publicani*, sought to evade the question by referring it to the Senate. When both sides sent representatives to Rome, Marcus Cicero, although believing that the merchants were in the right, nevertheless expressed himself as willing to address the Senate in behalf of the tax-farming company.

During the two decades that intervened between the economic reforms of Lucullus and the outbreak of the civil war between Pompey and Caesar, the bankers and other business-men from Italy carried on their activities in the province in increasing numbers.[51] Those of whom we hear most were the men who had money to lend. They included both the large banking-houses of Italy, which sent their agents to Asia, and the smaller private investors who had established themselves in the province and lent out their capital as they found opportunity.[w] Both categories made loans to cities as well as to individuals. Among the large bankers were the Fufii of Rome, whose agent in Asia collected money lent in Rome to the rhetorician Heraclides of Temnus,[x] Marcus Cluvius of Puteoli, who through a representative in Ephesus lent money to five Carian cities and held a mortgage on the house of a citizen of Alabanda,[y] and Lucius Egnatius Rufus, who had an agent at Philomelium and various interests both in Asia and in Bithynia.[z] Cicero's close friend, moreover, Titus Pomponius Atticus, had business-affairs in Asia which caused him to make a journey to the province in 54 B.C. and in 51 to maintain agents in Ephesus.[a]

The small investors included Castricius, a highly respected resident of Smyrna, who made a loan to Tralles,[b] a certain Sextilius of Acmonia, who lent 206,000 drachmae to Asclepiades, a somewhat disreputable citizen of the city,[c] and Gaius Appuleius Decianus, for twenty years a resident of Asia, who lent money on a mortgage at a high rate to a young man of Temnus and then acquired the estate by foreclosure.[52] Decianus, indeed, seems to have been none too scrupulous in his methods of acquiring property; for, if we may believe Cicero, he got possession of an estate at Apollonis by a transaction which in-

[w] Cicero *de Imp. Cn. Pomp.* 18. [x] Cicero *pro Flacco* 46f.
[y] Cicero *Epist. ad Fam.* XIII 56 and note 64; see also *ad Att.* VI 2, 3.
[z] Cicero *Epist. ad Fam.* XIII 43-45; 47; 73; 74.
[a] *Epist. ad Att.* IV 15, 2; 16, 7; V 13, 2; 20, 10.
[b] Cicero *pro Flacco* 54 and 75. [c] *Pro Flacco* 34f.

volved the hoodwinking of women, the appointment of a dishonest guardian and the fraudulent purchase of the property.

The bankers, however, although the best known to us of the Roman settlers in Asia, were probably not the most numerous element among them. Unfortunately, the ancient writers refer to these settlers by the general term of "business-men" (*negotiatores*) rather than by their specific occupations, and the inscriptions erected in their honour seldom make mention of their activities. We are, therefore, in ignorance as to the means by which they made their money. Sometimes, evidently, it was through speculation, as in the case of a certain Falcidius, who bought up the right to collect the revenues of Tralles for 900,000 sesterces and, according to Cicero, made a large profit from the transaction.[53] Others may have been exporters. As has been previously observed,[d] the wines of the Aegean coast and the islands, especially Chios and Cos, were shipped in large quantities to Italy, and of the many land-owners with Roman names who appear in the inscriptions from these places it is highly probable that some were vine-growers.[54] It is also possible that some were interested in the textile industries of Lydia, Ionia and southwestern Phrygia,[e] the fabrics of which were also exported to Italy. At Cos a man with a Roman name, Marcus Spedius Naso,[f] dealt in the purple silk for which the island was famous. But the majority were probably engaged in the ordinary small ventures of the cities in which they dwelt, like Publius Patulcius, a fuller at Magnesia-on-Maeander.[g]

It would be unfair to these settlers to suppose that they brought only harm and suffering to the province. Some of the banking fraternity, it is true, hand in glove with the *publicani*, won an evil name because of the ruinous rate of interest which they charged for the loans they advanced. But Castricius, after his death, received the highest honours at Smyrna,[h] and it may be assumed that many of the men who received letters of introduction from Cicero were honest enough. It is highly probable, too, that the capital which they brought into Asia was a boon to the province. Moreover, the presence of the merchants and the small business-men cannot be regarded as a detriment. It may well be that the enterprise of these men from the West stimulated trade and aided in the commercial development of many a city and that their energy had a salutary effect on the easy-going ways of the

[d] See Chap. II notes 60 and 111.
[f] *I.G.R.* IV 1071, see Chap. II note 113.
[h] Cicero *pro Flacco* 75.

[e] See above p. 47f.
[g] *Ins. Magn.* 111.

Asiatics. In many known instances they entered into the life of the community in which they resided, and the erection of monuments by grateful cities shows that many were held in high esteem.[55] Some of them even, becoming citizens of the cities in which they had settled, held local offices, bearing all the financial burdens which these entailed. At Priene, for example, in the early first century the high office of stephanephorus was held by four men who bore Roman names, although in the case of two a Greek surname indicates that their fathers had been natives of Greece or Asia.[56]

The career of one of these men, Aulus Aemilius Zosimus, son of Sextus, is instructive as showing how a stranger, perhaps a parvenu, could rise to high office in a Greek city. The form of his name suggests that his father was a freedman, and either father or son had evidently made a large fortune. The younger Zosimus settled at Priene, where he was presently made a citizen, apparently by decree of the Council, whereupon, "loving the city as his own fatherland and showing all the devotion of a native-born citizen," he entered upon a career distinguished alike for its high public offices and its acts of generosity. As Secretary of the Council and People, he caused the public records to be inscribed in duplicate on parchment at his own expense; as "head of the gymnasium of the Young Men," he reorganized that body and encouraged the use of the gymnasium by making the baths free of charge and by furnishing oil for the athletes from sunrise to nightfall, as well as by increasing the number of contests; acting also as "supervisor of the boys' education," he added to the usual sports certain contests in "philological studies," "wishing by the former to make the body resolute and by the latter to introduce the spirit to true excellence and to human experience"; as stephanephorus, he performed many public sacrifices at his own expense and entertained at banquets not only the Council and magistrates but also the whole body of citizens by tribes, those of the city's dependants and the resident settlers who had served their year among the *ephebi*, as well as all the Romans and the citizens of several cities of Greece and Asia resident in Priene. Closing his career, as we know it, by again holding the office of Secretary, he received the highest honours that the grateful citizens could bestow, including a golden wreath, a portrait in painting, three statues, of bronze, gold and marble respectively, and finally the promise of a state-funeral with a public procession.

The liberality of these men, who were able and willing to assume the office of stephanephorus with all the attendant expenses, may be regarded as an indication of a revival of prosperity in Priene. It is true that, being Italians, they may have made their money by loans to the provincials. There are, however, other signs of such a revival. Even before the intervention of Lucullus in 71, the citizen of Mylasa who invited the governor Silanus to visit the place gave the community "many gifts according to the needs which weighed heavily on the city, sometimes of oil and sometimes as a subsidy for the grain-supply."[i] During the decade that followed Lucullus's reforms, however, conditions improved greatly. This appears in the resumption of the celebration of important festivals, the cost of which was always a serious item in a city's expenditures. In Miletus the Didymeia, in honour of Apollo at Didyma, the celebration of which had ceased after the war, was held once more;[57] at Tralles the Olympia, in honour of Zeus, seems to have been renewed about 62 B.C. and to have been celebrated regularly thereafter;[58] and at Ephesus thirty-four men, who, over a period of as many years during the first century, conducted the festival of the Dionysia, are said to have done so at their own expense.[59]

The wealth of Tralles, moreover, is shown to have been very considerable by the fact that it was able to farm out the right to collect its revenues for the large sum of 900,000 sesterces.[j] We know of at least one rich citizen of the place, Pythodorus, apparently the son or grandson of that Chaeremon of Nysa who in the war against Mithradates had supplied the Roman army with grain and in consequence was proscribed by the King. In 48 B.C., it is said, Pythodorus, who had been a friend of Pompey, had amassed a property estimated at 2,000 talents, the foundation of which was presumably laid some time previously.[60]

Other fortunes also seem to have been made, or at least founded, during this period. Thus at Laodiceia, a certain Hiero not only adorned the city with many votive offerings but bequeathed to it more than 2,000 talents;[k] at Sardis, Iollas not only performed the duties of gymnasiarch and celebrated festivals at his own expense but also made many gifts to the city[l]; and at Mylasa, Euthydemus, an orator and political leader, inherited great wealth.[61]

There is evidence also of prosperity at Chios, where there seems to have been great commercial activity in the port.[62] Perhaps the best general indication, however, of some improvement in economic conditions in Asia is to be found in the issue, from 58 onward, of a new

[i] See note 43.   [j] See note 53.
[k] Strabo XII p. 578.   [l] *Ins. Sardis* 27 = *I.G.R.* IV 1757.

series of cistophori minted in five of the principal cities of the province.[63] Unlike the coins of the earlier series, these bore the names of governors, thus signifying presumably that they were issued under the authority and supervision of Rome.

It may not be supposed, however, that this prosperity was universal. The difficulty which the *publicani* experienced in 61 in collecting the taxes from the province, as the result of which they asked for the cancellation of their contract,[m] suggests that at least some of the communities were still in financial straits. In the middle of the first century, moreover, five of the cities of Caria—Mylasa, Alabanda, Heracleia, Bargylia, and Caunus—were in debt to an Italian banker.[64] Mylasa and Alabanda, it was hoped, would send their legal representatives to Rome to make a settlement of some kind, and the Caunians asserted that they had the money on deposit and ready for payment; but in the cases of Heracleia and Bargylia the creditor's expectation of recovering the amount of the debt seemed to depend chiefly on the seizure of the revenues of the two cities.

Thus in spite of instances of prosperity in many places, the exploitation of Asia by the Roman Republic wrought great harm to the inhabitants of the country. The tax-farming system, carried on by agents who wished to make the largest possible profit for their companies, could not fail to be a great drain on the province. The presence, also, of the bankers who had money to lend made it easy for a community to resort to the dangerous practice of mortgaging its future by borrowing for the present, and encouraged a people, naturally extravagant and as lavish in its spending as it was in its words, to raise loans rather than economize, and, in some cases, even to head for bankruptcy. The uncertainty of repayment naturally seemed to the lender to warrant the exaction of a high interest-charge; the known instances, in other provinces, of an outrageous rate[n] make it easy to suppose that, even after Lucullus had remedied the financial crisis caused by the Mithradatic War, iniquitous contracts may have been forced upon the cities of the province of Asia also. In justification for oppressive tax-levies the only plea that could be made was that Asia would be exposed to disaster brought about by attack from without or discord from within were she not subject to the rule of Rome[o]—the time-worn plea of the imperialist, who has always argued that security is to be preferred to liberty.

[m] See above p. 253.　　　　　　　　　　　　[n] See below p. 386.
[o] Cicero *Epist. ad Quint. Fr.* 1 1, 34.

CHAPTER XI

THE LANDS OF THE SOUTH

THE southern coast of Asia Minor, lying behind the Taurus Mountains, was but little affected by the vicissitudes undergone during the earlier Hellenistic period by the western part of the country. Except at its eastern end, it was far removed from the main thoroughfare which led from the Aegean to the Euphrates. The greater portion had seen little of the passage either of commerce or of armies, and it had constituted almost a world apart. Like the more northerly districts, it had been subject to the Persians, and Alexander, on the eastward march which led to the overthrow of their empire, had merely swept in and out again.[a] In the third century it was a bone of contention between the Seleucids and the Ptolemies.[b] Later, a portion of it was invaded by the usurper Achaeus.[c] But otherwise it had had slight contact with the struggles which led to the expulsion of the Syrian monarchs from western Asia Minor and the growth of the power of Pergamum.

This remoteness was the result of the peculiar geographical formation of the Anatolian Peninsula. The high Taurus range extends, under various names, in a mighty wall for about 250 miles westward from the Euphrates. North of it lie the broken mountain-masses of Cappadocia and the treeless high-lying plateau of Lycaonia. Toward this plateau the wall of the Taurus slopes down gently, but toward the Mediterranean the descent is steep and broken by deep river-gorges. The passes which lead across the range are both few and difficult. At the western end of this great length of almost unbroken ridge, the mountain-wall undergoes a striking change and breaks up into the wide highland-country of Pisidia and Milyas.[d] This region is part of the central plateau, though separated from it on the north and east by the high range of the Sultan Dağ and by lower mountains along the border of Lycaonia. It is a land of broad valleys and great lakes, Burdur, Eğridir and Beyşehir, with the lesser ones, Kestel and Suğla, lying farther south; into these the rivers flow from the mountain-ring around them. The extension of the Taurus separates this district from the Mediterranean littoral. Although more easily traversed than the high Taurus chain, this mountainous tract interposes a barrier, which, though crossed by two important routes leading to the Mediterranean,

---

[a] Arrian *Anab.* 1 24f.: Plutarch *Alex.* 17, 3f.   [b] See Chap. XII note 1.
[c] See Chap. I note 28.   [d] For Milyas see Chap. I note 56.

severed the interests of the districts forming the Pergamene Kingdom from those of the southern coast.

This coast consists of two great projections, formed by masses of the Taurus which extend far out into the Mediterranean and by two deeply indented bays, into which run the rivers flowing down from the mountains and forming rich alluvial plains at their mouths. Thus there are four divisions, each of which in the Hellenistic period was not only a geographical but also a political unit. The southwestern division, where the highlands of Pisidia are continued in rugged mountains, lies between the corner of Asia Minor, where the river Indus flows into the sea, and the Gulf of Antalya, the more westerly of the two indenting bays of the southern coast. This was Lycia; its interior, difficult of access, was peopled by highland folk, with an occasional city serving as a trading-centre and perhaps as a civilizing leaven; but its coast was fringed with a ring of Hellenized communities, which in the Hellenic fashion had prospered on trade. Of the federation which they formed and of their relations with Rome an account will be given in a later chapter.[e]

At the southeastern corner of Lycia lies Cape Chelidonia, forming with the more easterly of the two great projecting masses the deep Gulf of Antalya; the distance from the cape to the opposite shore is about one hundred miles and from the line thus formed the gulf extends inward for nearly seventy-five. At the head of the gulf is the plain of Pamphylia, in general appearance an irregular crescent, the arc of which is formed by the mountains of Milyas and Pisidia and the tips by the meeting of the two projecting masses with the sea.[1] The centre of the arc is distant about twenty miles from the head of the gulf, and the total area of the plain has been estimated at about 2,200 square miles.

The plain is well-watered. Two great rivers, the Cestrus and the Eurymedon, flow down from the mountains of Pisidia, dividing the lowlands into three approximately equal sections.[2] These in their turn are traversed by lesser streams, such as the Catarrhactes, which, bursting forth from underground channels, flows into the gulf in several mouths west of the Cestrus, and the Melas, near the eastern tip of the crescent. The land is correspondingly productive; although the alluvium from the rivers, especially the Cestrus, has caused much of the plain to become little more than a swamp, in ancient times it was very fertile and its olive-oil was exported to other countries. Even in its

e See below p. 524f.

present condition it is rich in fruit-trees and grain. In Antiquity, as also today, the surrounding mountains had great forests both of pines and of oaks; among the latter was the evergreen variety that yielded the kermes, an insect from the bodies of which a scarlet dye was prepared. The region also produced storax-gum as well as other substances used for perfumes and medicines.

Although the name of Pamphylia as the "Land of all tribes" was far from accurate, the inhabitants of the district included both natives and Greeks. While the myths which related that after the fall of Troy a miscellaneous throng of emigrants established themselves here are later attempts to explain the origin of the Hellenic element, it is probable that bodies of Greeks settled in Pamphylia at an early date.[3] Their language, even in the classical period, as shown by their coins and inscriptions, was a barbarous dialect, in one instance, at least, influenced by native elements. These Hellenic settlers naturally occupied the rich plain, while the folk who dwelt on the mountain-slopes seem to have remained comparatively free from outside civilizing influences; even at the beginning of the Christian Era they had a reputation for banditry.[f]

In the plain five great cities arose, Attaleia, Perge, Sillyum, Aspendus and Side, the first and last on the coast about forty miles apart, all of them forming an arc of a circle with Sillyum near its centre, about ten miles from the sea. The newest and greatest of all was Attaleia, which Attalus II of Pergamum founded during his control of Pamphylia, possibly on the site of some older settlement.[4] Provided with the best harbour on the coast, it soon surpassed the older cities of the district and became the chief port of the southern littoral. It retained its independence after the Romans organized Pamphylia into a province, for it was not until 77 B.C. that Attaleia was annexed to Rome's possessions.[g]

An older rival of Attaleia in commercial importance was Side, on a low peninsula at the opposite end of the plain.[5] Side claimed to be a colony of Cyme in Aeolis, but as late as the fourth century the legends on its coins were in some "quasi-Semitic" dialect, and in the time of Alexander its inhabitants spoke a language which was a mixture of Greek and native forms. In 192 and 190 it aided Antiochus III, but later, when Scipio Aemilianus was collecting a fleet for the final overthrow of Carthage, Side out of friendship for the Roman general contributed five vessels.[h] During the palmy days of Cilician piracy the city

[f] Strabo XII p. 570.   [g] See Chap. XII note 20.   [h] Appian *Lib.* 123.

put its shipyards at the disposal of the corsairs and permitted them to sell their captives;[1] doubtless it obtained a large revenue therefrom. Its general prosperity was also due to the road which led across the mountains into Lycaonia,[j] as well as to the fact that it was a port of call for vessels bound for eastern Cilicia.[k]

Of the three inland cities the oldest probably was Aspendus.[6] It also attempted to establish a Greek tradition, on the ground that it had been founded by Argives. If, however, there was any truth in the claim, the natives seem soon to have absorbed the foreign element, for the coins that the city issued in the fifth century before Christ show its name in the barbarous form *Estvedys*. Situated on a height above the navigable Eurymedon, it seems to have attained early to great prosperity, and its silver coins circulated far and wide. Important sources of its income were probably the salt yielded by a lake in its territory and the olives from the hills behind.[1] It agreed to pay Alexander a "contribution" of fifty talents and to give him in addition the horses which it furnished as a regular tribute to the Persian king; but the promise was not made good until the invader appeared before its walls and demanded, as a penalty for the city's faithlessness, not only the original requisition but fifty talents more. Unlike Side, its neighbour and rival, it submitted to Achaeus and contributed a contingent of troops for his campaign against Selge.[m] To a Roman invader it was equally submissive, for in 189, when Manlius appeared in Milyas, although the whole breadth of Pamphylia separated him from Aspendus, the city was intimidated by his threats into purchasing his "friendship" by the payment of fifty talents.[n] Under the Romans it seems to have flourished, for at the beginning of the Christian Era it had a large population.[o]

On a terrace rising above the western bank of the Cestrus and about five miles from the river stood Perge.[7] Its situation was perhaps due to the fact that up to this point the Cestrus was navigable and Perge was the point of departure for the roads leading into the interior. It was the seat of the cult of an ancient goddess, the "Lady of Perge," whom the Greeks identified with Artemis and whose likeness appears on the city's coins. A yearly festival held in her honour probably contributed much to the city's prosperity. Perge was occupied by Alexander, and in 218 it received Achaeus and served as his general head-

i Strabo xiv p. 664.
k Cicero *Epist. ad Fam.* iii 5, 3; 6, 1; 12, 4.
m Polybius v 73, 3.
o Strabo xiv p. 667.

j See note 18.
l Pliny *N.H.* xxxi 73: Strabo xii p. 570.
n See Chap. XII note 4.

quarters whence he sent envoys to the other cities of the district. After the battle of Magnesia the Seleucid commandant held out against the Romans until he was authorized by Antiochus to surrender.

On the eastern side of the Cestrus, north of Perge and near the mountains, was Sillyum, situated on a commanding hill.[8] Under the Persians it was an important stronghold, garrisoned by a force composed of both mercenaries and native troops. Consequently, Alexander made no attempt to storm it. In the third century coins show its name in a native dialectical form. If we may judge from an inscription written in unintelligible Greek, the language spoken in Sillyum in its earlier days was well-nigh barbarous.

These cities, whatever their origin and their original connexion with Greece, maintained the form of civic government which was characteristic of an Hellenic *polis*. A decree of the *demos* of Aspendus, enacted, probably, at the beginning of the third century before Christ by "the sovereign assembly," granted rights of citizenship and enrollment in the city-tribes to men of various nationalities—presumably mercenaries—who had served the city and King Ptolemy.[9] The eponymous official, as also in certain cities on the western coast and in Cilicia, was the "Artificer" or "Demiurge." In the second century Perge had a "Council and People" which conferred honours, and in this or the following century the city had a gymnasium and the customery associations of Young Men and *ephebi*, as well as its own courts, for which, on at least one occasion, it imported a judge from outside. The existence in the imperial period of a demiurge and city-tribes at Perge, Side and Sillyum may well have been an inheritance from Hellenistic times. Even the insignificant city of Seleuceia, in the mountains north of Side, evidently a royal foundation, had in the second century before Christ a "Council and People," which enacted decrees on motion of a board of *prytaneis*.

The Pamphylian cities, it would seem, were strong and flourishing when the Romans incorporated the district in their empire. Their continued prosperity under Roman rule is shown by the imposing remains, particularly the great theatres and stadia, which bear evidence to large and wealthy populations in the second century after Christ.[10]

High up on the mountain-ring and just across the indefinite line which separated Pamphylia from Milyas and Pisidia were two other great cities, Termessus, west of the plain, and Selge on the north. Termessus, situated on the western side of Mt. Solymus in a narrow valley over 3,000 feet high, approachable only from its northern end, had a situation that was as impregnable as it was magnificent.[11] Originally a Pisidian settlement, it had an old sanctuary of the "God of Solymus," but before our knowledge begins both city and god had become Hellenized, the latter under the name of Zeus.

The first appearance of Termessus in history was in 334 B.C., when, thanks to its inaccessible situation, it was able to offer such determined resistance to Alexander that he abandoned the idea of capturing the place.[12] In the third century it was so prosperous that it founded a colony near Oenoanda in Lycia, which, in the course of time, became independent. When the Roman Consul, Manlius, in 189 compelled Termessus to withdraw its troops from an attack on its neighbour, Isinda, he forced it, like Aspendus, to accept his "friendship" at a cost of fifty talents.

It was perhaps in view of this experience and the fear of possible encroachment on the part of the kings of Pergamum that early in the second century the Termessians fortified the pass at the northern entrance to their valley and thus established a control over the highway leading from Pamphylia to Pisidia. During this century also Termessus concluded a formal treaty of "friendship and alliance" with the Pisidian city of Adada, by which each of the contracting parties promised to come to the aid of the other in the event of an invasion of its territory or an attempt to overthrow its "democracy." The purpose of the compact was perhaps to guard against an attack by the Pergamene rulers, but it may have been to forestall a possible attempt to establish a tyranny in the city. In any case, the treaty shows that Termessus (as well as Adada) had been Hellenized—presumably in imitation of the cities of the Pamphylian plain—and had adopted the constitution characteristic of a Greek *polis*, in which the power was held by the *demos*, presumably with the usual Council. It may be that the city-affairs were administered at this time, as in the Roman imperial period, by a board of *probouloi*, twelve in number, whose presiding officer, the *archiproboulos*, was the eponymous official, charged also with the supervision of the public finances. Under Attalus II Termessus evidently maintained friendly relations with Pergamum, for the King presented it with a handsome portico. In the beginning of the first century it had an arrangement with Rome, by which Romans and Termessians enjoyed certain rights with regard to each other. Later, after Pamphylia had become a Roman province, the city was recognized as independent.

The situation of Selge was even more impregnable.[13] High above the western bank of the Eurymedon, it could be approached only by a long and toilsome ascent. But despite its altitude of 3,000 feet, it lay in a plain so level that it has been compared to a lake and so fertile that, together with the terraces which rise on its western side, it bore great quantities of grain and olives, and even today it is not unproductive. The city subsequently attempted to establish a Greek tradition by asserting that it was originally a settlement of Lacedaemonians. The assertion was fictitious, for at the beginning of the fourth century before Christ Selge was issuing coins on which its name appears in various native forms. These coins show that even at this time it had a civic organization. By the middle of the fourth century its name appears in the Hellenized form, and it soon became the most important of the communities of Pisidia. It is said at one time to have had a male population of twenty thousand. The importance of the city, we are told, was due to the lawful manner in which its government was conducted, for this enabled it to maintain its independence; but this freedom from outside control was perhaps equally due to the natural strength of its situation and its wealth, derived from its olive-orchards and the medicaments which it produced, as well as from its wide pasture-lands and the forests on the mountains round about. Selge made overtures of friendship to Alexander, largely, so it was said, because of an ancient enmity toward Termessus, but to later invaders it offered valiant resistance. It surrendered to Achaeus only after a narrow escape from capture through the treachery of a prominent citizen, and it steadily resisted the encroaching power of Pergamum. Even Rome's supremacy was accepted only on the definite understanding that the city should not be dispossessed of its territory.

For its communication with the rest of Asia Minor Pamphylia was mainly dependent on two routes which led in a northerly direction; for the roads along the coast to Lycia on the west and Cilicia on the east were dangerous and difficult.[14] The main traffic of the district, therefore, was to and from the north. These two routes diverged at the northwestern corner of the plain. The more westerly climbed the steep ascent to the mountains of Milyas, past the entrance to the valley in which lay Termessus, and over a pass 3,000 feet above sea-level into the plain of Isinda, near the headwaters of the Istanos Çay. From here it led over the mountains to the plain north of Cibyra and thence to Laodiceia on the Southern Highway.[15] This was presumably the route used by the army of Mithradates when it attacked Termessus and perhaps invaded Pamphylia.[p] It has previously been suggested

[p] See Chap. IX note 30.

that the desire to control it was Murena's chief motive for annexing Cibyratis.[q] The second of these routes, leading northward from Pamphylia over the mountains into the basin in which lies Lake Kestel, went on to Sagalassus and thence over a difficult pass to the modern Isparta.[16] From here an important road led to the east around Lake Eğridir, while another branch went northwestward east of Lake Burdur to Apameia. By this road the city of Sagalassus, one of the most powerful of the communities of Pisidia, was connected both with the Pamphylian coast and with the Southern Highway.[17] One branch was used by Alexander when, after marching from Termessus to Sagalassus and taking the city by storm, he advanced past Lake Burdur to Apameia, and Manlius led his army over at least the most northerly section of it, when, after his return from the neighbourhood of Isinda, he plundered the fertile territory of Sagalassus south of Lake Burdur and went on to Apameia.

These roads connected Pamphylia with the Southern Highway, and so not only with the Aegean ports near the mouth of the Maeander, but also with central Lydia and even Pergamum. With the northeast, too, Pamphylia had a means of communication; for a difficult route led up from Side across the mountains to Lake Beyşehir, from which could be reached not only the cities of Pisidia but also Iconium on the plateau of Lycaonia.[18]

The third of the divisions of the southern coast, formed by the great masses which project from the Taurus and from the highlands of Pisidia, extends far out into the Mediterranean. This was Cilicia "the Rugged" (Aspera), so called to distinguish it from the alluvial plain of Cilicia "the Level" (Campestris), which recedes on the eastern side of this mountain-region.

The eastern tip of the crescent to which the plain of Pamphylia has been likened is marked approximately by the promontory on which lay the town of Coracesium; this was the western boundary of Cilicia Aspera.[r] Its eastern boundary was the river Lamus, where the plain of Cilicia Campestris begins.[s] The distance between the two along the coast is about 130 miles, while that from the southernmost point at the high headland of Cape Anamur to the watershed far up in the Taurus is shown by approximate measurements to be about half as great. Along the whole coast-line the mountains descend precipitously to the sea, leaving little flat land for settlements, except where tiny plains are formed by the torrents which pour down from the slopes above.[19] Many of the ancient towns were perched on the steep mountain-side or on the bold promontories that jut out into the Mediterranean. These projecting headlands provided harbours, which were used by the natives, as will be shown, for their own nefarious purposes.[t] The interior extends upward in rocky terrace-like plateaus to the Taurus watershed with frequent open fertile patches of great beauty. It is broken by mountain-masses and seamed by mighty chasms, through which run the streams that lie deep down in the limestone. Chief among these is the Calycadnus, which, rising in the mountains of Pisidia, breaks through the Taurus and cuts the Rugged District with a great gash, finally emptying into the Mediterranean some twenty miles west of the mouth of the Lamus. Its yawning canyon, at one point several miles across and about 3,000 feet deep, and those of its tributaries, especially the greatest, which rises in the centre of the district and flows eastward, give this whole highland country a character which well deserves its name of Rugged. No less awesome is the gorge of the Lamus, which forces its way down to the sea in a similar chasm. The depth of these canyons is due, at least in part, to the presence of underground streams which have so weakened the rock that the river-beds have collapsed. This process is also responsible for the extraordinary phenomenon of the great bowl-like depressions, now totally dry, the so-called "Caves" near Corycus on the coast, the lair, according to one version of the legend, of the fire-breathing monster Typhon.

The natural wealth of this formidable mountainous district, where water is lacking and agriculture can be carried on only in the bottoms of the canyons, consisted almost exclusively of the great forests which covered its slopes in Antiquity and even in modern times have evoked the admiration of travellers.[20] The character of the routes in the interior prevented any extensive exploitation of the timber, but near the south-western coast, at least, the abundant cedar-forests were utilized for the building of ships, and the wood was exported for the purpose. As in Pisidia, the dwarf oaks furnished kermes-dye, and these mountains also produced storax-gum as well as various medicaments, including liquorice. More valuable still was the famous saffron, used both as a perfume and as a dye, the best variety of which was grown at Corycus. This and its timber were probably the chief commercial assets of this poor district. The only manufactured article was a coarse fabric woven

[t] See below p. 281.

from goats' hair, used for coverings of various kinds and apparently, as in the region nowadays, even for tents as well.

In a country where agriculture was difficult and industries lacking, there was little to attract settlers from outside. Consequently, there had been no penetration of Hellenism into this mountainous area. On the coast, however, a fringe of towns arose, and the Greek names borne by many of them indicate the presence of the ubiquitous Hellene and even the attempt to construct a community according to the Hellenic model.[21] The oldest of these places was probably Celenderis, a harbour-town northeast of Cape Anamur, regarded as a colony of Samos, which in the late fifth century before Christ was a member of the "Confederacy of Delos" and issued silver coins bearing legends in Greek. Another Samian colony was Nagidus, on a height somewhat west of Celenderis, with a harbour protected by an island lying off the shore. It issued silver coins in the fourth century, and its fortifications show a workmanship which is genuinely Greek. There was a Greek tradition also in the ancient town of Holmi on the coast west of the mouth of the Calycadnus; it had cults of Athena and Apollo Sarpedonius, and its coins, issued in the fourth century, also bear Greek legends. The community, however, ceased to exist when Seleucus I moved the inhabitants to his new foundation, Seleuceia-on-the-Calycadnus. This city, built on a height overlooking the only plain of any size on this coast, a tract of alluvial deposit brought down by the river, became the most important place in the Rugged Cilicia. "Differing much from the ways of the Cilicians and Pamphylians," it adopted the institutions of a Greek *polis*, and at the beginning of the Christian Era it was the home of two Peripatetic philosophers. On the coast northeast of Seleuceia was Corycus, situated on a promontory with a good harbour. The city was regarded as under the special protection of Hermes, and a temple of the God has been found in the neighbourhood. Corycus was also near the famous "caves," where there was an ancient sanctuary of Zeus. Off the coast, a short distance to the east, lay the island of Elaeussa, which in the second century was "sacred and autonomous," and about the beginning of the Christian Era was for a time the residence of a king.

In the interior, as contrasted with the coast, primitive conditions continued to predominate. There was no reason why towns of any size should spring up in a region so forbidding and remote, and the native inhabitants lived in villages which clustered around castles built of great polygonal blocks of stone and perched on the brink of ravines.[22] It was not until the Romans extended their influence north-ward and brought with them a certain degree of security and civilization that communities of any importance arose; these bore the names of princes of the imperial Claudian House.[u]

A remnant of primitive times was the temple-state of Olba, in the mountains some sixteen miles north of Seleuceia.[23] It was ruled by a princely dynasty whose members were priests of the great Temple of Zeus situated about three miles from Olba itself; around this temple grew up a settlement, which in the first century of the Christian Era became a separate city named Diocaesareia. The temple whose ruins are extant was probably built about 300 B.C., when, it is recorded, Seleucus I paid for the roof of a passage leading around the inner side of the enclosing wall. The cult of the God, however, was doubtless much older, although the assertion that both the sanctuary and the dynasty had been founded by Ajax, son of Teucer who fought at Troy and later ruled at Salamis in Cyprus, is clearly an invention of the Hellenistic period. The statement that most of the priests were named Teucer or Ajax evidently arose from the same desire to create a Greek tradition. The earlier priests, in fact, bore the name Tarkyaris, derived from that of Tarku, an ancient Asianic god, perhaps the deity originally worshipped at Olba. It was not until the late third century, apparently, that the priest's name was Hellenized into Teucer.

At the end of this century the dominions of these prince-priests extended down the mountain-slopes toward Elaeussa and perhaps even as far as the sea. With increasing power came greater self-importance, and whereas the earlier princes had been content with the simple title of Priest of Zeus, the later rulers assumed the pompous designation of "Great Archpriest." Their power, however, was not uncontested, for in the early first century their possessions were seized by various "tyrants," some of whom were probably nothing more than chiefs of pirate-bands. When one of these was overthrown and slain, his slayer was rewarded by the Seleucid prince, Philip II, who perhaps had found shelter at Olba when other members of his dynasty held the Syrian throne. Later, another chieftain, named Zenophanes, perhaps aided by the same tyrannicide, seized the priesthood. More shrewd than his predecessors, he married his daughter to a scion of the old priestly house. By this device he was able not only to hold the power in the capacity of her guardian but also to give to her descendants the semblance of a lawful claim to both the principality and the priesthood.

[u] See Chap XXIII notes 27 and 31.

The primitive character of Cilicia Aspera was due, at least to some extent, to a paucity of roads.[24] In such broken country it was difficult to construct the thoroughfares on which the development of a region depends, and in turn there was little incentive for road-building. Even in pre-Roman days, however, the coast settlements were connected; the remains of an ancient road, partly hewn in the rock and partly resting on "Cyclopean" substructures, have been found just east of Cape Anamur. But the cliffs which descend abruptly to the sea, as well as the projecting headlands, caused such rapid ascents and descents to and from the towns built on them that the route around the peninsula was no easy one. The Romans, nevertheless, maintained it as a thoroughfare between Pamphylia and the plain of eastern Cilicia.

Save for this one east-west route, the traffic went north or south; for the deep chasms of the rivers made the construction of roads running parallel to the littoral too difficult. What routes there were kept to the heights, and the deep ravines, for the most part, could be approached only by precipitous tracks. Even those which led from the coast into the interior ascended so rapidly that wheeled traffic was impossible, and they could be traversed only by pack-animals. Of these roads the most important were those which led northward from Seleuceia, the chief port of the district. One of them ran northwest, high above the western bank of the Calycadnus, to the site of the later city of Claudiopolis and thence over the Taurus to Laranda on the Lycaonian plateau, from which there was a route to Iconium and the Southern Highway.[25] The other led northward from Seleuceia to Olba, where it was joined by a road from Corycus. From Olba it went northward and westward to join the route from Seleuceia to Laranda; another branch may possibly have led thither also along the line of the modern highway. These roads leading inland from the coast, constructed, in the manner of ancient Alpine routes, of great stone slabs, made the ascent from the sea at terrific gradients. Another transverse route led northward from Cape Anamur to Isaura in the Taurus and thence onward to Iconium.

East of the mass of bleak highlands which constituted the Rugged Cilicia and between it and the mountainous littoral of northern Syria, lies a great indentation of the coast forming a deep recess. At the head of this is Cilicia the "Level" (Campestris), a luxuriant broad riviera, which contrasted both in nature and culture with its wilder neighbour on the west. Near the source of the river Lamus the broken masses of the western Taurus begin to form the great ridge, sometimes ten thousand feet in height, which extends to the Euphrates. This mighty range withdraws gradually from the sea, leaving a continually widening plain.[26] The mountain-wall, which thus describes a great curve about the Level Cilicia, consists of the Taurus itself and its southern extension, the Amanus, which runs down to the coast and constitutes a natural barrier between Asia Minor and Syria. Projecting westward from the Amanus is a spur—a miniature range with valleys and peaks having a maximum altitude of less than 2,500 feet—which forms an enclosing barrier at this corner also. Within this ring of mountains lies the Cilician Plain, at the mouth of the rivers which rush down from the Taurus into the Mediterranean and, little by little, have filled up the corner of the gulf. This land is divided into two levels by a line of hills which project from the north to meet the spur of the Amanus; through this ridge the river Pyramus breaks its way to the sea. The lower, southwesterly, portion—the Aleian Plain mentioned in the *Iliad*—is raised but little above the Mediterranean; it has been gradually formed by the deposit of the rivers, which are slowly increasing its area. Northeast of the barrier lies a higher level, completely surrounded by the mountains and their spurs. It consists entirely of the basin of the Pyramus and its tributaries and forms a recess, as it were, joined to the maritime plain only by an entrance between the projecting mountains. Thus it was but little affected by the busy intercourse between Syria and western Asia Minor which passed through the lower plain.

In the fifth century before Christ, the maritime plain was described as "large and fair, well-watered and full of vines and trees of every kind," and it bore all varieties of grain. In the Roman period it was still known for its wheat and its rice, its date-palms, its figs and its wines. Even now the ancient description holds good, for grain and fruit are still the products of this fertile land, perhaps the garden-spot of Asia Minor. The cereals of the region are exported in large quantities, and in its sub-tropical climate flourish fruit-orchards, the beauty of which is rendered all the more striking by reason of a background of snow-capped mountain-peaks.

The plain is traversed by three rivers, to which it owes its fertility and even its existence.[27] Of these the two greatest, the Sarus and the Pyramus, the former in three branches, rise in the mountains of Cappadocia far to the north and force their way through the chain of the Taurus in chasms of terrifying grandeur, sometimes with a depth of a thousand feet or more and comparable to the wildest scenery of

the Alps. The Sarus enters Cilicia from the north, the Pyramus at the
northeast corner; both are swelled by affluents which flow down from
the southern slopes of the Taurus or even, like the main streams, break
through the great chain. At the northwest corner of the plain is the
Cydnus, which, rising high up in the Taurus, flows southward, traversing a gorge so fear-inspiring that it is known today as the "Valley
of Hell." The water, after its long course through the mountain-
ravines, was noted in ancient times for a refreshing coolness, and one
noble Roman even asserted that it was a remedy for the gout.

Thus desirable for human habitation and cultivation, the Level
Cilicia contained cities which had been of importance since the time
of the Assyrian supremacy. With two exceptions, they were in the
lower portion of the plain, either on one of the rivers or on the coast
itself. The greatest and most famous was Tarsus, situated in the rich
and beautiful lowlands along the Cydnus backed by the foothills of
the Taurus.[28] A settlement of native origin, Tarsus was probably increased during the early days of Hellenic migration by colonists from
Greece; these were speedily amalgamated with the Asianic element,
but they nevertheless made it possible at a later time for the citizens
to assert that their city had been founded by three different Greek
heroes. When Cyrus and Xenophon marched through it with their
soldiers, Tarsus was the residence of the native ruler, a "large and
prosperous" place and the chief city of Cilicia. One of the earlier
Seleucids renamed it Antiocheia, and under the later monarchs of the
dynasty it seems to have had its own city-officials. Lying on the trade-
route which led from Antioch in Syria to the Aegean, Tarsus was
connected with the sea by the navigable Cydnus; for the river emptied
its waters into a lagoon, less than ten miles distant, which served as a
harbour. Tarsus, therefore, profited by traffic on both land and sea.
One of its chief industries was the weaving of linen made from the
flax which grew in the fertile plain, but tents, too, were manufactured,
presumably from the goat-hair obtained from the mountains of the
Rugged District. St. Paul, it will be remembered, was a tent-maker
of Tarsus. The perfumes prepared in the city were also well known.
With prosperity, as often, came culture and learning, and in the first
century before Christ Tarsus was the home of philosophers and poets.
The zeal of its inhabitants for education, we are told, surpassed even
that of the Athenians and the Alexandrians.[v]

At the eastern edge of the lower plain, on the Pyramus forty-five

[v] Strabo xiv p. 673f.

miles east of Tarsus, was the city of Mopsuestia.[29] Like Tarsus, it claimed a Greek hero as founder, the seer Mopsus, who was also accredited with the establishment of settlements in Pamphylia. The fanciful explanation of its name as "Hearth of Mopsus" appears on coins issued under the Roman emperors, some of which show the figure of the seer, while others have a representation of a flaming altar. Under the Seleucids Mopsuestia enjoyed the special privileges expressed by the epithet "sacred and autonomous." Its situation on the great trade-route, which crossed the Pyramus here, gave the city an important position commercially, and the ruins of a theatre and of a colonnade with columns of Egyptian granite, as well as other architectural remains, bear testimony to its splendour under Roman rule.

About half way between Tarsus and Mopsuestia, at the bridge over which the highway crossed the Sarus, lay Adana,[30] which, like Tarsus, still preserves its ancient name. Although a place of some importance in the earlier Seleucid period, during the first century before Christ it seems to have dwindled to such an extent that Pompey could reasonably establish in it some of the sea-robbers, whom, as will be shown, he settled in various cities of the plain. Apparently a rival of Tarsus in ancient times, it has since eclipsed it and now it is the chief city of Cilicia.

In addition to these three inland cities extending in a straight line across the northern part of the lower plain, there were three others on or near the coast, all, however, of less note. These were Soli, Mallus and Aegaeae. Soli was situated a few miles east of the river Lamus, which, as we have seen, was regarded as the western boundary of the Level Cilicia.[31] Actually colonized by the Rhodians about 700 B.C., it claimed at the beginning of the second century an older tradition; for in 189 the envoys of Rhodes, in presenting a plea to the Roman Senate that Soli should not remain subject to Seleucid rule but receive independence, based the request on the ground that, like their own city, it had been founded by Argives. Under the Persians Soli enjoyed the privilege of issuing its own coins, and so pro-Persian were the sympathies of the ruling faction when Alexander reached it on his eastward march, that he placed a garrison in the city and exacted a fine of two hundred talents; he then gave the citizens a new constitution, which established a government by the people and presumably ousted from power the aristocratic Persian sympathizers. The Seleucid rulers seem to have treated Soli with consideration; at least on one occasion a complaint that the city was unduly burdened by the quarter-

ing of soldiers brought from the monarch or his representative a rebuke
to the officer responsible for the action. During this period Soli could
boast of famous sons, for it was the original home, not only of Chry-
sippus, who became the head of the Stoic school and perfected its
philosophical system, but also of Aratus, whose astronomical poem in
epic metre was read far and wide in the Hellenistic world and was
twice translated into Latin. When, early in the first century before
Christ, the power of the Seleucids declined, many of the inhabitants, as
will be related, were carried away by Tigranes of Armenia to his
new city of Tigranocerta. Later, however, Soli was restored by Pompey
under the name Pompeiopolis. Of the new city there remain a theatre
and a colonnaded street, about 450 yards long, leading to the harbour,
where it ended in an extensive open space also enclosed by columns.
The foundations of the harbour-walls are still visible, but the port has
long been filled up with silt.

Somewhere on a height rising above the present swamp-lands on
the right bank of the Pyramus and not far from the mouth of the
river was Mallus, the ruins of which have entirely disappeared.[32] Here,
too, there was a Greek tradition, which related that the city was
founded, according to one version, by Amphilochus, a hero and seer
from Thebes, who was said to have accompanied Mopsus to Cilicia,
according to another, by a band of colonizing Argives. The memory
of the prophetically-endowed "founder" was perpetuated by a much-
frequented oracle, which in the second century after Christ was still
issuing responses in Amphilochus's name. Alexander had found Mallus
engaged in the factional strife all too frequent among cities of the
Hellenistic world. Not only did he succeed in bringing this to an
end, but he also freed the city from the payment of tribute to the
Persian monarch on the ground that he himself, as the reputed descendant of Heracles, was also of Argive stock. Soon after Alexander's
death, Ptolemy I, King of Egypt, invaded the Cilician coast in 315 and,
after taking Mallus, sold as slaves those of its inhabitants whom he
captured. Nevertheless, in the second century Mallus seems to have
had a civic organization with a "demiurge" as chief magistrate, and
in the first century, probably, its population included a group of
Italian settlers.

The most easterly of the coast cities was Aegaeae, situated on a point
which projects from the end of the previously mentioned mountain-
spur southward into the Mediterranean.[33] Like other Cilician cities,
it claimed kinship with Argos, "renewed" in the first or second cen-

tury after Christ. In the Hellenistic period it had a city-government of
its own, but the commercial development of the place must have been
greatly hampered by the fact that as late as the beginning of the
Christian Era its harbour was little more than an open roadstead.
Perhaps the city's chief claim to fame was its temple of Asclepius,
for early coins describe it as "sacred and autonomous" and "sacred
and inviolable," and others show the portraits of the God and of
Hygeia, his daughter. The Romans allowed Aegaeae to retain its
freedom and apparently improved its harbour; in the first century of
our era it had dockyards, and the title "Mistress of Ships," borne in the
third century, points to a certain importance in seafaring. Nevertheless,
it was described as a quiet place and well-suited for a student of
philosophy.

In contrast to the dense urban population of the lower plain, the
higher level contained only two cities of note. The more important
of these, Anazarbus, had a magnificent situation at the foot of a huge
rock rising precipitously from the floor of the plain, some distance
north of the great bend made by the Pyramus after leaving the mountains.[34] The natural strength of its citadel, as well as its position on
two main trade-routes, leading, respectively, to Syria and Cappadocia,
made it both a strategic and a commercial point of vantage. Nevertheless, Anazarbus seems to have been of little consequence under the
Seleucids, and its greatest development was apparently due to the
Romans. In the second century after Christ linen-weaving, as at Tarsus,
seems to have been an important industry. In the third century
Anazarbus rivalled Tarsus in the pretentiousness of its claim to the
rank of Metropolis, and the remains of two theatres, one of them cut
out of the rock which served as the acropolis, as well as an amphitheatre,
a stadium, and two colonnaded streets, show that its pretensions were
not without foundation.

The only other city of the upper plain was Hieropolis, situated at
the edge of the mountains where the Pyramus breaks forth.[35] Apparently originally called Castabala, it assumed the name of "City of the
Sanctuary" from the worship of the goddess Perasia, a cult-name for
the Persian deity assimilated to Artemis, and described itself on its coins
as "sacred and inviolable." In order to demonstrate a connexion with
Greece the claim was made, as in the case of many other similar cults,
that the statue of the goddess had been brought "from abroad" by
Orestes. At the beginning of the second century before Christ the
city was important enough to issue coins of its own. Under the Romans

it gained further prestige by becoming the residence of a dynasty of local client-kings.[w]

In striking contrast also to the remoteness of its neighbour on the west was the accessibility of Cilicia Campestris. Across it led the principal thoroughfare of Asia Minor—the southern extension of the great Southern Highway.[36] For centuries this road carried the traffic and the armies which passed from Syria and Mesopotamia to the Aegean coast, and even today its course through Cilicia is followed in part by the railway from Constantinople to Bagdad. From Cybistra, at the southeastern corner of the central plateau of Asia Minor, the road ascends to the watershed of the Taurus at an altitude of nearly 5,000 feet, descending rapidly on the southern side along the upper course of a river (Çakıt Su), which here bursts through the mountains in a narrow ravine with walls towering to a height of a thousand feet above the stream. At Podandus, in a small vale of great fertility, it leaves the river, which soon enters an impassable gorge, and ascends again through a side-valley to a point over 4,000 in height. From here it follows a tributary of the Cydnus flowing southward down through the Cilician Gates, in pre-Roman days the only waggon-road that led across the Taurus and through the ages the most famous of the passes of Anatolia. This gorge, a hundred yards long, with precipitous walls rising for over 500 feet and in width not more than fifty, is penetrated by the stream, which leaves a space of only a few feet for the road; this had, therefore, to be cut out of the wall of the rock and, where a cutting was impracticable, carried along on wooden planks. South of the Gates the road continues down the narrow river valley to Tarsus, about one hundred miles from Cybistra. From Tarsus its course lies through the lower level of the plain as far as the eastern end, where it crosses the Pyramus at Mopsuestia; there it enters the hills, passing through a fortified defile to the plain of Issus, in which the Persian East succumbed to the Hellenic West. South of this, it traverses a narrow strand enclosed between two spurs of the Amanus which reach down to the sea, the famous "Cilician-Syrian Gates," and then, at Alexandretta, it leaves the shore to wind its way over the mountains to Antioch, the Seleucid capital, and eventually to advance ever eastward to the Euphrates. Over the route through the Cilician Gates the younger Cyrus led his Grecian troops in his ill-starred attempt to secure the Persian throne, and over it also Alexander came to extend the power of Macedonia into the nearer East. Generals and traders,

[w] See below p. 377.

army-trains and caravans, climbed the toilsome mountain-sides which led to these famous Gates, and the Roman governors of Cilicia, among them even Cicero, were to follow in their steps. In later years Roman emperors and, after them, Crusaders traversed the same steep road.

Other routes also converged upon this populous plain. From the west came the coast-road from Seleuceia and Soli, the only means of communication with the city founded by Seleucus to maintain his hold on the southern coast.[37] From the east, over the range of Mt. Amanus to the higher level of the plain and along the course of the lower Pyramus past Anazarbus, led a road which brought the trade from northern Syria and the Euphrates beyond the crossing at Zeugma.[38] From the northwest, between the coast and the Gates, a short but difficult route crossed the high Taurus from Cybistra to Tarsus. The suggestion has been made that it was by this road that Cyrus's general, Menon, marched into Cilicia, thus turning the flank of the army of the native king in its attempt to bar the way.[39] Even from the northeast, through the almost impassable mountains, there was a road, at least in Roman times, from Cocusus in Cappadocia.[40] Leading from spur to spur above the gorge of the Sarus, descending at least once into the depths of the canyon and abruptly climbing again to a pass 5,000 feet in height, and finally emerging into the high level plain north of Anazarbus, it was probably the most toilsome in its ascents and descents of all the roads of Cilicia.

This long stretch of coast, from the great promontory of Lycia to the range of Amanus was acquired by the Romans, as will now be shown, during the first half of the first century before Christ. The establishment of their rule was no short process, for forty years intervened between the time when a Roman fleet first appeared off the southern littoral and the final acquisition of the lands of the South. The work was accomplished by the effort of two generals, who, by conquering the bold mountaineers, turned pirates, brought the coast districts under the sway of Rome.

CHAPTER XII

THE WINNING OF THE SOUTH

DESPITE the Seleucids' assured possession of the Level Cilicia in the early third century and their claim to the Rugged District, strengthened by the founding of Seleuceia-on-the-Calycadnus, the grandiloquent encomium written in praise of Ptolemy II by the poet Theocritus boasted that the King's possessions included "all the Pamphylians and the spear-bearing Cilicians."[1] The exaggerated character of the assertion is shown by the almost equally high-sounding record of the achievements of his son and successor, in which the monarch enumerated Pamphylia and Cilicia among his own conquests. Ptolemy II may, it is true, have had some slight claim to Pamphylia and Cilicia Aspera; for under his father, apparently, Aspendus conferred privileges on certain soldiers in the Egyptian service, and the two places on the coast which were called Arsinoe were presumably named in honour of his sister-wife. Ptolemais in Pamphylia, near the border of Cilicia Aspera, was evidently an Egyptian foundation. It was also true that Ptolemy III added to the possessions of Egypt on the southern coast; Soli, a Seleucid city, was occupied about 246 by a body of his soldiers. In general, however, the power of Egypt in southern Asia Minor was limited to certain places on the littoral west of Cape Anamur and never extended into the interior. Even though, about 220 B.C., Pamphylia was nominally an Egyptian possession, the cities were, in fact, independent states; for in 218 Perge received a lieutenant of Achaeus and Aspendus sent him a force of soldiers, and when the citizens of Side declined to support the rebel, their refusal was motivated by the wish to retain the favour of the lawful Seleucid monarch, Antiochus III.

Whatever claim the rulers of Egypt may have had to this coast was brought to an abrupt end when, in 197, Antiochus set out to recover the possessions which his predecessors had held in Asia Minor.[a] Sailing along the coast with his fleet, he compelled Soli, Corycus and the other Cilician places still subject to Egypt to submit.[2] Only Coracesium, relying on its impregnable position, offered resistance. Pamphylia also, falling into his hands, became a Seleucid possession, and in 188 Perge was held by a garrison of Antiochus's soldiers.

According to the terms of the Treaty of Apameia, by which An-

a See above p. 17.

278

tiochus was forced to cede all his dominions north of the Taurus, the southern coast should have remained in the possession of the defeated monarch.[3] Nevertheless, he was not permitted to retain the region in its entirety. The framers of the treaty, taking advantage of the fact that the range of the Taurus at its western end no longer constitutes a definite wall but breaks up into the mountainous masses of Pisidia, ruled that not only Lycia, lying west of the range regarded as the beginning of the Taurus, but also the highlands of Pisidia, with the region of Milyas, lay within the ceded area. Lycia, as has already been related, was awarded to the Rhodians, and Milyas with a part of Pisidia to Eumenes of Pergamum.

Even before the signing of the treaty, western Pisidia felt the hand of the conqueror. In the spring of 189 B.C. Gnaeus Manlius Vulso, successor of Scipio in the command of the army in Asia, set out on a punitive expedition against the Galatians, who had been allies of the defeated Antiochus. First, however, neglecting the primary object of the campaign for a more lucrative undertaking, he turned southward into Caria.[4] After forcing Tabae to surrender and mulcting the city of twenty-five talents and ten thousand measures of grain, he advanced across the mountains into the region around Cibyra, where he compelled the local tyrant, after protracted bargaining, to pay him one hundred talents and another ten thousand measures of grain for refraining from devastating the fields and attacking the city. Then, proceeding along the main route leading from Cibyratis to the southern coast and plundering as he went, Manlius exacted fifty talents from Termessus and like amounts from the distant cities of the Pamphylian Plain. Returning northward, still intent on plunder, he forced the wealthy city of Sagalassus to purchase immunity from the devastation of its lands by the payment of the same amount of money and forty thousand measures of barley and wheat. The whole procedure of levying what closely resembled the "black-mail" demanded by those Galatians whom he had undertaken to punish was a disgrace to the arms of Rome. To many it must have seemed a well-deserved retribution when, on his way to Italy after the conference at Apameia, Manlius and his army were attacked by the savage Thracians, who plundered the baggage-train and seized much of the money extorted from Asia.[b]

Scarcely had the treaty been signed when the question arose whether the plain of Pamphylia lay "within" or "without" the Taurus. Eumenes, presumably on the ground that spurs of the great range extend down

[b] Livy XXXVIII 40, 6f. = Polybius XXI 47: Appian *Syr.* 43.

to the sea on the eastern side of the plain, contended that Pamphylia was included in his new possessions.[5] Antiochus, on the other hand, maintained that the district still belonged to the Seleucid Empire. The dispute was necessarily submitted to the Romans for adjudication. The problem thus presented to the Senators was undoubtedly a difficult one, and they appear to have solved it in their usual temporizing fashion by declaring that Pamphylia—of whose existence many of them had probably been unaware—should be free and independent.

Eumenes's possession of Milyas next brought him into collision with the powerful city of Selge.[6] In 164 B.C., encouraged by Eumenes's enemy, Prusias II of Bithynia, Selge sent envoys to Rome to prefer charges against him, presumably of some kind of aggression. Whether the Senate intervened we do not know, but if so, its action could not have been very vigorous, for Eumenes's successor, Attalus II, whose policy it was to be guided in such matters by Rome's wishes, had scarcely ascended the throne of Pergamum when he invaded the city's territory. The Selgians stoutly withstood his attempt at conquest, but he was able to overrun at least the western portion of Pamphylia and to found the new port of Attaleia. Some of the cities, at least, entered into friendship with him, such as Termessus, to which he presented a portico.

By the loss of Pamphylia only the two districts of Cilicia were left to Antiochus. At the same time, his control over even this small remnant of his Asianic possessions was limited, for the Treaty of Apameia had crippled his power still further by means of the clause which forbad him to send warships west of the mouth of the Calycadnus.[c] Since the mountainous character of Cilicia Aspera made it almost impenetrable for armies, this prohibition of naval operations naturally resulted, for all practical purposes, in the exclusion of the Seleucids from the district. The rich plain of Cilicia Campestris, however, remained in their power for another century.

Under Antiochus Epiphanes, the brilliant son of the defeated monarch, who in general adopted a policy of Hellenization, a real effort seems to have been made to stimulate urban life by giving increased importance to the cities.[7] Following the example of his predecessors, who had refounded Tarsus and Mopsuestia as Antiocheia and Seleuceia, he gave the name of Antiocheia to both Adana and Magarsus. The native communities also in eastern Cilicia Campestris, Oeniandus and Castabala, became Hellenized as Epiphaneia and Hieropolis.

---

[c] Polybius XXI 43 (45), 14 = Livy XXXVIII 38, 9.

Several cities seem during his reign to have had a limited degree of local autonomy, for they issued bronze coins bearing the monarch's head, intended perhaps for general, as well as for local, circulation.

After the death of Antiochus Epiphanes, the power of the Seleucid dynasty, rent by dissensions among various claimants to the throne, steadily diminished. The little strength the monarchs possessed was devoted to the safeguarding of their eastern dominions, and their hold on Cilicia, as well as their interest in it, became gradually weaker. Before the end of the second century much of the interior, especially in the Rugged District, was free from all outside control. Whatever authority was wielded in these mountain-regions was in the hands of local rulers, such as the prince-priest of Olba.[d] In many places the tribes were subject to chieftains who dwelt in fortress-like castles[e] and frequently were little more than leaders of robber-bands.

The situation of Cilicia Aspera, in fact, made it well suited for brigandage both by land and by sea.[f] On the north, across the Taurus, lay unprotected farms, from which booty could be carried away without danger of pursuit over the mountain-passes. But it was especially the sea that gave these robbers an opportunity to seize their prey. The bold headlands sheltered many tiny harbours, often fortified and undiscernible to seafarers, which furnished a safe retreat to those who knew them, while the islands lying off the coast enabled pirate-vessels to lurk unseen by their intended victims. The mountains yielded an abundant supply of timber for ship-building, and from the watch-towers perched on the crags the approach of vessels could be seen from afar. Moreover, the great sea-lane from Syria to the Aegean and the western Mediterranean led along this coast. It was natural, therefore, that the inhabitants of this barren district, well supplied with opportunities for piracy, should have sought to enrich themselves by preying upon passing ships. So generally, in fact, were they engaged in this lucrative occupation that in the course of time the idea prevailed that all of them were free-booters, and the word "Cilician" became synonymous with "pirate."[g]

From the early years of Greek commerce the pirates had been the bane of merchants and travellers.[8] Athens, in the days of her supremacy in the Aegean, had taken effective measures to suppress the evil, but after the disastrous Peloponnesian War her diminished strength was no longer equal to the task. Although during the fourth century she

---

[d] See Chap. XI note 23.
[f] Strabo xiv p. 671: Appian *Mith.* 92.

[e] See Chap. XI note 22.
[g] Appian *Mith.* 92; see note 21.

made attempts to quell them, the depredations of the corsairs became a general menace. Alexander did much to establish order on the seas, especially by his policy of restoring to their homes the political exiles whom misfortune had turned into desperadoes. But during the struggles between his successors the sea-robbers not only infested the Aegean but even entered the service of the various monarchs. At the beginning of the second century, in the war waged by the Romans against Antiochus III, an "arch-pirate" named Nicander aided the royal admiral to capture a Rhodian fleet, and fifteen pirate-ships in the King's service, perhaps under the same Nicander, plundered the island of Chios.

In the course of this century piracy attained to alarming proportions, and among the most notorious were the robbers from Cilicia Aspera. As the dwindling power of the royal House of the Seleucids grew weaker, the activity of the pirates increased. They formed themselves into bands with which they raided the islands and the coast. There was none to hinder them, for there was no power ready to assume the burden of policing the eastern Mediterranean. The kings of Egypt, although in earlier years they had taken measures to repress the corsairs, were no longer willing or able to aid their Syrian enemies by fighting their battles for them or to protect a sea-traffic in which they felt but little interest. There was one state, indeed, which was vitally interested in the commerce of the Aegean, namely Rhodes.[9] Its efficient navy had done more than any other force to prevent the spread of piracy. Yet when, after 167 B.C., Rome's short-sighted policy of weakening the Republic caused its power to decline, the Rhodians were no longer able to control the sea-robbers, who even went so far as to attack the sanctuaries of the gods. It may be assumed that the reduction of the Rhodian supremacy on the seas was the prime cause of the growth of piracy in the latter part of this century.

Meanwhile the Romans did little to combat the danger. In fact, they seem tacitly to have encouraged it. After 167 B.C., when, in their desire to create a commercial rival to Rhodes, they declared Delos a free port, a great slave-market was established on the island.[10] In it, we are told, as many as ten thousand slaves could be sold in a single day. For this traffic the pirates furnished the material. Rome, enriched by the capture of Corinth and of Carthage in 146, proved an active buyer. The agrarian development of Italy, in which slave-labour on vast estates was rapidly replacing the small peasant-proprietor, as well as the increasing luxury of the great families of the city itself, created a demand for slaves which probably had no precedent in the ancient world—a demand of which the pirates were quick to take advantage.

One attempt, indeed, the Roman government did make to deal with the situation. About 140 B.C. a commission, consisting of Scipio Aemilianus and two other senators, was sent on a journey of good will to Egypt and the East to look into the affairs of the Senate's "allies."[11] By putting an end to internal dissensions, they were to establish these monarchs more securely on their thrones. In the course of their journey the three commissioners visited Syria and Rhodes and studied the causes of the piracy on the Cilician coast, and in their report they stated truly but uselessly the obvious fact that the trouble was due to the worthlessness of the kings. There is no record, however, of any resultant effort on the part of the Romans to crush the robbers or of any attempt to police the seas.

As time went on, however, and the operations of the Cilician pirates extended farther to the west,[h] their activity not only became a general menace but also interfered with the commerce between Rome and her new province of Asia and entailed losses on the Italian business-men who had established themselves there. Nevertheless, it was not until 102 B.C. that the Senate took any active steps to put down the evil. In this year the praetor, Marcus Antonius, grandfather of the later Triumvir and afterwards famous as an orator, was sent to Cilician waters with the rank of proconsul and the command of a war against the pirates.[12] He had once been quaestor of the province of Asia, but, as far as is known, he had had no military or naval experience. On his way to the East he stopped at Athens and at Rhodes, where he enjoyed conversations with the famous rhetoricians of the day, and in the latter city, at least, he appears to have collected some ships for his campaign. Indeed, he seems to have gathered a fleet from near and far, for more than a hundred and fifty years later the envoys of Byzantium boasted before the Senate that their city had given him aid in this war. With this fleet he defeated the enemy in a naval campaign, lasting perhaps two years, and captured some of their vessels, but there is no evidence that he took possession of the coast or annexed any part of it as a province of Rome. On his return he received the honour of a triumph—though afterwards, ironically enough, his own daughter was captured by pirates operating in the waters of the West.

Within a year, probably, of Antonius's campaign the Roman government again took action. This time, however, its move was rather diplomatic than military in character, although it is not unlikely that the military success of Antonius paved the way. A law, duly passed by the people, ordered the Consul to send letters to the free communities in alliance with Rome, bidding them do their utmost "to the end that Roman citizens and their Latin allies from Italy might transact their business without danger and sail the seas in safety."[13] Despatches were to be sent also to the kings of Cyprus, Egypt, Cyrene and Syria, "friends and allies" of Rome, requesting them to refuse the pirates admission to their dominions. The law was perhaps passed at the suggestion of the people of Rhodes, for the letters to the kings seem to have been given to Rhodian envoys. The publication in Delphi of this measure is evidence that it was put into effect, but unfortunately the document as preserved does not reveal what action the Romans themselves were preparing to take in the matter. There is no suggestion that any warlike measures were being considered.

This appeal to its allies in the East was all that the Roman government felt able to do for the protection of its citizens' interests. During the next decade it appears to have taken no steps to establish any permanent command in southern Asia Minor. It is true that Sulla, on the occasion of his mission to the East in 92 B.C., when he was ordered to restore Ariobarzanes to the throne of Cappadocia and, as far as possible, to thwart the designs of Mithradates, is referred to in certain of our late historical sources as governor of Cilicia.[14] This appellation has served as the basis for a view that at this time a province of Cilicia was in existence. But whatever title may have been given to Sulla officially for the purpose of his mission, there is no indication that this was concerned with any part of Asia Minor except Cappadocia. It would seem that if he ever set foot in Cilicia at all, his stay there was limited to the time needed for the journey through the Level District (then Seleucid) to his destination. There is no good reason for supposing that he exercised any military or administrative functions on the southern coast or that at this time the Romans made any attempt to police the eastern Mediterranean. Any concern they may have felt for the safety of seafarers in these waters was subordinated to more important considerations—the pretensions of Mithradates and two years of bitter warfare with the Italian Allies.

Even before peace with these allies was wholly restored, Mithradates burst upon the province of Asia. In the course of his triumphant march down the Maeander basin he ordered some of his generals to occupy Lycia and Pamphylia. This invasion, however, met with little success; for although the troops sent to Pamphylia overran the territory of Termessus, they failed to conquer the plain along the coast.[1]

Meanwhile the pirates had prospered. It has already been related that Mithradates, seeing their value as auxiliaries, aided them to gather a formidable fleet, which, even after the defeated King withdrew to his native Pontus, continued to plunder the cities along the Aegean Sea.[j] It was clearly necessary to take some steps to save the littoral of Asia Minor from their continued depredations, and to this end a permanent command was finally organized in the South. A pretext for the seizure of the coast district may have been found in Mithradates's invasion.

The suggestion has previously been made that Murena's annexation of Cibyra to the province of Asia may have originated in the city's submission to the Pontic generals;[k] Cibyra was in alliance with Rome, and an act of submission to the enemy could be construed as a breach of faith, entailing the forfeiture of the city's independence. The same pretext may have been used in Milyas and Pamphylia, for even though Termessus resisted the invader, some of the cities may have submitted when Mithradates's army entered these districts. Their action in so doing would afford a ground for annulling their status of freedom and reducing them to the position of subjects. Some favours, indeed, were granted, for Attaleia was permitted for a few years to retain its territory[l] and presumably also its freedom, and Selge, in accepting the supremacy of Rome, stipulated that it should not be deprived of its lands.[m] It is possible that privileges were granted to other cities as well, but if so, they were only isolated instances. The winning of a portion of the southern coast thus became an accomplished fact.

The new province was officially known as "Cilicia." The designation, however, was a misnomer, for the province included little or nothing of the district whose name it bore, and the power of the governors was limited to the districts of Pamphylia and Milyas and perhaps the adjacent portion of southern Pisidia.[15] The fertile plain with its wealthy cities and the hill-country behind it, through which led the routes to the north, naturally seemed to the Romans a much more valuable territory than the bleak mountains of Rugged Cilicia and the untamed tribes whose only wealth was the booty which they seized from others.

The arrangements made by Sulla or Murena for governing the new province are not known.[16] The earliest governor of whom we have definite information was Gnaeus Cornelius Dolabella, whose

i See Chap. IX note 30.   j See above p. 239f.   k See above p. 242.
l See note 20.   m See Chap. XI note 13.

participation in the scandalous trial of Philodamus was only one instance of his unfitness for office.[n] Of him Cicero remarked sarcastically
that he was one of those men of noble birth who, whether they did
right or wrong, did it so successfully that no one of humble origin
could equal them.[o] A more serious indictment against him, however,
may be found in his selection of the notorious Gaius Verres as legate
and later, after the death of the quaestor of the province, his appointment of Verres to the latter's post.

Dolabella was entrusted with the command of a military force to
be used against "the enemy"—evidently the pirates—but, since these
seem to have been especially active after his departure, it is evident
that he did nothing to restrain their operations. Like many another
Roman provincial governor, he was more interested in enriching
himself than in carrying out his official duties.

To what extent the extortion of which Dolabella was afterwards
accused was due to his own rapacity is uncertain. Cicero, in his prosecution of Verres, placed the main responsibility on the legate who became quaestor; the orator evidently desired to create the impression
that the governor was chiefly weak and complaisant and wholly under
the influence of his unscrupulous subordinate. But whosesoever the
guilt may have been, it seems assured that the province was shamelessly
exploited. Besides general allusions to the plundering carried on by
Verres and the specific mention of his thefts of works of art and golden
votive offerings at Aspendus and Perge,[p] the prosecutor made the
definite statement that it was with Dolabella's connivance that the
quaestor demanded from the various communities requisitions of
grain, hides and sacking, as well as the coarse fabric woven from
goats' hair which took its name from Cilicia.[q] These requisitions, however, were not accepted in kind but commuted into cash payments,
greatly, of course, to the pecuniary advantage of the governor and,
doubtless, his quaestor as well. According to the bill for damages later
presented at Dolabella's trial, the amount wrongfully extorted on these
articles alone was 750,000 sesterces.

The scandals of Dolabella's administration were so flagrant that on
his return to Rome there was no difficulty in bringing him to trial.
Evidence was readily forthcoming, not only from the communities of
the injured province, but from other places as well, as, for instance,
from Athens, where, it was proved, Dolabella had stolen a great

[n] See above p. 248.   [o] Cicero *pro Quinct.* 31.
[p] Cicero *II Verr.* 1 53f.; IV 71.   [q] See Chap. XI note 20.

quantity of gold from the Temple of Athena. Verres also was persuaded to give testimony against the accused, although his complicity in Dolabella's crimes was suspected because of the fact that by various excuses and acts of procrastination he succeeded in avoiding the presentation of his quaestor's accounts to the Treasury, as required by law. The prosecution was highly successful. Although the jury was composed of his fellow-senators, as Sulla's law ordained, Dolabella was convicted on the charge of extortion practised during his term as governor. Unable to pay the damages assessed, he left Rome and went into exile. Two hundred years later his name was still used as a synonym for a rapacious governor.

A great contrast to Dolabella's inactivity was afforded by the vigour and the military achievements of Publius Servilius Vatia, who had been praetor in 90 and in the following year had won a victory in his province for which he received the honour of a triumph.[r] The reputation which he gained thereby made it natural that at the expiration of his consulship, held in 79, he should be appointed to the task of suppressing the pirates.

The new governor sailed from Tarentum as early in the spring of 78 as navigation permitted.[17] Among his subordinates were the young Julius Caesar, who was later to have an adventure of his own with the pirates,[s] and Titus Labienus, afterwards Caesar's legate and finally his enemy.[t] Servilius spent four years in his province, and during this time he engaged in two separate campaigns, only the first of which was spent in the purpose for which he was sent to Cilicia—the suppression of the sea-robbers and their allies on the coast. His immediate task was the assembling of a fleet, for it can hardly be supposed that Dolabella and Verres had left one ready for his use.[u] The heavy ships which he succeeded in collecting were more than a match for the light craft of his enemies, and when he attacked the pirates off the Lycian coast he won a notable victory—the first gained over them by a Roman commander since the success of Antonius twenty-five years earlier—although his own losses were not inconsiderable.[18]

This victory over the enemy's fleet opened the way to the coast, and Servilius's next efforts were directed against the robbers who had established themselves on the land. The western shore of the Gulf of Antalya, from Cape Chelidonia northward, was under the sway of a pirate-chieftain named Zenicetes.[19] He had seized Olympus, "an ancient

[r] C.I.L. 1² p. 178 (88 B.C.).   [s] See above p. 249f.
[t] Cicero pro Rab. Perd. Reo 21.   [u] See above p. 247.

city embellished and adorned with works of art of every kind." At the end of the second century before Christ Olympus was autonomous and one of the members of the Lycian Federation; its seizure by the robber-chief could have taken place only through violence and must have brought misery to its inhabitants. Zenicetes used the mountain south of the city as a stronghold and from it dominated the neighbourhood. He had extended his power along the coast to include the cities of Corycus and Phaselis in Lycia and even some western outposts of Pamphylia. To these places also he had come as a conqueror. Phaselis, a Grecian settlement like Olympus, had an excellent harbour, and for this reason, presumably, Zenicetes forced it into what was euphemistically called an alliance. But after the defeat of the pirate-fleet he was no longer able to hold out on land. Servilius's forces captured Olympus and then its mountain, and the chieftain, abandoning all further resistance, set fire to his house and perished in the flames. With him fell the principality which he had formed by violence. Servilius, marching northward along the coast, took Corycus and Phaselis. Over them, as well as over Olympus, he exercised all the generally accepted rights of a conqueror; for he plundered their treasures and incorporated their territories in the Roman province.

Thus the western shore of the Gulf of Antalya was added to the dominions of Rome. Between this new acquisition, however, and the province of "Cilicia" lay the territory of the autonomous city of Attaleia. As we have already related, Attaleia had been on friendly terms with the Romans, and a few years earlier had probably furnished ships to Lucullus.[20] There is no reason to suppose that it had surrendered to Zenicetes or, by giving support to the pirates, had been guilty of any breach of friendship with Rome. But it possessed a good harbour, and through its territory ran the line of communication with the newly-acquired coast of Lycia. Servilius, therefore, in order to complete his conquests, annexed its lands to his province.

After his victory over the pirates' fleet and the destruction of one of their lairs, the Roman general, having increased his province by the annexation of Attaleia and the eastern coast of Lycia, seems to have made no attempt to conquer the maritime district of Cilicia Aspera which contained their fastnesses and had given them their usual appellation of "Cilician."[21]

Servilius's second campaign led him far, indeed, from the coast. Beyond the mountains which wall in Pamphylia on the northeast lies the basin of Lake Suğla, and southeast of this lake was Isauria, a wild and inaccessible region, broken by steep mountain-ridges and deep ravines, with occasional plains where grain can be grown.[22] The inhabitants of this part of Pisidia, unaffected by the spread of Hellenism and living in scattered villages, were loosely organized in clans, united chiefly for defence in time of war. There were, to be sure, certain towns, developed from strongholds, which served as rural centres, but in general the inhabitants were free mountaineers, who, when occasion offered, were ready to turn to banditry. In invading their district Servilius may have been led by the hope that an attack on this marauding folk might have an effect on the robbers of the coast. But it is perhaps more probable that he was moved by the desire of adding to his fame by the conquest of a region hitherto unsubdued. The enterprise was a difficult one, for it necessitated an ascent of the Taurus over a hazardous route, unfit for waggons, from sea-level to a pass perhaps as high as 5,000 feet and the penetration of a land where both Nature and man were hostile.[23]

The objective point of this adventure was the district that took its name from the two towns of Old and New Isaura.[24] These were evidently its chief centres, to which the other communities, described as "settlements of bandits," were subordinate. Isaura Vetus, dominating the region through which Servilius entered the enemy's country, presented a formidable obstacle. Built on a lofty hill, rising from the highest of the ridges between the Taurus and the Lycaonian plain and towering above the stream deep in the ravine below, the town was protected by precipitous cliffs and probably also by massive walls, of which, although in a reconstructed form, imposing remains are still in existence. Impregnable though it seemed to be, this stronghold was, nevertheless, captured by Servilius, though whether it was by storm or blockade is unknown. During the siege of another town, a desperate attack by a native force on the Roman camp was beaten off with great loss to the enemy, whereupon the town was forced by lack of water to surrender. It was then burned and its inhabitants sold into slavery. This act of terrorization had the desired effect. The people of Isaura Nova sent envoys to the Roman general to ask for peace, offering him hostages and promising to carry out his commands. Servilius, taking them at their word, led his army to Isaura and during his march thither forbad the soldiers to devastate the country or do any harm to the natives. But when the hostages had been delivered, the demand was made that the Isaurians should also surrender their arms and engines of war, as well as the refugees from other centres of resistance. This demand the younger men refused to carry out, and even the advocates of peace demurred. Servilius, thereupon, in the belief that only a threat would enforce the fulfilment of the promise made by the envoys, took up a position on a commanding hill. Even so, he seems to have forced the town to surrender only by diverting from its course the stream which supplied it with water. At the close of this vigorous campaign Isauria was at least nominally incorporated in Servilius's province, and in the course of time Roman settlers established themselves in its principal city.[v] The victorious leader, in the customary fashion, presently assumed the surname Isauricus derived from his conquest.

Apparently, however, the ambitious general was not yet satisfied. The very scant sources of our information suggest that he may have proceeded to an even more distant region—the highland country of eastern Pisidia east of Lake Beyşehir.[25] Protected by its isolation, it had hitherto remained unconquered. The city of Amlada, south of the Lake, had, it is true, been subject to the Pergamene kings, when it had some kind of a civic organization headed by a board of "Elders," but on the distribution of the various portions of the kingdom in 129 B.C. it had not been taken over by Rome. East of the Lake was the territory of the Orondians, a high plateau broken by gorges and sometimes rising into mountains. A part of this distant region may have been conquered by Servilius, as well as the lands of other, probably predatory, communities lying along the course of his return-march to Pamphylia.

When Servilius arrived in Rome, his friends of the Senatorial party, then still in power, acclaimed him as a great conqueror. In addition to his surname, later inherited by his son, he received the title of Imperator and the honour of a triumph.[26] It was said that he had taken prisoner more pirate-leaders than any Roman general before him, and men flocked from all sides to see his captives. He was praised for achieving outstanding success on both land and sea, and he gained lasting fame as the first Roman general to lead an army across the Taurus. He lived for thirty years after his return highly respected by all, and he was accredited by later historians with the conquest, not only of Isauria, but of Cilicia as well. But his achievements, when regarded impartially, seem more spectacular than real. He won for Rome the western coast of Lycia and an upland region north of the Taurus, to which remoteness lent the glamour of mystery. But the coast was only a narrow strip, cut off from the interior by almost impenetrable mountains and connected with Pamphylia only by a road along the coast which was difficult and even dangerous.[w] The district of Isauria had neither strategic nor economic importance, nor could the capture of its towns have contributed to the suppression of the pirates, since these towns were far removed from the sea. The banditry of its inhabitants was doubtless afterward restrained by Roman rule, but it is difficult to see how the raiding of these highlanders, far removed from the main arteries of trade and from any centres of wealth, could have wrought much damage to commercial interests, either Roman or Asianic. The only means of communication, moreover, between this outlying region and the province to which it was annexed led over difficult mountain-passes. The seizure of the territory of the friendly city of Attaleia did, indeed, round out Rome's holdings in the plain of Pamphylia, but the addition of a narrow coast on the southwest and a distant tract on the northeast resulted in the formation of a province which was neither a geographical nor an administrative unit.

Moreover, in spite of Servilius's destruction of a pirate-fleet and his capture of the mountain-fastness of Zenicetes, the evil had not been eradicated. At the very time of his return to Rome the corsairs were carrying on their wonted activities in the southern Aegean.[x] Ancient writers describe in vivid, although probably exaggerated, terms the power to which they attained and the outrages which they perpetrated.[27] It is said that their ships numbered more than a thousand and that they dominated not merely the eastern sea but actually the whole of the Mediterranean. They had discarded their traditional light craft for vessels of two and three banks of oars, and their chieftains, many of them men of illustrious descent and superior intelligence, were, in fact, generals of armies. So complete was their organization that they kept in captivity artisans who were chained to their tasks, and they possessed stores of timber and metals for the construction of ships and the manufacture of weapons. Disdaining the plunder to be obtained merely from those who travelled the seas, they had begun to lay siege to fortified towns. Temples were ruthlessly pillaged, and unwalled settlements and rural districts were wholly at their mercy. Even the western coast of Italy and Rome itself were terrorized. The crowning insult was the entry of a pirate-squadron into the port of Ostia and the attack and destruction of a Roman fleet lying at anchor there. In the very year in which Servilius was overrunning Isauria,

[w] See Chap. XI note 14.   [x] See Chap X note 44.

Gaius Cotta, the Consul of 75, is reported to have said publicly that the shores of Italy were beset by enemies.[y]

The situation was all the more perilous for the reason that in 74 B.C., when, probably, Servilius celebrated his triumph, it was generally known that Mithradates of Pontus was making ready for a second invasion of western Asia Minor, and there must have been many in Rome who remembered that the pirates had aided the King during his previous campaign.[z] Apart, therefore, from the desirability of safe-guarding Roman commerce and protecting the coast towns, it was evidently necessary to take vigorous action to prevent another com-bination between the pirates and the powerful enemy in the East. It was no mere coincidence that in the year in which the King was completing his plans for a new war the Senate took the step of creat-ing an extraordinary command for the purpose of removing a menace which had become intolerable.

The new command was magnificent in scale; it extended over the whole Mediterranean and included full authority to raise and man ships for the purpose of clearing the sea everywhere of the robbers who infested it.[28] The powers conferred were very different from those held by Antonius in 102 and recently by Servilius. No such command had ever been created before, and when, seven years later, it was again bestowed, this time at the demand of the people, upon the popular favourite, Pompey, an important step was taken in the development of senatorial government into monarchy.

The plan might have succeeded had a capable commander been selected. But the Senate's choice fell on Marcus Antonius, one of the praetors of the year. His only qualifications for the post, apart from his reputation as a man of good intentions and a generous nature, were his father's victory over the pirates and the fact that his wife was the daughter of Lucius Caesar, the distinguished Consul of 90 B.C. Gossip said that he obtained his appointment through the influence of Publius Cethegus, then all-powerful in the Senate, and the favour shown him by the Consul, Marcus Cotta. A later historian attributed the Senators' willingness to create a command fraught with danger to their own power to the reason that none of them feared the in-cumbent. The course of the campaign, however, showed that if he was not formidable to the Senators or, as it turned out, to the enemy, the provincials had reason enough to fear him.

After operations off the coast of Sicily, where he misused his power to oppress the farmers, and in Spanish waters, where he seems to have achieved little success, Antonius directed his efforts toward the East, apparently in the hope of exterminating the danger at its source.[29] On his way he stopped on the southern coast of Greece, where he forced the communities to make "contributions" to his campaign. One city was ordered to pay him the amount of 4,200 drachmae; unable to meet the demand from the public treasury, the citizens borrowed the money from resident Roman bankers at the ruinous rate of 48 per cent. In other places, such as Epidaurus in Argolis, he stationed troops, whose presence was a burden and a source of expense to the towns-people, and it was only after the earnest entreaties of a patriotic citizen to the "rulers," *i.e.* the governmental authorities, that the soldiers were removed.

The only campaign of this eastern expedition was directed against Crete. Its situation at the entrance to the Aegean gave the island a position which commanded the lanes leading both from the East and the West to the ports of this much-frequented sea. In consequence, from the fourth century onward, Crete had been the headquarters of the robbers of the eastern Mediterranean and had afforded them a place for the sale of their captives.[30] Although, in the course of time, the growing power of the Cilician pirates enabled them to worst their Cretan rivals, the robberies of the latter still continued, and the island ranked next to Cilicia as a "source of pirate-bands." Evidently the cities of its coast had done nothing to discourage these activities. Antonius, therefore, accused the Cretan communities of giving aid and shelter to the pirates and of promising mercenaries to Mithradates, and when his envoys could obtain no satisfaction, he invaded the island. But however good his grounds for attacking might be, his method of attack was sadly deficient. The enemy met him in a sea-fight in which they took most of his ships and captured many prisoners, among them the quaestor of the fleet. Antonius was forced to agree to terms which the Senate later refused to ratify, but before he could leave he was seized by an illness and died on the island, "having spent three years to no purpose." An attempt was made to gloze over his disgraceful failure by conferring on him posthumously the surname of Creticus, but the pirates continued to ravage the coast of Sicily, and two years after his death the Cretans, angered by the severe demands of the Senate, declared war on Rome. They were conquered only after a long and sanguinary struggle.

Antonius's campaign had not extended to Cilicia. About the time of his departure from Rome, Servilius's successor in that province, Lucius Octavius, who had been Consul in 75, went out to the East to take over his governorship. Any opportunity, however, of winning distinction either by a war against the pirates or by the administration of his province was taken from him by his death soon after his arrival.[a] His vacant post was eagerly sought by several applicants, for, in view of Mithradates's preparations for invasion, the command of Cilicia seemed to ensure military glory from the inevitable war.

The successful candidate was Lucius Lucullus. He had already won distinction in Asia both by his naval operations in the Aegean and by his merciful treatment of the communities threatened with financial ruin as the result of the indemnity imposed by Sulla.[b] As Consul in 74, he was the obvious choice in this emergency for a command in the East. Nevertheless, under the irrational Roman system of awarding provincial commands by lot, Lucullus had received Cisalpine Gaul; according to the gossip of the city, it was only by paying court to the mistress of the influential Publius Cethegus that he obtained the vacant proconsulship of Cilicia.[31] To this office was soon added the supreme command of the impending war against Mithradates. Some time later he was also made governor of the province of Asia.

At the end of 74 or the beginning of 73 B.C. Lucullus left Rome to take up the conduct of the war.[c] Not once during his seven years' command in the East did he enter the province of Cilicia, and the only use he made of his power there was to order the two legions that Servilius had left in the province to join him in Asia for the ensuing campaign.[32]

In the invasion of Mithradates, directed against northwestern Asia Minor,[d] the districts of the southern coast were left altogether untouched. The King, to be sure, had sent his general, Eumachus, who had once been "satrap" of the Galatians but had been driven out by them, to create a diversion in the region north of the Taurus.[33] After killing the Romans in Phrygia, Eumachus overran Pisidia and Isauria, but his expedition was evidently little more than a raid. On his return northward he was attacked and defeated by Rome's ally, the Galatian prince Deiotarus.

There were, nevertheless, two results of this war, each of which, in its own way, was of real importance in the history of the southern province. The first was an increased consideration on the part of the

---

[a] Sallust *Hist.* II 98 D Maur.: Plutarch *Luc.* 6, 1.   [b] See above pp. 228f. and 238.
[c] See Chap. XIV note 5.   [d] See below p. 324f.

Roman government toward the cities, an attitude which was adopted about the time when Lucullus was carrying out his economic reforms in the province of Asia and was perhaps not unconnected with his policy there.[e] It would seem that the King's invasion had demonstrated the expediency of establishing friendlier relations with the communities of the provinces. In any case, this policy was expressed in the enactment of a law recognizing the independence of Termessus, which had suffered during Mithradates's earlier campaign.[f]

As early as 91 B.C. the citizens of Termessus had enjoyed certain rights with regard to Rome, but now its status was more clearly defined. With the sanction of the Senate a bill was introduced by the board of tribunes, headed by Gaius Antonius, younger brother of the incapable "Creticus," which recognized the city's full liberty and autonomy.[34] The community became a "friend and ally" of Rome; full ownership of its territory was guaranteed as well as of all property, public or private, which the citizens had possessed prior to Mithradates's invasion in 88; all persons, free men and slaves, who had been carried away as captives during the war against Mithradates, were to be restored to the city, and Roman officials in the provinces were ordered to facilitate this restoration by legal decisions. The city was also promised immunity from the quartering of troops, save by express order of the Senate, and it was authorized to impose such customs-duties as it desired, with the sole provision that the produce of the public revenues of Rome transported through its territory by the *publicani* should be exempt therefrom. Unfortunately, the mutilated condition of the document does not enable us to determine all the rights conferred by the law or to discover whether a similar status was granted to other cities as well, but it is not improbable that the more liberal policy now adopted in the case of Termessus was extended to other communities also. Termessus, in any case, retained at least a nominal independence throughout the first three centuries of the Christian Era.

Whatever may have been the connexion between Lucullus's victory over Mithradates and Rome's recognition of the independence of Termessus, the second of these events in the South was the direct result of the continuance of the General's success in the war, for by it an enemy of Rome was driven out of Cilicia. Tigranes the Great, King of Armenia and son-in-law of Mithradates, had co-operated, as has already been related, with the King of Pontus by invading

[e] See above p. 252.   [f] See Chap. IX note 30.

295

Cappadocia.[g] He had taken no part, however, in Mithradates's invasion of the province of Asia in 88 and consequently had played no role in the concluding of the Treaty of Dardanus. His ambitions, in fact, had turned in a very different direction, namely the plain of Mesopotamia, where, after seizing the northern part of the country, he built a capital to serve as the centre and symbol of his enlarged empire, calling it, from his own name, Tigranocerta.[h] Then, not content with this great increase of territory, he turned westward and seized the Seleucid dominions in northern Syria and Cilicia Campestris.[35] In 83 B.C., two years after the conclusion of the Treaty of Dardanus, his power extended as far as the mountains of the Rugged District. The Seleucid capital, Antioch, became one of the royal residences of this "King of Kings," as he now styled himself, and Syria and Cilicia were governed by his deputy, Magadates.

Tigranes's rule over the conquered districts may have been no worse a calamity than that of the Seleucids of the time, but his advent meant disaster to twelve cities in the conquered territory; for he carried away a large number of their inhabitants in order to increase the population of his new capital, which he was desirous of making worthy of his own exaggerated claims to greatness.[36] Tigranes retained undisputed possession of his conquests until he provoked the enmity of the Romans by refusing to surrender Mithradates, and Lucullus, after defeating him near Tigranocerta, forced him to retreat to his native Armenia and abandon all his conquests south of the Taurus.[i] Magadates withdrew to join his king, and Cilicia and Syria were evacuated.[j] Lucullus then reinstated a feeble claimant on the Seleucid throne,[k] but the cities of Cilicia Campestris regarded the expulsion of the Armenian tyrant as the beginning of their independence.[37] It was, however, an easy step from Roman deliverance from a foreign invader to the establishment of Roman rule. Five years later, when the last king of Syria was deposed by Pompey, the Level Cilicia was formally annexed to the southern province.[38]

Within a year of Lucullus's defeat of the Armenian "King of Kings" his enemies at Rome—chiefly among the wide-spread business-interests —began to shear away the accumulation of provincial commands which he had long held.[l] The first of the provinces to be taken was Asia, but the loss of Cilicia soon followed. Before the end of 68 the Senate appointed a new proconsul for the province which Lucullus

g See above p. 205f.   h See Chap. XIV note 36.   i See below p. 344.
j Appian *Syr.* 49.   k See below p. 344.   l See below p. 345f.

had governed but never entered, namely Quintus Marcius Rex, one of the Consuls of the year.[39] In 67 Marcius, with three new legions, left for Cilicia, which he was, indeed, to enter but presently to leave without glory or gain. He was Lucullus's brother-in-law, for both had married daughters of the illustrious family of Claudius Pulcher. On his way to the East, Marcius stopped on the coast of Greece, and there he seems to have raised the hopes of the Italian settlers for deliverance from the dangers of piracy, which he was, in fact, to do nothing to allay. Even on his way to his province his attitude toward his kinsman and predecessor was made apparent. While travelling through Lycaonia on the Southern Highway, he was met with a request for assistance brought by messengers from Lucullus, who, although replaced in his command in Bithynia and Pontus by the arrival of his successor, Glabrio, was desirous of repelling Tigranes's invasion of Cappadocia. This request Marcius rejected, giving as his reason the probable refusal of his soldiers to follow—a reason which was perhaps true enough but scarcely to the credit of the general. This same attitude showed itself also after his arrival in Cilicia. For he entrusted the command of his fleet to his brother-in-law, Publius Clodius Pulcher, who during the previous winter had incited Lucullus's army to mutiny and had evidently found it expedient to change leaders.

Beyond a certain amount of diplomacy in dealing with the enemy, as when he gave a friendly reception to an officer of Tigranes who had deserted his master and apparently made overtures to the Romans, we know of no services rendered by Marcius to the province during his term of office.[40] The only action on his part of which there is any record was a journey to Antioch in Syria, where he demanded money from the Seleucid claimant Philip II, who had been put on the throne by an Arab chieftain. The payment was presumably the cost of an official recognition by Rome, but it was said in Marcius's favour that he contributed to the restoration of the hippodrome and the palace in the city. It is possible that the lack of any military activity on his part was due to the fact that before he had been long in Cilicia the most serious problem which faced a governor of the province—the suppression of the pirates—was solved by the great victory won by Pompey. He was soon superseded in office by the victor, who received supreme command not only over Cilicia but over all the provinces of the East. Nevertheless, Marcius aspired to the distinction of a triumph, so frequently granted to the members of the aristocracy for trifling services. But over three years later he was still waiting for the fulfilment of his hope, which, in fact, he was destined never to achieve.

About the time when Marcius departed for Cilicia a step was taken at Rome which was of great consequence, not only to his province but also to the whole Roman world. It has already been observed that after the ill-fated campaign of Antonius no action against the pirates, save for the war against their allies in Crete, was taken by the Senate. At the beginning of 67, however, a measure was enacted providing for the creation of another extraordinary command, which, it was hoped, would put an end to all their depredations.[41] Aulus Gabinius Capito, one of the tribunes of the year, who had already made himself hated by the aristocrats for his legislation depriving Lucullus of the conduct of the war against Mithradates, came forward with the proposal. Taking as his model the previous decree of the Senate which had bestowed unprecedented power on the unworthy Antonius, he introduced a bill to create a similar, but even more extensive, command. The incumbent was to have power for three years over the entire Mediterranean and equal authority with the provincial governors over its coast for fifty miles inland; all princes and communities were to furnish aid at his request; he was to have supreme control over the entire naval resources of Rome, the right to draw on the public treasury and full power to enlist both soldiers and crews; he might also name fifteen subordinates to act under his direction. The bill named no one to hold the new post but specified merely that an ex-consul should be appointed. It was clear to all, however, that the holder was to be none other than Gnaeus Pompeius Magnus. Gabinius was known to be acting in his interest, and the way was carefully prepared for his election. It was not until after the measure was carried in the teeth of violent opposition from the more conservative Senators that he appeared openly as a candidate. Then the further proposal was made that the command should be vested in Pompey. This met with an overwhelming response from the citizens. Despite the attempts of his opponents to have the proposal quashed by a tribune's veto or replaced by another bill creating a collegiate command, it was triumphantly carried, and even the Senate dared not refuse to ratify the action. Pompey was not only chosen to the newly-created office but empowered to raise a force almost twice as large as that contained in the original bill.

The new commander took action at once. His plan was brilliantly conceived and carefully carried out. His fleet consisted of all the naval forces of Rome and her allies, among them the people of Rhodes. The huge number of ships placed at his disposal he divided into thirteen separate squadrons, each under the orders of one of the lieutenant-commanders authorized by Gabinius's law. These were assigned to definite portions of the Mediterranean and made responsible for ridding the sea of the corsairs and destroying their strongholds on the coast. Simultaneous action on the part of all would necessarily prevent any co-operation among the enemies or the despatching of reinforcements by one pirate-fleet to another. Asianic waters were entrusted to three of these commanders, the Bosporus and the Propontis to Marcus Pupius Piso, the Aegean littoral to Lucius Lollius, and Pamphylia with the southern sea to Quintus Caecilius Metellus Nepos. It was the special task of Metellus, accordingly, to hold the Cilicians in check and prevent them from issuing forth to the aid of their comrades. All three of these men later served in the war against Mithradates.

Pompey himself, with a squadron of sixty ships—much the largest of the various units—acted independently. Setting forth to the West, he swept the sea, operating off the coasts of Sicily, Sardinia and Africa. The pirates, taken by surprise, were driven to their various lairs and thus forced into the grasp of Pompey's subordinates, who were then able to subdue them without difficulty. After clearing the entire western Mediterranean in the short space of forty days, the Commander turned his attention to the East. This was the most difficult phase of his campaign. Not only had his previous operations caused the Cilicians to scurry back to their home-land to await him with all their forces, but there were inaccessible strongholds to be captured. Consequently, he brought with him a supply of engines of war and the equipment needed for sieges. The pirates met him with all their ships off Coracesium on the western coast of Cilicia Aspera, and here a great naval battle was fought which resulted in a complete victory for the Roman fleet. The enemy, taking refuge on land, attempted to resist the invader. But they were unable to hold out against a siege, and when their envoys received favourable terms from the victor they agreed to surrender. Their example was soon followed by the rest of their fellow-countrymen.

In seven weeks from Pompey's departure for the East and less than three months from the beginning of his campaign, the war was brought to a close. The number of the pirates killed in battle was estimated by the Commander at ten thousand, and those who surrendered at twice that number. He asserted that one hundred and twenty settlements had been taken and more than eight hundred ships, large and small, destroyed or captured.[42] In addition, there fell into the victor's hands the Cilicians' stores of arms and their material for the construction of their fleets, as well as a vast number of captives.

The rapidity and the completeness of the Roman general's success were due in no small measure to the leniency with which he treated the enemy. Even before the battle off Coracesium the pirates who threw themselves on his mercy met with a kindly reception and were merely deprived of their ships.[m] This humane policy naturally had its effect, for it contributed largely to the readiness of many others not only to surrender themselves and their families but also to aid Pompey in seizing recalcitrants. His wisdom showed itself most of all, however, after his victory at Coracesium and the capitulation of the strongholds on the coast. In the belief that many had turned to piracy through lack of a definite occupation, he conceived the plan of establishing those who surrendered in permanent settlements. Here they might dwell at peace and earn a livelihood either in the occupations of the city or as tillers of the land. For these new settlers there was abundant room in the towns of eastern Cilicia, which at this time were in need of additional inhabitants.[43] With the surrender of the Rugged District there fell into his hands the neighbouring city of Soli, the population of which had been greatly reduced through the cruelties perpetrated by Tigranes. Here large numbers of the pirates were established, and Soli was "refounded" and called, from the name of its new founder, Pompeiopolis. It received, furthermore, all the rights of a free city. Its ancient glory was revived, and in course of time it developed into a magnificent port. In Cilicia Campestris, when entirely freed from the Armenian invader, other colonies of former pirates were established in the less populous cities, Mallus and Epiphaneia near the coast and Adana farther inland. Some were settled even in western Greece, at Dyme near the entrance to the Gulf of Corinth.

Some modern critics of Pompey have expressed the view that his victory was more specious than real, and that his purpose was to achieve a rapid success rather than a lasting settlement.[44] It has been pointed out that twelve years later the agents of the Roman tax-farmers in Syria complained that because of a pirate-raid they could not collect what was owed them. Sporadic outbreaks of piracy did, indeed, occur during the years which followed Pompey's Cilician campaign, particularly during the time when his younger son Sextus was so untrue to his

---

m Plutarch *Pomp.* 27, 4: Cassius Dio xxxvi 37, 4f.

father's memory as to organize a privateering fleet in his war against Rome. But the fact remains that, save for the depredations of this young man, Italy was never again subjected to raids or threatened with famine by the pirates, and no longer was the commerce of the eastern Mediterranean in constant danger of attack. It was Pompey who ended piracy on a large scale, ridding the Roman world of the evil and establishing Rome's supremacy on the sea.

He also established it on the southern coast. The little province of Pamphylia-Isauria was greatly enlarged by the addition of the Rugged Cilicia.[45] When the inhabitants surrendered to Pompey, this mountain-district came under the control of Rome, and the settlement of the pirates in the new Pompeiopolis meant Roman domination of the southern littoral. The establishment of these brave and hardy men in permanent homes assured not only an increase in the population and the economic prosperity of the region, but also its defence against disorder and invasion. The work of pacification begun by Servilius was completed by Pompey, and thus the entire southern coast from Lycia to the border of Cilicia Campestris was won for Rome. There remained only the fertile plain of the Level District on the east, and this Lucullus had already delivered from the grasp of the Armenian invader. The beginning of Roman penetration was effected by the colonies of former pirates established by Pompey in its depopulated cities, and after the completion of the great war against Mithradates, which he was now called on to bring to a close, this district also became subject to Rome.[n]

[n] See below p. 375f.

CHAPTER XIII

THE BEQUEST OF NICOMEDES

IN relating the efforts of the kings of Pergamum to extend their power, as well as in the narration of the events which preceded Mithradates's invasion of the province of Asia, mention has often been made of the Kingdom of Bithynia and the monarchs who ruled it. During the earlier part of the second century in particular, the Bithynian kings have been represented as the antagonists of the rulers of Pergamum, jealous of the favour shown by Rome to these monarchs and ready to resort to all possible intrigues to combat their rivals' power. In contrast to their enlightened neighbours they have not always appeared to advantage.

During the third century the monarchs of Bithynia had gradually increased their realm. At the time of the Romans' victory over Antiochus III in 190, it contained the entire northwestern corner of Asia Minor, an area of 18,000 square miles—approximately that of the modern country of Denmark.[1] The kingdom extended southward from the Euxine Sea to the soaring mass of the Mysian Mt. Olympus. On the west it included the shore of the Propontis from the Bosporus to the river Rhyndacus, which separated it from what was to become the Roman province of Asia; and on the east it was bounded by the great ranges which form the wall of the central plateau of Anatolia and divide Bithynia from the mountainous district of Paphlagonia.[a] On the coast of the Euxine it reached as far eastward as the territory of the free city of Heracleia.[b]

The one great river of the kingdom was the Sangarius. Formed by the union of several streams on the Phrygian plateau west of the temple-city of Pessinus, it describes a winding course, first eastward, then northward, then westward to the place where it enters the southeastern corner of Bithynia.[2] After a great bend, where it forces its way through the mountains continuing the range of Olympus toward the east, it traverses a series of precipitous gorges and flows northward into the Euxine. The broad basin of its lower course, known in late Antiquity as the Regio Tarsica and in modern times as Ak Ova, was the largest, as well as the most beautiful of the Bithynian plains. This region, together with the district that borders on the Euxine, abounding in grain and fruit, produced the rich harvests which caused Bithynia to be called "the greatest and best of lands."

The lower course of the Sangarius, for a certain distance a navigable stream,[c] divided Bithynia into two portions. On the west was the hill-country along the coast of the Propontis, deeply indented by the Gulf of Nicomedeia and, farther south, by the smaller Gulf of Cius. Here also were rich plains, such as those around Lake Ascania[d] and at the foot of Mt. Olympus. Though smaller in extent than the Ak Ova, they were likewise famed for their fertility. In this section of the country were the chief cities of the kingdom, all of them on or near the Propontis, for the coast of the Euxine had no harbours of importance.[3]

East of the lower Sangarius, beyond the plain of Ak Ova, are the great mountains. Towering up from the northern bank of the river along its course from east to west, they rise in majestic wall-like terraces and fantastic peaks to the mighty range of the eastern, or "Bithynian," Olympus and extend as far northward as the Euxine.[4] These huge masses are broken only by the tiny plains and the rock-bound defiles through which descend the smaller affluents of the San-garius, and, farther north, by the broader valley of the stream called in modern times the Mudurnu Çay, which joins the greater river in the Ak Ova. Through this rugged country extended the magnificent forests of firs, oaks and beeches which were famous in Antiquity and later caused the Turks to give to the mountains along the Euxine coast the picturesque name of "Mother of Trees." Even in modern times, though cruelly ravaged, they have evoked the admiration of travellers.

Beyond these mountains, to the east, are the beautiful plain of the upper Hypius, north of the Bithynian Olympus, and, still farther east, that of the Upper Büyük Su, a tributary of the Billaeus, in which lay, respectively, the cities of Prusias and Bithynium.[5] Beyond the latter was the Paphlagonian border.

Separated from Europe only by the narrow straits of the Bosporus and the Hellespont, the northwestern corner of Asia Minor had early fallen a prey to invaders from Thrace. About the end of the second millennium before Christ it was overrun by the "Mysians" and "Phrygians," who, spreading to the south and southeast, gradually amalgamated with the native population.[6] Later, another wave of Thracian immigrants, Bithyni and Thyni, crossed the Bosporus and

[c] Arrian *Bithyn.* frg. 20 Roos.   [d] Strabo XII p. 565.

settled in the fertile land to which they gave their names. In contrast to these were the Grecian settlers from Megara, who established themselves not only on the Bosporus, at Byzantium and Chalcedon, but also on the shore of the Euxine, and the Ionians, who founded colonies on the Propontis. These cities formed merely a fringe along the coast, for the interior of the country long remained unaffected by Hellenism. As in Pontus, the land in general probably belonged to the kings, and the cities which they founded, as well as certain of the Greek communities which they seized, were directly under their rule.

Of the Hellenic cities, the most favourably situated was Chalcedon, on the eastern side of the Bosporus, built on a small peninsula jutting out from the fruitful land along the coast.[7] The site, although more attractive to settlers than the hills on which Byzantium was placed, was, nevertheless, commercially less advantageous; for the currents of the Bosporus made the landing on the eastern side of the Strait more difficult and also swept the fish, which were one of the chief sources of the wealth of these cities, toward the European shore. Nevertheless, Chalcedon, although it never attained to the importance of its sister-city, profited by the trade that passed between the Euxine and the Aegean and also across the Strait; additional sources of wealth were the copper-mines and the semi-precious stones of its dependency, the island of Chalcitis.

During the fifth and fourth centuries, amid wars and other vicissitudes, Chalcedon, for the most part, preserved its freedom, although for a time after 387 it was subject to the Persians.[8] The city probably submitted to Alexander and later it was held in subjection by Lysimachus. After his overthrow in 281 Chalcedon again became free, and as an independent state it formed an alliance with Byzantium, Heracleia and Mithradates I, king of Pontus, against Seleucus I and later with Nicomedes I of Bithynia. Although forced by Philip V of Macedonia to become subject to his sway,[e] Chalcedon, like the other cities of Asia,[f] was made free when Philip was defeated in 197. In gratitude for this deliverance the city became an ally of Rome and contributed its quota of ships for the war against Philip's son, Perseus.[g] From this time onward Chalcedon succeeded in preserving its independence. As a Roman ally, it shared the terrible defeat of Rome's land and naval forces when in 73 Bithynia was invaded by Mithradates Eupator.[h]

[e] Polybius xv 23, 8f. [f] Polybius xviii 2, 4; 44. See Chap. IV note 44.
[g] Livy xlii 56, 6 (171 B.C.). [h] See below p. 325.

In contrast to Chalcedon's freedom, the other cities in Bithynia were subject to the kings. The most important of these was Nicomedeia, the seat of the royal court. It was the successor of the ancient Megarian settlement of Astacus, which had long been an independent community but at the beginning of the third century was destroyed by Lysimachus.[9] A few years after its destruction, the remnants of the population were moved by King Nicomedes I to a neighbouring site at the eastern end of the Gulf of Izmit. Here the King founded a new city, naming it, according to the custom of the Hellenistic monarchs, after himself and fortifying it by walls of which the foundations are still preserved.[10] Nicomedeia, in the innermost recess of the long narrow gulf, was built on a narrow strip of land lying between the water's edge and the curving hills which rise behind it like the tiers of a huge theatre. The situation was both picturesque and commercially advantageous. Not only did the gulf afford a deep-water harbour of unusual excellence, but the city lay at the end of the great trade-route which traversed the whole length of northern Asia Minor from the Propontis to Pontus and Armenia.[11] As a result, the carrying-trade of Nicomedeia developed rapidly, and its commerce, combined with its importance as the royal capital and the buildings with which it was adorned by the monarchs, gave the city a pre-eminence which lasted for centuries.[12]

Nicomedeia's rival for the primacy among the cities of Bithynia was Nicaea.[13] Originally founded by Antigonus on the site of an earlier settlement, it was enlarged and fortified by Lysimachus, who renamed it Nicaea after his wife. It lay at the eastern end of Lake Ascania, in a luxuriant plain framed by the mountain-ring that surrounds the lake. Without natural defences, Nicaea was protected by a massive wall, which, at the beginning of the Christian Era, had a circuit of nearly two miles; within this, the city was laid out on a rectangular plan, so that from the centre all four gates could be seen. This inland situation lacked the commercial advantages of Nicomedeia, and for its communications by sea the city was dependent on the harbour-town of Cius, about thirty miles distant. With this port it was connected by a road leading along the southern shore of the lake.[14] The eastern prolongation of this route afforded communication with the valley of the Sangarius and thus with Phrygia and Galatia. Another road, running across the mountain-range on the north, connected it with Nicomedeia. Thanks to the trade thus established, but perhaps also to the fertility of its immediate territory, Nicaea attained to great prosperity. Its industrial products included a scarlet silk, dyed by means of the kermes-gall, which during the Roman imperial period was a profitable article of commerce.[15]

Next in importance to these two cities was Prusa—which in modern times has greatly outstripped them both.[16] It may likewise have had a predecessor dating back to an early period, but its reputed founder was Prusias I, the fourth of the Bithynian kings, although there was also a tradition which connected the founding with Hannibal. Of all the cities on the western seaboard none has a more beautiful situation. Built on a low spur which projects to the northeast from the Mysian Mt. Olympus, it faces a rich and well-watered plain. On a flat-topped rock at its back rises the acropolis—perhaps the site of the original city—and behind this towers the majestic mass of Olympus, its lower slopes forest-clad, its higher peaks—one of them 8,000 feet above sea-level—capped with eternal snow. This great mountain protected Prusa from all assaults save in front, but it presented an effective barrier to communication with the interior. Nevertheless, the route which ran from east to west across the plain connected Prusa with the basin of the Sangarius, and the road which led along the coast of the Propontis to Cyzicus and thence to Pergamum and the cities of the Ionian coast was readily accessible; for Myrleia, on the Gulf of Cius, was only twenty miles distant, and Cius itself was but little farther away.[17] Under the later Bithynian kings Prusa seems to have had a Council vested with power for local administration, but the place was regarded throughout Antiquity as "a small city."[18] Among its chief assets were sulphur and other thermal springs, rising on the mountain-side west of the city, which appear to have made Prusa a centre for medical treatment; they are still a source of considerable wealth.

The two ports on the Gulf of Cius, Cius itself at the eastern end and Myrleia on the southern shore, were older by far than the cities of Nicaea and Prusa, whose commercial interests they served.[19] The former, colonized by Ionians from Miletus, had rapidly grown to importance because of the trade-routes which led eastward to the Sangarius and southeastward into Phrygia. It preserved its freedom until the latter part of the fourth century, when it fell into the hands of local tyrants, under whom it remained until the last of them, Mithradates by name, was murdered by Antigonus. Its freedom, as well as its very existence, however, came to an end in 202, when both Cius and Myrleia, a colony of Colophon, were captured and destroyed by Philip V of Macedonia.[20] He presented their sites to his brother-in-law,

Prusias I, who rebuilt Cius, renaming it Prusias, and probably also Myrleia, which he called Apameia in honour of his wife. Both were afterward favoured by Rome, for Prusias, resuming its ancient name, received its freedom, and Apameia was made a Roman colony.

In the mountainous portion of Bithynia that lies east of the Sangarius were two places of importance, a second Prusias, distinguished from the coast city by the name of Prusias-on-the-Hypius, and Bithynium. The former of these, originally the ancient community of Cierus, was perhaps a colony of the city of Heracleia, from which it was taken by Zipoetes, the first king of Bithynia.[21] It was afterward returned to Heracleia, however, by Zipoetes's son, Nicomedes, when, about 280 B.C., he needed the greater city's aid against Antiochus I. Nevertheless, nearly a century later Nicomedes's grandson, Prusias I, annexed Cierus to his kingdom, renaming it after himself, as he had done in the case of Cius. Standing on a hillside overlooking the mountain-girt basin around the lake from which issues the Hypius[1] and facing the great mass of the Bithynian Olympus, Prusias had a magnificent position. The remains of ancient walls, dating from the pre-Roman period, show that under the kings it was strongly fortified. The Roman theatre and the apparent expansion of the Hellenistic city from the hill to the plain below indicate that the place prospered under the rule of Rome.

Across the ridge which forms the eastern watershed of the basin of the Hypius lay Bithynium, the most easterly of the cities of the kingdom and on the great road leading to Pontus.[22] The remains of a wall of polygonal masonry which surrounded its acropolis show that the place was an early settlement. Built on the low hills which rise in the fertile plain of Salona, it resembled Prusias in its situation. The well-irrigated plain and also the lower slopes of the neighbouring mountains afforded excellent pasturage for cattle, and the cheese produced in the plain of Salona won particular fame. Another asset of commercial value may have been the thermal springs on the neighbouring Ala Dağ, which are much frequented in modern times.

In contrast to the state of subjection in which the communities of Bithynia were held by the monarchs of the country was the independence of the cities of the Euxine littoral. Chief among these was Heracleia, a city far more important than those of the kingdom of Bithynia and with a more distinguished history.[23] It had been founded about the middle of the sixth century by Megarian colonists, either from the mother-city itself or from Byzantium and Chalcedon. Front-

[1] See above p. 303.

ing on a bay which was protected on the northern side by a projecting headland, the city rose on a steep hillside from the water's edge to a citadel over six hundred feet above the sea. Its harbour was enclosed by moles, the remains of which are still to be seen, one extending from the point of the headland, the other from the city itself. In the neighbourhood was the famous Acherusian Cave, through which Heracles was reported to have dragged forth Cerberus from the Lower World; throughout its history the city regarded the Hero as its especial patron.

The plain around Heracleia was tilled by the native Mariandyni, who had been reduced to a form of serfdom.[24] Although narrow, this plain was very fertile, and it may have more than sufficed for the city's needs. In any case, the nuts grown in the neighbourhood were exported far and wide. A more important source of wealth, however, was the tunny-fishing in the Euxine, for the fish were salted and carried to Greece and Italy. Even more valuable for the purposes of trade were the magnificent forests which covered the coast-range on the south and furnished wood for the construction of ships as well as timber for export. At the same time, these mountains were a barrier to commerce with the interior.[25] The road, moreover, which led along the Euxine coast was toilsome, and transportation was correspondingly difficult. Consequently, the chief source of Heracleia's prosperity was the carrying-trade of its merchant-marine, which conveyed grain, timber and raw materials from the shores of the Euxine and brought back manu-factured articles from the ports of the Aegean. So rapidly did the city grow that at the end of the sixth century it was able to establish colonies on the western coast of the Euxine and even in the Crimea.[26]

After experiencing both the oligarchic and the democratic forms of government,[j] Heracleia, like most Greek states at one time or another, came under the power of tyrants.[27] This tyranny was es-tablished in 364 B.C. As frequently in ancient and modern states alike, it arose from ill-feeling between those who possessed and those who coveted. A citizen named Clearchus, recalled from banishment by the wealthy to quell their opponents, turned traitor, and, with the support of the masses and the aid of mercenaries, he murdered or exiled the better element and made himself military dictator. After ruling twelve years he fell by the sword which he himself had drawn, for a group of his exiled enemies assassinated him while he was performing a public sacrifice. The tyranny, however, continued and eventually de-

---

[j] Aristotle *Polit.* v 5, p. 1304 B and Aeneas Tacticus 11, 1of.

volved on Clearchus's younger son, Dionysius, who showed himself both a beneficent ruler and a master of diplomacy. By his marriage with Amastris, the divorced wife of Craterus, regent of Macedonia, he won recognition as a royal personage, and shortly before his death in 305 he assumed the title of King. His widow Amastris continued his policy. After joining the alliance formed by Lysimachus against Antigonus, she married her royal ally, and although the marriage proved to be of short duration, she made it possible for her two young sons to succeed to their father's power. They requited her devotion by causing her to be drowned but were in turn put to death by Lysimachus, when, in 289, he entered Heracleia with an army. Thus, after a duration of seventy-five years, the dynasty came to an end.

The tyranny, though founded in terror and oppression, brought prosperity to Heracleia, and the city grew in riches and power. Her territory was extended into the interior, where Cierus, if not actually a colony, at least came under her sway.[k] Her rule was also carried along the Euxine coast, where the ancient city of Tieium on a high promontory at the mouth of the Billaeus was annexed and provided with a harbour.[28] The astute Amastris, moreover, following the policy of her quondam husband, Lysimachus,[l] organized several smaller communities into a city to which she gave her own name.[29] This new city of Amastris lay on a rocky peninsula connected with the mainland by a narrow isthmus, on each side of which harbours were built, formed by gigantic moles. The trade of these ports must have added much to Heracleia's wealth, and the great forests behind them, especially those near Amastris and the neighbouring Cytorus, produced not only timber for ship-building but also the valuable boxwood, a hard, close-grained wood used for making musical instruments, statues, tools and costly furniture.

At the death of Lysimachus in 281 Heracleia recovered her freedom, which she retained for over 200 years. Entering into negotiations with Nicomedes I of Bithynia, she succeeded, apparently by purchase, in obtaining the freedom of Cierus and Tieium, which his father had seized.[m] With these cities and Chalcedon and Byzantium she joined Nicomedes and Mithradates I of Pontus in a league formed for the purpose of coming to terms with the Galatians and, presumably with their help, preserving the members' independence against Seleucid aggression.[30] Heracleia, by sending her navy to the aid, first of Nicomedes against Antiochus I, and, later, of Byzantium against Antiochus II, maintained good faith toward her allies and at the same time contributed to the weakening of the power of the Seleucids. In accordance with this policy, she entered into cordial relations with Ptolemy II—the chief enemy of the Seleucids—who in return sent the citizens a large quantity of grain and built a marble temple for their patron-deity Heracles.[n] Similar friendly relations were maintained with Pontus, for when the kingdom had been ravaged by the Galatians and famine threatened, Heracleia sent Mithradates II a present of grain for the use of his subjects.[o] This gift, as it turned out, was made at great sacrifice to the city, for the Celts, in revenge, attacked her territory and it was necessary to buy them off with a large ransom.

At the beginning of the second century Heracleia's long-standing friendship with the rulers of Bithynia was rudely brought to an end, when the ambitious Prusias I invaded her territory and not only captured Cierus and the basin of the Hypius but also extended his dominions as far as Tieium and the Euxine coast.[p] Thus Heracleia was surrounded by Bithynian territory, and of her extensive possessions she retained only the plain around the city. This and the city itself were successfully defended against the King, but it was probably only by the aid of a new and powerful ally that Heracleia's independence was preserved. For at this juncture the Roman army under the Scipios appeared in Asia.

In the coming of the Romans the statesmen who directed Heracleia's policy saw their opportunity. By a series of embassies to the Roman generals they succeeded in winning their good will and the promise of a recognition of the city's independence.[31] This promise was presently fulfilled and a formal treaty of alliance was duly drawn up and inscribed both in the Capitolium in Rome and the Temple of Zeus in Heracleia. True to her duty as ally, the city sent two ships to aid the Romans in their war against Perseus of Macedonia,[q] as well as on a later occasion, perhaps during the war against the Italians who were fighting to obtain citizenship.[r] But both the alliance and Heracleia's independence came to an end in 73, when Mithradates's admiral forced the city to contribute ships to the King's fleet.[s] At the same time some citizens, angered by the rapacity of the Roman *publicani*, who, in defiance of the rights of a free community, were attempting to collect taxes from Heracleia, took advantage of the occasion and put these aggressors to death. Three years later the city was captured and plun-

[n] Memnon 25, 1.   [o] See above p. 189.   [p] Memnon 27. See note 21.
[q] Livy XLII 56, 6.   [r] Memnon 29.   [s] See below p. 325.

dered by the Roman general, Cotta,[t] a victor more brutal than the Oriental potentate who had attempted to conquer western Asia Minor.

The Kingdom of Bithynia, which by the will of its eighth king became a province of Rome, was founded amid the general confusion which followed the death of Antigonus in 301.[32] Zipoetes, a local "dynast" whose ancestors for at least three generations had wielded some sort of power in the country, defeated Lysimachus and his generals in a series of battles and thereupon assumed the title of King. After enlarging his dominions by seizing part of the territory of Heracleia,[u] he defended himself successfully against an attack on the part of Antiochus I[v] and thus definitely established his power over Bithynia. When he died, about 279, his son Nicomedes succeeded to the throne.

For a century after the death of Zipoetes, Bithynia was ruled by a series of three competent and energetic monarchs, Nicomedes I, his son Ziaëlas, and his grandson Prusias I. During this period, by steadfast opposition to the Seleucid monarchs, the titular lords of Asia Minor, and by extending the boundaries of their kingdom by force or diplomacy, these rulers strengthened and consolidated their power, and through their efforts Bithynia grew from a small principality into an important independent state. Although ruthless in acquiring the territory of those Grecian cities whose harbours and lands they coveted, they maintained friendly relations with many which lay outside the scope of their ambitions, and, in general, endeavoured to take their place among the princes of the Hellenic world.

There was, it is true, little of the Hellene in Nicomedes, apart from his Grecian name.[33] His portrait, as it appears on his coins, shows a coarse-featured man of a barbarian type, but withal shrewd and energetic; it suggests the politician rather than the prince. At the outset of his reign, indeed, he showed himself no friend of Hellenism; for by his invitation to the lawless Galatians, whom he brought over from Thrace, nominally to aid him against his rebellious brother, but probably in reality to support himself and his allies against Antiochus I,[w] he introduced into Asia Minor a foe who for years to come terrorized the cities of the western seaboard. Nevertheless, Nicomedes played the part of a Greek king; for his coins show the likenesses of Greek gods, and his foundation of Nicomedeia, although his primary

---

[t] See below p. 341.   [u] See note 21.   [v] Memnon 15; 20, 3.
[w] In 277 B.C.; see Chap. I note 10. The brother's name appears as Ziboeta in Livy xxxviii 16, 8f.

purpose was doubtless to obtain a port on the Propontis, was, as has been observed, in conformity with the current Hellenistic practice.[34] He also succeeded in obtaining recognition in the Greek world; sacrifices were performed in his honour by a religious society in Cos, and an ivory statue of him was set up in Olympia. His alliance with Chalcedon and Heracleia showed a similar policy.[x] Although his object—a double one—was to strengthen himself against the Seleucids and to gain access to the Euxine, this alliance served to ensure the independence of these two Greek cities. This policy he continued to the end; for in his will he named as the guardians of his young children, born of his second wife, not only the kings of Macedonia and Egypt but also the free cities of Heracleia, Cius and Byzantium.[y]

The first act of his son Ziaëlas was to defy these guardians. Despite the opposition of the cities and many of the Bithynians as well, he drove out his half-brothers and made himself king.[35] In his means to this end he imitated his father by using for the purpose a band of Galatian mercenaries. Throughout his reign, indeed, he seems to have relied on their support—a policy which proved his undoing, for when they discovered a plan he had made to put some of their chieftains to death they forestalled it by killing him. But although he showed no hesitation in annexing to his kingdom a part of Paphlagonia and perhaps also of northern Phrygia, he seems to have made every endeavour to win the friendship of the Greeks. In a letter addressed to the "Council and People" of Cos, in which he agreed to recognize the inviolability of the Temple of Asclepius, he asserted his readiness to "exercise care for all the Greeks who might come to his kingdom"; he offered, in particular, to show favour to the Coans, promising safety to those seafarers who might enter his territory and protection to those who were cast on the Bithynian coast. He also took occasion to remind the Coans of his "friendship and alliance" with their protector, King Ptolemy, in this continuing the policy of Nicomedes, who had named Ptolemy's father as one of his children's guardians. By this alliance Ziaëlas also maintained his father's policy toward the Seleucids, the enemies of Egypt, even going so far as to marry his daughter to the rebellious Seleucid prince, Antiochus Hierax.[z]

Prusias I, who succeeded his father soon after 230 B.C., was as ambitious as his predecessors, but, if one may judge from his portrait, a

---

[x] See above pp. 305 and 309. [y] Memnon 22.

[z] Eusebius *Chron.* 1 p. 251 Schöne=p. 119 Karst. For the revolt of Antiochus Hierax see above p. 8.

man of greater refinement and intelligence.[36] At the outset he had little success in his attempts at expansion, for his first venture—an alliance with Rhodes against Byzantium—was a total failure. He did, indeed, conquer the Byzantine possessions on the Asiatic side of the Strait, but when the Rhodians made a separate peace with the enemy, he found himself unable to carry on alone and was forced to surrender all he had gained. His jealousy was then aroused by the growing strength of his neighbour, Attalus I of Pergamum. As long as Achaeus, the Seleucid general who had seized most of western Asia Minor, retained his power and menaced Prusias as well as Attalus,[a] both kings were constrained to be content with their ancestral dominions. But when Achaeus was finally overcome by the young Antiochus III, Prusias was free to carry out his intentions. The opportunity was offered by the outbreak of hostilities between the more powerful allies of each. In 211, when Rome, in conjunction with the Aetolians, declared war on Philip V of Macedonia, Attalus, as has already been described,[b] joined the coalition. Philip, in turn, called on his brother-in-law, Prusias, for help. The Bithynian King responded by sending some ships to the aid of his Macedonian ally,[c] but he also took advantage of Attalus's absence in Greece to increase his own dominions by invading the kingdom of Pergamum. This was, indeed, his chief contribution to the struggle; for the report of the invasion caused Attalus to return to Asia, and the withdrawal of his ships made it impossible for his allies to carry on warfare by sea.[37] But although Prusias seems to have defeated Attalus in one engagement, this attempt at expansion appears to have profited him nothing; for in 205 the Romans concluded a treaty with Philip, and Prusias, as an ally of the latter, had perforce to concur.[d]

There were, however, indirect results of the war. It won Prusias the friendship of Philip and the enmity of the King of Pergamum and, with this enmity, disapproval on the part of the Romans. For the moment, however, Prusias's alliance with Philip seemed to outweigh all other considerations. When the Macedonian monarch, three years after the conclusion of peace, invaded Asia Minor and, among other acts of cruelty, destroyed Cius and Myrleia, he presented his brother-in-law with their territories.[e] Thus Prusias not only gained additional ports on the Propontis but pushed forward the boundaries of his kingdom to the Rhyndacus and Mt. Olympus; and although by the treaty

a Polybius v 77, 1. See also above p. 10.   b See above p. 12.
c Livy xxvii 30, 16 (208 B.C.).   d Livy xxix 12, 13f. See also Chap. I note 35.
e See above p. 306f.

of peace imposed on Philip in 197, the Greek cities in Asia which he had captured were once more declared free,[f] the Bithynian King succeeded in evading the command of the Roman envoy to relinquish his new possessions.[g] About this time also, he enlarged his dominions toward the east by taking Cierus and Tieium from Heracleia.[38] We are told that it was only because of a fall which fractured his leg that he was prevented from capturing Heracleia itself.

The additions made by Prusias to his kingdom brought Bithynia to the greatest size that she ever attained. Now, at the height of his power, the King was compelled to face a difficult dilemma. Philip, his former ally, had been shorn of his strength. He was forced, therefore, to choose between his hereditary enemy, the Seleucid monarch, and Rome, the ally of his rival Attalus. Antiochus III, driven back from Greece to Asia and eager to strengthen his cause, approached the Bithynian ruler with an invitation to form an alliance.[h] At first Prusias was not averse to the proposal. He knew that his enmity toward Attalus had won him no favour in Rome and he feared that the coming of the Romans to Asia might result in the diminution of his power. But a counter-proposal from the Scipios, promising him security as the reward of neutrality, won him to their side. He thus saved his kingdom, but as he rendered no service which seemed to the Romans to deserve a reward, none of the prizes of the war fell to his lot. In fact, the arrangements made at Apameia provided that Phrygia Epictetus, which either he or his father had conquered, should be ceded to Attalus's son Eumenes, now King of Pergamum.[i]

This clause in the treaty provoked new hostilities.[39] Prusias was in no mind to comply with the demand contained in it and embarked on a war to keep what he considered to be his own domain. He also made use of Hannibal, who had fled to him for refuge after the defeat of Antiochus. His army was defeated by Eumenes's brother, Attalus, but Hannibal was successful in a sea-battle against the Pergamene navy. Eumenes, however, appealed to Rome, and the Senate sent a special commissioner to Prusias to demand not only his compliance with the terms of the treaty but also the surrender of Hannibal. The Carthaginian anticipated surrender by suicide, but Prusias was compelled to make peace and to give his rival the disputed territory.

Prusias reigned over Bithynia for about forty-five years. True to the

---

[f] See Chap. IV note 44.   [g] Polybius XVIII 44, 5 = Livy XXXIII 30, 4.
[h] Polybius XXI 11, 1f. = Livy XXXVII 25, 4f.: Appian *Syr.* 23.
[i] See Chap. I note 56.

traditions of his grandfather and father, he extended the boundaries of his kingdom. He followed the example of other monarchs of his time by founding or rebuilding cities and naming them after himself. Early in his reign, in imitation of Attalus of Pergamum, he established a great religious festival, called the Soteria, in which he expected the Greeks in general to participate.[j] But with all his efforts to appear in the light of an Hellenic prince, he was no true friend of Hellenism, and in his readiness to profit at the expense of the independent cities whose territory he desired, he presented a marked contrast to his neighbours, the monarchs of Pergamum.

With the death of Prusias I the succession of able and energetic rulers, who had brought Bithynia to a position of real importance, came to an end. Prusias II, who succeeded his father about 183, was a man of a very different type. While our most reliable historian's characterization of him as not deficient in mentality but cowardly and effeminate, as well as repulsive in appearance,[k] may be due, in part, to a hostile attitude, his coins show a sensuous face that is perhaps not repulsive but certainly weak and vicious.[l] Moreover, we know of no action of his which would justify a more favourable verdict. At the very outset of his reign he became involved in the war between Eumenes II and Pharnaces I of Pontus,[m] for the latter, amid his other conquests, captured Tieium,[n] which Prusias I had taken from Heracleia. Self-interest compelled the Bithynian King to ally himself with his father's rival, the ruler of Pergamum, but of his actual contribution to the cause we have no knowledge. When the war was brought to an end in 179, thanks rather to the military prowess of Eumenes than to the repeated embassies which the Roman Senate sent to the Pontian monarch, the provisions of the treaty included the return of Tieium, which Eumenes presently handed over to Prusias.[o]

Despite the probability that this unworthy monarch had no real interest in Hellenic civilization, he nevertheless imitated his father in trying to establish connexions with the Greek cities in Asia and with Greece itself. A year after the conclusion of the treaty with Pharnaces, Prusias presented gifts to the Milesians' Temple of Apollo at Didyma and about the same time he showed some favour to the Aetolians which led them to erect a statue in his honour at Delphi.[40] Later, like his father, he allied himself with the royal house of Macedonia and

---

j See note 36. k Polybius XXXVI 15 (XXXVII 7) = Diodorus XXXII 19.
l See *Receuil* 1 p. 220f. m See above p. 192. n Diodorus XXIX 23.
o Polybius XXV 2, 7. See Chap. I note 56.

315

married his cousin, the sister of King Perseus. This marriage, however, was not without its embarrassing consequences, for when war broke out between Perseus and the Romans, Prusias was faced with a serious dilemma. But fear of Rome proved more potent than the family tie, and he announced that he would remain neutral. Nevertheless, two years later, he abandoned this position to the extent of sending five warships to aid the Roman fleet in attacking the Macedonian coast.[p] Soon afterwards, while reminding the Romans of this assistance, he attempted at Perseus's request to negotiate a peace.[q] But after Perseus had been conquered at Pydna, fearing, apparently, that he had been too lukewarm in the Roman cause, the Bithynian King descended to a depth of adulation that won him general contempt. Not only did he receive the Roman commissioners arrayed in the garb of a freedman and professing that he was the freedman of the Roman people, but he even journeyed to Rome to present his congratulations in person and, prostrating himself at the threshold of the Senate-house, he did reverence to the Fathers, addressing them as gods and saviours.[41] However bad the impression this servility created, he nevertheless succeeded in obtaining a favourable reply to his entreaties.

Prusias's gift for intrigue, however, found greater opportunity after Eumenes fell from favour at Rome. His attempts to discredit the Pergamene King extended over a period of five years,[r] but they seem to have gained him nothing. However determined the Senate might be to curtail the power of Eumenes, this step was evidently not to be taken for the benefit of the servile and unreliable King of Bithynia. Nor had the Greek cities of the Aegean coast, whose gratitude Eumenes had won by lavish gifts,[s] any desire to further the interests of a monarch who had repeatedly shown himself the enemy of their benefactor. The Romans, to be sure, were slow to take measures against Prusias when after Eumenes's death his enmity toward Pergamum and his ambition to profit at its expense impelled him to open war against Attalus II.[42] Invading the Pergamene Kingdom, he not only plundered the sanctuary of Athena Nicephorus outside the capital but ravaged the northern part of Lydia as far east as Thyateira, sacking and destroying the temples. Attalus, true to his policy of making no move without the approval of Rome,[t] appealed to the Senate. The Fathers, however, taking no active steps to meet the situation, contented themselves with

---

[p] Livy XLIV 10, 12 (169 B.C.).

[q] Livy XLIV 14, 6f.

[r] 165-160 B.C. See above pp. 23 and 26.

[s] See above p. 24f.

[t] See above p. 27.

sending two separate commissions, one after the other, to Asia, and it was not until after the second of these, accompanied by Attalus himself, was treacherously attacked by Prusias and besieged in Pergamum that any effective measures were adopted. Then, angered by the insult, the Romans despatched a third commission with peremptory orders to Prusias to refrain from further acts of violence. When the King demurred at complying with the demand, the commissioners took the final step of severing the official friendship and alliance which existed between Rome and Bithynia. They also urged the cities of the Aegean coast to follow their example. Attalus was authorized to mobilize an army, although only for the defence of his borders. But his brother Athenaeus, with a fleet partly furnished by Pergamum's allies in Asia, ravaged the Bithynian coast, which was exposed to attack for the reason that Prusias's navy had previously been damaged by a storm. Finally, the pressure which Rome knew how to bring upon a dependent king was successful, and Prusias was compelled by a fourth commission to indemnify both Attalus and the cities whose territories he had plundered.[43] He had also to surrender to Attalus twenty of his remaining ships of war.

A client-king of this character was of little value to the Romans. Consequently, in 149 B.C., when Prusias's son, Nicomedes, setting out from Rome, where he seems to have been acting as his father's envoy, rebelled against the old monarch and entered Bithynia with an army, they took no active steps to prevent the invasion.[44] The aid of Attalus, as well as the moral support which his presence in person gave to the prince, can hardly be supposed to have lacked the Senate's approval. Commissioners were, indeed, appointed to protest, but they were feeble and incompetent, and, as was perhaps the Fathers' intention, they made no real effort to protect the discredited King. Moreover, the Bithynians themselves, who thoroughly hated and despised their ruler, welcomed Nicomedes; and when his emissaries had murdered Prusias in the Temple of Zeus at Nicomedeia, he made himself king without opposition either in Rome or in Asia Minor. The Senate was probably not unwilling to have an assurance of a stable peace between the two rival client-kingdoms.

Nicomedes II, surnamed Epiphanes, thus began his reign as the protégé of Attalus.[45] Except for his double crime of parricide and sacrilege, by means of which he ascended the throne, we know of nothing to his discredit. During his residence in Rome he had made many friends, among them Massinissa, the King of Numidia, to whom, soon after his accession, he erected a monument in Delos, testifying to the aged monarch's "fatherly affection and kindness." He seems to have been thoroughly imbued with respect for Rome's rule, and the example of Attalus probably contributed to his conception of his duties as a client-king. His fidelity was shown when he responded to the Senate's call for aid in the suppression of the revolt of Aristonicus.[u] Unlike his father, he cultivated friendly relations with the Greek cities; he was honoured by the Ionian Federation, and the city of Priene founded a cult for his worship, with a priest and a stated sacrifice; in another Greek town he erected a sanctuary for the worship of his deified mother.

About 127 B.C. Epiphanes was succeeded by his son, Nicomedes III, who, because of his many benefactions, received the surname of Euergetes.[46] At the beginning of his reign he seems to have become involved in a dispute of some kind with Mithradates V of Pontus, and the two monarchs appealed to Rome with the result that both were accused of trying to outbid each other in bribing the Roman voters.[v] Among his benefactions were gifts to the island of Delos and presents or other acts of generosity to the Society of Stage-artists at Argos[w] and to a citizen of Epidaurus,[x] in return for all of which monuments were dedicated in his honour. In his attitude toward the Hellenic world he seems to have emulated the monarchs of Pergamum.

His benefactions, however, brought little advantage to his own kingdom. In 104 the economic condition of Bithynia was so bad that many of its inhabitants had been seized as slaves by the Roman money-lenders to whom they had been forced to resort, and the Senate felt compelled to enact that no free man from an allied state should be held in servitude in any province of Rome.[y] Nevertheless, he maintained his benefactions to the end; not long before his death he and his second wife, Laodice, the sister of Mithradates Eupator, in response to a request from the officials of the Temple at Delphi, presented the God with thirty slaves, to be used as warders of the sacred flocks and herds and for other menial offices.[z]

Nicomedes's attempts to extend his power, first by a partition of Paphlagonia with Mithradates and then by his marriage with Laodice, the widow of Ariarathes VI of Cappadocia, have been described else-

---

[u] See above p. 150.   [v] See Chap. VI note 27.

[w] See *I.G.* IV 558, l. 25f. (115/14 B.C. see Wilhelm in *J.O.A.I.* XI [1908], p. 77).

[x] See *I.G.* IV² 591.

[y] Diodorus XXXVI 3, 1f. (see Chap. VIII note 57).

[z] See *Fouilles de Delphes* III 4, 1, no. 77 = *O.G.I.* 345 (see note 46).

where.[a] The former enterprise seems to have met with some success,[b] but his plan to gain control of Cappadocia was a total failure. When he died, not without the suspicion of poison,[c] about 94 B.C., he was discredited at Rome, his heir was impoverished, and his kingdom was a possible prey for the ambitious ruler of Pontus.

Nicomedes Euergetes left two sons. The elder, also named Nicomedes, born of his first wife, succeeded to the throne with the surname Philopator.[47] The younger, Socrates, the son of a concubine, the King had sent away, together with his mother, to Cyzicus with liberal provision for their maintenance. By this step he hoped to prevent any dispute for the throne. The new king, Nicomedes IV, was not unknown in the Hellenic world. While still crown-prince he had been honoured at Delos by a monument erected by the group of youths who had just completed the training in arms and discipline that was customary for a young Greek. It is possible that he had undergone this training with them. In any case, it may be assumed that he had at least a modicum of Hellenic culture; but so scandalous was his private life that in after years it was made a matter of reproach to Julius Caesar that in his youth he had spent some time at Nicomedes's court.

It is possible that a stronger man might have coped more successfully with the situation in Asia. As it was, Nicomedes speedily fell a victim both to the ambitions of Mithradates and to the demands of his—or his father's—creditors in Rome. The pretensions of Socrates, already described,[d] afforded the King of Pontus a welcome opportunity to place him as a puppet-king on the Bithynian throne, forcing Nicomedes to take refuge in Italy. Though reinstated by the Romans, the King was no longer his own master, for his debts were used to enforce the demands of the Roman commissioners in Asia. His invasion of Mithradates's territory, carried out at their command, ended in disaster and a second flight and, finally, in the seizure of Bithynia by a Pontic army.[e] His ultimate restoration by Sulla—one of the provisions of the Treaty of Dardanus[f]—made him an obedient vassal of Rome for the remaining eleven years of his reign. As an ally, he furnished some ships for the expedition against Mitylene, the last of the Asianic cities to hold out against the power of Rome.[g]

Like his father, Nicomedes IV was married twice. His first wife was his father's sister, after whose death he married the Cappadocian

---

[a] See above pp. 197 and 203.   [b] See Chap. IX note 14.   [c] Licinianus p. 29 Flemisch.
[d] See above p. 207.   [e] See above p. 208f.   [f] See above p. 230.
[g] Suetonius *Jul.* 2; see also above p. 246.

319

princess, Nysa, the daughter of his step-mother Laodice.[48] By arousing her husband's suspicions against his half-brother Socrates, Nysa seems to have afforded the latter a pretext for his appeal to Mithradates. She bore Nicomedes a daughter, named for herself, whose interests were later defended in Rome by Julius Caesar;[h] but, if she had a son at all, his father, apparently, was not the King, for there was no legitimate heir to the throne. It was natural, therefore, that Nicomedes, a subservient vassal of Rome, should follow the example set by Attalus III of Pergamum and bestow his kingdom on the power to which he owed it. When he died, in 74, it was found that he had bequeathed his kingdom to the Roman people.[49] The bequest, like that of Attalus, was not undisputed. A claimant appeared, who asserted that he was the lawful son of Nysa by Nicomedes.[50] Unlike the Pergamene Aristonicus, however, he made no effort to obtain his kingdom by warfare but merely attempted to make good his case by appealing to the Senate. His claim was examined but soon rejected, for natives of Bithynia itself appeared to testify against his legitimacy. The Senators, accordingly, accepted the bequest and ordered the governor of Asia, Marcus Juncus, to take over Bithynia and organize it as a province of Rome.[51]

Thus, within a few years of each other, two new provinces were acquired by the Romans in Asia Minor—Pamphylia on the southern coast and Bithynia at the entrance to the Euxine. The province of Asia was now flanked by two other dependencies. Both, as yet, were far inferior in size, as well as in wealth, to the bequest of Attalus; but both were destined within a few years to be greatly increased after the indomitable Mithradates of Pontus, the enemy of the last two Bithynian monarchs, was overthrown and his kingdom annexed to Rome's empire by the great conqueror and organizer, Pompey. But before this could happen Mithradates launched a second invasion on western Asia Minor.

[h] Suetonius *Jul.* 49, 3.

CHAPTER XIV

THE RETURN OF MITHRADATES

IT is not improbable that Nicomedes, when he bequeathed his kingdom to the Romans, realized that Bithynia would prove an apple of discord for them and for the ambitious King of Pontus. But long before the rupture was precipitated, the treaty which Sulla had forced on Mithradates at Dardanus must have seemed to both sides merely a temporary expedient. When Murena invaded Pontus in 83[a] this treaty had not received the formal ratification necessary to ensure its validity, and only the direct intervention of Sulla in 81 prevented further warfare. Two years later, Mithradates, desiring to forestall another such invasion and perhaps also to test the good faith of the Romans, sent ambassadors to the Senate to sign the treaty with all due formality.[b] His envoys, however, were confronted by a commission despatched by Ariobarzanes of Cappadocia, who again had a grievance to present. Although in 81 he had ceded a portion of Cappadocia to Mithradates,[c] he now complained that the King of Pontus was holding a part of his kingdom. Roman sympathy, as on previous occasions, favoured the Cappadocian monarch, and the Pontic envoys were informed by Sulla that before the treaty could be ratified formally, their master must evacuate the lands he had seized. Mithradates, accordingly, not yet ready for a struggle, complied with the demand. But before a second embassy sent to Rome to carry out the necessary formalities arrived in the city, Sulla had died. Amid the general confusion brought about by the revolt of the late Dictator's opponents, led by the Consul, Marcus Aemilius Lepidus, the Senators had neither the time nor the inclination to receive the envoys from Pontus. When these were refused an audience, Mithradates showed his anger, and probably also his insincerity, by encouraging his son-in-law, Tigranes of Armenia, to invade Cappadocia. Tigranes, accordingly, repeated his exploit of fifteen years earlier[d] and overran the kingdom, carrying off a large number of the inhabitants of its capital, Mazaca, as he had already done from Cilicia,[e] to swell the population of his new capital, Tigranocerta.[f]

Neither side, however, was ready for war. The Romans were involved

---

[a] See above p. 243. [b] Appian *Mith.* 67. [c] See above p. 245.
[d] See above p. 206. [e] See Chap. XII note 36.
[f] Strabo XII p. 539: Appian *Mith.* 67 (where those carried away are estimated at the incredibly large number of 300,000). For Tigranocerta see below p. 339.

in a difficult struggle in Spain, where Quintus Sertorius, a former general of Marius, was attempting to set up a rival state and had so far proved able to cope with the forces sent against him. In eastern Europe the robber-bands of Thrace, whom Sulla had chastised,[g] had broken out once more, and a stubborn war was in progress. Roman resources were further taxed by the elaborate armament with which Marcus Antonius made his unsuccessful attempt to crush the pirates.[h] The general situation was well described in the speech in which Gaius Cotta, the Consul of 75 B.C., is said to have told the Roman people that the Republic was beset by enemies both at home and abroad.[i]

Mithradates, likewise, was hampered in his plans to attempt another invasion of western Asia Minor. His previous failure made it necessary for him to restore his shattered prestige as well as to build up his broken forces. He had had to contend with a revolt of his subjects in the Crimea, which he finally subdued by creating his son Machares king of the district.[j] An attempt to connect this dependency with Pontus by the conquest of the tribes at the northeastern corner of the Black Sea met with complete failure, for attacks by the natives and the severity of the climate cost Mithradates two thirds of the army sent to subdue the region.[k]

It seems evident that at least some of the dangers in which the Romans were placed were due to the efforts of Mithradates to strengthen his position by abetting their enemies. His connexion with the pirates has already been noticed.[l] It is probable that he gave encouragement, if not actual aid, to the Thracians, for they had served under his standard in the former war, and in his new army they formed a numerous contingent.[m] He also entered into negotiations with Sertorius, using as agents two Roman renegades, Fannius and Magius, former soldiers in Fimbria's army who after the death of their leader had fled to the King.[1] It was said that for their voyages they bought from Verres, while acting as legate of Dolabella in Cilicia, the vessel which he had requisitioned from the Milesians for his own use. These men, appearing before the rebels' "Senate" in Spain, offered in Mithradates's name an official recognition of their cause and the more material help of money and ships. In return, the King asked this self-styled Roman government to recognize his claim to the whole of Asia Minor. Despite the protests of Sertorius against the cession of the province of

---

[g] See above p. 229. [h] See above p. 292f.
[i] Sallust *Hist.* II 47, 6 Maur. (see also p. 292); see also Appian *B.C.* I 111.
[j] Appian *Mith.* 67. [k] Appian *ibid.* [l] See above p. 239.
[m] Justin XXXVIII 3, 6f.: Appian *Mith.* 15 and 69.

Asia, the offer was accepted, and the two agents returned to Pontus, bringing with them a former Roman quaestor, who bore the name of Marcus Marius. He was to act both as Sertorius's representative and as military adviser to Mithradates in the impending war. The King, on his side, agreed to supply the rebels with the sum of three thousand talents and a fleet of forty ships.

The alliance proved valueless to Sertorius, for before the promised ships had gone far on their voyage to Spain he fell a victim to the treachery of some of his associates.[n] To Mithradates, on the other hand, it was not without benefit, for the traitorous Marius rendered him real assistance in the reorganization of the Pontic army, the formation of which was now begun in earnest. As in the previous war, he had at his disposal the man-power of Pontus and the mountains on the Armenian border. In addition to these forces he enlisted soldiers not only from the northern coast of the Euxine but also from the tribes of the lower Danube—among them the Bastarnians, the flower of his infantry—as well as from the Thracians of the Balkan Range. The number of his fighting-men was estimated at 120,000 foot and 16,000 horse, besides 100 scythed chariots; in addition, there was a great train of workmen and porters.[2] This force was smaller by far than the huge army with which he had conducted his former invasion. It was, however, much more effective. The King discarded the gorgeous armour and equipment and the Oriental military formation which he had previously used, and with the aid of Marius he armed his troops in Roman fashion and organized them after the Roman model.[o] Besides his land-forces he had a new fleet, well manned and well equipped with munitions of war and provisioned from granaries established on the coast. Its strength was estimated at four hundred fighting-ships, besides a large number of smaller craft.[p]

The creation of this armament was naturally not unknown at Rome, and a further struggle in Asia was regarded as inevitable. Marcus Cotta, one of the Consuls of 74 B.C., was made governor of the newly-acquired province of Bithynia, a post for which he proved wholly unfit.[3] He had under his command all the ships available in eastern waters and a force of infantry as well. His colleague, Lucius Lucullus, as has been already related, became proconsul of Cilicia and soon afterward received orders to take command of the war against the King. His army included two legions which had been trained by Servilius

[n] See below p. 326.
[o] Plutarch *Luc.* 7, 3f.: Appian *Mith.* 69.
[p] Memnon 37, 1: Appian *Mith.* 119.

Isauricus in his campaigns, as well as the two legions of Flaccus which had mutinied under the leadership of Fimbria and had been ordered by Sulla to remain in Asia. In addition, he was authorized to enroll a legion in Italy, which he took with him to the East. His total force, consisting of these five legions and native contingents, was estimated at about 30,000 foot and 2,500 horse, less than a quarter of the army of the King. He had under his orders at least six legates, who, when the need arose, could be vested with independent commands.[4]

Late in 74 or early in 73 the two Roman commanders crossed over to Asia Minor to prepare for the expected invasion.[5] Cotta took up a position at Chalcedon on the Bosporus, obviously with the intention of barring the Strait, while Lucullus, after marching through Greece, appears to have gone on to Ephesus, where he assembled his forces.[q] The first weeks of his stay were necessarily devoted to mobilizing his troops and organizing them into an army. The former legions of Flaccus, particularly, which had known no warfare for ten years, needed training and discipline. It is recorded that they were lawless and insolent but in a short time the new general curbed them so successfully that in him they found for the first time in their experience a true commander.[r] But not only were the soldiers garrisoned in Asia demoralized, but the province itself was in a wretched plight as the result of the exactions of Sulla.[s] The inhabitants of the cities, especially, were ready for an uprising, and there was every reason to fear that they might once more receive the King.

Soon after the arrival of the Roman commanders Mithradates struck his blow. In the spring of 73 he formally opened the war by a sacrifice to his protector, Zeus Stratius, and on the seashore, probably at Sinope, his naval base, he made a solemn offering to Poseidon by causing a chariot drawn by white horses to be driven into the Euxine.[6] He then gave orders to his fleet to begin its voyage along the coast. A detachment of the army under Diophantus was sent southward into Cappadocia to prevent any attack on Pontus from the south.[t] Then, with his generals, Taxiles and Hermocrates, and the great bulk of his forces, the King launched his attack. Proceeding through Paphlagonia, probably by the road leading through the valleys of the Amnias and the upper Billaeus, he burst upon Bithynia after a rapid march.[7] The terrified inhabitants had no means of resisting his vast array. Nor had they

---

q Plutarch *Cimon* 1, 5: see Reinach *Mith. Eup.* p. 321, note 1.

r Plutarch *Luc.* 7, 1f. s Plutarch *Luc.* 7, 5f. See also above p. 238f.

t Memnon 37, 1.

any motive for so doing, for even during the few months that Bithynia had been a Roman province the tax-collectors had won the hatred of the natives. To these, as to the cities of Asia fifteen years before, the King seemed a deliverer, and they welcomed him gladly.[u] Cotta, with his tiny land-force, was unable to offer any resistance and barricaded himself in Chalcedon. All the Romans present in Bithynia hastened to join him in his refuge.

Mithradates, wishing to follow up his success by an immediate victory over the enemy, at once sent a force against Chalcedon, and Cotta was foolhardy enough to attempt an engagement.[8] Unwilling to face the enemy in person, he placed Nudus, the commandant of the fleet, in charge of his land-forces and ordered him to occupy a strategic position on the hills which command the plain near the city. The attempted resistance proved a total failure. The Romans, unable to withstand the onslaught of the King's Bastarnian infantry, broke and fled. Cotta, panic-stricken, ordered the gates of the city to be barred, and the throng of fugitives was thus caught in a trap between the walls and the enemy. Nudus and some of the other officers were rescued by being hauled over the ramparts by ropes, but the great majority, despite their entreaties, were left outside and either killed or captured by their pursuers. The Roman loss was estimated at 5,300, while on the King's side about seven hundred fell, including only thirty Bastarnians.

Meanwhile the royal fleet arrived at the Bosporus. In the course of its voyage along the coast it had stopped at the free city of Heracleia.[9] The citizens, mindful of the treaty they had had with Rome since the coming of the Scipios to Asia, refused to admit the ships to the harbour, consenting only to sell the supplies demanded. The King's admiral, Aristonicus, however, contrived to seize two of the leading men of the city, and by holding them prisoner he forced Heracleia to contribute five ships for the war. By this act the citizens broke their treaty with Rome. The breach was then rendered irremediable by the action of some of the inhabitants, who seized the Roman *publicani* present in the city and put them to death. At the Bosporus Aristonicus met with no opposition, and on the very day of the disastrous defeat of the Romans at Chalcedon he entered the harbour of the city and captured or destroyed Cotta's entire fleet of sixty-four vessels. Among the prisoners seems to have been a force of three thousand men who manned the ships contributed by Rome's ally, the city of Cyzicus.

[u] Plutarch *Luc.* 7, 5.

Mithradates, having won a double victory at Chalcedon, felt little interest in capturing the city. Accordingly, leaving Cotta blockaded there, he proceeded to the occupation of Bithynia.[10] The prestige of his success,[v] as well as the general hatred of the Romans, made this occupation an easy matter. Throughout the province the various cities opened their gates to him and before the summer was over Bithynia was in his hands. On his march Marius went with him, apparently posing as the representative of Rome. Both Nicomedeia and Nicaea were forced to receive Pontic garrisons, Prusa, at the foot of Mt. Olympus, likewise surrendered, and the neighbouring ports on the Propontis, Apameia Myrleia and Prusias (Cius), were also seized, probably by the fleet. In fact, after the capture of Cotta's ships, the sea was wholly in the power of Mithradates. His navy advanced to the Hellespont, and, by capturing Parium and Lampsacus at the eastern end of the Strait, opened the way into the Aegean.[11] About this time the ships that had been promised to Sertorius were sent on their long voyage. Before they reached Spain the rebel leader had been killed by the treachery of some of his followers,[w] but the thought that the Mediterranean was now open to Mithradates's fleet caused panic in Rome.[x]

Lucullus, meanwhile, after bringing his soldiers into fighting trim, had set out from his headquarters, marching northeastward into Phrygia.[12] On reaching the river Sangarius, perhaps on his way to invade Pontus, he heard of the defeat of his colleague and Mithradates's successful seizure of Bithynia. There were many who urged him to continue his advance, since Pontus was now defenceless.[y] In particular, Archelaus, Mithradates's former general, who had left his master for Murena[z] and was now in Lucullus's army, declared that if the Roman general once appeared in the kingdom the whole country would surrender. This advice, however, Lucullus refused to accept. He gave as his reason the urgent need of rescuing his colleague, but, in fact, an advance into Pontus would have meant abandoning the province of Asia and its inhabitants to Mithradates and probably a repetition of the horrors that attended the King's previous invasion. He therefore turned about and marched into Bithynia to meet the enemy.

Lucullus, however, was too good a general to risk an engagement

[v] Cicero pro Mur. 33: Memnon 39, 3.

[w] Early in 72 B.C.; see Drumann-Groebe G.R. IV p. 390, note 2.

[x] Cicero de Imp. Cn. Pomp. 21; pro Mur. 33: Plutarch Luc. 13, 4.

[y] Plutarch Luc. 8, 3f.   [z] See above p. 243.

with a force so overwhelmingly superior to his own. Instead of a direct attack, therefore, he adopted the plan of weakening the enemy by guerilla warfare. Taking up a position in southern Bithynia, he used his cavalry for minor assaults as occasion offered, and in these he appears to have been generally successful.[13] Despite the murmuring of his soldiers, who demanded battle, he steadfastly refused to face the enemy in the field; and when the renegade Marius attempted to draw him into an engagement and his troops were about to attack, he used the appearance of some natural phenomenon, perhaps a meteor or a fire-ball, as an excuse for declining to fight. His plan was to cut off the enemy's supplies, for by adroitly questioning his captives he learned that the huge army was suffering from a shortage of food. He himself by cavalry forays was keeping his forces well provided.

Mithradates, meanwhile, was attempting to terrorize the province of Asia. He had a short time previously despatched Eumachus, as has already been related in connexion with the province of Cilicia,[a] to massacre and plunder in Phrygia and Pisidia. A cavalry-force under Metrophanes and Fannius was now sent into Asia, but before it advanced far into the province it was defeated by a subordinate of Lucullus.[14] The leaders themselves, together with two thousand horsemen, made their escape but were forced to retreat southward to Mysia and thence into the "Burned Country" in eastern Lydia;[b] from here, by roundabout routes and with adventures worthy of a romance, they made their way back to the King. Another of Lucullus's subordinates, Gaius Salluvius Naso, a legate with an independent command, successfully defended eastern Mysia and the borderland of Phrygia against a Pontic invasion.[15]

It was not Mithradates's way, however, to remain inactive when there were conquests to be made. Bithynia had fallen into his hands, but it was far from his purpose to stop with it. Accordingly, he began an advance into the province of Asia, which fifteen years earlier had proved so easy a victim. Leaving Phrygia and eastern Mysia to his subordinates and supported by his fleet, which now controlled the sea, he marched along the shore of the Propontis, intending to subdue the cities in the northwestern corner of the province. His first objective was Cyzicus, which had not been occupied during his previous campaign. As the citizens had not suffered from his cruelty then, they might be the more inclined to receive him now. They might also be more ready to surrender because they had suffered in the defeat of Cotta's

[a] See Chap. XII note 33.   [b] See above p. 36.

fleet at Chalcedon.[c] The capitulation of so important a city would add greatly to his prestige, and with Cyzicus in his hands the gateway to Asia would be secured. Therefore, although autumn was now at hand, he decided to advance against the city. Taking advantage of a rainy night, he evaded Lucullus and led his army from the neighbourhood of Prusa westward along the coast, intending to use both his land and sea forces for a double attack.

Cyzicus, however, proved to be no easy prey.[16] Situated on the southern side of what was practically an island connected with the coast by a narrow isthmus, it was defended by a wall of great strength which encircled the city and protected its harbours. It was also provided with abundant supplies of munitions and food. The townspeople, well aware of their strength and not daunted by the size of the Pontic army, made ready to resist; even the sight of their fellow-citizens captured at Chalcedon, whom the King led out in front of the city, failed to shake their resolution.

Disappointed in his expectation that the Cyzicenes would be ready to capitulate, Mithradates prepared to besiege the city. Seizing the southern end of the isthmus, he cut off this approach by a double wall. Meanwhile his fleet transported troops to the part of the island north of the city, and here a series of camps joined by moats was constructed. Thus the place was completely invested.

Lucullus, discovering that the enemy had outmanoeuvred him, followed on but steadfastly refused to give battle. Establishing himself on a hill south of the isthmus, he built a fortified camp and strengthened his position by a ditch between himself and the Pontic army.[17] Thus the King's communications by land were completely cut off, and while besieging Cyzicus he was in turn besieged by the small force of the Romans. He was entirely dependent on his fleet for the provisioning of his enormous array, and this, as winter advanced, became increasingly difficult.

Nevertheless, Mithradates prosecuted the siege with all the machinery known to ancient warfare. Mounds and towers with catapults and pent-houses with battering-rams were constructed for use against the ramparts; one especially large tower, mounted on two ships, was brought up to the sea-wall for the purpose of landing men from a drawbridge. Undismayed by these operations, the Cyzicenes continued to resist. They had been heartened by the news of Lucullus's arrival, made known to them by a soldier who, supported on inflated skins, swam over to the island, and they were still further encouraged when under cover of night some Roman troops were thrown into the city. Accordingly, when the King launched a joint attack by both sea and land they destroyed his battering-rams and quenched his fire-bearing missiles, and by pouring burning pitch upon the vessels that bore the great tower they repelled the assault.

This plan having failed, Mithradates, abandoning the attempt to attack by sea, decided to concentrate his efforts on the island-side of the city. For this his great force of cavalry was of no avail, and as the shortage of food had increased with the advent of winter, he resolved to reduce the number of mouths to be fed. Accordingly, learning that Lucullus was temporarily absent from camp, he sent away his wounded soldiers and almost all his horsemen, together with a large part of his baggage-train, including the transport-camels. Lucullus, learning of the move, pursued the retreating band during a snowy night, and overtaking them on the river Rhyndacus, the boundary between Bithynia and the province of Asia, he killed or captured almost the entire force.[18] About the same time came the news that Eumachus, in his invasion of Phrygia and Pisidia, had been defeated by the Galatians under their prince Deiotarus and driven back with great loss, a repulse which was of real service to Lucullus, for it relieved him of the necessity of diverting troops to protect the eastern part of the province.

As the winter advanced, Mithradates's efforts against Cyzicus grew increasingly unsuccessful. The besieged met his mines with countermines and burned his towers. His admiral, Aristonicus, while about to create a diversion along the shore of the Aegean, was entrapped by a pretended offer of surrender made by some former legionaries of Flaccus and delivered into the hands of Lucullus.[d] Worst of all, the shortage of food, which had been growing worse and worse, now became desperate, for Lucullus's policy of starving out the enemy was proving highly effective. Many Pontic soldiers died from malnutrition, and with hunger came also pestilence. Finally, the King was convinced that he could no longer continue the siege. With what remained of his fleet he set sail by night for Parium; at the same time he ordered Marius and Hermaeus to lead the army, now only 30,000 in number, to the neighbouring city of Lampsacus. The Romans, following along the coast, overtook the Pontic force as it was crossing the Aesepus, west of Cyzicus. In the battle that ensued many captives were taken and 20,000 of the enemy are said to have been killed; the remainder

[d] Plutarch *Luc.* 11, 5: Memnon 40, 1f. (where he is incorrectly called Archelaus, see note 9).

sought refuge in Lampsacus.[19] Here they were besieged by Lucullus, but before he could capture the city Mithradates arrived in the Strait. Taking the remnants of the army on board his ships, he made his way back to Nicomedeia, where he established his headquarters.

Lucullus then entered Cyzicus in triumph amid the joyous acclamations of the inhabitants.[e] As an expression of gratitude they founded a festival in his honour, giving it the name Lucullea. In reward for their fidelity to the Roman cause the victor granted them a large addition of territory.[f]

Despite the rescue of Cyzicus, however, the fact remained that Mithradates was still master of the sea, for the disaster at Chalcedon had cost the Romans their navy. In the panic which resulted from the King's seizure of the Hellespont in the previous autumn[g] the Senate had granted Lucullus the sum of eighteen million denarii for the construction of ships.[h] He, however, had refused the grant, replying that he could assemble a fleet from Rome's allies in the East. He had had experience in a similar mobilization fourteen years before, when he had collected a navy for Sulla. Now that spring had come it was possible to carry out his promise. Accordingly, after Mithradates's retreat he proceeded to the Hellespont and there began to gather and equip the much-needed ships.[20] They were promptly contributed by the cities of the Aegean littoral, still mindful of Lucullus's previous naval success against the King.

The newly-formed navy soon made the defeat of the enemy complete. Mithradates, apparently hoping to achieve some success by an attack on the Aegean cities, ordered Marius and two other trusted officers to take fifty vessels through the Hellespont. When word of their approach was brought to Lucullus, then in the Troad, he put out to meet the enemy and near the western end of the Strait he overtook a squadron of thirteen ships, which, probably because of a storm, had fallen behind the main body.[i] All of these he captured, killing their commander. Then hurrying after their comrades, he caught them at anchor off a small island near Lemnos. Although the skilful tactics of Marius and his colleagues, who beached their ships and ordered their men to fight from the decks, placed the Romans at a great disadvantage, Lucullus nevertheless succeeded in landing some of his best soldiers on the island. These, falling on the enemy from the rear,

[e] Plutarch *Luc.* 12, 1: Appian *Mith.* 76.   [f] Strabo XII p. 576; see Chap. III note 116.
[g] See above p. 326.   [h] Plutarch *Luc.* 13, 4 (3,000 talents).
[i] Plutarch *Luc.* 12, 2f.: Appian *Mith.* 76-77: Cicero *pro Arch.* 21 (see note 25): Memnon 42, 2: Sallust *Hist.* IV 69, 14 Maur.: Eutropius IV 6, 3; 8, 2: Orosius VI 2, 21f.

destroyed a large number of vessels together with their crews and forced the others to put out to sea, where they were at once attacked by Lucullus. Thirty-two fighting-ships, in addition to many transports, were captured, as were also the three commanders, one of whom succeeded in committing suicide, while another was reserved for a future triumph in Rome; Marius, who, as a former senator, could not be thus publicly exhibited, was put to death by order of the victorious general.

This success made the Romans masters of the sea. It was soon followed up by an advance against those cities of Bithynia which had surrendered to the King.[j] Prusa and Nicaea were occupied by Lucullus's subordinate, Barba; and his legate Triarius, with part of the fleet, captured Prusias and Apameia Myrleia, where Triarius slaughtered many of the citizens, even those who had sought refuge in the temples.[k] Other ships were placed under the command of Voconius with orders to guard the entrance to the Gulf of Nicomedeia and thus bottle up Mithradates.[l] Meanwhile Lucullus himself returned to Bithynia, while Cotta, now "liberated," came forth from his long imprisonment at Chalcedon to co-operate with Triarius in blockading Nicomedeia by land.[m]

Meanwhile Mithradates, dismayed by the loss of so large a part of his fleet and perhaps further disheartened by the news of Sertorius's death and the consequent break-down of the opposition to Rome in the West, had resolved on immediate flight.[21] Before Voconius, who had lingered in the northern Aegean, arrived off Nicomedeia, the King put out with the remnants of his fleet, now numbering somewhat over a hundred vessels—little more than a quarter of its original strength. His escape was successful, for there were no Roman ships to bar the way, and he sailed through the Bosporus without opposition. In the Euxine, however, he met with disaster, for a violent storm destroyed most of his ships, and he himself, it is said, was saved only by abandoning his leaking vessel for a small pirate-craft belonging to a chieftain named Seleucus. In this he made his escape to Heracleia, where he was received by the chief magistrate, but without the knowledge of the citizens. Leaving a Galatian officer with a garrison of 4,000 mercenaries to hold the city in his interest, he went on by sea to Sinope in his kingdom of Pontus.

Not since the time of Xerxes had so large an expeditionary force

[j] See above p. 326.
[l] Plutarch *Luc.* 13, 1.
[k] Appian *Mith.* 77: Memnon 41, 1.
[m] Memnon 42, 1 (see note 10).

been wrecked so completely in so brief a period. In the first war, although the campaign in Greece had cost Mithradates many thousands of lives and the Treaty of Dardanus had deprived him of most of his navy, he was still able to retire to Pontus with a large part of his army. Now, after a campaign of little more than a year, only a fraction of his huge armament remained. The lowest estimate places his loss at one hundred thousand men, and in view of the victories gained by Lucullus over isolated portions of the Pontic army and the still greater havoc wrought by starvation and storm, the number is probably not too large.[22] Mithradates had failed to take into account the fact that so great a force of men, especially when opposed by a general who knew how to prevent foraging, could not live from the country. Had he used a part of his fleet to bring supplies regularly from a base in Pontus— and had his navigators been more skilful in the event of storm—the results of the campaign might have been different. Had he been willing to isolate Cyzicus by a blockade, as he had done in the case of Chalcedon, and to advance into the province of Asia, while his fleet ravaged the Aegean coast, Lucullus, with the vastly inferior Roman army and without ships, would have found it impossible to cope with him, and once more Asia would have been at his mercy. As it was, his great force of cavalry proved only a burden and his sole naval success was that gained at Chalcedon. His great preparations had been squandered most wantonly.

After the flight of the King, in the summer of 72, the Roman leaders met in council at Nicomedeia.[n] Their decision was of the greatest importance for the future of Roman rule in Asia Minor. It was clear that the half-way measures to which Sulla had resorted at Dardanus could not be repeated with safety; the victors could not remain satisfied with the mere expulsion of the King from Roman territory, leaving him free, at some future time, to satisfy his ambition by a third invasion of western Asia Minor. The leaders decided, accordingly, to carry the war into the enemy's country and to crush him once and for all. In opposition to those who urged delay on the ground that the soldiers' strength had been exhausted by the recent campaign, Lucullus demanded an immediate advance. In response to this demand the council decided that the General with his five legions should invade Pontus, while Triarius with the fleet should remain in the Hellespont for the purpose of intercepting, on their return, the ships which had been

[n] Memnon 43, 1.

sent to Sertorius. Cotta was entrusted with the less important task of punishing Heracleia for its defection.

Lucullus set out at once, wishing to accomplish the long march before the summer came to an end.[23] In order to ensure an adequate supply of provisions for the journey, he took with him 30,000 Galatians, each of whom carried a *medimnos* of grain. But when the toilsome march had been accomplished without opposition, the invaders, on reaching the rich plain at the mouth of the Iris, found such an abundance of all things that not only could the army live on the produce of the country but those who had expected to enrich themselves by means of booty learned that the very abundance rendered their booty valueless.[o]

The region was dominated by the city of Amisus. Held by a royal garrison, it refused to surrender. The Roman general was therefore compelled to undertake a siege, while another division of his army invested Themiscyra near the eastern end of the plain.[24] Meanwhile the Roman cavalry plundered the open country, but, to the great discontent of the soldiers, all the captured strongholds or stores of treasure were by Lucullus's order saved from pillage. Thus the winter of 72-71 was passed. Themiscyra held out, though attacked by means of towers and mines, while the garrison of Amisus, besieged with less vigour and strengthened by the men and supplies which Mithradates sent in from the sea, made frequent sallies and successfully resisted the besiegers.

Save for the reinforcements thrown into Amisus, Mithradates appears to have left the invaded region to its fate. He had, indeed, few troops with which to defend it. On landing from his disastrous return-voyage, he had sent requests for assistance both to his son-in-law, Tigranes, and to his son, Machares, regent of the Crimea;[p] he even despatched an officer named Diocles, well provided with gold and other gifts, to gain the support of the Scythians—all of which measures were destined to prove fruitless.[q] He then hastened to Cabeira, the fortress which commanded the valley of the Lycus.[r] In this stronghold the King spent the winter of 72-71, with characteristic energy mobilizing a new army, which he placed under the command of Diophantus and Taxiles.[s] His efforts produced a force of 40,000 foot and 4,000 horse,[t] which, small as it was in comparison with the army he had led

[o] Plutarch *Luc.* 14, 1; Appian *Mith.* 78. For this plain see above pp. 182 and 186.
[p] Appian *Mith.* 78: Memnon 43, 2.   [q] See below p. 335.
[r] See above p. 180.   [s] See above p. 324.
[t] Plutarch *Luc.* 15, 1: Appian *Mith.* 78: Memnon 43, 3 (8,000 horse).

to Bithynia, was yet larger than that of Lucullus. With this he was prepared to defend his kingdom.

Meanwhile, however, the last remnant of the great armada with which Mithradates had expected to conquer Roman Asia was lost to him. When the ships which he had despatched to the aid of Sertorius heard of the rebel leader's death, they put about and headed for Pontus. Triarius, in accordance with the plan agreed upon at Nicomedeia, was awaiting them off the island of Tenedos at the entrance to the Hellespont, and here a desperate battle was fought.[25] The Pontic fleet was totally routed and almost all the ships were captured or sunk.

In the spring of 71 Lucullus, entrusting the siege of Amisus to his legate Murena with two legions, set out himself with the remaining three for Cabeira.[u] To those who had complained of his inaction while the King was gathering his new army, he is said to have replied that he was purposely refraining from an attack on Mithradates while defenseless, lest the King should be forced to take refuge with Tigranes and so bring the Armenians into the war.[v] As the Roman army marched southward, Eupatoria in the beautiful plain of Phanaroea, which the King had built at the confluence of the Iris and the Lycus and named for himself, opened its gates in surrender.[26] Some miles above Eupatoria, the road running high above the defile through which the Lycus flows was held by Phoenix, a member of the royal family, who had been ordered to signal the enemy's approach by lighting a beacon, the first of a series. He carried out his orders and then, together with his men, deserted to Lucullus. Thus the way was opened, and the invaders marched into the plain below Cabeira, where the King's horsemen crossed over from the left bank of the river, ready to meet them.[w] In the battle which followed, the Roman cavalry was badly defeated and its commander taken prisoner. Lucullus was apparently forced to withdraw up the slope rising from the river on the north. This defeat and the damage done to his cavalry demonstrated his inability to cope with the King on the plain, where the superior numbers of the Pontic horsemen placed the Romans at a great disadvantage. The General refused, therefore, to be drawn into further battle and retired to the mountains, where he established himself in a strong position on the heights overlooking Cabeira. Here he watched for favourable opportunities to harass the Pontic troops. A skirmishing-party, however, which met with some of the royal force was routed and driven up the

[u] See note 24.   [v] Plutarch *Luc.* 14, 4f.
[w] Plutarch *Luc.* 15, 2: Appian *Mith.* 79-80: Sallust *Hist.* IV 5 Maur.

mountain-side with serious loss; only the advance of Lucullus himself prevented the complete destruction of the panic-stricken soldiers.[27]

This success the King magnified into a great victory, spreading the news of his prowess far and wide. It was, in fact, necessary for him to redeem his prestige, for desertions had been frequent and the outside aid for which he had hoped was not forthcoming. Diocles, instead of using the treasure entrusted to him for the purpose of bringing Scythian auxiliaries, had long since gone over to Lucullus, and other officers also were ready to abandon the King's cause.[28] His request to his son Machares seems to have met with no response, and his envoy to Tigranes was able to get only a vague promise of assistance.

The King's boasting was not, it is true, wholly without foundation. Lucullus had been defeated twice, and in his purely defensive position he could do no real damage to the enemy. Worst of all, encamped, as he was, on a barren mountain-side, he was in great danger of suffering the same fate from starvation that the King had undergone at Cyzicus, the difference being that now the opposing royal force was exposed to a like danger.[29] The Romans could be fed only by supplies carried across the mountains from Cappadocia. This toilsome process, however, brought success to them and disaster to the King. First, Lucullus's legate Sornatius, who had gone with five thousand soldiers to bring in grain, was attacked by a body of Pontic horsemen. Facing about, the Romans gave battle and routed the enemy, inflicting serious losses. Later, when another legate, Hadrianus, was returning from a similar errand, he was attacked in a defile by a force of four thousand foot and two thousand horse, which Mithradates had stationed there to guard the road. On such ground, of course, the Pontic cavalry was useless, and the legate, hastily placing his men in battle-array, charged the infantry and the dismounted horsemen and gained a complete victory, killing or scattering the entire opposing force. The effect of the news of the disaster was greatly increased when Hadrianus marched past the royal camp, proudly displaying his waggons laden with grain and booty.

Then the inexplicable happened. Whether the decision was made by Mithradates himself or by some of his generals, whether it was due to the fear that Lucullus would attack at once or to despair at the loss of so large a body of troops or even to a shortage of supplies, our meagre sources do not permit us to determine; it can only be said that those in command of the Pontic army seem to have succumbed to panic. The resolve was taken to abandon the camp.[30] Presumably the retreat was to have been carried out on the following morning, but no sooner was the decision reached than a wild confusion broke out. The royal confidants, who were the first to hear of the decision, attempted to send their own possessions away before the general withdrawal, and their action attracted the attention of the troops. Supposing that they were about to be abandoned to their fate, the soldiers attacked those who were leaving and plundered their loads. The darkness increased the general excitement and terror, and in the universal panic men trampled down those who stood in what they thought was their way to safety. The King himself is said to have hastened forth from his tent in the hope of calming the frenzied mob. But he also was thrown to the ground in the commotion, and he was fleeing on foot with the rest when one of his eunuchs gave his horse to his master and led him out of danger. With a few followers and as much of his treasure as he could collect he fled away southward.

When the news of the panic was brought to Lucullus he set out at once in pursuit. Unfortunately for his purpose, however, the enemy's camp lay in his path. It was captured without a struggle, and the legionaries were ordered to kill those whom they found in it but to refrain from pillage. This order, however, was disobeyed; the soldiers in their greed began to plunder the camp, thus giving time for the men to escape. The cavalrymen sent on with all speed to seize Mithradates were equally remiss, and for the same reason. When the King was almost within reach, a mule laden with treasure fell in their way, by design, it was afterwards said, of Mithradates himself. While the men lingered over the rich booty, the inveterate enemy of Rome slipped from their grasp and escaped to the temple-city of Comana.[31] From here, after gathering around him the remnants of his cavalry, estimated at two thousand men, he went on hastily, probably southward to the neighbourhood of Sıvas on the upper Halys and thence to the Euphrates. Finally, Marcus Pompeius, ordered by Lucullus to pursue the fugitive monarch, learned that he had taken refuge in Armenia. Here Tigranes assigned him one of the royal estates as a residence, but not until a year and eight months had passed did he deign to grant his father-in-law a personal interview.[x]

With the King's flight from Pontus in the summer of 71 all opposition to the Romans, except in isolated places, collapsed at once. Cabeira surrendered and the other royal strongholds hastened to follow its

[x] See below p. 342f.

example.[y] In many of them treasures had been stored and these the Roman commander confiscated, everywhere ordering the legionaries, greatly to their discontent, to refrain from pillage. Lucullus, marching along the Euxine and through the back-country as far as the border of Armenia, met with little resistance to his arms.[32] To those commandants who surrendered he promised rewards and honours. The Greek cities of the coast, however, still held out, largely, so it would seem, because of the presence of the garrisons stationed in them by the King, but perhaps also because the citizens knew of the oppression suffered under Roman rule by their fellow-countrymen in western Asia Minor and had no desire for a like experience. Thus Amisus did not surrender to Lucullus's legate, Murena. The defence of the city had been ably carried on by Callimachus, the commander of the garrison, whose engineering skill had enabled him to employ every device for withstanding the siege. He could not, however, hold out against Lucullus and his army. The Roman general, after his demand for a surrender was refused, took by storm a suburb called Eupatoria and then by a surprise attack at night captured Amisus itself.[33] Callimachus and the garrison succeeded in making their escape by sea, but first, in order to cover their flight, they fired the city. The Romans, entering without resistance, killed all who came in their path. In vain Lucullus, wishing to save Amisus from destruction, ordered the soldiers to extinguish the flames. The men, however, in their eagerness for the booty they had long coveted, refused to obey and demanded the long-established privilege of plundering what they had captured by force. The General was compelled to give in, and the city was delivered over to pillage. All night long the soldiers sacked the houses amid the flames, and the torches which they left behind them spread the fire. Only a sudden rain prevented complete destruction.

The results of the capture of Amisus, an Hellenic *polis*, brought to Lucullus a deep feeling of grief and humiliation. On entering the ruins at daybreak, he is said to have burst into tears, lamenting that whereas he had hoped to imitate Sulla in his saving of Athens, Fate had made him a second Mummius.[z] He did his utmost, however, to make amends.[a] He gave orders to rebuild what the fire and the soldiers had destroyed and those of the citizens who had fled were restored to their homes. He also bestowed upon the city the rights of a "free

[y] Plutarch *Luc.* 18, 1: Sallust *Hist.* IV 12 Maur.: Memnon 45, 1.
[z] Lucius Mummius, whose army captured and sacked Corinth in 146 B.C.
[a] Plutarch *Luc.* 19, 4f.: Appian *Mith.* 83.

and independent" state and granted it a substantial increase in territory.

With the fall of Amisus most of eastern Pontus came under Lucullus's power. It was evident, however, that as long as Mithradates was alive the Roman occupation of the country was insecure and that no triumph would be complete without the seizure of the enemy in person. In fact, it had for some time been apparent that he could not be taken by force. Therefore, even before Amisus fell, Lucullus, deciding to resort to negotiation, had sent his wife's brother, Appius Claudius Pulcher, as an envoy to Tigranes with a demand for the surrender of Mithradates.[34] Meanwhile, as the season was now advanced, he resolved to await his envoy's return and suspend all further operations until the following summer. Accordingly, leaving the army in winter-quarters, the General withdrew to the province of Asia, of which he had been made proconsul, determined to relieve the economic distress which he had seen before setting out for the front.

The reforms carried out in Asia during the winter of 71-70 have already been described.[b] They won Lucullus the deep gratitude of the inhabitants, but they also won him the hatred of the Roman financiers who had been battening on the distress of the provincials; these men, with the co-operation of unscrupulous politicians in the Capital, were presently to take their revenge.

Appius Claudius, meanwhile, was attempting to carry out his mission to Tigranes.[c] After many wanderings east of the Euphrates, apparently on the Armenian plateau, he learned that the King was in Syria. Even here, however, Tigranes could not be found, for he was adding Phoenicia to his already swollen possessions, and the Roman envoy was forced to await his return. He employed the interval in opening negotiations with some of the chieftains who had yielded perforce to the King and had no desire to remain under his yoke, and in encouraging the representatives of the recently conquered cities to hope for deliverance at the hands of Rome.[35]

Tigranes was now the strongest potentate of the Near East, and he had all the insolence of one who had rapidly achieved great power. Having ascended the throne of Armenia in 95 B.C. at the age of about forty-five, he entered almost at once upon an ambitious career of conquest. After seizing the district of Sophene on the eastern bank of the Euphrates, he had invaded Cappadocia, and it was only the bold stand of the Romans in defence of their protégé Ariobarzanes that

[b] See above p. 252.
[c] Plutarch *Luc.* 21, 1f. For Tigranes's campaign in Phoenicia see also Josephus *Ant. Jud.* XIII 16, 4, §419f. and *Bell. Jud.* 1 5, 3, §116.

put an end to his plan of adding at least a part of the country to his dominions.[d] Then, devoting his energies to extending his realm toward the south, he wrested from the Parthians all northern Mesopotamia from the Euphrates to the mountains on the border of Media Atropatene in northwestern Persia.[e] Turning toward the west, he overcame the feeble prince who sat on the throne of the Seleucids and thereby annexed Syria and Cilicia Campestris to his kingdom.[f] Even in the distant Northeast, in the region of Trans-Caucasia, he made the rulers of the Albanians and Iberians his vassals. At the time of Mithradates's invasion of Bithynia the Armenian monarch's dominions extended from the Caspian to the Mediterranean.

For this vast realm the ancient Armenian capital, Artaxata, north of Mount Ararat, was too remote and perhaps too provincial. The now arrogant monarch, wishing to establish himself nearer the centre of his enlarged kingdom, and also, probably, to conform to the general custom of the Hellenistic rulers, founded a new city, named, after himself, Tigranocerta, providing inhabitants by transporting to it large numbers of Mesopotamians as well as settlers brought from twelve cities of Cilicia and Cappadocia.[g] Situated, apparently, in the hill-country between the Taurus and the upper Tigris, on a tributary of the latter, Tigranocerta was intended to rival the former magnificence of Nineveh and Babylon.[36] In order that the Hellenic culture which it was now customary for eastern potentates to affect might not be lacking, Tigranes and his wife Cleopatra, Mithradates's daughter, invited to their court not only Greek players but men of learning as well. If these were sometimes killed or imprisoned it was merely due to the emergence, for the time being, of the Oriental despot.

The pretentiousness of this monarch, now nearly seventy years of age, and his passion for display were in keeping with the suddenness with which he had risen to power. He assumed the titles of "God" and "King of Kings," and when he appeared in public, arrayed in purple and wearing on his head a tiara encircled with the royal diadem, he was attended by the "kings" he had conquered, now serving as menials.[37] Nevertheless, when Appius Claudius stated his errand with true Roman bluntness, informing the monarch that should the request for the surrender of Mithradates be refused, Rome would declare war, Tigranes showed no anger and even treated the envoy with courtesy.[h] But when

[d] See above p. 205f.
[f] See Chap. XII note 35.
[h] Plutarch *Luc.* 21, 6f.: Memnon 46, 2f.

[e] Plutarch *Luc.* 26, 4: Eutropius VI 8, 4: Strabo XI p. 532.
[g] See Chap. XII note 36 and above p. 321.

Claudius returned to his general, probably in the early summer of 70, it was with the answer that Tigranes would not give up the King of Pontus and that if the Romans made war on him he would take measures for defence.[38] This response certain ancient authors attributed to Lucullus's failure to address him as "King of Kings," adding that in retaliation Tigranes was careful not to use the title of Imperator in his reply. These writers failed, however, to understand that the surrender of Mithradates would have been tantamount to a confession of vassalage intolerable to the arrogant Armenian and wholly inconsistent with his pretensions.

The reply of Tigranes made it evident to Lucullus that the war must be resumed. But before embarking on a further campaign, it was necessary to complete the subjugation of Pontus. Heracleia, to be sure, had recently fallen after a long siege.[i] In the summer of 72, it will be recalled, the task of reducing the city had been assigned to Marcus Cotta.[j] On his march thither the city of Prusias-on-the-Hypius surrendered, but when he appeared before the walls of Heracleia, the citizens, remembering the breach of their treaty with Rome and encouraged by the presence of Mithradates's garrison, refused him admittance. An attempt to take the city by storm was a total failure, for Cotta's engines of war had no effect on its massive walls. It was therefore necessary to resort to a blockade. Throughout the following winter the city's ships brought provisions from southern Russia, but the supplies were insufficient for the needs of both the citizens and the soldiers of the royal garrison, with the result that the latter resorted to violence to obtain what they considered their share.

During the summer of 71 conditions grew worse. Triarius, having destroyed the Pontic ships which had returned from their voyage toward Spain,[k] was now master of the sea. When he appeared in the Euxine with forty-three warships the fleet of Heracleia was unable to cope with him. A naval battle cost the citizens more than half of their ships so that it was now possible for Triarius to enforce the blockade. The second winter of the siege (71-70 B.C.) was therefore spent in great misery. Pestilence accompanied famine and carried off a third of the garrison. Finally, in the spring of 70, the royal commandant, together with the chief magistrate, entered into secret negotiations with Triarius, by which it was agreed that Heracleia should be surrendered but the garrison permitted to sail away to safety. The soldiers, accord-

---

[i] For the siege of Heracleia see Memnon 47-52. [j] See above p. 333.
[k] See above p. 334.

ingly, embarking on the remnant of the city's fleet, departed to the coast cities of Tieium and Amastris and the magistrate opened the gates of Heracleia to Triarius.

In spite of the fact that Heracleia had capitulated, a general massacre followed. Cotta, learning that the city had been entered by his colleague, hastened thither with his troops, eager for a share in the plunder, and a battle between the two Roman forces was averted only by Triarius's promise to divide the booty with him. Then Triarius with part of the fleet sailed away to Tieium and Amastris, while Cotta, after pillaging Heracleia and loading certain ships with captives and spoils, set fire to the city, thus completing a career of inefficiency with an act of the utmost brutality. As though in retribution, a part of his squadron was sunk by a storm on the way to Italy. He himself, after his return to Rome, was brought to trial for his treatment of Heracleia and, having been convicted, was deprived of his senatorial rank.[39] His province of Bithynia was added to Lucullus's command.

With Triarius's capture of Tieium and Amastris[1] the conquest of the coast of western Paphlagonia was complete. There remained, however, Sinope far to the north and Amaseia in the interior. Lucullus, therefore, set out from Ephesus in the summer of 70 with the determination of taking both cities.

Thus far, Sinope had been able to hold out against a Roman blockade.[40] The narrow isthmus which connected the city with the mainland was well protected by formidable walls, and attacks from the sea were impossible because of the steep rocks with which the peninsula was girt. Food was supplied by importing grain from the Crimea, the safe delivery of which was assured by the city's fleet. This fleet, in fact, was strong enough to defeat a Roman squadron of fifteen vessels which was convoying grain-ships to the besiegers. The land-force consisted of the royal garrison of about 10,000 "Cilician" mercenaries, some of them perhaps former pirates, including the chieftain, Seleucus, who once had rescued Mithradates from death by storm in the Euxine.

On Lucullus's arrival the commandant Leonippus entered into secret negotiations with him. This act of treachery, however, was detected and Leonippus himself was assassinated by a eunuch named Cleochares, who had been associated with him in the command. The defence was now pushed vigorously, but the rigour of Cleochares's rule caused the townsfolk to regard him as almost a second enemy. Then starvation

---

[1] Memnon 52, 3: Appian *Mith.* 82 (where the capture of Amastris, as well as of Heracleia, is incorrectly attributed to Lucullus).

threatened. Machares, the ruler of the Crimea, who had been selling the citizens the grain on which they depended, made overtures to Lucullus, accompanying his request for Roman friendship by a wreath of gold valued at a thousand talents.[41] The request was quickly granted, and Mithradates's son was included among the friends and allies of Rome, but on condition that he should send to Lucullus the grain which he had formerly furnished to Sinope. Then the story of Amisus and Heracleia was repeated. Cleochares, despairing of further resistance, decided to abandon his post. Before setting sail, however, he sacked the city and after killing many of its inhabitants set it on fire. Part of the garrison escaped with the commander, but Lucullus, seeing the flames, hastened at once to the attack. Entering the city without resistance, the Romans killed a large number of the mercenaries and perhaps some of the citizens as well.[m] Lucullus succeeded, however, in preventing a general massacre and gave orders to extinguish the fires. As at Amisus, he showed the citizens that his war was directed against Mithradates and not against them, for he restored their private property and granted Sinope the status of a free and independent city.[42]

After the capture of Sinope, Amaseia, the ancient capital of the Pontic kings, surrendered after a brief resistance.[43] Thus before the end of the year 70 the entire kingdom was in the hands of the Romans, and Lucullus was able to report his conquest to the Senate and ask for the appointment of the usual ten commissioners, who, in co-operation with the General himself, would arrange for the organization of the new province.[n]

Tigranes had meanwhile remained strictly on the defensive. He has been blamed for stupidity in not realizing that his reply to Lucullus was equivalent to a declaration of war.[o] But, in fact, the real threat came from the Roman general and there was no good reason why the King should make the first move. With what seems much more like caution than stupidity he spent the interval in strengthening his hold over his newly-acquired dominions in northern Mesopotamia. Learning of negotiations between Appius Claudius and the prince of Gordyene in the northeastern part of this district,[p] he forestalled any move on the part of the latter by putting him to death, together with his wife and children.

It was therefore not until the early spring of 69 that Mithradates,

[m] 8,000 in all, according to Plutarch *Luc.* 23, 3.
[n] For the arrival of the commission in 67 see below p. 349.
[o] So Reinach *Mith. Eup.* p. 354.   [p] See note 35.

after waiting in quasi-exile for twenty months, was finally summoned to his son-in-law's presence.[44] He was received with all honours and even a show of affection, and the two monarchs in the course of a three days' interview renewed their previous cordial relations. Tigranes promised his father-in-law a force of 10,000 men with which to recover Pontus, and it was reported to Lucullus that both kings were preparing to enter Lycaonia with a view to an invasion of Asia.

Lucullus now decided to take the offensive. He appears to have spent the winter of 70-69 in Pontus,[q] and in the early spring he set out on his advance into the land of the enemy. It was a bold move, for no Roman general save Sulla, in his famous interview with the Parthian envoy in 92,[r] had ever seen the Euphrates, and all that lay beyond the river was an unknown country. The General doubtless justified his invasion to himself and his staff on the ground that their conquests would never be assured as long as the arch-enemy was alive, and now that this enemy was about to resume operations for the recovery of his kingdom—perhaps even to attack the Roman provinces—it was necessary to be the first to strike. It was harder to justify it to the troops, who had heard rumours of long marches, deep rivers and mountains covered with perpetual snow. Always prone to complaint and even disobedience and after years of hard fighting eager for their discharge, they resented the order for a further advance.[s] It was hardest of all, however, to justify it to the voters at Rome; for the enemies whom Lucullus had made by his deliverance of the province of Asia from the clutches of the financial interests were ready to adopt any means to discredit him. Politicians, quick to make use of this hostility, began, with all the dishonesty of their kind, to charge him with needlessly prolonging the war in order to gratify his ambition and add to his wealth; the persistent repetition of these charges, combined with the machinations of those who envied him, was destined in time to bring about his recall and consequent humiliation.[t]

Before his departure for Armenia, Lucullus made adequate preparation, as he thought, for safeguarding the Roman provinces. His legates Sornatius and Hadrianus, whose courage and enterprise had been conspicuous in the encounters leading to Mithradates's panic and flight, were left with an army of 6,000 men to defend Pontus; Triarius, who was probably still in command of the fleet, was deputed to protect Rome's sovereignty in Asia and Bithynia.[u]

q See note 34.
r See above p. 206.
s Plutarch *Luc.* 24, 2f.
t See below pp. 345f. and 348.
u Plutarch *Luc.* 24, 1; 35, 1: Appian *Mith.* 88: Cassius Dio XXXVI 9, 2; 10, 1.

The story of the expedition which led Lucullus far beyond the confines of Asia Minor may be related briefly.[45] Taking with him an army of about twenty thousand men, including three thousand cavalry, he made a swift march through Cappadocia and crossed the Euphrates at Tomisa. This stronghold, which a former Cappadocian monarch had sold to the ruler of Sophene, was now presented to Ariobarzanes, and the control of this strategic point was thus assured. From the river Lucullus, advancing rapidly and without resistance through Sophene, crossed the Taurus and descended past the head-waters of the Tigris into Mesopotamia.

Two years were to pass before Lucullus returned to the provinces committed to his charge. In his first campaign, after dispersing the forces sent by Tigranes to oppose his advance, he defeated the King himself in a great battle near Tigranocerta, driving the Armenians from the field in total rout. Soon afterward, aided by "Greeks" who had been forcibly transported to Tigranocerta, he captured the city, which he then pillaged and destroyed. This double success won him great prestige, and envoys from princes near and far came to him with gifts and offers of submission. Among them was Antiochus I, ruler of the district of Commagene, which lay west of the Euphrates, extending from the chain of the Taurus to the border of Syria.[46] The victory also had its effect elsewhere, for Magadates, whom Tigranes had made governor of Cilicia and Syria, withdrew to join his master.[v] Thus Cilicia Campestris was freed from the Armenian yoke and soon fell beneath the sway of Rome. In Syria, the Seleucid prince Antiochus XIII was recognized by Lucullus as king and restored for a brief time to the throne of his ancestors.[w]

After spending the winter of 69-68 in Gordyene, Lucullus set forth on a second campaign, bolder and more ambitious than any he had as yet attempted.[47] This was nothing less than an advance into the heart of the Armenian plateau, where Tigranes had taken refuge.[48] Here the defeated monarch had been joined by Mithradates, and during the winter the two kings had mustered a new army of carefully picked men, organized in the Roman fashion. Mithradates had also learned how to use Roman tactics, and when, in the early summer, Lucullus appeared with his army, the two monarchs employed against him the methods he had practised so successfully in Bithynia. Entrenching themselves in a fortified camp, they refused to meet their opponent in the field, while at every opportunity their cavalry attacked

---

[v] See above p. 296. [w] Justin XL 2, 2: Appian *Syr.* 49. See below p. 360.

the Roman foragers. It was only by the device of beginning a march onward under the pretext that he intended to advance across Armenia to Artaxata that Lucullus succeeded in drawing out Tigranes to battle. Here again the superiority of the Roman legions made itself evident, and once more the Armenian King and his army fled in panic. The victory, however, was followed by Lucullus's first defeat—administered by the soldiers of his own army. For after an advance of only a few days on his northward march, his men, alarmed by the approach of winter and demoralized by the rumours they had heard of the rigours of the country and its climate, broke out into mutiny.[49] Despite their leader's appeals and entreaties, the soldiers refused to follow him farther, and he was forced to turn back and withdraw to Mesopotamia.

Although cheated of his hope of adding Armenia to his conquests, Lucullus, nevertheless, was resolved to wrest from Tigranes the last of his possessions south of the Taurus. Advancing southward beyond the Tigris, he laid siege to Nisibis,[x] a strongly fortified city under the joint command of Tigranes's brother and Mithradates's general, Callimachus, who had defended and then fired Amisus.[y] After a siege of many weeks the Roman army forced its way over the ramparts and captured the place, together with a great amount of booty. Then at last the weary soldiers were permitted to go into quarters for what remained of the winter.[50]

Lucullus's downfall, however, had already begun. His enemies in Rome, ready to take advantage of any opportunity for an attack, used even his victory at Tigranocerta as material for their charges.[51] Wholly ignoring the facts, they accused Lucullus of allowing Tigranes to escape in order to enrich himself and retain his command. Even in the Senate there were many envious of the general who was governor of the three provinces of Asia, Cilicia and Bithynia—all of them lucrative posts which the greedy coveted for themselves. Other senators combined with Lucullus's enemies among the business-men, either because their own interests had been affected by his reforms in Asia or because they were themselves in debt to the money-lenders and hence were under pressure to give these men their support. Popular demagogues also, currying favour with the voters, began to attack the aristocratic general. Among these was a praetor, Lucius Quinctius, who, when tribune of the Plebs during Lucullus's consulship in 74, had attempted

x Plutarch *Luc.* 32, 3f.: Cassius Dio xxxvi 6f.: Orosius vi 3, 7: Eutropius vi 9, 1: Festus *Brev.* 15, 3.
y See above p. 337.

to make himself conspicuous by harangues against the senatorial oligarchy then dominant but had been tactfully quieted by the Consul; this man now attacked Lucullus again, accusing him of greed and ambition. As a result of this agitation, the Senate early in 68 voted that the province of Asia should be taken from Lucullus and placed once more under a governor annually appointed by the Fathers. Later in the year it was further decreed that Cilicia also should be withdrawn from him and assigned to the Consul Quintus Marcius Rex, who was Lucullus's own brother-in-law.[z] Thus Lucullus's command was reduced to Bithynia and the recently conquered Pontus.

The report of these measures, when it reached Mesopotamia, naturally lessened the authority of Lucullus over his already disaffected army. His influence is said to have been further weakened by the conduct of his young brother-in-law, Publius Clodius Pulcher, who went about the winter-quarters at Nisibis sympathizing with the soldiers, especially the former legions of Flaccus, in the hardships they had endured, thereby inciting them to mutiny.[52] As though in answer to their complaints, the news arrived in the spring of 67 that the opponents of Lucullus in Rome had succeeded in enacting a law granting these legions their long-desired discharge. About the same time, however, the further news was brought that war had broken out in Pontus and that Lucullus's legates who had been stationed there were in urgent need of assistance.[a] Confronted by this situation, the soldiers agreed to forego temporarily their discharge in order to rescue their comrades; and their leader, sacrificing his hopes of victories beyond the Euphrates, withdrew from the territory he had conquered and began the long return-march northward.

The Roman hold on Pontus had indeed been seriously weakened. After his defeat in Armenia, Tigranes, doubtless eager to create a diversion outside his kingdom, aided Mithradates to return to his own land.[b] In the autumn of 68, therefore, with a force of only 8,000 men, half of whom had been furnished by Tigranes, the old monarch arrived in the kingdom from which he had fled precipitately three years before. He was gladly received by his subjects, who had begun to resent the demands made by the Roman army, and he had no difficulty in increasing his little force. His sudden arrival caught his

[z] See Chap. XII note 39.

[a] Plutarch *Luc.* 35, 1: Appian *Mith.* 88 (where Lucullus's withdrawal from Mesopotamia is attributed to a lack of provisions).

[b] Plutarch *Luc.* 34, 5; 35, 1: Appian *Mith.* 88: Cassius Dio xxxvi 8, 2—11, 1: Cicero *de Imp. Cn. Pomp.* 24; *pro Mur.* 33: Sallust *Hist.* v 1-3 Maur.: Eutropius vi 9, 2.

opponents off their guard. Isolated detachments of Romans were surprised and cut to pieces, and even some strongholds were forced to surrender. When Hadrianus, whom Lucullus had left in command, marched out against him, Mithradates issued a proclamation promising freedom to all slaves present in the Roman camp. Consequently, when Hadrianus, deceived by a false report brought in by a scouting-party, was suddenly attacked by the King, many of the slaves aided the enemy. The Romans were driven from the field with considerable loss. Hadrianus attempted to remedy the situation by freeing the remaining slaves, but in a second engagement the Romans were again defeated. Only the wounding of Mithradates himself and his withdrawal from the battle saved them from complete destruction. Hadrianus and his men then took refuge in Cabeira, where they were besieged by the Pontic forces. From this predicament they were rescued by the arrival of Triarius, who, on hearing of his colleague's plight, gathered the remaining Roman soldiers in Pontus and hastened to the relief of the beleaguered troops. Mithradates, not daring to face this new army, withdrew to Comana, whither he was followed by Triarius, now in command of the combined Roman forces. Wishing to attack him while on the march, the King, advancing with part of his army across the river Iris, which flows near the city, ordered the remainder to cross by a bridge. In the crowding, however, the bridge collapsed, and a terrific storm added to the general confusion.[53] Mithradates was forced to withdraw, while Triarius marched down the Iris to the fortress of Gaziura,[c] where, after sending a messenger to inform Lucullus of the situation, he ensconced himself for the oncoming winter. Meanwhile Mithradates took a position in the mountainous country south of the river, probably not far from Zela.[d]

In the spring of 67 the King, drawing up his forces near Gaziura, attempted to provoke Triarius to a battle, eager to defeat him before Lucullus's arrival.[54] The Roman leader, however, knowing that he need only wait until his general appeared, refused to leave his position. But when Mithradates, in an effort to draw him out, sent a body of men to lay siege to a stronghold in which the booty of the Romans was stored, Triarius was compelled by his soldiers to march to the rescue. Caught by a surprise-attack at daybreak near Mt. Scotium, some three miles from Zela, he and his men were overcome by the superior numbers of the enemy. The Romans, forced back into a swamp, were com-

[c] See above p. 180.
[d] So Munro in *J.H.S.* xxi (1901), p. 58, followed by Guse in *Klio* xx (1926), p. 336f.

pletely at their opponents' mercy and a terrible slaughter ensued. Only a remnant was saved, again because of the wounding of the King. Triarius himself, with some of his cavalry, escaped from the carnage, but seven thousand Romans, it is said, were left dead on the field. When Mithradates, later in the same day, led his troops to the Roman camp, he found that the men who had been left to hold it had fled in terror.

The indomitable monarch was once more in possession of his kingdom. When, shortly after the battle, Lucullus and his army arrived in Pontus, he could do nothing but take the wretched Triarius under his protection and thus save him from the angry soldiers.[55] Mithradates, not willing to risk a battle with an army superior in number, established himself in an entrenched position, refusing to fight. He had heard that Tigranes was on the way to support him, and in fact, although the King's coming was delayed, an advance-guard under the command of his son-in-law inflicted a defeat on some Roman foragers.

In the meantime, however, Lucullus had been deposed from his command. In the opening weeks of 67, the tribune of the Plebs, Aulus Gabinius Capito, had carried a bill which completed the revenge of the General's enemies.[56] This measure deprived Lucullus of Bithynia and Pontus, the last of his provinces, and bestowed them on Manius Acilius Glabrio, one of the Consuls of the year. The bill also provided for the discharge of the legions of Flaccus, whose term of service had already expired.

Glabrio, whose command appears to have begun with the passage of the law, hastened to his province before his consulship expired. In the summer of 67 Lucullus, while still vainly attempting to draw out Mithradates to battle, was officially informed by the new governor that his term of office had come to an end and that Glabrio himself was now in command.[57] Another proclamation informed the legions of Flaccus that they were discharged, and ordered them, under penalty of confiscation of the booty they had gained, to depart from the camp. However lacking this order may have been in courtesy to Lucullus, there was no doubt of its validity. The troops now refused to obey the commander whom they regarded as an ordinary citizen; the discharged legions, especially, felt free to leave the service. Nevertheless, when word was brought that Tigranes had entered Cappadocia, Lucullus, although his command automatically expired with his successor's arrival and he himself was bound by law to leave the province within thirty days,[e] made a last attempt to save the situation. After vainly requesting help from his brother-in-law, Quintus Marcius Rex, who with three legions was proceeding through Lycaonia on the way to his new province of Cilicia,[f] he endeavoured to persuade his own troops to follow him against Tigranes. They marched as far as the boundary of Cappadocia but there they halted, refusing to proceed farther. Their leader's appeals and personal entreaties had no effect; he was able only to exact from them a promise to remain in camp during the summer, in order to repel any actual invasion on the part of the enemy.

It seemed the irony of Fate that during this crisis the ten commissioners, whom the Senate, on receiving the report of Lucullus's victories, had appointed to organize the new province of Pontus, should arrive on the scene.[58] Among them were the General's brother, Marcus, and Murena, probably his former legate. They were all well disposed to Lucullus and ready to endorse his actions. But there was no province for them to organize. Mithradates, taking advantage of Lucullus's enforced inactivity, proceeded to re-establish his power and make himself master of his own kingdom.[59] Gaining control of his strongholds, he punished those places which had opened their gates to the Romans. At the same time Tigranes crossed the Euphrates and ravaged Cappadocia, driving out once more the unhappy Ariobarzanes. Lucullus, meanwhile, was forced to sit by idly until autumn, when the soldiers' agreement came to an end and the legions of Flaccus were disbanded and the other troops handed over to Glabrio. The latter, although he had been eager to rob Lucullus of the fruits of his victories, was content, now that Mithradates was again in arms, to remain quietly in Bithynia on the plea that he was not sufficiently equipped for a war.

In the wreck of his hopes and the collapse of his conquests, Lucullus lingered on in Asia through the winter of 67-66, conferring with the senatorial commissioners on the various measures which needed their ratification.[g] The results of their conference, however, were destined never to be put into effect.[h]

Lucullus had fulfilled the mission entrusted to his charge. He had successfully defended Asia and Bithynia against the enemy. He had been a conscientious administrator and had saved the provincials from

[e] Cicero *Epist. ad Fam.* III 6, 3; see Mommsen *R.St.R.* II³ pp. 205f. and 254.

[f] See above p. 297.

[g] Plutarch *Luc.* 36, 1; *Pomp.* 31, 1; 38, 1: Cassius Dio XXXVI 46, 1.

[h] See below p. 353.

bankruptcy. His conduct of the war had invariably shown ability and courage: his consistent employment, when necessary, of the policy of wearing out the enemy by skirmish and hunger; the strategic skill which enabled him to win pitched battles against superior forces; the boldness with which he assaulted strongly fortified cities; and the dauntless spirit with which he had unhesitatingly entered regions never before visited by a Roman army. But with all his virtues he had one outstanding fault which frequently appears as their concomitant, namely the haughty dignity of the ancient Roman which made it impossible for him to win the devotion of his soldiers and inspire them to follow him to the end.[1] He failed in his ambition to crush his formidable opponent and left Mithradates in full control of his kingdom and able to offer successful resistance to a Roman army.

This sense of failure Lucullus carried back with him to Rome. It is true that, despite the attempts of his enemies to prevent it, the Senate ultimately granted him a triumph for his successes over Mithradates and Tigranes.[60] The spectacle was an impressive one. Sixty of the Kings' generals and friends, many mail-clad horsemen and ten scythe-bearing chariots, the bronze beaks of one hundred and ten warships, couches of gold and litters of silver bearing vessels and ingots of precious metals, famous works of art, and, to crown all, a life-sized golden statue of Mithradates himself were displayed to the eyes of the populace. But after it was over, Lucullus withdrew into private life, giving little attention to politics and devoting himself to literature and art and to the luxurious mode of living which, more than his achievements as a general, has made his name famous. Yet without his achievements his illustrious successor could not have won the victory which overthrew the great enemy of Rome.

[1] Plutarch *Luc.* 33, 2; 36, 5: Cassius Dio xxxvi 16.

CHAPTER XV

POMPEY THE ORGANIZER

THE collapse of Lucullus's offensive against Mithradates and the inefficiency of his successors, Marcius Rex and Acilius Glabrio,[a] caused great dissatisfaction and even alarm at Rome. It was inevitable that the inactivity of the two generals now commanding in Asia and the triumphant position of Mithradates should be contrasted with the spectacular success which had been won in Cilicia by the energy of Pompey and with his suppression of the pirates whom no previous Roman commander had been able completely to subdue. Public opinion in the Capital, therefore, called for action providing for a new move against the enemy, and a legislative proposal for a resumption of hostilities was soon forthcoming. At the beginning of 66 B.C. Gaius Manilius, tribune of the Plebs, brought forward a bill designed to remedy the existing situation.

This new measure was modelled on the law of Gabinius enacted in the preceding year, but it was wider in its provisions.[1] Once more Pompey was named supreme commander, this time for the prosecution of a war against the two royal enemies of Rome, Mithradates and Tigranes. He was vested with unlimited powers over all Asia Minor and the surrounding seas, and the governors of the Asianic provinces were ordered to resign in his favour both their posts and their armies. He was also authorized to appoint legates in addition to those who had served against the pirates.

The proposal was bitterly attacked by the leaders of the conservative element in the Senate. Although wise enough to refrain from opposing Pompey personally, these men contended that the bestowal of such vast powers was contrary to all precedent and should not be granted to any one man.[b] Their opposition, however, was fruitless. It was easy to secure the votes of the populace, ready to listen to those who inveighed against the ruling oligarchy and under the spell of Pompey's fame and achievements. It was equally easy to gain the support of the financial interests, desirous of establishing peace in Asia and assuring the safety of their investments. The bill was also advocated by many of the senators.[2] These included Servilius Isauricus, Marcus Cicero and perhaps Julius Caesar: Cicero, because he genuinely admired Pompey and wished to become more closely associated with him;

---

[a] See above pp. 297 and 349.   [b] Cicero *de Imp. Cn. Pomp.* 52f.

Caesar, it was said, because he hoped by supporting the measure to gain the favour of the populace and to establish a precedent for the bestowal of similar powers on himself at some time in the future.

The voters who listened to Cicero's eloquent arguments for the proposed law were assured that the alliance of the Kings was a formidable one, fraught with great danger to Roman Asia.[c] They were reminded of the cruelties perpetrated by Mithradates twenty-two years earlier both on Greek cities and on Roman commanders, as well as of his more recent depredations in Bithynia. The business-men, in particular, were urged to take the only possible course to save from total ruin both their own investments and those of their fellow-countrymen in the eastern provinces. Cicero's hearers were not told, however, that the present situation in Asia Minor was due to the folly of themselves and their government in displacing an able commander and sending incapable men to posts in the East, and that Lucullus's final failure was largely due to the recklessness of his legates and the insubordination of his soldiers.[d] Nor were they informed that Mithradates, although he had succeeded in establishing himself in his ancestral kingdom, was now nearly sixty-five years old and in the present state of his resources[e] could scarcely hope to carry out another invasion before old age came upon him. It was likewise left unmentioned that Tigranes's invasion of Cappadocia had been but a brief occupation, for the reason that during his absence his son, also called Tigranes, had attempted a revolt and the King had returned to Armenia to drive out the rebellious young man.[f]

The news of the unanimous passage of the bill was brought to Pompey with all possible speed. He was in Cilicia, occupied in settling the recently-conquered pirates in the towns of the coast. Although the measure had been passed with his full knowledge and even at his suggestion, he affected, with characteristic dissimulation, to feel oppressed by the new burden thrust upon him.[3] Nevertheless, he assumed that burden with great alacrity.

Before making any hostile move, the new commander seems to have sent an envoy to Mithradates in order to ascertain whether his intentions were those of a friend or a foe.[4] Finding that the King scorned his overtures, he at once began the war. At the head of the three legions which Marcius Rex had brought to Cilicia, he crossed the Taurus—probably by way of the Cilician Gates—as early in the spring of 66 as

[c] Cicero *ibid*. 4f.
[e] Appian *Mith*. 97.
[d] These facts are glozed over by Cicero *ibid*. 23-25.
[f] Appian *Mith*. 104: Cassius Dio xxxvi 51, 1.

the snow permitted. He also summoned to his standard the troops which Lucullus had perforce placed at Glabrio's disposal as well as the contingents furnished by Rome's allies.[g] Such was the magic of his fame that even the two discharged legions of Flaccus re-enlisted in his service. His army consisted of about 50,000 legionaries and, in addition, the Asianic contingents.[5] Mithradates, on the other hand, had not more than 30,000 foot and 3,000 horsemen.[h]

Leaving the three Cilician legions in Cappadocia to repel any possible invasion from Armenia,[i] Pompey marched northward into Galatia. Immediately after assuming the command, he had issued a proclamation annulling all the arrangements made by Lucullus and the ten commissioners sent out from Rome.[6] This procedure naturally aroused great ill-feeling on the part of Lucullus. He was still in eastern Galatia, and it was hoped by the friends of both generals that a personal meeting might effect a reconciliation. Their interview, however, although begun with politeness, ended in recrimination and even abuse, and the rivals parted on worse terms than before. It seemed to Lucullus and his partisans a real injury that Pompey did not permit him to take more than 1,600 soldiers to Rome to march in his triumph.

Mithradates, aware that his force was inferior to Pompey's in both numbers and training, was counting on help from outside. It soon became apparent, however, that he could expect nothing from Tigranes. That selfish and unreliable monarch, either because he was alarmed by Pompey's reputation and the size of his army, or because he feared further trouble from his son, who had taken refuge with his father-in-law, the King of the Parthians, refused to become embroiled in this new war. Mithradates then set his hopes on the Parthian monarch, Phraates III.[j] Here, however, he was forestalled by Pompey, who sent a message of friendship to this ruler, encouraging him to invade Gordyene, which, since Lucullus's departure, Tigranes had regarded as once more part of his dominions.

The result of this diplomacy was twofold. Not only was Tigranes definitely prevented from any hostile move against Asia Minor, but Mithradates could no longer hope for aid from either of his fellow-monarchs in the East. The King therefore sought to find out what terms could be obtained from Pompey by negotiation.[k] But when his

[g] Plutarch *Pomp.* 31, 1; *Luc.* 35, 7: Cassius Dio xxxvi 16, 3; 46, 1.

[h] Appian *Mith.* 97: Plutarch *Pomp.* 32, 1 (2,000 horse).

[i] See Reinach *Mith. Eup.* p. 382. For their later presence in Pontus see below p. 354.

[j] Cassius Dio xxxvi 45, 3: Livy *Per.* c: Justin xlii 4, 6. See also Chap. XIV note 47.

[k] Cassius Dio xxxvi 45, 3f.: Appian *Mith.* 98.

envoys returned with the reply that he must surrender unconditionally, such an uproar arose in his camp that he was compelled to promise his troops that he would never make peace with Rome.

Now that war was inevitable, Mithradates decided that his only hope of success lay in wearing down the enemy by hunger and stealthy attacks.[7] Accordingly, he fell back into the mountainous district of eastern Pontus, devastating the land as he went. While our sources, abounding in omissions and even mutually contradictory, do not permit of an adequate reconstruction of the campaign, it would appear that the King entrenched himself in the mountains, perhaps near Zara, not far from the headwaters of the Halys. Here he hoped to maintain a resistance and to weaken the enemy by cutting off his supplies and by sudden cavalry-onslaughts. Pompey, not daring to attack the King's camp, took up a position in wooded country not far off, where he was protected from the Pontic horsemen and archers. Wishing to draw out the enemy, he placed his light-armed troops and some of his cavalry in hiding and sent out the remainder of his horse toward Mithradates's encampment. When the King's cavalry, however, came forth against the Romans, the latter fell back slowly, drawing their pursuers into the ambush. Thus attacked on both sides, the Pontic force suffered serious loss, but when Mithradates advanced with his infantry, the Romans were compelled to retire.

The loss of a large part of his cavalry made it more difficult for Mithradates to pursue his plan of starving out his opponents. Pompey, moreover, gained control of the road which led eastward toward the Euphrates. By subduing the region of Anaïtis on the upper course of the river, he succeeded in obtaining adequate supplies. At the same time, Mithradates, unaware that the mountain on which he was encamped contained underground springs, was suffering from lack of water. For this reason and discouraged by his failure to starve out his opponents, the King decided to withdraw from his position. Falling back northward across the mountains toward the basin of the upper Lycus, he again established himself in camp on a hill near Dasteira, southwest of the plain of Endires, through which flows a tributary of the greater river. Pompey followed and again took up a position facing the enemy. His army was now increased by the addition of the three Cilician legions, which, after all fear of an invasion of Cappadocia had vanished, had received orders to join him in Pontus. But still unwilling to attack a fortified camp, he proceeded to surround it with a ring of redoubts, said to have had a length of 150 stades (approximately eighteen miles), an operation which the enemy was unable to prevent. The Roman army was well supplied with food, but Mithradates, completely hemmed in by his opponents, was unable to forage. He held out for forty-five days, finally feeding his men on the carcasses of slaughtered pack-animals. Then, on the point of starvation, he resolved on flight.

The flight was, indeed, a desperate move and the prelude to complete disaster.[8] Mithradates, after killing the sick and disabled, led out his army under cover of night, leaving his camp-fires burning. Having thus succeeded in escaping observation, he hastened eastward on the road toward the Euphrates. Pompey, on discovering the trick, hastened after the King. An attack on the Pontic rear-guard was repulsed, but Mithradates refused to be drawn into battle and on the following day took up a strong position, where he encamped. Pompey, following him closely, also encamped, and early next morning (perhaps at daybreak) he engaged the enemy's light-armed troops and cavalry in a gorge outside the Pontic entrenchments. The assault caused a panic among the enemy, and in the narrow defile a terrific confusion prevailed, in which men, horses and camels trampled one another to death. The nature of the ground prevented escape, and the Pontic army was cruelly slaughtered. At least ten thousand men are said to have been slain. Mithradates himself, with a few companions and a concubine dressed as a man, fled from the general massacre.

In his retreat the King was joined by some horsemen and a body of 3,000 foot, and with these he took refuge in the fortress of Sinoria, where he had accumulated a vast hoard of treasure.[9] Here he paused long enough to give rewards and a year's pay to the soldiers who accompanied him; then, taking with him about six thousand talents for his own use, he set off again on his journey.

In the course of his flight Mithradates sent messengers to Tigranes, announcing his defeat and presenting a request for refuge. But on arriving on the Armenian plateau near the sources of the Euphrates (not far from the modern Erzurum), he found a welcome very different from the one for which he had hoped.[1] He was met with the news that his son-in-law not only forbad him to enter the kingdom of Armenia but had thrown his messengers into chains and even put a price of one hundred talents on his head. This hostile attitude on the part of Tigranes may have been due to the suspicion that Mithradates had encouraged his son to invade his kingdom, but, as will appear, he had

[1] Plutarch *Pomp.* 32, 9: Appian *Mith.* 101: Cassius Dio XXXVI 50, 1.

suffered serious loss in that invasion, and, thoroughly impressed by Pompey's great victory, he was in no mood to provoke an attack by the Roman army.

The rebuff left Mithradates without a refuge in Asia. His only recourse was to seek shelter in his dominions in southern Russia, now under the rule of his traitorous son, Machares. Accordingly, after spending three days in equipping the soldiers he had with him, he set out on his long march.[m] While making his way through the mountain-district north of Armenia, he was attacked by the natives, and it was only with great difficulty that he finally succeeded in reaching the plain of Colchis at the eastern end of the Euxine.[10] Passing northward through the plain, he went on to the former Milesian colony of Dioscurias, the last outpost of Greek civilization. Here, during the winter of 66-65, he and his escort found a resting-place.

The fugitive's goal, however, was over 300 miles away and could be reached only by land, since the sea was controlled by the Roman fleet. It was a bold adventure, for the route was both difficult and dangerous.[11] It led around the eastern end of the Euxine, where the Caucasus forms a great barrier, descending abruptly to the shore and in some places leaving only a narrow passage. The region was held by savage tribes, whom Mithradates in his palmy days had once vainly tried to subdue. But the indomitable old man, setting forth in the spring of 65, overcame all obstacles. By conciliating one hostile tribe, avoiding another by coasting along its territory in native boats, and forcing his way through where he found opposition, he finally completed the circuit and arrived at the Strait of Kertch. Here, before he could be assured of safety, he had to deal with an unfaithful son.

In the short space of a few summer-months Mithradates had been completely vanquished and driven out of Asia forever. The monarch who had appeared in the Roman province as a deliverer from the oppression of the Romans and, after showing himself an oppressor more cruel than they, had been defeated and sent back to his own land; who later, in an attempt to prevent the further extension of Rome's dominions, had a second time invaded the Aegean littoral, only to be driven from it in a humiliating rout; who, when his own kingdom was invaded, had fled from it in panic but had returned again and defeated his opponent, had now fled for the last time.

m Plutarch *Pomp.* 32, 9: Appian *Mith.* 101f.: Livy *Per.* ci: Cassius Dio xxxvi 50, 2: Cicero *pro Mur.* 34: Strabo xi p. 496; xii p. 555.

After a vain attempt to overtake the fugitive Mithradates,[n] Pompey, carrying out the rest of the mission enjoined on him by the law of Manilius, advanced into Armenia to confront Tigranes.[12] That arrogant potentate was now in a humbled frame of mind. The invasion of his Mesopotamian dominions by the Parthian Phraates, accompanied by the younger Tigranes, had driven him back from Gordyene to the Armenian table-land; but the enemy, not content with this, advanced through the centre of the plateau as far as Artaxata itself. Tigranes took refuge in the mountains; but when the Parthians, finding it impossible to storm the massive walls of the Armenian capital, withdrew to Mesopotamia, leaving the prince to face his father unaided, the old monarch suddenly reappeared and forced his rebellious son to flee for his life. The young man's first thought was to join his grandfather, Mithradates, but on learning of the latter's flight, he adopted a bolder course. When Pompey, marching along the upper Euphrates, arrived on the Armenian plateau, the prince presented himself. Tendering his submission, he offered to escort the Roman army through his father's kingdom. The offer was accepted, and as Pompey proceeded eastward the towns along the route opened their gates. The King, now thoroughly alarmed, made overtures to the invaders; he even attempted to prove his complete severance of relations with Mithradates by delivering up his father-in-law's envoys in their chains. These overtures, however, met with no response, for the Roman general was not to be put off by any such gestures and continued his march to Artaxata. When he was within a few miles of the city, Tigranes himself appeared, ready to surrender.

The purpose of the campaign was thus achieved; for the second of the two kings with whom the Romans were at war now made a complete submission. Pompey was well aware that Tigranes would be of more value to Rome as ruler of his ancestral kingdom than as an exhibit in a triumph and that the enmity existing between him and Phraates would prevent either monarch from becoming a menace to Roman rule. Tigranes, therefore, was received into the camp, where, after making obeisance, he was informed of the terms imposed by the conqueror. His kingdom of Armenia was granted to him, and he was promised the title of Friend and Ally of Rome. On the other hand, he was compelled to resign all claim to Asia Minor and all his conquests of the past thirty years, including Mesopotamia and Gordyene, Syria and Cilicia. Even Sophene, the first of the districts he

[n] Cassius Dio XXXVI 50, 3.

357

he annexed, was taken from him and given to his son. In addition, an indemnity of six thousand talents was demanded. The terms were accepted, and Tigranes, now hailed as King by the Roman army, showed his pleasure by presents of money both to the soldiers and to their officers.

The younger Tigranes, however, was less well satisfied.[o] It seems to have been arranged that on his father's death he should succeed to the throne of Armenia, but he had evidently expected to have it at once. Not content with the kingship of Sophene, he demanded also the treasure stored in the district, and when the demand was rejected, he grew angry and made plans to escape. Thereupon he was placed under guard. Pompey himself made two attempts to collect the treasure as part of the indemnity owed by the elder Tigranes, and when both proved fruitless he not only deprived the young man of the promised kingdom but also threw him into chains. Later, a request from Phraates, asking that his son-in-law might be freed, was flatly rejected, and the prince was eventually sent to Rome to be led in the conqueror's triumph.

In his march to Artaxata—distant nearly a thousand miles from the Hellespont—Pompey had advanced farther from Rome than any general before him. He had surpassed the achievement of Lucullus's expedition into Mesopotamia and he had led an army across the table-land of Armenia. Even so, however, he was not satisfied. Though it was now autumn, he resolved to go forward. Leaving his legate Afranius with a garrison in Armenia,[p] he marched from Artaxata across the mountains to the broad basin of the lower Kur in what is now Azerbaijan. Here he and his army spent the winter of 66-65 in the country of the Albani.[13]

A year was to pass between Pompey's departure from Armenia and his return to Asia Minor.[14] During this time he defeated in battle not only the Albani but also the Iberi, whose lands lay along the course of the middle Kur. Advancing westward from the neighbourhood of Tiflis, he descended to Phasis in the plain of Colchis. Here he met Servilius with the Roman fleet which was guarding the Euxine, and he seems even to have considered the feasibility of extending his march still farther in order to follow Mithradates to the Crimea. But on hearing of the length of the journey and the obstacles in the way, he contented himself with the capture of some Colchians and some tribes-

[o] Plutarch *Pomp.* 33, 5f. (= Zonares x 4): Appian *Mith.* 105: Cassius Dio xxxvi 53.
[p] Plutarch *Pomp.* 34, 1.

men from the northern shore of the Euxine to lend glamour to his expected triumph. The pursuit of Mithradates was entrusted to Servilius, who was ordered to blockade the Crimean ports.

From the plain of Colchis Pompey, returning over the mountains of northern Armenia, followed the Kur through the land of the Iberi until he came to the borders of the Albani.[15] Here, near the junction of the Kur and the Abas (probably the Alazan), he again defeated the tribesmen. After the battle Pompey made a formal treaty with the vanquished Albanian prince, who presented him with costly gifts. So great, in fact, was the conqueror's prestige that even remote nations from the Caucasus and the countries south of the Caspian Sea sent envoys to him to profess their submission.[16] In his desire to reach the end of the known world he planned to march on to the Caspian, but when only three days distant he abandoned his purpose, for the reason, we are told, that the region was infested by poisonous reptiles. Turning back, perhaps along the course of the lower Aras (Araxes), he made his way to Armenia and thence on to Pontus.

Pompey's motive for embarking on this long expedition, in the course of which he traversed the entire district of Trans-Caucasia, can hardly be regarded as other than selfish. The reason assigned by his ancient biographer, namely, that he must necessarily take this route in his pursuit of Mithradates, is, of course, without basis.[17] Equally unsatisfactory is the explanation that the King, in his flight to the Crimea, entered into negotiations with the tribes of the district; for it is hard to believe that these were ready either to send him reinforcements or to divert Pompey's pursuit by an offensive against the Roman force in Armenia. It would appear, therefore, that while Pompey may have been led to make this march partly for the purpose of impressing these distant tribes with the greatness of Rome and the fear of her arms, his motive was more probably the desire to gain greater prestige for himself and the glory of having advanced into lands that lay beyond the bounds of Roman experience. The names of the Kings of the Albani and Iberi and the trophies won in the course of the expedition were afterward prominently displayed in his triumphal procession in Rome.

After returning from this adventurous journey, Pompey devoted himself during the winter of 65-64 to the more useful task of reducing those fortresses of Mithradates which had not made formal surrender.[18] Among these was Sinoria, to which the King had fled after his last disastrous battle in Pontus. In its underground vaults lay a vast hoard of treasure. After holding out until its supplies of food were exhausted, the place surrendered to Pompey's legate, Manlius Priscus. In another stronghold the private archives of the King were discovered, including lists of those to whom poison had been given. In Taulara,[q] apparently the richest of all these treasure-houses, was found such a store of vessels, furniture and trappings for horses, all studded with jewels and gold, that the removal of it continued for a whole month.[r] These and other strongholds which were captured were rendered unfit for the use of future rebels by filling up the wells with great blocks of stone.[s]

In the spring of 64 Pompey advanced to Amisus, and here, as the arbiter of Asia Minor, the conqueror announced his plans for the disposal of his conquests. As will presently be shown,[t] they determined the destiny, for some years to come, of the northern and eastern portions of the Anatolian Peninsula.

On the conclusion of the deliberations at Amisus and the division of the spoils of war among those who were to have their shares of the dominions of Mithradates, Pompey turned his steps toward the south. After pausing at Zela to bury the bones of Triarius's soldiers,[u] slain three years earlier, he marched on rapidly across the Taurus into what remained of the former Seleucid Empire. Ignoring the restoration of the royal house, which Lucullus had re-established on the throne in the person of Antiochus XIII,[v] he declared that Tigranes by his submission at Artaxata had surrendered Syria and Cilicia Campestris to himself and that therefore these countries now belonged to Rome.[19] The young Seleucid monarch was brusquely told that there was no good reason why his dynasty, which had been expelled by Tigranes, should now rule in Syria rather than the Romans who had conquered the Armenian King. The victorious general then deposed the last of the ancient line from his insecure throne and annexed his dominions to the Roman Empire. Thus Rome acquired not only the district of Level Cilicia, now added to the province which had long borne its name,[w] but also the great expanse of territory which reached southward from the Gulf of Issus along the coast of the Mediterranean and included all the land as far as the Euphrates, the ancestral kingdom of the Seleucid monarchs, henceforth the province of Syria. Even Antiochus, the ruler of Commagene, who had made formal submis-

q See Chap. XIV note 31.
s Strabo XII p. 561.
u Plutarch Pomp. 39, 1.
w See below p. 376.

r Appian Mith. 115.
t See below p. 368f.
v See above pp. 296 and 344.

sion to Lucullus after the fall of Tigranocerta,[x] surrendered to the conqueror, thus swelling the list of the monarchs over whom he triumphed.[20]

Meanwhile, trouble had arisen with the Parthians. The rebuff administered to Phraates when he asked for the return of his son-in-law, the younger Tigranes,[y] had put a strain on the relations which probably became still less cordial when the Parthian monarch saw his enemy Tigranes seated securely on the throne of Armenia and acknowledged as an ally of Rome. Pompey, in fact, was not unwilling to have Phraates actively embroiled with the Armenian King. He gave orders, accordingly, to his legate Afranius, who during the commander's Trans-Caucasian expedition had remained in Armenia,[z] to seize Gordyene, driving out Phraates and the army with which he had entered it, and to claim the region for Rome's new ally.[21] Meanwhile another legate, Aulus Gabinius, entered Mesopotamia from the west, advancing as far as the upper Tigris. Angered by these attacks on his kingdom, the Parthian ruler sent a protest to Pompey, but against Tigranes he took more active measures and entered the disputed territory with an army. Although defeated in the first engagement, he was later victorious. But by this time Pompey had arrived in Syria, and the two Kings hastened to send their representatives to him, the one asking for aid in obtaining the territory which the Romans had claimed for him, the other protesting against the enforcement of this claim. Phraates's protest naturally reflected on the Romans' complicity in Tigranes' attempt to seize a region to which he had previously resigned all right.[a] Pompey, in fact, could not support the demand of his Armenian ally without provoking hostilities with the Parthian King, and this was not included in his mandate from Rome. Furthermore, he had no desire to embark on another war, lest his now great prestige should in some way be lessened. Accordingly, he resorted to the device of suggesting the appointment of arbitrators to settle the quarrel, thus establishing east of the Euphrates a practice long since adopted by the cities of the Aegean coast, which had learned to submit their disputes to the arbitration of Rome. A formal treaty concluded with Phraates guaranteed peace for the present.[22]

In Syria, Pompey was joined by Afranius, who, after conquering Gordyene for Tigranes, had set out to meet his general.[b] In the course

[x] See above p. 344.   [y] See above p. 358.
[z] See above p. 358.   [a] See above p. 357.
[b] Plutarch *Pomp.* 39, 2 (=Zonaras x 5): Cassius Dio xxxvii 5, 5.

of his wanderings westward, he fought with the tribes living in the mountain-range of Amanus, the eastern border of Cilicia Campestris,[c] and by defeating them established the nominal supremacy of Rome in that remote region.[d]

For another year Pompey remained outside the borders of Asia Minor, concerned with the affairs of the new province of Syria.[e] In the spring of 63 he set out on a triumphal progress, in the course of which the communities received him without opposition, for they welcomed relief both from the exactions of Tigranes and from the constant strife between Seleucid claimants. Acting with all the rights of a sovereign, he founded new cities, granted freedom to many already in existence and settled the disputes submitted to him for decision.

Of the various disputes which he was called on to arbitrate the most important was that which had arisen between the brothers Hyrcanus and Aristobulus, princes of the Maccabean House, each of whom, at the head of a faction, was striving to become King of the Jews and High Priest of Jehovah.[23] The adjustment of the quarrel occupied a large portion of the summer of 63, involving, as it did, the siege of the Temple at Jerusalem, where the partisans of Aristobulus took refuge. The great walls of the sacred enclosure enabled them to offer a stubborn resistance, and for three long months the siege dragged on. Finally, on a holy day, when the defenders were engaged in a religious ceremony, a breach was made, and the Romans poured into the enclosure. A general slaughter followed, in which 12,000 Jews are said to have lost their lives. Hyrcanus was then declared High Priest and his brother carried away in chains to be shown to the Roman populace.

Before the capture of the Holy City, however, Pompey had embarked on a new adventure. The first Roman general to penetrate to the extreme north of the Orient, he wished also to be the first to advance to the farthest south and to visit the Red Sea.[f] Accordingly, on the pretext of punishing Aretas III, King of the Nabataeans, who, more than twenty years previously, had invaded southern Syria and recently had led an armed force into Judaea, he set out for Petra, the monarch's rock-bound capital.[24] On arriving at Jericho, near the mouth of the Jordan, he entrusted the command of the expedition to the quaestor Marcus Aemilius Scaurus, who, before reaching Petra, persuaded the

c See above p. 271.   d See below p. 377.
e Plutarch *Pomp.* 39, 2f.: Strabo xvi pp. 751 and 755: Josephus *Ant. Jud.* xiv 3, 2, §38f.: Eutropius vi 14, 2.
f Plutarch *Pomp.* 38, 2f.

Nabataean ruler to save himself and his territory by a show of submission and the payment of three hundred talents. The name of Aretas was added to the list of kings whom Pompey claimed to have conquered.

From Jericho Pompey returned to Jerusalem to lay siege to the Temple. Jericho therefore was the farthest point in his advance to the southeast. But the place assumed a significance in the General's eyes greater than that lent by its geographical position, and his return was due to a motive more important by far than the desire of seizing the Jewish capital. For while he was encamped at the mouth of the Jordan, a courier arrived with a laurel-bound spear, bearing the tidings that no longer was there any cause for war: Mithradates was dead!

During the two years which had passed since the old monarch had arrived in southern Russia as a fugitive, his career had been a stormy one.[25] First of all, he had had to deal with the faithless son who had made submission to Lucullus and in return had received the title of King and Ally.[g] On reaching Phanagoreia on the eastern side of the Strait of Kertch, Mithradates was met by an envoy sent by Machares to ask for his father's forgiveness. When these overtures received no response, the young man barricaded himself at Panticapaeum on the other side of the Strait. But Panticapaeum soon opened its gates to the King, and Machares, abandoned by his followers and now without hope of resistance, perished either by his own hand or by that of one of his associates. So in a brief time Mithradates made himself master in his northern kingdom. By the prestige of his name, by lavish gifts and by promises of marriage with his numerous daughters, he won the support of the neighbouring chieftains. Encouraged by their adherence, as well as by the submissiveness of his own dominions, he set himself once more to the familiar task of creating a powerful armament. By dint of great exertions and lavish expenditures an army of over 36,000 men was raised and a fleet was constructed and manned.

At some stage in these preparations, perhaps before they had been carried on very far, the King made an attempt at negotiation. Sending an envoy to Pompey, he asked for the restoration of his kingdom of Pontus, binding himself, in return, to pay tribute to the Romans as their vassal. The proposal, however, did not accord with the views either of the Roman government, determined that Mithradates should

g See above p. 342.

cease to be a menace to the provinces of Asia, or of the General himself, who would not brook the restoration to power, even as a vassal, of the enemy he had set out to conquer. Accordingly, the answer was given him that he must come and present his petition in person. But the King, knowing better than to entrust himself to the Romans, refused to comply with the demand, offering, however, to send some of his sons to act in his stead—a proposal, of course, unacceptable to Pompey.

Meanwhile the active and ambitious brain of the old monarch was devising a new plan, namely the invasion of Europe. He dreamed of marching up the course of the Danube, and then, with the help of allies among the Gauls, launching an attack across the Alps on Italy, supposedly defenceless by reason of the absence of Pompey's legions in the East. This visionary plan, however, aroused little enthusiasm among his followers. In fact, enforced military service and increase in taxation, combined with the extortion practiced by his officials, were causing growing distaste for his rule. The dissatisfaction broke out first at Phanagoreia, where Castor, prefect of the garrison, called upon the citizens to revolt. The citadel was captured, and four of Mithradates's sons were seized and eventually handed over to the commandant of the Roman fleet. The example of Phanagoreia was followed by many other strongholds in the Crimea; even the King's own troops, acting as escort to the daughters whom he had promised to the Scythian chieftains, killed the eunuchs in charge of the princesses and delivered the latter to the Romans.

These various acts of revolt and betrayal infuriated Mithradates almost to the point of insanity. A reign of terror set in; not only were the guilty detected and punished, but many others, including, apparently, some of the royal family, were put to death merely on suspicion. This procedure aroused the fears of Mithradates's son, Pharnaces, who had been named heir to the throne. A conspiracy which the prince formed to overthrow his father was detected and further executions followed. The old monarch agreed to spare his son, at least for the moment, but Pharnaces, putting no faith in the promise, persuaded the troops to crown him King. Then Mithradates, after vain appeals both to Pharnaces and to the soldiers, resolved by drinking poison to avoid the shame of a surrender to his unfilial son. The drug, however, failed to take effect, and so, turning to a Gallic officer, the old monarch besought deliverance from the fate of appearing in a Roman triumph. The Gaul, in pity, granted the request.

The announcement that the king who for a quarter of a century had troubled Asia Minor would endanger it no longer left Pompey no further pretext for carrying on the war. He remained in Judaea, therefore, only long enough to establish Hyrcanus as the ruler of a much-diminished land[h] and then hastened northward. Travelling rapidly through Syria and Cilicia and over the Taurus, he accomplished the long march to the coast of the Euxine before winter set in.[26] At Amisus he found envoys from Pharnaces. They brought gifts and hostages, together with the men of Mitylene who twenty-five years previously had surrendered Manius Aquilius to his enemy.[i] They also brought a strange offering—the body of Mithradates himself, which Pharnaces had caused to be embalmed for transportation. The gifts were accepted, and the King was laid away with all due ceremony in the royal tomb at Sinope. Pharnaces's offer of surrender was likewise accepted, and, in gratitude for the act of faithlessness which had freed Rome from the terror of twenty-five years, he was recognized as ruler of the Crimean kingdom with the rank of a King and Ally of the Romans. Only the city of Phanagoreia, because it had begun the last insurrection against Mithradates, was declared free and independent, and on its commandant, Castor, was bestowed the title of Friend of Rome.[27]

The winter of 63-62 Pompey spent in Pontus, in taking over the few strongholds which had not already come into the power of the Romans and in completing the plans for the future of the conquered lands. In the spring, after distributing among his army the unprecedented amount of sixteen thousand talents,[j] the General set forth on the long march to the Aegean coast. In all the cities he was received with pomp and acclaim.[28] In Mitylene he attended a contest of poets whose theme consisted of the greatness of his exploits. The city, in disgrace because of its surrender of Aquilius, had been kept in subjection since its capture in 80;[k] but now Pompey, for the sake of the historian Theophanes, a native of the place, who composed a chronicle relating his achievements, granted it freedom. Finally coming to Ephesus, he set sail for Greece and after stopping in Athens reached Brundisium in December.[l]

In Rome the news of Mithradates's death and the sense of freedom from the fear he had so long inspired had caused the greatest rejoic-

[h] Josephus *Ant. Jud.* XIV 4, 4, §73f. = *Bell. Jud.* I 7, 6, §153f.
[i] See above p. 215.   [j] See note 5.   [k] See above p. 246.
[l] Cicero *Epist. ad Att.* I 12, I (I Jan. 61 B.C.), written before Pompey's arrival in Rome.

ing.[29] On the motion of the Consul, Marcus Cicero, the Senate voted a festival of thanksgiving to be held for ten days, and in the following year, when Pompey's report of his successes arrived, a similar festival of twelve days was proclaimed. As time went on, however, there were many who began to fear the return of the conqueror. They reflected that, with an army so devoted that it had followed him through the entire Orient, he might easily establish himself as master of Rome, and, like Marius and Sulla, take revenge on his opponents. To their surprise and relief, Pompey, as soon as he landed at Brundisium, dismissed his legions, merely bidding them join him later to march in his triumph. On his journey through Italy he was everywhere received with acclamation, and when he arrived near Rome, after an absence of nearly six years, the populace poured out in welcome. Even his enemies joined in the throng.

These enemies, nevertheless, and particularly the friends of Lucullus, who had not forgiven the slights he had suffered, were not ready to lay aside their resentment.[m] They could not, however, prevent the decree authorizing Pompey's triumph. Although not held until more than eight months after his arrival in Rome, it surpassed in magnificence all that had ever been seen. Having previously celebrated triumphs over Africa and Spain,[n] he now seemed to be adding a third continent to his achievements. For two whole days the populace was dazzled by the display of the conqueror's exploits, including both his successes against the pirates and his victories over the kings of the East.[30] Placards boasted that in addition to destroying the forces and ships of the corsairs, the General had conquered fourteen nations, extending from the Crimea to the Red Sea, Pontus and Armenia, Cappadocia and Paphlagonia, Cilicia and Mesopotamia, Syria, Phoenicia, Judaea and Arabia, Media and the districts of Trans-Caucasia. Six kings besides Mithradates had been overcome in war, eight hundred and forty-six pirate-ships had been destroyed or captured[o] and fifteen hundred and thirty-eight towns and strongholds taken. The amount of gold and silver, in money and plate, that accrued to the public treasury was set at one hundred and twenty million denarii, and the annual revenues from the newly-acquired provinces were estimated at eighty-five millions—nearly twice the total amount that Rome had hitherto received from her dependencies. Waggons and litters bore ornaments and trophies, jewelled vessels and crowns, golden chariots

---

m Plutarch *Luc.* 36, 1; *Pomp.* 46, 3.
n In 79 and 71 B.C. respectively; see *Acta Triumphorum, C.I.L.* I^2 p. 178.
o But see Chap. XII note 42.

and banqueting-couches, among them a couch said to have belonged to the Persian monarch Darius, son of Hystaspes, also golden statues of the gods, silver statues of Pharnaces I of Pontus and Mithradates, besides a colossal statue of the latter, made of solid gold. On the second day of the triumph—Pompey's own birthday—were displayed the notable captives, three hundred and twenty-four in number: pirate-chieftains, royal women taken from the Scythians, hostages given by the princes of Albania and Iberia and by Antiochus of Commagene, Menander, chief of cavalry in the Pontic army, the Colchian ruler Olthaces, Aristobulus, the vanquished claimant to the Jewish High Priesthood, together with three of his children, five sons and two daughters of Mithradates, and Tigranes, the prince of Armenia, with his wife and daughter and one of his harem. Paintings of Mithradates and Tigranes the elder were exhibited, showing them in battle or in flight, and the death of the Pontic monarch was also depicted. Finally, attended by the officers who had shared in his wars, came the Conqueror himself, riding in a four-horse chariot, bedecked with jewels and arrayed in a cloak which, it was said, once belonged to Alexander the Great. After the triumph most of the illustrious captives were sent to their homes at the state's expense. Aristobulus escaped to stir up further trouble in Judaea, while Tigranes was kept in captivity in Rome.[31]

Then came the anticlimax. Pompey was eager to secure the Senate's ratification of all the arrangements made at Amisus for the future government of the districts he had conquered, and he also hoped to obtain grants of Italian land for the soldiers he had discharged. He found, however, that he had neither friends nor supporters in the Senate and that his position was one of complete isolation.[32] He had obtained his command in the East by the aid of the popular leaders and in spite of opposition among the Conservatives. They, wishing to thwart him, now rallied around Lucullus, ready to avenge the wrongs he had suffered. Pompey had asked for a general approval of all the measures he had taken in Asia, and in this request his enemies saw their opportunity. They protested that all he had done could not be approved by one single vote, and that each measure must be separately discussed, in order that the Senate might ratify them singly. Thus the entire year 60 dragged on with nothing accomplished, and the once mighty conqueror found himself unable to achieve the results of his conquest. Fearing to submit the question to the Assembly of the People, he was ready to abandon the entire programme.

Then a new opportunity offered itself. Julius Caesar, returning from Spain, had been elected Consul for the year 59. Well aware of the Senate's hostility toward him and of his own need for assistance in his plans for the year, he formed a combination with Pompey and Crassus, in which the three men agreed each to support the measures desired by the others. Then, backed by his fellow-Triumvirs, Caesar proposed to the Senate a bill for the bestowal of lands on the citizens— among whom were included the soldiers of Pompey. But finding the senators resolved to obstruct the passage of the measure, he brought it before the Assembly. Here, not only the land-bill but also his other proposals, including the ratification of Pompey's actions in Asia, were all successfully passed. Thus, through the machinations of an able politician, all that had been done at Amisus was finally ratified.

These arrangements for the organization of northern and eastern Asia Minor as well as of Syria, begun by Pompey at Amisus in the winter of 65-64 and completed at Antioch in 64-63 and again at Amisus in the following winter, resulted in important alterations in the government of large portions of the East.[33] The task of determining the future status of so wide an expanse of territory was a great one, involving the solution of many problems. It was necessary not only to provide for the conquered kingdom of Pontus, including the Greek cities of the Euxine, but also to decide upon the future of many native rulers. Some of these had aided Rome in the struggle and now expected rewards, while others, overawed by the victor, had merely made submission, hoping to retain through Rome's grace the lands they had previously held. These princes now gathered about the conqueror, paying their court to the Roman general who had prizes to bestow. The speed and efficiency with which the task was accomplished cannot but call forth real admiration. Aided, perhaps, by competent advisers who were acquainted with local conditions, Pompey proceeded to make arrangements for the future which showed that his ability as an organizer was in no way inferior to his skill as a general. Having conquered three new provinces for Rome, he had now to arrange for the administration of his conquests. Assuming that the law of Manilius empowered him to organize the newly-won territory without consulting the usual senatorial commission, he established himself as arbiter in the allotment of the lands he had gained, either annexing them outright to the Roman Empire, or granting them to those who in his judgement would rule them in the interest of Rome.

Of the prizes of the war the greatest was taken for Rome herself. The core of the kingdom of Mithradates, extending along the Euxine coast from the Bithynian border at Heracleia to Pharnaceia, east of the promontory of Iasonium, and as far south as the mountain-ranges which formed the frontier of Cappadocia,[p] was made the new province of Pontus and placed under the command of the governor of Bithynia.[q] It comprised not only the ancestral realm of the Pontic kings, including that portion of the coast of Paphlagonia which they had annexed,[r] but also the valley of the Amnias, which Mithradates had seized at the time of the partition of the district in 104 and, despite the provisions of the Treaty of Dardanus, had probably succeeded in retaining.[s]

The reorganization of Pontus carried out by Pompey revolutionized the political and economic conditions which had hitherto prevailed in the district. It has been previously observed that in the interior of Pontus the old Asianic system of domain-land, royal and sacred, and rural communities with village-centres had held out against the growing influence of Hellenism,[t] while the cities of the Euxine littoral had preserved the Hellenic tradition of self-government. This long-established system, lost by Sinope and Amisus under Mithradates but recently restored to them by Lucullus,[u] Pompey now introduced with some modifications in the communities throughout the newly-organized province of Bithynia-Pontus, giving them uniform constitutions.[34] Under this system a community was composed of all citizens, it being permitted to enroll among them any who were not already citizens of another community in the province. The government consisted of popularly elected magistrates—none to be under thirty years of age—and a Council composed of those who had held magistracies, the members to be enrolled by duly appointed censors and subject to ejection by these officials on grounds which were carefully specified. This method of local administration, based on the usual Hellenic model but including the characteristically Roman element of a revision of the Council by censors, established by virtue of the ordinance known as the *Lex Pompeia*, became the standard form of government for the communities of the new province. With a slight modification, it was still in force in the second century after Christ.

As organized by Pompey, the urban centres of Pontus were, so we

---

[p] See Chap. VIII note 4.

[q] Livy *Per.* CII: Strabo XII p. 541: Velleius Paterculus II 38, 6. See also Niese in *Rh. Mus.* XXXVIII (1883), p. 577f.

[r] See above p. 189f.

[t] See above p. 179f.

[s] See above p. 197 and Chap. X note 2.

[u] See above pp. 337f. and 342.

are told, eleven in number.[35] They included, doubtless, the three ports of Amisus, Sinope and Amastris and the ancient capital, Amaseia. The others were presumably the seven new communities which Pompey at his triumph claimed to have founded. These communities were placed either on the site of a settlement which had grown up around a royal residence or an important sanctuary or in a locality of historic significance; in each case the existing population was probably increased by including the villages situated in the surrounding rural district, which became the city's territory. To signify the change that had been made in their condition, most of the new communities received Hellenic names. Thus in the basin of the Lycus Mithradates's residence at Cabeira and the new Eupatoria, which he had left unfinished, became, respectively, Diospolis and Magnopolis. Near Dasteira, in commemoration of the final victory over Mithradates in the mountains toward the southeast, was founded the new city of Nicopolis, and here Pompey established some of his soldiers, discharged from service because of their wounds. In the rich district of Phazimonitis was placed the city of Neapolis, and in the far south lay Megalopolis, commanding the valley of the upper Halys. Zela also, the sacred town of Anaïtis, near which Triarius had suffered defeat at the hands of Mithradates,[v] was made one of the new communities—the only former settlement to retain its ancient name—the rule of the priest being replaced by a civic organization and the estates of the Goddess forming the territory of the new city. Far in the west, in Paphlagonia, Pompeiopolis was founded in the fertile plain along the Amnias, where in 88 B.C. the Pontic generals had defeated Nicomedes IV of Bithynia.

The sites of these communities, however, were not chosen merely because of the existence of an earlier settlement or on the grounds of an historic interest. The organizing skill of the conqueror of Pontus caused him to select places of outstanding strategic significance for his new foundations. Thus of the seven, five—namely, Nicopolis, Diospolis, Magnopolis, Neapolis and Pompeiopolis—lay on the great trade-route which traversed Asia Minor from Bithynia to Armenia,[w] while Zela and Megalopolis were situated on the road which led from the Euxine coast through Amaseia to the valley of the upper Halys and over the mountains to the Euphrates at Tomisa.[x] Thus the trade both from east to west and from north to south was carried through these communities. With urbanization and commerce came increasing prosperity;

[v] See above p. 347f. [w] See Chap. VIII note 33.
[x] See Chap VIII note 25.

at the beginning of the Christian Era Nicopolis, at least, had a large population, and in the second and third centuries it had the rank of metropolis.[y]

One great Pontic centre, however, was not thus Hellenized. This was the prosperous settlement around the Temple of the Mother-Goddess at Comana,[z] where the priest of the deity exercised sovereign power over the serfs belonging to the sacred domains. Whereas smaller temples, like that at Zela, might conceivably be merged in an urban centre of the western type, it was obvious that this wealthy and important sanctuary could not be reduced to a mere appanage of one of the new communities. Pompey, therefore, with a wise regard both for traditional sanctity and for oriental prejudice, abstained from any attempt at Hellenization. He preserved the high-priesthood of the Goddess but appointed to the office a man who would be an obedient vassal of Rome. The new incumbent was Archelaus,[a] son of the Pontic general of that name who had negotiated the Treaty of Dardanus and later fled from Mithradates's anger to join Murena.[b] A Pontian by birth, he had grown up under Roman influence, and so would be both acceptable to the native population and amenable to the commands of a provincial governor. Although ambitious and adventurous, as his later career proved, he seemed a suitable compromise between the traditions of the East and the West.[36] The possessions of the Temple, in a fertile valley on the upper Iris, were increased by a gift of land sixty stades in circumference, perhaps part of the rich plain of Dazimonitis farther down the course of the river; the inhabitants were made subject to the new priest, now the ruler of an hereditary semi-independent principality within the confines of the province.

Thus Pompey adopted the system of placing those conquered regions which could not be easily Romanized under the rule of princes of native stock ready to yield obedience to Rome's commands. This principle was not a new one, for as early as the second century the monarchs both of Pergamum and of Bithynia had been in a position of somewhat similar dependence, but it had never been applied as widely as in Pompey's appointment of client-princes throughout the East.

Among the regions where the creation of a native ruler of this type

[y] Strabo XII p. 555: *C.I.G.* 4189 and *B.C.H.* XXXIII (1909), p. 35, no. 13.

[z] See above p. 181.

[a] Strabo XII p. 558; XVII p. 796: Appian *Mith.* 114.

[b] See above pp. 229f. and 243.

seemed highly advisable was Paphlagonia. While, after the conclusion of the Treaty of Dardanus, part of the district had been given to Nicomedes, Mithradates seems to have retained at least the eastern portion.[c] In any case, Paphlagonia, along with the rest of the defeated King's dominions, had become part of the spoils of war, to be disposed of by Pompey. Both the seaboard and the valley of the Amnias, in which lay the new community of Pompeiopolis, were now annexed to the province of Pontus. The remainder, comprising not only the basin of the Devrek, together with Gangra and that portion of the region of Pimolisene which lay south of the junction of the Devrek and the Halys, but also the western section, which included the valley of the upper Billaeus and the mountains of Timonitis, was assigned to princes of native stock.[37] Two claimants were found, Attalus and Pylaemenes, "members of the house of Pylaemenes," though whether of the earlier kings of the name or of their Bithynian namesake, we are not informed. Paphlagonia was divided between them, and it was expected that in return for this boon they would rule in the interest of Rome. In the course of time the new order brought the usual influx of Roman business-men, who established themselves in the district.[d]

Beyond the mountains which formed the southern boundary of Paphlagonia lay the land of the Galatians, whose territory reached from the borders of Pontus as far west as the upper Sangarius and the frontier of the Roman province of Asia. At least a portion of the district had been seized by Mithradates,[e] and Galatian tribesmen served in the armies with which he invaded western Asia Minor and Greece.[38] But his brutal slaughter of their princes[f] and his subsequent attempt to reduce their nation to subjection aroused a general revolt against the King. Led by the princes who had escaped from the massacre, they drove out the Pontic "satrap" Eumachus and the garrisons he had placed in their country.[g] Less than a year later, the Treaty of Dardanus compelled Mithradates to resign all claim to Galatia. In 73, when for the second time he invaded western Asia Minor, some of the Celts, like Connacorix, who commanded the garrison imposed on Heracleia,[h] entered his service, but, in general, they supported the cause of Rome.[39] In the new organization of Asia Minor it was necessary to make some arrangement by which the relations of these tribes with Rome might be more definitely established and a means devised for securing their submission in the future.

[c] See Chap. X note 2.
[e] See above p. 198.
[g] See above p. 226.

[d] See Chap. XIX note 47.
[f] See above p. 223.
[h] Memnon 42, 5; 49f. See above p. 331.

Of the Galatians who had rendered service to Rome the most notable was the able and energetic Deiotarus, a "tetrarch" of the Tolistobogii, one of the three tribes which composed the nation. He had won high commendation from Sulla and Murena in their wars against Mithradates,[i] but his most conspicuous achievement was the repulse of Eumachus, the old enemy of the Galatians, who in 73 was sent by the Pontic monarch to plunder Phrygia and the newly-won districts of Pisidia and Isauria.[j] Deiotarus's success on this occasion and his apparent readiness to act in Rome's interest recommended him to Pompey. In a dominant position among his fellow-countrymen, he would ensure their fidelity to Rome, and as a client-prince he would prove a suitable ruler of part of those dominions of Mithradates which it seemed inadvisable to include in the new province of Pontus.

To provide for this position of supremacy among the Galatians, a change in their method of government was necessary. According to their long-standing system, each of the three great tribes, the Tolistobogii, the Tectosages and the Trocmi,[k] was divided into four clans and each one of these had its own "tetrarch," as well as its judge and minor officials; the twelve princes, all of them, apparently, regarded as members of the royal house, ruled the nation in common. It was manifestly impossible, however, to have twelve rulers as vassals of Rome. Pompey, therefore, simplified the ancient system by replacing the twelve tetrarchs by three, one for each of the tribes.[40] The reduction in number was doubtless made easier by Mithradates's massacre of some of the tetrarchs at Pergamum. Deiotarus was made sole tetrarch of the tribe of the Tolistobogii, and his son-in-law, Brogitarus, was appointed ruler of the Trocmi. Brogitarus also received the fortress of Mithradatium, which Mithradates had built in the southwestern corner of his kingdom, presumably for the purpose of holding in subjection the territory he had taken from the Galatians. The tetrarch of the Tectosages is not definitely known; he may have been Castor Tarcondarius (or Saocondarius), another son-in-law of Deiotarus, or perhaps a certain Domnilaus (or Domnecleius).

Deiotarus, although his rule over the Tolistobogii remained only a "tetrarchate," was exalted by the bestowal of the title of King, and, in addition to his ancestral dominions in Galatia, a kingdom was formed for him in territory taken from Mithradates but not incorporated in the new province of Pontus.[41] This kingdom consisted of a

[i] Cicero *Phil.* XI 33; *pro Rege Deiot.* 26 and 37.
[j] See above pp. 294 and 329. [k] See Chap. I notes 11 and 13.

long stretch of coast on the southern side of the Euxine, including the western part of the plain of Gazelonitis at the mouth of the Halys and, much farther east, the district that contained the ports of Pharnaceia and Trapezus. It was a rich and valuable possession, not only for the fisheries of the coast but also because of the great natural resources of its mountain-country, the deposits of iron, copper and silver,[1] and the wealth of timber from its forests. In addition to this region, Deiotarus received also the valleys which contain the headwaters of the Lycus and the Çoruh and all the northern portion of Armenia Minor, which Mithradates had wrested from its native ruler and added to Pontus.[m] His new kingdom, accordingly, extended from the Euxine to the northern border of Cappadocia, including all the mountainous tract lying between Pontus and the upper Euphrates. On the northeast, peace was assured by the recognition of the local dynast Aristarchus as the ruler of Colchis.[42]

By this new arrangement in Galatia the ancient tribal division was preserved, but each tribe was placed under a ruler who would act in Rome's interest. At the same time, Deiotarus, a man possessed of real intelligence and even a modicum of Hellenic culture, received a position of supremacy over the others, which was intended to secure the allegiance of the whole nation to Rome.[43] Harmony, indeed, was not accomplished, for in the course of time Deiotarus quarrelled with both his sons-in-law and in the end put one of them to death.[n] Toward Rome, however, he maintained unbroken fidelity,[o] and such was his loyalty to Pompey that when the General armed himself for the final struggle with his rival at Pharsalus, the Galatian prince appeared in person with a body of horsemen for his army.[p]

Of all the rulers who, during the great struggle, had been Rome's allies in the East, the most faithful and also the most long-suffering was Ariobarzanes I, King of Cappadocia. Ever since his elevation to the kingship in 95[q] he had resisted the encroachments of Mithradates; he had been repeatedly thrust from his throne by the Pontic King and he had had to endure the ravaging of his country by the latter's Armenian son-in-law.[r] He had sent provisions to Lucullus when the Roman army was in danger of starvation at Cabeira,[s] and he had also borne aid when the General set out through Cappadocia

---

[1] See above p. 179.   [m] See above p. 195f.   [n] See below p. 426.
[o] Cicero de Har. Resp. 29; Epist. ad Fam. xv 1, 6; 2, 2; 4, 5; Epist. ad Att. vi 1, 14; Phil. ii 93; Brut. 21.
[p] See below p. 402.   [q] See above p. 205.   [r] See above pp. 321 and 349.
[s] See above p. 335.

to the Euphrates on his adventurous march into Mesopotamia.[t] Thus far, Ariobarzanes's only reward had been the strategically important stronghold of Tomisa at the crossing of the river, which he had received from Lucullus.[u] Now, however, his dominions were greatly increased. In addition to Tomisa, he obtained the whole district of Sophene, on the eastern bank of the Euphrates from the mountains north of the Arsanias (Murat Su) across the Taurus to the upper Tigris.[44] By this gift the pass of Ergani,[v] which led across the Taurus into northern Mesopotamia, was held by an ally and the control of this route was thus assured to Rome.

On the west also, Ariobarzanes received an extension of territory, namely the region of Cybistra in southeastern Lycaonia.[45] Nominal possession of Lycaonia, it is true, had already been given by Rome to the Cappadocian monarchs in 129 B.C.,[w] but their hold on the southern portion had been rendered precarious by the Isaurian bandit-chieftains, one of whom, a certain Antipater, was now brought into the position of a Roman vassal by the gift of a territory containing Derbe and Laranda on the northern side of the Taurus between Isauria and Cybistra.[46] The most valuable part of Lycaonia, however, was that which was now assigned to Ariobarzanes, for the region of Cybistra was fertile and well-suited to the growing of grain and in the neighbouring Taurus there were rich mines of silver and lead.[47] This region was strategically even more important, for it commanded the approach to the Cilician Gates through which passed all traffic from the north and the west to the plain of Cilicia and onward to Syria.[x] Thus the two great routes to the East were controlled by a vassal-king and through him by Rome.

Ariobarzanes, however, was not destined to rule over his enlarged kingdom for long. Before Pompey left Asia the monarch, we know not why, at a formal gathering in the presence of the General abdicated his crown in favour of his son, Ariobarzanes II.[48] He was recognized in his father's stead as a friend and ally of Rome but after only a few years' reign he met with a violent death.[y]

Pompey was credited with the distinction of having gained two other provinces for Rome in addition to Pontus—Syria and Cilicia.[49] The *coup de grâce* by which the Seleucid dynasty was brought to an end

---

[t] Memnon 56, 1.
[v] See Chap. XIV note 45.
[x] See Chap. XI note 36.

[u] See above p. 344.
[w] Justin xxxvii 1, 2; see above p. 154f.
[y] See below p. 390.

and their kingdom of Syria made a Roman province has already been described.[z] The same act made it possible definitely to annex the district of Level Cilicia—if, indeed, it had not been already annexed by Lucullus[a]—to the province, thus finally justifying the name by which this had long been known. Pompey's victory over the pirates had won Rugged Cilicia for Rome, and now, with the further addition of the Level District, the province extended along the whole southern coast from Cape Chelidonia to the Gulf of Issus; its capital henceforth was Tarsus in the rich plain of the Cydnus. How far northward of the Taurus the enlarged province was carried is uncertain, but it seems evident that at least the highland-country of Isauria, which had been overrun during the brilliant expedition of Servilius Isauricus,[b] was still included within its boundaries. Six years after Pompey left Asia Minor, the three judiciary "dioceses" of which Phrygia consisted —Cibyra-Laodiceia, Apameia and Synnada[c]—were taken from the province of Asia and transferred to Cilicia,[d] an addition which presupposes the inclusion also of at least the western part of Lycaonia with its judiciary centre, Iconium, as well as the neighbouring Phrygia Paroreius. But whether this region was added to Cilicia by Pompey or whether it was incorporated later, together with the three Phrygian dioceses, cannot be determined. In any case, the great extension brought about by the addition of the two Cilicias to the small province of Pamphylia-Isauria seemed to justify the claim that Pompey had acquired this third province for Rome.

As the new province of Pontus was guarded by the client-kings of Cappadocia and Armenia Minor, so the Greater Cilicia also was protected by princes who ruled henceforth as vassals of Rome. Of these, Antiochus I, King of Commagene, had already made submission to Lucullus, but on Pompey's appearance in Syria he hastened once more to acknowledge Rome's supremacy.[e] The descendant of a long line of princes, one of whom, about 162 B.C., made himself independent of Seleucid rule and perhaps even assumed the royal title, he ruled over a kingdom which extended from the Taurus to the northern border of Syria.[50] It was rich by reason both of the fertile land on the western bank of the Euphrates[f] and of the forests which clothed its mountains and produced the oak-galls widely used for tanning and dyeing.[g] His capital, Samosata, on the Euphrates below the great

[z] See above p. 360. [a] See Chap. XII note 38. [b] See above p. 288f.
[c] See above pp. 171 and 242. [d] See below p. 383f. [e] See above p. 360f.
[f] Strabo XVI p. 749.
[g] Josephus *Ant. Jud.* XIV 15, 8, §441: Pliny *N.H.* XVI 27; XXIV 9.

gorges in which the stream breaks through the Taurus, was a station on the route to the East which led down the western bank of the river and crossed here into Mesopotamia.[51] Thus Commagene, apart from its natural wealth, had great strategic importance. Separated by mountains from Cappadocia and Cilicia and with a distinct national tradition, it could not readily be included in a Roman province and was obviously a separate realm. The "conquered" Antiochus, therefore, was allowed to retain his kingdom.[52] His royal title was recognized by Pompey and he was added to the list of Rome's client-kings. He was even presented with the city of Seleuceia, on the eastern bank of the Euphrates not far from Samosata, and a small district around it. Thus the bank of the river and the important crossing at Samosata, like that at Tomisa also, were placed under the control of a vassal of Rome.

Southwest of Commagene, another dependency of Rome was established along the Cilician border. Here the range of Amanus, projecting southward from the Taurus, from which it is separated by the gorges of the Pyramus, extends to the Mediterranean at the entrance to the Gulf of Issus.[h] This region had been overrun by Afranius in the autumn of 64,[i] but, peopled in part by bandit-tribes, it was ill-suited for incorporation in a Roman province. It was therefore left under the rule of a local dynast, Tarcondimotus, who was now recognized as friend and ally of Rome.[53] He seems to have established his residence at Castabala on the upper Pyramus in eastern Cilicia, and from here he and his descendants ruled at least the northern part of the mountain-district. His realm also included a port somewhere on the Gulf of Issus, and through it ran the route which connected the Cilician plain with the Euphrates.[j] A "notable man" and distinguished for his courage,[k] Tarcondimotus remained faithful to Pompey and, like the other royal clients in the East, aided him in the final struggle with Caesar.[l]

Pompey's enemies in Rome may have said in his disparagement that the Mithradatic War was waged against weak women,[m] and Caesar, after his victory over Mithradates's son, may have commented on his rival's good fortune in being able to win such great fame from the conquest of so unwarlike a foe.[n] Lucullus and his friends may have asserted that Pompey had merely robbed his predecessor of the prizes

---

h See above p. 271.
j See Chap. XI note 36.
l Cassius Dio XLI 63, 1; see below p. 403.
n Suetonius *Jul.* 35, 2.

i See above p. 362.
k Strabo XIV p. 676.
m Cicero *pro Mur.* 31, quoting Cato.

of victory and compared him to the carrion-bird which preys on the bodies of those whom others have slain.[o] It is true that Lucullus had had to deal with the King at the height of his power, while he himself had an army far inferior in size and always ready for mutiny. It is true that by Lucullus's victories the enemy's power was broken and his prestige diminished, and that the army which he put into the field, when compared with the vast hosts led into Asia in 88 and Bithynia in 73, was pitiably small.[p] It is true that the great reputation which Pompey had won by his success in the West disheartened his opponents in the East and thus made it less difficult to defeat them. It is also true that Pompey in the record of his achievements which he displayed at his triumph may have magnified fishing-boats into pirate-vessels and hamlets into fortresses and claimed victories over kings whom he had never even seen. He did, indeed, reap where others had sown, and he grossly exaggerated the amount of the harvest. Nevertheless, the fact remains that he succeeded where his predecessor had failed. It may be that at the outset it was Pompey's prestige that won him the allegiance of the soldiers who had refused to follow Lucullus into Armenia, but no prestige alone could have induced those selfsame troops to advance to the Caspian and to the mouth of the Jordan, supporting their leader in his wish to carry far and wide the terror of Rome's arms. Lucullus had, indeed, been prevented from carrying out whatever plans he and his commissioners were making for the disposal of the conquered lands; but it is evident that these plans never contemplated the annexation to Rome's dominions of the vast amount of territory which was added by his successor. Pompey's wide-spread conquests and, still more, his organization of those conquests—the foundation of Hellenized communities in eastern Asia Minor and the creation of vassal-kings in remote regions—carried Roman influence and power to the Euphrates and even beyond. Although nowhere save in northern Syria did a Roman province touch this stream, nevertheless a line of client-princes held for Rome not only the Euphrates frontier, with the crossings of the river, but also the border of the Syrian Desert. Even on the farther bank of the river, the submission of the rulers of Armenia and Osroene safeguarded the approaches from the East and held the Parthians in check. Not since the days of the Scipios had a Roman general contributed so greatly to the extension of the far-flung Empire, exacting the toll of blood and suffering which the glory won for Rome by a policy of imperialism demanded from enemy and citizen alike.

[o] Plutarch *Luc.* 35, 7; *Pomp.* 30, 3; 31, 6f.   [p] See above p. 353.

CHAPTER XVI

FROM POMPEY TO CAESAR

IN the year 62, the summer of which Pompey spent in organizing his new conquests, the province of Asia was governed by Lucius Valerius Flaccus, the son of the unfortunate general who was to have replaced Sulla in the command against Mithradates but was murdered by his subordinate, Fimbria.[1] Flaccus had had a good record in public office,[2] and as praetor during the year before his governorship he had rendered valuable service to the cause of law and order by arresting the Gauls who were acting as agents for Catiline's associates.[a] Like many another Roman, however, he regarded his governorship as an opportunity for self-enrichment and he seems to have shown little hesitancy in exploiting the province entrusted to his care.

We are told that under the pretext of constructing a war-fleet Flaccus levied a money-assessment on the cities; as no fleet was needed at the time, he was able to keep a large part of the funds contributed.[3] On various grounds not known to us he extorted money from the communities of Acmonia, Dorylaeum and Temnus.[4] At Tralles he appropriated a sum which the cities had collected years before for the purpose of founding a festival in honour of his father.[5] Not even Romans residing in the province were spared. Asserting that a certain Valeria, who died intestate, was under his guardianship, Flaccus diverted her property from her husband to a young relative of his own,[b] and when a speculator named Falcidius had paid a sum equivalent to thirty-seven and a half talents, apparently for the privilege of collecting the revenues of the city of Tralles, Flaccus extorted fifty talents from him as the price of his ratification of the transaction.[c]

These were among the charges brought against Flaccus when in 59, two years after his return from Asia, he was accused by a certain Decimus Laelius of extortion practised during his administration of the province. Laelius was a young man, and he was probably actuated more by the hope of gaining a reputation through a successful prosecution than by a genuine interest in justice. It is possible, too, that the trial was political in character and part of a plan to discredit all who had been active in the suppression of Catiline's conspiracy.[6] The evidence against Flaccus, moreover, was neither extensive nor weighty,

---

[a] Cicero *in Cat.* III 5f.; *pro Flacco* 102f.: Sallust *Cat.* 45f.
[b] Cicero *pro Flacco* 84f. [c] *Pro Flacco* 90f.; see Chap. X note 53.

for, with the exception of Tralles, the cities which gave adverse testimony were of little importance and were represented by citizens whose standing—if we may believe the counsel for the defence—was none too high. Nevertheless, the fact that Cicero, in attempting to refute the charges, was forced to resort to evasions, coupled with heavy sarcasm, and, by accusing the Asianic witnesses of mendacity, to adopt the expedient of appealing to national prejudice, inevitably leads to the suspicion that Flaccus was far from innocent.[d] His acquittal was clearly due rather to the skill of his advocates than to the strength of his case.[7]

In the year in which Flaccus was brought to trial, a new law was carried by Julius Caesar which was designed to restrain corruption on the part of public officials with special reference to those stationed in the provinces.[8] This measure—the *Lex Julia* concerning restitution—applied to "all moneys received by anyone holding a magistracy or a position of power or responsibility or the post of legate or any other public charge or office or by any member of his staff." Its provisions were extensive and at the same time specific. A public official might not receive money from any person except from certain designated relatives. He was expressly forbidden to accept gifts in administering justice or in approving public contracts or in arranging for requisitions of grain, under penalty of a fourfold restitution—which might be claimed from his heirs or other assigns—and the loss of his senatorial rank. Time-limits were imposed on missions involving travel at the public expense, and no one, while on an official journey, might accept anything from the inhabitants of the country save shelter, firewood and salt, hay for his animals and perhaps a limited amount of rations. With a view, presumably, to preventing provincial governors from lending their services—doubtless in return for a financial consideration—to outsiders, a provision contained in a previous law of Sulla's was re-enacted, and a governor was forbidden, without authorization by the Senate, to enter a foreign kingdom, to wage war or, in fact, to leave his province for any reason. He must, moreover, at the expiration of his term of office, deposit copies of his accounts in two of the principal provincial cities as well as a copy in the Treasury at Rome. The passage of this law by the public Assembly may perhaps have resulted from the exposure of the evils which the trial of Flaccus revealed, but however much a conscientious official, like Cicero, might comply with its provisions, it did not put an end to the practice of extortion.

[d] Macrobius *Sat.* II 1, 13.

It was unfortunate for Flaccus that the year of his governorship of Asia was a time of financial stringency. The economic situation, in fact, seems for some time previously to have been none too good. It has been suggested that a law carried, probably as far back as 67 B.C.— the year of Pompey's victory over the pirates—by Aulus Gabinius which forbad loans to provincial cities was intended, at least in part, to check the flow of money from Italy; and it may have been no mere coincidence that in Asia in this year a saving of silver was effected when the issuing of cistophori in Ephesus—the last city to continue the minting of these coins—was brought to an end.[9] But whatever the purpose of the law and the effort to save silver, the situation was not improved, for in 63 B.C. Catiline, in his campaign for the consulship, offered as part of his programme a general cancellation of debts.

It was necessary, accordingly, to take some steps to remedy the shortage of money, and in this same year the Senate, in the hope of conserving the existing supply of precious metals, prohibited the exportation of all gold and silver from Italy.[e] This measure, adopted in the year preceding Flaccus's governorship, may well have been the cause of an action taken by him in Asia, which brought him no little ill-will.[10] It was customary for the Jews of the province, like their co-religionists in all other lands, to make annual contributions, consisting of two drachmae for each member of their body, toward the expenses of their Temple. In Asia, at least, their payments were converted into gold before they were sent to Jerusalem. The exportation of this money was forbidden by Flaccus's command, and the gold—apparently exceeding two hundred pounds in weight—which had been already collected in four cities of the province for shipment to Judaea was seized by his agents.[11] He then sent it to Rome to be deposited in the public Treasury, thus aiding in the desired conservation of bullion.

The successor of Flaccus in office was Quintus Cicero, the younger brother of the orator, who governed Asia for three years—a term, as far as we know, of unprecedented length.[12] A treatise on the art of governing a province, which purports to be a letter to him from his brother written at the beginning of his third year in Asia, contains certain statements, which, if the document may be regarded as genuine and not the work of some moralizing rhetorician, yield some information concerning Quintus's career as governor.[13] The letter is largely composed of excellent, if somewhat obvious, precepts emphasizing the need of practising integrity and self-control; of using firmness tempered

[e] Cicero *pro Flacco* 67; *in Vat.* 12.

by kindness in the administration of justice; of reconciling the divergent interests of tax-farmers and tax-payers; and finally of restraining a violent temper. Wedged in among all this good advice is the information that under Quintus's administration the communities incurred no new debts and many discharged those formerly incurred; that city-governments were brought under the control of the upper and more responsible classes; that taxes were imposed more equitably; that the communities were freed from the obligation of contributing money for the celebration of the aediles' spectacles at Rome;[f] that certain decayed cities, notably Samos and Halicarnassus, were rehabilitated; that brigandage had been abolished, particularly in Mysia, where it had been especially rife; and that law and order were established throughout the province.

More reliable, however, is the information that, while Quintus gained favour in the province by remitting that part of the ship-tax imposed by Flaccus which was to provide for rowers[g] and won the gratitude of the people of Magnesia-near-Sipylus by withstanding the demands of a certain Lucius Sestius Pansa, he made many enemies among the provincials as well as among the resident Romans.[14] Described by his brother as affable and agreeable but with a disposition quick both to take offense and to forgive,[h] Quintus had, in fact, a violent temper and a bitter tongue, and in punishing he was ruthlessly severe.[i] He threatened, although perhaps only in jest, two Roman citizens—one of them a man of Equestrian rank—with burning alive. He also caused two men from Mysia, probably parricides, to be sewn up in a sack, a punishment which he likewise wished to inflict on a certain Zeuxis of Blaundus, who was convicted of murdering his mother. So many complaints of Quintus's severity were brought to Rome both by Romans and by natives that his brother deemed it necessary to placate the complainants by every means in his power. On the other hand, with that affability which formed the other side of his self-contradictory character, Quintus was over-complaisant in granting requests for official orders, even in cases where the facts did not warrant the action.

Among other reasons why Marcus Cicero wished his brother to establish a good record in Asia was the fear that a reputation for violence might cause him to be compared unfavourably with his presumptive

f Subsequently forbidden by Marcus Cicero in Cilicia (see note 49).
g Cicero pro Flacco 33.   h Epist. ad Att. 1 17, 2.
i Cicero Epist. ad Quint. Fr. 1 2, 4f.

successor, who—although he lacked certain of Quintus's qualities—was regarded as a "mild-mannered" man.[15] This successor was Titus Ampius Balbus, who had been an adherent of Pompey's and when tribune of the Plebs in 63 had collaborated in enacting a measure permitting Pompey to wear a gold wreath at the public games.[j] On his return to Rome from Asia in 57, Balbus was succeeded in the province by Gaius Fabius, who was followed in 56 by Gaius Septimius.[16] His successor was Gaius Claudius Pulcher, a member of one of the most distinguished families of Rome and the older brother of Publius Clodius, Caesar's political henchman and Cicero's enemy. He was governor for a second year, but the suggestion of Cicero that he remained because of the entreaties of the entire province, "prevailed upon to do so by the business-men and the tax-farmers and by all the provincials and the Roman citizens,"[k] sounds highly ironical in view of the fact that after his return he was convicted of extortion—and this in spite of having entered into collusion with his accuser by means of a large bribe.[17]

As was probably to be expected, most of the men who governed the province of Asia during this period were bound to the cause of the political group known to history as the First Triumvirate, whose power was shown by their provincial appointments, as well as by their legislation in Rome. Not only was Balbus devoted to Pompey's interests and favoured by him in return, but both Quintus Cicero and Fabius became legates of Caesar and fought under his leadership during his war in Gaul, where it so happened that Fabius took part in rescuing Quintus when besieged by the enemy. Even Flaccus, in spite of Cicero's insinuations that the Triumvirs were supporting his prosecution, was appointed legate by Caesar's father-in-law Piso when governor of Macedonia.[l]

Another supporter of the Triumvirs was Publius Cornelius Lentulus Spinther, who had obtained his consulship in 57 by the aid of Caesar and with it an appointment as governor of Cilicia. This province, it will be remembered, had been greatly increased in size when Pompey added the fertile Cilician plain and perhaps the district of Lycaonia also.[m] Now, under Lentulus, it was still further increased by the incorporation in it of the districts of Phrygia and Cibyratis, consisting of the three judiciary dioceses of Laodiceia-Cibyra, Apameia and Synnada,

[j] Velleius Paterculus II 40, 4. See also Cicero *Epist. ad Fam.* VI 12, 4.
[k] Cicero *pro Scauro* 35.　　　[l] See note 7.　　　[m] See above p. 376.

which had hitherto been part of the province of Asia.[18] By the addition of this territory—extending from the southern watershed of the Sangarius on the north to the frontier of Pisidia on the south and as far west as the upper reaches of the Tembris and the junction of the Maeander and the Lycus—the province of Cilicia was nearly doubled in size.[19] It was now not only the most extensive of the eastern provinces, but, occupying a large part of central Asia Minor between the districts of the Aegean seaboard and the Euphrates frontier and containing a long section of the Southern Highway, it had a position of both commercial and military importance.[n]

Two years previously, Cilicia had received another addition, namely the island of Cyprus. Since the time of Ptolemy I, this island had been subject to the rule of the Egyptian kings, and repeated attempts of the Seleucids to capture it had been successfully repulsed. In 80, when the possessions of Ptolemy VIII Lathyrus were divided between his two illegitimate sons, the older, nicknamed "Auletes," succeeded to the throne of Egypt and Cyprus fell to the share of the younger.[20] The claims of these two princes, however, to their respective thrones were not over-secure, for there were many at Rome who asserted that the dominions of the royal house of Egypt had been bequeathed to the Roman People by the young men's cousin, Ptolemy Alexander II, who, as the protégé of Sulla, had ruled in 80 B.C. for the brief space of nineteen days. The question of the succession to Egypt was settled in 59, when Ptolemy Auletes paid Caesar and Pompey the sum of six thousand talents for a senatorial decree and a law which recognized him both as king and as friend and ally of Rome.[21] His brother in Cyprus, however, took no such precautions to secure his crown, and in 58 the Triumvirs, taking advantage of the alleged will of Ptolemy Alexander, decided to annex the island.[22] The principal reason for this step was probably the desire to complete the subjugation of the eastern Mediterranean, which the annexation of Cilicia and Syria had brought under Roman control, as well as to safeguard the sea-route to the latter province. An additional motive was doubtless the desire to possess the rich mines of copper, which were henceforth the property of the Roman state.[23] The pretext, however, was that the King had given aid to the pirates in their operations off the Cilician coast and that the annexation of Cyprus was necessary to the future security of the seas. Accordingly, a bill was carried by the Triumvirs' supporter, the tribune Publius Clodius (who, it was said, bore a grudge against Ptolemy for

[n] See R. Syme in *Anat. Stud. Buckler*, p. 302f.

contributing only a small amount to his ransom from the pirates), ordering that the rule of the King should be brought to an end and declaring that both his kingdom and his treasures were the property of Rome. The bill also provided that the act of seizure should be carried out by the Triumvirs' opponent, Marcus Cato, who was thus removed from the Capital. Seldom was a measure more high-handed or an act of robbery more flagrant. The Cypriots, however, were unable to resist, and the King, on hearing of the passage of the bill, committed suicide by taking poison. It is said that the sale of his property brought the sum of nearly seven thousand talents to the Roman Treasury. Cyprus itself was incorporated in the province of Cilicia. As regularly happened in the case of annexation, Roman business-men established themselves in the island.[24] An opportunity also was afforded to the capitalists of the City to lend money at exorbitant rates to needy communities, in one instance, at least, greatly to the sorrow of the community concerned.

The city of Salamis, on the eastern side of Cyprus, facing the Syrian coast, with a history that went back to the sixth century, was the most important of the Hellenic communities of the island. Under the Ptolemies it was subject to a royal prefect, but in the second century it had a local government of the usual Hellenic type, which remained in existence after Cyprus was annexed by the Romans.[25]

In 56 B.C., two years after this annexation, the Salaminians found it necessary to raise a loan.[26] Cato, during his stay in Cyprus, had been accompanied by his nephew, Marcus Junius Brutus,[o] at that time twenty-seven years old, a member of one of the most distinguished families of Rome and an ardent student of philosophy. Despite his family connexions and his studious tastes, Brutus was not unwilling to increase his wealth. The Salaminians, moreover, were officially under his and his uncle's protection.[27] Accordingly, when they needed funds, he was ready to arrange for a loan. Such a loan, to be sure, was illegal, for the Gabinian Law of 67 forbad the lending of money to provincials.[p] Brutus's friends in the Senate, however, found a remedy for this difficulty, and a special decree was passed which provided that, in the event of a loan to the Salaminians, neither they nor the lenders should be liable to punishment under the Gabinian Law.[28] But since by the terms of this measure the amount of any bond of indebtedness could not be recovered by application to a court, a second decree was passed, providing that this particular bond should be actionable. Brutus, ac-

o Plutarch *Brut.* 3; *Cat. Min.* 36.　　　　p See note 9.

cordingly, advanced the amount desired—at the lowest estimate nearly fifty-five talents. He himself, however, was careful to remain in the background, and the loan was made in the name of two agents, Scaptius and Matinius, who carried out all the details of the transaction. In view, perhaps, of the unusual circumstances which preceded the lending of the money, the bond called for compound interest at the rate of 48 per cent.[q]

The loan was made after Lentulus—shortly before the expiration of his consulship—had left Rome for Cilicia.[29] There is no reason to suppose that he was involved in the favour shown by the Senate to Brutus, of whose uncle, Marcus Cato, he, as a supporter of the Triumvirs, must have been a determined opponent. His government of the province, in fact, afterwards won commendation from Cicero.[r] During the first year of his administration, however, he appears to have been less concerned with the welfare of the provincials than with his hopes of restoring King Ptolemy Auletes of Egypt to the kingdom from which he had been driven by his much-oppressed subjects. The question of the restoration of this "ally" of Rome had been brought up in the Senate during Lentulus's consulship, and, as it was known that Ptolemy was prepared to pay liberally for the recovery of his throne, the mission to reinstate him was regarded as highly desirable. Devising a plan for securing it for himself, Lentulus had made a bid for Pompey's support by proposing a law, in conjunction with his fellow-consul, by which Pompey was vested with unlimited power over the grain-supply of the entire Empire for five years.[30] Popular gossip, to be sure, asserted that the purpose of conferring this post on Pompey was to forestall any desire on his part to restore the King, but, nevertheless, the proposal won Lentulus the support for which he had planned, and by decree of the Senate he received the coveted appointment.

Lentulus's hopes, however, were destined never to be fulfilled. After his departure for his province, some of Pompey's followers began to urge that the restoration of the King should be entrusted to their leader, and their action gave rise to the belief that he himself desired the mission. Pompey's enemies, on the other hand, headed by a certain Gaius Cato, a tribune of the Plebs, wishing to deprive him of the prestige and the profit which he would derive therefrom, determined to prevent the restoration altogether. Accordingly, they produced an oracle from the sacred Sibylline Books, which declared that if an

[q] For another loan at the rate see Chap. X note 45.
[r] *Epist. ad Fam.* XIII 48 (47 B.C.).

Egyptian king were aided with an army it would bring great danger on Rome. In order to keep Lentulus also from any action in the matter, Cato even proposed his recall from Cilicia. This proposal, to be sure, was unsuccessful, but Cato was able to bring about the passage of a decree forbidding a restoration by means of an armed force. Lentulus, accordingly, in spite of Cicero's advice—in which Pompey was said to concur—to reinstate the King in the hope that success would justify the action, dared take no steps in the matter. Ptolemy, nevertheless, recovered his kingdom; for later in the year Pompey's faithful supporter, Aulus Gabinius, now governor of Syria, tempted by an offer of ten thousand talents to disregard the oracle, led an army into Egypt, and in the spring of 55 he conducted the King triumphantly to Alexandria.[31]

Lentulus, greatly to his credit, returned from Cilicia a poor man.[s] His three years' stay in the province, however, brought him, if not pecuniary gain, at least some military glory; for he performed some exploit—not necessarily of importance—by which he obtained the title of Imperator and, eventually, a triumph. He seems also to have shown a commendable, although dangerous, firmness in restraining the tax-farmers.[t] Nevertheless, at least in the three dioceses transferred to Cilicia from Asia, the communities suffered so greatly from poverty or mismanagement that it proved difficult to collect the taxes levied in accordance with the contracts made in 58, and eight years later they were still in arrears.[u]

In the spring of 53 Lentulus was succeeded by Appius Claudius Pulcher, who eighteen years previously had been Lucullus's envoy to King Tigranes of Armenia.[v] He was a brother of the Gaius Pulcher who had just returned from the governorship of Asia. Like other members of noble Roman families, he showed to a marked degree the ignoble traits of vanity and cupidity. During his consulship in 54, an office which he held by the favour of the Triumvirs,[32] his reputation suffered in consequence of the exposure of a plan by which two of the candidates for the following year expected to purchase the help of Appius and his colleague in winning the election. Appius's self-assurance, however, enabled him to face the scandal imperturbably. He doubtless felt more secure because of his family-alliances, for he had married one of his daughters to Pompey's elder son and another to Marcus Brutus.[33]

---

[s] Cicero *Epist. ad Att.* VI 1, 23.   [t] Cicero *Epist. ad Fam.* I 9, 26.
[u] *Epist. ad Att.* VI 2, 5; *ad Fam.* II 13, 4.   [v] See above p. 338.

During the two years of Appius's administration the economic condition of the province of Cilicia, especially of the dioceses recently added to it, went from bad to worse.[34] The communities were unable to pay the current taxes and many owed arrears for the previous period.[w] In a desperate effort to raise money they sold all their revenues and imposed special levies, such as a poll-tax and a tax on house-doors, which proved a heavy burden.[35] Some, forced to borrow money at ruinous interest-rates, were crushed by their debts. In certain cases, it is true, their plight was due to the inefficiency and even the dishonesty of the local magistrates, who actually stole public funds.[x] In general, however, the desperate financial situation which Cicero found in 51—"the savagery of some cruel wild beast," as he called it—was the result of the demands made by Appius, who "gave the province treatment by the reducing-method and practiced blood-letting," with the result that he left it in a state of exhaustion.[y] One of the means which he used was the extortion of large sums of money from the richer communities as the price for refraining from quartering troops on them during the winter.[z] The cities of Cyprus alone paid 200 talents for such an exemption, and the Salaminians later declared that Cicero's refusal to take the perquisites which they had been accustomed to give to their governors would make it possible for them to discharge the amount—which they estimated at 106 talents—of their indebtedness to Brutus.[a]

Another source of great expense to the communities was the practice of sending envoys to Rome to convey resolutions in praise of a retiring governor. While not profitable to him financially, such delegations gratified his vanity, and were he threatened with prosecution for maladministration, their testimony might aid in refuting the charges against him. In spite of the cost which the sending of these delegations entailed upon the impoverished communities—the plight of which was all the more serious because of a wide-spread failure of the harvests of 51[b]—Appius, before he left the province, arranged that at least six of them should send envoys to the Senate to sound his praises.[36]

It was not only Appius himself, however, who was guilty of wrong done to the province. His subordinates, both civil and military, outdid their chief in plunder, insults, and licentiousness.[c] Among them was Marcus Brutus, who accompanied his father-in-law to the province

w See above p. 387.
x Epist. ad Att. VI 2, 5; ad Fam. III 8, 5.
y Epist. ad Att. V 16, 2 and VI 1, 2; see also V 15, 2 and 17, 6.
z Epist. ad Att. V 21, 7.
a Epist. ad Att. V 21, 11. See below p. 394.
b Epist. ad Att. V 21, 8.
c Epist. ad Att. VI 1, 2; ad Fam. III 8, 7.

in the capacity of quaestor.[37] His presence there made it possible for him to take more active measures for the recovery of the money owed him by the Salaminians.[d] Still keeping himself in the background, however, he persuaded Appius to appoint his agent Scaptius to the post of prefect of a body of cavalry, a command which enabled him to proceed more vigorously against the debtors. During a session of the city-council the prefect surrounded their chamber with his troopers and kept the unfortunate councillors imprisoned until five of them died of starvation. This act of brutality, however, accomplished nothing, and both principal and interest remained unpaid.

Not content with acquiring money, Appius wished also to gain glory as a soldier. Although to judge from his career, as far as we know it, he had had no military experience since his service in Lucullus's army, he succeeded in performing some warlike exploit by virtue of which he was able to assume the title of Imperator.[38] His management of his army, however, left much to be desired. It is true that the two legions stationed in Cilicia were depleted in strength and that Appius himself appreciated the need of additional men, especially as he considered that some of those in service should be discharged.[39] He had also to cope with a mutiny, which he succeeded in quelling, perhaps by giving the soldiers the arrears of their pay—for, with all his shortcomings as a governor, he paid the troops in full up to the time of his departure from the province. Nevertheless, in consequence of his lax methods, the army was disorganized and scattered, and for a time, at least, three cohorts disappeared entirely.[e] The situation was all the more serious because the provincials, weakened and embittered by the harshness of Roman rule and the wrongs inflicted upon them, were neither willing nor able to face an enemy.[f] In the event of a sudden need for additional troops, therefore, the governor must apply to the native kings for assistance.

Of these rulers, the most powerful were Deiotarus of Galatia and Ariobarzanes of Cappadocia. Deiotarus, appointed tetrarch of the Galatian Tolistobogii by Pompey and afterward made ruler also of part of Armenia Minor with the title of King,[g] was a faithful ally. He had an army consisting of 12,000 foot-soldiers armed in Roman fashion and 2,000 horse, equal in number to the force maintained by Rome in Cilicia.[h] In contrast to the veteran Deiotarus, the King of Cappadocia,

---

[d] See above p. 386.
[f] *Epist. ad Fam.* xv 1, 5.
[h] *Epist. ad Att.* v 18, 2; vi 1, 14.

[e] *Epist. ad Att.* v 14, 1; *ad Fam.* iii 6, 5; xv 4, 2.
[g] See above p. 373.

Ariobarzanes III, was a young man, who had recently ascended the throne. He was the grandson of that Ariobarzanes who had been the ally of Rome during three wars against Mithradates and who because of his fidelity had received from Pompey an addition to his kingdom.[i] On the old ruler's abdication in 62 his son, Ariobarzanes II, had become king.[40] He seems to have been beset by enemies, some of whom he succeeded in removing by bribing Aulus Gabinius, while on the way to Syria in 57, to put them to death. Nevertheless, he fell a victim to those who remained, and died a violent death, probably about 54, leaving his son the kingdom but little else besides.

Ariobarzanes III, in fact, had neither army nor money.[41] He was overwhelmed by debt, contracted perhaps by his grandfather or his father. His principal creditor was Pompey, to whom, by a special arrangement with Cicero, he later promised to make a monthly payment of thirty-three talents, although even this large sum did not meet the total interest on the debt. He also owed money to Brutus, but, in view of the size of his payments to Pompey, his less influential creditors had to be satisfied with whatever amounts they could obtain.

This legacy of misery and bankruptcy prevalent in the province of Cilicia under Appius fell to Marcus Cicero, when, much against his will, he assumed the governorship on the last day of July, 51 B.C.[j] Although he was evidently not wholly aware of the condition of the province, his formal "edict," or proclamation of the principles in accordance with which he intended to govern, drawn up, as was customary, before he left Italy, contained measures which, if enforced, would remedy at least some of the evils.

Many of the provisions of this edict were taken from the traditional body of principles used by Cicero's predecessors.[42] In particular, the edict of Scaevola, rightly regarded as one of Rome's greatest provincial governors, served as the model for a clause which granted to a community having a municipal government of the Hellenic type the right to conduct trials according to its own laws. Another clause taken from Scaevola provided that a business-contract should be invalid if it contained some provision by which it was impossible to abide honourably. One section of the edict was added later at the request of the tax-farmers, who met Cicero when, on his way to Asia Minor, he stopped on the island of Samos.[43] This, taken from the edict of Appius—whose professions, as often in political life, differed widely from his practice—dealt with the difficult problem of

---

i See above p. 375.   j *Epist. ad Att.* v 15, 1; *ad Fam.* xv 2, 1.

reducing the expenses of the local communities. Their relations with the *publicani*, accordingly, were included, as were also their budgets and their bonded indebtedness. Moreover, with a view to bettering their financial condition, a clause was inserted limiting interest-charges to 12 per cent; this was the rate which, twenty years earlier, Lucullus had established, probably temporarily, in the province of Asia, but with the difference that Cicero permitted interest to be compounded annually, whereas Lucullus had ordered that it should be simple.[44] Cicero's edict, furthermore, contained the usual provisions with regard to inheritances and sales of property, and—what was apparently less usual—the statement that in his decisions he would be guided by the edicts issued by the praetor in Rome.

From the very beginning Cicero showed a readiness to interest himself in the affairs of the provincials which seems to have presented a marked contrast to the practice of many governors. At all times he was accessible to their representatives. On his initial journey through the northern dioceses in August, 51, he received deputations from the various communities and listened to their grievances.[k] In the following February, establishing himself at Laodiceia, he spent two and a half months in hearing cases not only from these dioceses but also from the distant Pamphylia and Isauria.[l] Both in the Phrygian districts and in the Level Cilicia, especially in Tarsus, the capital, his rule, within six months of his arrival, won great admiration. The communities were pleased by his fulfilment of the promise contained in his edict that he would permit them to have their own courts—a privilege which made them think that they were indeed autonomous. The shortage of food, moreover, which was due to the failure of the harvests of 51, was alleviated when the governor appealed personally to those—both Romans and provincials—who had stored up supplies, and they, yielding to his persuasion, agreed to share what they had with their fellow-townsmen. Most important of all was the great improvement in the financial condition of the communities of the northern dioceses—where the situation had been especially bad—; many were now entirely free from their indebtedness and others were relieved to a large extent from their burdens.

Economy and integrity were, indeed, the watchwords of Cicero's administration. That his government was not causing the province a farthing was his repeated boast.[45] He had successfully impressed upon

[k] *Epist. ad Att.* v 16, 2; *ad Fam.* iii 8, 5f.; xv 4, 2.
[l] *Epist. ad Att.* v 21, 7f.; vi 1, 15; 2, 4f.; Plutarch *Cic.* 36, 3. See also Larsen in *C.P.* xliii (1948), p. 187f.

his legates—his brother Quintus and three others—that they must practise a like restraint.[46] Only once did one of them offend by taking some food for the day's needs, as indeed may have been permissible under the Julian Law.[m] Cicero himself, on his journey through the province, did not even accept hay, which this law did allow to a governor when travelling, or firewood or anything except a lodging and four beds, and, in fact, he and his staff often used a tent—all to the amazement of the provincials.[n] He doubtless caused astonishment also by his refusal to permit any community to erect a statue or a chariot or a shrine in his honour.[o]

It was not, however, merely a matter of the integrity of the governor and his staff. The improvement in the condition of the bankrupt communities which Cicero found in the spring of 50 was due entirely to his personal interposition. On learning that one cause of the evil was the peculation committed by local magistrates, he conducted an examination of the men who had held office for the past ten years and persuaded the guilty to confess and, on receiving promises of pardon for their offences, even to make restitution to their communities.[p] In those towns where he found that the local taxes were intolerable he issued an order that none should be levied until an investigation had shown that it was necessary and he had given his official sanction.[q] When several communities asked to be freed from the burden of sending delegations to Rome to eulogize his predecessor, Cicero advised strongly against this practice and even forbad them to send the envoys without his express approval.[47] Great relief also was given by his forbearance in refraining from the demand, made by previous governors, that the cities should pay heavily for exemption from the quartering of troops.[r]

It was difficult to gain the favour of both the provincials and the tax-farmers. Nevertheless, Cicero accomplished it. On his arrival in his province, he found that the sub-contracts between the *publicani* and the communities had already been drawn up, a fact which made it possible for him to avoid offending either side.[s] There was, however, the question of the arrears not only for the current tax-period but for the previous one as well. As a remedy Cicero adopted the principle that these arrears, if paid before a certain day, were subject to the interest-charge of 12 per cent specified in his edict, but if not so

[m] *Epist. ad Att.* v 21, 5 (*pransitans*, see note 8).
[n] *Epist. ad Att.* v 16, 3.
[o] *Epist. ad Att.* v 21, 7.
[p] *Epist. ad Att.* vi 2, 5: Plutarch *Cic.* 36, 4.
[q] *Epist. ad Fam.* iii 7, 2f.
[r] See above p. 388.
[s] *Epist. ad Att.* v 13, 1; 14, 1.

paid, to the rate named in the contract, however high that might be.[t] By this measure, combined with the relief from burdensome requisitions and the economy forced upon the communities, he was successful in collecting large amounts of unpaid taxes, greatly to the satisfaction of the *publicani*, who regarded him, so he himself wrote, as "the apple of their eye."

This policy of honesty and economy was carried out only in the face of protest and petition from men influential in Rome. Appius Claudius was aggrieved at the encouragement given to the cities to withhold their delegations.[u] He also protested against the prohibition to impose new levies, angry because the citizens of the Phrygian town of Appia were thereby prevented from constructing a certain building in the erection of which he was for some reason interested.[v] Pompey and Aulus Torquatus, whom Cicero greatly respected, wishing to protect their business-interests in Cilicia, presented requests for the appointment of their agents to military prefectures, and it was necessary for Cicero to inform them that he had made it a rule to refuse a military command to any man engaged in business in his province.[48]

It became necessary also to refuse appeals from personal friends. One of these, Marcus Caelius Rufus, had made an arrangement, or so he supposed, whereby some of the communities were to contribute money toward the cost of the spectacles he planned to give as aedile; these contributions Cicero felt it his duty to forbid.[49] Caelius, moreover, with a view to presenting a wild-beast hunt in connexion with his spectacles, importuned Cicero repeatedly for a gift of panthers from the mountains of Cibyratis, a request which the governor refused to fulfil on the ground that an official panther-hunt in his province would not conduce to his reputation.[50]

A further request was made by Caelius on behalf of a friend, namely, that the revenues from the lands of certain communities which this man, a member of the Equestrian Order, had bought up should be declared exempt from taxes.[51] Caelius urged that such a procedure would be "easy and honest," but although Cicero's action in the matter is unknown, it seems improbable that he granted the exemption. From Syria came a request from the acting quaestor of the province, Sallustius, who asked for a loan of 100,000 drachmae, whether for himself or someone else is not stated, to be taken, apparently, from the proceeds derived from the sale of the booty obtained

[t] *Epist. ad Att.* VI 1, 16; 2, 5; 3, 3; *ad Fam.* II 13, 4.
[u] See note 47.
[v] *Epist. ad Fam.* III 7, 2f.; 9, 1.

from the enemy during Cicero's one military campaign.[52] The reply, however, was that, as the soldiers' share was being managed by their prefects and Cicero's by the quaestor, there was no money to lend. Even the members of his own staff hoped to divide among themselves the surplus of one million sesterces which remained from the appropriation allowed for the year's expenses; and when Cicero, who carried out conscientiously the provisions of the Julian Law ordering a retiring governor to deposit copies of his accounts in two cities of the province, returned this balance to the Treasury in Rome, it was regarded as a real grievance.[53]

The strongest pressure, however, came from Brutus; it was exerted not only directly but also through Cicero's closest friend, Atticus. Brutus was, of course, chiefly concerned with the debt owed him by Salamis.[w] The outrage which Scaptius's cavalry had perpetrated on the city-councillors was related to Cicero with great emotion by a delegation of the leading men of Cyprus, who were waiting to meet him on his arrival in Asia. In answer to their plea and without any knowledge as to who was actually responsible, he ordered the troopers to leave the island at once, and the grateful Salaminians extolled him to the skies. During the following winter, however, he was approached by Scaptius, who, presenting a letter of recommendation from Brutus, asked for aid in recovering the money owed by the Salaminians, a favour which for Brutus's sake Cicero promised to grant. But when Scaptius made the further request for reappointment to his post as prefect of cavalry, Cicero refused outright, reminding him of the rule that no military command should be given to a business-man in his province. At the same time he reassured him with regard to the collection of the debt and presently summoned the representatives of Salamis to Tarsus. On ordering them to discharge their indebtedness, he was told, apparently to his surprise, that they could easily do so, since what they owed Scaptius was, in fact, less than the amount of the perquisites usually given to their governor.[x] But when, at Cicero's bidding, they and Scaptius proceeded separately to calculate the sum that was actually owed, their estimate proved to be 106 talents, while that of Scaptius was 200, an amount which horrified Cicero, for the payment of so much money would mean financial ruin for the city. The difference between the two estimates arose from the fact that the Salaminians calculated the interest due at 12 per cent compounded annually, as specified in Cicero's edict, whereas Scaptius demanded 48, according to the terms of the original bond. When Cicero pointed out that so high an interest-charge could not be demanded under his edict, Scaptius produced a copy of the decrees of the Senate validating the original contract. He also showed a letter from Brutus, from which Cicero learned for the first time who the real creditor was. The dilemma was a difficult one. The outrageous contract had been validated by the Senate and would be hard to annul. Moreover, Cicero was reluctant to incur the enmity of Brutus as well as that of his uncle, Cato. At the same time, he was unwilling to abandon the principle he had laid down in his edict. He took refuge, accordingly, in a makeshift that was none too creditable. Although the Salaminians offered to deposit the amount of their debt, as they computed it, in a temple—where it would be available for the creditor at any time, while they would be freed from all further payment of interest—he forbad them to do so and at Scaptius's request asked them to leave the matter as it stood. His action in so doing was all the less praiseworthy as he was fully aware of what might happen to the Salaminians under his successor, especially if, as seemed to him probable, that successor should be Lucius Paullus, whose brother had married Brutus's half-sister.[54]

Brutus was also concerned over the debt owed him by King Ario-barzanes,[y] but, in this case, with less dire results to the debtor. In fact, it was essential that the King should be maintained on his throne. Consequently, Cicero, before leaving Rome, was charged by the Senate, acting on Cato's motion, with the duty of protecting the King, whose safety, so the decree read, was a matter of great concern to the Senate and People.[55] Ariobarzanes, in fact, was in greater danger than had been supposed. Cicero, soon after his arrival in the province, was told by the young monarch of a conspiracy which he had just detected. His mother, Athenais, he said, after driving his father's counsellors into exile, had formed a plot to dethrone him in favour of her younger son, Ariarathes. She had the support, it seemed, of the Priest of the Temple at Comana, who, ranking in importance next to the King,[z] was well provided with both followers and money. The story was confirmed by Ariarathes himself, who, although he had not been ignorant of the plot, now accompanied the King to the interview and protested vehemently that never while his brother was alive would he accept the throne. The conspiracy seems to have been easily suppressed. Cicero, having restored the exiled counsellors and, according to his own statement, persuaded the Priest to leave Cappadocia, established

Ariobarzanes in his kingdom. He gave the young monarch some good advice but not the Roman troops for which he asked.

Mindful of Brutus's interests, Cicero laboured with Ariobarzanes to obtain the payment of at least a part of his indebtedness.[a] In addition to pleading by letter, he even went so far as to appoint two agents of Brutus, another Scaptius and a certain Gavius, to the command of some Roman soldiers stationed within the frontiers of the kingdom, appointments which did not violate the rule he had established, since they were not in his own province. Ariobarzanes was also approached by Deiotarus, acting in Brutus's behalf. But the Cappadocian King had nothing in his treasury and few sources of revenue. Pompey's claims outweighed all others, and the tribute which Ariobarzanes wrung from his subjects scarcely sufficed to meet the monthly payments of interest. Nevertheless, before the end of his term of office Cicero succeeded in obtaining for Brutus the comparatively large sum of about a hundred talents as one year's payment, which, he wrote proudly, was at least larger in proportion to the loan than the amount promised to Pompey, namely, two hundred talents for a period of six months.

A matter much more serious than the debts owed to influential Romans was the threat of an invasion by the Parthians.[56] Their defeat of Marcus Crassus in the early summer of 53 and the slaughter of a large part of his army had caused the Romans to regard them as a source of great danger. Consequently, when, a month after his arrival in the province, Cicero was informed by messengers from King Antiochus of Commagene that a large Parthian force was about to cross the Euphrates, he could not but feel alarmed for the general safety.[57] Some remnants of Crassus's army, which Gaius Cassius Longinus, quaestor of the defeated general, had collected in Antioch, appeared unable to repel an invasion of such magnitude, even though in 52 Cassius had succeeded in driving back some Parthians who had crossed over into Syria.[58] The Roman force in Cilicia, consisting of two undermanned and disorganized legions and about 2,600 horsemen, was wholly inadequate;[59] and, although Deiotarus offered to contribute all his forces, thereby doubling the troops in the province,[b] even their strength could afford little assistance in resisting so dreaded a foe.

The largest part of the scattered and disorganized army was encamped outside Iconium, and Cicero, travelling through the province, had reached this place when the news of the Parthian invasion arrived.

[a] *Epist. ad Att.* VI 1, 3f.; 2, 7; 3, 5.
[b] *Epist. ad Att.* V 18, 2; *ad Fam.* XV 1, 6; 2, 2; 4, 5.

He had had no military experience and knew nothing of warfare, but his legates, Quintus Cicero and Pomptinus, had both served in Gaul, and Anneius also had apparently commanded troops. At first there was doubt whether the enemy would cross the Euphrates into Syria or join forces with Artavasdes, the king of Armenia, whose sister was married to Pacorus, son of the Parthian king, and, in conjunction with him, invade Cappadocia.[60] It was necessary, therefore, to provide for either contingency. Cicero, accordingly, presumably acting on the advice of his legates, collected the various detachments of his army, enlisted additional troops from among the Roman citizens in the province as well as from the natives, and gathered in all the available grain.[61] He planned to take up a strategic position at Cybistra, north of the Taurus and just within the border of Cappadocia,[c] a place which commanded the two main routes leading, respectively, southeastward through the Cilician Gates and northeastward through Cappadocia to the Euphrates. But in approaching the place, he received further news, this time from Tarcondimotus, whom Pompey had made ruler over part of the mountain region of the Amanus,[d] and Iamblichus, an allied Syrian chieftain. According to these despatches, a large Parthian army, under the leadership of Pacorus, had actually crossed the Euphrates into the northernmost district of Syria, adjoining the Level Cilicia on the east. All danger of an invasion through Cappadocia being thus removed, Cicero led his forces across the Taurus, ready to defend Cilicia against the enemy.

In little over a fortnight after leaving Cybistra, Cicero and his army arrived at the range of Amanus, which separated his province from Syria.[62] Before his arrival some Parthian horsemen, who had ridden over into Cilicia, were attacked and killed by a troop of Roman cavalry and a cohort in garrison at Epiphaneia in the southeastern corner of the province.[e] But meanwhile a greater victory had been won in Syria. The Parthians had advanced as far as Antioch but, falling back again, had been caught in a trap by Cassius and badly defeated, and Osaces, their commander—for Pacorus's command was merely nominal—had been mortally wounded.[63] Their army, however, remained on the Roman side of the Euphrates, and a further attack in the following spring seemed highly probable.[f]

Cicero, however, was not to be balked of military laurels. The tribesmen who lived in the Amanus a day's march east of Epiphaneia had

c See above p. 375.   d See above p. 377.   e *Epist. ad Fam.* xv 4, 7.
f *Epist. ad Fam.* ii 10, 4; *ad Att.* v 21, 2; vi 1, 14.

397

never submitted to Rome and could therefore be regarded as "eternal enemies." Within three days of his arrival at the mountain-range, Cicero invaded their territory in a night-attack.[64] His army under the four legates, catching the mountaineers off their guard, killed a considerable number and took many prisoners. Several village-strongholds —one of them having even the "appearance of a city"—were captured and burned. After this campaign, which lasted from dawn until the late afternoon, the army withdrew triumphantly to Issus on the sea-coast, where it encamped on a site once used by Alexander, and at a place called Alexander's Altars the new victor was hailed as Imperator.[65]

Meanwhile the army plundered the nearest part of the Amanus region, but the commander was not yet satisfied. A week after his victory he advanced against the "Free Cilicians," a vigorous mountain-folk who had never been wholly subject, even to the Seleucids. The exact situation of their country is uncertain, but it may have lain somewhat north of the region just conquered, perhaps not far from the route which led across the Amanus from Cilicia into northern Syria.[66] These people had a capital, Pindenissus, in a strong position on a well-fortified height. They had received some fugitives and were thought to be in sympathy with the Parthians. Cicero, accordingly, under the plea that to put a check on their audacity would enhance the reputation of Rome, laid siege to their town. All the paraphernalia used in ancient siege-operations were brought into play—an encircling wall and ditch, six redoubts, a mound, mantlets, towers and engines both for hurling stones and for discharging arrows. Against all this array Pindenissus held out for fifty-six days, but finally it was forced to capitulate—as it chanced, on the first day of the festival of the Saturnalia. The town was destroyed and the booty presented to the soldiers, but the captives were sold off as slaves, the proceeds from the sale amounting to over 12,000,000 sesterces. As the campaigning-season was now over, the army took up winter-quarters in the newly-subdued area, Quintus Cicero being placed in command.[g]

An administration characterized by such honesty and uprightness as Cicero's, if by no means unique, was at least rare under the Roman Republic. Yet, with all his refusal to reap profit unrighteously, he amassed by legal means the large sum of 2,200,000 sesterces, which, on leaving Asia Minor, he deposited in the form of silver cistophori in

g *Epist. ad Att.* v 20, 5; 21, 6; *ad Fam.* xv 4, 10.

the tax-farmers' bank at Ephesus.[h] High-minded though he was, he yielded to pressure from men of importance in Rome—perhaps to the consideration that they might be of use to him in obtaining the recognition he coveted—even though it meant the financial ruin of a community; and he could not withstand the temptation to win a paltry military title and cheap military glory, whatever the cost might be in human life and suffering. Although conscientious in the fulfilment of his duties, he showed no hesitation—in fact, the utmost impatience—in departing from his province before the appointment of a successor and on the very day when his year's term expired, leaving as his substitute, not his brother Quintus, who, he felt, could not be asked to take charge of the province, but a quaestor, newly arrived, young and without experience, even frivolous, perhaps, and lacking in self-restraint.[67]

During Cicero's term in Cilicia, the province of Asia was governed by Quintus Minucius Thermus, an honourable man, according to Cicero, and deserving of praise.[i] He was gracious in consenting to further Atticus's interests, and Cicero's relations with him were so cordial that while proconsul he recommended to Thermus's care four different men who had business in Asia. His colleague, Publius Silius, the governor of Bithynia-Pontus, Cicero likewise held in high esteem, and on at least five occasions he asked him to protect the interests of Italian business-men.[j]

The province of Bithynia, in fact, had rapidly fallen into the hands of exploiters from Rome. It has already been noted that the activities of the tax-farmers, who descended upon the country immediately after it became a Roman province, caused the inhabitants to welcome Mithradates when, in 73 B.C., he invaded western Asia Minor.[k] Ten years later we hear of them particularly as exploiting the territory which had formerly been the property of the kings but now belonged to the Roman People.[l] A year afterward, as has been already related,[m] the province was greatly increased by Pompey, who attached to it the former kingdom of Pontus, thus giving further scope for the activities of Roman financiers.

One of the early governors of the enlarged province was Gaius

---

[h] *Epist. ad Att.* XI 1, 2; 2, 3; *ad Fam.* V 20, 9.

[i] *Epist. ad Att.* VI 1, 13. For Cicero's relations with him see also *ad Att.* V 13, 2; 20, 10; 21, 14; *ad Fam.* II 18; XIII 53-57.

[j] *Epist. ad Att.* VI 1, 13; *ad Fam.* VII 21; XIII 61-65.

[k] See above p. 325.

[l] Cicero *de Leg. Agr.* II 40 and 50; see also Chap. XV note 34.

[m] See above p. 369.

Papirius Carbo, the successful prosecutor of Marcus Cotta, notorious for his sack of Heracleia.[n] His term of office, beginning in 61, the year of Pompey's return from the East, lasted for at least two years.[68] With regard to his administration we know only that, presumably finding a shortage of currency of low denominations, he encouraged the communities to issue copper coins, and as many as eight separate places responded with coins bearing his name. Nevertheless, at least some of his actions rendered him liable to prosecution, for on his return from Bithynia he was charged with dishonesty in the province.[o] The accuser, to be sure, was Cotta's youthful son, but his action in bringing Carbo to trial seems to have been more than a mere attempt to take vengeance, for the defendant was convicted of the charge.

Carbo was followed—although not immediately—by Gaius Memmius, governor in 57, and he, in turn, by Gaius Caecilius Cornutus in 56.[69] Memmius, "versed in letters, but only Greek, and scornful of Latin,"[p] and famous for the bitterness of his speeches against Julius Caesar,[q] took with him to Bithynia as members of his staff two young poets of the new school, Catullus and Cinna. The former had only scorn for the province, because there was nothing there "for natives, governor or staff,"[r] a jibe which, perhaps, is a tribute to the governor's honesty. Memmius won some military success, in consequence of which he took the title of Imperator,[70] but his chief claim to fame lies in the dedication to him of Lucretius's great poem *On the Nature of Things*.

During this period the Roman money-lenders were active in Bithynia, as elsewhere. Under the administration of Cicero's acquaintance, Publius Silius, a certain Pinnius lent 8,000,000 sesterces to the city of Nicaea, and a Marcus Laenius, presumably the man who represented Torquatus's interests in Cilicia, had "business" in Bithynia which, we may infer, also had to do with the lending of money.[71] Even members of the Roman aristocracy seem to have had interests there, for the young Tiberius Claudius Nero—father of the later Emperor Tiberius—had "bodies of clients" in the province whom he hoped, with the support of the governor, to attach more closely to himself. The *publicani* also continued their activities. In 51 the deputy-manager of the company which farmed the pasture-tax, apparently experiencing difficulty in

[n] See above p. 341.
[o] Valerius Maximus v 4, 4: Cassius Dio xxxvi 40, 4.
[p] Cicero *Brutus* 247.
[q] Suetonius *Jul.* 23, 1; 49, 2; 73: *Scholia Bob.* pp. 130 and 146 Stangl.
[r] Catullus 10, 9f.

drawing up agreements with some of the communities, secured the interest of Cicero with the governor of the province.[s] The "Bithynian Corporation," moreover, was so large and influential that it could be described as a "very great factor" in the Roman state, important both because of its position and because of the kind of men who held its shares.[72]

Meanwhile the Parthians were still regarded as dangerous, and during the early summer of 50 Cicero and his troops remained in camp on the river Pyramus in eastern Cilicia, prepared to repel an invasion.[t] In Syria, Antioch was closely invested and the governor, Bibulus, did not dare make a sally against the enemy.[73] Then suddenly, during the first half of July, by "incredible good fortune," as Cicero described it, the Parthian army retired from Syria, recalled by the King, apparently because of the threat of a revolt, in which even his son seems to have been involved.

The invasion of the Parthians, although in itself it came to nothing, was of the greatest importance by reason of its effects on the political situation in Rome and the struggle which this ultimately brought to pass. As early as the autumn of 51 various proposals were made for meeting the danger,[u] and the supporters both of Pompey and of Caesar attempted to secure for their respective leaders the command of an army to be sent to the East. It was generally expected in Asia that Pompey would receive the appointment and this was his expectation also;[v] but after months of discussion the only decision reached by the Senate was the order that each of the two leaders should detach one legion from his army for service against the enemy.[74] This order was utilized by Pompey to demand the return of a legion which he had lent to Caesar two years previously; he, accordingly, lost no troops through the transaction, while two legions were taken from Caesar.

The retirement of the Parthians put an end, for the present, to any plan for sending an army to the East; but the ill-feeling caused by the withdrawal of the two legions from Caesar served to loosen further the already weakened tie between the two leaders. For some time Pompey, increasingly jealous of his associate's growing prestige, had been seeking a means to undermine Caesar's position. Now, by attaching himself more and more closely to his rival's enemies, he became

[s] *Epist. ad Fam.* XIII 65.
[t] *Epist. ad Fam.* II 13, 4; 19, 1; III 11, 1 (May-June, 50).
[u] *Epist. ad Fam.* VIII 10, 2 (17 Nov. 51).
[v] *Epist. ad Att.* VI 1, 3 and 14 (Feb. 50).

their most powerful instrument in their manoeuvres to effect Caesar's ruin by forcing him out of his governorship of the Gallic provinces and, by means of some trumped-up charge, sending him into banishment before he could carry out his expectation of securing the election to the consulship for the following year. The plan miscarried, for Caesar, after various offers with a view to compromise, decided to oppose legalized violence with physical force, and on the 11th of January, 49, he led his army across the Rubicon. The die was cast.

During the ensuing Civil War the actual fighting came no closer to Asia Minor than southern Thessaly. The effects of the war, however, were felt throughout the eastern provinces. In the course of the nine and a half months which elapsed between the time when Pompey, abandoning Italy, set sail across the Adriatic and the landing of Caesar in Epirus, the man-power of the East was mobilized to defend the cause of its former organizer.[75] Although the peoples of the Hellenic world were in no way responsible for this conflict between two Roman leaders and derived no benefit from it, they were expected to bear a large part of the cost. But to many of them the conqueror of Mithradates was still a hero, and when he issued a call for assistance, Greece and the islands, Asia Minor and Syria responded to his demands.

In the province of Asia, where Gaius Fannius, an adherent of Pompey, was governor and Lucius Antonius, youngest brother of the later Triumvir, proquaestor, soldiers were enlisted from among the Roman citizens—tax-gatherers, land-owners, bankers and other business-men—by Lucius Lentulus Crus, one of the Consuls of the year, aided by Titus Ampius Balbus, once governor of the province.[76] So vigorous and so successful were Lentulus's efforts that he was able to raise two legions. During this year, and perhaps in connexion with this enlistment of soldiers, the three Phrygian dioceses were retransferred from Cilicia to the province of Asia.[77]

Troops were mobilized in the other provinces also. In Cilicia, the two skeleton legions which Cicero had commanded were combined into one of full strength, and in Syria, Quintus Metellus Scipio, the father of Pompey's latest wife, took over the soldiers who had served under Cassius and Bibulus.[w] The client-kings, too, who owed their thrones to Pompey, were ordered to furnish troops, and there was none who failed to respond.[78] Deiotarus of Galatia came in person with six hundred horsemen, Ariobarzanes of Cappadocia sent five hundred, and Antiochus of Commagene two hundred, many of them mounted

[w] Caesar *Bell. Civ.* III 4; Appian *B.C.* II 49.

archers. The two Galatian chieftains, Castor Tarcondarius and Dom-nilaus (or Domnecleius), together furnished three hundred soldiers,[x] and Tarcondimotus, ruler in the region of Mt. Amanus, supplied timber for ships.

Every effort, in fact, was made to collect a fleet, and the cities along the coasts of Asia Minor from Pontus to Cilicia, as well as those of the islands, above all the Rhodians, whom Cato had persuaded to take up Pompey's cause, were ordered to furnish whatever ships they had and to build a further supply.[79] Ready money, too, was demanded, especially from the inland cities, which could not provide ships. The princes also were ordered to contribute, and the tax-farmers were forced to turn over to Pompey's subordinates whatever funds they had on hand.[y] This means of raising money was used with especial rigour in Syria, where Metellus Scipio, not satisfied with the arrears owed by the *publicani* for the previous two years, forced them to advance the expected amount of the taxes for the current year as well.[z]

Scipio, indeed, appears to have been ready to oppress the provinces in every way possible. After winning some sort of victory over the tribesmen of Mt. Amanus, who had furnished Cicero with easily-gained laurels, he also assumed the title of Imperator.[80] He then led his army to Asia, where he established himself in Pergamum for the winter of 49-48, quartering his soldiers in the various cities of the province and, in order, probably, to meet current expenses, issuing silver cistophori bearing his own name. The inscription from a statue erected to him by the Pergamene people calls him "Saviour and Benefactor," a title which accords so ill with the account of his actions in Asia given by Caesar[a] that we must suppose either that it was given to him out of fear rather than gratitude or that he has been much traduced by his opponent. According to Caesar's narrative, certainly far from impartial and probably over-coloured, Scipio bled the province of Asia without mercy or restraint. The groups of Roman citizens and the Hellenic communities were alike forced to pay fixed sums, farcically called loans authorized by a decree of the Senate. The money was raised, as in Cilicia under Appius Claudius,[b] by poll-taxes, imposed on both free men and slaves, and by taxes on house-doors and on porticos. Requisitions of grain and arms were made, and there was a conscription of soldiers and sailors and even of labour for trans-portation. The tax-farmers, whose current income had already been

x See Chap. XV note 40. y Caesar *Bell. Civ.* III 3, 2. z Caesar *Bell. Civ.* III 31.
a *Bell. Civ.* III 31f. b See note 35.

seized, were compelled to advance the taxes they hoped to collect during the following year. Even the money deposited in their bank by private persons like Cicero was confiscated. To enforce these demands, soldiers were stationed in communities of every size, city and hamlet alike. Thus the province was filled with military officials, who, in addition to the levies imposed by Scipio, collected for themselves also, on the plea that, having been forced to leave their homes, they lacked the ordinary necessities of life. To meet the requirements, the communities, as usual, were forced to resort to the money-lender. As was inevitable, the rates of interest were raised, and within two years the total indebtedness of Asia was doubled. If we may regard as historic what may be an over-dramatized incident, Scipio, ready to commit the sacrilege of seizing the money deposited from remote antiquity onward in the Temple of Artemis at Ephesus,[e] had actually entered the sanctuary to carry out his purpose when he received a message from Pompey, bidding him hurry to Greece, for Caesar and his army had crossed the Adriatic.

In the following June—August, according to the calendar—on the plain of Pharsalus in southern Thessaly, Pompey and his followers went down in defeat and his motley army was scattered. The leader himself with three senators—of whom two were Lentulus Spinther and Lentulus Crus—and a few horsemen fled to the coast at the mouth of the river Peneius, where he boarded a merchantman just putting out to sea.[81] Deiotarus, joining him, escaped on the same ship. Landing at Mitylene, where his wife and son were awaiting him, Pompey declined the citizens' invitation to make the city his refuge and went on by way of Attaleia, Syedra in Cilicia and Paphus in Cyprus to Egypt, where, on the anniversary of his triumph over Mithradates, he was treacherously murdered by two renegade Romans at the bidding of a eunuch-minister of the boy-king.

Caesar, in pursuit, sailed down the coast of Asia from the Hellespont as far as Ephesus. Here he tarried to receive the submission of Asia, and here he received the representatives of the eastern provinces who gathered in suspense, not knowing what fate they would meet at the hands of the new conqueror.

e See Chap. V note 67.

CHAPTER XVII

THE END OF THE OLD RÉGIME

THE representatives of the provinces who met Caesar at Ephesus came to the audience in a spirit far different from that in which the leading men of Asia had gathered around Pompey at Amisus.[1] There, those who presented themselves had fought on the side of the victor against the common enemy and were expecting their several rewards. Here, they had, indeed, fought on the side of the same leader, but he was no longer the victor, and they came fearing punishment for their opposition to the new conqueror and in their fear remembering that his success had been portended by strange phenomena. These men had now to face their hero's triumphant rival, a man who had not been in Asia since his youth and who, if known at all to its inhabitants, was famous chiefly for bloody victories over the distant Gauls.

Caesar, in rapid pursuit of his fleeing opponent, arrived in Ephesus in the late summer of 48 B.C., probably less than three weeks after his victory at Pharsalus.[2] Some of Pompey's adherents had lingered in the city, among them Ampius Balbus, who, if we may believe Caesar's own statement, was on the point of seizing the money deposited in the Temple of Artemis when he was frightened away by the victor's approach.[a]

Although Caesar came as a victor, he showed no intention of punishing the vanquished. He was prepared to extend to those in Asia who had supported Pompey the same clemency with which he treated all his opponents who were willing to forego further resistance.[3] The cities not only were pardoned but even received kindly treatment at his hands. At Ilium, perhaps before his arrival in Ephesus, he confirmed the city's ancient privileges of freedom and immunity from taxation and gave it additional territory, including land along the coast as far as Dardanus. Pergamum also obtained some favour, described as a "restoration of the city and its territory to the gods." This act may have resembled in some way the recognition of inviolability received by various Asianic cities during the later third century,[b] but it was scarcely identical with the grant of freedom which was accorded to Pergamum at least a year later.

This "restoration" seems to have been obtained for Pergamum

---

[a] Caesar *Bell. Civ.* III 105. [b] See Chap. IV note 29.

through the good offices of a man named Mithradates, the son of a Pergamene citizen by the Galatian princess Adobogiona (the sister of the Tetrarch Brogitarus) but rumoured to be an illegitimate child of Mithradates Eupator.[4] He was highly regarded by Caesar, who, when hard pressed in Egypt a few months after his stay in Ephesus, sent Mithradates to obtain reinforcements and later conferred on him the titles of Tetrarch and King. Meanwhile the Pergamenes, in gratitude for his service, erected statues of Mithradates as their "New Founder," ranking him with the eponymous hero, Pergamus, and with Philetaerus, the first of their former royal dynasty.

Another friend of Caesar's was also able to obtain privileges for his native city. This was Gaius Julius Theopompus of Cnidus, who seems to have acquired some fame as a mythographer and with the aid of Caesar had received Roman citizenship together with the *nomen* of his sponsor.[5] During Caesar's stay at Ephesus or, perhaps more probably, on the occasion of a visit to Cnidus, this man obtained for his city a grant of freedom and exemption from taxation, a status which soon afterward was guaranteed by a formal treaty of alliance, to observe which representatives of both contracting parties bound themselves by oaths. Favours were evidently granted also to Cos, where a priest for the worship of Caesar was created, as well as to Chios and Samos, in both of which the victor was honoured as patron of the city and its benefactor.[6]

Caesar, however, needed money for the expenses, past and future, of his campaign against Pompey and his partisans. There is no record of his having mulcted the communities of Asia, but he did not hesitate to make demands on individuals, particularly on those who had supported his rival.[7] Deiotarus, who, after leaving Pompey, had made his way back to Galatia, was ordered to pay a large sum, so large, in fact, that, if we may believe Cicero, he was finally forced to hold three auctions of his property in order to raise the amount demanded. Another victim was Pythodorus of Tralles, who had been received into "friendship" by Pompey; his property, estimated at over 2,000 talents, was now confiscated by Caesar and sold. He succeeded, however, in buying it back again, and he ultimately bequeathed it to his children, one of whom afterward became queen of Pontus.

The most notable of Caesar's measures, however, dealt with the taxation of the province of Asia.[8] Perceiving, apparently, that the amounts previously paid to Rome were excessive, especially in the present depleted state of the province, he remitted one third of

406

the amount which Asia had hitherto paid. Then, taking a step of much greater consequence, he abolished the old method of collecting the taxes through contracts with the tax-farming corporations. This was now replaced by a new system, by which amounts were raised by the communities themselves and paid directly to the quaestor of the province. This change, to be sure, affected the direct taxes only; the indirect levies, such as the customs-duties, were still collected, like the income from the state-owned properties and utilities, by the agents of the old corporations.

In gratitude for the benefits received from Caesar, the cities and tribal districts of the province erected a monument at Ephesus in which he was honoured as "the descendant of Ares and Aphrodite, a god made manifest, and the common saviour of all human life."[9] The dedicators appear to have constituted an organization similar to that of the "peoples and tribes in Asia," which in the early part of the century honoured the governor Mucius Scaevola and other worthies. It is probably to be identified also with the "Commonalty of the Hellenes," to which a Roman official about the middle of the century sent a letter intended to correct some prevalent abuse. While we know of the activities of this federation only under the emperors, it evidently existed during the late Republican period, when it was officially recognized as a body through which communications could be sent by the Roman government to the provincials.

After the conference at Ephesus, Caesar left the mainland of Asia Minor for Rhodes.[10] The Rhodians had furnished ships to Pompey; but recently, refusing shelter both to the defeated leader and to some of his partisans in their flight from Pharsalus, they had sent an envoy to the victor.[11] After spending not more than a few days on the island, Caesar set sail for Alexandria with ten Rhodian warships and a small fleet contributed by the cities of Asia, to which other vessels were added later. He remained in Egypt until the spring of the following year, when he received an urgent call to deliver northern Asia Minor from invasion by a son of Mithradates Eupator.

It seems one of the many ironies of the history of political combinations that Pompey's followers should have tried to enlist in their cause the son of the monarch whom their leader had conquered. It will be remembered, however, that Pharnaces, after murdering his father and seizing his kingdom in southern Russia, had made peace with Pompey and received recognition as king and ally of Rome.[c] Now,

c See above p. 365.

Pompey's supporters, if we may believe the historian Appian, at a council held after their defeat at Pharsalus devised the plan of detailing a certain Lucius Cassius to proceed with some ships to the Crimea and persuade Pharnaces to take up arms against Caesar.[12] The mission of Cassius, whatever its purpose, was a failure, for he and his ships, meeting Caesar while crossing the Hellespont, surrendered without striking a blow.

Pharnaces, however, learning of the struggle between the two Roman generals, had already begun to take advantage of the opportunity to recover his father's Asianic dominions. His first move was directed against the district of Colchis at the eastern end of the Euxine Sea, which had been placed by Pompey under the rule of the dynast Aristarchus but now submitted without a struggle.[13] From here he advanced into Armenia Minor, the kingdom of Deiotarus, whose absence—for he had not yet returned from his expedition in behalf of Pompey—made it easier for the invader to take possession of his dominions. Then, proceeding farther to the south and west, Pharnaces overran also the nearest portion of the kingdom of Cappadocia.

On setting out from Asia Minor to Egypt, Caesar left his legate, Gnaeus Domitius Calvinus, in general charge of the Roman provinces east of the Aegean.[14] Deiotarus, accordingly, his kingdom occupied by an invading army, turned to Calvinus for assistance. He could not, he said, pay Caesar the money he had promised unless his realm was restored to him. The force of this argument was not lost on Calvinus and, moreover, Pharnaces's occupation of the kingdom of an allied monarch was an affront to Rome. Calvinus, however, had only one legion, for two of his original three had been summoned by Caesar in his predicament at Alexandria. He therefore sought to gain time by sending a messenger to Pharnaces with an order to withdraw from Cappadocia and Lesser Armenia. Meanwhile, mobilizing his manpower to supplement the force he had with him in Asia, he enrolled a second legion from among the unorganized soldiers in Pontus. There were also auxiliary troops in Cilicia, and Deiotarus had two legions of his own, armed and organized in Roman fashion, and both he and Ariobarzanes were ready to furnish some cavalry. These forces were ordered to assemble at Comana in Pontus. Pharnaces, meanwhile, in consequence of the order he had received, consented to evacuate Cappadocia. He refused, however, to relinquish Lesser Armenia until Caesar himself rendered a decision on the validity of his claim to this portion of his father's former dominions. Even before this message was received, Calvinus, in the belief that his presence nearer the scene of action would give more weight to his demand, had resolved on an advance into Pontus. His decision was strengthened by Pharnaces's reply, and, hastening eastward with his legion, he assumed command of the forces at Comana.

Pharnaces, meanwhile, had taken up his position at Nicopolis, the city which Pompey had founded in commemoration of his final victory over Mithradates.[15] The place, near the border between the Roman province of Pontus and the kingdom of Lesser Armenia and some eighty miles east of Comana, was situated on the main route that led from the Euphrates to Pontus.

In the autumn of 48, nearly four months after the battle of Pharsalus, Calvinus with his somewhat makeshift army set out from Comana against Pharnaces. Having refused various offers to negotiate and having delayed at a defile seven miles from Nicopolis, in the hope of peace according to our far from impartial source, but more probably because he had detected a very evident plan to ambush his army, he advanced to the town and encamped near the ramparts. At this juncture, despatches arrived from Caesar, urging Calvinus to hasten in person to Alexandria with reinforcements.[16] Accordingly, he resolved to fight at once.

The battle resulted in the total defeat of the Romans. The legion brought from the province of Asia succeeded in driving back some of the enemy's troops, but the other, enrolled in Pontus, caught in a trap while crossing a ditch on its flank, was almost annihilated, and the troops of Deiotarus were routed at the first onslaught and suffered heavy loss. Calvinus, although he was able to rally the men of his legion, who, after their success, had been thrown into disorder by the defeat of their comrades, was forced to abandon the struggle; with what was left of his army he retired to the province of Asia.

This victory made Pharnaces master of Pontus. Following up his success, he overran the kingdom of his ancestors, plundering the property of native Pontians and Roman settlers alike and even seizing the slaves belonging to the tax-farmers.[17] Many of the cities were forced to surrender, among them Sinope and Amisus, the latter only after a long siege. It is said—in the hostile sources at our disposal—that Pharnaces behaved everywhere with the greatest cruelty, killing the men of fighting-age and mutilating the youths. After six months this career of conquest and brutality was interrupted by the arrival of Caesar himself.

The news of Pharnaces's invasion had been brought to Caesar in Egypt, and as soon as the government of that distraught kingdom was provided for by the appointment of Cleopatra and her younger and only surviving brother as joint rulers, he hastened northward to recover Rome's lost possessions.[18] After stopping in various places in Syria to attend to the affairs of that province, he went on to Tarsus. Here he arrived about the 1st of July 47, according to the calendar, but actually soon after mid-April.

Caesar's purpose in coming to eastern Asia Minor was, in reality, a double one. He had not only to expel the invader but also to set in order the affairs of these regions, still in upheaval as a result of the Civil War. For the accomplishment of the first of these ends he was badly equipped; for he had brought with him from Egypt only one legion—the Sixth—which constant fighting and long travelling had so reduced in size that when it reached the battlefield it numbered less than one thousand men.[d] To supplement this tiny force, despatches were sent to Calvinus, ordering that the troops under his command, which he seems to have built up to a force of two legions, should proceed at once to Pontus.

In order to facilitate the arrangements to be made in the province of Cilicia, Caesar—probably before his arrival—issued a summons to the various communities, bidding them send representatives to meet him in Tarsus. In a series of sessions held in the city he made the necessary provisions for the future of the province. Among those who were present was probably King Tarcondimotus, for it may be supposed that the pardon he received from Caesar was granted to him here.[19] Privileges seem also to have been conferred on certain cities, as, for instance, Aegaeae, which henceforth used a new era, reckoned from this year.

From Tarsus, Caesar with his Sixth Legion, on the way northward, crossed the Taurus by the great route through the Cilician Gates. His first objective was Mazaca, the capital of Cappadocia, which Pompey had rebuilt after Lucullus's capture of Tigranocerta made it possible for the Cappadocians transported thither by Tigranes to return to their home.[e] Here pardon was granted to King Ariobarzanes for his support of Pompey, and an attempt was made to satisfy the ambitions of his brother, Ariarathes, who, four years previously, had been the unwilling instrument of a group of conspirators against the King.[20] The young man now received either territory or power—it

---

[d] *Bell. Alex.* 69, 1.   [e] See Chap. XV note 35.

is uncertain which—but on condition that he should hold it as his brother's vassal.

During a two days' stay at Mazaca, Caesar seems also to have dealt with the question of the succession to the priesthood of the Mother-Goddess worshipped at Comana in Pontus. By bestowing this office as a semi-independent principality on the younger Archelaus, Pompey had made the priest a vassal of Rome.[f] Archelaus, after his death in Egypt in 55, had been succeeded by his son, but the latter was now for some reason deprived of the priesthood. In his place Caesar named a certain Lycomedes, a native of Bithynia but in some way related to the Cappadocian kings.[21] His purpose was evidently to have someone in this office who would prove a firmer adherent than a member of a family which owed its fortunes to Pompey.

From Mazaca Caesar set out to meet the enemy. He appears to have travelled by the route leading northward through northern Cappadocia and over the mountain-range which formed the southern boundary of Pontus.[22] At the place where his line of march approached most closely to the border of Galatia, Deiotarus appeared in the camp. He came without his royal insignia and in the garb of a mourner, asking forgiveness for having taken up the cause of Pompey.[23] He was spared on the score of his age, his previous services, and his long-standing friendship with Rome, but a rebuke was administered on the ground that he should have known that Caesar held supreme power in Rome and Italy. At the same time, he was kept in suspense as to his future status, for the complaints of the other Galatian princes that, acting contrary to both law and precedent, he had made himself ruler of almost the whole of Galatia were reserved for a future hearing. He was ordered meanwhile to send Caesar all his cavalry as well as his foot-soldiers who had survived the battle of Nicopolis and were now organized as one single legion.

On arriving in southern Pontus, Caesar found the two legions sent, according to his order, by Calvinus. Deiotarus's troops also appeared, led by the King in person. With these forces and the veteran Sixth Legion, Caesar advanced, ready to face the enemy. Pharnaces wished to make terms or at least to temporize. He knew that Caesar was needed in Italy and in haste to return there, and he hoped that by making a show of surrender he could persuade his opponent to accept a nominal submission in lieu of a trial of force. It is possible, besides, that he may already have heard of a revolt which had broken out in

[f] See above p. 371.

his Crimean kingdom under the leadership of Asander, one of his satraps, and that for this reason he wished to conserve his strength.[24] Caesar, however, had not made his long march merely to go through the form of receiving a surrender. Pharnaces's envoys, who came bearing a golden wreath, were told that their peace-offering would be accepted only when their master restored what he had stolen from Roman citizens and provincials and removed himself and his army from Pontus.[25] Further offers and attempts to procrastinate were rejected with similar firmness.

Pharnaces was encamped just north of Zela, where, twenty years previously, his father had annihilated the army of Lucullus's legate, Triarius.[26] It is said, in fact, that he had placed his camp on the site which Mithradates had occupied on that occasion. Caesar, advancing by night from the position he had taken five miles to the south, was in the course of constructing an entrenchment on a hillside separated by a deep valley from Pharnaces when, to his surprise, the King's army, after descending into the valley, began to charge up the steep slope against him. So extraordinary was the manoeuvre that the ancient historian did not know whether to attribute it to Pharnaces's conviction that the locality was a lucky one, to encouragement by favourable auspices, to his knowledge that Caesar's army was inferior in size to his own, or, finally, to over-confidence in his soldiers and contempt for the Romans, inspired by his previous victory over Calvinus. At first, the charge was successful. Caesar's men were caught off their guard and the enemy's cavalry and scythed chariots, advancing rapidly, wrought considerable havoc. These once repulsed, however, by a discharge of missiles, the Roman infantry, from their superior position, drove back the King's forces in total rout, the Sixth Legion setting an example to the less seasoned troops. The remnants of the enemy's army fled to their camp, closely pursued down into the valley and up the opposite hillside by the Roman force. The camp was captured and plundered. Amid the wreck of his army and his hopes, Pharnaces, with a body of horsemen, fled from the field. Making his way to the sea-coast at Sinope, he tried to hold the city against Calvinus but finally capitulated on the condition that he should be allowed to take ship for the Crimea.[g] Caesar's victory, won on the fifth day after his arrival in Pontus and after only four hours of fighting, was afterward described on placards displayed in his triumphal procession in the famous words, "I came, saw and conquered."[27]

g Appian *Mith.* 120; *B.C.* II 92: Cassius Dio XLII 47, 5.

After the victory, Caesar remained in Zela only long enough to divide among the soldiers the great amount of spoils found in Pharnaces's camp and to arrange for the erection of a trophy large enough to outdo the one which Mithradates had constructed after his defeat of Triarius.[h] He left the very day after the battle, we are told, taking with him only some lightly-equipped horsemen. The general supervision of Pontus was entrusted to Calvinus together with the two legions he had furnished to Caesar, while the veterans of the Sixth were ordered back to Italy, there to be discharged with honours and rewards.[28] With Caesar, apparently, went Deiotarus. He had taken part in the battle, and on the long journey to western Asia Minor the Roman leader was a guest in two of his castles.[29] Without lingering anywhere on the way, Caesar continued onward rapidly to Nicaea in Bithynia, where he arrived perhaps a fortnight after his victory.[30] Here he spent another fortnight in dealing with various matters. Again in need of money, he proceeded, as previously, to collect large amounts from all available sources.[i] All those who had promised to make payments to Pompey were ordered to give these to him, and every pretext was used to raise the needed funds. It may be assumed that even the golden wreaths presented to him by various rulers were turned into ready money. Decisions had also to be made in regard to several questions, of which the most important were the charges against Deiotarus and the future status of the Euxine cities.

The case of Deiotarus, as both king of Armenia Minor and Galatian tetrarch, presented special complications. His offence in supporting Pompey, already punished by the imposition of a large fine,[j] had been partly atoned for by the aid he had rendered at Zela. It was necessary, however, to deal with the complaint which the Galatian princes had presented to Caesar, namely, that he had made himself master of almost their entire country. The interests of the old ruler were represented by Marcus Brutus, who delivered a plea in his behalf.[k] Despite the efforts of his advocate, however, Deiotarus did not go unpunished; for although the dominions along the Euxine coast, which had been assigned to him in 62 by Pompey but had recently been overrun by Pharnaces, were restored to him, and both he and his son and namesake were allowed to retain the title of King, he was deprived of part of his possessions, and the portion of Lesser Armenia which bordered on Cappadocia was taken from him and given to Ariobarzanes.[31]

h *Bell. Alex.* 77, 2: Cassius Dio XLII 48, 2.   i Cassius Dio XLII 49, 1f.
j See note 7.   k See note 30.

The complaint of the Galatians, when reduced to fact, was apparently based on Deiotarus's seizure of the tetrarchate of the Trocmi on the death, a few years previously, of his son-in-law Brogitarus, whom Pompey had appointed ruler of this tribe.[1] Fortunately, an answer to this complaint was easily found, although Deiotarus once more lost by the decision. Mithradates of Pergamum, who had obtained privileges for his native city from Caesar and later rendered him signal service in Egypt, was nephew on his mother's side to Brogitarus and consequently had a claim to the latter's tetrarchate.[32] By appointing him to his uncle's position, Caesar was able not only to reward a faithful and valued adherent but also to satisfy the Galatians by creating as tetrarch of the Trocmi a man whose claim could be represented as more valid than that of Deiotarus. It was, to be sure, unfortunate for the outcome that later, in a desire to advance Mithradates's fortunes still further, Caesar proclaimed him king of the Crimean possessions of Pharnaces, who, shortly after his return, was killed by the rebellious Asander; for Mithradates, in an attempt to wrest his new kingdom from Asander, was defeated and presumably killed.

On the Euxine coast, Amisus and Sinope, both of which had been declared free by Lucullus,[m] had surrendered to Pharnaces. For yielding to the enemy and breaking faith with Rome they were liable to punishment and especially to the loss of their freedom. It was apparent, however, that Amisus had surrendered only after a siege and had suffered cruelly at Pharnaces's hands. In view of the fidelity shown by this resistance, the city was pardoned and its former status of freedom and autonomy was confirmed.[n] Sinope, after it had finally been evacuated by Pharnaces, obtained an even better status, for within two years of the victory at Zela Caesar settled in it a group of Romans, who, established alongside of the old Hellenic *polis*, constituted a colony of Roman citizens with the official name of Colonia Julia Felix Sinopensis.[33]

This policy of colonization was not confined to Sinope. While it is probable that the actual foundation of the other colonies was delayed for some time, it seems most natural to connect the plan for their foundation with this stay of Caesar's in Asia Minor. A colony was established at the eastern end of the Propontis at Apameia Myrleia, the Greek city of Myrleia destroyed by Philip V and afterward rebuilt, probably by Prusias I,[o] now in the province of Bithynia, and perhaps

---

[1] See Chap. XV note 40.
[n] Strabo XII p. 547: Cassius Dio XLII 48, 4.
[m] See above pp. 337f. and 342.
[o] See above p. 306f.

also at the western end, at Parium in the province of Asia, once a free Hellenic *polis* and apparently a member of the Federation of the Troad.[p] The new Romanized communities received the names, respectively, of Colonia Julia Concordia Apamea and Colonia Julia Pariana.[34] A group of Roman settlers seems to have been sent also to Heracleia Pontica, where they occupied a portion of the city and its land.[35] The old *polis*, however, still continued in existence. Although reduced to a shadow of its former greatness as the result of the brutality of Cotta in 70, it obtained its freedom from Caesar through the efforts of a patriotic citizen, who, we are told, followed him about the world in order to gain his plea.[q]

These communities of Roman citizens thus settled in the provinces differed wholly from the groups of resident Romans which already existed in many of the cities of Asia. In distinction from an Hellenic *polis*, such a community was a political organization of a purely Italian type, a replica of those which Rome had founded in Italy and the western provinces. The settlers continued to be Roman citizens, enrolled in one of the tribes of which all Romans were members. In Parium certainly, and in Sinope and Apameia apparently, they had full "Italic rights," including the outright ownership of the land they occupied and exemption from the payment of any taxes to Rome.[36] These communities had two chief magistrates called *duoviri*, who were assisted by two aediles, and a council consisting of *decuriones*, a system of government modelled on that of Rome.

Thus Caesar, who, by bestowing Roman citizenship on the inhabitants of Cisapline Gaul, began the process of lessening the distinction between ruling-city and subject-province, inaugurated the new policy of transplanting Roman institutions to Asia Minor and created a miniature Rome in the East.[37] It was a step of great significance in the progress of Roman imperialism.

Having taken the necessary measures with all possible despatch, Caesar left Asia Minor for Italy, travelling by way of Greece.[38] Somewhere in the course of his journey he was approached by a delegation from Mitylene. The city, it will be remembered, had received its freedom from Pompey in 62, and in his last campaign it had sheltered his wife and son and during his flight even offered him a refuge.[r] In refusing this offer, Pompey had advised the citizens to yield to the victor,[s]

p See Chap. III note 53. q Memnon 60, 3.
r See above pp. 365 and 404. s Plutarch *Pomp.* 75, 2.

415

and in conformity with this advice they now sent a deputation of at least eight leading men, headed by the orator Potamo, to offer their submission to Caesar and to announce the bestowal of honours.[39] Unwilling, because of his haste to reach Italy, to stop at Mitylene, Caesar responded by a courteous letter, granting pardon to the citizens and expressing appreciation of their good will with the assurance of his readiness to be of service to their city.

Whatever plans Caesar may have had to improve further the condition of the eastern provinces were frustrated by the critical situation in the West. After a stay in Italy of not more than two months, he hurried to Africa, where the followers of Pompey had rallied to continue their opposition. During the five months' campaign which resulted in the total defeat of the Pompeian forces, the cities of Asia seem to have sent him aid. Cyzicus contributed at least one quadrireme, with the auspicious name of "Deliveress," of whose company one man was captured by the enemy.[t]

Although Caesar himself was prevented by his many activities from doing more for the betterment of the Asianic provinces, he appointed as governors men who had been associated with him and so were presumably ready to continue the liberal policy he had instituted at Ephesus. In 47 B.C. Bithynia was placed under the command of Gaius Vibius Pansa, a "serious and reliable man," who was a personal friend of Caesar's; and Cilicia was perhaps entrusted to Quintus Philippus, presumably a relative of the Philippus who had married Caesar's niece, and a man with whom Cicero claimed a friendship of long standing.[40] Save that under Pansa certain cities in Bithynia were allowed to issue bronze coins of their own, there is no information concerning the administration of these men in their respective provinces. Asia, on the other hand, is known to have had an excellent governor in Publius Servilius Isauricus, a son of the famous conqueror of the Isaurians and in 48 B.C. Caesar's colleague in the consulship.

At the outset of his political career, Servilius, in conjunction with Marcus Cato—whose niece he had married—had been instrumental in introducing into a senatorial decree a section which in some way protected free communities against excessive demands on the part of Roman capitalists.[41] As proconsul of Asia, he showed a similar desire to promote the welfare of his province and "safeguard that badly treated part of the commonwealth." Well aware that there were many

[t] *I.G.R.* IV 135 = *Syll.*[3] 763.

in the province who had reason to be grateful to him, Cicero wrote him at least six letters recommending various persons, both Romans and provincials, whose interests he hoped that Servilius would further.

The gratitude of the Greek cities to Servilius is amply attested by inscriptions honouring him and various members of his family.[42] At Pergamum he restored "the ancestral laws and the democracy subject to no one" and received from the *demos* the title of Saviour and Benefactor of the city. He also won the citizens' gratitude by rendering a decision in favour of the Temple of Asclepius against a Roman in a case involving the Temple's right of inviolability. It is probable that a similar restoration of the city's "ancestral laws" took place at Ephesus, for the citizens added the worship of Servilius to that of the Goddess Roma with a priest for the combined cult. At Aegae the people erected (or restored) a temple of Apollo in gratitude for "having been saved" by Servilius, and the Proconsul himself "restored" at least two buildings. At Magnesia-on-Maeander a monument in honour of Servilius's father testified to the benefits conferred by the son on both the city and the Temple of Artemis, and the Proconsul also guaranteed the inviolability of the sanctuary of the Persian Goddess worshipped in the Lydian town later known as Hierocaesareia. At Mitylene and Cos inscriptions honouring his wife, Junia, and a dedication to Asclepius by Junia herself, as well as "restorations" carried out by Servilius on the islands of Tenos and Calymnos, in the latter case offerings to Apollo, show a like interest both in the communities and in their gods. Apart from the bestowal of political rights and the recognition of privileges belonging to temples, Servilius, unlike many governors, who seized secular and sacred property alike, seems actually to have taken measures to protect and improve both public and sacred possessions.

Servilius appears to have remained in Asia until the spring or summer of 44, having been in office for a term of two years. Meanwhile Caesar, after his return from Africa in the early summer of 46, resumed his interest in the affairs of the East. A deputation from Mitylene, under the leadership of the same Potamo who had headed the envoys sent to Caesar in 47, appeared before the Senate, requesting the "renewal" of the city's friendship and alliance with Rome and the privilege of sacrificing to Jupiter Capitolinus.[43] When these men returned to their home they brought a letter to their Council and People from Caesar himself, in which, assuring the citizens of his good will, he promised that they should enjoy the full revenues from their city and territory and that Rome would exempt no one from the taxes they imposed. Similarly, the Temple of Aphrodite at Aphrodisias in Caria obtained a "letter" from Caesar, guaranteeing the inviolability of the Goddess's sanctuary, and shortly before his assassination he issued an order adding two miles to the inviolable area of the Temple of Apollo at Didyma. Samos also received some favour which caused the citizens to erect a statue of Caesar's wife, Calpurnia, in gratitude for what her husband had done for their city.

It is not improbable that Caesar originated the plan for the dismemberment of the large and unwieldy province of Cilicia which seems to have been put into execution after his death.[44] The process had begun in 49, when, as has been related, the three Phrygian dioceses were retransferred from Cilicia to Asia. Further reductions were made when Pamphylia also was combined with Asia and with it, doubtless in order to connect the two, a portion of the mountain-region of Milyas and Pisidia. Cyprus, once a possession of the Ptolemaic dynasty, was returned by Caesar to Cleopatra, who stationed a prefect on the island. Finally, apparently in the course of 44, the district of Cilicia Campestris was attached to the province of Syria.

When, on 15 March, 44, Caesar was assassinated in the Senate-chamber attached to the great portico which Pompey had built, the inhabitants of the provinces lost a ruler whose general policy, for all his seizure of individual fortunes, had been considerate and even beneficial. In exchange, they became subject to the Dictator's assassins and their like, men of the stamp of the governors chosen from among the old senatorial oligarchy, whose chief conception of a province was a place from which they could extort money.

Among the conspirators who had been selected by their victim for high office were Gaius Trebonius and Lucius Tillius Cimber, appointed governors, respectively, of Asia and Bithynia.[45] Both appointments were confirmed by the Senate a few days after Caesar's death, and within a month the two men left Rome for their provinces. Their departure was hastened by the attitude of the Roman populace, whose anger at the Dictator's murder was inflamed by the harangues of Mark Antony, his colleague in the consulship and the would-be heir of his power.

It soon became evident that the policies of the two new governors did not include the conferring of benefits on their provinces. The leaders of the conspirators, Marcus Brutus and Gaius Cassius, had neither money nor an armed force. Each, as has been noted,[u] had previously spent some time in the eastern provinces in an official capacity, and in the traditional Roman way they regarded these as an inexhaustible source of wealth and power. Accordingly, both Trebonius and Tillius were instructed to raise money for their associates and to force the cities to furnish ships for a fleet.[v] Among those whom Trebonius despoiled of their property was Caesar's friend, Theopompus of Cnidus, who was compelled to take refuge in Alexandria.[w] What means were taken to obtain these new levies—whether the imposition of additional taxes or the seizure of private property—is unknown, but, added to the demands of Metellus Scipio in 49[x] and those made by Caesar, they must have been a heavy burden to the province. Nevertheless, money and ships were collected, to be delivered to Brutus and Cassius, who in the autumn of 44 occupied, respectively, Macedonia and Syria, provinces to which neither until somewhat later had any lawful claim.[46] Syria was especially valuable to them on account of the troops by which it was protected. Cassius, taking command of these, extended his power over Cilicia also, where he forced the people of Tarsus, much against their will, and also King Tarcondimotus to join him as allies.[y]

The lawful governor of Syria was the young Publius Cornelius Dolabella, who, after a highly discreditable early career, had been selected by Caesar to serve as his substitute in the consulship of 44, which he himself intended soon to resign. While his appointment to the province may have been arranged by the Dictator, it is probable that, according to the ordinary procedure, the Senate, after Caesar's death, named two provinces for the Consuls of 44 and that Syria fell to Dolabella in the usual casting of lots.[47]

Leaving Rome before the expiration of his consulship, Dolabella, on his way to Syria, arrived in Asia early in January, 43, escorted by one legion.[48] He evidently expected to collect money in the course of his march through the province. Trebonius, the governor, who was fortifying the towns in the interest of Brutus and Cassius, received him with some appearance of cordiality but apparently not without suspicion, for he forbad him to enter Pergamum or Smyrna. He nevertheless permitted Dolabella to buy provisions for his troops outside the walls of the two cities and promised to admit him to Ephesus,

---

[u] See above pp. 388f. and 396.

[v] Cicero *Epist. ad Fam.* XII 13, 3: Appian *B.C.* III 6: Cassius Dio XLVII 21, 3 and 26, 1 = Zonaras x 18.

[w] Cicero *Phil.* XIII 33.   [x] See above p. 403f.

[y] Cassius Dio XLVII 26, 2 = Zonaras x 18.

sending a body of soldiers to escort him on his way. But when night came on, Dolabella, having escaped from the surveillance of his escort, returned to Smyrna, which, left unguarded, he captured without difficulty. Seizing Trebonius in his house, Dolabella, if we may believe Cicero, tortured him for two days, hoping to get from him the money he had collected for Cassius. Finally, crowning his brutality with an act of the utmost barbarity, he broke the wretched man's neck, and, cutting off his head, had it carried about the city on a pike, while the body, mangled by being drawn through the streets, was at last thrown into the sea.

This savage murder of the Proconsul of Asia caused the Senate to declare Dolabella an enemy of the state. Nevertheless, he remained in Asia during the remainder of the winter, raising money and forces for the inevitable struggle in Syria against Cassius.[49] The funds which Trebonius had collected, as well as the ordinary public revenues, were seized, new levies were imposed on the cities, and even the property of Roman citizens was not spared. Soldiers were enlisted and a legion was added to the one which had accompanied Dolabella to Asia, while he himself assumed the title of Imperator. A special effort was made to add to the fleet, which Dolabella planned to use for the transportation of men and supplies to Syria. He himself went to the maritime cities of Lycia, where he forced or paid the ship-owners to put more than a hundred merchantmen at his disposal. The Rhodians also supplied him with a number of vessels. They sought to gain his favour, fearing, as they afterwards said, for their mainland possessions, and, although they refused to let him come to the island, they nevertheless sent two separate delegations to meet him. They also refrained from aiding his opponents; for when Trebonius's quaestor, the young Lentulus Spinther (son of the former governor of Cilicia), pursuing Dolabella with some of the ships collected by the murdered Proconsul, arrived at Rhodes, he was forbidden to enter the harbour and even his request for water and food was rejected.

Dolabella's fleet did not reach Syria without incurring both loss and delay. Lentulus, according to his own statement at least, dispersed the Lycian merchantmen and restored them to their owners. Other vessels, under the command of Lucius Figulus, were pursued along the southern coast of Asia Minor by Cassius Parmensis, acting in the interest of his kinsman, with ships obtained from the maritime cities of the province of Asia and by those which, during the previous year, Tillius Cimber had collected in Bithynia. Acting in co-operation, the two fleets forced Figulus to take refuge in the harbour of Corycus on the Cilician coast.

Meanwhile, Dolabella himself and his two legions, after being defeated in battle by Tillius Cimber with the aid of Deiotarus, marched overland to Cilicia.[50] Crossing the Taurus as soon as the pass was free from the winter's snow, he arrived in Tarsus about the first of May. Here he was welcomed by the inhabitants, who even allowed him to enlist additional soldiers. Advancing through Cilicia, he overwhelmed the garrison placed by Cassius in Aegaeae and thus made his way into Syria, where he established himself at Laodiceia on the coast. Here he was closely invested by Cassius with a vastly superior force. For some weeks he succeeded in holding out, but defeat, famine, desertion and the treachery of his officers made further resistance impossible, and, at his own demand, he was killed by one of his soldiers.

The disastrous campaign of this violent and unprincipled young man ultimately brought ruin upon the people of Tarsus.[z] While he was still beleaguered in Laodiceia, they opposed Tillius Cimber when hastening to Cassius's aid. At first they tried to prevent Tillius from crossing the Taurus; then, frightened by his apparent strength, they entered into an agreement with him. Later, finding him weaker than they had supposed, they refused to receive him into the city or supply him with provisions, and when he passed on into Syria they made a successful attack on a body of soldiers he had left in a certain Cilician fort. They even took advantage of the situation to invade the territory of their rival, Adana, on the ground that it was supporting Cassius. Finally, however, losing courage, they surrendered without resistance to one of Cassius's subordinates. Nevertheless, they did not escape punishment; for Cassius, coming to Tarsus after his victory at Laodiceia, imposed a fine of fifteen hundred talents on the citizens. The money was exacted by a body of soldiers, apparently with great ruthlessness. Since the funds in the city's treasury did not suffice to meet the demand, the gold and silver offerings in the temples were melted down and the metal coined. Private property also was confiscated and, according to the highly-coloured narrative contained in our source, boys and girls of free birth and even older men and women were sold into slavery by the city-magistrates in an effort to raise the required amount. Not until Cassius himself remitted the balance of the fine were the exactions discontinued.

The chief sources of wealth for both Cassius and Brutus were the

<hr>

[z] Appian B.C. IV 64: Cassius Dio XLVII 31, 1f.

revenues accruing to Rome from the provinces of the East. These they acquired by forcing or persuading the quaestors to deliver the money they were conveying to Italy.[51] Brutus, in particular, while in Macedonia, received from Marcus Appuleius, a quaestor returning, apparently, from the province of Asia, a sum amounting, it was said, to sixteen thousand talents, obtained from the revenues from his province.

Brutus may perhaps have made a preliminary expedition from Macedonia to Asia in the spring of 43, hoping to find allies and to obtain supplies of money and soldiers, but if so, his stay there was a brief one.[52] In the autumn, after learning that on 19 August Caesar's great-nephew and adopted son, Octavian, had taken the consulship and that the lives and property of those who had conspired against the Dictator had been declared forfeit, he led his army across the Hellespont and took possession of western Asia Minor.[53] During the following weeks he not only visited the cities in the capacity of governor but even carried on negotiations with local rulers. He also compelled or persuaded Cyzicus and the Bithynian cities to provide him with a fleet.

Some information about Brutus's dealings with the cities is contained in a collection of letters in Greek, which purport to have been written by him to several of the communities of Asia.[54] The genuineness of these compositions is highly doubtful, but it is not impossible that whoever wrote them and attributed them to Brutus may have used material of historical value. One of these letters relates that the Cyzicenes' fleet was used to convey arms from Bithynia to the Hellespont, which Brutus was holding, and that as a reward the city received the marble-quarries on the island of Proconnesus.[a] Later, apparently, they asked to be freed from the obligations entailed by their alliance. Another letter contains the statement that the Bithynians, when a certain Aquila, acting for Brutus, demanded fifty merchantmen and two hundred warships with sailors and rowers and four months' rations, were so slow in complying with the demand that they were fined the large sum of four hundred talents. It is related also that the Coans were ordered to build ships and that Pergamum gave Brutus two hundred talents, while Tralles was told to refuse a reception to Dolabella and to banish his friend Menodorus, sending to Brutus the money which Dolabella had left in the latter's care.[55] The letters addressed to Caunus, Smyrna, Miletus and Samos, on the other hand, merely contain general exhortations to be zealous in Brutus's cause.

a See above p. 44.

During the early winter of 43-42, Brutus, having summoned Cassius from Syria, met him in Smyrna for a discussion of further plans.[56] The conference was evidently necessitated by the union formed by the young Octavian, Mark Antony and Marcus Lepidus, Master of Horse during Caesar's later years as Dictator, for the purpose of seizing supreme power over the Roman world. The combination of these three men was legalized on 27 November, 43, when a law proposed by a tribune created them "Triumvirs for ordering the State," and their power was soon established by sentencing a large number of their opponents to death. Brutus and Cassius, therefore, were faced with certain war. Intending to fight in Macedonia, they meanwhile used Asia as a source of supplies. Sending their emissaries through the province, they visited many of the cities in person, in search of both money and troops.[b]

Although, after many exactions, the wealth of the province was well-nigh exhausted, there were sources still untapped, namely, the Rhodian Republic and the free cities of Lycia. Both, after supplying Dolabella with ships, had refused them to Cassius, saying that they would form no alliance with him or with Brutus and that they had furnished the ships to Dolabella merely as an escort and not to be used in war.[c]

Their action, however, could be interpreted as giving aid to the enemy and thus used as a pretext for seizing the needed supplies. The two leaders, therefore, agreed to proceed against them; it was decided that Cassius should attack the Rhodians, leaving Brutus to deal with the Lycians. In the spring of 42 both set out on their respective campaigns.

Cassius had brought a fleet from Syria, numbering at least eighty large vessels.[57] Stationing it at Myndus, he made preparations for proceeding against his intended victims. The Rhodians were divided in their sentiments, the wealthier class favouring negotiation, while the lower element, under the influence of two demagogues, clamoured for war. This party prevailed to the extent of equipping a fleet of thirty-three warships, but the advocates of peace succeeded in having envoys sent to Cassius to urge him to refrain from violating the Rhodians' treaty with Rome. The embassy was wholly unsuccessful. Cassius retorted that the Rhodians had already violated the treaty by supporting Dolabella and that if they did not promptly yield to his demands they should suffer punishment. A second, more personal, plea, brought

[b] Cassius Dio XLVII 32, 4.   [c] Cassius Dio XLVII 33, 1: Appian B.C. IV 61.

to the Roman leader by his former teacher, met with a similar response.

The demands made by Cassius are not definitely known, but it is highly probable that, determined as he was to provoke a war and to profit pecuniarily by it, they were wholly unacceptable. In any case, the Rhodians sent out their fleet, which met the enemy off the promontory of Myndus. They were, however, at a great disadvantage; for Cassius's ships, heavier and far more numerous, were able to prevent them from using their customary tactics of ramming and immediately putting about. The result, in consequence, was a decisive victory for the Romans.

Cassius's next move was to concentrate his land and naval forces at Loryma, the point on the mainland nearest to Rhodes. Then, transporting troops to the island, he invested the city of Rhodes both by land and by sea. A second naval battle likewise resulted in a Roman victory, and Rhodes seemed doomed to succumb either to assault or to famine, when some of the peace-party opened a gate and Cassius with a band of soldiers suddenly appeared inside the walls. The true purpose of the campaign then became apparent. Issuing strict orders to his soldiers to refrain from any violence, Cassius, after condemning fifty citizens to death and twenty-five others to banishment, announced his demands: all gold and silver in the city, whether the property of the state, the gods or private citizens, was to be brought to him before a certain day under penalty of death for those who attempted concealment. The sum obtained from all sources, public and private, is said to have amounted to 8,500 talents. Thus the city which had received Roman fugitives when Mithradates invaded the province of Asia and had valiantly resisted the forces of the King was, forty-four years later, mercilessly robbed of its wealth by a Roman general on the pretext that its citizens had furnished ships to the lawful, although violent, governor of Syria, when he wished to transport troops to his province.

The campaign of Brutus against the Lycians will be described elsewhere.[d] The obstinate defence of Xanthus, which resulted in the destruction of the city and the death of many of its citizens, caused much greater bloodshed than Cassius's attack on Rhodes, but the amount of money obtained was far smaller; for, after taking all the gold and silver from the communities of Patara and Myra, Brutus demanded from the federated cities of the district the comparatively small sum of a hundred and fifty talents. At the same time, commanding the

---

[d] See below p. 528.

Lycians to place all their ships at his disposal, he sent these to the Hellespont to be used for transporting his army across the Strait to Thrace.

Like the Rhodians, the two principal client-kings of central and eastern Asia Minor, Deiotarus and Ariobarzanes, had also declined to furnish aid to Cassius. In the case of Ariobarzanes, this refusal was fatal, for the Roman leader, after the capture of Rhodes, sent a troop of cavalry to Cappadocia to seize the King and put him to death.[e] He was accused of having plotted against Cassius, but the fact that the soldiers brought his treasure back to their commander suggests that there was in fact another motive for the murder.

Deiotarus, on the other hand, was persuaded by Brutus, who had once pleaded his case before Caesar, to retract his refusal and form an alliance.[f] During the five years which had elapsed since the loss of part of his possessions,[g] the shrewd ruler had succeeded in remaining in the good graces both of the Dictator and of his opponents. In the summer of 45 he had sent envoys to Caesar, at the time in Spain, to ask for some favour, evidently, from the distance traversed, a matter of considerable importance.[58] It may be assumed that this mission concerned the tetrarchate of the Trocmi, which had been conferred by the Dictator on Mithradates of Pergamum but had become vacant at the latter's death. The envoys returned with Caesar to Rome in the early autumn, having apparently reason to hope for a favourable answer to their request. Any decision in the matter, however, was postponed on account of the accusation that Deiotarus had once plotted against the Dictator's life.

This charge was brought by the King's grandson, Castor, a son of his daughter and the Galatian chieftain Castor Tarcondarius (or Saocondarius), who, like Deiotarus himself, had taken part in the battle of Pharsalus on the side of Pompey.[59] The accuser alleged that his grandfather had planned to murder Caesar during their journey together in 47 from Zela to Nicaea.[h] The King was defended by Cicero in a speech delivered before the Dictator himself, in which the orator showed that there were no grounds for the accusation and denied the more definite allegations that his client hated Caesar and had raised an army to be used against him.

Before the King's request could be granted and perhaps even before his innocence was established, Caesar fell before the daggers of his

---

[e] Appian *B.C.* IV 63: Cassius Dio XLVII 33, 1 and 4 = Zonaras X 18.
[f] Cassius Dio XLVII 24, 3.   [g] See above p. 413.   [h] See above p. 413.

assassins. The answer to the question at issue, therefore, had devolved on Antony, who, claiming to have possession of the Dictator's papers, was rendering decisions in his name. Deiotarus, to be sure, seems, on hearing of Caesar's death, to have attained his end by means of violence, but his action was confirmed by Antony—in return, it was said, for a note for 10,000,000 sesterces signed by his envoys in Antony's house.[i]

Even this addition to his power did not satisfy the old monarch's ambition. Coveting the possessions of his son-in-law, Castor Tarcondarius, but probably no less eager to obtain revenge for the accusation brought against him by the latter's son, Deiotarus attacked Gorbeus, the residence of Tarcondarius, and after killing both his daughter and his son-in-law, levelled the place to the ground.[60] Despite his bargain with Antony, he had supported the opponents of Caesar and aided Tillius Cimber in the latter's successful attack on Dolabella.[j] Now, through the death of Tarcondarius, he was sole ruler in Galatia and, as the most powerful of the client-kings, a welcome ally for Brutus in the projected campaign against Octavian and Antony. Too old himself to accompany the army to Macedonia, he sent a body of cavalry under the command of his secretary, Amyntas.[61]

Cassius, meanwhile, was continuing to extort money for the impending war. Not content with having despoiled the Rhodians, he issued an order that all the provinces should contribute amounts equal to the estimated taxes of the next ten years, a demand which, so the representatives of the cities are said to have declared later, compelled the provincials to surrender not only all their money but even their plate and their personal ornaments.[k] It may be suspected that not all these funds were used for the purpose for which they were intended; for we are told that Cassius, when two members of his staff were found guilty of peculation, merely rebuking them, retained them in his service.[62] Brutus, on the other hand, adopting a sterner attitude, condemned and disgraced a former praetor against whom the people of Sardis brought a similar charge.

On the eve of the campaign the two leaders met at Sardis for a conference.[63] Then, in the middle of the summer of 42, they set forth, each bearing the title of Imperator, for Macedonia with an army nearly 100,000 strong. Before the end of October, in two battles with the Triumvirs' forces on the marshy plains of Philippi, this huge army was defeated and scattered, both leaders were slain, and the cause which claimed to be that of the old Roman Republic was lost forever.

[i] Cicero *Phil.* ii 95; see note 58.   [j] See above p. 421.   [k] Appian *B.C.* iv 74; v 6.

CHAPTER XVIII

THROUGH MONARCHY TO PRINCIPATE

THERE was no reason why the death-blow administered at Philippi to the Roman Republic should have been lamented by the provinces of the East. The client-princes, to be sure, had sent contingents to the army which represented the republican cause. But even the troops contributed by Deiotarus, in spite of their master's alliance with Brutus, felt no zeal for that cause, and after the first engagement at Philippi they and their leader, Amyntas, deserted to the Triumvirs.[a] The cities, although they too had furnished aid, could hardly, after experiencing the methods of Brutus and Cassius, have done so without the greatest reluctance. Caesar had indeed punished both princes and private individuals for supporting Pompey; but both he and some of those whom he appointed as governors had granted favours and privileges to the cities which evoked wide-spread gratitude. Those, on the other hand, whom their admirers called Liberators and Tyrannicides had proved merciless oppressors, using every pretext to demand money from the much-maltreated provincials. The total amount of their extortions during a period of a little over a year has been estimated at more than 25,000 talents.[b]

At first, the victory of the Triumvirs brought no relief from extortion and suffering, and the new ruler seemed as great an oppressor as the so-called restorers of the Republic. Mark Antony, crossing over to Asia Minor to take command of the East, gradually assumed a power as absolute as those of a monarch.[1] Entering Ephesus in triumph, he took up his quarters in the city with great pomp and luxury, allowing the citizens to hail him, as they had once hailed Mithradates, as the incarnation of the beneficent god Dionysus. In fact, however, he proved to be as little of a benefactor as his predecessor in the title. Summoning the representatives of the communities, he informed them that to make it possible for him to pay what he owed to his soldiers the province must give him during the current year the estimated amount of the taxes due during the next ten years, the same sum which a few months earlier had been levied by Brutus and Cassius. For a country drained dry by previous exactions, the fulfilment of this exorbitant demand was clearly out of the question. The communities, protesting vehemently against such severity, begged for mercy. In response to their

[a] Cassius Dio XLVII 48, 2.   [b] See Broughton in *Econ. Surv.* IV p. 584.

entreaties, the sum was reduced to the amount of nine years' taxes and a second year was granted in which the payment might be completed. For collecting the money definite regions were assigned to Antony's agents, some of them, apparently, the adventurers who succeeded in winning his favour like Anaxenor, a lyre-player of Magnesia, to whom four cities were allotted. It is hard to believe, however, that in the ruined condition of the province the payments, even on the less rigorous terms which were granted, were ever made in full.

In Antony's demands were included not only the cities, both free and subject, but also the client-kings and the minor rulers, who were evidently forced to pay for retaining—or receiving—their power.[c] One of these may have been a certain Nicias of Cos, a philologist, who, after spending several years in Rome as the friend of many leading men, had returned to his native island.[2] Becoming tyrant of Cos, he remained in power, evidently with Antony's support, for at least eight years and was honoured as the friend of his fatherland and benefactor of the city.

On the other hand, some of those who had resisted—even though in vain—the demands of the Triumvirs' opponents, now received their reward. The Rhodians, in return for what they had suffered, obtained the city of Myndus as well as the islands of Andros, Naxos and Tenos, the Lycian Federation was released from whatever remained of the payments demanded by Brutus, and the people of Xanthus were encouraged to rebuild their ruined city.[3]

At Ephesus the "New Dionysus" was prevailed upon to grant extensive privileges to the famous organization of poets, musicians and actors who regarded themselves as under the special patronage of his divine prototype.[4] The Society of the "Artists of Dionysus," the Ionian branch of which had flourished under the Pergamene kings, had become part of a larger organization, a "world-wide" society of the victors in "sacred" contests, namely those in which the prizes were wreaths. The Artists had enjoyed various rights in the past, a ratification of which had been obtained from Sulla; but now, fearing for these, as well as desiring further privileges, the priest of the larger organization, a native of Ephesus, appeared before Antony with a recommendation from the latter's "friend," Marcus Antonius Artemidorus. In a reply, addressed to the "Commonalty of the Hellenes in Asia," the Roman general not only confirmed the existing status of the association but in specific terms granted it exemption

[c] Appian B.C. v 6.

from military service, from civic burdens (liturgies) and from billeting, as well as an assurance against attack or violence during the festival of Artemis and even the right to wear purple robes, privileges which were afterwards ratified by the emperors.

At this time also Antony, following the example of Mithradates, courted the favour of Artemis by increasing the inviolable area belonging to her temple.[d] By this addition its extent was doubled and, greatly to the advantage of those who sought refuge, even a part of the suburbs of the city was included within its limits. Showing all respect for the rights of sanctuary enjoyed by the Temple, he even spared those partisans of Brutus and Cassius who had fled to it as suppliants, except in the cases of one of the conspirators against Caesar and a certain man who had betrayed Dolabella to Cassius.[e] Later, it is true, under the influence of Cleopatra, he did not scruple to kill Arsinoe, her sister, who had taken refuge in the Temple, and to summon to his presence the Chief Priest of the Goddess, who had received her, an order rescinded only after the Ephesians had appealed to the Queen.[5]

From Ephesus Antony set out on a triumphal journey through Asia Minor, in the course of which he levied further contributions.[6] On reaching Tarsus in the course of this progress, he rewarded the city for its sufferings under Cassius, granting it exemption from taxes and liberating those persons who had been sold into slavery in order to raise the amount of the penalty which Cassius had imposed. Here also he gave a public office to one of his favourites, a demagogue named Boethus, who had courted him by writing a poem in celebration of the victory at Philippi. Appointed to the office of gymnasiarch, this man, despite an habitual dishonesty which led him to steal even the oil provided for the athletes, succeeded in retaining his post until after Antony was overthrown.

During this visit to Tarsus, in the autumn of 41, occurred an event, which, insignificant in itself, was destined to be of great consequence, cleaving the Roman world once more into two factions and pitting East against West. Among those whom Antony summoned to the city to be rebuked for aiding Cassius was Cleopatra, Queen of Egypt. The brilliant scene staged by this astute woman on her appearance before her would-be judge has captured the imagination of writers both ancient and modern.[7] The new Dionysus, fascinated by this second Aphrodite, went on through Syria to Alexandria, where he spent the

d Strabo xiv p. 641.   e Appian B.C. v 4 and 7.

winter of 41-40 amid the allurements which the Queen knew how to provide. His stay there marked the beginning of the transformation of the Roman general into an oriental monarch.

Early in the summer of the following year a new disaster fell upon Asia Minor from a source with which the country had hitherto had no experience.[8] Brutus and Cassius were dead, but the evil they had done lived after them. Several months before the battle of Philippi, the "Liberators," seeking to strengthen their cause by entering into negotiations with Rome's most formidable enemies, the Parthians, had sent an envoy to King Orodes to ask for assistance. Their messenger was the young Quintus Labienus, son of Titus Labienus, once Caesar's legate in Gaul but later in Pompey's service. Although unable to carry out his mission by bringing back troops in time to be of aid to his leaders, Labienus nevertheless persuaded Orodes to embark upon a war against Rome. Taking advantage of Antony's absence in Egypt, the Parthian monarch sent an army across the Euphrates under the joint leadership of Labienus and the prince Pacorus, the nominal commander of the force which had invaded Roman territory ten years previously.[f] Having defeated Lucius Decidius Saxa, the governor of Syria, and compelled him to flee for his life, the two leaders took possession of the province.

After this success, the renegade Labienus, now intent on the conquest of Asia Minor for his Parthian allies, left Pacorus to complete the conquest of Syria and advanced across the Taurus. In addition to Parthian troops, he seems to have had some soldiers of Brutus and Cassius, who, left by Antony in Syria, had deserted to their former comrade. Saxa, who had taken refuge in Cilicia, was put to death, and Plancus, the governor of Asia, unable to oppose the invaders, withdrew to the Aegean islands.[9] As Labienus proceeded along the Southern Highway, the various places, all unarmed, yielded to his superior strength. Only the Laodiceans, under the leadership of Zeno, a teacher of oratory, offered resistance, but whether successfully or not is unknown.

Bands of soldiers seem to have been sent through the defenceless province, demanding money from its inhabitants and even robbing the temples. One such band met its match in the person of a certain Cleon, a native of Gordiucome in the southeastern corner of Bithynia, who, as the leader of a company of brigands with headquarters in the wild region of Mt. Olympus, successfully attacked the marauders and

[f] See above p. 397.

checked any further operations.[10] The brunt of the invasion, however, seems to have fallen on the district of Caria, which was overrun by the main part of the army under Labienus himself, now turned wholly Parthian and officially styled Parthicus Imperator. Aphrodisias may perhaps have succeeded in holding out against him, but when he turned southward up the valley of the Marsyas, Alabanda capitulated and received a garrison of his soldiers. Mylasa also surrendered, but only after some resistance inspired by the rhetorician Hybreas, who, before the city fell, succeeded in making his escape to Rhodes.[g] At both places the citizens, in an effort to free themselves, massacred the Parthian garrisons, but by so doing they only brought punishment upon themselves. Mylasa suffered especially, for "it lost many of its citizens who were taken prisoners, not a few who were slain and certain ones who were burned together with the city, the cruelty of the enemy sparing neither the temples nor the holiest sanctuaries"; its territory was pillaged, the farmsteads burned and the city itself partly destroyed.

Stratoniceia, however, was successful in resisting the invaders, although the city's territory was devastated, and at Lagina the sanctuary of Hecate was profaned and the celebration of her quadrennial festival suspended. At Panamara, on the other hand, it was believed that Zeus by a miraculous intervention repulsed the enemy by means of fire-bolts, fog and storm and finally drove them off in panic.

The invasion of Labienus was possible only because Asia Minor had been left wholly unguarded. Meanwhile Antony, tearing himself away from the allurements of Alexandria, made his way to Italy in the summer of 40, and in October, meeting Octavian at Brundisium, he formed a compact with his associate which gave him the command of Macedonia, Greece and the eastern provinces.[11] In the following spring, setting himself to the task of providing for the defence of Asia Minor, he sent Publius Ventidius Bassus, Consul during the closing months of 43, across the Aegean with an army.[12] Labienus and his forces were unable to oppose a really formidable enemy, and, evacuating the province of Asia without a battle, they withdrew in haste to the Taurus. Here, probably near the Cilician Gates, both Labienus and Ventidius, who had pursued him, remained in camp for some days, each waiting for reinforcements. When these arrived, the Parthian troops, without joining forces with their commander, charged up the mountain-side against the Roman entrenchments. Driven back in

[g] Strabo XIV p. 660.

great disorder and with considerable loss, they fled down into Cilicia, and Labienus, while withdrawing from his post, was attacked by Ventidius from ambush and lost his force through death and desertion. Compelled to flee in disguise, he concealed himself for a time in Cilicia, but finally he was seized by Antony's representative and promptly put to death.

By this brief campaign Ventidius cleared Asia Minor of the Parthian invaders. Using a stratagem to defeat a force which was holding a pass at the border of Cilicia and Syria, he made his way into the latter province and took possession of it without opposition.[13] A second battle, in the spring of 38, against another Parthian army, which Pacorus had brought across the Euphrates, resulted in complete victory, and in the flight the leader was killed. This was followed by a general move against those who were said to have sympathized with the enemy, among them Antiochus of Commagene, whose rule had been confirmed by Pompey.[h] He was accused of having sheltered fugitive Parthians, but it is probable that the real reason for attacking him was a desire to obtain some of his great wealth.[14] Ventidius besieged Antiochus in his capital, Samosata, but the siege made little progress, for the reason, according to gossip, that the King was bargaining with the Roman commander, even offering him a thousand talents to withdraw. At this juncture Antony himself arrived and, displacing Ventidius, took command in person. Finally, Antiochus capitulated and surrendered the city, but again gossip mentioned collusion, attributing the surrender to a secret agreement which made it possible for Antony to withdraw without disgrace.

Meanwhile an attempt, somewhat belated, was made to improve conditions in western Asia Minor, particularly with regard to the position of the cities.[15] In August, 39, an embassy from Stratoniceia, coming to Rome, obtained a senatorial decree apparently granting the city its freedom, presumably in recognition of its resistance to Labienus in the preceding year. During the following winter, probably, Miletus, also after sending an embassy to Rome, recovered its ancient status of freedom and autonomy. About the same time an envoy from the united communities of Aphrodisias and Plarasa obtained a senatorial decree, confirmed by a law, declaring them free and granting them all rights enjoyed by the most favoured nation, including exemption from tribute to Rome and from the imposition of taxes on any of their possessions. The sanctuary of their goddess Aphrodite

[h] See above p. 377.

and the surrounding land were also declared inviolable and vested with the rights and sanctity enjoyed by Artemis at Ephesus. A law, moreover, supported by Antony, conferred Roman citizenship on certain inhabitants of Cos who had been loyal to their alliance with Rome.

In dealing with the cities, the form appears to have been preserved of referring action to the Senate. But after Antony's rule over the East had been established in consequence of the compact of Brundisium, the senators seem to have ratified in advance all the measures that he might take.[16] Of these perhaps the most important were his arrangements concerning the client-kingdoms. The first problem to be presented was the disposition of the dominions of Deiotarus, whose adventurous life came to an end about the time when the compact was formed. His possessions in Galatia were inherited, as was natural, by his grandson, Castor, who had once accused him of a plot to murder Caesar. Castor also obtained, presumably by gift from Antony, the interior of Paphlagonia, whose ruler Attalus, appointed by Pompey, died about the same time as Deiotarus. The portion of Pontus, on the other hand, which had belonged to the late King, namely the coast region of Pharnaceia and Trebizond with its rich *hinterland*, was assigned to the Pontic prince Darius, son of Pharnaces whom Caesar had vanquished at Zela.

Of greater significance because of the royal positions to which these rulers later attained, were the appointments of the Galatian Amyntas, the former secretary of Deiotarus who had deserted to the Triumvirs at Philippi, and the Laodicean Polemo, son of that Zeno who had encouraged his fellow-citizens to defend their city against Labienus and the Parthians. Both men were evidently chosen as fitting instruments for ruling lands as yet little affected by the influence of Rome, and the subsequent advancement of both, as well as their retention in power by Octavian, shows that the choice was a wise one.

It has been previously observed that the province of Cilicia was probably dismembered soon after Caesar's death.[i] In any case, the separation into its component parts had been completed in 38, when the Level District was subject to Gaius Sosius, the governor of Syria.[j] Of what remained, the hill-country of northern Pisidia was now given to Amyntas and the arid steppe of Lycaonia together with the city of Iconium and perhaps the adjacent part of Cilicia Aspera to Polemo.[17] Farther south, in the mountains of the Rugged District, the former

[i] See Chap. XVII note 44. [j] Cassius Dio XLIX 22, 3.

433

temple-state of Olba was ruled by Aba, a daughter of the bandit-chieftain Zenophanes who, after making himself master of Olba, had married his daughter to a member of the old princely family, the hereditary prince-priests of the Temple of Zeus.[k] This woman, by courting the favour of Antony and Cleopatra, succeeded in retaining her power, and under Augustus her descendants continued to rule this mountain-region.[l] In the East, the border country near the range of Mt. Amanus was left to Tarcondimotus, who had obtained pardon from Caesar and now assumed the titles of King and "Friend of Antony."[18]

The dominions parcelled out to Amyntas and Polemo probably appeared neither to them nor to anyone else to be of any great value. Their rule over their respective assignments, however, proved to be of short duration, for three years later each received a kingdom which greatly increased his prestige and power.[19]

In 37/6 B.C. Castor, ruler of Galatia and Paphlagonia, died or was deposed from his throne. His dominions in Paphlagonia, including the capital, Gangra, and, in the northern part of the district, the basin of the river Amnias with the city of Pompeiopolis, were inherited by his son, Deiotarus Philadelphus, who, perhaps later, received additional territory in Phazimonitis, east of the Halys, including the city of Neapolis.[20]

Galatia, on the other hand, did not pass to Castor's heir. Antony, evidently regarding Amyntas as a more valuable supporter, presented the district to him, conferring on him also the title of King.[21] His kingdom was increased by the addition of Lycaonia, and he seems also to have received part of the Pamphylian coast, including the harbour-town of Side, where he minted silver coins. Thus enlarged, his rule extended from the mountains of northern Galatia to the shore of the Mediterranean.

The extension of Amyntas's dominions to Lycaonia meant, of course, that the district was lost to Polemo. Whatever portion of Cilicia Aspera this prince held or hoped to hold, was likewise lost to him, for the region was now presented by Antony to Cleopatra, to whom its timber was especially valuable for building a fleet.[22] Polemo, however, was provided with other dominions, namely that portion of Pontus which lay east of the river Iris, and he also received the title of King.[23] Part of Polemo's kingdom had previously been assigned to Darius, the son of Pharnaces, now either dead or deposed, whose possessions included

[k] See Chap XI note 23.   [l] See Chap. XXI note 12.

434

the region of Phazimonitis, farther to the west. When this was claimed by a certain Arsaces, perhaps another son of Pharnaces, Polemo, aided by Lycomedes, the Priest of Comana, captured and killed him. Thereby the new King of Pontus acquired additional territory, for although western Phazimonitis seems to have been given to Deiotarus Philadelphus, Polemo obtained the eastern portion of the region. Later, Antony further enlarged his kingdom by the gift of both Lesser Armenia and Colchis.

It is highly probable that, together with eastern Pontus, Polemo obtained from Antony the cities of Amaseia and Amisus and, with the latter, a stretch of the Euxine coast.[24] Nevertheless, he did not receive all of the province which Pompey had formed out of the former Pontic kingdom. Apart from the bestowal of western Phazimonitis on Deiotarus Philadelphus, Lycomedes retained his independent position as Priest of Comana, and Zela seems to have resumed its former status as a temple-city under its own priest. Both now received additional grants of land.[25] A small principality was created also for the Galatian chieftain Ateporix, who obtained lands in southern Pontus, probably the valley of the upper Halys and the mountain-region on the north. This division of the province put an end to the most important of Pompey's innovations, namely the formation of cities of the Hellenic type.[m] Of those which he founded east of the Halys, the communities of the Lycus valley came, like Amaseia and Amisus, under the rule of Polemo, Neapolis was assigned to Deiotarus, and Megalopolis, probably, to Ateporix.

In Cappadocia also an appointee of Antony's became king. On the murder of Ariobarzanes III by order of Cassius, his younger brother, Ariarathes, who had received some position as a royal vassal from Caesar but presently arrived in Rome in search of a kingdom,[n] became the lawful ruler. Antony, however, wishing to have Cappadocia, like Galatia and Pontus, ruled by a follower of his own, deposed Ariarathes and installed as king a certain Sisines, a grandson of that Archelaus whom Pompey had created priest of the Pontic Comana.[26] Assuming the ancestral name Archelaus, to which was added later the surname Philopatris, this young man took the throne of Cappadocia, which he held for a half-century, enjoying the favour not only of Antony but also of Augustus, from whom he received an addition to his kingdom.[o]

Besides the appointment of these kings, minor princes also were created by Antony either at this time or in the course of the next two

---

[m] See Chap. XV note 35.   [n] See Chap. XVII note 20.   [o] See Chap. XX note 24.

years. The Galatian chieftain Adiatorix, son of the tetrarch Domnilaus (or Domnecleius) who followed Pompey to Pharsalus, received a grant at Heracleia Pontica consisting of that part of the city and its territory which had not been assigned by Caesar to the colonists from Italy.[27] Even the bandit-chieftain Cleon, who had resisted Labienus's raiders, was rewarded, and, however incompatible a sacred office might seem to be with his previous career, he was made Priest of Zeus Abrettenus, whose temple in the mountain-country of northeastern Mysia possessed a considerable territory.

In consequence of this distribution of provincial territory in Asia Minor, only the provinces of Asia and Bithynia in the west and the district of Level Cilicia in the southeast were directly subject to the rule of Rome. The rest, save for the cities of the Lycian Federation, was now governed by princes of Asianic birth acting as instruments of Roman rule—a policy used twenty-five years previously by Pompey but now applied more widely. It is indeed probable that this new arrangement made for increased efficiency in the government of these regions and that the natives were more content under the rule of their own kings, whose knowledge of local conditions and consideration for local customs doubtless far surpassed that of a Roman proconsul.[28] In Pontus, particularly, where urban life was but little developed, Pompey's foundation of cities with Hellenic civic institutions may have been premature. There was the further advantage that the position of Antony, wishing to set forth on an expedition against the Parthians to avenge the defeat of Crassus, was strengthened by the bestowal of these dominions on men who, he had every reason to believe, would be loyal to the bestower. Nevertheless, the more extensive use of this method of government could not but retard both the cultural and the economic development of a large part of Asia Minor and its emancipation from the ideas and the methods of the East.

Unlike Pompey, Antony was not obliged to submit his new measures to the Senate for ratification, for, as has been observed, that body had approved in advance whatever he might do in his capacity as ruler of Rome's eastern possessions. In fact, these measures, taken arbitrarily and subject to no restraint, were characteristic of the policy followed by Antony in the last five years of his life, during which he held the power and played the part of an Hellenistic monarch.

The turning-point in Antony's career was his marriage to Cleopatra in the early winter of 37-36, which marked, as has been aptly observed, "the beginning of his breach with the West."[29] After acknowledging as his own the twin children whom the Queen had borne some three years previously, he presented Cleopatra with marriage-gifts of Roman provincial land, including not merely Cilicia Aspera but also portions of Syria, Phoenicia and Palestine. By this action and by his appointments in Asia Minor, Antony became the overlord of rulers, like the oriental potentates, a "King of Kings," a grandiose position which was to be surpassed less than three years later, when this title was conferred on Cleopatra's children, and Antony himself aspired to an even higher distinction.

With Antony's disastrous expedition against the Parthians in 36, in the course of which he and his army marched through Armenia into Media Atropatene (northwestern Persia) and back again with great loss and suffering, this narrative is not concerned.[30] This expedition, however, had an aftermath which was of great consequence in the history of Rome's participation in eastern affairs; for eighteen months after his return, Antony, accusing the Armenian king, Artavasdes, son of Tigranes the Great, of treacherous dealing during the Parthian campaign, invaded Armenia and carried off Artavasdes as a prisoner to Alexandria. The consequent enmity toward Rome of the monarch's son, Artaxias, who, having escaped from Antony, was made king by his fellow-countrymen, ultimately led to his murder and to the establishment of his Romanized brother as ruler. Thus arose the "Armenian question," which, for a century after Artavasdes's capture, played an important part in Roman diplomacy.

About the time of Antony's return from Media, western Asia Minor was the scene of the last act in the stormy life-drama of Sextus Pompeius, the younger son of the conqueror of the East. Since the defeat and death of his older brother in Spain in 45, Sextus had carried on warfare against Caesar and those whom he regarded as the Dictator's successors, in the course of which he and his fleet terrorized the coast of Italy by frequent depredations. A formal reconciliation with the Triumvirs in the spring of 39 was soon followed by a renewal of his war against Octavian. In this struggle, after winning a victory over his opponent, Sextus, in the autumn of 36, was finally defeated in a naval battle off Naulochus at the northeastern corner of Sicily. In this campaign, apparently, ships sent from the East by Antony fought on Octavian's side.[31]

His power destroyed and his hope of further resistance lost, Sextus with a few ships fled to Asia Minor.[32] He was cordially received in

Mitylene, where the citizens still thought of his father with gratitude. Learning of the losses suffered by Antony during the Parthian campaign, Sextus dreamed of re-establishing himself in power and began to refit his ships and train a body of fighting-men. In the hope of gaining support from one side or the other, he sent envoys both to the Parthian King and to Antony, who by this time had returned to Alexandria. But apparently without waiting for any result from these missions, Sextus in the spring of 35 crossed over to the mainland. The governor of Asia, Gaius Furnius, permitted him to land but soon, perceiving his warlike preparations, suspected violence. As at the time of Labienus's invasion, the province was unarmed, but Furnius was able to enlist a small force and sent messengers both to Gnaeus Domitius Ahenobarbus, governor of Bithynia, and to King Amyntas, asking for assistance. Sextus thereupon, throwing aside all pretence of friendly relations, seized Lampsacus by treachery. By promising large bounties to the inhabitants, especially to the Romans settled in the city, he induced many to join him, thereby raising his army to the strength of three legions. An attack on Cyzicus failed, partly on account of the strength of the city and partly because of the presence of a troop of Antony's gladiators and some soldiers guarding them; but in a battle in the plain of the lower Scamander Sextus drove Furnius's army from the field. Then entering the Propontis, he carried the war into Bithynia, where Domitius was powerless against him. A landing-party, making a raid into the interior, entered Nicaea, where the soldiers seized a large quantity of booty, and the ships even sailed up the long gulf to Nicomedeia, which also was captured.

About this time, a fleet of 120 ships, under the command of Marcus Titius, sent by Antony to the aid of the two helpless governors, arrived in the Propontis. Sextus retreated before it, and after fruitless negotiations carried on near Nicomedeia—where he seems to have been entrapped in the gulf—he formed the desperate resolve of burning his ships and with his soldiers and sailors withdrawing into the interior. It was believed that his plan was to take refuge in Armenia. Titius and Furnius, following him along the highway which led through Phrygia Epictetus to Galatia,[p] overtook him at Midaeum, where they were joined by Amyntas and his cavalry. After a parley, in which he refused to surrender to Titius, Sextus attempted flight under cover of darkness. His plan, however, was betrayed, and, pursued by Amyntas and the horsemen, he was forced to yield without con-

[p] See Chap. II note 21 and Chap. XIX note 9.

ditions to the Galatian King. He seems to have been taken to Miletus and there killed by Antony's order. It was one of the ironies in which history abounds that the son should have met a traitor's death in that portion of the Empire which his father had delivered from an invader.

The breach with the West, opened by Antony's marriage to Cleopatra and his bestowal on her of lands which the Romans regarded as theirs, was greatly widened in the late autumn of 34 at the completion of the campaign in Armenia in which Artavasdes had been carried away as a captive. The victory was celebrated in Alexandria by a magnificent procession, modelled on the triumph held in Rome by a successful general, and in connexion with it Cleopatra's son Caesarion was declared the lawful son of Julius Caesar and made co-ruler of Egypt with his mother under the title "King of Kings."[33] This title seems to have been conferred also on the two boys who had been born to the Queen and Antony and who now were made titular rulers of the East. The elder—one of twins—received Armenia and all else east of the Euphrates, while his sister obtained the Roman possessions in Cyrenaica and Libya, and the younger boy, still a small child, was presented with Phoenicia and Syria, together with Cilicia and all that lay west of the Euphrates "as far as the Hellespont." Henceforth, Antony himself was to be no mere "King of Kings" but the supreme ruler of the inhabited world. This ambitious programme, when known at Rome, aroused great indignation. It was at once utilized by Octavian, who, in his resentment at the behaviour of his former associate, was ready to employ any means of propaganda.[34] Cleopatra, on her side, in her desire to extend her rule, caused Antony to involve himself to the point where war became inevitable.

The two spent the winter of 33-32 at Ephesus.[35] The legions which had served in the Armenian campaign were ordered, on their return, to assemble here, and preparations were begun in earnest for the impending struggle. Above all, a huge fleet was mobilized, which eventually consisted of five hundred warships and three hundred transports. A quarter of this number was supplied by Cleopatra, and it may be assumed that the coast cities of Asia were forced to furnish their contingents. At Cos one of Antony's subordinates even went so far as to cut down a grove sacred to Asclepius in order to get wood for the construction of vessels. In the spring, headquarters were moved to Samos.[q] Here, amid further mobilization, there was much feasting, enlivened by entertainments given by the Artists of Dionysus, who

[q] Plutarch *Ant.* 56, 3f.

were ordered to appear on the island and in return for their services were presented by Antony with the city of Priene as an official residence. To Cleopatra he gave three colossal statues of Zeus, Athena and Heracles, the works of Myron, which had stood in the Temple of Hera.[r]

During the summer of 32 B.C. the huge fleet and an army of about 75,000 infantrymen, besides cavalry supplied in part by the client-kings, were taken across the Aegean and onward to the western coast of Greece. In September of the following year, after his forces had been weakened by illness, desertion and minor defeats, Antony and his ships, with at least 35,000 legionaries on board, met Octavian's fleet off the promontory of Actium. The sudden withdrawal of Cleopatra and her squadron, followed by Antony, and the subsequent surrender of the land-forces brought it to pass that the ancient world was ruled not by an oriental monarch but by a Roman *Imperator*, who, astutely maintaining the form of a republican government, called himself *Princeps* or Foremost Citizen.

In the late autumn of 31 B.C., a few weeks after the battle at Actium, the victorious Octavian—at the age of thirty-two the unquestioned ruler of the Roman world—crossed the Aegean Sea and landed at Samos.[36] After a visit to Ephesus he returned to the island, remaining there until after the first of the following January, when he entered upon his fourth consulship. His stay was celebrated by the introduction of a new era, by which the years were reckoned from "Caesar's victory."[37] Intended, presumably, both as a compliment to the new ruler and as expression of the general hope for improved conditions under his rule, this method of computing time, although in general it did not replace the older era of Sulla, was afterward adopted by some of the cities of Lydia.

At the end of the year, after the surrender of Alexandria and the suicide, first of Antony and then of Cleopatra, Octavian paid a second visit to Samos, where, having assumed the consulship for the year 29, he stayed until the middle of the summer. In the course of these two visits the communities and princes that had supported Antony made their peace with the new ruler, and the necessary measures were taken for the future government of Asia Minor.

Like his adoptive father seventeen years earlier, Octavian came to Asia as a victor, but it was to a land which had suffered cruelly during

[r] Strabo XIV p. 637.

that interval. It is true that prior to Caesar's arrival in the summer of 48 the resources of the eastern provinces had been weakened by the exactions of the partisans of Pompey,[s] but in comparison with the depredations which followed, these must have appeared negligible. The assessments which Caesar himself laid upon certain of his rival's supporters were followed a few years later, first by the exactions ordered by Brutus and Cassius, then by the wholesale robberies committed by the "Liberators" themselves, and after these by the ruinous levies mercilessly imposed by Antony.[t] In addition, extensive portions of the country had been ravaged during the invasion of Labienus and the Parthians; the raid of Sextus Pompey, though limited to a small area, must have brought damage to the region around the Propontis; and Antony's recent mobilization of troops and, especially, a fleet could not but have entailed great expense upon the provincial communities. It needs but little imagination to picture the general economic distress which must now have presented a serious problem to the victor.

It is related that Octavian, after his victory, punished the cities which had sided with his opponent by levying payments of money and by suspending their governmental assemblies,[u] by which is evidently meant that he deprived them of their freedom and autonomy. The sum of money demanded from Cos, of which Octavian is said to have remitted one hundred talents in payment for Apelles's painting of Venus rising from the sea,[38] was perhaps a fine imposed on the Coans for allowing Antony to seize timber for the construction of ships. But, with this possible exception, there is no definite record that Octavian imposed any penalties on the cities, and indeed in the ruined condition of Asia, it is improbable that any large sums of money could have been collected. The Rhodians, to be sure, seem to have been deprived of Myndus and the islands which they had received from Antony, but this action is ascribed, not to a desire to punish them for a friendly attitude toward Octavian's enemy, but to the harshness with which they were ruling these new possessions.[v]

On the other hand, there is positive evidence of Octavian's interest in the cities' welfare. In Caria, to which, particularly, Labienus's invasion had brought great suffering, Stratoniceia and Mylasa were treated with all consideration.[39] To the former, by his care for the Temple of Hecate at Lagina, Octavian gave a "true conception of the gods among men," confirming the inviolability of the sanctuary of the

---

[s] See above p. 403f.
[u] Cassius Dio LI 2, 1.

[t] See above pp. 406, 419 and 421 and note 1.
[v] See note 3.

Goddess, as well as that of Zeus at Panamara, and praising the citizens for the steadfastness they had shown during the invasion and for their loyalty to Rome. In his letter to Mylasa, written on his arrival in Asia at the end of 31 in a reply to an embassy which described the city's plight and doubtless asked for some favour in recognition of its attempt at resistance, Octavian courteously expressed his sympathy, and, although but little of his letter is preserved, it may be assumed that he granted the request. The fact that his letter is addressed to the "Magistrates, Council and People" indicates that he recognized the city's right of self-government. The brave orator Hybreas, who, when Labienus captured Mylasa, was forced to take refuge in Rhodes, had probably by this time returned and begun the work of restoring the place. Recovery, however, was slow. Some time after Octavian's letter was written, the financial condition of the city was so bad that it seemed necessary to a Roman official, presumably the governor of the province, to condemn a method of collecting taxes which would bring some persons into virtual servitude and to comment on the fact that, because all of the public funds had been pledged, it had proved necessary, in order to repair the damage wrought by Labienus, to bring the city into debt by borrowing money from individual citizens.

With the intention, presumably, of improving the economic condition of the province, Octavian, during his visit to Asia in 29, began an issue of gold and silver coins, minted at Ephesus and Pergamum and perhaps in other places also.[40] Antony had, indeed, caused silver pieces to be minted, but merely for the purpose of paying his soldiers, and it is probable that those first issued by Octavian were similarly used. The fact, however, that his issues continued for over a decade indicates that they were intended for general circulation and for the purpose of supplying the need for ready money. These coins, bearing Octavian's portrait, show various types and legends, one issue, intended to glorify the victory at Actium, being inscribed "Asia Recovered." Of these issues, the most important were the cistophori, which at first bore the traditional representation of the mystic *cista* but afterward showed other types. Similar coins, all with the ruler's head, were issued by later emperors also; they became the standard for circulation in the East and served as a general medium of exchange.

In addition to the problem presented by the economic condition of Asia Minor, Octavian was confronted with the question of the future of the client-kingdoms created by Antony, whose rulers had supported their benefactor's cause in the campaign ended at Actium.[w] Amyntas of Galatia, to be sure, had gone over to the opposing side before the final battle, Deiotarus Philadelphus of Paphlagonia had likewise deserted after Antony's cavalry was defeated in a preliminary encounter, and Tarcondimotus of the Amanus had fallen during a minor engagement.[x] In the cases of the others, Polemo, Archelaus and Mithradates, who had succeeded Antiochus in Commagene, there was reason to expect that they might be deprived of their thrones.

The reverse proved to be the case. Not only did Octavian take no vengeance on those who had supported his rival, but, with a few minor exceptions, he adopted Antony's policy of using these native princes to govern the less Hellenized countries.[41] It was natural enough that the two rulers who had decided before the battle to throw in their lot with him should be rewarded, and both Amyntas and Deiotarus Philadelphus were confirmed in the possession of their kingdoms. The dominions of the former, in fact, were greatly enlarged. On the south of Lycaonia, he was permitted to attack the dynast Antipater, ruler of Derbe and Laranda, and, after killing him, to seize this Taurus region, as well as part of the neighbouring Isauria. Octavian, furthermore, presented him with that portion of the coast of Cilicia Aspera which Antony had given to Cleopatra. These additions to an already extensive kingdom made the former secretary of Deiotarus the Galatian the most powerful of Rome's client-princes.

In accordance with this policy of retaining Antony's appointees in their positions of power, Archelaus and Polemo were likewise permitted to keep their kingdoms of Cappadocia and Pontus. Polemo, indeed, was punished by a delay in confirming his position, for it was not until four years later—in 26 B.C.—that he was formally declared a "friend and ally" of Rome.[42] He lost, moreover, the territory which had been given to him in Armenia Minor. This was presented to Artavasdes, the former king of Media Atropatene, who, after his kingdom had been invaded by Antony, became reconciled to him and, in consequence, was driven out by the Parthians. As the enemy of Artaxias, the ruler of Greater Armenia, who was a bitter foe of Rome, Artavasdes could be entrusted with the guarding of the Euphrates frontier.

While the four principal monarchs who owed their power to Antony retained their kingdoms, a few changes were made among rulers of

[w] Plutarch *Ant.* 61, 1.
[x] Plutarch *Ant.* 63, 3: Cassius Dio L 13, 5 and 8; 14, 2: Velleius Paterculus II 84, 2: Horace *Epodes* 9, 17f.

minor importance. Lycomedes, whom Caesar had made priest-ruler of Comana in Pontus and Antony had retained in power, with the gift of additional territory, was now deprived of his office.[43] Presumably on his deposition, but perhaps a little later, the priesthood of the Goddess was conferred on the former bandit-chieftain Cleon, who, after his resistance to Labienus, had been made priest of Zeus in eastern Mysia. His present reward was given in return for his services in persuading the Mysians to abandon the cause of Antony for that of Octavian. Cleon's lawless nature, however, led him to disregard the rules either of health or of the Goddess and this disregard brought punishment upon him. He died within a month of his arrival in Comana, as the result, some said, of gluttony, but according to the pious, because he was stricken by the Great Mother, whose anger he had incurred by bringing a pig into her sacred city in transgression of the divine law. It is, however, not impossible that the Goddess acted through the agency of some partisan of the previous incumbent of the priestly office.

Other recorded changes seem to have been due to the desire, not so much to punish Antony's partisans, as to right some existing wrong. The city of Amisus, which had been given to Polemo by Antony but had fallen under the power of a tyrant named Strato, was delivered from its oppressor and restored to the status of independence granted by Caesar.[44] In commemoration, the city afterwards used a system of dating reckoned from this "year of freedom." At Heracleia, Adiatorix, who, after receiving from Antony the rule over the Greek portion of the city, had attacked the Romans placed by Caesar in an adjoining settlement, was punished for his violence and for the slaughter he had committed. Octavian deprived him of his power, and caused both him and his sons to be led as captives in the triumphal procession held in celebration of the victory at Actium. Adiatorix himself and his younger son were then put to death; the older, Dyteutus, a youth of outstanding ability, apparently, and of great strength of character, was afterward made priest-ruler of Comana.

In addition to the changes thus made on the northern coast, it seemed necessary to take certain measures also in southeastern Asia Minor. The death of Tarcondimotus had left the Amanus region without a ruler, but his son Philopator expected to succeed to the throne.[45] This expectation, however, was cut short by a misfortune which could not have been anticipated. Antony's band of gladiators stationed at Cyzicus, who had helped to defend the city against Sextus Pompey, hearing of their master's defeat at Actium and wishing to join him, had set out on the long march across Asia Minor to Egypt. In Galatia, Amyntas tried to bar their advance, but they succeeded in fighting their way through and, apparently without further opposition, arrived at the border of Syria. Here they asked for aid from Philopator and his brother, since the young men's father had fought for Antony. The princes, however, wishing to gain favour with the new ruler, refused, and the gladiators were compelled to take matters into their own hands and force the governor of Syria to admit them to his province. They found a temporary refuge at Daphne, near Antioch, but although this place was well outside the boundaries of the kingdom of the Amanus, the sons of Tarcondimotus did not escape the suspicions of Octavian. Philopator was not permitted to succeed to his father's power, and the kingship of this region was for a time suspended.

In Commagene, on the other hand, King Mithradates II, even though he had fought on Antony's side, was retained in power. So ready, in fact, was Octavian to uphold him against his brother Antiochus, who had designs on the throne, that when this prince murdered an envoy sent by Mithradates to Rome, Octavian had him brought before the Senate for trial and, when he had been declared guilty, caused him to be put to death.[46] This incident, if correctly reported, is the first known example of the subjection of a foreign prince to the jurisdiction of the Roman Senate; it constituted a precedent repeated nearly forty-five years later, when King Archelaus of Cappadocia was brought to trial before the same tribunal.

Two years after Octavian, during his second visit to Samos, became Consul for the fifth time, the Roman Empire was reconstituted on a new basis. In January, 27 B.C., the *Imperator* who was now master of the Roman world, going through the form of "restoring the Commonwealth to the Roman People," resigned his irregular and extraordinary command and emerged with greater powers veiled under the term "authority" and with the name Augustus. The change brought with it a new and important arrangement with regard to the government of the provinces.[47] Like the other administrative functions, they were divided between the Senate and the self-styled *Princeps*, who, vested with military *imperium*, was the commander of all the military forces of Rome. In the division, the general principle was adopted that the provinces which, long included in the Empire and ordinarily at peace, did not need the permanent presence of troops should fall to the share of the Senate; they were governed, as in the time of the Republic, by former consuls or praetors, holding office for one year, and the revenues from them, still managed by quaestors, accrued to the Senate's treasury. Those provinces, on the other hand, which had been more recently acquired and which needed troops either for maintaining order within or preventing invasion from without, became the *provincia* of the holder of the *imperium*; a representative of his, a "legate of Augustus acting as praetor," governed in his name for as long a time as he wished to keep the appointee in office, and the revenues were collected by his special agents, the procurators.

Under this arrangement, the provinces of Asia and Bithynia, peaceful in themselves and with no frontier exposed to an enemy, remained under the power of the Senate. A distinction was made between them, however, in that Asia, like Africa, the only other province of similar importance, was placed under an ex-consul, while Bithynia, like all the other senatorial provinces, was governed by an ex-praetor, who, to be sure, enjoyed the courtesy title of Proconsul.

Almost from the beginning, however, the inhabitants of Asia and Bithynia thought of Augustus rather than the Senate as their ruler. To them he was not so much *Princeps* as monarch, taking the place of the kings who had ruled Asia Minor in the past. As these, from Alexander onward, had, while still living, received divine honours in the Hellenic cities, so, within two years of the victory at Actium, the communities of the two provinces, taking action in their general assemblies, requested permission to establish sanctuaries in which the new Roman *Imperator* should likewise be worshipped as a god.[48]

Apart from the dynastic cults established by the Seleucids in their kingdom, the divine honours which the city-states had bestowed on the rulers were the result of measures taken by the citizens themselves and on their own initiative.[49] Conferred, at least at first, on these rulers rather as benefactors than as monarchs, they were intended to express the citizens' gratitude for the recognition of privileges and perhaps, as has sometimes been supposed, to find some place of honour for the king in a democratically organized city-state. In many cases, doubtless, they were motivated by the hope of obtaining favours in the future. The recipients of such honours had not, indeed, always been of royal rank; for after the rule of the kings had given place to that of Rome, individual cities retained the custom of conferring them on those who were considered to have deserved well of the community, as Manius

Aquilius and Diodorus Pasparus, for whom the Pergamenes created priests, and Servilius Isauricus, whom the Ephesians worshipped in conjunction with Roma.[50] United action, however, was taken for the first time when the representatives of the cities, peoples and tribal districts of Asia, meeting in Ephesus, declared Julius Caesar a "god made manifest."

A ruler-cult of the Hellenistic type, however, played no part in the policy and purpose of Augustus. In full knowledge of the distaste with which the bestowal of divine honours on his adoptive father during the latter's lifetime were viewed in Rome, but none the less emphasizing the deification of the dead Caesar, he had already shown the Romans his attitude toward any possible proposals of a similar nature by incorporating in his name the patronymic of "Son of the Deified."[51] Nevertheless, making a concession to the traditions of the Asianic communities, he granted their petitions. At the same time, lessening his own distinction and furthering the glory of Rome, he stipulated that he should be worshipped only in conjunction with the deified Roma, a cult of whom was already in existence in at least eleven places in the province of Asia.[y] For this compromise there was a precedent in the combined worship of Roma and Servilius Isauricus at Ephesus. As the seats of the new cult, the *Princeps* named Pergamum and Nicomedeia. In the former, the province of Asia erected a temple to "Roma and Augustus," and it may be supposed that the Bithynians founded a corresponding sanctuary in the latter.[52] The Roman citizens resident in the two provinces, who had no part in the action of the Hellenic communities or share in their cult of Roma and the Emperor, were permitted to build temples in Ephesus and Nicaea, where they might worship Roma in conjunction with the Deified Julius.[53]

In each of the two provinces the maintenance of the cult which gave the Roman *Princeps* a permanent place among the gods and thereby established his position as monarch was entrusted to the "Commonalty of the Hellenes." In Asia this organization had been in existence under one name or another since the beginning of the first century, when the "peoples and tribes" of the province conferred honours on Scaevola and other illustrious men.[x] About the middle of this century and again in Antony's time the Commonalty of the Hellenes in Asia had served as intermediary for communications addressed to the cities by Roman officials.[a] But with these exceptions

[y] See Appendix III A 1.   [z] See Chap. VII note 48.
[a] See Chap. VII note 41 and above note 4.

447

nothing is known of its actions during the period prior to the foundation of the cult of Roma and Augustus, the supervision of which greatly increased both its activity and its importance.[54]

From this time onward the Commonalty of Asia held annual meetings for the worship of the new deities and for the transaction of business by its Assembly.[55] At first these meetings seem to have taken place at Pergamum in connexion with the worship in the provincial temple. About 10 B.C., however, the Assembly met in Smyrna, and after A.D. 26, when a second temple for the province was erected there, the sessions must have taken place in both cities, possibly alternately. Later, Ephesus, where another temple was built, was added as a meeting-place, and in course of time the Assembly was held also in Sardis, Cyzicus, Philadelpheia, Laodiceia-on-Lycus, Miletus and Tralles. The deputies were evidently chosen by the member-cities, and if, as is not improbable, the method used by the federation of the Lycian communities was employed, it may be supposed that each city sent from one to three representatives, according to its size.[56] At a meeting held about 4 B.C., 150 deputies were present.

In addition to maintaining the worship of Roma and the Emperor, this organization celebrated a "common" festival with a "sacred" contest, held at regular intervals, perhaps of one year, in honour of the two deities.[57] This was called, from the names of both, *Romaia Sebasta*, and it soon became one of the great festivals of the eastern portion of the Empire, drawing contestants from far and wide. Connected with the temple at Pergamum was also a celebration of Augustus's birthday, at which sacrifice was offered and a hymn sung in his honour by a choir of "hymnodists."[58] These singers formed a province-wide organization which was carried on by their descendants, the expenses, according to the provisions of an order of Augustus, being defrayed by an assessment imposed on the province as a whole. Even in the second century these "hymnodists of the Deified Augustus and the Deified Roma," apparently forty in number, were still in existence, with officials and a building of their own.

The principal official of the Commonalty was the Chief Priest of Roma and Augustus, commonly called the Chief Priest of Asia, who was chosen at the annual meeting of the Assembly for a term of one year, probably from among the deputies sent by the cities.[59] Since the six Chief Priests who are known to have held office during the principate of Augustus and whose homes are recorded were citizens of six different cities, both large and small, it is evident that none of the member-communities had any prior claim to the office. The principal duty of the Chief Priest was to conduct the worship of Roma and the Emperor, but he had also secular functions; he made proposals for action by the Assembly and arranged for the execution of its enactments, including the formal communication of its transactions to the cities concerned. He might also serve as "agonothete" of the *Romaia Sebasta*, but since this office was frequently held for life, it seems to have had no necessary connexion with the priesthood. From the middle of the first century onward the Chief Priest's wife enjoyed the privilege of being called Chief Priestess.

The Commonalty had also one or more annually elected "advocates" who acted as its envoys to the emperor and on one occasion were made responsible for the publication of the Assembly's decrees in the member-cities.[60] Other officials included a secretary, who might preside over the contests at the provincial festival, and a treasurer, whose duties, it may be assumed, included the management of the funds needed for the maintenance of the provincial temples and the festivals, the various expenses incurred in connexion with the meetings of the Assembly and perhaps also for the minting of the coins issued by the Commonalty.

It has frequently been supposed that there was a connexion between the Commonalty of Asia and the dignitaries who held the title of Asiarch, of whom a large number are known from the inscriptions and coins of the first three centuries of the Christian Era.[61] This title is first heard of in the work of Strabo, who relates that some of the citizens of Tralles, called Asiarchs, were prominent in the province, among them the famous Pythodorus, formerly a friend of Pompey. It is also recorded that St. Paul had many friends among the Asiarchs at Ephesus. In the opinion of most modern scholars this term was either an alternative designation, used less formally, for the Chief Priest of the province or a distinction held by the official who presided over—and bore the cost of—the provincial festival. Neither of these views, however, is supported by convincing evidence, and the fact that only a small proportion of the Asiarchs whose names are extant appears in the list of the known Chief Priests seems to show that the two offices were not identical. Still another view, namely, that the Asiarchs were the deputies sent by the various cities to represent them in the provincial Assembly has likewise not been established.

While it must be admitted that no positive knowledge can be obtained from our available sources concerning the nature and functions of the Asiarchate a few inferences regarding the office are possible. The brief statement of Strabo and the remark about the friends of St. Paul suggest that at a given time there were several who bore the title. On the other hand, the bearers did not form a permanent, merely honorary, group, for in several cases the holder of this title is described as Asiarch for the second or the third or perhaps even for the fourth time. Another was Asiarch for only four days. There seems, moreover, to be more reason to connect the Asiarchs with individual cities than with the province as a whole, for whereas one man is called Asiarch of Asia, others appear as Asiarchs of Ephesus and of Pergamum, as well as of the temples in these places and in Smyrna.

The Asiarchs, in fact, appear chiefly as benefactors of the cities. At Miletus a certain man repaired one of the public baths "in return for the Asiarchate," and in at least nineteen places, which include not only Pergamum, Smyrna and Cyzicus, but also a majority of relatively unimportant cities, bronze coins were minted bearing the names of Asiarchs, who, it may be supposed, paid the costs of the respective issues. The fact that a municipal title, such as *strategos, archon* or *grammateus*, is also found on these coins shows that a local office might be held simultaneously with the Asiarchate. Perhaps the most conspicuous service, however, performed by the Asiarchs was the bearing of the expense of local contests or spectacles in the arena. In several cases they had the additional title of agonothete, and of one Asiarch it is recorded that he gave a spectacle at Ephesus lasting for thirteen days, in which "African beasts" (panthers?) were slain and thirty-nine pairs of gladiators fought to the death. On the famous occasion when Polycarp, Bishop of Smyrna, was burned alive, an Asiarch presided over the wild-beast hunt which formed part of the local festival, and monuments record the existence of bands of gladiators of at least five Asiarchs. Even in the late fourth century an imperial letter to the governor of the province ordered that a man from a smaller city who wished to win fame might obtain an Asiarchate by giving a public spectacle at Ephesus but in so doing he might not abandon his native community. If, from the meagre information available, a conjecture be permissible, it might be supposed that this title was conferred on those who performed some public service—usually, apparently, the giving of a spectacle—and that it was renewed at each repetition of such a service; but whether the bestowal was an act of the Commonalty or of a city—or the temples of a city—or of some outside authority is beyond even the realm of conjecture.

Concerning the Commonalty of Bithynia there is much less information than for its counterpart in Asia.[62] There is no mention of a Chief Priest of the province corresponding to the holder of this title in Asia, and the conduct of the worship of the emperor was probably the duty of the "Sebastophant and Hierophant of the mysteries" of the "common temple of Bithynia." The provincial Assembly had also an *Archon*, probably a presiding-officer, whose tenure of office was limited, and the "common festival" was celebrated periodically at Nicomedeia. The province had also Bithyniarchs, on one of whom the title was conferred three times.

The activities of these provincial assemblies were by no means confined to the worship of Roma and the emperor and the celebration of their festivals and contests. On several occasions they took action in matters affecting the provinces they represented, particularly those which concerned their relations with the government at Rome. At a session held about 9 B.C.—the earliest of which there is actual record—the Commonalty of Asia enacted a decree by which the member-cities adopted a new calendar, proposed by the proconsul.[b] A few years afterward, on three separate occasions, this organization sent an "advocate" to Rome,[c] who not only acted as a special envoy to convey its congratulations to Augustus's grandson on his assumption of the man's toga but also "honestly and carefully watched over the interests of Asia, neglecting no opportunity for the advantage of the Hellenes and using all zeal in their behalf," a eulogy which suggests that the business he transacted may have been of real significance.

A much more important function of these organizations was the presentation of charges against Roman officials who abused their powers in the provinces. In A.D. 22 the Commonalty of Asia brought an accusation for cruelty and extortion against the proconsul of the province, and in the following year it caused an imperial procurator to be prosecuted for usurping the command of troops; in both cases the defendant was found guilty of the offence.[63] Similarly, the Bithynian Assembly, during the first century and the opening years of the second, brought charges against four proconsuls, two of whom were convicted. Other complaints also were presented. When, at the end of the first century, the Assembly of Asia protested against an imperial edict, designed to increase the production of grain, which commanded the provincials to destroy half of their vines, the order, as it concerned this province, was promptly rescinded. Somewhat later,

b See Chap. XX note 39.   c See note 60.

451

in a time of "the direst need," this assembly sent an embassy to the emperor to plead for the remission of "the 5 per cent tax," and the honours paid to one of the envoys seem to show that the mission was successful. As late as the third century the Bithynian Assembly protested successfully against the illegal action of officials who attempted to prevent appeals to the emperor.[d]

As has been already observed, the creation of the imperial cult and the assignment of its administration to the Commonalties of the provinces greatly increased the importance of these organizations. Their position was further strengthened by the recognition of the right to deal in a corporate capacity with the Roman government in matters affecting the interests of their provinces. This, in turn, added dignity to the member-cities vested with what must have appeared to be an addition to their powers. It also gave prestige to their representatives in the common Assemblies, who in the course of time acquired a distinction that gradually led to the formation of a provincial nobility.[64] The sons of the Chief Priests, admitted to the Equestrian Order, held office under the Roman government, and their sons, in turn, even became members of the Senate.

The new cult, furthermore, provided a means, hitherto unknown, of establishing a general loyalty in which all could participate, the worship of the God-Emperor. In his "common festival" all might take part, and in worshipping him, together with Roma, the province as a whole placed itself under the protection of Rome and professed allegiance to the *Imperator* who ruled the known world. This method of maintaining the loyalty of Rome's subjects, which originated in western Asia Minor, was gradually extended to the other provinces as well. The institution of provincial Assemblies and of the imperial cult, not only in the East and in Greece and Macedonia, but also in Africa, the Danube region, Spain, Gaul and even Britain, became a successful political expedient to weld the far-flung dominions of Rome into a unified empire.

[d] *Digesta* XLIX 1, 25.

CHAPTER XIX

THE GALATIAN PROVINCE

WHEN, after the victory at Actium, Octavian not only confirmed the power given by Antony to King Amyntas but
even extended it, there was every reason to suppose that this
monarch's rule over most of central Asia Minor would prove a
lasting arrangement. After five years, however, a complete read-
justment was made necessary by Amyntas's death.[1] With the purpose
of establishing his power in the country recently assigned to him in
the Taurus region, the King had undertaken the fortification of
the natural stronghold of Isaura, which had been captured for Rome
by the elder Servilius Isauricus some fifty years earlier. The work—
a massive wall, about two and a half miles in circumference—appears
to have been all but finished when the King was called away to
suppress the turbulent mountain-folk who bore the name of Homonadeis.[2] This formidable people, considered unconquerable, lived in
the rugged Taurus country, probably west or southwest of Isaura, and
may well have endangered the route which connected the city with
Side, Amyntas's port on the Pamphylian coast. In spite of the difficulty of the country and the ferocity of its inhabitants, Amyntas
had killed their chieftain and taken possession of a number of
their strongholds when he himself was captured by a stratagem of
the chieftain's widow and promptly put to death by the mountaineers.

Amyntas left sons, but they were not permitted to inherit his kingdom and the lion's share of the late monarch's dominions was now
incorporated in the Roman Empire.[3] By this step a new province was
created which contained not only the district of Galatia, the home of
the Celtic tribesmen, but also the steppe of Lycaonia, extending to the
northern slopes of the Taurus, and, farther west, the highland country
of Pisidia, from the border of the province of Asia to the mountains
back of the Pamphylian plain. The inaccessible and undeveloped district of Cilicia Aspera was given either at this time or shortly afterward
to King Archelaus of Cappadocia.[a] It is uncertain whether Amyntas's
possessions on the coast of Pamphylia were incorporated in the new
province or organized as a separate administrative unit.[4]

The new addition to Rome's dominions seems to have been officially

[a] See Chap. XX note 24.

called the "Galatian Province," a name taken from the land which had formed the principal part of Amyntas's kingdom, but indicating that other districts as well were included within its boundaries.[5] A comparison of its outline to an irregular trefoil may indicate its general configuration as well as the relative positions of its three component portions. These were clustered about the high peaks of the Sultan Dağ, the northernmost point of the great range which, under many names, extends northwestward from the Taurus and, after forming an obtuse angle above the wide plain of the Phrygian Caÿster, bends back toward the southwest to Apameia in Phrygia.[6] Rising somewhat southwest of the true centre of a circle enclosing the three districts, this mountain may nevertheless serve as the point with reference to which their several situations can be determined.

Farthest to the north and northeast of the angle of the Sultan Dağ, lay Galatia proper. Reaching northward as far as the mountain-range which formed the natural frontier of Paphlagonia and extending across the Halys, it is an upland region, broken into separate valleys by groups of low mountains. Its northern portion, in particular, well watered by the tributaries of the Halys and the Sangarius and by their affluents, is a fertile country, capable of bearing rich crops and affording abundant pasture, and the mountain-range along the Paphlagonian border contained extensive forests.[7] In the south, on the contrary, the land, as also in modern times, seems to have been treeless and bare. On the southeast of this barren region, a high undulating plateau, described as "dreary and forbidding," the borderland between Galatia and Lycaonia, stretched as far as the northwestern corner of the great salt lake, Tatta, beyond which lay the kingdom of Cappadocia.[8]

From early times northern Galatia had held a position of strategic importance. Situated between the eastern and western portions of Asia Minor, it lay on the line of communication which the Hittites and their various successors maintained from Armenia to the Aegean. During the Hellenistic and Roman periods also, roads from Phrygia and Bithynia led through the district, connecting its chief towns, Ancyra and Tavium, not only with the western coast but also with Pontus and Cappadocia.[9] One of these, in the fourth century after Christ, became the route of pilgrims from Europe to Jerusalem. Nevertheless, in spite of the presence of these thoroughfares, urban life had been little developed, and in this respect, especially, Galatia presented a great contrast to the Aegean littoral. Little was done by the Celtic tribesmen to stimulate the growth of cities, for they lived chiefly in

and around their castles, lording it over the villages which they possessed.[b] The ancient town of Gordium, said to have been in existence
as early as the second millennium before Christ and in Alexander's time
a place of some size, was in the second century only a market-town
and at the beginning of the Christian Era a mere village.[10] Pessinus,
to be sure, famous for its sanctuary of the Great Mother and once
an independent temple-state, probably developed early into a trading-
centre of importance.[11] Having come under the power of the tetrarchs
Brogitarus and Deiotarus, it finally became, if not under Amyntas, at
least under Roman rule, a secularized community of the *polis*-type.
The principal place in the district, however, was the great road-junction
Ancyra, the chief settlement of the Tectosages.[12] This community,
Romanized, probably, without having been Hellenized, became the
administrative centre of the new province and soon outstripped the
other towns of Galatia. East of the Halys, Tavium, the principal town
of the Trocmi, situated in a fertile region and near the point of diver-
gence of several roads leading to Pontus and Cappadocia, was, like
Pessinus, a centre of trade.[13] It was famous for a sanctuary of a god,
Hellenized as Zeus, whose sacred precinct had the privilege of inviolability.

On both sides of the southeastern extension of the range of the
Sultan Dağ itself, lay the region known as Phrygia Paroreius, "along
the mountain."[14] Well watered by the descending streams, it was fertile
and thickly populated; but on the northeastern side the inhabited
country was little more than a narrow fringe, for the streams soon
lose themselves in a number of lakes, beyond which lies the salt wilderness extending to Lake Tatta.

Farther to the south and east, Lycaonia extended eastward to the
mountains which border Cappadocia.[15] On the northwest, its limit was
perhaps the low range which runs from Lake Tatta to the chain of
the Sultan Dağ, and on the southwest, reaching across the lower extension of this mountain-chain, it met Pisidia and Isauria on boundaries which were never well-defined. The eastern portion, an undulating plain, was treeless, like the country farther north, and, for the most
part, arid; there were occasional streams, but, in general, water had to
be obtained from wells, often of great depth. The soil, impreg-
nated with salt, produced grass which made excellent pasture.
Amyntas, it is said, had over three hundred flocks of sheep in this
general region, and wild asses from the herds found here were prized

[b] See Chap. I note 13.

for breeding. The salt from Lake Tatta, the water of which has a higher saline content than that of any other lake of its kind, was used not only for ordinary purposes but also medicinally. The Sultan Dağ, moreover, besides timber, especially oak, contained mineral wealth; cinnabar, used as a pigment, was mined at Sizma, north of the city of Iconium, and copper and lead were also found in this region.

In the narrow fertile strip of Phrygia Paroreius which flanked the mountain-range on the northeast and extended on into Lycaonia,[16] there was a long line of urban settlements—Philomelium, Thymbrium, Tyriaeum, Laodiceia, Iconium and, in a more remote region in the mountainous country, Lystra and Derbe. All but the last two owed their development to the Southern Highway which led from Apameia around the northern angle of the Sultan Dağ to Laodiceia and thence by one fork through Cappadocia to the Euphrates, by the other through the Cilician Gates to Syria.[c]

Of these towns, Thymbrium, Tyriaeum and Iconium were of sufficient importance at the beginning of the fourth century before Christ to be referred to in the narrative of Xenophon as *poleis*.[17] Philomelium and Laodiceia, on the other hand, were evidently of Hellenistic origin. The former was perhaps founded in the third or early second century by a Macedonian soldier of fortune called Philomelus; the latter, distinguished from other cities of the same name by the epithet Catacecaumene or "the Burned," was presumably named for the wife of a Seleucid monarch, either Antiochus II or Antiochus III.

On the southwestern side of the range of Sultan Dağ, Pisidia, a land of lakes and rugged mountains, extended far to the west and the south. The northeasterly corner, that portion of Phrygia Paroreius which lies around the lakes of Beyşehir and Eğridir and is sometimes called Pisidian Phrygia, was probably the most fertile part of the district.[18] If, as has sometimes been supposed, a very ancient route led from Apameia around the north of these lakes and from the southern end of Beyşehir to Lycaonia, this region must in early times have had great commercial importance.[19] In the Hellenistic period, however, its natural connexions were with Apameia and the West. It was natural, therefore, that the possessions of Pergamum should include all this portion of Pisidia, and, in fact, under Attalus II they extended to Amlada, south of Lake Beyşehir,[d] but this remote part of the Pergamene dominions had not been taken over by Rome.

In "Pisidian Phrygia," the Hellenic *polis* was represented by the cities

c See Chap. II note 18.　　　　　　　d See Chap. I notes 56 and 77.

456

of Apollonia and Antioch. The former, perhaps a Seleucid foundation, was situated on a ridge on the northern side of a mountain-chain overlooking the plain of an affluent of Lake Eğridir.[20] Not more than twenty miles east of Apameia, it was in close contact with western Asia Minor, and by way of the lake-region it had a connexion with Lycaonia and the East. Its inhabitants, in the second century after Christ, regarded themselves as descendants of "Lycian Thracian colonists," perhaps meaning thereby Thracians who had settled in Lycia.

Antioch, with the distinguishing epithet of "near Pisidia," lay about fifty miles northeast of Apollonia in the inner angle of the Sultan Dağ.[21] Situated on a plateau which rises from the plain and is cut off from the mountains on the east by a defile two hundred feet in depth, the city was a place of considerable natural strength. It was founded, evidently, by one of the early Seleucids with the aid of emigrants, according to tradition from Magnesia-on-Maeander, and presumably for the purpose of controlling the region and, particularly, the route around the lakes. On the expulsion of Antiochus III from Asia Minor in 188, the city was not assigned to Eumenes of Pergamum but declared a free and independent community, and it seems to have preserved this status until it came under the power of Amyntas. Probably antedating the Hellenistic foundation was a sanctuary of the god Men, standing high up on a hill some fifteen miles south of the city.[22] Like other ancient Asianic deities, Men owned sacred estates and temple-slaves, and his surname Ascaënus, derived from Ascaea, an old name, evidently, of the plain in front of his hill, suggests that he was regarded as its lord.

The region of the lakes contained also various cities of minor significance, such as Seleuceia, later distinguished from other towns of the same name by the addition of the epithet Sidera, or "the Iron," and Prostanna, the former southwest of Lake Eğridir, the latter perhaps at the southern end.[23] Other places were Timbriada, between this lake and Lake Beyşehir, and Anabura in the hill-country south of Antioch.

In Pisidia proper, farther west and south, the principal cities were Sagalassus and Selge, both of which have already been mentioned.[24] The former, in a well-fortified position on a mountain-terrace commanding the pass which led southward from the lake-country, was included in the new province of Galatia; the latter, in an even stronger situation, which had enabled it to defy both the Pergamenes and Amyntas, was likewise incorporated in the province. In the wild and mountainous country between Selge and Lake Eğridir, Adada, which in the second century before Christ had made a treaty for mutual defence with Termessus, had also a strong position on a slope descending to a deep ravine.

In parts of southern Pisidia groups of villages had been organized for common action into communes, one of which, the Commune of the Milyades, had taken part in 78 B.C. in the prosecution of the governor Dolabella.[25] Some of them may have existed in the imperial period, but even at the beginning of the first century before Christ their chief centres had developed into what could be called cities. One of these, Cremna, east of Lake Kestel, perched on a rocky peak, three sides of which were formed by precipitous cliffs, was a place of such extraordinary strength that Amyntas succeeded in capturing it only after a stubborn resistance.

As thus formed, the "Galatian province" from the Paphlagonian mountains on the north to the Taurus on the south measured not less than two hundred and fifty miles. Its width varied from 175 miles, the approximate distance through Galatia from the latitude of Tavium to that of Pessinus and through Lycaonia and Pisidia from the frontier of Cappadocia to the border of Cibyratis in the province of Asia, to the comparatively short stretch of 100 miles that separated Lake Tatta from the eastern border of Phrygia. With its irregular configuration and the diverse positions of its three component districts, partially connected, to be sure, by the Southern Highway as well as by the route that led through "Pisidian Phrygia" to Lycaonia, but nevertheless separated from one another by the great mountain-range near the centre and by the salt wilderness, the province has been aptly described as "a fantastic conglomeration of territories."[e]

The inhabitants of the province were as varied as the districts of which the province was composed. Including Greeks and Celts, half-Hellenized Asiatics, peasants of native Anatolian stock and fierce mountaineers whose independence had never been curtailed, they presented a motley array of different races, most of whom were not yet Romanized and some even hostile, so that it became necessary to take arms against them.

It is evident that Galatia, bordering on the client-kingdoms of Pontus and Cappadocia, was a frontier-province. On its governor, as formerly on the proconsul of Cilicia, a province which had occupied much the same strategic position, devolved the responsibility of carry-

e Syme in *Anat. Stud. Buckler* p. 330.

ing on relations between the emperor and these rulers.[f] It was therefore natural, on the principle governing the assignment of the provinces to the supervision, respectively, of Augustus and the Senate, that the Galatian province should be placed in the care of the former and be ruled by a "legate" chosen by him.

As the first governor of the new province, Augustus appointed Marcus Lollius, who was destined later to fill other posts of responsibility and even of danger but to die in disgrace and apparently by his own hand.[26] He seems to have held office until 22 B.C., when he returned to Rome to take the consulship for the following year, and it may be assumed that he began the work of Romanization which would bind together this heterogeneous conglomeration of lands with so few ties of their own.

Of the many changes that were effected to this end during the next score of years, it is impossible definitely to attribute any to Lollius. If it may be supposed that he selected Ancyra as the provincial capital —a choice due to the fact that of the component parts of the province, the district of Galatia was regarded as the most important—he may also be credited with the establishment of the worship of Roma and Augustus in this city.[27] Instituted during the lifetime of the Emperor, this cult was carried on in a temple dedicated to the two deities, which, even in its ruined condition, is still an important architectural monument of modern Ankara. On its walls was afterwards carved in both Greek and Latin a copy of the record of Augustus's "Achievements," which, composed by himself, was inscribed on two pillars in front of his Mausoleum in Rome. The supervision of the cult was entrusted to a "Commonalty of the Galatians," modelled, evidently, on those of Asia and Bithynia and having, like them, a Chief Priest and a festival.[28] In the course of time, not only Ancyra but also Pessinus and Tavium expressed their loyalty to the Emperor by adding Augusta (*Sebaste*) to their names.[29]

In Pisidia the process of Romanization was begun by creating Antioch a Roman colony.[30] This was in accordance with the policy of Caesar, who, by founding colonies at Sinope, Apameia and probably Parium, had set a precedent for establishing in the East a group of communities modelled on those which Rome had founded in Italy. The colonists at Antioch included veterans of the Fifth Legion, surnamed the Gallic, and apparently of the Seventh also. As Roman

[f] See Ramsay *Hist. Comm. Epist. Galatians* p. 113.

citizens, they were enrolled in the tribe *Sergia*, and, like the settlers established by Caesar, they had a status of full liberty. Even at the end of the first century after Christ, a distinction was still drawn between "colonists" and "natives."

The new colony was officially called Colonia Caesarea.[31] It seems to have been intended to discard the old name of the city, but tradition was too strong, and before the end of the first century Antiochea appeared by the side of the official name. Since, as will presently be shown, each of the other colonies founded by Augustus in Pisidia bore the adjective *Augusta* as part of its name, the word Caesarea applied to Antioch points to a different, and evidently earlier, date of foundation, probably soon after the annexation of the province. It may perhaps be supposed that Amyntas had already renamed the city in honour of his overlord and that when the place became a colony the new name was retained.

Every effort was exerted to make the new colony as Roman as possible. As in other colonies, a temple was built for Jupiter Optimus Maximus in imitation of the famous sanctuary on the Capitolium in Rome.[32] The principal square of the city was called Augustea Platea, and, later, one adjoining it received the name Tiberia Platea. In the second century, as many as seven precincts (*vici*) of the city had Latin names, some of them taken from places in Rome. Distinction was sought for its public offices by the device of electing some prominent Roman as one of the *duoviri* (the colony's chief magistrates), such as Drusus, stepson of Augustus, and, afterward, Sulpicius Quirinius, the conqueror of the Homonadeis, each of whom, as might be expected, named a substitute to hold the office.[33] After Augustus's death, a record of his "Achievements," as also at Ancyra, was inscribed on a wall or on the base of a statue at one side of the *Platea* named after him, but, as befitted a Roman colony, only the original version in Latin was presented. The "Achievements" were also inscribed at Apollonia, but here, as was natural in a Greek *polis*, only the translation into Greek was used for the purpose.

Another measure, namely the formation of a new legion composed, at least in part, of inhabitants of the new province, was taken soon after the annexation of Galatia. Deiotarus, it will be remembered, brought to the battle of Zela a body of soldiers organized and armed on the model of a Roman legion,[g] and in view of the fighting in Pisidia undertaken by Amyntas, it may be assumed that this force had

[g] See above p. 411.

not been disbanded. This veteran unit appears to have been taken over and incorporated into the Roman army as the Twenty-Second Legion.[34] It was soon sent to Egypt, where it is known to have been stationed in 8 B.C., and while at first it was probably not officially so called, it acquired in time the surname of the "Deiotarian," thus perpetuating the memory of its founder. Some of its members appear in a fragmentary list which contains the names and places of origin of thirty-six soldiers of two legions (probably the Third and the Twenty-Second) serving in Egypt about the beginning of the Christian Era. Of these soldiers, ten are recorded as natives of Ancyra and ten as coming from other places in the former kingdom of Amyntas, including Paphlagonia, Pisidia and Pamphylia; of those from Ancyra two bear the name Marcus Lollius. It seems evident that recruits from Galatia remained (or subsequently enlisted) in the legions stationed in Egypt, not only in the Twenty-Second but in the Third as well.

During the fifteen years which followed the governorship of Lollius the work of strengthening Rome's supremacy was continued. It soon became evident that the unsubdued Homonadeis, a victory over whom had cost Amyntas his life, must be put down with a strong hand.[35] Publius Sulpicius Quirinius, Consul in the year 12 B.C., who, either before his consulship or immediately after it, had brought the wild Berber tribes of Libya under the power of Rome, was selected for the task. His success in Africa was now repeated in eastern Pisidia. On his approach, the tribesmen seem to have taken refuge in their mountain-strongholds, which could not be stormed without great loss on the part of the attacking force, especially as Quirinius had been prevented by the nature of the country from bringing the necessary siege-train. The Roman general, accordingly, resorted to blockade, and by closely investing the various fortresses he compelled the defenders to surrender through gradual starvation. This tedious process accomplished, he cleared the country of the enemy by destroying their strongholds and carrying off the captive warriors, estimated as 4,000 in number, to be settled, as Pompey had once settled the captured pirates, in various cities of the province. Quirinius's success against the tribesmen was hailed as a victory of great importance, and he was rewarded by the bestowal of the insignia granted to a general at his triumphal procession—a purple toga and a laurel-wreath, which might be worn on festal occasions. Nevertheless, only a few years later, the mountaineers of Isauria, undaunted by the experiences of the Homonadeis, turned from their accustomed banditry to open warfare, making it necessary to use force for their suppression.[36]

Rome, however, used other means than conquest to establish her power, and the methods employed by Caesar in western Asia Minor and by Augustus in the case of Antioch were now applied on a much wider scale. Among the "Achievements" of which Augustus boasted in the record inscribed in three cities of the new Galatian province, was the founding of military colonies in Pisidia.[h] In addition to Antioch there were five communities in this part of Asia Minor on which this status was conferred. Three were in the mountainous district of central and western Pisidia, one much farther east, near the border of Lycaonia, while the situation of the fifth is uncertain. Of the Pisidian group, Cremna, henceforth Colonia Julia Augusta Felix Cremnensium, was presumably selected because of its almost impregnable position, commanding central Pisidia.[37] Farther west, Comama, previously, like Cremna, a self-governing community, was situated southwest of Lake Kestel in the broad valley of the chief affluent of the Lake.[38] Under its new name it appeared as Colonia Julia Augusta Prima Fida Comama (or Comamenorum). Still farther west, in the region of Milyas, lay Olbasa in a well-fortified position high up on the slope of the mountain-range which forms the southeastern border of the valley of the Lysis, the principal affluent of Lake Burdur.[39] Its acropolis-wall shows that this place also was a Hellenistic settlement. Whatever importance Olbasa may have had was probably due to its situation on a cross-route which, following the Lysis, connected northern Pisidia with the road from Laodiceia-on-Lycus to Pamphylia. Romanized under the name of Colonia Julia Augusta Olbasene (or Olbasenorum), it expressed its loyalty to Rome by establishing the worship of Jupiter Capitolinus and a festival called Augusteius Capitoleius, held every four years. At Cremna and Olbasa (and presumably at Comama also) the colonists had the full liberty enjoyed by Roman citizens. Despite the attempts to Romanize these communities, however, and the continuation of Latin for certain official purposes, as for instance, the legends on coins, the earlier speech finally prevailed, and, as time went on, at both Comama and Olbasa inscriptions recording the bestowal of honours by the city-council were written in Greek.

Of the other colonies, Parlais and Lystra, the site of the former is not definitely known. The meagre geographical information availa-

[h] Augustus *Res Gest.* c. 28.

ble, however, places it near the none too exactly determined border-
line between Lycaonia and Pisidia.[40] Coins of the city issued before
Parlais became a Roman colony, showing a galley with a helmsman
and rowers, indicate a situation on a lake, which was possibly Lake
Beyşehir but may perhaps have been Lake Eğridir. Lystra, situated
about thirty-five miles east of the southern end of Lake Beyşehir on
a low hill rising from a fertile plain, had a position which was advantageous because of the richness of the land but for purposes of
commerce too remote from the main trade-routes.[41] The choice of
this place, therefore, as a colony, named Julia Felix Gemina Lustra,
is difficult to explain, and, in fact, Lystra never attained to a position
of importance. The settlers of a later time included discharged soldiers,
and inscriptions show that Latin was widely spoken, but when, somewhat more than a half-century after the foundation of the colony, the
inhabitants hailed St. Paul and his fellow-missionary, Barnabas, as
Hermes and Zeus, they used, we are told, "the speech of Lycaonia."

In addition to the foundation of Latin-speaking centres, another
means of Romanizing Pisidia was employed, namely the construction
of roads. This method of binding the Empire together had been used
in the Balkan Peninsula and western Europe, and on the formation
of the province of Asia, Aquilius had constructed, or perhaps rebuilt,
a series of roads through the new dependency.[i] In pursuance of this
policy, Augustus caused two great roads to be laid out from Antioch
as a centre, each called after himself, but by the hybrid name of *Via
Sebaste*. One, leading around the northern end of Lake Eğridir, presumably to Apollonia, and then turning southward, crossed the mountainous district of Pisidia to the colony of Comama, a distance of
122 miles.[42] From here it probably joined the highway from Laodiceia-
on-Lycus to Pamphylia. The other, running in a southeasterly direction
from Antioch—in general along the line of the ancient route leading
from Apameia around the northern ends of the two lakes—traversed
the rolling country between Lake Beyşehir and the range of Sultan
Dağ, gradually turning eastward to the ancient city of Pappa, at the
western end of a long narrow defile.[43] After passing through this defile,
the main road probably led on over a low pass to Iconium, while a
branch seems to have crossed the hill-country on the south to the
colony of Lystra.

These roads were completed, as the milestones testify, in 6 B.C.
during the governorship of Cornutus Aquila. It may be assumed, how-

[i] See above p. 157.

ever, that the execution of so elaborate a programme, involving the construction of over two hundred miles of road, extended over a period of several years. Consequently, although no definite date can be determined, the plan for the Romanization of Pisidia may well have been adopted during the decade which followed the formation of the Galatian province, and as this plan included not only the construction of roads but also the foundation of colonies, the latter may be dated about this time.

It has often been held that the colonies established by Augustus were provided with territories obtained by the Emperor at the death of Amyntas and that large tracts of land thus acquired, but not so distributed, continued to be imperial domain, with the result that the Roman emperors owned great estates in Pisidia and Lycaonia. It must be remembered, however, that of the six colonies which Augustus established in these regions, at least three—Antioch, Cremna and Parlais—were already in existence as organized *poleis*, and it is therefore improbable that they had to be provided with territories. The view, moreover, that Augustus acquired these estates is based partly on the unfounded belief that Amyntas had gone through the form of making a will in his favour and partly on the theory that certain large landed properties known to have been in existence in the third century after Christ were owned by the emperors.[44] It is true that a boundary-stone shows that an imperial estate was situated northeast of Lake Burdur, but the date of the stone is uncertain, and the acquisition of the property cannot be traced to Augustus. There were perhaps other estates belonging to the emperors east and south of Lake Beyşehir, but their existence is very questionable. Farther to the northeast, on the Lycaonian side of the mountains, the presence of the emperor's freedmen and slaves in the neighbourhood of the "Burned" Laodiceia suggests that there was imperial property in this region, but, again, there is no reason to suppose that it was acquired by Augustus or, in fact, before the second century.

While it is evident that far more attention was given to the colonization of Pisidia than of any other portion of the Galatian province, the other districts were not wholly neglected. In Galatia proper the process of Romanization was furthered by the creation of a colony in the extreme west, near the border of Phrygia. Here the Colonia Julia Augusta Felix Germenorum was established in an older settlement called Germa.[45] Its position at the junction of roads leading from Dorylaeum and Pessinus, respectively, to Ancyra gave the place a commercial importance which may well have determined its selection as the site of a colony. An attempt was made also to carry out this policy in the Taurus region far to the south, where, perhaps near the border of Lycaonia but more probably in northern Cilicia Aspera, Augustus seems to have founded a colony of veterans at a place named Ninica.[46]

Just at the time when Cornutus Aquila celebrated the completion of the great Pisidian road-system by erecting his series of milestones, the province received a notable addition on the north. Here the dynasty of Deiotarus the Galatian ruled a considerable kingdom, which Antony had granted, and Augustus confirmed, to Deiotarus Philadelphus, the old monarch's great-grandson.[j] On his death (or that of his heir) in 6/5 B.C., his dominions, like those of Amyntas, were annexed to Rome's Empire. Not only eastern Paphlagonia, including Gangra, the capital, and the valley of the Amnias, with the city of Pompeiopolis, but, east of the Halys, the region of Phazimonitis as well became part of the Galatian province.[47] An oath of allegiance to Augustus and his house, sworn before "Zeus, the Earth, the Sun, all other gods and goddesses and Augustus himself," was taken by the native inhabitants of Paphlagonia and the Romans resident both in Gangra and in the various communities of the kingdom, each of which convened in its "Sebasteium" to perform the ceremony. The inclusion of Augustus among the deities in whose name the oath was taken was a distinct advance in the conception of the Emperor as a god; for only in Egypt, as far as is known, was the living ruler named among the deities called upon to witness an oath and punish its violation.[48] Under the Seleucids—as well as under the earlier Ptolemies—it had been customary to swear by the "Fortune" of the monarch, and the Romans, in imitation, had introduced the practice of taking oaths by the *Genius*, or guardian-spirit, of Julius Caesar and perhaps even of Augustus. It is indeed possible that the Paphlagonian kings, like the Egyptian, caused themselves to be included among the gods so invoked, and that the formula used upon the present occasion was merely the one established by long tradition. But the action of Roman citizens, who, in professing their allegiance to their *Princeps*, took an oath by the same Princeps together with Zeus and other deities, suggests that the plan for Romanizing the Asiatics was accompanied by a seeming orientalization of the immigrants from Italy.

Three years after the annexation of Paphlagonia and Phazimonitis,

[j] See above pp. 434 and 443.

a further addition was made to the Galatian province.[49] This was the region, south of Phazimonitis and east of Galatia proper, which included Amaseia, the old capital of the kingdom of Pontus, situated on the upper Iris, and the city henceforth called Sebastopolis, near the headwaters of the Scylax. It seems highly probable that, together with the two cities, the land that lay between them, the basin of the Scylax, was also incorporated in the province. This annexation not only added the rich and fertile territory belonging to Amaseia, but it also straightened this section of the eastern frontier, which was now formed by the mountain-range extending along the right bank of the Scylax and separating the river-basin from the territory of Zela and the rest of the Pontic kingdom. South of Sebastopolis, the new southern boundary of the province ran westward as far as Lake Tatta, the city and its immediate territory being thrust forward toward Lesser Armenia. With these additions on the north and the northeast, the area of the Galatian province, now extending across Asia Minor from the mountain-range bordering the Euxine coast to the crest of the Taurus—and perhaps even farther south—was about equal to that of the province of Asia and more than twice the size of Bithynia.

The history of the growth of this province during the thirty years which preceded the beginning of the Christian Era is highly illustrative of the policy and methods of Augustus. As has been previously observed,[k] he took no step, on coming to power, which would be subversive of the existing position of the Asianic client-rulers. As occasion offered, however, first at the death of Amyntas, then, apparently, at the death, or perhaps the deposition, of the lesser princes, their dominions were annexed to the Empire and became part of the province governed by the Emperor's legate. Eastern Pontus continued to be ruled by the dynasty of Polemo and Cappadocia by Archelaus, but, save for these two client-kingdoms and the still independent Lycian Federation, all Asia Minor was now directly subject to Rome. A deliberate plan was adopted, whereby the newly annexed districts were to be Romanized by founding colonies with civic institutions modelled on those of Rome, established, especially, in that part of the province which had been least affected by contact with the Graeco-Roman world. Through these regions also roads were constructed to serve as the means whereby this contact might become increasingly closer. In great contrast to Antony, who, by strengthening the influ-

[k] See above p. 443.

ence of the East, aspired to become "King of Kings," Augustus, in incorporating the territories of those kings whose overlord Antony had wished to become, set himself the task of substituting the influence of the West for that of the East by bringing these lands directly under the power of the Roman "Princeps."

CHAPTER XX

THE FIRST PRINCEPS

THE annexation of the large part of Asia Minor which had formed the kingdom of Amyntas inevitably increased the administrative cares of the already burdened Augustus. His health, never rugged, had been impaired by an arduous campaign against the Cantabrian mountaineers in northwestern Spain, and after his return to Rome in 24 B.C. a serious illness seemed to make it advisable for him to free himself from a part of his responsibilities by appointing a colleague as administrator of the provinces of the East.

For this post he chose his able friend and counsellor, Marcus Agrippa, who had commanded his fleet at Actium and more recently, during the war in Spain, had represented him in the conduct of affairs in Rome. Now, as the ruler's deputy in the eastern provinces, Agrippa was vested with a proconsular command superior to the powers of the imperial governors of Galatia and Syria and in fact, although not in law, to those of the senatorial proconsuls of Asia and Bithynia.[1] Like Pompey, during his tenure of unlimited military command, he was assisted by several legates.

Leaving Italy in the course of the year 23, Agrippa sailed to Lesbos, where he spent the following winter at Mitylene.[2] The city had been recognized by Caesar as a friend and ally of Rome, and in 25 B.C. the usual formal treaty of alliance had been concluded with the Senate, by which Rome and Mitylene bound themselves by oaths to assist each other in the event of war and to preserve the *status quo*. Thereupon the citizens sent envoys to Rome to present a golden wreath, and in honour of Augustus they established a festival at Mitylene, modelled on that of Zeus, and erected a statue of the Emperor with an inscription characterizing him as the common benefactor and the saviour and founder of the city. As a free state and a well-disposed ally, Mitylene was well-suited to serve as the residence of Augustus's personal representative in the East.

Except for an audience granted, while at Mitylene, to Herod the Great, King of Judaea, and perhaps a journey to Antioch in Syria, nothing is known of Agrippa's actions during the two years in which he held his extraordinary command.[3] The mere creation of this command and the precedent thus established for the division of power over the West and the East between the emperor and an associate were of far greater importance than anything that was done by this first incumbent of the office.

A few months after Agrippa's return to Rome, Augustus himself, now recovered from his illness, came to Asia. Taking up his residence in Samos in the autumn of 21 B.C., he spent the following winter as well as that of 20-19 on the island.[4] In the course of his stay he restored to their places in the Temple of Hera the colossal statues of Athena and Heracles which Antony had given to Cleopatra, and the citizens, in gratitude, erected a monument to the Goddess Roma and the God Augustus. He also indicated his position as ruler by holding the semblance of a court on the island, where he received envoys sent both by the Queen of Ethiopia and by one of the princes of India.[5]

The summer of 20 B.C., which intervened between Augustus's two visits to Samos, was devoted to an inspection of the eastern provinces, first those of Asia Minor and, later, Syria.[6] Although the government of the provinces of Asia and Bithynia was a prerogative of the Senate, the Emperor appears to have assumed the right to carry out whatever reforms he considered desirable. Some communities were ordered to increase the amount of the tribute they paid to Rome, while others, which seemed to be in need of aid, received payments of money. Among the latter were the cities damaged by a great earthquake which had occurred a few years before, during Augustus's absence in Spain. Of these, Tralles, which seems to have especially suffered, had appealed to the Emperor for assistance.[7] In response to its plea the city was rebuilt with the aid of some Italian settlers and in gratitude assumed the name Caesareia. Similar appeals in consequence of like damage, probably at this time, which Laodiceia, Thyateira and Chios presented to the Senate, also received a favourable hearing.[8]

While other benefactions to cities cannot be definitely placed at this time it seems probable, in view of the fact that Augustus, after his departure in the summer of 19 B.C., never returned to Asia Minor, that the honours conferred upon him in many places are to be connected with favours granted during this visit to the East.[9] Thus at Ilium he rebuilt the ancient temple of Athena and in return was honoured by the Federation which used it as their common sanctuary as "kinsman, patron, saviour of the citizens and benefactor of all." At Pergamum he erected a monument in the Temple of Athena and received honours from the Pergamene people as "greatest benefactor and founder." At Miletus a building, apparently the theatre, was dedicated to Augustus, Apollo and the *demos*, and the Emperor was elected to the office of stephanephorus for the year 17/16, an honour which was conferred on him also at the neighbouring Heracleia. He seems likewise to have held the eponymous office at Mitylene. Even the people of Cos, whom, perhaps, he had punished for their enforced support of Antony, dedicated a "propitiatory offering" for his safety and, calling him "Founder of the City," established a contest in which a prize was given for an encomium in his honour.

Among the "Achievements" of which Augustus afterward boasted was his restoration to the temples in "all the communities of the province of Asia" of the works of art which Antony had seized for himself.[a] These included, besides the statues at Samos, another work of Myron, a bronze statue of Apollo, which had been taken from the Ephesians, and a statue of Ajax from the sanctuary of the hero at Rhoeteium on the Hellespont.[b] At Ephesus he righted, perhaps on some later occasion, another wrong by revoking Antony's addition of a part of the city to the inviolable precinct of Artemis.[10] This grant, which exposed Ephesus to danger from the evil-doers seeking refuge in the sanctuary, had proved harmful to the city, and its revocation was in the interest of law and order. To compensate Artemis for the loss, the Emperor restored certain revenues of which she had been deprived, among which were perhaps the lands in the plain of the Caÿster, northeast of the city, of which inscriptions record that they were returned to her by Augustus. In order to determine more accurately the inviolable area, a wall was built "from the revenues of Artemis," which enclosed not only the Temple of the Goddess but also the Augusteum, a building erected by the city for the worship of the Emperor.

A cult of Augustus instituted and maintained by a single community must be distinguished from the cult which was carried on by the province as a whole.[c] The various cities of the province of Asia, following the example set by the Commonalty, quickly adopted the practice of establishing the local worship of the emperor, and twenty years after the institution of the provincial cult each of the centres of the various judiciary dioceses of the province had a temple dedicated to Augustus.[11] Besides these centres, at least seven cities are known in the province of Asia in which he was worshipped during his lifetime. To these must be added the colonies of Antioch-near-Pisidia and Sinope and various places in Paphlagonia, including Neapolis. In no less than

[a] Augustus *Res Gest.* c. 24. [b] Pliny *N.H.* xxxiv 58: Strabo xiii p. 595.
[c] See above p. 447f.

eleven of the cities in Asia he was worshipped in conjunction with Roma. Since four of these are known to have had cults of Roma already, it may be supposed that the worship of Augustus was merely combined with these. In cities where no such cult existed, the community might, like the Commonalty of the province, establish a joint cult or, did it prefer, worship the Emperor alone. In certain places he was identified with Zeus as either the Liberator or the Olympian or the Guardian of the city, as well as with Apollo in the aspect of Liberator.[12] After his death he was known also as Zeus of the Fathers.

There can be little doubt that these cults were established with the consent of the Emperor. As in the case of the commonalties, he was willing to permit the communities of the eastern provinces to show their loyalty by according him the divine honours traditionally conferred on their ruler. The value of this loyalty and the importance of securing the cities' co-operation in the administration of the provinces had been perceived by Caesar. He, it will be remembered, had assigned to the several communities the duty of collecting the taxes levied by Rome, substituting the payment of definite amounts for the old tax-farming system.[d] This method, by which fixed taxes were imposed on land and on personal property, was not only continued by Augustus but placed on a more stable foundation by the institution, at least in the imperial provinces, of a periodic census, which, affording a basis for assessment, enabled the communities to determine the amounts to be collected.[13] The change from the uncertain and often burdensome levies by the *publicani* did much to increase the prosperity of the cities, and Augustus's policy of making use of their services as instruments of Roman rule gave them a more definite position in the organization of the Empire. It has been aptly said that he planned to make the Empire "a commonwealth of self-governing cities."[e] This policy was followed by many of his successors, who wished to promote the prosperity of the provinces and found the officials of the communities, because of their knowledge of local conditions, better qualified than minor governmental agents for local administration, and at the same time, as the result of the control exercised by the wealthier and more responsible citizens, both more efficient and perhaps more honest.

The adoption of this policy by Augustus led to a development of urban life and with it to the spread of Hellenism. This is apparent in the number of cities which bore the Emperor's name in its Greek form.[14] In Pontus, two cities already mentioned, which were annexed

d See above p. 407.   e See Rostovtzeff S.E.H.R.E. p. 50.

to the Empire about the beginning of the Christian Era, received the names Sebastopolis and Sebasteia. In Caria, another Sebastopolis was founded on the route which led through the mountains from the eastern part of the district to Cibyratis. Still another city named for the Emperor was Sebaste in Phrygia, situated in a fertile plain watered by streams flowing into a tributary of the Maeander and on a route which led southward from Acmonia (on the line of the Royal Road) to Eumeneia and the plain of the Maeander. According to a local metrical chronicle, the city was formed from a number of settlements of the old Asianic type by Augustus in person, acting in obedience to the command of an oracle of Apollo; but it is not improbable that the community was an older one which changed its name.

Like Caesar, Augustus extended the influence of Rome by the foundation of colonies. His efforts thus to Romanize the districts which composed the new Galatian province have already been described.[f] In addition to these, he established a colony at Alexandria Troas.[15] The situation of this city, commanding the western entrance to the Hellespont, and its resultant commercial importance marked it as a suitable place for a colony, and the fact that it was a Hellenistic foundation, without an ancient Greek tradition, made it more receptive of the process of Romanization. As far as is known, Alexandria, henceforth Colonia Augusta Troadensium, was the only colony founded by Augustus in western Asia Minor; but it must be remembered that there were two other cities of this status—Apameia and Parium—on the southern shore of the Propontis, and it might have proved difficult to transform any of the old Greek cities of the Ionian-Carian coast into a Romanized community.

One of the effects of the stimulus given by Augustus to urban development appears in the number of cities which, presumably with the authorization of the imperial government, issued their own coins. Whereas, as has been observed, the principal Asianic communities had regularly minted bronze coins for local use—and in Caria, especially, even the smaller places, when freed from the rule of Rhodes, had issued similar pieces[g]—there was now a great increase in the number. Under Augustus and his successor, Tiberius, at least ninety-four cities in the Asianic provinces, exclusive of the colonies, are known to have had a local coinage.[16] Of these, seventy-three, some of them comparatively small communities, were in the province of Asia, where, naturally, the development of local autonomy was greatest. In Bithynia-Pontus

[f] See above pp. 459f. and 462f.   [g] See Chap. IV note 86.

and the districts forming the Galatian province, on the contrary, where urban life had progressed to a much less degree, coins were issued only in the chief centres.

The great majority of these communities whose coins are known possessed a very limited autonomy, which, however much their civic organizations served the purpose of the central government, hardly exceeded that of the subject cities under the Hellenistic kings. They included, however, as might be expected, the free cities as well, whose existing rights Augustus, in general, appears to have recognized. While it is impossible, from the available information, to present a complete catalogue of those which possessed this status during his principate, some information may be derived from the lists preserved in Pliny's *Natural History*, which are now generally supposed to have been taken from the official "Commentaries" compiled by Agrippa as an accompaniment to his great map of the Roman Empire.[17]

In these lists the following places are described as free: On the islands, Rhodes, Astypalaea, Chios, Samos and Mitylene; in Asia, Ilium, Caunus, Cnidus, Mylasa, Alabanda, Stratoniceia and Aphrodisias; in Bithynia-Pontus, Chalcedon and Amisus; in Cilicia, Tarsus, Aegaeae and Mopsuestia. In the case of Samos, freedom was granted by the Emperor himself during his visit in 19 B.C., and the city celebrated the event by again instituting a new era, designated, wholly incorrectly, as the "year of the colony."[18] He had previously, in 26 B.C., confirmed the free status of Chios and in the following year made a treaty with Mitylene; still earlier, on his arrival in Asia in 31, he had restored the independence of Amisus and perhaps recognized the freedom of Mylasa. The ancient rights of Ilium, recognized by Caesar, were, as a matter of course, preserved. The treaties, moreover, which had been concluded with Astypalaea in 105 B.C. and Cnidus about 45 were evidently still in existence, and the freedom of Stratoniceia and of Aphrodisias, recognized by senatorial decrees under Sulla and in 39 B.C., respectively, remained unquestioned. In Cilicia, Tarsus, where a Stoic philosopher, Athenodorus, formerly a teacher of Augustus, had delivered the city from the rule of the adventurer Boethus, one of Antony's favourites, recovered its status of freedom, and the grateful citizens erected a monument in honour of the Emperor. This restoration of the city's rights had presumably occurred before Augustus's stay in Cilicia while on his way to Syria in 19 B.C., when Anazarbus assumed the name of Caesareia and adopted a new era in honour of the occasion. The freedom of Aegaeae may likewise have been recognized at this time, for the citizens dedicated an altar to the God Augustus Caesar and to "Poseidon the Preserver and Aphrodite the Giver of Fair Voyage," the deities who were expected to guard the Emperor on his travels.

The lists of Pliny, however, are evidently incomplete, especially as regards the province of Asia, where, except for the islands and Ilium, only the district of Caria seems to have been taken into consideration. There is no reason to suppose that Pergamum and Ephesus, which had obtained their freedom from the younger Servilius Isauricus, or Miletus, which had been recognized as independent in 39/8 B.C., or even Phocaea, declared free by Pompey a decade earlier, had been deprived of this status.[19]

The status of freedom, however, as possessed by these cities, differed materially from its earlier conception. They were, indeed, free in so far as the local administration was concerned, and they might still elect their own officials and make their own laws. But Pliny's specific characterization of Ilium as exempt from taxation and the similar exemption granted to Tarsus by Antony and to Cos in A.D. 53 suggest that even free cities might now be required to make regular payments to the treasury in Rome.[20] A much greater infringement, however, of their ancient rights was the danger to their existence as city-states which was implied in the fact that their freedom had become practically dependent on Rome's favour. By an extension of the principle—widely employed after the First Mithradatic War[h]—that a city which received an enemy of Rome might be regarded as having forfeited its freedom, even some act of constructive disloyalty might now be considered sufficient ground for depriving it of independence.

The application of this principle led in 20 B.C. to the loss of the freedom of Cyzicus.[21] The city was accused of having caused (or permitted) some Romans to be scourged and then put to death, apparently in connexion with a riot. There is no indication, however, as to whether the city-government or a mob was responsible for the deed. The murder of Roman citizens did, in fact, call for some penalty, but the interpretation of an act of violence of this kind as a breach of the city's obligations implied by its alliance with Rome and the punishment inflicted in retaliation indicate the extent of the power which might be wielded by the Emperor over even the free city-states in depriving them of the independence which they had long possessed.

[h] See above p. 233.

It has already been pointed out that Augustus, after his victory at Actium, adopted in general the policy of Antony by which those countries of the East which had never been completely Hellenized were placed under the rule of native princes.[22] The sole exception was the kingdom of the Amanus, where he did not permit the heir of Tarcondimotus to succeed to his father's throne. In 20 B.C., however, wishing to avoid a further extension of the Empire in the East, Augustus restored the kingdom to one of the late monarch's sons. A stretch of coast, to be sure, which had been part of the kingdom was not included among the restored dominions, perhaps out of a desire to prevent the new ruler from becoming too strong. His dynasty, nevertheless, continued in power for at least thirty-seven years after the restoration.

About this time a change of ruler occurred also in the neighbouring kingdom of Commagene, where Mithradates II, recognized as king by Augustus,[i] had either died or been deposed. The heir to the throne was a child, also named Mithradates, whose father is said to have been murdered by the late King, but whether the murderer was Mithradates II or a usurper cannot be determined. In any case, the boy was now recognized as ruler.[23] His dynasty remained on the throne until A.D. 17 and again, after an interval, ruled over a somewhat enlarged kingdom for another period of thirty-five years.

The most favoured of the client-kings, however, was Archelaus, whom Antony had made ruler of Cappadocia.[j] He was not, to be sure, wholly beloved by his subjects, some of whom appear to have brought an accusation against him at Rome.[24] His defence was conducted by the Emperor's stepson, the young Tiberius Nero, with the result that he was acquitted. The grounds for the charge are unknown, but evidently there was no reason to doubt Archelaus's efficiency as a ruler or his loyalty to Rome. He now received the coast region which had formerly belonged to Tarcondimotus and—a much greater gift—the district of Cilicia Aspera, formerly part of the kingdom of Amyntas. Included in it was the former principality of Antipater, consisting of Derbe and Laranda, as well as the island of Elaeussa. In this pleasant place, which was evidently more to his liking than the mountainous region of Cappadocia, Archelaus built a royal residence, and on the adjacent coast he founded a new city, which he called Sebaste from the name of his imperial patron. His possessions were further increased by the addition of at least the southern part of Armenia Minor, the throne of which had become vacant through the recent death of Artavasdes the Mede. As the result of this gift, Archelaus's kingdom extended from the mountains of Armenia to the shore of the Mediterranean. Thereby the task devolved upon him of guarding the Euphrates frontier.

Beyond the Euphrates, the table-land of Greater Armenia was ruled by Artaxias, son of the monarch whom Antony had taken as a captive to Alexandria.[k] A bitter enemy of Rome, he had slaughtered the Romans in his kingdom and was obviously ready to side with the Parthians, should any war arise.[25] Fortunately for Rome, a means of setting up a rival was available, for his younger brother, Tigranes, had been kept in captivity after his father's death and could now be used as a claimant. A pro-Roman party in Armenia was encouraged—or created—with the result that a petition was produced requesting that Tigranes might be sent out as king. The task of escorting him to Armenia was delegated to Tiberius Nero, a young man of twenty-one years, and in 20 B.C., accompanied by a body of Roman troops and by Archelaus, Tiberius and the claimant advanced into Armenia. A civil war was averted by the murder of Artaxias at the hands of some of his relatives, and Tiberius, acting for the Roman government and in the presence of his army, crowned Tigranes II as King. A series of coins was issued at Rome bearing the legend "Armenia Captured," and Augustus boasted in the record of his "Achievements" that whereas he could have made Armenia a province, he preferred, following the precedent of his ancestors, to hand it over as a kingdom to Tigranes. Thus the policy was adopted of making Armenia a client-kingdom, ruled by a monarch who would act in the interest of Rome and serve as a bulwark against the Parthians. As later events showed, however, this policy was to prove a total failure.[l]

After Augustus's return from Asia to Rome in 19 B.C., it seemed advisable again to divide the cares of empire by appointing a deputy to act as supreme commander in the eastern provinces. Once more the choice fell upon Agrippa, now the husband of the Emperor's daughter, Julia. Accordingly, having been formally vested with a five years' proconsular command and a share in the Emperor's tribunician power, Agrippa, probably in the spring of 16 B.C., accompanied by Julia and their two little sons, set out for the East.[26]

As in the case of Agrippa's former stay in the East, little is known

[k] See above p. 437.   [l] See below p. 485.

concerning his actions or his policy. During the summer of 15 he visited Syria, and in the course of his travels there he again met Herod the Great, in some of whose cities he was formally received. He also accompanied the King to Jerusalem, where he invited the populace to a banquet and even offered sacrifice in the Temple.

In general, Agrippa seems to have adopted a policy favourable to the Greek cities in the province of Asia. One of his first measures was the revocation of the action of Augustus in regard to Cyzicus, which he restored to its former status of freedom.[27] He appears, indeed, to have acted arbitrarily and harshly in the case of Ilium, on which he imposed a fine on the ground that the citizens had neglected to bring aid to Julia when she was almost drowned by a sudden freshet in the Scamander. Otherwise, however, there is evidence of the good will of the cities in the homage paid both to him, as in the festival named for him at Cos, and to Julia, whom the Samians and the Coans honoured with statues and the Lesbians called Benefactress and a New Aphrodite.[28]

One ambitious undertaking on the part of Agrippa, to be sure, is recorded, namely a project for extending the power of Rome across the Euxine by creating Polemo of Pontus King of the Crimea. Caesar, it will be remembered, had made a similar effort when he proclaimed Mithradates of Pergamum ruler of this region; but the plan had been thwarted by the native leader Asander, who, having previously killed Pharnaces, the son of Mithradates Eupator, prevented the new claimant from taking possession of the kingdom.[m] Thereupon Asander assumed supreme power, calling himself at first Archon and afterward King.[29] He strengthened his position by a marriage with Dynamis, the daughter of Pharnaces, and finally received Roman recognition, probably from Augustus. He proved himself a capable ruler, protecting his kingdom against invasion from the barbarians by a wall across the northern part of the Crimea and extending his power along the shore of the Sea of Azov as far as the river Don. But after a reign of at least twenty-nine years, he died, apparently about the time of Agrippa's arrival in Asia, on the eve of a battle against a rebel who bore the Roman name Scribonius. This man, evidently an adventurer, claiming to be a grandson of Mithradates Eupator, married Dynamis, asserting that Augustus had recognized him as king.

The overthrow of Asander, a protégé of Rome, and the impudent assertion of Scribonius afforded a ground for interference in this distant

[m] See above p. 414.

region, for Agrippa could assert that Roman prestige was at stake. Probably, however, the real reason for his action was a desire to control the commercially important cities of Panticapaeum and Phanagoreia on either side of the Cimmerian Bosporus. In any case, he called upon Polemo to take an army across the Euxine and restore order in the Crimea. In the meantime Scribonius had been killed by his subjects, but these, having no desire to be ruled by Polemo, offered armed resistance on his arrival and, although defeated in battle, refused to accept him as king.

It seemed necessary, accordingly, for Agrippa to take action. Setting out in the early spring of 14 B.C., he advanced with his ships and, presumably, troops as far as Sinope, intending to support his nominee by force.[30] The Crimeans, however, intimidated by his evident purpose, laid down their arms and submitted to Polemo. Thus the two portions of the kingdom of Mithradates, which his son Pharnaces had in vain tried to combine, were once more united under a single ruler. Dynamis, who had married first her father's slayer and then a rebellious subject, now became the wife of Polemo, thereby giving a sort of legitimacy to his new position.

Thus Rome's power was extended to the northern shore of the Euxine, and in honour of this achievement the city of Phanagoreia was renamed Agrippea.[31] When the news of this success was brought to Rome, Agrippa, who by his mere presence at Sinope seemed to have accomplished it, received the honour of a triumph—which, to be sure, he never celebrated—and sacrifices of thanksgiving were offered in his name.[n]

The new arrangement, however, was short-lived. The opposition to Polemo continued, and when he attempted to subdue the country as far as the Don, Tanais, a Greek settlement, refused to yield and was pillaged by his troops in punishment.[o] Later, when, under a pretence of friendship, he advanced into the region lying east of the Cimmerian Bosporus, his stratagem was detected, and the tribesmen, taking him prisoner, put him to death.[32] Henceforth Rome had to be content with exercising a merely nominal supremacy in the Crimea by giving a formal recognition to the man who proved strong enough to maintain himself in power.[33] The first king of whom there is record after Polemo's death, a certain Aspurgus, who was ruling in A.D. 16, was dignified by the titles "Friend of Caesar" and "Friend of Rome."

While at Sinope, Agrippa was joined by Herod of Judaea, who had

[n] Cassius Dio LIV 24, 7.　　　　　　　　　　[o] Strabo XI p. 493.

travelled by sea, having been detained by contrary winds at Chios and, during his stay in the city, paid for the rebuilding of a portico.[34] The two rulers then set out together on what must have seemed a triumphal tour, visiting Paphlagonia and Cappadocia. Then, turning westward, they travelled to Ephesus, from which they took ship for Samos. Herod, in addition to his former gift to the Chians, presented them with a sum of money which they apparently owed to Augustus, and he made gifts to other cities in Ionia. He also won the gratitude of the Ilians by prevailing on Agrippa to remit the fine which had been imposed because of their alleged neglect of Julia. It may perhaps be supposed that he was responsible for a letter which Agrippa wrote to the Council and People of Ephesus, ordering that the care of the money contributed by the Jews to the Temple of Jerusalem should be left in their own hands and that no Jew should be required to appear in court if the day called for in his bail should chance to be the Sabbath.

The following winter, 14-13 B.C., Agrippa spent in his favourite Lesbos.[35] In the spring or summer he left Asia for Italy, where he died a year later. It was not until eleven years had passed that Augustus again appointed a deputy with plenary power in the East.

In the year after Agrippa's return to Italy another earthquake, severe even beyond the usual character of those which occurred in the country, brought disaster to some of the cities of the province of Asia.[36] They found it necessary, therefore, to apply to Rome for relief. Since Asia was subject to the Senate, the appeal was made to that body, which, accordingly, was forced either to help the afflicted communities or to forego the taxes which these would ordinarily pay. The problem was solved by the Emperor, who from his own funds deposited in the Senate's treasury an amount equal to the cities' taxes for the current year, thus making it possible to give the needed aid. At the same time, presumably to save the expense entailed by a change of governor, he stipulated that the present incumbent of the office should remain in the province for a second year. The cities, if the coins issued by Clazomenae and Teos which gave Augustus the title of "Founder" may be connected with this incident, expressed their gratitude for the Emperor's generosity.

In general, however, Augustus refrained from any interference in the administration of the Senate's province of Asia. When a controversy arose at Thyateira, apparently concerning some "sacred funds," the question at issue was settled by the proconsul of the province in a letter addressed to the magistrates of the city.[37] On another occasion, a certain Eubulus, a citizen of the free city of Cnidus, accused before the city-court of homicide because one of his slaves, in an attempt, at his command, to repel an enemy who hurled abuse at Eubulus and his wife, had accidentally killed the man's companion, and finding the court hostile, appealed to the Emperor.[38] The Cnidians, on their side, sent envoys to Rome to present charges against the appellant. Augustus, however, referred the case to the proconsul of the province of Asia, Gaius Asinius Gallus, for examination and decision. He himself merely reported Gallus's verdict of acquittal to the city-authorities in a letter in which, however, he expressed disapproval of the evident prejudice of the court against the defendant. Apart from the action of Augustus in referring the question to the senatorial proconsul, the incident is of interest in showing that a citizen of a free city, which had its own courts, might, if likely to suffer injustice, bring his case to the Emperor for decision.

Meanwhile, about 9 B.C., another proconsul, Paullus Fabius Maximus, had devised an arrangement which seemed to combine practical convenience with an expression of loyalty to the Emperor. He proposed to harmonize the Julian Calendar, as used in Rome, with the Macedonian system employed generally throughout the East except in those cities which still preserved their ancient month-names.[39] Fabius's plan, submitted during his proconsulship to the Assembly of the Commonalty of Asia, won the wreath offered as a prize for the best means of honouring Augustus. In his new calendar the first day of the year was to fall on the Emperor's birthday, the 23rd of September. The change, indeed, was not very drastic, for under the systems generally in vogue in the East the year—as the result, Fabius pointed out, of the desire of the gods to honour Augustus—began at the time of the autumnal equinox. The first month was henceforth to be called Caesar instead of Dius, as heretofore; the names and order of the others were retained as in the Macedonian Calendar but synchronized with the Roman system by the arrangement that each month should begin on the ninth day before the Calends of the Julian month to which it corresponded and should have the same number of days. In response to the Proconsul's letter, written in both Greek and Latin and filled with extravagant flattery of the Emperor, the Assembly passed decrees adopting the new system and commanding the cities to set the dates of their elections at a time which would allow the interval required by law to elapse before the successful candidates entered office at the opening of the new year. Both the letter and the decrees, so it was ordered, were to be inscribed in the several centres of the judiciary districts, and the fact that of the five places in which copies of the document have been found, only one, namely Apameia, was a district-centre shows that the publication was carried out even more widely than the order required. Nevertheless, despite the advantages of a uniform calendar synchronized with that of Rome, and despite the enthusiasm of the provincial Assembly for the Proconsul's "recommendation," tradition triumphed, and the principal cities of the province, Miletus—although ready to honour Augustus by creating him stephanephorus for the year 7/6 B.C.—as well as Ephesus, Smyrna, Cyzicus and some of less importance, did not give up their old calendars for the new system.[40]

For twelve years after Agrippa's departure from Asia no further attempt was made to appoint a supreme commander over the eastern provinces. Then the experiment was repeated by conferring extraordinary powers on the young Gaius Caesar, the eldest son of Agrippa and Julia, whom Augustus, eager to found a dynasty, had formally adopted. When, at the age of fifteen, Gaius had assumed the white toga of manhood and was appointed to a consulship to be held five years later, he was regarded as the Emperor's heir and his successor in the imperial power. The occasion was utilized by the Commonalty of Asia as well as by individual cities to express their loyalty both to Augustus and to his adopted son.[p] The people of Sardis, in particular, decreed that the day on which he assumed the toga was thenceforth to be celebrated as a holy day, on the annual anniversary of which all should wear wreaths and festal clothing and sacrifices should be performed and prayers offered for Gaius's welfare, and that furthermore an image of the young man should be installed in his father's temple—these honours to be announced to Augustus by special envoys sent to Rome for the purpose.

The extraordinary command conferred on Gaius in 1 B.C. included, like that formerly held by Agrippa, full proconsular power and authority over the governors of the eastern imperial provinces. At his early age, however,—for he was only nineteen years old—he could hardly be expected to assume the entire responsibility which his duties involved. He was therefore provided with advisers, among them Marcus Lollius, who twenty-five years earlier had organized the Galatian province and

p *Ins. Sardis* 8 = *I.G.R.* IV 1756 I-VI.

hence was regarded as an authority on eastern affairs, and Quirinius, famous for his success against the Homonadeis.[q]

It was evident that at least part of Augustus's purpose in bestowing this high office on Gaius was to introduce his heir to the provinces of the East. The cities, accordingly, conferred on him the honours appropriate to the Emperor's son.[41] Both at Miletus and at Heracleia he was named stephanephorus, and at Ilium he was hailed as kinsman and benefactor. Even divine honours were accorded to the young man, for an altar was dedicated to him at Cos, at Mylasa there was a priest for the worship of his guardian-spirit together with Augustus, and at Halicarnassus sacrifices seem to have been performed to both him and the Emperor. Festivals also were instituted in his honour at Cos and at Sardis, as well as at Pergamum, where he and his younger brother, Lucius, seem to have shared the festival held for Dionysus. His superior position was also acknowledged by Augustus's stepson, Tiberius Nero, who, after being married, against his will, to Agrippa's widow, Julia, had withdrawn from Rome to live privately in Rhodes but now came to Samos, or possibly Chios, to pay his respects to the Emperor's heir.[42] Archelaus of Cappadocia also came, at some time during Gaius's visit to Asia, to do him homage.

After a short stay in Asia, Gaius, presumably in furtherance of the Emperor's purpose in sending him to the East, sailed to Egypt, whence, after visiting northern Arabia, he took ship for Syria. Here, on 1 January, A.D. 1 he entered upon the consulship to which he had been appointed five years previously, taking office in the province, as Augustus had twice done in Asia. While in Syria, Gaius advanced to the Euphrates, and here he held a conference with the new Parthian monarch, Phraataces, concerning the question of the succession to the throne of Armenia.

It is highly probable that Augustus, in appointing Gaius as his deputy in the East, was in part impelled by the hope that the appearance of his personal representative might bring about a settlement of the Armenian problem and prevent the country from falling under the control of the Parthians. The question of the succession had again been raised a few years previously, perhaps about 6 B.C., by the death of Tigranes II, whom Tiberius had enthroned as king.[43] He was succeeded by a son named after him, who reigned with his sister Erato, in the fashion of the eastern monarchs, as man and wife. For some reason he was unacceptable to the Romans. Accordingly, when Ti-

[q] See above pp. 459 and 461.

berius, withdrawing to Rhodes, refused to undertake another mission
to Armenia, Augustus himself attempted to provide another ruler
for the country in the person of a certain Artavasdes, presumably a
member of the Armenian royal house, who was sent out to his kingdom
with an escort of Roman troops. Artavasdes, however, was not acceptable to his subjects. Some sort of civil strife arose, and his opponents,
apparently with the help of the Parthians, succeeded in defeating him,
"not without disaster" to his supporting force of Romans. He himself
presently died of disease.

This "disaster," while undoubtedly negligible as far as the Romans'
military strength was concerned, did damage to their prestige in the
East. Tigranes and Erato, resuming the royal power, were naturally
not disposed to recognize any overlordship on the part of Augustus,
and they seem to have given encouragement to the quartering of
Parthian troops in their kingdom. It had become a question whether
Armenia, "now in strife and rebellion,"[r] as Augustus himself phrased
it, was to be an appanage of the Parthians or of Rome.

At this juncture, fortunately for the success of Roman diplomacy,
there was a change of rulers among the Parthians. Shortly before Gaius
was sent to the East, the old king, Phraates IV, was killed as the result
of a plot formed by his youngest son and the latter's mother, a former
slave of Italian birth.[44] This son, Phraataces, succeeding to the throne
but none too sure of his position and perhaps disturbed by the news
of Gaius's departure from Rome, was ready to compromise with
regard to Armenia and opened negotiations with Augustus. At first,
nothing was accomplished, for, in a process of bargaining which was
not infrequent among the rulers of the East, Phraataces demanded
the return of his four older half-brothers, who were being held at
Rome as hostages, and Augustus insisted on the withdrawal of the
Parthian troops from Armenia.[s] But Tigranes also, fearing that the
support of the Parthians would fail him, began to make overtures to
Rome. Sending gifts to Augustus with a letter in which he punctiliously
refrained from calling himself King, he requested the Emperor to
recognize his claim to the Armenian throne.[45] This action, which
implied the acceptance of Rome's suzerainty, was sufficient, and
Augustus, in accepting the gifts, indicated his readiness to grant the
petition. For form's sake, however, he bade Tigranes present his request to Gaius, holding out the hope of a favourable response.

Finally, Phraataces, realizing from Gaius's presence in the East that

[r] *Res Gest.* c. 27.   [s] Cassius Dio LV 10, 20.

Rome would enforce her claim to suzerainty over Armenia and doubt-less alarmed by Tigranes's submission, agreed to abandon his demand for the surrender of his brothers and to withdraw his troops. It was arranged, accordingly, that he and Gaius should meet on an island in the Euphrates, and here the Roman prince and the Parthian mon-arch, after acting as host to each other on their respective banks of the river, agreed upon terms.[46] Thereby not only did the questionable status of Phraataces receive Roman endorsement, but the Parthian Empire was recognized as the equal of Rome. An unexpected result of the conference was the fall of Lollius. Gaius was told by the Parthian King that his trusted adviser had accepted bribes from the princes of the East, and, believing the charge, he renounced the old man's friend-ship. Within a few days Lollius was dead, as the result, it was gen-erally supposed, of a self-administered dose of poison. His place as chief adviser to Gaius seems to have been taken by Sulpicius Quirinius.

With Phraataces's surrender of Parthian pretensions to Armenia and Rome's recognition of Tigranes as king, it must have seemed that the chief problem which had confronted Gaius in the East was solved. But scarcely had the agreement been reached when Tigranes met his death in a war against "barbarians"—perhaps some of his own rebellious subjects—and his consort Erato deemed it advisable to resign her royal power.[t] It was necessary, accordingly, to find some new candi-date for the vacant throne who would be willing to rule as a client-king of Rome. With the death of Tigranes III, however, the royal house of Armenia seems to have become extinct, and Gaius and his advisers were forced to look elsewhere for a possible ruler. The choice fell on Ariobarzanes, King of Media Atropatene, apparently a son of that Artavasdes who had once been made ruler of Lesser Armenia by Augustus and had died shortly before 20 B.C.[47] He is said to have been handsome in person and of a noble spirit and acceptable to some, at least, of his future subjects.

The precedent set by Tiberius, however, in the case of Tigranes II made it necessary for Gaius to proceed in person to Armenia and place the royal diadem on the head of the new monarch. But on reaching the country, in the late summer of A.D. 2 or in the following spring, instead of a peaceful ceremony he found a civil war. A faction among the Armenians, refusing to submit to the Median King, rose in revolt, and it was necessary to suppress the rebellion by force of arms. Gaius himself, taking an active part in the campaign, invested a stronghold

[t] See note 45.

called Artagira.[48] During the siege, however, at a conference to which the commandant had enticed him by the promise of information concerning a hoard of treasure belonging to the Parthian King, the Roman prince was attacked and gravely wounded. The besieging force punished the act of treachery by killing the perpetrator and destroying the stronghold; but Gaius, stricken in mind as well as in body, made his way back to the Syrian coast, where he embarked for Italy, with the purpose, it was said, of withdrawing from all public life. While sailing along the southern coast of Lycia, he stopped at the city of Limyra, and here, on 21 February, A.D. 4, the young man, not yet twenty-four years old, succumbed to the effects of his wound.

Augustus did, indeed, achieve a temporary success in placing a Roman client-king on the Armenian throne, but at the cost of the life of his heir. This success, moreover, was short-lived, for Ariobarzanes died soon after his coronation, and his son Artavasdes, whom Rome recognized as king in his stead, was disliked by the Armenians and soon murdered by the malcontents.[49] After this failure, another attempt was made to establish a Roman vassal in the person of a prince who, according to Augustus, was a scion of the royal family of Armenia and bore—or assumed—the national name Tigranes.[50] If, as is generally believed, his parents were Alexander, a son of Herod the Great, and Glaphyra, daughter of Archelaus of Cappadocia by an Armenian princess, his connexion with the land which he was sent to rule was remote indeed. It was perhaps for this reason that he, too, proved unable to hold Armenia and was soon forced to flee from his kingdom. An attempt seems then to have been made—perhaps by a nationalist faction—to restore the former queen, Erato, but she, as unable to hold the throne as any Roman candidate, was "shortly expelled" from the kingdom, leaving the Armenians "unsettled and disorganized, without a master rather than free."[u]

Thus the various efforts of Augustus to reduce Armenia to the position of a client-kingdom ended in failure. No pro-Roman, whether a member of the ancient royal house or a ruler from a neighbouring kingdom, could hold his own against nationalist sentiment, stimulated, probably, by Parthian aid and sympathy. Even when the prince Vonones, the eldest of Phraataces's half-brothers, who for a short time held the Parthian throne but because of his Romanized ways was deposed by his subjects, sought to take the Armenian crown, he could obtain recognition neither from Rome nor from his successful

[u] Tacitus *Ann.* II 4, 3.

rival in Parthia nor from the Armenians themselves.[51] Nevertheless, the policy of Augustus was continued by his successors, and it was not until sixty years after the useless sacrifice of Gaius that the Romans finally perceived that only by consenting to recognize a Parthian prince as king of Armenia was it possible to maintain a Roman vassal on the throne.[v]

In regard to the client-kingdom of Pontus, on the other hand, Augustus's policy was more successful. Polemo, to be sure, had met his death in southern Russia;[w] but his widow, Pythodoris, who had ruled Pontus during Polemo's absence in the Crimea, was now recognized as queen in her own right.[52] Evidently a woman of real ability, she was presumably of great service in maintaining Rome's hold on eastern Asia Minor. Her realm, it is true, was somewhat reduced in size, for, about the time of Gaius's mission to the East, the city of Amaseia and the valley of the upper Halys, with the place renamed Sebasteia were taken from Pontus and annexed to the Galatian province. Pythodoris, however, still retained the greater and more valuable part of her husband's kingdom, both the southern littoral of the Euxine with the rich land of Colchis and the mining-region back of Pharnaceia and Side (renamed Polemonium) and the mountainous country as far as the Euphrates, as well as the valley of the Lycus, where she established a royal residence at Cabeira, renamed Diospolis by Pompey but now called Sebaste in honour of the Emperor. Even in the south she may have still held a part of the former dominions of the Temple of Zela.

In ruling Pontus, Pythodoris was aided by her eldest son, who, it is narrated, bore no title but was content with the position of a private citizen.[53] Her other children attained to high rank; for her daughter, Antonia Tryphaena, became the wife of Cotys, King of Thrace, and her younger son, Zeno, achieved the distinction of ruling Armenia for sixteen years, the first of Rome's appointees to the kingship of this country to hold the sceptre with the full approval of his subjects.

The position of Rome in eastern Asia Minor was further strengthened by the marriage of Pythodoris to Archelaus of Cappadocia,[54] a union doubtless the result of Roman diplomacy, for it may be presumed that it took place with the consent, if not at the suggestion, of Augustus. This marriage brought under the joint sway of the two rulers a kingdom which included all eastern Asia Minor from the Euxine to the Mediterranean, a territory nearly as large as that once ruled by

v See below p. 561.   w See note 32.

Amyntas, rich on account of the mines both in the Pontic mountains and in the Taurus and powerful enough to serve as a formidable barrier to any invaders from the Parthian side of the Euphrates.

The combination of the two kingdoms, however, was to prove of short duration. Archelaus, as will presently be shown, fell into disfavour with Augustus's successor and died in Rome under the suspicion of treason.[x] Pythodoris survived him, but as the ruler of Pontus only, for Archelaus's dominions became a Roman province. The length of her reign is unknown, and, in fact, nothing is recorded about the fortunes of Pontus until A.D. 38, when Pythodoris's grandson was made king of the country by the Emperor Gaius.[y]

As to the Asianic provinces themselves, little is known during the last fifteen years of Augustus's principate. Two years before his death, the Emperor issued an order which many cities probably regarded as detrimental to their interests, namely that no one who had been formally banished from Rome might live in any city on the mainland of Asia Minor or on any island less than fifty miles from it, excepting only Lesbos, Rhodes, Samos and Cos.[55] The purpose of the order, it was said, was to prevent the banished from living in places other than those to which they had been relegated and to check the luxurious living of the wealthy; but it is perhaps more probable that the real reason was a desire to exercise a stricter supervision over those who were political offenders and, therefore, possible traitors. While this regulation may have freed some cities from undesirable visitors, many of those who took up their residence in them were men of wealth, whose expenditures must have been of material benefit and whose debarment resulted in serious financial loss.

Another measure taken by Augustus, although useful in itself, nevertheless brought hardship to the provinces, namely the establishment of an imperial post to provide an efficient means of communication between distant portions of the Empire and the Capital.[56] Relays of runners or—somewhat later—of vehicles, were maintained in the principal stations on the great roads for the use of state-officials or even of private persons who were influential enough to obtain governmental passes for their own transportation. The system, however, became a great burden to the cities, for the expense of providing the necessary vehicles and animals fell upon them, and it was not until the opening of the third century that an attempt was made to transfer the cost of maintaining the service to the imperial treasury.

Nevertheless, the institution of this service was of advantage in that it ensured the maintenance or construction of the highways which led through the provinces. The roads which Augustus caused to be built in the newly-annexed district of Pisidia have already been described.[z] While in western Asia Minor no milestones have preserved any similar record, an inscription found in Ionia indicates that the road which led from Ephesus to Smyrna was rebuilt under his direction,[57] and from the middle of the first century onward the construction of roads, even in the senatorial provinces, devolved on the imperial government.

The most beneficial of the measures taken during the later years of Augustus for the welfare of the provinces was an effort to prevent extortion on the part of the governors. In 4 B.C. a new form of procedure was introduced by a decree of the Senate with the Emperor's concurrence for the prosecution of a governor charged with having exacted money wrongfully either from a province or from individual inhabitants.[58] It was intended to render reclamation easier and less expensive; for the former system, according to which such cases were tried by the praetor and his court, was cumbersome and, because of the necessity of bringing large numbers of witnesses from a distant province, often very costly. Under the new method, which was to be used in the prosecution of ordinary cases of extortion involving no capital charge—that is, one punished by exile or by loss of the rights of citizenship—but only the recovery of the money itself, the plaintiffs brought their cases to one of the higher magistrates. He thereupon convened the Senate for the purpose of presenting the accuser, together with the special advocate assigned him at his request. After this preliminary hearing, the matter was referred to a commission of nine senators, chosen by the magistrate who had received the indictment. This commission, after its number had been reduced to five by the challenges allowed to the plaintiff and the defendant, conducted the trial under the presidency of the magistrate who had appointed it, hearing the evidence of the witnesses, not more than ten in number. In the event of a decision against the defendant, the commission ordered him to repay the sum that was proved to have been wrongfully exacted.

In addition to this attempt to deter officials from oppressing the provincials, an effort was made to forestall extortion by instituting the system of paying fixed salaries to governors.[59] These, in the cases of the

---

[z] See above p. 463.

proconsuls of Asia and Africa—the most highly paid of the provincial posts—amounted, in later times at least, to 1,000,000 sesterces for a year of service. It was hoped that the substitution of regular salaries for the perquisites previously granted by the government at Rome would lessen the temptation to extort money from the provincials. The fact that a governor, in order to recoup himself for the expenses of his previous political career, was no longer dependent on what he could wring from his province at least seemed likely to prevent this method of self-enrichment from being a foregone conclusion.

It is probable that, in general, these measures did much to deter governors from oppressing their provinces. In the closing years of Augustus's principate, however, a flagrant case of misrule and even cruelty occurred in the province of Asia. The guilty man was Lucius Valerius Messalla Volesus, Consul in A.D. 5 and proconsul of Asia perhaps some six years later.[60] He was a member of a family long famous in Rome, and his father before him had governed Asia. It was said of him that he executed three hundred persons in a single day and gloried in the deed as one worthy of a king. However exaggerated this charge may be, there is no reason to doubt that he was brought before the Senate for trial and that his case was not one of ordinary extortion. Augustus himself, despite his great age, took part in the proceedings to the extent of sending the Fathers a recommendation which evidently urged that no mercy be shown, and Messalla was condemned by formal decree of the Senate. His successor in the proconsulship, Gaius Vibius Postumus, won the gratitude at least of the communities of Samos and Teos, which hailed him as their benefactor, and inscriptions in honour of his brothers show that they shared in the esteem in which he was held.[61] His term of office, extending over the unusually long period of three years, lasted beyond the death of Augustus into the principate of Tiberius.

Meanwhile Augustus's own interests in the provinces were placed under the care of special officials charged with the supervision of the property belonging to the emperor.[62] It has already been noted that in the imperial provinces the collection of the taxes and other revenues which accrued to the emperor devolved on a "procurator of Augustus," who, like the procurators concerned with imperial finances in Italy, was, strictly speaking, not a public official but a personal agent of the emperor. The post was analogous to that of a steward in a private household. Accordingly, while Augustus as a rule filled the more important procuratorships, particularly many of those in the provinces, with free-born men of Equestrian rank, for the lesser posts he employed largely imperial freedmen—former slaves in his own household and so directly dependent on him—and this practice, as will appear, was more widely adopted by his successors.

In the senatorial provinces, although the taxes were collected under the supervision of the proconsul for the Senate's treasury, the emperor, nevertheless, had extensive financial interests of his own. It was evidently to supervise these that Augustus appointed Pompeius Macer, son of Theophanes of Mitylene, the friend of Pompey and chronicler of his eastern campaigns, to the post of procurator of the province of Asia. A similar position was held during the principate of Tiberius by a certain Lucilius Capito, and later, under Claudius, there was also a procurator of Bithynia. Under Tiberius the sources of the income managed by the procurator of Asia are said to have been "slaves and private funds." Since this somewhat indefinite statement may refer either to agriculture or to industry, the precise nature of the properties under the procurator's charge cannot be determined. It may, however, be supposed that they included landed estates as well as the mines and quarries which in later times are known to have belonged to the emperor.

On 19 August, A.D. 14, Augustus died at Nola, near Naples, and a month later the Senate formally declared him a god, granting to him after his death the worship which the eastern provinces had accorded him during his life. His official deification in Rome, announced in Asia, caused new honours to be conferred on him, as at Samos, where the citizens, who had once celebrated his recognition of their freedom by using the date for reckoning time, now introduced a new system based on the "year of the apotheosis."[63] None of the honours bestowed on him after his death could exceed those which he had received during his life from many a community which had cause to be grateful to him, and of all these none could surpass the decree of the citizens of Halicarnassus, fulsome in expression but evidently sincere in its gratitude, praising the Emperor as Father of his Fatherland, Zeus of our ancestors and "Saviour of all mankind in common, whose provident care has not only fulfilled but even surpassed the hopes of all; for both land and sea are at peace, the cities are teeming with the blessings of concord, plenty and respect for the law, and the culmination and harvest of all good things bring fair hopes for the future and contentment with the present."[a]

[a] I.B.M. 894 = S.E.G. IV 201 (after 2 B.C.).

CHAPTER XXI

THE HEIR OF AUGUSTUS

FOR fifty-four years after Augustus died the imperial power remained in the possession of members of his family—the dynasty which he had planned to found. These were his stepson Tiberius, finally adopted as his son; his great-grandson Gaius, nicknamed Caligula, born to Germanicus, son of Tiberius's younger brother Drusus, by Agrippina, daughter of Agrippa and Julia; Claudius, younger son of Drusus; and, finally, Augustus's great-great-grandson, Nero the weakling and degenerate, the last and least worthy of the line.

Within a year of the old Emperor's death Rome acquired a new province in Asia Minor—the kingdom of Cappadocia. After a half-century of rule, King Archelaus, now approaching the age of eighty, was accused by Tiberius of some treasonable design and summoned to Rome for trial by the Senate.[1] The old man—so weakened by age and the fatigue resulting from his long journey that it was necessary to carry him into the Senate-house in a litter—was not convicted of the charge, but whether he was acquitted or the case abandoned has not been recorded. Exhausted, however, by the humiliation and strain, he was unable to return to his kingdom and died in Rome soon after the conclusion of his trial.

As Augustus, at the death of Amyntas some forty years earlier, had incorporated the King's dominions in the Empire,[a] so now, by joint action, apparently, of the Emperor and the Senate, Archelaus's kingdom of Cappadocia was taken over as a Roman province.[2] This new province—the fifth to be formed in Asia Minor—consisted of the realm of the old Cappadocian monarchs, extending from the range of mountains on the north which formed the border of the kingdom of Pontus as far south as the crests of the Taurus, and in an east-to-west direction from the Euphrates to Lake Tatta and Lycaonia. The area thus included amounted to about 33,000 square miles.

Strategically, Cappadocia was of the greatest importance on account of the roads by which it was traversed.[3] Through the centre of the kingdom, the ancient route which diverged from the Southern Highway in Lycaonia led by way of the capital, Mazaca, and the temple-city of Comana to Melitene and the crossing of the Euphrates at Tomisa. Through the western end ran the "Pilgrims' Road," connecting Ancyra

---

[a] See above p. 453.

with Tyana and the Cilician Gates, and from Mazaca routes radiated
northward to Tavium, northeastward to Sebasteia (Sıvas) and southwestward to Tyana. As one of the principal thoroughfares of Asia
Minor, the road to Melitene received especial care from the emperors
who ruled during the third century after Christ, and numerous milestones erected by them record the repair of the pavement and the rebuilding of the bridges, evidently for the purpose of making this
road serviceable for the passage of troops to and from the Euphrates
frontier.

Economically, the country was valuable for its natural resources.[4]
The most fertile portion was the region of Melitene, a high-lying plain
watered by tributaries of the Euphrates and famous for its fruits, among
them the olive and the grape; from the latter a wine was made which
was said to rival the wines of Greece. Farther west, Cataonia included
a plain of considerable size, where several streams unite to form the
Pyramus. Save for this plain, however, Cataonia is a rugged area filled
with the great mountain-masses—the so-called Antitaurus—which, projecting from the Taurus range, extend northward to meet the mountains of Pontus. The region is broken by deep narrow valleys: in
the north, by the gorges of the Tohma Su, which, cutting down deep
in the rock, flows through precipitous chasms toward the Euphrates; in
the south, by the upper courses of the streams tributary to the Pyramus
and the Sarus, which rush down through stupendous canyons to
Cilicia and the Mediterranean. It was probably chiefly in the plains
of Melitene and Cataonia and in the fertile regions in the western
part of the country, both along the Halys and farther south as far as
the Taurus, that agriculture was carried on. Cappadocia was said to
be rich in grain, but in certain places, at least, grain seems to have been
none too plentiful, for the inhabitants were accustomed to store it in
underground caverns, where, because of the altitude and the airiness
of the region, it could be preserved for many years.

Another source of wealth was the breeding of all kinds of cattle.[5]
These were reared particularly in the western portion, probably along
the Halys, as in modern times, but especially in the volcanic region
around Mazaca, where the shallow soil produced abundant grass, a
fact which, it was said, led to the choice of this place as the royal capital,
since the kings were interested in the breeding of stock. The live-
stock of Cappadocia had, indeed, been famous since the days of the
Persian supremacy, when the country paid the Great King a yearly
tribute of 1,500 horses, 2,000 mules and 50,000 sheep, and although at

the beginning of the Christian Era sheep-breeding seems to have decreased, the horses of Cappadocia continued to be famous as late as
the third and fourth centuries.

The greatest wealth of the country, however, lay in its mineral resources. The red ochre (*miltos*) which, it has already been related,[b]
was exported through Sinope, was the earliest of its products to be
known to the western world. There were quarries of stone in the
vicinity of Mazaca, but the neighbouring marshes made it difficult to
work them.[c] More valuable were a variety of alabaster, apparently
found in the western part of the kingdom, south of the middle Halys,
and a translucent marble, used in Rome for the construction of a shrine,
the interior of which, as the result, was brightly illuminated.[6] These
were perhaps the crystal and onyx of which, it is said, slabs were found
in northwestern Cappadocia by Archelaus's miners. In addition, the
country yielded sheets of mica or talc, used for glazing windows,
which, although more clouded than those from other countries, particularly Spain, excelled them in size. Most important of all, however,
were the rich mines of silver and lead in the Taurus, of which those
near the Cilician Gates were included in the territory given by Pompey
to Ariobarzanes I. They were presumably the source of the silver coins
which, after Cappadocia became a province, were issued by the great
imperial mint at Mazaca-Caesareia.

Under the rulers of the old dynasty of Ariarathes,[d] Cappadocia consisted of ten "prefectures."[7] Later, an eleventh was added, formed out
of the region included in the country by Pompey.[e] It seems highly
probable that these were dominated by vassal-lords or by the priests
of the rich and semi-independent temples at Comana and Venasa.[f]
In a country thus organized according to the Asianic, as opposed to
the Hellenic, system, the communal centres were mere villages.[g] If
the account of Strabo may be believed, there were at the beginning
of the Christian Era only two places which could be characterized
as *poleis*, Mazaca and Tyana, both in the western and, therefore,
less backward portion of the kingdom.[8] An attempt to Hellenize these
cities had been made, probably about the middle of the second century, by the Philhellene King Ariarathes V Eusebes Philopator, who
called each of them Eusebeia either from his own honorary surname
or that of his father. In Tyana, at least, this attempt was successful to
the extent that under Ariarathes VI the city celebrated a festival in

[b] See Chap. VIII note 22.   [c] Strabo XII p. 538.   [d] See above p. 201f.
[e] See above p. 375.   [f] See above p. 201.   [g] See above p. 180.

honour of Hermes and Heracles and maintained a gymnasium organized in the Greek method under a gymnasiarch.

This Hellenizing policy was continued by Archelaus. He renamed Mazaca, calling it, in honour of his patron, Caesareia, a name which it still bears.[9] Following, moreover, the custom of the Hellenistic monarchs, he "refounded" the old town of Garsaoura, which he called after himself, Archelais. In a well-watered, fertile situation and on the great road which led from Lycaonia through central Cappadocia to the Euphrates, this city grew in importance so rapidly that before the middle of the first century it was made a Roman colony. Even the temple-village at Comana became an organized community, the *demos* of which erected a monument lauding Archelaus as "Founder and Saviour."

Of the dominions which had been ruled by Archelaus, his original kingdom of Cappadocia, and with it, possibly, that portion of Armenia Minor which he had received from Augustus,[10] became the new province. Pontus, including the mountainous country between the range of Paryadres and the upper Euphrates, often regarded as part of Armenia Minor, which Archelaus's wife, Pythodoris, had inherited from her first husband, Polemo, remained a separate kingdom, governed by the Queen.[h] Only the district of Cilicia Aspera, with, perhaps, Derbe and Laranda in Lycaonia, and the island of Elaeussa were given to the late King's son, also named Archelaus, who twenty years after his father's death was still ruling with the title of King.[11]

As under the old monarch, the royal dominions in Cilicia did not include the temple-state at Olba, the rule of which Antony had granted to Aba, the daughter of a bandit-chieftain, and her husband, a member of the old priestly family of the place.[i] A half-century later, shortly before the death of Augustus, the position of Chief Priest of Zeus was held by a young man named Aias, son of Teucer, who may well have been Aba's grandson.[12] Olba itself had by this time become nominally autonomous with coins and a *demos* of its own, but Aias, besides his priesthood, had the title of "toparch" of the tribes of the Cennatae and the Lalasseis, of whom the former lived in the region around the Temple. Presumably Augustus had recognized the temporal power of the prince-priest and, while confirming his sacred office, dignified him further with a secular title. His principality, lying between the kingdom of Archelaus II and the district of Cilicia Campestris, was evidently not absorbed in the new province of Cappadocia.

Nothing, however, is known of its history until the time of the Emperor Claudius, when the region passed into the possession of a ruler named Polemo, presumably a relative of the royal family of Pontus.[j]

On the annexation of Cappadocia, a form of government was established for the province which as yet had not been employed in Asia Minor. In Egypt, to be sure, on the principle that the country was not a province of the Roman people but an annexed kingdom, Augustus, as the successor of the Ptolemies, was represented by a "prefect," who acted as viceroy.[13] The smaller central-European districts of Rhaetia and Noricum, on the other hand, also annexed to the Empire by Augustus, were placed, either by him or Tiberius, under the charge of a procurator, whose position, corresponding to that of the agent of a private proprietor, indicated that the revenues from these districts belonged to the Emperor personally. The same arrangement was now introduced into Cappadocia by Tiberius, presumably on the theory that the Emperor was the direct successor of Archelaus and so lord of the land. The income from the new province was assigned to the military treasury, which Augustus and Tiberius had founded jointly in A.D. 6 for the purpose of supplying the funds needed for the rewards paid to veterans on their discharge from the army; and so large were the expected returns that the Emperor announced that one of the sources of income for this treasury, namely the 1 per cent sales-tax, against which there had been vigorous popular protest, could now be reduced by one-half.[k] In Cappadocia itself, moreover, it was found that the taxes which had been paid to the King could likewise be reduced, a measure which contributed greatly to the popularity of Roman rule—the purpose, it is recorded, of the reduction.[l]

About the time when Archelaus died, the situation at the southeastern corner of Asia Minor was complicated by the death both of Antiochus III, King of Commagene, and of Philopator, King of the Amanus.[14] The former was presumably the son of Mithradates III, whom Augustus had made king in 20 B.C., the latter possibly the prince of this name who was raised to the throne in the same year, but perhaps his son or nephew. In Commagene the problem of the future status of the country was especially difficult. Antiochus left a son and a daughter, and it was the desire of the people in general that the royal line should continue to govern a country nominally independent. The upper classes, on the other hand, wished to have Commagene annexed to the Roman Empire. Each faction, sending representatives to Rome,

[j] See Chap. XXIII note 26.   [k] Tacitus *Ann.* II 42, 6.   [l] Tacitus *Ann.* II 56, 4.

495

presented its case, with the result that the claim of the children of Antiochus was disregarded and Commagene added to the province of Syria. It may be assumed that a similar disposal was made of the kingdom of Philopator.

The termination of the royal power in Cappadocia, Commagene and the Amanus marks an advance in the process, begun by Augustus, of reversing the policy of Antony whereby a large part of Asia Minor was formed into client-kingdoms. As Augustus, from the death of Amyntas onward, gradually merged the various kingdoms and principalities, as they fell vacant, into the Galatian province, so Tiberius, following his adoptive father's policy, continued the process in eastern and south-eastern Asia Minor, with the result that, save for the kingdoms of Pythodoris in Pontus and the younger Archelaus in Cilicia Aspera and the principality of Olba, all the client-states west of the Euphrates were now provincial territory of the Roman Empire.

Beyond the Euphrates, however, a difficult problem still presented itself, namely that of the control of Armenia and the relations with the Parthians that this involved. Augustus, in compiling for his heir an elaborate statement of the population and the resources, military and financial, of the Empire, appended the advice that the frontiers should not be extended.[m] Tiberius, accordingly, who at the very beginning of his principate adopted the policy of rigidly observing the instructions of his predecessor and the precedents established by him, must necessarily have been averse to expansion across the Euphrates, the eastern boundary of the Empire. But Augustus had made repeated attempts to reduce Armenia to the status of a client-kingdom, and it seemed, therefore, not merely permissible but even mandatory to follow his example.

The plan of Augustus with regard to Armenia, had resulted, as has already been observed, in utter failure.[n] Even the Romanized Parthian prince Vonones, who, shortly before the old Emperor's death, tried to seize the Armenian throne, was forced to abandon the attempt and finally to give himself up to the Roman governor of Syria, retaining only his royal title and perhaps the semblance of royal pomp.[15] Meanwhile the Parthian monarch bestowed Armenia on one of his sons.

The continuance of such a state of affairs was not only inconsistent with the maintenance of Augustus's eastern policy but was also damaging to Rome's prestige in Asia. The Emperor, accordingly, determined to remedy the situation by appointing a supreme commander over the

[m] Tacitus *Ann.* I 11, 7: Cassius Dio LVI 33, 2f. [n] See above p. 485.

eastern provinces, who was charged specifically with the installation of a Roman candidate as king of Armenia. As Augustus had bestowed extraordinary powers on his grandson Gaius, so Tiberius chose, as his deputy in the East, Germanicus Caesar, his brother's son, whom he himself, when formally adopted by Augustus, had adopted in turn. The young man had spent four years in command of the legions in Germany, where he led his soldiers far beyond the Rhine with none too great success and considerably to the embarrassment of the government at Rome. It was common knowledge that his own desire for military glory was stimulated by his ambitious and domineering wife, Agrippina, a daughter of Agrippa and Julia. Gossip, in fact, asserted that Tiberius, in sending him to Asia, was moved by the wish to remove from a command of such importance and of such proximity to Italy a man, who, as a result of his own and his wife's ambition, might prove a formidable candidate for the imperial power.[o]

After a triumph held in May, A.D. 17, to celebrate the victories of Germanicus over the tribes of Germany "as far as the Elbe,"[p] the Senate, at Tiberius's request, conferred an extraordinary command on the prince, allotting to him the "provinces beyond the sea," in which he was to have powers superior to those held by the governors.[16] Before the end of the year he set sail for the East, where, during the spring, he visited the Aegean islands as well as some of the mainland towns, bringing aid and encouragement to the cities "exhausted by internal strife or the wrongs inflicted by magistrates."

The communities were prepared to welcome the new "Benefactor" with extravagant honours. Before his arrival, probably, the Commonalty of Asia issued a coin on which Germanicus and his cousin (and brother by adoption) Drusus were described as the "New Gods of Brotherly Love."[17] Stopping at Mitylene in the course of their voyage, Germanicus and his wife were received with all marks of respect, the prince being hailed as a "New God" while Agrippina was called the divine Harvest-bringer of Acolis; monuments were even erected to the sons who accompanied them. Their travels took them as far as the Euxine Sea, perhaps even to the colony of Sinope, where the community erected a statue of Agrippina.[q] In southern Bithynia the small city which had recently adopted the name Caesareia added Germanice to its name as a mark of honour to the prince.[18] Skirting the coast of the Troad, Germanicus and his wife visited Ilium out of

o Tacitus *Ann.* II 5, 1; see also Cassius Dio LVII 6, 2f.
p Tacitus *Ann.* II 41, 2.   q *I.G.R.* III 94.

regard for its ancient connexion with Rome and also Assus. Then proceeding onward toward the south, they touched at Samos, where the community erected statues of them both, and at Notium, where Germanicus consulted the famous oracle of Apollo at Clarus. The election of the prince to the office of stephanephorus at Priene and the honours conferred on him at Iasus suggest that he visited these places also, and even far in the interior, at Eumeneia in southwestern Phrygia and at Alabanda in Caria, he was hailed as "Benefactor of the People."

On his way to Syria, Germanicus evidently stopped on the island of Rhodes, where a statue of him was erected by the community of Cameira.[19] He also visited the coast of Lycia, where, although the federated cities were not subject to Rome, a priest for his worship and a festival bearing his name were established at Patara, and the *demos* of Myra erected statues both of Germanicus and of Agrippina, honouring the prince as "Saviour and Benefactor."

In the search for a candidate for the throne of Armenia who would terminate the anarchy which prevailed in the country and could be trusted to rule in the interest of Rome, the choice had fallen upon Zeno, the younger son of King Polemo of Pontus and his wife, Pythodoris.[20] The scion of two Hellenized families, Zeno was by race and tradition wholly alien to those over whom he was destined to rule. Brought up, however, in his father's kingdom of Pontus, he had from childhood, it is recorded, "imitated the manners and customs of the Armenians, and by hunting and banquets and all else in which barbarians indulge had won the attachment of nobles and commons alike." The enjoyment of such popularity in Armenia, coupled with the loyalty of both his father and his mother to the rule of Rome, seemed to make him eminently suitable for the vacant kingship. Germanicus, accordingly, escorting the young man to Artaxata, formally crowned him King of Armenia, and as an indication of his devotion to his new country the new monarch assumed the Armenian national name Artaxias.

Once more the Armenian problem seemed to have been solved by the enthronement of a Roman vassal-king. The new Artaxias did, indeed, remain on the throne for the next sixteen years, but, as in the installation of a Roman protégé by Gaius Caesar, the diplomatic success was followed by tragedy. The coronation accomplished, Germanicus repaired to Antioch in Syria, where he remained during the early winter of 18-19, making the necessary arrangements through his legates for the annexation of the kingdoms of Commagene and the

Amanus.[r] He also carried out his duties as governor by presiding over the law-courts and receiving foreign princes or their representatives, among them the envoys sent by the Parthian monarch, Artabanus III, to renew the friendly relations formed with Augustus.[21] In the following spring Germanicus left Syria for Egypt where, in tourist fashion, he travelled up the Nile as far as the First Cataract. But on returning to Antioch, he was stricken with an illness which, after seeming to abate, attacked him with greater intensity and soon proved fatal. He died on 10 October 19 at the age of thirty-three, the second imperial prince to fall a victim to a supreme command in the East.

Another tragedy was to follow. Gnaeus Piso, the imperial governor of Syria, resenting his position as the subordinate of a much younger man, had refused to carry out Germanicus's orders and even rescinded some of his measures.[22] Finally, on the point of withdrawing from the province in anger, he received a message from Germanicus renouncing his friendship and perhaps even ordering him to depart from Syria. In the course of his voyage to Italy, Piso stopped at Cos and here he learned of Germanicus's death. Thereupon, forming the ill-advised plan of returning to his province, he mobilized a small force, including contingents furnished by some of the princes of Cilicia Aspera, and seized the stronghold of Celenderis on the coast. His motley army, however, proved no match for the troops brought against him by Germanicus's legate, Gnaeus Saturninus, now acting governor of Syria, and after a brief resistance he agreed to surrender on condition of receiving safe passage to Rome.

On his arrival in the city, Piso was brought to trial before the Senate on the multiple charge of having poisoned Germanicus, shown insubordination toward his superior and employed force to effect a return to the province from which he had been commanded to depart. The prosecutors were friends and associates of Germanicus, the most conspicuous being Publius Vitellius, recently governor of Bithynia, and Quintus Veranius, who had organized Cappadocia as a province. The charge of poisoning was quickly refuted, but it was easy to arouse a general feeling against the defendant, and the unhappy man, foreseeing the outcome of the trial, anticipated evident condemnation by suicide.

About the time of Germanicus's appointment to the supreme command of the East, an earthquake of unusual intensity, even in a country

[r] Tacitus *Ann.* II 56, 4f.

subject to such disturbances, wrought widespread destruction in the Hermus basin from Philadelpheia to the Aegean.[23] In one single night, it is said, twelve communities were stricken, including Cyme and Myrina, some distance north of the most seriously affected region. Like Augustus on a similar occasion, Tiberius promptly took steps to aid the sufferers. To Sardis, which seems to have received the most damage, he presented the large sum of 10,000,000 sesterces, granting at the same time a five years' remission both of all taxes due to the senatorial treasury and of all payments owed to himself. To the other communities sums of money were given, and payments owed to the government were remitted for the same length of time. By action of the Senate, moreover, a special commissioner was appointed to carry out these measures for relief. Ephesus, which was stricken probably somewhat later, seems also to have received assistance. When, six years afterward, a like disaster befell Cibyra, the Emperor requested the Senate to decree a three years' remission of taxes, and the city, in return for this favour, introduced a new era for reckoning time.

In gratitude, Sardis, Mostene, and Hyrcanis in the Hermus basin and probably Cyme also assumed the name of Caesareia, and Philadelpheia that of Neocaesareia. Others honoured Tiberius as their Founder, and all fourteen united in erecting a colossal statue of the Emperor in Rome, the base of which was surrounded by figures representing the donors.

Besides the cities which called themselves Caesareia in recognition of Tiberius's benefactions, there were two which took their names from him as their founder. One of these, Tiberiopolis, lay in the sparsely settled hill-country of northwestern Phrygia near the Mysian border, to which Hellenism had not fully penetrated.[24] The creation of this community of the *polis*-type, with the usual "Council and People" was evidently an attempt to bring this remote region under the influence of the West. The other city, Tibereia—also called Tiberiopolis—was a refoundation of the old community of Pappa in southeastern Pisidia, on that branch of the Via Sebaste which led from Antioch to Iconium.[25] Situated near the western end of a long defile which was traversed by the road, the place had a position of considerable strategic importance. The creation of this city is an indication of Tiberius's purpose of continuing Augustus's policy of Romanizing this part of Pisidia.

Tiberius's desire to maintain the policy of his predecessor appears also in his attitude toward the worship of the Emperor. The cults instituted in 29 B.C. by the provinces of Asia and Bithynia were continued, and Tiberius and Roma were worshipped together in the cities in which temples had been erected. In the year 23, however, a problem presented itself when the communities of the province of Asia, after adopting a resolution for the erection of a second temple, to be dedicated jointly to the Emperor, his mother and the Roman Senate, made formal application for permission to build the new sanctuary.[26] The authorization formerly given by Augustus serving as a precedent, Tiberius granted the request. The permission thus accorded, however, did not settle the matter, for the cities could not come to an agreement as to which should have the honour of possessing this new temple. At last, after three years of discussion, they agreed to refer the question to the Senate, and the representatives of eleven rival cities appeared before the Fathers, urging their several claims. Of the foremost communities of the province, Pergamum was rejected because of its already existing temple of Augustus and Roma, and likewise Ephesus and Miletus on the ground that their respective cults of Artemis and Apollo must inevitably receive the citizens' principal attention. Sardis and Smyrna were the most favoured competitors, and the decision was finally awarded to the latter on the ground of the antiquity of its relations with Rome, as shown by the fact that as early as 195 B.C. the city had erected a temple to the Goddess Roma. Further action by the Senate provided for the appointment of a special commissioner to assist in the work of construction.

On the other hand, when no precedent existed, Tiberius, with a characteristic scorn of what he interpreted as flattery, refused to permit the erection of provincial temples in his honour.[8] When, in 25, two years after the authorization granted to the cities of Asia, representatives of the province of Farther Spain presented a similar request, the Emperor, declaring that, while in view of Augustus's action he had not opposed the previous petition, he would regard it as an act of arrogance were he to receive worship in all the provinces, firmly refused to grant his permission. He seems, moreover, to have made every effort to discourage individual communities in the provinces from establishing local cults in his honour, in this respect, at least, proceeding counter to the practice of Augustus. For although before his adoption, he had received divine honours both at Pergamum and at Nysa, where priests had been created for his worship, after he became emperor he dis-

[8] Tacitus *Ann.* IV 37f.

couraged such cults, declaring that no community might erect a sanctuary or a sacred image in his honour except by special authorization,
which, he added, he would not grant.[27] In keeping with this declaration
was his reply to the city of Gytheium in the Peloponnese; for when
an envoy came to him asking for permission to bestow divine honours
both on Augustus and on himself, Tiberius accepted them for his
adoptive father but replied that for his part he was satisfied with those
which were "more moderate and suited to men."

Nevertheless, despite these professions and prohibitions, there are
numerous instances of the worship of Tiberius by communities in the
East.[28] The city of Lapethus in Cyprus, in direct disregard of his expressed desire, dedicated to him both a temple and a sacred image. There
were priests for his worship on the islands of Cos and Thera, and at
Sardis, Tralles and, apparently, Aphrodisias. Priesthoods for him were
created also at Iconium in the new Galatian province and even by the
federation composed of the free cities of Lycia. He was also called
"God" during his lifetime at Eresus, Mitylene, Cos, and by the people
of the Lycian city of Myra, and, toward the close of his principate, he
was referred to in a decree of Cyzicus as the "greatest of the gods."

Besides these instances of actual worship, Tiberius was hailed as
"Saviour" or "Benefactor," titles appropriate to a ruler.[29] These were
given to him not only in several places in the province of Asia, but
also in the temple-state of Olba, whose priest he had confirmed in
what was now a secular power, and at Myra he was even called the
"Benefactor and Saviour of the whole Universe." At Aphrodisias a great
monumental square surrounded by colonnades was dedicated to him
and his mother, Livia, together with Aphrodite and the Deified
Augustus.

It is, of course, possible that these appellations, like the expression
of gratitude on the part of the cities which had been aided after the
great earthquake of A.D. 17, arose from a genuine sense of obligation
to the Emperor for actual benefactions. In view, however, of the general practice of the Greeks of the Hellenistic period, whereby, in the
words of the Gospel,[t] "Those who exercise power over them are
called Benefactors," it is perhaps more probable that at least in part
they were bestowed on Tiberius as conventional titles appropriate to
the ruler who represented the supreme power of Rome over her subjects in the East. Evidence, in fact, of the present complete subjection
of the formerly free cities is not lacking. Under Augustus, it will be

[t] Luke XXII 25.

remembered, Cyzicus had been deprived of her independence on the ground that Roman citizens had been put to death, but the city's freedom had subsequently been restored by Agrippa.[u] Again in A.D. 25, however, an accusation was brought against the city, on this occasion because certain Romans had been imprisoned.[v] But in order to present the defendants in a more unfavourable light, it was further alleged that the citizens had failed to complete the Temple of Augustus which they had begun to build. The case was tried before the Senate with the result that Cyzicus was once more deprived of her independence. The fact that so trivial a charge might lead to the loss of an ancient freedom indicates that there was no longer any essential difference between a free city and provincial territory.

Another example of the cities' status of dependence on the ruling power appears in the action which was taken on the claim to the right of sanctuary asserted by the principal temples of Asia Minor.[30] Long regarded as a valuable prerogative, this privilege had been greatly abused, and the temples were thronged with refugees accused of various offences, including even those regarded as guilty of capital crimes. Consequently, the cities in which sanctuary was extended had become centres of disorder. It was evident that the citizens themselves could not control the situation and that measures must be adopted for the maintenance of law and order by the curtailment, if necessary, of the rights of the temples. The initiative in the matter was perhaps taken by the provincial governor, but in any case, the decision was reached that the cities in which the temples in question were situated should send delegations to Rome to present their claims and, if these were allowed, to obtain the confirmation of their ancient rights, but subject to a reasonable restraint.

In the years 22 and 23, accordingly, the envoys of twelve cities of the province of Asia appeared before the Senate. Some of these spokesmen, notably those from Ephesus, Miletus and Hierocaesareia, traced their cities' privileges of inviolability back to the Persian, or even the Lydian, period; other communities, such as Smyrna and the Island of Tenos, based their claims on the bidding of the oracle at Delphi, or, like Samos, on the recognition accorded by the Amphictyonic Council; Sardis could pretend to no earlier source than Alexander, or Pergamum than its native kings, while Magnesia-on-Maeander, Aphrodisias, Stra-

u See above pp. 474 and 477.
v Tacitus *Ann.* IV 36: Cassius Dio LVII 24, 6: Suetonius *Tib.* 37.

toniceia and Cos could cite only the authorization of various Roman generals or services rendered to Rome.

The several claims were considered and weighed, some of the cases, when the Senate grew weary, being referred to the Consuls for more minute examination. Although certain of them, especially those which depended on the authorization of the Delphic oracle, seemed dubious, no drastic action appears to have been taken. In a series of decrees, couched in polite language, the Senate strictly defined the bounds within which each temple might possess the right of sanctuary, presumably reducing those areas which were unreasonably large; and in order to prevent extension in the future by communities attempting to rival one another, it was further ordered that each temple should display a bronze tablet stating exactly the limits within which sanctuary could be claimed.

It is true that in the Hellenistic period both monarchs and communities had frequently recognized the inviolability of temples and even, in some cases, of the cities in which these were situated,[w] and that Roman generals, notably Sulla, Caesar and Antony, had confirmed sacred rights and even extended the limits of inviolable areas. The assurance of this status by an outside power, which, in the prevailing lawlessness, guaranteed sanctuaries and cities against violence, was the response to a request originating in the community itself, which hoped in this way to safeguard its position. In the present case, however, the possessors of long-established rights were compelled to show cause why these rights should be allowed and to accept a decision as to the bounds within which they might be exercised, a limitation of their powers which, however politely phrased, placed them in the category of subjects.

At the same time, it must be taken into consideration that conditions differed greatly from those of the period when the recognition of inviolability was essential to the safety of a temple. The supremacy of Rome had put an end to the wars which kept the Hellenic world in constant turmoil, and while piracy still existed sporadically, even in the Hellespont, it was held in check by the ruling power.[31] Consequently, neither temples nor cities were in need of protection from an enemy. With the cessation of internal factional strife, moreover, there was no longer any necessity of seeking refuge from political opponents. The conception of inviolability, accordingly, had undergone a great change, and it was doubtless true that the refuge which

[w] See above pp. 98f. and 102.

the temples afforded was often misused for the protection of guilty persons to the detriment of the administration of justice. Some limitation of their privileges was therefore justified; and there can be little question that the checking of what had become an abuse, however damaging it might be, from the sentimental standpoint, to the long-established rights of the temples, and, from the economic, to the pecuniary profits resulting from the presence of the refugees, was a means of combatting lawlessness and was conducive to the general welfare of the province.

An effort to prevent lawlessness of a different kind was made in the cases of governmental officials who had practised extortion during the administration of their provinces or had exceeded the limits of their power. As early as the second year of Tiberius's principate, Marcus Granius Marcellus, whom the Senate had appointed governor of Bithynia shortly before the death of Augustus, was accused before the Fathers by the quaestor who had been associated with him in his administration.[32] The actual charge was extortion, but the accuser, aided by a professional prosecutor, sought to strengthen his case by allegations of disrespect toward Augustus's memory and of disloyalty to Tiberius. The evidence for this charge of constructive treason was too trivial to merit serious consideration, and on this count the defendant was acquitted. The charge of extortion was referred, according to the form of procedure adopted in 4 B.C., to a special commission, which appears to have found Marcellus guilty of having taken money unlawfully from his province and to have ordered him to make restitution.

Seven years later—just at the time when the temples' rights of sanctuary were restricted—a more conspicuous case was brought before the Senate, that of Gaius Junius Silanus, who had been proconsul of Asia a year or two previously and was now accused by the province of maladministration.[33] Although the prosecution was actually conducted by a former Consul in co-operation with other men of senatorial rank, namely Silanus's former quaestor and one of his legates, permission was formally given to the "most eloquent orators of all Asia," who had come to Rome for the purpose, to appear against the defendant. The charges of cruelty and extortion were easily proved, and after Tiberius had paved the way for a condemnation by reading the indictment of Augustus against Messalla Volesus and the Senate's decree dealing with his case,[x] Silanus was punished by banishment to the island of Cythnos in the Aegean.

[x] See above p. 489.

The following year saw another case of official lawlessness, that of the imperial procurator of Asia, Gnaeus Lucilius Capito, who was accused by the province of having arrogated to himself the authority of a governor and especially of having made use of troops to enforce his commands.[34] As an official of the Emperor, he would normally have come before the latter for trial. Tiberius, however, referred the matter to the senators, requesting them to listen to the evidence presented by the provincials. As a result, Capito, like Silanus, was sentenced to banishment.

On the other hand, where there was no actual guilt, no steps were taken against an accused person. In the year 21 an attempt was made by a personal enemy to prevent the appointment of Marcus Aemilius Lepidus to the governorship of Asia on the ground that he was generally incompetent and had failed to live up to the standard set by his ancestors.[35] The Senate, however, refused to consider the reasons alleged and Lepidus was sent to the province, where he remained for two years. Similarly, a little later, when Gaius Fonteius Capito, after returning from his proconsulship of Asia, was brought to trial by a professional accuser, the Fathers, finding the charges false, returned a verdict of acquittal.[36]

Despite such efforts to deal justly both with the provinces and with their governors, the provincial policy of Tiberius met with bitter criticism. It was said that he appointed men to gubernatorial posts and then refused to allow them to depart from the Capital, leaving the provinces to be administered by their legates, and that both imperial and senatorial governors were often kept in office for an undue length of time, sometimes even for a term of six years.[37] This policy was attributed by the Emperor's critics to an habitual procrastination or to his fear of disloyalty on the part of appointees; it was even alleged that the number of those qualified to serve as governors had been greatly diminished by the murder of many members of the Senatorial Order. Tiberius, on the other hand, justified himself, now by declaring that only a few men were available because so many refused to serve as governors, and again by pointing out that, in view of the extortion practised by the men placed in command of provinces, these suffered less from governors of long standing, whose greed had presumably been satisfied, than from new incumbents who had still their fortunes to make. But, whatever policy Tiberius may have followed with regard to appointments to the imperial provinces, there is little doubt that in those which belonged to the Senate he retained men in office for terms far exceeding the usual one year; for in the latter part of his principate Asia was governed by Publius Petronius for six consecutive years and Africa by Marcus Silanus for the same length of time.[38] The fact that Tiberius prevented Gaius Sulpicius Galba, a man notorious for his extravagance, from participating in the assignment by lot of these two provinces[y] is an indication both of his interest in their welfare and of his control over the appointments made by the Senate.

Nevertheless, in spite of his supposed procrastination or the difficulty of finding those who would (or could) serve as provincial governors, Tiberius, in his old age, when he seemed especially indifferent to the welfare of the Empire, showed an unexpected energy and knowledge of men by appointing Lucius Vitellius governor of Syria.[39] This efficient and adroit man, it is recorded, was "placed in charge of all plans that were being made for the East," a statement which seems to imply that his powers exceeded those of an ordinary provincial governor, but how far they extended beyond the limits of Syria cannot be determined. They did, however, include the supervision of the client-kingdom of Armenia.

The problem which Germanicus was thought to have solved sixteen years previously was again brought to the fore by the recent death of King Zeno-Artaxias, apparently without leaving an heir. The opportunity was promptly seized by the old Parthian monarch, Artabanus III, who, by entering into treaty-relations with Germanicus, had tacitly acknowledged the appointment of Artaxias but, now that the latter's death had left the throne vacant, proceeded to declare his oldest son monarch of Armenia. He was emboldened to take this step by the mistaken belief that Tiberius was no longer capable of taking vigorous action, and, in the same spirit of contempt, he went so far as to claim the treasure left in Syria and Cilicia by his former rival, Vonones, who had been killed fifteen years previously. He seems also to have made some kind of threat against Cappadocia, and he talked in a vainglorious fashion of conquering the whole empire of Cyrus and Alexander.

But the arrogance and cruelty of Artabanus had aroused much dissatisfaction among the Parthians, and, as on other occasions, the malcontents appealed to Rome. Their appeal offered an excellent opportunity for thwarting Artabanus's designs on Armenia by creating trouble in his own kingdom. In reply to a request presented by representatives of the disaffected faction, the Parthian prince Phraates,

y Tacitus *Ann.* VI 40, 3 (A.D. 36): Suetonius *Galba* 3.

Vonones's brother, who had lived in Rome for nearly a half-century, was sent by Tiberius to claim his ancestral throne. He soon succumbed, however, to his attempts to live like a Parthian, whereupon his younger and more vigorous brother, Tiridates, was deputed to take his place as claimant. It was part of Vitellius's duty to ensure the success of the undertaking but without involving Rome in a Parthian war.

The project naturally included the eviction of the Parthian prince from Armenia and the bestowal of the kingdom on someone who would rule as the protégé of Rome. A candidate was finally found in the person of Mithradates, the brother of Pharasmanes, King of the Trans-Caucasian Iberians, a people which had submitted to a legate of Antony and afterward sent envoys to Augustus.[z] In response, doubtless, to instructions received from Rome, the two brothers entered Armenia with a large force, and, after bribing the attendants of the Parthian claimant to assassinate their master, they took possession of Artaxata.

Artabanus, undaunted by this reverse, selected another of his numerous sons, Orodes, as ruler of Armenia. Accompanied by a Parthian army, the prince entered the country. The Iberians, however, had meanwhile mustered a larger force, and the Parthians, after compelling their leader to join battle, were thrown into great confusion by the superior strength of the enemy. Orodes himself was wounded by Pharasmanes and forced to withdraw from the field. A report that he had been killed completed the demoralization of the Parthians and they yielded the victory to their opponents.

This defeat Artabanus tried to retrieve by marching into Armenia in person at the head of a large army. His attempt to seize the country, however, was thwarted by Vitellius, who, so far, had taken no active part in the struggle for Armenia. Now, however, mobilizing his troops, he spread the rumour that he was about to lead an army across the Euphrates. The feint was wholly successful. Artabanus, alarmed for the safety of Mesopotamia, abandoned the Armenian venture and returned for the defence of his own dominions.

This retreat, however, greatly damaged the old monarch's prestige and afforded an opportunity to his opponents. Encouraged—or bribed—by Vitellius's agents, they succeeded in driving him from his kingdom to seek refuge among the Scythian tribes on the Caspian Sea. Tiridates, accompanied as far as the Euphrates by Vitellius and the Roman legions, entered Mesopotamia in triumph and, welcomed by the

[z] Cassius Dio XLIX 24, 1: Augustus *Res Gest.* c. 31.

opponents of the late ruler, he was crowned king at Ctesiphon, the royal residence of the Parthian monarchs. Once more Roman diplomacy seemed to be successful. A Roman nominee was king of Armenia and a Romanized Parthian sat on the throne of his ancestors.

In the case of Tiridates, however, this success was short-lived. Showing greater interest in taking possession of his predecessor's treasures and concubines than in winning his subjects' allegiance, he soon lost prestige, and those who opposed him seized upon the opportunity to recall Artabanus. On his arrival the old King found ready support, and Tiridates, deeming it wise to withdraw from Ctesiphon into northern Mesopotamia, rapidly lost his followers and finally, with only a few attendants, took refuge in the province of Syria.

Even this reverse, however, was turned to advantage by Vitellius; for Artabanus, humbled by his misfortunes, was ready to make concessions. The Roman governor, accordingly, advancing to the Euphrates, met the Parthian King on a bridge of boats, and here a treaty between the two great powers was concluded. In return for his recognition as ruler, Artabanus, sending one of his sons to Italy as a hostage for his fidelity, agreed to accept Mithradates as ruler of Armenia. When the latter was afterward removed from his throne, the removal was not the act of the Parthians but of Tiberius's successor in the imperial power.[a]

Meanwhile, in the year 36, another success, of much less importance, it is true, but involving a military campaign, was achieved by Vitellius through the agency of a legate, Marcus Trebellius.[40] The Cietae, a rugged people living in the rough mountain-country of eastern Cilicia Aspera, had been assigned to King Archelaus II when he succeeded to a portion of his father's dominions. An attempt on his part to reduce them to the position of subjects by ordering them to furnish statements of their property—analogous to the census in Rome—and to pay taxes in accordance with these statements met with bitter resistance. Withdrawing into the inaccessible fastnesses of the region, they defied the King's troops, who were powerless to cope with either the tribesmen or their difficult country. It became necessary, therefore, for Archelaus to appeal to Rome for help, and, since the neighbouring district of Cilicia Campestris was attached to Syria, the governor of which had an army at his disposal, the task of furnishing the required aid devolved upon Vitellius. His legate, therefore, with four thousand legionaries and some auxiliary troops, was sent to Cilicia. Employing the

[a] See below p. 514.

same methods of warfare that Quirinius had used against the Homonadeis,[b] Trebellius blockaded two rebel strongholds, investing them
so closely that none could leave them and no relief could be brought.
Their water-supply exhausted, the defenders capitulated and with their
surrender the rebellion was crushed.

Scarcely had this exploit been reported in Rome when the principate
of Tiberius came to an end with the death of the Emperor in his
seventy-eighth year.[c] His rule of over twenty-two years had been cheer-
less and gloomy from the beginning, but his last eight years, by reason
of the succession of punishments inflicted on those suspected of
treason, were regarded by Roman writers as a reign of terror. In the
provinces of the East, on the other hand, where there was no one to
antagonize the diffident and even irritable Emperor and none to arouse
his suspicions, his government had been honest and beneficial. In his
efforts to prevent extortion and cruelty and to maintain law and order,
in his acceptance of divine honours, in his reduction of the number
of client-kingdoms while maintaining a Roman vassal on the Armenian
throne, and finally in his preservation of nominally peaceful relations
with the Parthians, Tiberius, without initiative or plans of his own,
was content to abide by the precedents set by his adoptive father. His
death meant the end of the type of principate which Augustus had
founded and Tiberius in his earlier years had attempted to maintain.
While the form of government by the Senate aided by the Foremost
Citizen continued to exist, the actual power was henceforth held by one
man, and the monarchical rule by which the Roman Empire was henceforth governed was established by Tiberius's youthful successor, who
on 18 March, A.D. 37, two days after the old Emperor's death, was
hailed by the Senate as *Imperator*.[d]

On the accession to power of Gaius Caesar, popularly known as
Caligula, the youngest son of Germanicus, an oath of allegiance was
taken by various cities in the Empire.[41] In the East, the Council and
People of Assus celebrated the beginning of a new and blessed epoch,
"when the Universe found unmeasured joy and every city and every
nation has striven to behold the God," by passing a formal decree containing an oath in the name of Zeus the Saviour, Athena the Virgin
and the Deified Augustus, by which all swore to show good will to the
new *Princeps* and his house and to consider his friends as friends and

[b] See above p. 461. [c] Tacitus *Ann.* vi 50, 7f.: Suetonius *Tib.* 73.
[d] *C.I.L.* vi 2028 = Henzen *Acta Frat. Arv.* p. xliii.

his foes as foes. In token of this allegiance, five envoys were appointed to go to Rome and, taking a vow for the Emperor's safety, to sacrifice to Jupiter Capitolinus in the name of their city. At Jerusalem, Vitellius, as governor of Syria, administered an oath of allegiance to the Jews. In the West, the citizens of Aritium, in what is now Portugal, swore, in much the same terms as the people of Assus, to regard the enemies of Gaius as their own and to defend him with arms both on land and on sea. Such expressions of loyalty to the Roman *Imperator* signify the unity of the Empire as well as the subjection of communities which once were independent.

The dream of a new age did, indeed, seem justified when, wishing to create the appearance of a reaction against the harshness of Tiberius, the young Emperor promised to bring back the banished, to punish false informers, and to defer to the power of the Senate—in short, to restore all that the Romans regarded as "liberty."[e] Nowhere was there greater enthusiasm for the new régime than in the cities of Asia. At Cyzicus Gaius was elected to the highest civic office, that of Hipparch, and in a decree of the city he was hailed as the "New Sun," who "has wished to illumine with his rays the kingdoms that are the body-guards of his Empire, to the end that the greatness of his immortality might be the more august."[42] At Chios a festival called Caesareia seems to have been celebrated on his birthday, and at Cos an inscription was dated in the first year of his "epiphany," as though he were a deity incarnate.

But the dream of a just and beneficent ruler was soon shattered. Whether Gaius's mind was suddenly affected by a serious illness which seized him six months after his accession to power or whether (more probably) he now put into effect a previously formed policy of setting himself up as a despot has long been a matter of dispute.[43] To the ancient writers his behaviour suggested a psychopathic case afflicted with delusions of grandeur.

At the beginning of his rule, Gaius had issued an order forbidding both the erection of statues of himself and the offering of sacrifices to his Genius.[44] A letter to the commonalty of some of the states of Greece contained a similar prohibition concerning statues save on the occasion of the great festivals. It is questionable whether his order was ever observed, but, in any case, dedications at Mitylene to Gaius himself as God, Benefactor and Founder and to his dead brothers and two of his sisters show that it soon fell into abeyance. These titles conferred

e Cassius Dio LIX 6: Suetonius *Cal.* 15.

on the Emperor, to be sure, were presumably merely the conventional appellations which had also been given to Tiberius.[f] Even that of New Aphrodite, conferred on his favourite sister, Drusilla, not only at Mitylene but also at Cyzicus and Magnesia, was analogous to a similar title received by his mother, Agrippina. At Rome, however, Gaius broke with long-established tradition, not merely in the deification of Drusilla after her death, which raised her to the position of divinity held by Caesar and Augustus, but especially by his claim to equality with Jupiter.[45]

Even in the East Gaius's claim to godhead must have seemed extravagant; for, whereas Augustus and Tiberius, with a show of reluctance, had given permission to the provincial commonalties to erect temples for their worship, Gaius, if we may believe an ancient historian, issued a command to build a temple for himself at Miletus.[46] It must, indeed, be admitted that this "command" may have been nothing more than an assent to a proposal for the construction of a new temple in the city. But the correctness of the historian's statement seems probable in view of Gaius's order to Publius Petronius, when governor of Syria, to erect a colossal statue of Zeus, bearing the Emperor's features, in the Temple of Jehovah in Jerusalem, a command which aroused such bitter opposition among the Jews that a rebellion would have ensued had not Petronius succeeded in postponing its execution until it was rendered unnecessary by Gaius's death.[47]

The grandiose ideas of Gaius and his evident desire to play the part of an Oriental ruler were attributed to the influence both of a prince of Judaea, Julius Agrippa, a grandson of Herod the Great, and of Antiochus, the son of the King of Commagene at whose death in A.D. 17 the district had become Roman provincial territory.[g] These two men were coupled together in the minds of the Romans as the young Emperor's "tutors in tyranny."[h] Whatever be the truth with regard to this belief, it is evident that both enjoyed the close friendship of Gaius and likewise profited by it, for to each a kingdom was granted. By the gift Agrippa obtained the regions of Batanaea and Abilene, south and west of Damascus, the dominions, respectively, of his uncle Philippus and the tetrarch Lysanias, the last known member of a dynasty which had ruled in central Syria since the middle of the first century before Christ.[48] Antiochus was not only restored to his ancestral throne but received also 1,000,000 sesterces as a reimbursement for the taxes and other revenues from his kingdom, which during the twenty years

[f] See above p. 502.   [g] See above p. 495f.   [h] Cassius Dio LIX 24, 1.

512

that had elapsed since his father's death had accrued to the imperial treasury.[49] His dominions were enlarged by the addition of territory in Cilicia Aspera; for the death of Archelaus II, whom Tiberius had made ruler over part of this district, made it possible for Gaius to bestow the late King's possessions on his so-called Tutor.

New monarchs were appointed also in the northeastern part of Asia Minor. The death of Pythodoris during the principate of Tiberius appears to have left the kingdom of Pontus without a ruler, for it is nowhere recorded that the Queen was succeeded by her elder son, and her younger son, Zeno, had become King of Armenia.[50] Pythodoris's daughter, Antonia Tryphaena, had married the Thracian king Cotys, by whom she had three sons, Rhoemetalces, Polemo and Cotys.[51] Her husband, described as a mild-mannered and kindly ruler, had been treacherously murdered about A.D. 19 by his uncle, Rhascuporis, whom Augustus had recognized as ruler of a part of Thrace. The murderer, cajoled into surrendering to a Roman official, was brought to trial before the Senate, the formal accusation being presented by Tryphaena herself. By vote of the Fathers, Rhascuporis was deposed and banished. The portion of Thrace which had belonged to Cotys was granted to his three sons, but, since they were minors, it was placed under the care of a Roman, who was appointed by the Senate as their guardian.

After the condemnation of her husband's murderer Tryphaena took up her residence in Cyzicus. Here she became the priestess of Livia and did much for the improvement of the city, including among her benefactions the dredging of the lagoon between Cyzicus and the mainland as well as of the canals which connected this with the harbours. It was perhaps partly because of her generosity that the city, despite the loss of its freedom, still enjoyed great prosperity. Her three sons, on the other hand, seem to have remained in Rome, and, although presumably somewhat older than Gaius, they became, if a decree of Cyzicus may be believed, his "foster-brothers and comrades."[1] By the time of Gaius's accession to power, eighteen years after Rhascuporis had been condemned, the princes had long since attained their majority. The dilatory Tiberius, although about the year 34—perhaps on the occasion of Pythodoris's death—he had reduced the size of the kingdom of Pontus by annexing the city of Comana to the Empire,[52] seems to have taken no steps to restore the young men to the realms once held by their father and by their maternal grandmother.

[1] I.G.R. IV 145 = Syll.³ 798.

It was natural, therefore, that Gaius should recognize these brothers as rulers of the lands to which they had an hereditary claim. Rhoemetalces, as the eldest, succeeded to his father's dominions in Thrace, while Polemo received Pythodoris's kingdom of Pontus.[53] A portion, at least, of the territory in southern Russia which his grandfather had obtained from Augustus was also granted to the young man, but, as will be shown, it was soon taken from him, and his claim to the region seems never to have been completely established. Cotys, the youngest of the three princes, was made ruler of Armenia Minor, part of which also had once belonged to Pythodoris, while another part, perhaps, may have been attached to the province of Cappadocia.

In Greater Armenia, on the other hand, Gaius nullified the arrangement made by Tiberius. Summoning Mithradates the Iberian to Rome, he detained him there under guard, allowing the Armenian throne to remain vacant.[54] Even in his own arrangements he showed no consistency, for he took away from Antiochus Epiphanes the district of Commagene, which he had given him only a short time previously.

The appointment of these client-kings in Judaea and Asia Minor, together with the restoration to power of Gaius Julius Laco, who had been deprived by Tiberius of his position as a local ruler at Sparta, and the creation of a certain Sohaemus as ruler of a part of Ituraea, which, like Abilene, had once belonged to the house of Lysanias, suggests that Gaius abandoned the policy, initiated by Augustus and continued by Tiberius, of merging client-states in the Empire.[55] The view has even been expressed that he reverted to Antony's method of parcelling out the East among native princes, wishing to rule as a "King of Kings," surrounded by vassal-monarchs.[56] It is, of course, impossible to tell how far the Emperor, had he lived longer, would have carried out such a policy, but his actual performance does not seem to warrant this view. It is true that Commagene, when assigned to Antiochus, and perhaps Armenia Minor, when assigned to Cotys, were provincial territory, but both regions had belonged to the dynasties represented by the two princes and their restoration to these young men does not imply any general plan for increasing the number of vassal-states. Thrace and Pontus were merely given back to the heirs of their late monarchs, Batanaea was handed over to the nephew of its former ruler, the coast of Cilicia Aspera was transferred from one client-prince to another, while Abilene and Ituraea, belonging to a dynasty of native princes, had never been incorporated in the Roman Empire. However whimsical Gaius may have appeared in regard to Commagene and however ready he was to sacrifice what had been gained in Armenia—and there may perhaps have been cause for both actions—it does not appear that he formed any plan for the creation of a number of vassal-kingdoms of which he was to be the overlord.

There is no reason, moreover, to suppose that, except perhaps for the temple at Miletus, the provinces of Asia and Bithynia were affected by Gaius's pretensions. The adulatory titles conferred on him were presumably, as has been observed, merely conventional, and his election to public office in a city, as in the case of the stephanephorate in Priene,[j] held probably in 40/1, which had been bestowed also on Tiberius and Germanicus, was likewise only a traditional compliment. His ruthless cruelty, however, was shown in the case of Gaius Cassius Longinus, a descendant of the conspirator against Caesar, who in 40/1 was pro-consul of Asia.[57] The Emperor, so it is told, warned by a prophecy to beware of a man named Cassius, leaped to the conclusion that the namesake of Caesar's assassin was the source of his danger. Whatever be the truth of this explanation, Gaius, overriding any authority that the Senate had over the governor of a province committed to its charge, gave orders that Cassius should be brought to Rome under guard, intending, so it was believed, to put him to death. The Proconsul, however, was saved; before his arrival in the city, the prophecy had been fulfilled, for on 24 January, 41 Gaius was murdered by a Cassius— a certain Cassius Chaerea, a tribune of the Praetorian Guard, who, as a frequent butt of the Emperor's jests, bore him a personal grudge.[58]

Under the rule of Gaius, lasting but three years and ten months, the policies and methods which Augustus had used in the East and Tiberius had scrupulously observed underwent no serious change. However much this irresponsible young man may have wished to assume in Rome the role of an oriental ruler, he found little opportunity to play that part in the Orient itself.

[j] *Ins. Priene* 142 ii.

CHAPTER XXII

LYCIA: FEDERATION AND PROVINCE

IN the course of this narrative incidental mention has been made of
Lycia and the cities which it contained, especially those of its coast.
No detailed account, however, has been given of this district, for it
was not until the time of the Emperor Claudius that it became a part
of Rome's empire in the East.

A rugged tract of mountain-country, thrust forward at the southwest
corner of Asia Minor and, as it were, separating the Aegean and the
Mediterranean, Lycia is broken by huge masses of the Taurus into
narrow valleys with an occasional broader plain. Difficult of access
from the interior, it depends for its intercourse with other lands chiefly
upon the sea, and here Nature has compensated for the lack of land-
communications by providing a succession of excellent harbours extending around the entire circuit of the coast.

The northern boundary of the district originally corresponded
roughly to a line drawn from the head of the Gulf of Antalya westward to the mouth of the river Indus.[1] The territory controlled by
the Lycians, however, was increased and a more definite boundary
established in 84 B.C., when Murena, having dissolved the "Tetrapolis"
headed by Cibyra, incorporated the latter into the province of Asia
and attached to Lycia the region of Cabalis with the three remaining
cities, Bubon, Balbura and Oenoanda.

On the east, Lycia, regarded politically, extended only as far as the
mountain-range, called by Strabo Solyma, which, running parallel to
the coast, extends northward from the projecting headland of Cape
Chelidonia.[2] The narrow strip of land between this range and the
Gulf of Antalya was held by the Greek cities of Olympus and Phaselis.[3]
The former was probably a Hellenistic foundation; the latter was a
Rhodian colony, settled in the early seventh century, which, thanks
to an advantageous position and a triple harbour, developed into a
place of great commercial importance.

On the west also the political and natural boundaries did not coincide,
for Lycia, while including the stretch of coast between Mt. Cragus
and the sea, did not extend to the Indus. The Rhodian possessions in
southern Caria, reaching across this river, included Daedala, some distance to the east.[a] Even Telmessus, on the coast still farther east, the

---

[a] See Chap. II note 15.

most important city of the region, possessing one of the largest and best natural harbours in Asia Minor, although it was conquered in the early fourth century by a Lycian ruler and in this period used the native language, was not included in Lycia.[4] Like the cities of the district, however, Telmessus during the third century was controlled by Egypt, but in 188 B.C. after the defeat of Antiochus III the Romans gave it to the kings of Pergamum, and it seems not to have joined the Lycian cities until after the First Mithradatic War. From this time onward Lycia was regarded politically, as well as geographically, as extending to the Indus. Including both the eastern and the western coasts, with the region as far as the Indus, the area of the district was somewhat over 3,500 square miles.

The chief geographical feature of inland Lycia is the great mountain-range, in outline comparable to a horse-shoe, which occupies the entire centre of the district.[5] Reaching down from the northeast, this extension of the Taurus forms a wide curve bending back from its greatest peak, the huge massif, nearly ten thousand feet high, now known as Ak Dağ ("White Mountain"), and returning to the northeast under various names (including another "White Mountain") until it is merged in the range called Solyma. From this principal mountain-group, to which the name Massicytus was applied somewhat indefinitely, minor ranges stretch forward both toward the northwest and toward the south. In the centre of the curve is a wide plain, in which the cities of Podalia and Choma were situated, abundantly watered by the streams which descend from the surrounding peaks but, in some cases, finding no means of exit, lose themselves in marshy lakes or in underground channels.[6]

Besides this great range in the centre of Lycia, there are other mountain-districts, separated from it by deep river-valleys. Along the western coast, towering up from the sea, stretches the long line of Mt. Cragus, with a maximum height, at its northern end, of nearly 6,000 feet. On the south, along the Mediterranean, a plateau, broken by a succession of ridges and valleys, lies between the central mountain-ring and the sea, often descending steeply to the water's edge.[7]

In this central ring rise the three main rivers which, flowing in a generally north-south direction, drain the district, the Xanthus, the Arycandus and the river now called Alakır Çay. In the south, the Myrus, formed by several streams in the western part of the coast plateau, flows northeast and then southeast, frequently through deep gorges, and separates the lower slopes of the central range from the broken hill-country along the Mediterranean.[8]

Of these rivers, by far the most important was the Xanthus, the valley of which, a much-used thoroughfare, was the centre of Lycian culture. Rising on the northern side of the great mountain-ring and augmented by the streams which pour down from it, the river breaks through the northwestern extension of the Ak Dağ, flowing through a chasm of great depth into a wide plain.[9] Here, much increased by the water flowing from copious springs, it bends sharply to the south and traverses a valley about forty miles in length and in places as much as three miles wide, flanked on the east by the precipices of the Ak Dağ and on the west by the gradual slopes of Cragus, until it finds its way into the Mediterranean. In eastern Lycia, the Alakır Çay, formed by streams which unite between the central ring and the range of Solyma, flows through a narrow romantic valley, closely hemmed in by mountains, until it reaches the plain of Finike, through which it empties into the sea. Between these two principal rivers and shorter than both, the Arycandus, rising near the pass which leads southward from the plain of Podalia across the range of Ak Dağ, takes a southeasterly course into the same littoral plain.

The products of Lycia were, naturally, mainly those of a mountain-region. Its principal source of wealth was its forests, containing the pines which still clothe the sides of the great ranges, as well as a variety of cedar used for ship-building and, on the lower levels, cypress.[10] A species of thorny shrub was also valuable, for a juice used in medicine was produced from its roots. No mines, however, seem to have been known except a variety of chalk (*creta*) found near Bubon in the extreme north, which also was supposed to have a medicinal value. On the other hand, the region around Telmessus exported a wine favourably known in Italy, and it is probable that the fertile plain of Podalia, which now produces large amounts of fruit, was rich in ancient times and that the broad valley of the Xanthus bore grain. The only industry known was the production of goats' hair, used especially in the manufacture of rope. Off the coast, there were valuable fisheries, especially near the Chelidonian Islands, and the sponges from Lycia were regarded as especially good.

It is evident that the utilization of the resources of this rugged country was hampered by the difficulty of transportation. There were, nevertheless, certain roads by which communication was maintained. The great route which ran southward through Caria to Physcus on the

Strait of Marmaris led on past Calynda to Telmessus, whence, turning eastward into the interior to the valley of the Xanthus, it followed the river to Patara on the coast.[11] From here, continuing across the southern plateau to the mouth of the Myrus and over a high, steep mountain to the plain of Finike, it crossed the range called Solyma to the Gulf of Antalya. A particularly difficult section led on from here past Phaselis to the Pamphylian plain.

The interior of Lycia also was traversed by a route from northwest to southeast. Entering the mountain-country from the plain of Cibyra— whence routes ran northward to Laodiceia-on-Lycus and southeastward into Pamphylia[b]—this road led to Balbura and Oenoanda, and thence across the central mountain-ring into the plain of Podalia.[12] Leaving this plain at the southeastern corner, it crossed the watershed into the valley of the Arycandus, which it followed past Limyra to the plain of Finike on the Mediterranean.

Another road led up the valley of the Xanthus from the point where it was entered by the main route from Telmessus as far as Araxa, where the river breaks through the mountains northwest of the Ak Dağ.[13] From here it perhaps went onward through the very difficult country which lies between Araxa and Tabae in Caria. In eastern Lycia also there may have been a road leading to the northeast up the valley of the Alakır Çay and over the northern end of the range called Solyma to Pamphylia.

As might be supposed, most of the cities of Lycia were either on or near the coast, where communications could be carried on either by sea or by the great route which ran parallel to it, or on one of the roads which led from the north through the valleys of the Xanthus and the Arycandus. On the main route lay the six cities regarded as the largest of the twenty-three communities which, about 100 B.C., comprised the powerful federation formed by the cities of the district, an organization which will presently be described in detail.[14] These six cities were Tlos, Xanthus, Pinara, Patara, Myra and Olympus, of which the first four were important places in the fourth century before Christ.[15] The first two stood above the left bank of the river Xanthus, Tlos on an elevated terrace on the side of the height which served as its acropolis, "bounded by perpendicular precipices and deep ravines," with the cliffs of the Ak Dağ towering up behind, Xanthus on an isolated hill, rising steeply from the river, some fifteen miles below Tlos and about eight miles from the Mediterranean. Pinara, somewhat more remote, on the eastern side of the range of Cragus about six miles from the river Xanthus, had a situation of extraordinary grandeur at the foot of an acropolis described as "a stupendous tower of rock, faced by a perpendicular precipice." Patara, on the seashore, east of the mouth of the Xanthus, with an excellent harbour (now a marsh) flanked by a hill on which there appears to have been a lighthouse, was one of the principal ports of Lycia. Myra, on the other hand, lay a few miles back from the coast on the eastern edge of the southern plateau, where the river Myrus breaks through the hills to the sea. Its territory included the smaller community of Trebenda and the port of Andriace, some four miles to the southwest, from which St. Paul set forth on his fateful voyage to Italy. The sixth city of the series, Olympus, lay beyond the original confines of Lycia on the shore of the Gulf of Antalya, where a stream breaks through the mountain-range in a narrow defile below the acropolis of the city high on a projecting headland.[16] Toward the north, on a small plateau on the mountain-side, is the famous "Chimaera," a niche in a wall of rock giving vent to a highly inflammable gas, the burning jets of which—"an everlasting fire"—caused wonder in Antiquity as well as in modern times.

While it is impossible definitely to identify all the remaining seventeen cities which belonged to the Lycian Federation at the beginning of the first century before Christ, it may safely be said of eleven that they were connected with this group; for not only does their use of the Lycian language show that they were in existence in the fourth century before Christ, but their coins indicate that during the second and first centuries they were members of this organization.[c]

These cities occupied a fairly limited area, chiefly in the southern and central portions of the district. In the west, the only community which can be definitely named as a member of the group was Sidyma, lying in a little plain high up on the western side of Cragus, about 2,600 feet in altitude and (in an air-line) slightly over three miles from the sea.[17] In southern Lycia, there were three cities situated directly on the Mediterranean. Of these, Phellus and Antiphellus lay on opposite sides of a broad and beautiful bay some twenty miles east of the mouth of the Xanthus, protected on the south by the large island of Megiste, Phellus in a recess at the southeastern corner, Antiphellus on the northern shore, on the neck of a long tongue of land which, separating the bay from a narrow inlet, provided the city with two harbours. Farther east, Aperlae stood on the narrow isthmus of a short but broad peninsula, extending toward the Mediterranean and almost entirely filled by a mountain-range.

Somewhat farther inland, about four miles from the sea, Cyaneae stood on a high hill which formed a natural fortress of great strength dominating the plateau between the river Myrus and the Mediterranean.[18] The city seems to have possessed a large territory, including, probably, the port of Teimiusa on a small, but almost completely land-locked, bay.

East of the mouth of the Arycandus three cities bordered the plain of Finike.[19] Of these, Limyra and Rhodiapolis were some miles back from the Mediterranean, the former at the northwestern corner of the plain in an elevated position at the end of the range which forms the eastern side of the Arycandus valley, the latter high up in the mountains on a sort of terrace terminated at each end by a deep ravine. The third city, Gagae, at the southeastern corner of the plain, lay close to the sea, partly on level ground and partly on the side of a hill on the top of which was a strongly fortified citadel.

Another city, Arycanda, was far removed from the shore and near the head-waters of the river to which it gave its name. Built on a series of terraces on the steep side of the central mountain-ring, it stood in a strong position dominating the pass which led from the central plain into the river-valley and eventually to the coast.

Two other inland cities, Cadyanda and Araxa, may also be added to the number.[20] The former, about ten miles northeast of Telmessus, had a situation of great beauty and natural strength on a flat-topped mountain; the latter stood on a low hill at the mouth of the gorge through which the Xanthus rushes to enter the broad valley leading to the sea. Both cities were evidently autonomous communities. As early, apparently, as the second century before Christ Cadyanda issued coins of its own, and in the first century the citizens were wealthy enough to subscribe to a fund for some public purpose, amounting to over ten thousand drachmae. At Araxa, probably in the third century, a decree was passed by the Assembly in the name of the *polis* and the magistrates, mentioning an embassy sent to Rhodes.

Of the three cities in the region of Cabalis, Bubon, Balbura and Oenoanda, which were not attached to Lycia until 84 B.C., Bubon had an imposing situation on a series of terraces rising steeply from the eastern bank of a stream flowing northward into the plain of Cibyna.[21] The natural communications of the city, accordingly, were in this direction, although a route leading southward over the mountains may have connected it with the valley of the Xanthus at Araxa. About eleven miles to the east, Balbura lay on a branch of the Xanthus, "which issues from a deep gorge beneath a high and steep hill, crowned by the acropolis of the city." The third of these communities, Oenoanda, on the road connecting Balbura with the plain of Podalia, stood high above the south bank of the upper Xanthus on the end of a mountain-spur. Strongly fortified by Nature, the city was protected also by a massive wall interspersed with frequent towers. The construction of one section is so similar to the walls of Pergamum built under Eumenes II that it may well date from the same period. The resemblance, indeed, may be due to the extension of the influence of Pergamum—which is found at Termessus under Attalus II[d]—to this autonomous city in a remote region. In any case, the power of Termessus penetrated to this neighbourhood, for, probably during the third century before Christ, it founded a colony, called, in order to distinguish it from the mother-city, Termessus-near-Oenoanda, which seems to have lain on the north bank of the Xanthus not more than two miles from Oenoanda.[22] Separated from the greater Termessus, perhaps in the second century, it appears to have attached itself to Oenoanda and, although preserving its identity, to have entered into a close combination with the latter, a connexion which continued down to the third century after Christ.

After the addition, soon after the First Mithradatic War, of Telmessus and the three communities of Cabalis, the Lycian cities may be supposed to have been twenty-seven in number. This, to be sure, does not agree with the statement, found in the *Natural History* of Pliny, that there were thirty-six towns in Lycia.[23] The author's list, however, contains some places for whose independence there is no evidence, and it is probable that this list may have included smaller communities which had entered into a political combination or "sympolity"—a process known to have occurred at Aperlae, as well as elsewhere—with some more important city.[24] By such a combination these communities, while retaining their names and, probably to some extent, their civic organizations, were merged with the larger cities for all political purposes, including presumably membership in the Federation.

The Lycians were recognized as belonging to the Hellenic world as early as the middle of the fifth century, when, in 446/5 B.C., they jointly paid a contribution to Athens supposedly for the use of the "Confederacy of Delos."[e] Before this time, however, they had appeared in the *Iliad*, fighting as allies of the Trojans under the leadership of the heroes, "godlike" Sarpedon and "blameless" Glaucus, in whose honour at Xanthus and Tlos buildings were afterward erected and divisions of the community named.[25] In the early fourth century, although nominally subject to the Persians, the cities of Lycia seem to have been ruled by their own "dynasts," apparently a loose federation of princes, but soon after 360 B.C. Maussolus of Halicarnassus extended his sway over at least a part of the district.[26] During all this period the Lycians were evidently but little affected by Hellenic influences, for the use of the native language was general.

When Alexander arrived in Lycia in the winter of 334-333, Pinara, Xanthus and Patara, as well as thirty additional places, it is said, submitted to him, and others which sent envoys were ordered to surrender to officers designated for the purpose.[27] Later, he appointed Nearchus, one of his most trusted "companions," as satrap of the district.

In the division of Alexander's empire after his death Lycia fell to the share of Antigonus "the One-eyed."[28] In 309, however, Antigonus's enemy, Ptolemy I of Egypt, invading the district, captured Xanthus as well as Phaselis. Ptolemy, to be sure, did not succeed in retaining his conquests, for four years later Patara was held by Antigonus's son, Demetrius, one of whose vessels was burned in the harbour by an attacking force of Rhodians.

After Antigonus's death, Ptolemy, again invading southwestern Asia Minor—perhaps in 295 B.C.—seized Caunus in Caria and with it Telmessus and the western part of Lycia. Twenty years later, his son, Ptolemy II, was in possession of both Xanthus and Patara, the latter of which, in the manner of the monarchs of the time, he renamed Arsinoe in honour of his sister-wife. His son was able to boast that on succeeding to the throne (in 247) he had inherited both Caria and Lycia.

The supremacy of Egypt in Lycia, while nominally based on a system of alliances with the several cities, was, in fact, as also in Caria, an outright rule.[29] The collection of the cash revenues from the district and of certain taxes or monopolies was farmed out to agents, presumably of the royal treasury. It is significant also that the cities dated their decrees by the regnal year of the king. Nevertheless, as a result of the process of Hellenization which had led to the abandonment of

[e] See notes 3 and 4.

their native language in favour of Greek, they developed civic institutions with "sovereign assemblies," which were able to grant citizenship and even exemption from local taxes, thus preserving what has been aptly called a "façade of autonomy."

The rule of Egypt over Lycia lasted throughout the third century.[30] Under the incompetent Ptolemy IV, however, it grew rapidly weaker, and when, in 197 B.C., Antiochus III set out to regain his ancestors' empire in western Asia Minor, he had no difficulty in occupying Limyra, Andriace and Patara and apparently Telmessus as well. Xanthus also surrendered, but through some sort of compromise, by which the King went through the form of consecrating it to Leto, Apollo and Artemis, the fiction of its independence was preserved.

The submission of these cities to Antiochus and their support during his war with Rome were regarded by the victors as sufficient ground for treating Lycia as conquered territory.[31] Except for Telmessus, given to Eumenes II of Pergamum, the district was assigned to the Rhodians, to whom, dependent on ships both for their commerce and for their political power, the timber from the forests was of great value.

A description has already been given both of the determined and continued opposition to Rhodian rule and of the Senate's action, taken in 167 B.C. after various attempts at a compromise, by which Lycia was finally declared free. By this action the various communities became independent city-states, possessing the same rights as the Greek autonomous cities of the Aegaean seaboard. Their gratitude to Rome and the assurance of her protection were expressed on a monument, presumably erected at this time, which records that the "Commonalty of the Lycians, having recovered its ancestral democracy," made an offering to Jupiter Capitolinus and the Roman People in acknowledgement of the benefits conferred upon it.

It may be presumed that this "Commonalty," or Federation, of the Lycian cities had been formed during the third century, perhaps during the period when the power of Egypt was growing steadily weaker.[32] It seems to have been in existence in 188 B.C., when the Lycians took joint action in sending envoys to Rhodes to present a plea for an alliance,[f] and before the death of Ptolemy V in 181 it erected a monument, probably in Alexandria, to one of the King's officials.[g] In any case, its importance was greatly increased after the liberation of Lycia from the rule of Rhodes. At the end of the second century, when it was at the height of its power, it is said that there were twenty-three

[f] Polybius XXII 5, 8f.   [g] O.G.I. 99.

member-cities.[h] Of these, at least eighteen, during the second and first centuries, issued silver or bronze coins, uniform in type and inscribed with the word "Lycians" as well as with the initials of the individual city.[33]

The affairs of the Federation were managed by a congress composed of representatives of the member-cities, which cast votes in proportion to their size and importance, the six largest having three votes each, while those of medium size had two and the smallest only one.[34] Since no city was ever named as a permanent political centre, the delegates convened in whatever place they might choose. The chief function of this federal Assembly was to discuss and decide questions pertaining to the common interests of the member-cities, particularly the declaration and prosecution of war, the conclusion of treaties and the formation of alliances. While action on these matters was necessarily curtailed as the increasing power of Rome exercised a greater control over the foreign policy of even independent communities under her protection, there can be little doubt that at least until the time of the wars against Mithradates the Assembly had full power to arrive at such decisions.

The expenses of the Federation were met by assessments which the Assembly levied upon its members. The payments were imposed in the proportion in which the votes were allocated to the several cities, and the funds obtained were placed under the care of a treasurer.[35] These expenses included the maintenance of a navy and an army. An "admiral of all the Lycians," in the early first century, gained the victory in a sea-fight off the Chelidonian Islands, and also as commander of the army won three battles in the enemies' country. The titles of admiral, general and commander of cavalry which appear in inscriptions indicate that naval and military forces were maintained permanently and not used merely in this one campaign.

The Federation had also a court of law, consisting of a body of judges, elected from the various member-cities.[36] Its decisions were probably rendered in accordance with a legal code drawn up by a body of jurists. The primary functions of this court may have been the settlement of matters of issue between the Federation and a city or the adjudication of disputes between members. It is possible also that it dealt with lawsuits between the citizens of a single city, but in some cases, at least, these seem to have been settled, in the usual practice of the cities of Asia, by an impartial imported court.

The Federation chose its own officials.[37] The most important of these

[h] See above p. 519.

was the Lyciarch, who, elected annually, presided over the meetings of the Assembly and was responsible for the execution of its decisions and, in general, was regarded as the head of the Federation. Next in rank, apparently, was the Secretary, whose office during the period when Lycia was a Roman province was held by men of high position and great influence.

Action was frequently taken by the federal Assembly in the bestowal of honours. The recipients were, of course, largely citizens of the member-communities, but from the beginning of the second century before Christ onward, the Federation conferred honours on distinguished strangers, such as an official of Ptolemy V of Egypt, an Athenian admiral, and Ptolemy, king of Mauretania.[38]

The patron-deity of the Federation was "Apollo of the Fathers," whose head appears on the coins issued during the second and first century before Christ by many of the member-cities.[39] In the Roman period his priest was regarded as one of the federal officials. The Lycian Federation, however, unlike those of Ionia and the Troad, appears to have had no common place of worship, unless the Temple of Leto, Apollo and Artemis near the mouth of the Xanthus was not, as seems probable, the seat of a local cult belonging to the city of Xanthus but a federal sanctuary. A quadrennial "national festival" was held, presumably with contests of various kinds, but there is no definite evidence to show that it was connected with this temple.

During the second century, presumably, after the liberation from the rule of Rhodes, the Federation, as well as individual communities, established the worship of the deified Roma.[40] As in the cities of the later province of Asia, this cult, like the offering made by the Federation to Jupiter Capitolinus soon after 167 B.C., was a symbol of the protectorate implied in the Romans' restoration of the Lycians' independence.

The first real test of the fidelity for which this protectorate called came with the invasion of western Asia Minor by Mithradates of Pontus. In contrast to the cities of the province of Asia, the Lycians seem to have held out against the invader.[41] The army which the King sent into the district during his march on Ephesus appears to have been unsuccessful, and when the combined Pontic army and fleet attacked Rhodes, a body of Lycians, whatever ill-will they might have cherished against their former oppressor now forgotten in the face of the common danger, joined the Telmessians in aiding the island-republic.[i] The successful defence of Rhodes did not, it is true, save Lycia from attack, for Mithradates next led his forces against Patara.[j] Here he destroyed the sacred grove attached to the neighbouring sanctuary of Leto, but he soon desisted from his attempt on the city itself, leaving the prosecution of the siege to one of his generals. Of this man's success or failure there is no record, but the Lycians' fidelity in the war against Mithradates was acknowledged by Sulla when, in his reorganization of western Asia Minor, he formally recognized their independence.[42]

The danger which threatened the Lycian cities from Mithradates's invasion, however, was overshadowed by the greater menace of the depredations of the pirates of Cilicia. It was said to the Lycians' credit that they had no desire to share in the "shameful profits" gained by these sea-robbers,[k] but whether they took any active part in aiding the Rhodians in attempting to suppress the evil is unknown. There is no record of an attack on any of the cities of Lycia proper, but the capture and occupation of Olympus by the pirate-chieftain Zenicetes resulted in the destruction of one of the members of the Federation.[l] But Olympus and Phaselis, which Zenicetes had also seized, were taken from him, as has already been related, by Publius Servilius Isauricus, who incorporated all this stretch of coast in the Roman province of Pamphylia-Cilicia. Nevertheless, the danger of attack was not wholly removed until piracy in the eastern Mediterranean was finally suppressed by Pompey.

Of any participation of the Lycians in the civil war waged between Pompey and Caesar nothing is known, but during the latter's Alexandrian campaign there were five Lycian ships in his fleet.[m] Somewhat less than five years afterward, the infamous Dolabella, on his way to Syria, stopped on the coast of the district, where he mobilized a large number of vessels, obtained from the cities as well as from the Rhodians for the purpose of conveying troops to his province.[n] The support thus given to a prominent adherent of Caesar's, coupled with a refusal to aid the self-styled Liberators, brought down vengeance on both Rhodes and the Lycians. It was not only a wish for vengeance, however, but also the desire for money that in this case, as in many other measures of Brutus and Cassius in Asia, prompted the act of violence. At the conference which the two leaders held in Smyrna it

[i] See note 4.
[k] Strabo XIV p. 664.
[m] *Bell. Alex.* 13, 5.
[j] Appian *Mith.* 27 (see above p. 219).
[l] See above p. 287f.
[n] Cicero *Epist. ad Fam.* XII 14, 1; 15, 2 and 5: Appian *B.C.* IV 6of. See above p. 420.

was decided that in the spring of 42, while Cassius attacked Rhodes, Brutus should lead an army into Lycia.[43]

The invading army was opposed by a force despatched by the Lycian Federation to bar the way. This opposition, however, was unavailing, for the defenders were routed and most of them captured, with the result that several places surrendered. Some men from Oenoanda actually took service in the Roman army, but it is not clear whether they were a contingent sent by their city or (more probably) an independent body of adventurers. After this initial success Brutus marched on Xanthus. The citizens, refusing to submit, destroyed the suburbs in order to prevent the Romans from obtaining either shelter or material from them and strengthened the defences of the city by surrounding it with a deep trench. They were thus able, by means of arrows and darts, to ward off attacks. By the utmost diligence on the part of his soldiers, however, Brutus soon succeeded in filling enough of the defenders' entrenchment to bring up his battering-rams. A large section of the fortifications had been thus destroyed when the Xanthians, during a sally, set fire to the besiegers' engines of war, inflicting serious damage. Meanwhile, however, the gates had been left open, and when the Xanthians fell back, a body of Roman soldiers, pressing close behind, entered with them. The peril of these men roused their comrades to immediate action, and the city was taken by storm. In the confusion which followed, Xanthus was set on fire, either by the Roman soldiers or by the inhabitants. Even then, Brutus seems to have made an effort to persuade the townspeople to surrender, but, preferring death to captivity, they threw themselves into the flames or continued fighting until they were slain. The victor captured, it was said, only 150 men and a few women.

The fate of Xanthus served to intimidate the other cities. Patara, after a show of resistance, opened its gates. Myra, when Lentulus Spinther, quaestor of the province of Asia, had captured its port Andriace and the leader of its troops, likewise surrendered. In both cities the announcement was made that under penalty of death all gold and silver, from public and private stores alike, must be handed over to the victor. Moreover, when the Federation itself, three of its members having fallen into the enemy's hands, sent envoys to ask for peace, the price was set at 150 talents. At the same time, the coast cities were ordered to place all their ships at Brutus's disposal, to be used, if necessary, in the impending campaign against Antony. In this campaign, however, there was no fighting by sea, and, consequently, the Lycian vessels suffered no damage. Moreover, the money which Brutus demanded from the Federation—evidently still unpaid—Antony remitted during his visit to Asia after his victory, at the same time urging the Lycians to unite in rebuilding Xanthus.[44]

During the period of nearly seventy-five years which intervened between the battle of Actium and the annexation of Lycia to the Roman Empire various cities conferred honours on the emperors, perhaps out of gratitude for favours actually received but in some cases, perhaps, merely as an expression of friendship for Rome. At Xanthus a "temple of Caesar" was erected and a priest created for the cult.[45] But whether the sanctuary was dedicated to the Dictator or to his successor before the latter took the name Augustus is not clear. If it was the latter who was thus honoured, it suggests that while in Asia in 30/29 B.C. he aided the Xanthians to rebuild their city. At Tlos, Augustus was honoured in extravagant terms as "Founder of the whole Universe," and at Myra the community bestowed the even more grandiloquent title of "Imperator of land and sea, Benefactor and Saviour of the whole Universe" on him as well as on Tiberius after the latter's accession to the principate.[46] Before Augustus's death both of them were honoured with statues by the little city of Apollonia, near Aperlae, and the Federation itself established the worship of Tiberius, which was in existence as late as the third century.

The good relations, of which these honours and compliments bear evidence, seemed to assure the long continuance of the friendship between the Lycians and Rome. Nevertheless, in A.D. 43, a little over 200 years after liberating Lycia from the rule of Rhodes, the Senate, evidently on instructions from the Emperor Claudius, declared the district a Roman province.[o] This high-handed action, in accord with Claudius's desire for the glory of extending the Empire which led to the annexation of Mauretania, Britain, Thrace and Judaea,[p] was justified on the specious ground that no other means could be found of preventing the Lycians from quarrelling with one another; a further pretext—often used on other occasions—was found in the charge that Roman citizens had wrongfully been put to death.

The new province was included among those assigned to the Emperor and governed by a legate of his appointment, and the annexation was celebrated by an issue of coins, both silver and bronze, for local use.[47] Smaller than any of the provinces of which Asia Minor consisted,

[o] Cassius Dio LX 17, 3: Suetonius *Claud.* 25.   [p] See below p. 547f.

529

it was considerably increased in size by the addition of Pamphylia, which, whatever connexion it may hitherto have had with one of the other provinces, was now combined with Lycia in a single administrative unit.[48] The new province seems to have been increased on the north also by the incorporation of the region around Cibyra, which had previously been a part of the province of Asia.[49] As far as Pamphylia was concerned, however, the arrangement was not permanent, for in A.D. 69 the district was detached from Lycia and combined with the large Galatian province. What disposal was then made of the Lycians is uncertain. It has been generally believed—although the evidence is of doubtful value—that they were declared free.[50] If so, however, their independence was short-lived; for the fact that we know the names of at least three men who were governors of Lycia in the course of the ten years' rule of the Emperor Vespasian shows that the district was a province during a large part of the latter's principate. At this time it was again combined for administrative purposes with the neighbouring Pamphylia.[51]

It may perhaps be supposed that Vespasian, whose rule was marked by a much-needed policy of fiscal reform, accompanied by devices for raising money by any expedient,[q] exercised a closer supervision over the finances of the Lycian cities with a view to enforcing measures of economy.[52] At Cadyanda an inscription records that he built or equipped a public bath with money which he had "saved for the city," and at Patara a bath was erected by the governor from "preserved funds" obtained from the city as well as from the Federation. In any case, a general prosperity is indicated by the construction of other buildings, such as a triumphal arch at Xanthus, honouring Vespasian as Saviour and Benefactor of the Universe, an aqueduct at Balbura, erected from funds of the city, and a bath dedicated by Aperlae and its associated towns to Titus in A.D. 80 but presumably begun under his father.

With the loss of independence resulting from the formation of Lycia as a Roman province, the activities of the Federation were necessarily restricted and, in consequence, the organization lost some of its power. Nevertheless, it continued to play an important part in local affairs and it appears to have retained a degree of self-government which exceeded that possessed by the provincial assemblies of Asia and Bithynia. In fact, under Roman rule its structure seems to have grown more complicated. This development will become apparent if it be

q See below p. 566.

530

permitted to depart from the principle of strict chronological sequence and describe the Federation in the second century after Christ, when a large number of decrees and testimonials of honour, in particular a long series of resolutions concerning a certain Opramoas, a citizen of Rhodiapolis and the holder of several federal offices, may be utilized to throw light on its form and officials as well as on the general condition of Lycia.[53] During this period there were two deliberative bodies, a "Council" and an "Elective Assembly," the latter apparently a large group of delegates, who chose the various officers of the Federation for the ensuing year, the former a smaller group evidently different in personnel from the Assembly. While it may have been customary for the Council to take preliminary action with regard to measures presented to the Assembly, with the result that these were passed conjointly, it seems also to have been possible, as, for instance, in the conferring of honours, for either body to act independently of the other.

As in the period of independence, the highest official of the Federation was the Lyciarch.[54] Another dignitary of great importance was the Chief Priest of the Augusti, who was elected annually and usually gave his name to his year of office. His chief function was obviously, as in the province of Asia, to carry on the worship of the emperors, but with this important difference that in Lycia there seems to have been no provincial temple for this cult. In many cases the Chief Priest held the additional office of Secretary of the Federation. Of lower rank were the "Chief-guardian" (*archiphylax*) and the "Under-guardian" (*hypophylax*), charged with the maintenance of peace and order, posts held by young men.[55] The former was regarded as the first step in the career of federal office. In some cases, at least, the incumbent was responsible for the payment of taxes accruing to the imperial treasury; he seems to have advanced the necessary amount and to have reimbursed himself by exacting what he could from the tax-payers, a process which resulted in his being entrusted with a certain amount of jurisdiction. Unfortunately, nothing definite is known as to the size of the region for which any one "Guardian" was held responsible; in one case only it is recorded that his sphere of duty was a group of communities near Mt. Cragus.

There is also a lack of definite information about the office of federal treasurer which existed in the period of Lycian independence. The existence of some financial officer, however, may be inferred from the fact that the Federation owned very considerable funds. Opramoas was praised for having presented it with the sum of 55,000 denarii, of which 50,000 constituted an endowment, the interest to be used for annual gifts of money to the "Electors and Councillors and federal officials and the others who customarily received them."[56] About the same time, Licinius Longus, a member of a wealthy family of Oenoanda, gave twice this amount to serve as a fund for a similar purpose. Besides these endowments, there were many outright gifts of money for similar presents to the "Councillors and Electors" as well as for the general expenses of the Federation, such as the sacrifices offered in connexion with its festival.

It is probable that, apart from the ordinary costs of the annual meetings of the delegates (presumably borne by the member-cities), the chief expenses of the Federation were those entailed by this festival and by the honours which it conferred.[57] The former, now called the "Common Festival of the Lycians," was presumably a continuation of the "national festival" celebrated by the Federation in the period of independence. In addition, there were various contests which, although held under the auspices of the Federation, were supported by endowments made by private persons and bore the names of the donors.

The honours conferred by the federal Council or Assembly consisted of golden wreaths, portraits painted on a gilded background and bronze statues.[58] A mark of especial distinction, as also in other cities of Asia Minor, was the privilege, sometimes granted for life, of wearing a purple robe and occupying a foremost place at the national festival. As a rule, the recipients of these honours were federal officials, who received them at the expiration of a term of office, but they included also other persons who had deserved well of the Federation. In several cases they were renewed at intervals, although presumably without a repetition of the bestowal of wreaths and statues. The highest number of such renewals on record was that of Opramoas's father, who received them for the sixth time, but in the case of Opramoas himself the extraordinary distinction was granted of a yearly renewal, apparently for the remainder of his life.

The number of cities which were members of the Federation during this period greatly exceeded the twenty-three of which it was composed at the beginning of the first century before Christ and was somewhat larger than the thirty-six "towns" known to Pliny.[r] In the record of the gifts presented by Opramoas to the communities of Lycia

---

[r] See above pp. 519 and 522.

there are thirty names, all of them presumably member-cities, and ten others also are known, which during the period of Roman rule had the organization of an Hellenic *polis*.[59] Of these cities, forty in all, as many as twenty in the third century issued their own coins. Of the six which, at the beginning of the first century before Christ, were regarded as the principal Lycian communities, four—Myra, Patara, Tlos and Xanthus—still retained their position of prominence, with the official rank of "Metropolis of the Lycian Nation," a title now held also by Telmessus.[60] Pinara, on the other hand, perhaps because of its remote situation, appears to have declined in importance, and Olympus, though rebuilt after its destruction in the time of Servilius Isauricus, seems never to have attained to its former greatness.

As the provincial assembly authorized by the Roman imperial government to conduct the affairs of Lycia, the Federation was still powerful enough in A.D. 57 to institute proceedings against Titus Clodius Eprius Marcellus, a former governor of the province.[8] During his term of office he had granted some favour to the city of Tlos, which appears to have erected a statue in his honour, but nevertheless the charge against him was extortion. The Lycians were unsuccessful in the prosecution, but Marcellus's acquittal, it was said, was due rather to the influence he wielded than to his innocence. So great, in fact, was this influence that some of his accusers were actually punished by exile on the ground that they had caused danger to an innocent man, but whether these accusers were Lycians or prosecutors from Rome is not recorded.

In the second century, on the other hand, the activities of the Federation were closely controlled by Rome. How much supervision was exercised over its expenditures is not known, but in a matter of much less importance—the bestowal of honours—its action had to be ratified by the imperial governor.[61] That this ratification was not a mere formality is shown by the case of Opramoas; for the special honours voted to him by the federal Assembly during his term as Lyciarch were disallowed by the governor, and it was not until after appeals had been made to the Emperor both by envoys of the Federation and by representatives of the city of Xanthus that an imperial order overrode the governor's ruling and bade his successor confirm the Assembly's action. There was a certain advantage, on the other hand, in such supervision, as in the case of the Lyciarch Jason only a few years after the vindication of Opramoas. When, at the expiration of

---

[8] Tacitus *Ann.* XIII 33, 4: *T.A.M.* II 562 = *I.G.R.* III 553.

Jason's term, the Assembly voted him the usual honours, an enemy wrote to the governor, presenting a charge against Jason and asking for a rejection of the proposal. The governor referred the matter to the authorities in Rome, and the Lycians, on their part, sent an envoy to present the case to the Emperor. After an examination of the evidence, the decision was reached that the charge was false, and a letter was written to the Federation in the Emperor's name absolving Jason and endorsing the bestowal of the honours.

This governmental control of the measures taken by the once powerful federal Assembly shows the extent to which the process of Romanization progressed during the century after Lycia became a province. Another mark of the same process was the spread of the worship of the emperor. In addition to the federal cult of the "Augusti," both the dead and the living, and the worship of Tiberius and a festival in honour of his mother, Livia, also established by the Federation, individual cities likewise founded cults of the emperors.[62] After the annexation of Lycia as a province a priest of Claudius was created at Aperlae and a temple built for the "Saviour-gods, the Augusti," at Sidyma. So widely was the divinity of the emperors recognized that by the end of the second century at least thirteen communities in Lycia had priests for the worship of the "Augusti," a term in which were included all holders of the imperial power. This priesthood, which, like the civil offices, was held for a limited term, was one of the most highly honoured posts which a city could bestow.

This process of Romanization appears also in the introduction of spectacles of the kind popular in Italy. It is true that the traditional Greek practice of holding athletic contests was maintained at the federal festival and that in individual cities similar contests, such as the pancratium and, more specifically, wrestling-bouts, were held at regular intervals and often bore the names of the founders.[63] But after Lycia was made a Roman province, it became customary for wealthy men to present gladiatorial combats as well as wild-beast fights and hunts for the entertainment of their fellow-citizens. Spectacles of this kind were given at Oenoanda for two days by Licinius Longus on the occasion of his election as Lyciarch, at Myra and Patara by Opramoas at the time when he held this office, and at Telmessus and the Temple of Leto near Xanthus, respectively, by a federal and a local priest of the Augusti.[64] The presence of gladiators at Telmessus and Xanthus, moreover, is shown by monuments erected after their death.

There are other indications also of increasingly close contact with

Rome during the first and second centuries of Lycia's existence as a province. Not only did the federal Assembly, as has already been noted, send envoys to the emperor, but the several cities also, when occasion arose, despatched their representatives to Rome.[65] The fact of having acted in this capacity is regularly listed among the achievements of an honoured citizen, especially if it might be added that he performed this mission at his own expense as a "gift" to the community.

The same tendency is shown in the names borne by prominent Lycians. The large number of those called Claudius bears out the statement of an ancient historian that the Emperor made extensive grants of Roman citizenship with the understanding that the recipients would take his name.[t] But the names of early governors also are found, such as that of Quintus Veranius, borne by men of prominence at Sidyma and Xanthus as well as at Cibyra, and of Gaius Licinius, evidently from Gaius Licinius Mucianus, governor under Nero, borne not only by a family of great importance at Oenoanda, whose genealogy is known through seven generations, but also by several other Lycian notables.[66] It was natural that these newly-made citizens and their descendants should place the designation "Roman" at the head of the list of the various city-rights which they enjoyed and that they should regularly specify in the official forms of their names the Roman city-tribes of which they severally became members.[67] Roman names, however, were borne also by Lycians who neither called themselves "Roman" nor added the name of a Roman tribe, and it can only be supposed that many assumed these names who did not receive citizenship.

In the course of time, these Romanized families, whose members were federal Chief Priests and Lyciarchs, became a group of special distinction, and, as was the case with the delegates to the provincial assembly in the province of Asia,[u] they developed into a kind of provincial nobility. As men of importance and social position in their several cities, and, above all, wealthy enough to bear the financial burdens entailed, they filled the municipal offices and sat in their local councils, forming a definite class, higher in rank than the "commoners."[68] Many of this class who had received Roman citizenship were gradually admitted to public office in Rome, becoming members of the Senate and even Consuls. Of the rise of such a family there is an excellent example in the descendants of Gaius Licinius Musaeus of Oenoanda, who, probably in the time of Nero, was Chief Priest of the Augusti and Lyciarch.[69] His grandson, Gaius Licinius Longus,

[t] Cassius Dio LX 17, 5f.   [u] See Chap. XVIII note 64.

married the daughter of Marcius Titianus, who was military tribune in the Roman army and chief centurion in a legion and, after the expiration of his military career, a Lyciarch, while Longus's sister, by marrying into a similar family, became the wife of Julius Antoninus, a military prefect and tribune of the Fourth Legion, the son of an imperial procurator who was also federal Chief Priest of the Augusti and a Lyciarch. Their daughter, in turn, by a marriage with Claudius Dryantianus, a Lyciarch, was the mother of Tiberius Claudius Agrippinus, who was Consul at Rome; through the marriages of her daughter and her son's daughter to men of senatorial rank, she became the grandmother and great-grandmother of senators and consulars, one of the latter being governor of the province of Lycia-Pamphylia.

A similar advancement appears in the case of the family of Claudius Telemachus, federal Chief Priest in the early second century, whose descendants, natives of Xanthus, became senators and consulars, one of them even receiving the coveted post of proconsul of Africa.[70] Such, in fact, was the prestige attached to these offices that kinship with those who held them became a source of great pride, and the laudatory inscriptions of members of their families include such honours as "father of a senator" or "a consular," "mother and grandmother" or "grandfather and great-grandfather of senators," "cousin and uncle of senators and consulars." Even Opramoas, whose family, by reason of benefactions and high offices, had many claims to distinction, included among the marks of honour enjoyed by his father and his wife those of great-great-grandfather and great-grandmother of senators, while he himself in formal decrees composed in his honour by the Lycian Federation was called uncle of a senator's wife.

It is hardly a coincidence that the families which thus attained to a position of social and official prominence also included men of great wealth. Mention has already been made of the generosity of both Licinius Longus and Opramoas to the Lycian Federation and of their presentation of gladiatorial spectacles, as well as of other gifts to the Federation and the endowments and presents which were made by public-spirited citizens for similar spectacles and athletic contests in their cities.[v] This, however, is only a partial statement of the liberality of these men. Opramoas in the years 140-143 presented various sums of money to twenty-eight different cities to repair the havoc wrought by an earthquake which had devastated Lycia.[71] The aggregate amount of these gifts was not much less than 500,000 denarii, to which must be

---

[v] See above pp. 531f. and 534.

added the cost of building two temples at Rhodiapolis, a distribution
of grain at Corydalla, and an earlier gift of 20,000 denarii for the oracle
of Apollo at Patara. His benefactions, moreover, continued even after
his death; for he bequeathed a farm to the city of Tlos, yielding an
annual income of 1,250 denarii, which was to be used for a festival
held every four years and a distribution of one denarius to each citizen
on the list of those receiving doles of grain. With regard to Longus
there is less information, but his gifts are known to have included
10,000 denarii to Myra and 50,000 to Tlos and a bequest to his native
city of Oenoanda of an endowment for a yearly present of four
measures of grain and two denarii to each member of "the Five
Hundred" (apparently the members of the local ruling body), besides
a sum for the use of certain boys and girls. His generosity found a
parallel in the action of his brother, who presented ten denarii to each
resident of his native city and on two separate occasions distributed
doles of grain.

These are the more conspicuous examples of liberality in Lycia in
the second century, but other gifts abounded, though they were perhaps
less munificent.[72] Some of these were public buildings, such as a bath
at Xanthus, two porticos at Telmessus, exedras and the stage and
proscenium of the theatre at Patara, the conversion of a gymnasium
into a public guest-house at a cost of 30,000 denarii at Arneae, two
gifts of 10,000 denarii for building a portico and a theatre at Myra and
a gateway at Balbura. Others were endowments, such as the sum of
56,058 "light drachmae" to be used for the expenses of the gymnasium
at Telmessus, a gift of 60,000 denarii to the city of Cadyanda, and a
bequest, the income of which was to be used for doles of oil, to the
people of Lydae. Amounts were also given from which largesses or
banquets or doles of oil were to be presented to the citizens at Termessus
Minor, Balbura, Xanthus, Telmessus and Phaselis, and especially at
Sidyma, where, in addition to endowments for public buildings and
annual largesses, money and banquets were given to the populace, oil
was furnished for the gymnasium and the bath, and estates were
bequeathed to the "sacred college of the Thirty" and to the city itself.

The discrepancy between an economic condition which led to gifts
of doles and largesses and the possession of the wealth which made
possible these doles as well as benefactions of greater value need cause
no more surprise when found in Lycia than when it appears in other
parts of the ancient or the modern world. What does, however, seem
surprising is the apparent existence of large fortunes in a land pos-

sessed of but few natural resources, in which there seems to have been little opportunity for accumulating wealth. Moreover, since trade by sea appears to have been a principal means of building up such fortunes, it might be supposed that what wealth there was in Lycia would be found in those cities which either lay directly on the coast or had ports within easy access, and particularly in those which had the rank of metropolis. This, however, appears not to have been the case. Rhodiapolis and Oenoanda, the homes, respectively, of Opramoas and Licinius Longus were places of only moderate size. The latter, perhaps, was prosperous because of its situation on the route which connected Lycia with the north, but the former possessed neither extensive territory nor harbour nor direct connexion with the interior. Sidyma, high up on the side of Mt. Cragus, was likewise inaccessible, yet here also there was a generous use of wealth. In some of the larger cities, on the other hand, as Tlos, Patara and Myra, the paucity of public gifts on the part of the citizens, even if allowance be made for a greater destruction of inscriptional records, seems difficult to explain.

Some credit, at least, for this prosperity—sometimes, perhaps, as will presently be suggested,[w] more apparent than real—must be given to Rome and the *Pax Romana*. Although in the palmy days of the Lycian Federation there was frequent co-operation among the cities, and the allegation of discord in the early first century after Christ may well have been exaggerated—or even invented—in order to justify Rome's annexation of the district, nevertheless there can be little doubt that in the days of independence there existed in the cities a certain separatism. The gradual disappearance of this separatism in favor of a spirit of solidarity is particularly evident in the inscriptions recording the bestowal of titles and honours. In cases too many to enumerate, the recipient was not only designated by the name of his native community, as well as by those of others which had conferred citizenship on him, but was also described as "having received citizenship in all cities throughout Lycia." It was characteristic of this spirit, too, that the Xanthians erected a monument to the city of Tlos as a "kindred" people "in token of perpetual harmony."[x] Furthermore, it will be remembered, Licinius Longus, in addition to his gifts to his native city, presented money to Myra and Tlos as well, and Opramoas did not confine his benefactions to Rhodiapolis and his mother's birthplace, Corydalla, but extended his generosity to twenty-eight other communities.

w See below p. 591.   x *T.A.M.* II 555.

It is true that with the disappearance of separatism and a greater feeling of solidarity among the Lycians there was increased subjection to Rome.[73] While the form of the Federation continued as late, even, as the beginning of the fourth century, so wholly submissive was it that, in obedience to an imperial edict which ordered the communities to take such action, the "Nation of the Lycians and Pamphylians" addressed a petition to the Emperors requesting that they would at length suppress the Christians, "rebellious of old and now still afflicted with the same disease."

CHAPTER XXIII

THE CLAUDIAN EMPERORS:
BUREAUCRACY AND WAR

IN the confusion which prevailed after the assassination of Gaius, his elderly uncle, Claudius, was declared emperor by the soldiers of the Praetorian Guard, who thereupon, if we may believe the ancient writers, forced the Senate to accept their choice.[1] Awkward and uncouth both in manner and in speech, perhaps as the result of an illness in his childhood, Claudius had been kept in the background under Augustus and Tiberius. Not until Gaius, upon his succession to the imperial power, made him Consul, had he held any public office. His enforced leisure had been devoted to study, particularly history, with the result that he developed learned, if somewhat pedantic, interests, to which may be traced his later capacity for giving meticulous attention to the most minute details concerned with the administration of the Empire.

Beginning his rule with great moderation, Claudius pardoned all who had opposed his election, punishing only the assassins of Gaius.[a] Toward the Senate he showed a deference which recalled the attitude of Augustus. By declining to accept unusual honours and in general repudiating the excesses of Gaius, he gave every appearance of intending to restore the principate as conceived by its founder. This appearance, however, proved to be illusory. Those whom Claudius chose as his principal advisers were without regard either for Roman tradition or for the prerogatives of the Senate; for on the principle, sometimes observed by Augustus in the management of the imperial property,[b] that a Roman used his freedmen as stewards for the administration of his affairs, Claudius employed as his agents in governing the Empire a group of his former slaves. These men, of Hellenic birth, became the heads of the chief departments of the state, forming a sort of cabinet.[2] Of more ability, evidently, than the Roman nobles, they exercised a far greater influence on the Emperor and in consequence were hated and feared by the Senators. As capable ministers of state, they seem to have been largely responsible for the efficiency of Claudius's administration; but the possession of great power by the Emperor's personal agents and the development of the bureaux committed to their charge inevitably led to a form of government under which the Princeps became an absolute ruler.

[a] Suetonius *Claud*. 11f. [b] See above p. 489f.

In the provinces the extension of this bureaucracy was apparent chiefly in the increased importance of the procurators, both those who managed the emperor's private property and those who supervised the collection of the revenues accruing to the imperial treasury, the *fiscus*, now definitely organized and placed in the charge of one of the members of Claudius's cabinet.[3] With this increase in importance came greater power when, in the year 53, a decree of the Senate, enacted at the Emperor's request, conferred on these agents full civil jurisdiction in fiscal cases, a grant of magisterial functions altogether alien to the conception of the office as instituted by Augustus. Consequently, not only were those who collected the income from the imperial provinces empowered to enforce payment, but in the senatorial provinces also the emperor's agent became a judicial officer, able to render decisions in claims made for the benefit of the imperial property. The bestowal of such a function was not merely an infringement on the powers of the senatorial proconsul but it might easily result in serious abuse, involving bribery and corruption.

In one case this charge was actually preferred when Junius Cilo, the procurator of the imperial property in Bithynia, was accused by the province of having accepted bribes.[4] Cilo was acquitted, but only, so it was said, because the Emperor's deafness prevented him from hearing the testimony of the Bithynian witnesses, and his office was extended for two years longer. On the other hand, two of Claudius's procurators in the province of Asia, of whom one held office before the grant of civil jurisdiction, the other after it was conferred, were presumably men of good character, honoured for the gifts which they made, respectively, to the cities of Miletus and Ephesus.[5]

In general, efforts were made to promote the welfare of the provinces. Among these was some plan intended to relieve the communities of the duty of supplying vehicles for the imperial post, which, as has already been observed, had become a great burden.[c] This attempt, however, was unsuccessful, as the result, so Claudius expressed it in an edict, of "the iniquity of men."[d] Another, more effective, measure, designed to keep senatorial governors from lingering in Rome and so failing to discharge their duties, was an order from the Emperor commanding them to leave the Capital by the middle of April of their year of office.[e] An attempt was made also to prevent extortion on the part of governors by the adoption of the principle that none, at the

---

[c] See above p. 487.
[e] Cassius Dio LX 11, 6; 17, 3.
[d] *C.I.L.* III 7251 = Dessau 214.

expiration of his term, might be appointed immediately to another post, thus affording an interval during which he might be prosecuted.[f] In one case, at least, an offender of this kind was punished; for Gaius Cadius Rufus, proconsul of Bithynia, who was accused by the provincials of extortion, was convicted and expelled from the Senate.[6]

Minor officials also were punished for misdeeds. At Cibyra, when a petition was presented to the Emperor by a special envoy from the city, asking for the removal of a treasury-agent who had ordered the citizens to pay an exorbitant sum of money annually in lieu of an assessment of grain, the request was granted.[7] An arrangement, furthermore, was adopted whereby in the future the grain should be assessed openly in the market-place on the basis of a definite amount for each taxable land-unit in the city's territory.

With regard to the cities in the provinces, Claudius appears to have maintained, in general, the liberal policy of his predecessors. A letter of the Emperor addressed to the magistrates of Mitylene, praising the loyalty of the citizens to the imperial house, indicates that the autonomy of the city, however limited it was, received official recognition.[8] The grant of exemption from taxation which Ilium had obtained from Caesar was confirmed by the Senate in A.D. 53, after the Emperor's young stepson, Nero, had delivered an oration advocating the measure. The Council and People expressed their gratitude by erecting statues of the young man as "kinsman of the city" as well as of the children of Claudius in a portico dedicated to the Emperor and his wife, the younger Agrippina, daughter of Germanicus, whom he married in A.D. 49 and in the following year honoured with the name Augusta.

In the year in which the exemption of Ilium was confirmed, the same privilege was granted to Cos as a "sacred island, the servant of the God," namely Asclepius.[9] This action, taken by the Senate, was a response to a direct request from the Emperor; for Claudius used this means of doing honour to his personal physician, Gaius Stertinius Xenophon, a native of the island. In return, the Coans included Claudius in a cult already created for Tiberius with a priest for the two Emperors and established a festival in his honour, besides giving him the name of Zeus the Saviour and Agrippina that of Demeter the Harvest-bringer.

Measures were also adopted for the relief of cities which had been affected by some disaster. Thus, in the year 53, after Apameia had been

[f] Cassius Dio LX 25, 4f.

damaged by one of the earthquakes which frequently devastated the valley of the Maeander, the action of Tiberius on a similar occasion was repeated and all taxes payable to Rome during the next five years were remitted.[10] At Samos, where also an earthquake had wrought havoc, Claudius restored a temple of Dionysus and received honours from the community as a "New Founder." Smyrna and Ephesus, too, are said to have suffered and to have been helped by the Emperor. It was perhaps also in gratitude for some assistance received in connexion with an earthquake that the city-council at Tralles assumed the name Claudia, which it still bore in the late second century.

Other cities also, even though they had suffered no damage, received various benefits.[11] At Sardis Claudius bore the expense of completing an aqueduct and was honoured by the community with a statue. At Cibyra the governor, at the Emperor's command, constructed some "Augustan works"; in return, the title of "Founder of the City" was given to Claudius and a monument was erected to his son. Elsewhere, as at Cyzicus, where an arch was built in honour of Claudius, together with Augustus and Tiberius, the dedication of various public works to the Emperor suggests some act of generosity on his part, and the bestowal in many places of the titles "Saviour" and "Benefactor," as well as monuments erected both by communities and by individuals, may have been more than merely conventional honours.

Among the favours granted to the provincials by Claudius was his recognition of the privileges long enjoyed by the "world-wide" society of the Artists of Dionysus, the ancient organization whose favoured status had been confirmed by Antony.[g] In A.D. 43 these stage-artists presented a petition to the Emperor, in which, after reminding him that Augustus, with concurrent action by the Senate, had guaranteed their rights, they asked for an assurance that these would be respected.[12] Not only was this request granted, but five years later, on the presentation of a second plea, commended, apparently, by one of his officials, Claudius promised that, since the Artists were so "piously disposed toward his house," he would make an effort to increase the favours they had already received. A similar guarantee of privileges had already been given to the "sacred guild" of the "hymnodists of all Asia," which had been formed to sing the praises of Augustus on his birthday, and in gratitude the choristers dedicated a monument for the Emperor's welfare.

Another "world-wide" society, the "Itinerant Athletic Association"

[g] See above p. 428f.

under the special patronage of Heracles, an organization whose privileges had been extended by Augustus, also sought the Emperor's favour. Sending envoys to congratulate him on the conquest of Britain, this society presented Claudius with a golden wreath, which was accepted as a token of its devotion. In a second letter, a year later, the Emperor wrote of his pleasure at the Society's expression of gratitude to the Kings of Commagene and Pontus, at whose festivals, held in his honour, the athletes had competed and had "received every attention and kindness."

In recognition of his position—and perhaps of the benefits he had conferred—several of the cities of Asia, following the precedent established under Augustus and Tiberius, instituted the worship of Claudius. The Emperor, to be sure, at the outset of his rule had issued an edict requesting the people of Alexandria in Egypt to refrain from creating a priest or constructing a temple for him.[13] Nevertheless, the Prefect, in his introductory proclamation, referred to the Emperor as "our God," and the provinces generally failed to observe this request. The cult of Claudius at Cos has already been mentioned. He had also a priest at Magnesia-on-Maeander, at Mylasa and at Aphrodisias, while at Aezani he was worshipped together with Zeus, at Acmonia he received the title of the New Zeus, and festivals named after him were founded at Magnesia, Laodiceia and Aezani. At Prusa in Bithynia a citizen, on bequeathing his house to Claudius, imposed the condition that a shrine of the Emperor should be built in the courtyard.

In addition to the worship of the Emperor himself, a new form of the imperial cult arose in the eastern provinces. From the time of Claudius probably—certainly from that of his successor, Nero—onward there was in many of the cities of Asia and Greece a priest, usually a "Chief Priest," of the Augusti in general.[14] He was charged with the collective worship of all the deified Emperors together with the actual holder of the imperial power, an arrangement by which the provincial communities showed their loyalty to their rulers both past and present.

Together with the bestowal of benefits, steps were taken to put an end to abuses. The privilege of an appeal to the emperor, of which a citizen of Cnidus had availed himself under Augustus,[h] appears to have been seriously misused. Cases with which the local courts should have dealt were referred to Rome for decision, and the dignity of these courts was thereby impaired. An attempt to remedy this evil was made by Gnaeus Domitius Corbulo, proconsul of Asia.[15] In re-

[h] See above p. 480.

sponse to a decree of the Council and People of Cos, protesting against
an appeal which a citizen of the place had made to Claudius, Corbulo ruled that the appellant's action had been taken "for the purpose of calumny" and hence on illegal grounds. In order to check
the abuse, he issued an order that every appeal to the emperor must
first be examined by the proconsul and receive his approval; a second
clause contained the provision that in the event of an appeal made to
the proconsul the appellant must first deposit a sum of money as a
pledge of his *bona fides*, a measure intended to protect the governor
against trivial or malicious proceedings.

A more conspicuous attempt to remedy an evil was made early in
Claudius's principate by Paullus Fabius Persicus, the proconsul of
Asia, in an edict intended to put an end to inefficiency and even corruption at Ephesus, in consequence of which the revenues of the
Temple of Artemis had been greatly diminished.[16] It was a common
practice, according to the Proconsul, for the city-officials to sell priesthoods—a long-established custom in Asia Minor[17]—at what was practically a public auction on terms by which the buyer obtained not only
the perquisites of the office but also the right to draw large sums from
the temple-revenues. While this arrangement increased the purchase-
price and, consequently, the amount of money received by the city,
the Goddess had thereby suffered serious loss. Her income had been
further impaired by the practice of hiring free labour for services
which might have been performed by the public slaves at the disposal
of the Temple, by the illicit support obtained for the substitutes employed by these slaves and by the excessive hospitality furnished to the
victors in the contests held at the sacred festival. Both the priests and
the city-officials, moreover, were in the habit of borrowing money to
be charged against the revenues of the following year, with the result
that the annual budget was left unbalanced.

The Proconsul was naturally more concerned with the condition
of the Temple's finances than with the fact that priesthoods had been
bought by men unworthy of the post. Nevertheless, his decree implied
a rebuke to those who were responsible for this evil. While on account
of the condition of the inscription it is not wholly clear what action
was taken against those who had obtained priesthoods on these terms,
it seems evident that they were discharged from office; for the city
was ordered to reimburse them to the extent of 1 per cent of the price
which they had paid—a larger amount being considered too great a
burden for the municipal finances. The priests and city-councillors,

furthermore, were prohibited in the future from giving and receiving money in connexion with these sales. The abuses which had led to the waste of the temple-income were forbidden and the amount of money which might be expended on the quadrennial festival of the Goddess was strictly limited. As another measure of economy, the city was ordered to use volunteers as choristers instead of those who received pay for their services.[18] The edict also declared that a loan negotiated by a public official must be repaid out of the revenues of the current year, the official otherwise to be personally responsible for repayment to the lender. Funds, moreover, which were bequeathed for endowments must be duly invested and the income might not be diverted to any other purpose than that specified by the testator.

In issuing this edict, Persicus declared in high-sounding words that he was under obligation "to make provision for the welfare, not only for his year of office but for all time also, both of the province as a whole and of the several cities." At the same time he admitted that he was impelled by the example of the Emperor, "who, having received the whole human race under his own protection, has granted among his foremost benefits, dearest to all men, this boon, namely, that each should enjoy his own." It seems probable, therefore, that the order emanated from Claudius himself. In this instance, as in the action taken by Augustus in limiting the inviolable area of the Temple, the Emperor's intervention in the administration of a senatorial province was based on his "greater" *imperium* extending over the whole Empire.[19]

Attempts were made also to develop urban centres in regions where Rome's influence appeared to need strengthening by this civilizing process or where a stimulus to the trade passing along the chief highways was considered advisable.[20] In eastern Bithynia the ancient town of Bithynium on the great route leading through Paphlagonia to Pontus was renamed Claudiopolis. The organization as a *polis*, with a "Council and People," which the place possessed in the second century after Christ, may perhaps date from this time. Communication with the coast of the Euxine was rendered easier by improving the road to Amastris, cut through rock by Gaius Julius Aquila, a prefect of engineers, who dedicated the work to Claudius. Much farther east, on the other side of the Halys, in the region of Phazimonitis, which had been annexed to the Galatian province in 6/5 B.C., the old settlement of Andrapa on the road running through Pontus to Armenia, at or near which Pompey had placed his city Neapolis, was refounded as Neoclaudiopolis.

In the new province of Cappadocia Claudius, adopting the policy of Romanization used by Augustus in Pisidia, gave the town of Archelais the status of a colony.[21] A place named Claudiopolis in the southeastern corner of the province, apparently near the Euphrates, was presumably founded about this time. In the district of Lycaonia, now part of the Galatian province, the Seleucid community of Laodiceia and the ancient city of Iconium, both on the main road to the East, obtained some advantage, perhaps the authorization of a civic administration, which impelled them to add the Emperor's name to their own as Claudiolaodiceia and Claudiconium. A similar change took place at Seleuceia in northern Pisidia, perhaps on the branch of Augustus's road which led to the southern part of the district, which now called itself Claudioseleuceia. A statue of Claudius as a "god made manifest" was also erected in the city.

In the neighbouring district of Pamphylia communications were improved in A.D. 50 by a general repair of the roads.[22] This work, undoubtedly a boon to the inhabitants of the province, was done in the name of the Emperor by the procurator charged with the supervision of the finances. In the following year the great highway which led from Smyrna to Ephesus and thence up the Maeander to Tralles was also repaired in the name of Claudius. While it is not surprising that the construction of roads in the imperial province of Pamphylia was carried out by the Emperor through the agency of his procurator, the fact that he assumed the responsibility for those in a senatorial province—an example followed by many of his successors—indicates that the imperial government now accepted the general care of the roads as of importance to the whole Empire rather than to any single province.

In comparison with the conservatism of Tiberius, the foreign policy of Claudius's administration was, in general, marked by aggression and expansion.[23] In the West, his conquest and annexation of southern Britain and Mauretania were definite departures from the principle that the boundaries of the Empire should not be extended. In the Balkan Peninsula, the client-kingdom of Thrace, long disturbed by quarrels among the members of the royal family, was abolished and the country made a Roman province. In the East, Agrippa was, to be sure, rewarded for his services to Claudius by a considerable addition to his kingdom, but on his death in A.D. 44 his young son was permitted to retain only a small portion of his father's dominions and the greater part was incorporated into the Empire as the province of Judaea.

In Asia Minor, the Lycian Federation, as has already been narrated, was forcibly annexed in A.D. 43 on grounds which can be regarded only as a pretext for adding this, the one remaining free part of the mainland, to the Empire.[i] In the following year a similar charge, namely, that Roman citizens had been put to death, apparently in some local disturbance, was brought against the Rhodians.[24] In their case also the punishment was the loss of independence, and the proud republic, once one of the great powers of the East and the mistress of the seas, which for over two hundred years had had treaty-relations with Rome, was reduced to the position of a subject and, together with the possessions she still retained on the mainland, incorporated in the province of Asia.

The subjection of the Rhodians, it is true, was not of long duration. Nine years after the loss of their freedom a delegation sent to Rome by the citizens was received by the Senate. Their plea for the restoration of their freedom, supported by a speech in Greek by the youthful Nero, was granted, and the envoys returned, bearing the "prayed-for response." The Rhodians' "ancestral constitution and laws" were restored and they recovered their mainland possessions south of the Gulf of Cos. Less than two years later, after Nero had become emperor, a letter written in the name of the Consuls contained some statement which caused them to fear for their newly-obtained freedom; but after an embassy had been sent to Rome, the "Magistrates, Council and People" were assured that the letter had been "mistakenly conveyed" to them and that the Emperor's good will was undiminished.

In contrast to the policy adopted with regard to the Lycians and the Rhodians, no steps were taken to annex the client-kingdoms in eastern and southern Asia Minor. Polemo II, whom Gaius had made king of Pontus, retained his throne and his Asianic dominions. He did, however, lose the territory in southern Russia which had been given to his grandfather under Augustus and was assigned to him by Gaius.[j] It is probable that the natives of the region, angry at the loss of their own king, Mithradates, resented the domination of a foreigner. In any case, one of the first acts of Claudius was to remove Polemo from Russia and restore the native ruler.[25]

In Cilicia Aspera, a small kingdom, apparently in the eastern part

[i] See above p. 529.　　　　　　　　[j] See Chap. XXI note 53.

of the district, was ruled by another Polemo, presumably related to the royal house of Pontus; but, since he bore the name Marcus Antonius Polemo, he is evidently to be distinguished from Julius Polemo, the Pontian king.[26] He seems to have begun his career as Chief Priest of Olba and dynast of the neighbouring regions and only later to have received the title of King. If, as seems probable, he founded the city of Claudiopolis, deep down in the valley of a tributary of the Calycadnus, he was evidently an enlightened man, desirous of extending the influence of Hellenism in this primitive mountain-region.[27] He also formed the tribes over which he ruled into a "commonalty," an organization which presumably gave them a limited autonomy.

The other client-ruler in Cilicia, Antiochus IV, who had been deprived of his dominions in Commagene by Gaius, was restored to the throne of his ancestors.[28] For the next thirty-five years he continued to rule over his two kingdoms, separated by the district of Cilicia Campestris. His Cilician possessions included the coast from the island of Elaeussa—once the residence of Archelaus—to the border of Pamphylia. In the interior, where the respective positions of his kingdom and Polemo's cannot be definitely determined, he seems to have ruled in the central and western parts of the district; his dominions probably extended also across the Taurus into Lycaonia.

Like Polemo, Antiochus adopted the policy of extending the influence of Hellenism by founding cities—or perhaps by giving new names with civic institutions to places already in existence. In Commagene, the city of Germaniceia, a name evidently derived from the honorary surname borne by both Gaius and Claudius, was presumably a foundation of Antiochus.[29] Situated in the extreme west of the kingdom, near the borders of Cappadocia and Syria, on the southern slope of the mountains descending to a well-watered plain, the city had an easy communication on the southwest with the road over Mt. Amanus to Anazarbus in Cilicia. Toward the east and southeast routes led, respectively, to Samosata, the old capital of Commagene, and to Zeugma at the crossing of the Euphrates.

On the coast of Cilicia, although there were many cities already in existence, Antiochus, wishing to bring the western part of his dominions more completely under his control and, perhaps, to follow the example set by many Hellenistic monarchs, founded two new cities, named, respectively, after himself and his wife. These were Antiocheia, with the distinguishing epithet "upon Cragus" taken from the precipitous rock on which the city stood, and, somewhat farther northwest, Iotape, situated on a projecting peninsula.[30] Each city, evidently organized on the model of a Greek *polis*, had, by the middle of the second century, the usual Council and various public officials.

Antiochus's rule, however, was not altogether peaceful. Ten years after his reinstatement by Claudius, the turbulent Cietae, who had resisted the attempts of Archelaus II to reduce them to subjection, invaded his dominions in force.[k] Occupying the mountain-slopes above the seaboard, they swept down to the coast, attacking both farmers and townspeople as well as the seafarers who had put into port. Growing more daring, they actually laid siege to the city of Anemurium. A troop of horsemen was sent by the governor of Syria to repel the invasion, but while it was possible by this means to relieve Anemurium, the horsemen could not follow up this success by pursuing their opponents into the mountain-fastnesses over roads scarcely practicable even for infantry. It was, in fact, only by the diplomacy of Antiochus himself that the enemy was finally defeated. "By offering inducements to the rank and file," it is related, "and by using trickery against their leader, he broke up the barbarians' forces." Capturing those who were responsible for the invasion, he put them to death; the tribesmen, accepting an offer of pardon, submitted to his rule.

This region Antiochus sought to bring under his control by founding the city of Philadelpheia, evidently named in honour of his wife, Iotape Philadelphus.[31] The process of Hellenization was furthered by the foundation of two other cities, Eirenopolis, the "City of Peace," intended, perhaps, to signify the pacification of some mountain-region, and Germanicopolis, named, like the city in Commagene, after one of the King's imperial patrons. The growth of these cities, which in course of time became prosperous enough to issue their own coins, indicates that Antiochus was successful in creating urban centres among the "barbarian" Cilicians and seems to justify his appointment as ruler of this hitherto undeveloped district.

On the eastern frontier, the policy of the government, unlike its course of action in the West, was conservative and in keeping with the precedent established by Augustus and continued by Tiberius.[32] On the advice, doubtless, of the astute Lucius Vitellius, who had governed Syria during the last years of Tiberius and was Claudius's chief counsellor in eastern affairs, peace was maintained with the Parthians. At the same time, an army stationed on the Roman side

---

[k] Tacitus *Ann.* XII 55; see above p. 509.

of the Euphrates was kept in readiness for an invasion of Mesopotamia, should a threat become necessary, and strife between rival princes was fomented even to the extent of again sending a Romanized Parthian to claim the royal power.

In Armenia, the policy of Augustus called for the rule of a Roman client, whatever efforts might be made by the Parthians to control that much-disputed country.[33] Mithradates the Iberian, accordingly, whom Gaius had deposed, was sent back to his former kingdom with a detachment of Roman soldiers to protect him. His reinstatement, to be sure, was not accomplished without opposition. An army led by a certain Demonax, apparently a native Armenian, made ready to resist, and Cotys, whom Gaius had made king of Armenia Minor,[1] was persuaded to set himself up as a claimant for the rule. Demonax's army, however, was soon defeated in battle, and Cotys, on the receipt of orders from Rome, abandoned his pretensions. All resistance was stamped out by the Roman soldiers acting in co-operation with troops sent by Mithradates's brother, Pharasmanes, and the new monarch, although soon hated for his cruelty, was maintained in power by a Roman garrison stationed in the country.[34]

The rule of Mithradates, however, was destined soon to end in treachery and murder. Pharasmanes's son, Radamistus, who, pretending that he had quarrelled with his father, appeared in Armenia and was cordially received by the King, used his position at court to stir up discontent among the nobles.[35] When the preparations for a revolution were thus effected, Pharasmanes sent an army to invade Armenia, and Mithradates was forced to take refuge in the stronghold held by the Roman garrison. An attempt to capture this place having failed, Radamistus, resorting to negotiations, found the commandant, Caelius Pollio, ready to listen to his proposals. Under the pretext that, should peace not be made, the soldiers would surrender, Pollio compelled the King to leave the stronghold. A pledge made by Radamistus that he would use neither the sword nor poison against his uncle was observed to the extent that Mithradates and his wife were put to death by suffocation.

Meanwhile, word that the client-king of Armenia had been attacked was brought to Julius Paelignus, the imperial procurator who was governing the province of Cappadocia. Collecting some soldiers, Paelignus advanced into Armenia, presumably for the purpose of restoring order and relieving the Roman garrison.[36] His troops, however, ill-disciplined

[1] See above p. 514.

and intent on plunder, fled at the first attack of the enemy, and Paelignus, learning that Mithradates was now dead, accepted the situation
and gave his official sanction to the crowning of Radamistus as king.

The strife in Armenia and the murder of Mithradates were soon
reported to Gaius Ummidius Quadratus, the governor of Syria and
commander of the only Roman army in the East. At a meeting of his
staff the view prevailed that it made but little difference who ruled
over Armenia, and the decision was reached that no active steps should
be taken against the invader. Possible censure from Rome, however,
was avoided by sending a note to Pharasmanes, ordering him to
remove his son and his army from the country. This course left it
open to the Emperor either to recall Radamistus and recognize him as
king or to order the enforcement of the demand contained in the note.

The announcement, however, that Radamistus, far from complying
with this demand, had been crowned king of the country and that the
act of investiture had been sanctioned by a Roman official after
his troops had been dispersed by a native force altered the situation. Quadratus, finally considering it necessary to repair the damage
to Roman prestige, ordered a legion to proceed to Armenia, instruct-
ing its commander, Helvidius Priscus, to "take such action with regard
to the disturbed state of affairs as circumstances should demand."[37]
Using this discretionary power, Priscus accepted the situation and, apparently refraining from ordering Radamistus to leave the country,
"had settled more matters by diplomacy than by force" when he received orders to return to Syria. It was feared that his further presence
in Armenia might embroil Rome in a Parthian war.

Meanwhile an able and far-sighted prince, Vologases I, had in
A.D. 51 become ruler of the Parthians.[38] Unlike most of their monarchs,
he began his reign by conciliating and not murdering his brothers.
The elder of the two he made king of Media;[m] the younger, Tiridates,
he planned to place on the throne of Armenia, thereby satisfying any
ambitions which this prince might cherish and at the same time
strengthening his own position.

The state of affairs in Armenia offered a favourable opportunity
for the execution of this plan, and in the spring of 52 Vologases led an
army into the country. At the report of his advance the legion of
Priscus was withdrawn and Radamistus's Iberian troops fled without
offering serious resistance. The Parthian King, marching across the
whole extent of the Armenian plateau, seized the capital, Artaxata,

[m] Josephus *Ant. Jud.* xx 3, 4, §74.

which immediately received the invader. But the intensity of an Armenian winter and a failure to provide a sufficient store of food wrought havoc in the Parthian army. Vologases, consequently, was forced to abandon his conquest and withdraw into Mesopotamia, leaving Armenia unguarded.

This withdrawal made it possible for Radamistus to return to his kingdom. Having never learned, however, that it was necessary to conciliate his subjects, he proceeded, with the savagery characteristic of his family, to punish the Armenians as betrayers, expecting thereby to stamp out any likelihood of a future rebellion. But the reverse of this expectation took place. Refusing to endure his cruelty, the Armenians revolted, compelling the King to take refuge in the royal palace, to which they then laid siege. Although successful in effecting an escape, Radamistus could find no support in Armenia and was forced to flee in haste to his native Iberia. Here, a few years later, his father, in an attempt to gain the favour of Rome, put him to death as a traitor.[n]

Once more the Augustan policy of maintaining a Roman nominee on the throne of Armenia met with failure. But this failure was more disastrous than any of those which preceded it; the ruler chosen by Rome was murdered by a kinsman, and he, after receiving a semblance of Roman endorsement, was driven from the country by his angry subjects. The prestige of Rome in the East had received a shattering blow and Armenia lay open to the first invader.

This was the situation in the East when, in October, A.D. 54, Claudius was succeeded by Nero, who, through the intrigues of his mother, Agrippina, and in spite of the claim of Claudius's son, Britannicus, was hailed *Imperator* by the Praetorian Guard and accepted as ruler by the Senate. The new Emperor, not yet seventeen years of age, was obviously incapable of administering the Empire without advice. Claudius's powerful freedmen, however, were removed from their positions of power, and Nero, although for a time subject to his mother's influence, depended for guidance on Agrippina's former protégé, Seneca, a brilliant man of letters, and Burrus, a sturdy old soldier, the commander of the Praetorians. Nevertheless, there was no change in the power of the ruler. The emperor's sovereignty was still supreme and his sway continued to be absolute.

Scarcely had the new régime been established when it was reported in Rome that Vologases, taking advantage of the unprotected condi-

n Tacitus *Ann.* XIII 37, 3 (A.D. 58).

tion of Armenia, had again seized the country, evidently intending it as a kingdom for Tiridates.[o] About the same time, an Armenian delegation arrived in the Capital to "plead the cause of their nation."[p] It was apparent that the Parthian supremacy was not universally acceptable and that steps must be taken not only to support Rome's adherents but also to restore Roman prestige in the East.[39] But nearly nine years passed before the Armenian problem was solved, and then the solution was reached by a compromise.

Fortunately, the right man was available for the task of "retaining Armenia."[40] Gnaeus Domitius Corbulo, chosen by Nero's advisers as supreme commander, had won fame by a successful campaign in Germany and later, as proconsul of Asia,[q] had acquired some knowledge of the East. A vigorous and powerful personality, although in an estimate of his achievements allowance must be made for the dependence of the extant historical sources on his own account of his campaigns, Corbulo stands out as the central figure in all the events which led to the re-establishment, however nominal, of Rome's suzerainty over Armenia.

In order to give Corbulo a position of authority commensurate with the task assigned to him, a special command seems to have been created, with headquarters in the province of Cappadocia, which, as the nearest of Rome's possessions to Armenia, was a convenient base of operations. At his disposal were placed the four legions stationed in Syria, together with a complement of auxiliary forces and some soldiers quartered in Cappadocia. Additional troops were obtained from King Antiochus IV of Commagene and the Jewish prince, Agrippa II, now the ruler of the region bordering on the Syrian Desert.[41] Measures for protecting the frontier were taken by replacing Cotys, the king of Armenia Minor, who had once shown a desire to take the Armenian crown, by Aristobulus, a great-grandson of Herod the Great, and by assigning Sophene, on the eastern side of the Euphrates, to a certain Sohaemus as client-king. This region was of great strategic importance, for it commanded both the crossing of the river at Tomisa and the route leading by the pass of Ergani across the Taurus into Mesopotamia.

Actual hostilities, however, did not begin until three years had passed. Vologases, occupied with the suppression of a rebellion, perhaps on the part of his son, was forced to withdraw his troops from Armenia and appeared ready to consent to a peaceful settlement of the dispute.[42] When Corbulo and Quadratus, the governor of Syria, each acting

[o] Tacitus *Ann.* XIII 6, 1. [p] Tacitus *Ann.* XIII 5, 3. [q] See note 15.

independently of the other, despatched envoys requesting him to maintain friendly relations and give hostages, the King complied, sending some members of the royal family in proof of his good faith. Nevertheless, nothing was done in regard to Armenia, where Tiridates seems to have retained possession of the throne.

This interval was utilized by Corbulo for training and hardening his troops, especially the legions from Syria, ill-disciplined and enervated by luxurious living and a mild climate and unfit for serious fighting and severe winter-weather.[43] Finally, however, in the spring of 58, the General, abandoning all pretence of peace, took the offensive by advancing across the Armenian plateau. Tiridates, unable to offer effective resistance, avoided any direct encounter, resorting to guerilla warfare and eluding any force sent against him. His tactics forced Corbulo to alter his plan of campaign by dividing his army into small units, which attacked several places simultaneously and so prevented the enemy from coming to the relief of any. At the same time Antiochus IV was instructed to create a diversion from the direction of Commagene, and both Pharasmanes the Iberian—who now showed his zeal for Rome's cause by killing his son Radamistus—and the tribesmen of the mountains between Armenia and the plain of Colchis were instigated to attack from the east and north.[44] Meanwhile, by seizing the route which led up from Trapezus on the Euxine Sea over the Zigana Pass to the table-land of Armenia, the Roman general provided his army with supplies.

Thus placed at a great disadvantage, Tiridates made overtures for peace. His envoys presented to Corbulo a list of his grievances based on the plea that he and his brother had done nothing to disturb the friendly relations into which they had entered with the Roman commanders. He added, however, that, were Corbulo to persist, the power of the Parthian ruler would again assert itself. In reply, Tiridates was told that he had only to present his plea to the Emperor and that if he would take the course which circumstances dictated, his success would be achieved without bloodshed and his throne would be secure.

This suggestion, which seems to have been made by Corbulo on his own initiative rather than in consequence of instructions received from Rome, presents a conspicuous contrast to the policy hitherto followed.[45] If accepted, it would mean that the ruler of Armenia would be a member of the Parthian royal house, selected by the Parthian monarch, and that Rome's suzerainty would henceforth be purely nominal. This compromise, to be sure, was finally adopted, but not until five years had passed. For the present, all hope of an immediate settlement disappeared when a conference arranged between Tiridates and Corbulo was abandoned as the result of mutual suspicion.

The invasion of Armenia, accordingly, proceeded as before. Capturing and destroying the strongholds as he advanced, Corbulo, probably in the autumn of 58, arrived at Artaxata.[46] After a vain attempt to defend his capital, Tiridates fled to his brother in Media, and the city opened its gates to the victor. Unable to hold the place and unwilling to leave it to be reoccupied by the enemy, the Roman general, after wintering in the city, razed it to the ground.

In the spring Corbulo continued his campaign by a long march southward across the Armenian plateau. Finally, after many dangers and privations, due to the hostility of the inhabitants and the lack of provisions, he arrived at Tigranocerta, founded by Tigranes the Great in the hill-country south of the Taurus.[r] The city, perhaps after a show of resistance, soon capitulated, and the garrison of a neighbouring stronghold, which attempted a defence, was overpowered by a detachment of Roman troops.[47] With its surrender all that part of the Armenian kingdom which lay south of the Taurus fell into Corbulo's hands.

Tiridates, nevertheless, was unwilling to yield, and, apparently in the spring of A.D. 60, he brought an army from Media into Armenia. The advance of the Roman auxiliary troops, however, followed by the General and his legions, soon put an end to his hopes and he was forced once more to take flight. His partisans were ruthlessly put to the sword, and before the summer was over Corbulo could boast that at last he had subjugated Armenia. In recognition of his achievements he was made governor of Syria, a post left vacant by Quadratus's recent death.

This subjugation of Armenia led the government at Rome to revive the policy of Augustus by again bestowing the crown on a Romanized Oriental. The nominee was a member of the royal house of Judaea, a certain Tigranes, who was a great-grandson of Herod the Great and through his grandmother a great-grandson also of Archelaus I of Cappadocia.[48] On his arrival in his kingdom, probably toward the close of A.D. 60, Tigranes was welcomed by the faction opposed to Parthian rule. But since there were still some who supported Tiridates, a Roman force, amounting to about 2,500 men, was stationed in the

[r] See Chap. XIV note 36.

country to protect the new monarch. As a means of ensuring support in the event of a Parthian attack a sort of partition of northern and western Armenia was effected, by which the interest of the neighbouring client-kings in the new arrangement might be secured. Territory bordering on Iberia was given to Pharasmanes, while the western part of the country was divided between Polemo of Pontus and Aristobulus of Armenia Minor and the region nearest to Commagene was assigned to Antiochus.

All this time Vologases seems to have done nothing to aid his brother, partly because he had been occupied in suppressing a revolt of the Hyrcanians in the distant part of his dominions bordering on the Caspian Sea. He might, indeed, have felt compelled to acquiesce in Rome's action with regard to Armenia had not Tigranes, apparently in the year following his arrival in the East, provoked him by invading the district of Adiabene, between the Tigris and the mountains of Media.[49] Since this was a Parthian vassal-state, the invasion was tantamount to an attack on the Parthian kingdom. Angered by this act of aggression, Vologases replied by formally crowning Tiridates King of Armenia and sending one of his generals, Monaeses, to drive out the invader. He himself mobilized an army in northern Mesopotamia, whence he could either bear aid to his brother or threaten the Roman province of Syria.

Meanwhile Tigranes, falling back before Monaeses's rapid advance, had taken refuge in Tigranocerta. Its massive walls and the Roman soldiers in the city afforded sufficient protection against the Parthian besiegers. Corbulo, moreover, ordered two legions to cross the Euphrates and relieve the beleaguered city, stationing three others along the river to guard Syria against a possible invasion. At the same time he sent a message to Vologases expostulating with him for laying siege to a city in which were present a friend and ally of Rome and a force of Roman soldiers, and threatening that, should the siege not be raised at once, he himself would invade the Parthian kingdom.

The bold tone of this message produced the desired result. Vologases, yielding to the situation, promised to refrain from further hostilities. As a solution of the question at issue, he offered to send envoys to Nero asking for the recognition of Tiridates as King of Armenia and the conclusion of a lasting peace. Under the terms thus proposed, the Parthian troops were to be withdrawn from northern Mesopotamia and Tigranocerta evacuated by Tigranes and the Roman force.

This offer was not essentially different from the proposal made by

Corbulo to Tiridates early in the war.[s] It was, of course, wholly at variance with the policy recently adopted by the government at Rome in sending out Tigranes, a measure which had resulted only in stirring up further trouble. Corbulo, however, hoping that the question of the Armenian succession might be settled without a renewal of the war, accepted Vologases's proposal.[50] Soon afterward, probably in the early winter of 61-62, a Parthian embassy set out for Rome.

About the time of these envoys' arrival in Rome, a change in Nero's advisers took place which gravely affected the character of the government; for the year 62 saw the death of Burrus and the retirement of Seneca and the elevation of the unscrupulous Ofonius Tigellinus, the new prefect of the Praetorian Guard, to the position of power which they had held. To what extent he was responsible for the disregard of Vologases's proposal is unknown, but in any case, the envoys could obtain no definite reply and returned to the King with their mission unaccomplished. A Parthian war now seemed inevitable.

Corbulo meanwhile had brought it to the government's attention that, engaged as he was in protecting the Syrian frontier, he could not also defend the upper course of the Euphrates and the approaches to Cappadocia, still less carry the war into Armenia.[51] He therefore urged that a special commander be appointed for the post which he himself had previously held in this area. His advice was taken, and Lucius Caesennius Paetus, one of the Consuls of 61, was chosen for this command. In order that he might have an army, Corbulo was ordered to assign him two of the five legions stationed in the East as well as the local militia of Galatia and Cappadocia. The order was carried out, but Corbulo kept for himself the veterans who had served in Armenia, assigning to Paetus a legion which had seen little or no active warfare and one which had recently been transferred to Syria from Europe.[52] In addition to these, a legion stationed on the lower Danube received orders to join the newly-appointed general.

Early in the summer of A.D. 62 Paetus arrived in Cappadocia.[53] He announced that, after conquering the Armenians, he would "subject them to tribute and laws and, instead of the semblance of a king, to the jurisdiction of Rome," in other words, annex Armenia as a Roman province.[54] This programme was at once put into effect. Taking command of the troops sent him by Corbulo but without waiting for the arrival of the legion from the Danube, Paetus crossed the Euphrates into Sophene, proclaiming that his purpose was the recovery of

[s] See above p. 555.

Tigranocerta. Advancing over the Taurus, he captured some strong-holds, sufficient in number and importance to serve as the basis of a boastful report to the Emperor. Falling back, however, as autumn approached, he prepared to encamp for the winter in the plain of the Arsanias, the southern arm of the Euphrates which joins the north-ern and greater branch of the river some distance above the crossing at Tomisa. The place of encampment, Rhandeia by name, was ill-chosen; for it lay on the northern bank of the Arsanias and its com-munications with Tomisa and Cappadocia could easily be cut by an army advancing across the Taurus.[55]

Considering that this position in a client-kingdom was secure, Paetus took no special measures for defence, even granting furloughs to some of his legionaries. Consequently, he was caught off his guard when the news was brought that Vologases with a large army was advancing up the southern side of the Taurus. Unwisely dividing his forces, he sent a body of legionaries to hold the pass of the Taurus and stationed his cavalry in the plain south of the Arsanias, detailing other troops to defend the stronghold of Arsamosata, where his wife and son had sought refuge. It was so evident that an army thus scattered could not cope with the enemy that the members of his staff compelled him, much against his will, to apply to Corbulo for reinforcements.

On receiving this appeal, Corbulo gave orders that a relieving force should make ready to go to the aid of his colleague. The preparations, however, were made in so leisurely a way that the General was sus-pected of wishing to add to his fame by making a last-minute rescue. It is perhaps more probable that, having every reason to suppose that Paetus was in a fortified camp, he saw no need for haste. But when a second and more urgent message arrived, Corbulo, calling out addi-tional troops, advanced by forced marches through Commagene to the crossing of the Euphrates at Tomisa.

Meanwhile Paetus's campaign had ended disastrously. The Parthians, having destroyed the legionaries guarding the pass and scattered the cavalry in the plain, had crossed the Arsanias and invested the camp at Rhandeia. Although disheartened by the arrival of the fugitives who had escaped the slaughter of their comrades, the Romans made ready to resist, remaining strictly on the defensive.[56] But as time went on, the soldiers became increasingly demoralized, and finally Paetus was compelled to enter into negotiations with the enemy. At first these came to nothing, but after a second envoy was despatched to the King a conference was arranged between the Roman general and two

Parthian officers. It was agreed that Paetus should surrender the camp and its supplies and withdraw the Roman forces from Armenian soil and that Parthian envoys should go to Rome to ask for official ratification of the surrender of the country.[57]

The remnants of the army, withdrawing from Rhandeia in shame and humiliation, met the relieving force at Tomisa. Rejecting Paetus's proposal for a joint invasion of Armenia, Corbulo returned to Syria. At Vologases's demand he evacuated the forts he had built on the left bank of the Euphrates, but at the same time he insisted that pending negotiations the Parthian troops should be withdrawn from Armenia.

On their arrival in Rome in the spring of 63, the Parthian envoys presented a proposal which was practically identical with that which the King had made to Corbulo two years previously and a former embassy had fruitlessly conveyed to Rome, namely, that Tiridates, after doing homage to the Emperor's statue before the military standards, should be recognized as King of Armenia, of which, they added, he was now in full possession. Nero's advisers, however, refusing to treat with a victorious enemy, decided to renew the war. Nevertheless, the way for further negotiation was left open; for gifts were presented to the envoys and the hint was given that should Tiridates offer to come to Rome in person, his petition might meet with acceptance.

In accordance with the government's decision, preparations were made for resuming the attack on Armenia. Corbulo's forces were increased by the addition of still another legion brought from the Danube and by detachments from Dalmatia and Egypt. He himself was made general-in-chief of all the Roman troops in Asia, and by this measure the whole eastern frontier was brought under one unified command.[58]

With his increased army and authority Corbulo, in the summer of 63, crossed the Euphrates. While advancing through Sophene toward the pass of Ergani, evidently with the intention of carrying the war into the enemy's country, he was met by an embassy from the now alarmed Vologases bringing new proposals for peace. Replying with what was virtually an offer to accept Tiridates and enter into an alliance with the Parthians, the Roman general sent the envoys back to the King. As an object-lesson, however, he attacked and destroyed the castles of those Armenian magnates who had opposed the Romans, thus "filling with fear the strong and the weak alike."

The conciliatory tone of Corbulo's reply and his evident ability to use force, if necessary, accomplished its purpose. Vologases went through the form of requesting a truce and Tiridates asked for a meeting with Corbulo in person. This, by common consent, was held at Rhandeia, the scene of the Romans' humiliation but now of their triumphant success. Here, after elaborate ceremonies, Tiridates laid down the crown of Armenia before the Emperor's statue, binding himself not to assume it again until he received it from Nero's own hand. The condition, however, was imposed that a Roman force should remain in Sophene until the terms of the agreement were fulfilled.[59] But in Rome the compromise was hailed as a great victory, and, "peace having been won on land and sea," the doors of the Temple of Janus were officially closed.[60]

Finally, in the year 66, Tiridates, accompanied by a huge retinue, arrived in Rome. After various preliminary ceremonies, he was received by Nero, seated on the Rostra and accompanied by the Senators and the Praetorian Guard.[61] Here the Parthian prince, having addressed the Emperor as master and done reverence to him as Mithra, was solemnly invested with the royal diadem and declared King of Armenia. As a vassal of Rome, he was granted permission to rebuild Artaxata and received a large sum of money and the services of the artisans needed for the work.[t] In return, the city was called—temporarily—Neroneia.

Thus the compromise originally proposed by Corbulo to Tiridates and on two later occasions offered by Vologases, only to be rejected, was finally adopted. It left to Rome merely the shadow of the power which Nero's predecessors had claimed over Armenia, but it saved Rome's prestige and at the same time it satisfied the aspirations of the Parthians. By providing at long last a solution of the Armenian problem, the new arrangement brought to the East a peace which was to endure for half a century.

Shortly after the ceremony at Rhandeia in which Tiridates went through the form of relinquishing the crown of Armenia, Rome acquired further territory in northeastern Asia Minor by the annexation of the kingdom of Pontus.[62] On the retirement—at least nominally voluntary—of Polemo II in A.D. 64, his dominions were incorporated in the large and unwieldy Galatian province. The territory thus added included not only the mountain-region of interior Pontus with the city of Zela and the valley of the Lycus with Neocaesareia but also the coast of the Euxine from the free city of Amisus to Colchis with Cerasus-Pharnaceia, Polemonium (founded by Polemo II on the site

t Cassius Dio LXIII 6, 5f.

of Side) and Trapezus, also a free city. Besides this territory, Rome acquired the royal naval vessels, the nucleus of the Pontic fleet which later patrolled the Euxine. Its headquarters were at Trapezus, where there was also a garrison consisting of former soldiers of Polemo, now enjoying the rights of Roman citizens and retained in Rome's service for the protection of this remote corner of Asia Minor.

The possession of this region assured the control not only of the port of Trapezus with the route leading into Armenia but also of the whole line of sea-communication between the Thracian Bosporus and the mouth of the river Phasis at the eastern end of the Euxine. Its annexation may have had a further purpose as part of a plan to extend the rule of Rome toward the northeast by an expedition whose objective, it was said, was the "Caspian Gates," presumably the Dariel Pass leading over the Caucasus north of Tiflis.[63] By this somewhat impressive term may have been meant merely the annexation of the kingdom of Pharasmanes the Iberian. In any case, the plan was not carried out, for while preparations were being made, Nero's principate came to an end, and it was not until after the close of the civil wars which followed his death that the Romans appeared in Trans-Caucasia.[u]

In the general administration of the provinces the bureaucratic methods of Claudius, under which the imperial procurators possessed increased power and influence, seem to have been continued by his successor. It is true that the measure which gave the procurators jurisdiction in fiscal cases was rescinded by an edict of Nero enacting that claims against tax-payers should come under the jurisdiction of the governor of the province, who, since no claims might be admitted if not presented within a year, was ordered to give such cases a special hearing.[64] But in the district of Pisidia in the imperial province of Galatia the procurator acted in conjunction with the governor in determining, on instructions from the Emperor, the boundary between the territories belonging, respectively, to the city of Sagalassus and a village-community.[65] In Bithynia the repair of the road from the colony of Apameia to Nicaea by the procurator Julius Aquila—who as prefect of engineers had formerly improved the road to Amastris on the Euxine coast—indicates that even in the senatorial provinces the construction of the highways had been taken over by the imperial government. The fact also that the procurator of Asia, Publius Celer,

[u] See below p. 575.

was accused by the province of extortion, suggests that he occupied a position of sufficient power to enable him to exact money from the provincials.[66]

In the trial of Celer no verdict was ever pronounced, for the case dragged on until, so it was said, he died of old age. It was asserted that he was protected because of the service he had rendered in killing Marcus Junius Silanus, proconsul of Asia in A.D. 54, whom, as the great-great-grandson of Augustus, Agrippina feared as a possible rival of her son and immediately after Nero's accession had poisoned through Celer's agency.[67] Influence at court, as has already been observed, also saved Eprius Marcellus, the governor of Lycia, when accused by the province.[v] On the other hand, in some cases dishonest officials were brought to justice. In the same year in which Celer and Marcellus were accused, Cossutianus Capito, notorious as a prosecutor, who was charged by the Cilicians with extortion, was convicted and punished by the loss of his seat in the Senate.[68] Three years later, Marcus Tarquitius Priscus, governor of Bithynia, prosecuted for the same offence, was also declared guilty.[69] Nevertheless, when Publius Suillius Rufus, also a well-known prosecutor, was accused of maladministration during his proconsulship of Asia, although there was evidence that he had robbed the provincials and stolen public funds, his accusers found it easier to have him tried on the ground that by false charges he had caused the death of many prominent Romans.[70]

Action was also taken to prevent an official from escaping a possible prosecution for misdeeds committed in his province. In A.D. 57 an imperial edict forbad a governor or a procurator to present any kind of spectacle, whether gladiatorial combat or wild-beast hunt, by which he might court popularity and so gain supporters.[w] Some years later, the Senate, with Nero's approval, prohibited the provincial assemblies from sending delegations to Rome to eulogize retiring propraetors or proconsuls, a measure intended not only to prevent governors from referring to such testimonials in the event of a prosecution but also to reduce the expenditure of money on the part of the provincials.[71]

Similar measures adopted for the benefit of the provincials were the prohibition of illegal exactions by which tax-farmers had fraudulently extorted money and the exemption of merchant-ships from any property-tax in order that the transportation of grain to the provinces might be encouraged.[x] Some favour, furthermore, was granted to the

[v] See above p. 533.   [w] Tacitus *Ann.* XIII 31, 4.
[x] Tacitus *Ann.* XIII 51, 2f. (A.D. 58).

Commonalty of Asia which elicited a decree, praising, in the fulsome terms characteristic of such documents, the Emperor's "forethought and solicitude."[72] On the other hand, Laodiceia, when, together with Colossae and Hierapolis, it was damaged by an earthquake in A.D. 60, received no assistance, and the inhabitants were forced to rebuild the city at their own expense.[73]

Like his predecessors, Nero received the appellation of "God"—and his mother that of "Goddess"—which appears on the coins of several cities of the province of Asia.[74] In other places he was identified with the patron-deity, as at Cos, where he was Asclepius Caesar, and at Sagalassus, where he was the "New Zeus."[75] At Ephesus and Nymphaeum buildings were dedicated to him in conjunction, respectively, with Artemis and Apollo, and at Aezani, a citizen presented the city, in honour of Nero, with a gift of such munificence that the Emperor wrote a letter expressing his gratification.

But whatever popularity Nero may have enjoyed in the East must have been greatly damaged when, wishing to beautify Rome with works of Greek art, he sent his freedman, Acratus, to pillage the cities of Greece and Asia.[76] Delphi and Olympia were robbed of much of their sculpture, and at Pergamum, although the citizens attempted to prevent by force the removal of their art-treasures, the statues commemorating their rulers' victories over the Galatians were seized and carried off to Rome to adorn the Emperor's new palace.

No effort to oppose the Pergamenes' resistance to Acratus's robberies was made by the proconsul, Barea Soranus, an upright man, who, during his term of office displayed "justice and vigour."[77] His interest in improving the economic condition of the province was shown by his activity in dredging the harbour of Ephesus. But when, a few years after his return to Rome, his enemies brought him to trial on a trumped-up charge of treason, they accused him, among other alleged offences, of attempting to incite the cities of Asia to violence with a view to his own aggrandizement. Despite the weakness of the evidence against him, his accusers—presumably with Nero's support— won their case and both Soranus and his daughter were condemned to death.

Soranus was, in fact, the second proconsul of Asia to meet with death in the course of a short time. In the previous year, Lucius Antistius Vetus, who governed the province soon after Soranus, was accused by a thieving freedman in conjunction with a provincial whom Vetus had punished during his term of office.[78] The actual charge is unknown, but, whatever it was, the defendant had no hope of acquittal; for, as the father-in-law of Gaius Rubellius Plautus (the grandson through his mother of Tiberius's son Drusus), who had been recently murdered by Nero's order, he was an object of suspicion to the Emperor. His villa was surrounded by a body of soldiers, and after a vain appeal to Nero, Vetus, with his mother-in-law and daughter, forestalled condemnation by suicide.

The deaths of these men were but incidents in the reign of terror, which, encouraged by Tigellinus, prevailed during the last years of Nero. Nevertheless, though hated for his acts of cruelty and despised for his vices and follies, the Emperor was protected by the Praetorian Guard, and his opponents were powerless as long as it remained loyal. The common folk, moreover, entertained by such spectacles as that which attended the coronation of Tiridates, were diverted from any outbreak. But when, after Nero had crossed the Adriatic in the autumn of 66, it was announced that after an oration in Corinth in which he declared Greece free and exempt from taxation,[y] the Emperor had taken part in the four great festivals of Greece—all held in one year at his demand—appearing not only as a charioteer but even as a lyre-player and a tragic actor, there was wide-spread contempt and sense of outrage. His return to Italy at the end of 67 did not avail to allay the general indignation. A revolt of the troops in Gaul and Spain was followed by the mutiny of the Praetorians, now willing to support the Senate in a declaration that Nero was an enemy to the state. Abandoned by all save a few attendants, the wretched man fled from the city and in one of the suburbs was aided by a freedman to drive a dagger into his throat. By the Romans he was ever afterward held in abhorrence, but in the East, little affected by his cruelty and follies, he was regarded almost as a supernatural being, destined to reappear and rule once more.[79]

[y] *I.G.* VII 1, 2713 = *Syll.*[3] 814 = Dessau 8794.

CHAPTER XXIV

CENTRALIZATION AND PROSPERITY
UNDER THE FLAVIANS

THE provinces of Asia Minor were but little affected by the series of murders and battles in Italy which followed the overthrow of Nero—the violent death of Galba, named emperor by the Senate, the defeat and suicide of Otho, chosen by the Praetorian Guard, and the disastrous war in which the forces of Vitellius, the candidate of the legions in Germany, were crushed by the armies of eastern Europe acting in behalf of Vespasian. As the commander of the Roman army in Judaea, engaged in the suppression of the revolt of the turbulent people of that province, Vespasian was well known in the East. His chief adviser, moreover, and the prime mover in the intrigues which led to his seizure of the imperial power was Mucianus, governor of Syria, who under Nero had been imperial legate of Lycia-Pamphylia.[a]

The new Emperor, Titus Flavius Vespasianus, proclaimed at Alexandria on 1 July, 69, was promptly accepted by the eastern provinces. While his legions, under the command of Mucianus, marched through Asia Minor from the Syrian frontier to the Bosporus, doubtless at great cost to the provinces, Vespasian himself, travelling by ship, touched at various cities on the coasts of Lycia and Ionia, where the inhabitants took the usual oath of allegiance.[1] The only opposition of which there is record was the seizure of Trapezus in the name of Vitellius by a former freedman of Polemo II, who had once commanded the royal fleet, but this attempt at rebellion was promptly crushed by a detachment of legionaries.

On his accession to power, Vespasian found a bankrupt treasury, exhausted by the extravagance of Nero and by the civil wars which followed his death. In an attempt to rehabilitate the public finances, the Emperor adopted a general policy of economy by which governmental expenses were greatly reduced, and he sought also to increase the income of the state by every possible means, especially by compelling the people of Rome to pay new and often ingeniously contrived taxes.[2] In the provinces, a change in the management of the revenues of the imperial government, namely the transference of the collection of

[a] See Chap. XXII note 48.

certain taxes from agents of the *publicani* to governmental officials, which was in effect in the early second century, is perhaps to be attributed to this practical and competent ruler. The adoption of this new method was a step in the trend toward centralization which had appeared in the bureaucratic policy of Claudius.

This system, it will be remembered, had been introduced in the province of Asia by Julius Caesar, under whom the collection of the direct taxes was transferred from the tax-farming syndicates to the communities themselves,[b] and it seems to have been subsequently adopted in the other senatorial provinces. The direct tax, or *stipendium*, appears to have been levied on the province as a whole but to have been actually raised by quotas imposed on the communities.[3] In the imperial provinces, it seems probable that the direct tax, or *tributum*, levied on individual holdings of land, had from the beginning been collected by agents of the government.

The occasional and indirect taxes, on the contrary, which the imperial government had taken over from the Republic, notably the 5 per cent tax on the manumission of slaves and the $2\frac{1}{2}$ per cent tax on exports and imports, were still collected under Tiberius and Claudius by tax-farming syndicates.[4] Even the new 5 per cent tax on inheritances, which Augustus levied on all Roman citizens, both at home and abroad, was similarly collected by agents of the *publicani*.

By the beginning of the second century, on the other hand, the *publicani* seem to have disappeared and the collection of these taxes in the eastern provinces had been taken over by governmental officials with the title of *promagister*, who, in the case of the manumissions-tax, appear to have been attached to a central bureau in Rome, apparently in charge of a special procurator. In the course of time, however, the *promagister* seems to have been replaced in the provinces by a subordinate procurator, responsible for a certain district. Thus, as early as the time of Trajan, while the collection of the inheritance-tax was under the general supervision of a procurator stationed in Rome, in the provinces there were procurators of lower rank, each in charge of a district, sometimes formed, as in the combination of Asia and Lycia-Pamphylia or in that of Asia, Lycia and Galatia, of two or more provinces. In the later years of the second century, moreover, the collector of customs in the district composed of Asia and Bithynia also had the title of procurator.

An increase in the importance of the office of procurator, which

[b] See above p. 407.

began, as has already been noticed, under Claudius,[e] may also be attributed to the centralizing tendencies of Vespasian's rule. It is not surprising that in the imperial province of Lycia-Pamphylia the names of the governor and the procurator should appear together in inscriptions on an aqueduct at Balbura and a public bath at Aperlae, each of which was built at the expense of the city.[d] The great development of this office in the senatorial province of Asia, however, is more remarkable. Both the duties of this imperial agent and the personnel subordinate to him grew henceforth more and more complicated.

This development, suggesting a greater control of this province by the emperor, was presumably due, at least in part, to an increase in the amount of imperial property in the province and to the need of special officials for its management. Unfortunately, no information is available with regard to the source of the payments made from the Flavian period onward into a special branch of the imperial treasury known as the *fiscus Asiaticus*, which was under the charge of a special procurator (who might be a freedman of the emperor) with headquarters in Rome.[5] It may perhaps be assumed, however, that the collection of the money paid into this *fiscus* devolved upon the provincial procurator and that the special agent in charge was one of his subordinates. Other officials who, with a higher degree of certainty, were subject to his orders were the procurator of the marble quarries near Synnada, known from the end of the first century onward, the procurator of Phrygia, which in the late second century seems to have formed a separate unit for the administration of the imperial revenues, and, somewhat later, the procurator of the *region* of Philadelpheia, who was evidently in charge of a single estate.[6] As freedmen of the emperor, these men had evidently a lower status than the procurator of the whole province. Subordinates of a lower degree, also imperial freedmen, described as "assistants" were likewise attached to his office.[7] During the second century, moreover, there were in Ephesus large numbers of lesser functionaries who formed a numerous staff attached to the *Tabularium*, or record-office, evidently the central bureau of the procurator. These men included both clerks, who were imperial freedmen, and accountants, a lower grade composed of slaves born in the emperor's house. The system was presumably adopted from that used in the imperial provinces, as in Galatia, where the procurator,

[e] See above p. 541.
[d] *I.G.R.* III 466 and 690 (= 1523 = Dessau 8796).

568

charged with the collection of all the revenues, was assisted by a similar staff of clerks in the record-office at Ancyra.

The tendency toward an increased control of the senatorial provinces on the part of the emperor is suggested also by the appointment of Eprius Marcellus to the proconsulship of Asia for three successive years.[8] Marcellus, it will be remembered, had been brought to trial for extortion by the Lycians but had escaped punishment. As the successful prosecutor of Thrasea Paetus, a leader of the conservative opposition to Nero, who was put to death in 66, he won the hatred of the supporters of that opposition and immediately after Nero's overthrow and again in the first year of Vespasian's rule he was bitterly attacked before the Senate by Paetus's son-in-law. Since it seems improbable, therefore, that his enemies in the Senate would of their own free will have allowed those who would normally have become proconsuls of Asia to be passed over in his favour, it may be supposed that this unusual prolongation of his office was due to Vespasian. This step, however much it curtailed the rights of the Senate in favour of the central imperial authority, was perhaps intended to secure a more efficient government of the province. Marcellus was undoubtedly an able man, and it may have seemed to Vespasian that the great wealth which he possessed would render him less susceptible to the temptation to enrich himself at the provincials' expense. The erection of a statue of him during his second year, the cost of which was paid out of the taxes of the community of Dorylaeum, and the appearance of his name on the coins of at least four of the cities of the province of Asia suggest that his governorship was not altogether unacceptable. The Emperor could not foresee that in the last year of his rule this brilliant, if unscrupulous, man would enter into a conspiracy against him and, after its failure, die by his own hand.

A somewhat similar tendency toward centralization appears in the suppression of the independence of Rhodes and perhaps of Samos as well.[9] There was a precedent, to be sure, for such action, for under Claudius the Rhodians had lost and then regained their freedom.[e] The reason for this step on the part of Vespasian is unknown; at least an effort to win his favour had been made by the community of Ialysus, which erected a monument to him as its Benefactor.[f] As under Claudius, however, the Rhodians soon recovered their freedom; for Vespasian's son and successor, Titus, restored their former independence and received divine honours in one of the communities of the island.

---

[e] See above p. 548. [f] *I.G.* xii 1, 679 = *I.G.R.* iv 1138.

The Rhodians also regained possession of their mainland dominions on the Peninsula of Loryma, together with Syme and other neighbouring islands, and they were still able to maintain at least the semblance of a navy. While the statement of the orator Dio the "Golden-mouthed," a native of Prusa in Bithynia, that they were the wealthiest of all the Greeks was doubtless exaggerated for the purpose of pleasing his audience, he was probably justified in saying that they derived large revenues from their possessions on the mainland as well as from the islands under their rule.

It is probable that the island-city of Cos, to which Claudius had granted full exemption from taxation,[g] was likewise deprived of its freedom despite the honour paid to Vespasian by one of the *demes* of the community, which, in the year 74, erected a statue of the Emperor.[10] In this case also, however, Titus reversed his father's action by restoring the city's independence.

While depriving these cities of their independence, Vespasian, like Claudius, adopted the policy of developing urban centres. The old town of Crateia, which lay at the fork of the roads leading through the valleys, respectively, of the Devrek and the Amnias to the Halys, was refounded under the name Flaviopolis and perhaps received the rights of a city.[11] Particular attention seems to have been given to eastern Lydia. Both Daldis, in the hill-country southeast of Thyateira, and Temenothyrae, near the border of Phrygia, were also refounded as Flaviopolis, and the important city of Philadelpheia, as well as the ancient town of Grimenothyrae, east of Temenothyrae, assumed the name Flavia. Under Vespasian's younger son, Domitian, Sala, also in the border-land of Lydia and Phrygia, became Domitianopolis.

This policy was furthered by a general improvement in the means of communication; for Vespasian continued to bear the responsibility for the construction of roads both in senatorial and imperial provinces which had been assumed by Claudius.[h] In the province of Asia this improvement appears in the construction, in the year 75, of the highways which led from Pergamum southward along the coast by way of Smyrna to Ephesus and through northern Lydia to Thyateira and Sardis.[12] This work was continued after Vespasian's death by Domitian, who "restored" not only these roads but also a section of the route leading through central Phrygia to Prymnessus and thence to a junction with the Southern Highway.

In Bithynia, the road connecting the city of Prusa with the Propontis

[g] See above p. 542.   [h] See Chap. XXIII note 22.

was "constructed anew" in 77/8 under the supervision of the procurator, Lucius Antonius Naso.[13] He also rebuilt the route leading to Tieium on the Euxine coast, the easterly extension of which had been improved under Claudius. The use of a procurator for this purpose, as previously under Nero in Bithynia, is indicative of the extent to which the maintenance of the roads in this senatorial province had become the concern of the imperial government. Farther east, the difficult route which connected Sinope with the great road leading through the valley of the Amnias was likewise rebuilt by order of Vespasian and the accessibility of this important colony materially increased.

The greatest attention, however, was given to the repair of the roads in central and eastern Asia Minor, by which the Euphrates frontier was made more accessible from the Aegean and the Propontis and the transportation of troops and supplies facilitated. It appears to have been part of the general plan to strengthen this frontier which led, as will presently be shown, to a great enlargement of the Galatian province.[1] This construction was begun in A.D. 76, when the governor of Galatia, Gnaeus Pompeius Collega, rebuilt the road through Lesser Armenia which connected the highway leading up the Lycus with the region of the upper Euphrates.[14] It is possible that he also began the development of the route which afterward led along the right bank of the river to Samosata in Commagene. Shortly afterward, in 80-82, another governor, Aulus Caesennius Gallus, initiated a more ambitious plan for a general repaving of the roads in the province. Milestones bearing his name show his work on the routes from Ancyra southwest to Pessinus and the colony of Germa and southeast to Tyana and the Cilician Gates, and an inscription records also his repair of the road in southwestern Lycaonia which seems to have led from Iconium to Lystra. In Cilicia Aspera also an attempt was made to improve the means of communication by building a bridge over the Calycadnus to carry the road leading along the coast eastward to the Level District and Syria and westward to the cities beyond Cape Anemurium and to Pamphylia.

An attempt was made, furthermore, to secure the good will of the provincials by the bestowal of privileges. Following the example of Claudius, Vespasian confirmed the exemptions enjoyed by the World-wide Association of Athletes, for, "knowing their high repute and distinction," he promised to safeguard all the rights they had previ-

[1] See below p. 574.

ously received.[15] A measure of greater importance was the grant of a privileged status to teachers, a step in accord with Vespasian's adoption of a system whereby those who taught rhetoric at Rome should receive regular salaries from the imperial treasury. In an edict issued in A.D. 74, a copy of which has been found at Pergamum, the Emperor ordered that not only teachers but also physicians (in this, following a precedent set by Augustus) and gymnastic trainers should be exempt both from the obligation of providing lodging for officials or troops and from the payment of taxes, any violation of this order to be punished by a fine payable to Jupiter Capitolinus. Nearly forty-five years later the provisions of this edict were re-enacted by the Emperor Hadrian, who specified as the civic duties from which exemption should be granted the office of gymnasiarch, the supervision of the markets, the local priesthoods, the necessity of serving as judges, envoys or soldiers or providing billets or supplying the public with grain or oil—an immunity which, as will be shown, was subsequently greatly abused.

The general success of Vespasian's efforts to ensure the allegiance and contentment of the cities of Asia appears in the honours conferred on him in several places giving him the usual title of Benefactor, sometimes even Benefactor of the World and Saviour and Benefactor of all Mankind.[16] At Aphrodisias a priest was created for his worship, and both here and at Bargylia Titus also had a priest.[17] He, too, was honoured in several cities, most conspicuously at Laodiceia, where a stadium, amphitheatrical in form, dedicated to him was presented to the community by a wealthy citizen.

In addition to these honours, mention must be made of the handsome temple of the Augusti erected at Ephesus by the province of Asia.[18] Although, except for the fact that it is known to have been in existence in the early years of Domitian's rule, the time of its construction cannot be determined, its later designation as the Temple of Vespasian suggests that it was built during his principate rather than, as has been supposed, under either Claudius or Domitian.

It has already been suggested that Vespasian's repair of the roads leading to the Euphrates may have been connected with a general plan for strengthening the eastern frontier of the Empire. The need for such a measure had been demonstrated in Nero's war for the "retention" of Armenia; for, since the procuratorial province of Cappadocia was unarmed save for the local militia, and the levies of the client-kings of Commagene and Armenia Minor were unable to offer any real resistance to an enemy from the East, the defence of this frontier depended entirely on the legions stationed in Syria. To meet the obvious need of protecting eastern Asia Minor without relying on assistance summoned from so great a distance, Vespasian adopted a plan for increasing both the size and the strength of the Galatian province, the most recent addition to which was the kingdom of Polemo of Pontus.

The first step in carrying out this plan was the annexation of the two client-kingdoms which bordered on the Euphrates. Antiochus IV of Commagene, "great in his long-standing power and the richest of the vassal-kings," had been among the first to swear allegiance to Vespasian and had brought troops to assist the Emperor's son Titus in his siege of Jerusalem.[19] Epiphanes, the King's eldest son, moreover, also had a claim to consideration; for he had been wounded in fighting for Otho against Vespasian's enemy, Vitellius, and he had accompanied his father when the latter bore aid to Titus. Nevertheless, in the year 72 both the old monarch and his son were accused of having formed a plan to throw off their allegiance to Rome and enter into an alliance with the Parthians. The fact that the accuser was the vain Caesennius Paetus, who, in spite of his capitulation at Rhandeia ten years previously, was now governor of Syria, casts some doubt on the truth of the charge. The Emperor, however, finding it convenient to give credence to the allegation, authorized Paetus to carry out whatever measures seemed expedient. Accordingly, with a small army composed of but one legion and some auxiliary forces, he invaded Commagene. Antiochus, taken by surprise and unable or unwilling to withstand the power of Rome, offered no resistance and, withdrawing together with his wife and daughters to his Cilician dominions, allowed his capital, Samosata, to be occupied by Paetus's troops. His two sons, however, met the Romans in battle, fighting not without success, but, on the flight of the King, their troops refused to continue the struggle. The young men themselves sought refuge with the Parthian monarch, Vologases. Although at first they were treated with all honour, Vologases soon surrendered them to a Roman officer, evidently acting for Paetus, who, promising a safe-conduct, escorted them to Rome together with some of their adherents.

Antiochus, meanwhile, had been arrested by Paetus's order at Tarsus and sent to Italy in chains. Although deposed from his royal power and position, he was received with respect by Vespasian, who ordered the removal of his bonds, and, on the arrival of the two princes, gave permission to them all to take up their residence in Rome. The kingdom of Commagene was once more annexed to Syria and its incorporation in the Roman Empire was celebrated by an issue of bronze coins minted in the district.[20] By this annexation the province of Syria was made contiguous with Cappadocia, and Rome obtained full possession of the crossing of the Euphrates at Samosata.

In the same year a similar step was taken with regard to the kingdom of Lesser Armenia.[21] Aristobulus, whom Nero's government had made ruler in 54, was removed from his throne and the country was annexed to the new province which was to comprise all eastern Asia Minor. By this action the whole frontier from the Euxine to Syria, including the region north of the great bend of the Euphrates as well as the western bank of the river, was brought directly under the rule of Rome.

The new administrative unit now created was a vast one. Formed by combining the Galatian province as enlarged by the Pontic kingdom of Polemo with Cappadocia and Lesser Armenia, it reached from the eastern borders of Bithynia and Phrygia to the Euphrates and, save for the narrow strip of Paphlagonia and Pontus which, bordering on the Euxine as far eastward as the city of Amisus, was attached to Bithynia, it extended from the northern coast to the crest of the Taurus.[22] Including the districts of Galatia, northern Pisidia, Lycaonia, Paphlagonia and Cappadocia and the former kingdoms of Pontus Polemoniacus and Lesser Armenia, it covered almost the entire central plateau of Asia Minor with an area of hardly less than 112,000 square miles. With a permanent garrison, probably of two legions, it became a province of the higher class, ordinarily governed by an imperial legate of consular rank.

This notable increase in military strength was said to have been due to "the constant inroads of barbarians."[j] It is difficult to suppose that this statement refers to the Parthians, if only for the reason that King Vologases, satisfied by the Armenian compromise, was disposed to be friendly toward the Romans, as is shown by his readiness to surrender the two princes of Commagene and especially by an offer to supply Vespasian with a force of 40,000 mounted archers to aid him in gaining the imperial power.[23] It is also unlikely that mere raids by brigands are meant, for these could have been repelled by the Cappadocian militia. The most reasonable explanation, therefore, of this addition to the strength and importance of Cappadocia is that Vespasian, in

[j] Suetonius *Vesp.* 8, 4.

continuance of the plan, formed by Nero's government, of preventing attacks by the Alans and other Caucasian tribes, resolved, by fortifying the frontier, to forestall an invasion from the northeast.[24] About the time of the formation of the greater province, a band of these Alans, with the connivance of the Hyrcanians—long-standing enemies of Vologases—carried out a raid into Media and Armenia in the course of which they forced the Median king to buy them off with one hundred talents and almost succeeded in capturing Tiridates, the ruler of Armenia. It seems probable that this attack aroused in the Roman government the fear of a similar inroad into Lesser Armenia or Cappadocia. Three years later, Vologases, either in the face of another raid or, perhaps more probably, wishing to take the field against the barbarians, asked for some Roman troops to be used against the Alans, a request which Vespasian, apparently wishing to remain on the defensive, refused to grant. It may have been, moreover, a consequence of the same policy of warding off these inroads that in 75 the Emperor, presumably by sending troops, helped the king of Iberia to strengthen the walls of a fortress near Tiflis, which commanded the southern end of the Dariel Pass, the Alans' chief avenue of approach toward the region east and southeast of the Euxine Sea.

The actual defence of the eastern frontier alone did not, it is true, necessitate the formation of so vast a province, for—as was afterward discovered—it was possible to ward off invasion by maintaining a sufficient force in Cappadocia. It may have seemed, however, that the construction of the roads, already described, which led to this frontier could best be carried out were all eastern Asia Minor placed under a unified command. Whether, when this construction was accomplished, it was found that the continuance of this huge province was no longer necessary, or whether the burden of administration proved too great for a single governor cannot be determined. In any case, the existence of this greater Galatia was not of long duration.[25] The exact time of its division into its component parts cannot be definitely established, but inscriptions of the governors who held office during the early years of the second century indicate that it took place between 107 and 113. Under this arrangement, as will presently be shown,[k] the Galatian province, reduced to its earlier size, once more consisted of the districts of Galatia proper, inland Paphlagonia, northern Pisidia and Lycaonia, of which it was composed under Augustus.

[k] See below p. 605.

On the enforced abdication of Antiochus IV and the annexation of Commagene, the King's dominions in Cilicia Aspera were left without a ruler. A small portion of them was given to the monarch's daughter, Iotape, now married to Alexander, one of the numerous descendants of Herod the Great of Judaea and a son of that Tigranes who for a short time under Nero had tried to rule Armenia.[26] Both the situation and the amount of this portion, however, are uncertain; in any case, it was insignificant, and Cilicia Aspera as a whole was taken under the direct rule of Rome. In order to provide for its administration, Cilicia Campestris, which, as far as is known, had long been under the charge of the governor of Syria, was detached from this province and combined with the Rugged District to form the province of Cilicia.[27] In connexion, doubtless, with the formation of this new administrative unit, the city of Flaviopolis was founded in the northeastern corner of the Level District, probably as a means of extending Roman influence in this region. In the Rugged District, too, there seems to have been a corresponding attempt at urbanization; for about this time, probably, the village around the Temple of Zeus near Olba became the city of Diocaesareia, with the result that there were henceforth two separate *poleis* situated only three miles apart.

In connexion with the great enlargement of the Galatian province by its union with Cappadocia, a minor administrative change was brought about when Pamphylia, which for a short time after Nero's death had been placed under the command of the imperial legate of Galatia, and perhaps part of southern Pisidia were combined with the neighbouring Lycia.[1] This combination, however, was purely an administrative one, effected solely for the convenience of the Roman government, for there was no real amalgamation of these districts. The Pamphylian cities did not become members of the Lycian Federation but formed (or continued) an organization of their own, evidently modelled after that of the Lycians, which conferred the usual honours and created Pamphyliarchs and other officials.[28] Nevertheless, there was a real advantage in the arrangement, for with the formation of the two imperial provinces, Cilicia in the East and Lycia-Pamphylia in the West, the whole of southern Asia Minor between the Taurus and the Mediterranean was composed of two well-defined administrative units.

The rule of Domitian, who succeeded his elder brother, Titus, in September, 81, marked a great advance in the process of centralization,

---

[1] See Chap. XXII notes 48 and 51.

bringing with it a despotism greater than that exercised by any of the Emperor's predecessors. By seizing power unscrupulously and ruthlessly employing every means for the furtherance of his purposes, Domitian obtained a position of complete mastery over Senate, army and people and succeeded in establishing himself as an autocrat. It was character-istic of the man and his methods that he allowed and even desired his courtiers to address him as "Master and God" and, so it was said, him-self assumed these titles.[29] The aristocrats and conservatives, on the other hand, weakened, intimidated, and punished by exile and, in some cases, by death, branded him as a merciless tyrant.

An echo of such execration was, indeed, heard in the East, where the orator Dio of Prusa—who, be it said, suffered exile under Domitian—in a speech delivered after the Emperor's assassination referred to him as "violent and overbearing, called Master and God of both Greeks and barbarians, but in reality a spirit of evil."[30] In the provinces of Asia Minor, moreover, there was a general compliance with the decree of the Senate, passed after Domitian's death, which ordered that the name of the hated Emperor should be erased from all public monu-ments.

Nevertheless, in these provinces there is little evidence of cruelty on the part of Domitian or even of exaggerated pretensions to grandeur. In the East, to be sure, the appellation of "God" which grated on the ears of the Romans had long since been accepted as normal. Even the fulsome title of "God invincible, Founder of the City," which was inscribed on the pedestal of a statue of the Emperor at Priene, was no more extravagant than those given to many of his predecessors, and the bestowal of the title of "Founder" seems to indicate that he actually conferred some benefit on the city.[m] The various statues and altars, moreover, as, for example, those erected in the Temple of the Augusti at Ephesus, and the dedication of buildings, as a city-gate at Laodiceia, while they were probably merely the usual honours which had been ac-corded to earlier emperors, may also have been expressions of gratitude for favours received.[31]

In fact, in his administration of the provinces Domitian seems to have shown both vigour and intelligence.[32] It is related that he exercised such control over the governors that they were never more honest or more just. One case, to be sure, may appear to have been marked by the cruelty of which he has been accused; for Civica Cerialis, pro-consul of Asia about A.D. 89, was put to death by his command. The

---

[m] *Ins. Priene* 229.

ground for this act of violence was alleged participation in a conspiracy to overthrow the Emperor. If, as has been supposed, the procurator Gaius Minicius Italus, who "by command of the Emperor" governed Asia "in place of the deceased proconsul," was made acting-governor on the occasion of Cerialis's death, a step so unusual as the appointment of a personal agent of the emperor to the governorship of a senatorial province suggests that there was indeed a situation which necessitated vigorous action. This appointment may well have been considered high-handed by the Senators, but in fact it had no real significance. There is no reason to suppose that Italus was not promptly replaced by a senatorial governor, and no precedent was created by his appointment, for there is no other known instance until the early third century of a procurator serving in Asia "in place of the proconsul."

In general, the statement regarding the excellent character of provincial governors under Domitian is borne out by what is actually known of the men who held office in the provinces of the East. It is true that the number of those available for appointment to these posts was in large measure due to the discernment of Vespasian; for during his command in Judaea he had had opportunity to mark men of outstanding ability, whom he subsequently enabled to enter an official career.[33] One of these, for example, a Spaniard by origin, Marcus Ulpius Trajanus, father of the later Emperor, became proconsul of Asia in Vespasian's last year. His term of office was marked by the construction of public works in various cities, not only the stadium at Laodiceia already mentioned and an aqueduct at Smyrna, but also by the rebuilding of the wall surrounding the precinct of the old Temple of Augustus at Ephesus as well as by monuments at Miletus and Myndus on which he was called "Benefactor."

It was presumably by retaining in service the men selected by Vespasian that Domitian was able to find provincial officials of high character. Of those who, having begun their careers under his father, were promoted by him from one administrative post to another were the natives of Asia, Celsus Polemaeanus and Julius Quadratus, both of them, during Trajan's principate, governors of the province. Tacitus, the historian, whose career was "greatly advanced" by Domitian, afterward governed Asia; and Pliny, whom Trajan later chose as his own personal representative in Bithynia, owed Domitian both his elevation to the Senatorial Order and his promotion in office.

Among the governors of Asia during Domitian's principate were Lucius Mestrius Florus, a scholarly man and a friend of Plutarch, proconsul in the year 83/4; Sextus Julius Frontinus, perhaps Florus's predecessor in the proconsulship, later supervisor of the aqueducts of Rome and the author of books on the city's water-supply and other subjects; Lucius Luscius Ocrea, who had governed Lycia under Vespasian; Lucius Junius Caesennius Paetus, who had served as tribune of a legion under Corbulo in Armenia; and Publius Calvisius Ruso Julius Frontinus, who had been enrolled by Vespasian among the patricians and was later (about 107) governor of the united province of Galatia-Cappadocia.[34]

For the appointment of these proconsuls the Senate was, of course, nominally responsible, but in view of Domitian's domination of that body, it may be supposed that he had a voice in their selection. In the imperial provinces, however, for whose governors Domitian was directly responsible, those of his appointees who are known appear to have been able and competent men. In the huge province of Galatia-Cappadocia, the credit for appointing the great builder of roads, Aulus Caesennius Gallus, belongs to Titus, not to Domitian.[n] But the latter chose Tiberius Julius Candidus Marius Celsus, twice Consul and "Master" of the priestly college of the Arval Brethren;[o] L. Antistius Rusticus, who, after commanding the Eighth Legion, stationed on the Rhine, had been, successively, governor of one of the Spanish provinces and prefect of the senatorial treasury;[p] and Titus Pomponius Bassus, who, retaining his office under Domitian's successors, continued the construction of roads begun by Gallus,[q] and, in his old age, was said to "have held most important offices, to have commanded armies and to have devoted himself, for as long a time as befitted, to public affairs."[r]

In Lycia-Pamphylia men of similar character held the office of governor. Gaius Caristanius Fronto, a native of Antioch-near-Pisidia, who had commanded a legion in Britain, was appointed governor of the province by Titus but continued to hold office under Domitian.[35] His successor, probably, was Publius Baebius Italicus, in office in the year 85, who had commanded the Fourteenth Legion, stationed in Germany, and had been decorated in Domitian's war against the Chatti; during his incumbency in Lycia he was honoured by the city of Tlos as "Founder and righteous Governor." If, as has been supposed, he was the Baebius Italicus who, perhaps in his youth, wrote the *Latin Iliad*, an epitome (with variations) of the Homeric poem in 1,070 hexameter lines, he was not without pretensions as a versifier.

---

[n] See note 14. [o] *C.I.L.* III 250; See *R.E.* x 539f. [p] See note 22.
[q] See below p. 595. [r] Pliny *Epist.* IV 23.

Other governors were the distinguished Pergamene, Gaius Antius Aulus Julius Quadratus, the holder of important offices in all the eastern provinces, who was in Lycia probably immediately before his consulship in 93, and Lucius Domitius Apollinaris, a friend of Pliny and presumably the Apollinaris described by the poet Martial as a learned man but a fair and kindly critic.

A special consideration for the economic welfare of the eastern provinces was shown about A.D. 92, when Domitian, in an effort—repeated in modern times—to lessen the dependence of Italy on imported grain by increasing her ability to supply herself, issued an edict prohibiting any further planting of vines in the country.[36] Its purpose, probably, was to make more land available for the production of grain. In the provinces, according to the terms of this edict, not more than one half of the present number of vines might remain in existence. The order was generally unpopular, but nowhere more than in the province of Asia, where, particularly in Ionia, the production and exportation of wine played an important part in the economic life of the people. The matter was taken up by the provincial Assembly, and a special delegate, the orator Scopelianus of Smyrna, was despatched to Rome to protest. He was successful in his plea and Asia was exempted from the application of the edict; he even persuaded the Emperor, it is said, to impose a fine on those who failed to plant additional vines.

Nevertheless, there is reason to believe that, even in its application to the eastern provinces, the prohibition contained in this edict was not without wisdom. The procuring of an adequate supply of grain had always constituted a serious problem for the cities of Asia Minor, and even with the improved means of communication the danger of a shortage which had constantly been imminent during the Hellenistic period continued also under Roman rule.[8] Despite the increased centralization, the task of providing for the needs of a local population devolved upon the municipal authorities, for the imperial government concerned itself only with the requirements of the city of Rome. At best, the produce of a city's territory barely sufficed for the needs of its inhabitants, and in the event of the failure of a harvest it became necessary to import grain from elsewhere. This process was not only expensive but often difficult, for the causes of the failure were frequently wide-spread: and for the importation of grain from Egypt, the great granary on which Italy depended, a special authorization from

[8] See Rostovtzeff *S.E.H.R.E.* p. 137f.

the imperial government was ordinarily demanded. In fact, there is striking evidence to show the need of stimulating production in Asia Minor during this period.

The dearth existing at the end of Vespasian's principate in the Bithynian city of Prusa is shown by the situation known from a speech of the orator Dio.[37] Angered by the high prices, the city-proletariat was incited by its leaders against the rich and privileged class and especially against Dio, who, having recently invested money in the construction of a handsome portico with workshops to be rented out to tenants, became the principal object of their rage. The mob attacked the Orator's house with stones and firebrands, and only a sudden panic in the crowd saved the inmates. The general anger, however, persisted, and Dio, in order to allay it, deemed it necessary to promise that he would himself assume the burden of supervising the city's supply of grain.

A somewhat similar situation in the Roman colony of Antioch-near-Pisidia, which, by a striking coincidence, occurred just at the time of Domitian's order, brought about drastic action on the part of the governor of the province, Lucius Antistius Rusticus.[38] In consequence of a particularly severe winter, the harvest had been a failure, with the result that grain prices soared and the magistrates and Council of the city presented a petition to the Governor requesting him to make it possible for the people to purchase necessary supplies. In response to this request, Rusticus issued an edict ordering that every inhabitant of Antioch (citizens of the colony as well as mere "residents") should report to the magistrates within thirty days the quantity of grain in his possession and the amount which he needed both for the support of his household during the current year and for his next planting; the penalty for failing to make this declaration was confiscation by the government. All grain not needed for these two purposes was to be offered for sale to the people of the city at a price not to exceed one denarius per *modius* (quarter-bushel) or double the ordinary purchase-price.

How wide-spread this dearth may have been is not known. If, as has been suggested, this was the famine represented by the third of the Four Horsemen of the Apocalypse, who announced "a measure of wheat for a denarius and three measures of barley for a denarius,"[39] it may be conjectured that the severe winter affected the harvest in a large portion of Asia Minor. In any case, as time went on, a shortage of grain was a not infrequent calamity, and during the second century, as will presently be shown,[t] there were numerous cases in which it became necessary for an official to assume the burden of providing his fellow-townsmen with an opportunity for buying the grain they needed at a price which they could afford to pay.

With the assassination of Domitian in September of the year 96 the Flavian dynasty came to an end, for the Emperor left no heir. The century and a quarter which had elapsed since the victory of Augustus at Actium had seen a cessation of the strife which had brought economic ruin to the eastern provinces; for, except for the forays of the Cilician mountaineers, there had been no fighting west of the Euphrates. The establishment of the *Pax Romana* and the rise of a spirit of confidence in the *eternity* of the Roman Empire as ensuring general peace and happiness,[40] accompanied by a wide-spread improvement in world-conditions, had made it possible to develop the great natural resources of western Asia Minor and had introduced an era of prosperity such as the country had never known even under its native kings. A versifier at the end of the first century, expressing in the form of an oracle the actual conditions of his time, described it thus: "Great wealth shall come to Asia, wealth which once Rome, having gained it by rapine, stored in a house of surpassing riches, but anon she will make a twofold restitution to Asia; then there will be a surfeit of strife."[41]

Of this prosperity there is an apparent indication in the expenditure of money in the cities of the province of Asia in the late first and the early second centuries. This appears in the construction of buildings financed from the municipal incomes but chiefly in the gifts presented by generous individuals.[u] Of these donors, some were natives of the province who had attained to office under the Roman government, like Servenius Cornutus, the legate of a proconsul of Asia under Vespasian, who received the title of Benefactor at Acmonia, apparently the home of his family,[v] and Julius Quadratus and Aquila Polemaeanus, both of whom were Consuls in Rome and benefactors, respectively, of Pergamum and Ephesus, their native cities. Most of the donors, however, although in some cases Roman citizens, were members of the various communities, who gave liberally of their wealth for the benefit of their fellow-citizens.

These gifts included money used for the construction, improvement

t See Chap. XXVII note 42.
u See Broughton in *Econ. Surv.* iv p. 746f. and A. H. M. Jones *Greek City* pp. 237 and 356.
v *I.G.R.* iv 644 = *O.G.I.* 482 = Dessau 8817.

or repair of public buildings; for the maintenance of social centres, especially the gymnasium, for which funds were provided for lighting and for heating as well as for the purchase of the oil needed by the bathers; for the foundation of festivals, accompanied by contests at which prizes were given to the victors; and for the demoralizing practice of bestowing doles, not only on the lower orders of the populace but on those of the upper classes as well. Usually, the gifts were made outright, but sometimes they were in the form of an endowment, the income from which was to be used for a specified purpose.

Of the cities which thus profited from the prosperity of the time, the most conspicuous example was Ephesus, the official residence of the proconsul of Asia and the seat of the great Temple of Artemis. It was said of Ephesus early in the second century that "it had increased in size beyond all the cities of Ionia and Lydia and, having outgrown the land on which it was built, had advanced into the sea," and again that it was regarded by all as "the common treasury of Asia and her recourse in need."[w]

The city itself, besides contributing to the cost of constructing the magnificent Temple of the Augusti, already described, supplied the money needed for repairing the theatre.[42] In the time of Nero, probably, a wealthy freedman presented public buildings as well as endowments for the distribution of money to the citizens. During the Flavian period a great gymnasium was built and, adjoining it, a triple colonnade enclosing a large open space for exercise. Other colonnades were decorated with mosaics and variegated marble, exedras were embellished by various donors, and two citizens not only erected harbour-buildings but also gave money for improving the theatre, besides presenting funds for gladiatorial combats and for distributions and banquets for the populace.

An especially generous donor was Gaius Vibius Salutaris, a member of the city-council at Ephesus and of the Equestrian Order in Rome.[43] His gifts to the city, made in 104 and by a subsequent bequest, consisted of thirty-one gold and silver statuettes, including those of Artemis, the Emperor Trajan and his wife and personifications of the Senate, the Equestrian Order and the Roman People, and also, in two installments, the capital sum of 21,500 denarii for an endowment, the income of which was to be distributed yearly among the city-councillors, the members of the Elders' Association, the ephebi and their president, the boys and their supervisors and the citizens enrolled in the six

---

[w] Philostratus *Vit. Apoll.* VIII 7, 28: Aristides *Orat.* XXIII 24 Keil.

city-tribes, with appropriations for choristers, sacred bards, and others connected with the worship of Artemis.

The most famous of all the gifts to Ephesus during this period was perhaps the great public library dedicated to the memory of Tiberius Julius Celsus Polemaeanus, a native of the city, who, after having held various administrative posts, had been proconsul of Asia.[44] The building was erected and endowed in the early second century by Polemaeanus's son and completed by the latter's heirs. Contemporary with it was another large structure, fronting on one of the streets leading to the harbour and consisting of a great hall with a room at either end, which has been regarded as either the *Mouseion*, a centre for the instruction of the youth and the headquarters of the physicians of the city, or a sort of bazaar for the exhibition and sale of merchandise.[45]

In Smyrna, the chief commercial rival of Ephesus, with a far superior harbour, there is evidence of a similar prosperity. The place itself was famous for its beauty, which led an orator to declare that "were the likeness of any city to appear in the heavens, as did, according to report, that of Ariadne's crown," it would indeed be the likeness of Smyrna; for "all the way down to the shore it is resplendent with gymnasia, market-places, theatres, sacred precincts and harbours, beautiful works of nature vying with those wrought by man, and there is nothing which does not serve both for ornament and for use."[x]

Under the proconsul Trajanus, in the year 79/80, the Temple of Zeus was provided with an aqueduct, which, although it bore the Proconsul's name, was probably constructed by the city.[46] About the same time a citizen presented the Temple of Apollo with a statue of the god himself and other gifts, including a colonnade for the use of the temple-attendants. Another colonnade and a monumental gate were built with money bequeathed by a former tribune of a Roman legion, an association, apparently athletic in character, was presented with an endowment for a yearly distribution of money to its members, and a fund for the improvement of the harbour was raised by a number of contributors.

Like Ephesus, Smyrna had a *Mouseion*, frequented throughout the second century by scholars and men of letters, who gave instruction in both rhetoric and law.[47] The presence of some of these is known from the tombstones of two "philologians" and the mention of Herodotus, a "philosopher of Smyrna." Among them was also a certain Theon, described as a "Platonic philosopher," who was, in fact,

[x] Aristides *Orat.* XVII 8 and 11 Keil.

the author of an extant treatise "On the Use of Mathematics for the Study of Plato." The city had also an Asclepieium, a resort of physicians, one of whom, Hermogenes, although ridiculed by two of his contemporaries, was evidently a man of both learning and industry; for it is said that during a lifetime of seventy-seven years he wrote seventy-seven books on medicine as well as seventeen others on various subjects, including the "Origins" of cities in Asia and Europe, a history of Smyrna and the "Wisdom'" and "Native City" of Homer.

In Pergamum, which, although less of a commercial centre than either Ephesus or Smyrna, was still a place of prime importance, "by far the most renowned of Asia,"[y] the chief benefactor was Julius Quadratus, a native of the city who crowned an illustrious career as a Roman official by becoming proconsul of Asia.[48] His gifts included a restoration of the sanctuary of Dionysus Cathegemon, whose priest he was, and an endowment for a festival held in connexion with the temple erected in honour of Zeus and the Emperor Trajan. One of his freedmen, following his example, contributed to the adornment of the Temple of Asclepius. Other indications of the wealth of the city were the rebuilding, apparently by a general subscription, of the gymnasium of the Young Men—one of the six or seven in Pergamum—including a portico and an anointing-room, and the gift of new columns and vaulting for another portico, the architect of which, Julius Nicodemus, father of the famous physician Galen, used part of the structure for his office as supervisor of the city's markets.[49] Other gifts were a contribution of 70,000 drachmae, apparently for the festival in honour of Zeus and Trajan, a bequest to the city of 100,000 drachmae, and the benefactions of C. Julius Maximus, a former legionary tribune, who, after retiring to Pergamum, held various offices, including those of priest for life of Apollo Pythius and gymnasiarch of all the gymnasia, and, honoured by the Young Men for his "unsurpassed generosity" to their association, "strove by means of his offerings to beautify his native city."

These three cities, each with a population of at least 200,000, were the richest and the largest in the province of Asia.[50] But in Miletus also, although it had yielded its former primacy to Ephesus and Smyrna, it was possible, at the end of the first century, to rebuild one side of the great North Market, with the addition of a large number of rooms for the use of merchants, and to erect a public bath and, a little later, an ornamental fountain known as the Nymphaeum.[51]

[y] Pliny N.H. v 126.

At the sanctuary of Apollo at Didyma, moreover, the sacred officials not only enlarged and improved the buildings but gave entertainments and distributions of money both to residents of the sacred precinct and to the councillors and citizens of the city itself.

In the interior of Lydia the cities enjoyed a corresponding, if more moderate, degree of prosperity. This appears in a modest gift of 1,575 denarii and the bequest of an endowment for distribution of money at Sardis and in gifts and an endowment for distributions at Philadelpheia.[52] At Thyateira both the *demos* and private donors erected various buildings, including a group of dwellings surrounded by colonnades with an ornamental gateway, and a certain Tiberius Claudius Socrates, a gymnasiarch, and his son beautified their native place by erecting public works. Even a slave-dealer, who held the office of supervisor of markets and streets, presented gifts to the citizens on the emperors' birthdays. At Tralles also much was done for the benefit of the city. Of two men who had held public office, one gave twenty columns for the market-place with marble incrustation and mosaics for an exedra, as well as an endowment for an annual present of 250 denarii to each councillor, the other erected a colonnade in the form of a peristyle with rooms in the upper storey, the rentals from which were to serve for the maintenance of the building. Another citizen, who had been gymnasiarch, paid the expenses of the three gymnasia of the city for four months.

In Phrygia, Laodiceia, in spite of the damage resulting from the earthquake in the time of Nero,[z] could be represented as boasting, "I am rich and increased with goods and have need of nothing."[a] In addition to the stadium and the city-gate, already mentioned, which were dedicated to Titus and Domitian,[b] several gifts, among them the white marble pavement in front of the Temple of Zeus, were presented to the city by a Roman citizen who had held various local offices, and two other men, an uncle and nephew, bequeathed money to the Council as an endowment, the interest of which was to provide garlands for their tombs.[53]

In Caria the principal cities also enjoyed a high degree of prosperity. At Aphrodisias the Ionic temple of Aphrodite, now in ruins, to which contributions were made by many citizens, was erected in the second century, and a great public bath dates from the same time.[54] During the Flavian period, however, aqueducts and reservoirs were constructed, and later various donors made generous gifts. Among

[z] See above p. 564. [a] *Apocalypse* III 17. [b] See above pp. 572 and 577.

them was Attalus Adrastus, who presented the Goddess with the sum of 122,000 denarii, part to be used for a building containing a place for sacrifice and a hall for public banquets and part to create an endowment for its maintenance. Other gifts of his, supplemented by a bequest, amounting to 264,174 denarii, were devoted to enlarging the area of a gymnasium and endowing the posts of gymnasiarch and stephanephorus. Another benefactor, Marcus Ulpius Carminius Claudianus, treasurer of the Commonalty of Asia, provided the "Gymnasium of Diogenes" with an anointing-room and a great hall supported by marble columns; he also presented the city with money, in all 110,000 denarii, to be spent on public works, which included seats for the theatre and a square surrounded by colonnades, besides making presents on various occasions to all the citizens and the strangers in the city and creating an endowment for the distribution of money to the councillors and the members of the Elders' Association. Another endowment was bequeathed by Titus Flavius Lysimachus to found a quadrennial musical and dramatic contest named after himself.

At Stratoniceia there is little record of the construction, during this period, of public works in the city itself. The theatre, to be sure, which dated from Hellenistic times, seems to have been repaired or rebuilt in the early second century, a public bath was erected, and an "atrium for a bath," "costing not a few myriads," was presented by another donor.[55] At the temples of Panamara and Lagina in the city's territory, however, there was lavish expenditure on the part of the priests. At Panamara a priest of Hera and his wife not only repaired the Temple itself but also gave a vaulted building with various embellishments, some of which were made of white marble, and other priests of the Goddess decorated or repaired both the Temple and buildings connected with it, including a colonnade and a banqueting-hall. At Lagina Tiberius Flavius Menander, who gave the atrium at Stratoniceia, built the atrium of the Upper Gymnasium, and other priests of Hecate restored colonnades.

Both at Panamara and at Lagina, moreover, it was incumbent on the priests on the occasion of the great festivals to give banquets and even presents of money to those attending, including not only citizens and resident Romans but strangers as well.[56] They had also to act as gymnasiarchs on certain days, when they furnished oil to those who came to the gymnasia in the sacred precincts and even provided theatrical entertainments. The priest of Zeus at Panamara was expected to give banquets in Stratoniceia itself, at which he presented the guests with money as well as with food and wine to be taken away; at two such banquets about the middle of the second century each citizen received twelve pounds of pork, beef and mutton and eight pounds of bread. The ability of these priests to meet the heavy expenses which their offices entailed indicates the long-continued existence in Stratoniceia of families of great wealth, which held the sacred offices from generation to generation.

In Bithynia the economic conditions prevailing at the end of the first and the beginning of the second century are known chiefly from the speeches of Dio Chrysostom, a native of Prusa, and from the letters of the younger Pliny, who was appointed governor of the province by Trajan about 110 and wrote frequently to the Emperor concerning problems arising in connexion with his administration.[c] The extant writings of both show an apparent wealth and prosperity not dissimilar to those which existed in the province of Asia. At Nicomedeia, which, as the centre of the worship of the emperors and the usual residence of the Roman governor, arrogated to itself the right to be called the "First City" and the "metropolis" of Bithynia, there was at this time a building-activity which suggests abundant riches.[57] The ship-owners, who, thanks to the excellent harbour and the roads leading into the interior, were evidently a prosperous group, erected a "house" to be used for the purposes of their business but perhaps containing a sanctuary of Vespasian, to whom the building was dedicated. The city itself, moreover, was ready to spend money freely. A project was formed to construct a canal connecting Lake Sophon, on the road to the East, with the harbour—a distance of some twelve miles with a difference in altitude of 120 feet—for the purpose of avoiding the transshipment of heavy materials brought from the interior and thus facilitating transportation to the sea. Again, in order to provide space for a new building, the citizens voted to demolish some ancient monuments, including even the tomb of King Prusias;[d] and when a second market-place was added to the one already in existence, there was no hesitation—except on the part of the Roman governor—in taking down the Temple of the Great Mother and removing it to another site.[e] The city also spent more than three and a half million sesterces on aqueducts, an outlay which was wasted, for before completion they were allowed to collapse, so that the water-supply was insufficient for the citizens' needs.[f]

[c] See below p. 596.
[e] Pliny *Epist. ad Trajan.* 49-50.

[d] Dio *Orat.* XLVII 16f. (A.D. 101).
[f] Pliny 37-38.

The neighbouring Nicaea, "inferior to none of the cities which were famous either for nobility of origin or for the number of inhabitants,"[g] also asserted the right to be entitled First City of Bithynia, a claim which caused a long-protracted antagonism between it and Nicomedeia.[58] Although somewhat over thirty miles from the Propontis, Nicaea had easy access to the sea through the port of Cius, and the roads leading eastward to Galatia and Phrygia ensured a thriving trade. A large part of the city's wealth, however, was derived from the fertility of its extensive territory, the cultivators of which paid tithes on the produce.

Evidence of building-activity under Vespasian appears in the erection of a city-gate shortly before the end of his principate. Somewhat later, the city spent ten million sesterces on a new theatre but without completing the building, and certain citizens promised to provide a colonnade around the top of the rows of seats as well as halls connected with the place.[h] Also, when the gymnasium had been destroyed by fire, the city-authorities began the construction of a new one on a much more extensive scale. Legacies bequeathed by citizens included one of 2,500 denarii willed to the Elders' Association to provide a "rose-festival" in memory of the testator.[59]

Of the other cities of Bithynia perhaps the foremost in interest and importance was Prusa at the foot of Mt. Olympus, a prosperous place which numbered many rich men among its citizens.[i] Among these was Dio, under whose influence, apparently, an ambitious building-programme was adopted in the hope that the city might be enlarged by the addition of people from the neighbourhood; for the plan, it was argued, would give Prusa "shade in summer, sun and shelter in winter and high buildings, worthy of a great city, in the place of low and mean ruins."[60] For carrying out these operations, both Dio himself and many other citizens promised to contribute money, and after an endorsement by the Roman governor the project was formally adopted by the public Assembly. The Orator even produced a letter from the Emperor—evidently Trajan—which seems to have given approval and expressed the wish that Prusa might increase in size. A beginning was made by removing some unsightly buildings and constructing a colonnade to flank the principal street of the city. The improvements, however, met with opposition, probably from those who feared expropriation, and Dio's enemies, taking advantage of this ill-feeling, criticized him bitterly in public on the ground that he wished to destroy

---

[g] Dio XXXIX 1.　　　　[h] Pliny 39.　　　　[i] Dio XL 30 and XLVI 6.

the city and even its holy places. Many of those, moreover, who had agreed to give the money necessary for the execution of the project were unable or unwilling to make their promises good. Ten years later, although a public building, containing a library, had been completed under Dio's supervision, the machinations of the Orator's enemies had prevented its formal transfer to the city.[j] At this time, in fact, much of the plan for beautifying Prusa was still unaccomplished. The public bath was old and squalid, and a once handsome house, which had been bequeathed to Claudius but under terms providing that the rental of the building should accrue to the city and a temple of Claudius should be built in the peristyle, had been allowed to fall into ruin.[k] Moreover, funds belonging to the community—so the governor, Pliny, reported—had been retained not only by the curators of public works but by certain private citizens as well.[l]

With regard to the smaller cities of the province information may be obtained not only from the letters of Pliny but also from inscriptions.[61] At the colony of Apameia Myrleia a colonnade and its site were dedicated by a Roman to Asclepius, and at Prusias-on-Hypius a bath was built, apparently from the bequest of a man who had been prefect of two auxiliary cohorts in the Roman army and tribune of two legions. At Claudiopolis (formerly Bithynium) a bath was begun, the cost of which was to be met from the fees paid by the newly-elected members of the Council, and two pieces of property in the neighbourhood of the city were bequeathed as an endowment for a rose-festival at the testator's tomb. At Amastris, "a handsome and well-equipped city," money was available for covering over a stream which had become a noisome sewer, and there was a "house of the ship-owners," built, presumably, for their use. A fund for the benefit of the poor was raised by a general subscription at Amisus, and there was a project for an aqueduct at Sinope, which also was to be built by contributions from the citizens. An unknown admirer of Pliny, moreover, leaving him a legacy of 50,000 sesterces, directed that the remainder of the estate should be divided between the cities of Heraclea and Tieium, to be used, as Pliny might decide, either for public buildings dedicated to Trajan or for contests bearing the Emperor's name.[m]

While it is undoubtedly true that, to a large extent, the liberality with which individual citizens gave money or buildings to their native

[j] Pliny 81-82. See below p. 602.   [k] Pliny 23 and 70.
[l] Pliny 17 and 23.   [m] Pliny 75.

cities was due to public spirit and a genuine desire to contribute to the general welfare, there were other reasons for their gifts.[62] Apart from the custom which made the payment of fees by those who held public offices practically compulsory, a long-established principle that a wealthy citizen should spend money on the community or make a bequest for the common good amounted almost to a real obligation. The example set by the more generous made it difficult for others to fail to live up to the precedent thus established. It was also expected that a citizen whose wealth made it possible would assume his share of the various "liturgies" or public services, as, for instance, the expenses of the gymnasium or the cost of a festival or of an official mission, such as an embassy to Rome.

The expenditure of money by a city, moreover, may not be regarded as affording definite proof that the municipal finances were in a healthy condition.[63] An apparent abundance of ready money, to be sure, is suggested by the statement of Pliny that on account of a lack of purchasable farm-lands—regarded generally as the safest form of investment[n]—and a dearth of borrowers at the prevailing interest-rate of 12 per cent the communities were unable to find ways of using their surplus funds.[o] Nevertheless, there was a recklessness, indeed often dishonesty, on the part of those in authority which must frequently have proved detrimental to the economic welfare of the community concerned. The waste of the money spent on the aqueducts at Nicomedeia, whether due, as the Emperor suggested,[p] to a desire to benefit certain contractors or to a general incapacity, indicates a lack of conscientiousness in managing the public finances, and a similar carelessness was shown in the failure of the city-authorities to provide for any apparatus for extinguishing fires.[q] It was presumably also through a like irresponsibility at Nicaea that the construction of the theatre was so faulty that the building soon began to settle and fall apart and that the money provided for a new gymnasium was in danger of being wasted because the plan was bad and the walls had been pronounced too weak.[r] There was mismanagement also at Prusa, where, as has been previously noted, public money was not only spent illegitimately but even permitted to remain in the hands both of certain citizens and of those in charge of the buildings of the city.[s]

Recklessness and extravagance in the management of the public finances had long existed in the Hellenic communities of Asia Minor,

[n] See *e.g. I.G.R.* IV 915. [o] Pliny 54. [p] Pliny 38.
[q] Pliny 33. [r] Pliny 39. [s] See above p. 590.

the wealth of whose natural resources enabled the local authorities to spend money lavishly and often unwisely. Such a course, however, was highly precarious, and in the event of a decline of these resources it might easily lead to bankruptcy. This, indeed, might possibly be averted by the control exercised by a strong, centralized rule, salutary perhaps for communities no longer able to make the right use of the liberty they had once enjoyed, but at the same time destructive of the sense of responsibility which is wont to disappear under the imposition of regimentation.[64]

CHAPTER XXV

TRAJAN, ADMINISTRATOR AND CONQUEROR

WITH the accession to power of the elderly senator, Marcus Cocceius Nerva, whom his colleagues proclaimed Emperor after the assassination of Domitian, the Roman imperial system entered upon a new phase. Hitherto, save for the disastrous year after the death of Nero, when claimants to the Empire rose and fell in civil war, each new ruler had assumed the power on the basis of a dynastic succession. But when Domitian died without heirs no such claim could be advanced, and a new principle was introduced, namely, that the man best fitted to rule should be chosen by the emperor through the process of adoption.[1] When, after eighty-five years, this adoptive principle gave way to the dynastic, the principate was soon replaced by a military monarchy.

The rule of Nerva, of only sixteen months' duration, was characterized, in contrast to the despotism of Domitian, by an observance of constitutional forms, a policy which even impelled him to spare professional accusers hated for the charges they had preferred against the victims of his predecessor's cruelty.[a] But perhaps the greatest benefit which he conferred on the Empire was the adoption as his successor of Marcus Ulpius Trajanus, commander of the legions stationed along the upper Rhine and son of the Trajanus who under Vespasian had been proconsul of Asia.[b] A man of outstanding ability and energy, in fact no less of an autocrat than Domitian but without the latter's cruelty, Trajan administered the provinces carefully and with a firm hand, continuing the centralizing tendencies which marked the rule of the Flavians. At the same time, adopting an aggressive policy of expansion, he extended the Empire by annexing countries hitherto beyond its boundaries.

Despite the process of centralization, the free cities of Asia still preserved a semblance of their former status. The character of this status, however, was expressed in the paradoxical description of Aphrodisias and Stratoniceia in Caria as "free and autonomous from the beginning by grace of the Augusti" which appears in dedications erected by the two cities at Ephesus under Domitian and reveals the extent to which their liberty was dependent on the emperor's will.[2] A similar status

a Pliny *Epist.* I 5, 15; IV 22, 4f.: Cassius Dio LXVIII I, 3.
b See Chap. XXIV note 33.

appears to have been granted to Mazaca-Caesareia in Cappadocia, a place which had no traditional claim to independence; a coin was issued bearing Nerva's portrait and the legend "Freedom of the People." Nevertheless, the right of a free city to make and enforce its own laws was respected; when it was proposed at Amisus to form an association for aiding the poor, Trajan ruled that, provided the laws of the city permitted the existence of such organizations and the members used their funds for legitimate purposes, any interference on the part of the government was unjustified.[3]

It may be inferred, moreover, from the honours and the extravagant titles, characteristic of the later Greeks, which were conferred on both Nerva and Trajan that favours were granted to many of the cities. The former was called Common Benefactor, Saviour of the province and the city and Patron at Teos; a building was dedicated to him at Thyateira, a priest was created for his worship—perhaps after his death—at Aphrodisias, and statues of him were erected in several places.[4] Instances of honours conferred on Trajan are much more numerous. On a statue erected at Pergamum he was called Lord of Land and Sea, and at Chios and Eresus he had the more extravagant title of Saviour of the World.[5] At Mitylene, toward the end of his principate, as many as eleven "thank-offerings" record expressions of gratitude, perhaps due to aid in repairing the damage resulting from an earthquake which caused great destruction in the cities on the neighbouring coast of Aeolis. At Miletus at least six statues of Trajan testified to the gratitude of the Council and People for his action in rebuilding the "Sacred Way" from the city to the Temple of Apollo at Didyma. He and his wife and other relatives received honours also in other places in the province of Asia, among them Ephesus, Magnesia, Aphrodisias and Apameia, at Apollonia and Sagalassus in Pisidia, and in some of the cities of Lycia.[6]

Of the many monuments in honour of Trajan by far the greatest was a magnificent temple at Pergamum.[7] This sanctuary, a large peripteral building with columns of the Corinthian order, was placed in a conspicuous position on almost the highest point of the great rock on which the city stood. Erected, presumably, by the province of Asia, it was shared by Zeus "the Friendly," who was worshipped here together with the Emperor. A quadrennial festival, with contests held in honour of the two deities, was endowed by the wealthy Pergamene, Julius Quadratus, whose gift was formally accepted by the Senate. The possession of this second temple dedicated to an emperor made it possible for the title-loving people of Pergamum to assume, doubtless with the Senate's endorsement, the honorary appellation of "Twice Temple-warden of the Augusti," a distinction likewise obtained some years later by both Smyrna and Ephesus.[c]

Following the example of previous emperors, Trajan adopted a policy of urbanization by founding or refounding cities, which he named after himself.[8] One of these, a new community, was placed near the ancient city of Grimenothyrae on the border of Lydia and Phrygia. The other was the Seleucid city of Epiphaneia in Cilicia, which, to be sure, retained its new name for only a brief time. Each was but a short distance from a place which Vespasian had called Flaviopolis. This was probably no coincidence but the result of the wish of both emperors to place the cities in strategic positions. The Lydian Trajanopolis was on or near the line of the Royal Road, and the Cilician city commanded the road leading through the depression in the hills west of the range of Amanus to the province of Syria, a route of importance to Rome during Trajan's war—to be described presently—against the Parthians.[d]

The development of the country, promoted by this urbanization, was furthered also by the construction of roads. The work, begun by the Flavian emperors, of "restoring" the road which led from Sardis to Thyateira and ultimately to Pergamum was continued by Nerva, and Trajan seems to have repaired at least one road near Cyzicus.[9] Much more important, however, was the construction carried on in eastern Asia Minor by Titus Pomponius Bassus, who, appointed imperial governor of the united provinces of Galatia and Cappadocia by Domitian, remained in office until the year 100 or later.[10] In the southern part of his province he repaired the road leading from Mazaca-Caesareia to Tyana and the Cilician Gates, but a far greater achievement was his work in Pontus. Here he "restored" the routes from Ancyra in Galatia to Amaseia in Pontus and from here either to the valley of the Lycus or through southern Pontus to Cappadocia, as well as a road along the lower Lycus. He seems also to have rebuilt a section of the great highway which led from the Lycus through Phazimonitis to Paphlagonia and Bithynia.

With all the readiness shown by the emperors to confer privileges and favours on the cities, it appeared necessary to take measures which, however conducive to their welfare, could not but seem to curtail their right of self-administration. The general recklessness in expenditure

[c] See below pp. 615 and 619.   [d] See below p. 606f.

and irresponsibility in managing the public finances, already noticed, were a matter of concern to the imperial government; for the impoverishment of the communities might easily render it difficult for them to pay the taxes demanded by Rome and even necessitate grants of subsidies to local treasuries.[e]

Some effort had been made by the Flavian emperors to check the tendency toward extravagance. Vespasian, as has already been noticed, caused certain of the cities of Lycia to practise economy,[f] and, in order to lessen generally the expenses of communities, he issued an edict ordering that no delegation sent to the emperor should consist of more than three members.[g] Under Trajan, however, there were more systematic attempts to exercise a supervision over the financial affairs of cities, including even those which still retained their freedom. It was evidently for this purpose that, about 108, the Emperor despatched a special legate to Greece "to set the affairs of the free cities in order."[11] Bearing, unofficially, the title of *Corrector*, this commissioner was vested with full authority, symbolized by a right to use the *fasces*. Shortly afterward, about 110, Trajan took the further step of causing the Senate to transfer to him temporarily the control of the province of Bithynia-Pontus, where, as will be shown, conditions were in great need of reform, in order to appoint a special commissioner to act as *corrector* of the whole province. To this post the Emperor named Gaius Plinius Caecilius Secundus as imperial legate vested with consular power.[12] Both Trajan and Pliny himself regarded the position as that of a deputy, "sent to the province in the Emperor's place." Whatever administrative problems, therefore, however trivial they might appear, seemed to involve any principle of wider application were referred to Trajan for decision.

The special task assigned to Pliny by the Emperor was "to examine the accounts of the cities, for it is well established that they are in a state of disorder."[h] To this task, accordingly, he devoted much attention. In order to prevent a further waste of money on the construction of the aqueducts at Nicomedeia, he proposed to utilize old material as far as possible and to employ an engineer to supervise the work.[i] A similar waste at both Nicaea and Claudiopolis, where large sums had been spent on public buildings of faulty construction or in an unfavourable situation, might also be obviated, he suggested, by obtaining expert advice.[j] At Prusa he pointed out that if an architectural

---

[e] Pliny *Epist. ad Trajan.* 24 and 91. [f] See above p. 530. [g] *Digesta* L 7, 5, 6.
[h] Pliny 18, 3. [i] Pliny 37-38. [j] Pliny 39-40.

survey were made, "no small sums might be recovered from the cura-tors of public works" and that if he could recover the city's funds which had fallen into the hands of certain persons, it would even be possible to build a bath.[k]

It was Pliny's duty also to effect economies in the more highly-privileged communities—a task of greater difficulty because in these the management of the public finances was a long-established right. Finding that the free city of Byzantium, which had been committed to his care, was spending a large amount of money each year on send-ing envoys with congratulatory messages both to the Emperor and to the neighbouring governor of Moesia, he forbad this practice and arranged for the transmission of the messages in a less costly manner.[l] In the Roman colonies it was even more difficult to prevent resent-ment at what might have been regarded as interference on the part of the governor of the province. Nevertheless, at Sinope Pliny under-took to obtain contributions from the citizens for the construction of the aqueduct.[m] At Apameia he found it advisable to carry out the formality of requesting the local officials to permit him to examine the colony's accounts.[n] The request was granted, but with a protest to the effect that hitherto no governor of the province had made such an examination, since the colony had the right to administer its own affairs; and, in fact, when Pliny asked the Emperor to confirm the proposed action, Trajan, while endorsing this inspection, emphasized the general principle that the city's rights should be observed.

The careful attention to the financial affairs of the provincials which impelled Trajan to appoint a *corrector* for free cities and a represen-tative of his own to govern Bithynia led him also to name a special agent with the title of *Curator* for the purpose of supervising the property and finances of communities.[13] It was the duty of this official, when necessary, to remedy bad economic conditions by causing the civic organizations to conduct their affairs with greater efficiency and economy. This post, to be sure, may have been created under Domitian, but in any case it was developed by Trajan, who appointed auditors of this kind in cities both in the eastern and in the western provinces, and it was widely employed by his successors. Unlike the *corrector*, whose duties included a number of communities, or indeed a whole province, the curator in almost every known instance was charged with the care of a single city; it was considered a matter for special

k Pliny 17, 5 and 23.   l Pliny 43.
m Pliny 90; see Chap. XXIV note 61.   n Pliny 47-48.

mention when an important imperial official served as curator at the same time of the three Bithynian cities, Nicomedeia, Nicaea and Prusa. In the larger communities the curator was usually a member of the Equestrian, or even the Senatorial, Order. In those of less importance, on the other hand, he was ordinarily a provincial, and in the course of time, as a result of the growing practice of appointing Asiatics to high office, natives of the provinces acted in this capacity in the principal cities also. Ordinarily named for a definite term, the curator might be reappointed, and one man is known to have held his post for life. As time went on, the office tended more and more to become permanent, differing little from a local magistracy, so that inscriptions were sometimes dated by the name of the curator of the current year.

Entirely independent of the civic officials and subordinate only to the governor of the province, the curator was charged with the general supervision of the property belonging to the community. He was responsible for the investment and legitimate use of communal funds, including legacies bequeathed for civic purposes and money expended in the purchase of grain, as well as for the maintenance and the leases of public lands and the construction and care of public buildings. Although without judicial powers, so that he was unable to impose fines, he had authority to veto not only illegal appropriations of money made by local councils to private persons but also the remission of debts owed to the community. A curator at Ephesus, for example, about the middle of the second century was charged by the emperor with the task of auditing the accounts of city-officials for the purpose of taking over any balances which they might owe the city. At Aphrodisias, later in the same century, a curator endorsed the use of the prize-money won by a victorious athlete for the erection of a statue by the young man's father, and authorized the local council and magistrates to use for a public festival a fund bequeathed some time previously to the city, since the income had now reached the requisite amount. The curators of Phellus in Lycia were named by the owner of a tomb both as the recipients of information concerning any violation of the monument and as collectors of the fine to be paid to the city by the violator. During the second century, moreover, a curator occasionally supervised the finances of a society, such as a local Elders' Association, the Artists of Dionysus and a musical society at Rhodes; in one case a man was even appointed curator of a city-council. It is probable that the powers of the office were left somewhat vague and undefined, in order that, should the need arise, the curator, as an imperial commissioner, might take whatever action seemed likely to ensure the execution of the emperor's will. The activity of such an appointee, however, conducive though it might be to efficiency in administration, encroached on the powers of the local officials and hence could not fail to appear detrimental to the principle of self-government. The creation of this office, in fact, was an important step in the extension of the central authority. Since, however, it gradually developed into what amounted to merely another local magistracy, it finally brought about what has been described as "a certain centralization of local government from within."[o]

In addition to extravagance and irresponsibility in dealing with the public finances, the cities suffered from other serious evils, arising from the age-old inability of the Greeks to live in harmony with one another. In some cases, rivalry between cities and even petty jealousy caused bitter feuds. The enmity between Nicomedeia and Nicaea, known from the speeches of Dio Chrysostom, which arose from the resentment of the citizens of the former at the Nicaeans' claim to the title of First City of Bithynia has already been described.[p] There was enmity also between Prusa and the neighbouring colony of Apameia, which in spite of an economic interdependence—for Prusa needed the harbour-facilities of Apameia and the latter the timber of Mt. Olympus —was of long standing and hard to allay.[q] While the cause of this quarrel is not definitely known, it was evidently a question of money, perhaps income from lands but more probably the payment of harbour or customs dues by the one city to the other. So bitter was the feeling that Dio, although he deprecated the state of affairs and urged his fellow-townsmen to put an end to the feud, believed that he could not respond to the overtures which the Apameians made to him personally as enjoying the rights of citizenship in their city until the Council of Prusa named him as a member of a commission appointed to restore harmony between the two places.

There was similar enmity in the other provinces also. In Asia there was a feud between Ephesus and Smyrna.[r] In Cilicia the claim of the wealthy city of Tarsus to pre-eminence as well as to certain lands of which the ownership was disputed aroused the hostility of other communities, notably Aegaeae, Mallus, Soli and Adana.[s]

[o] C. Lucas in *J.R.S.* xxx (1940), p. 70.   [p] See above p. 589.
[q] Dio *Orat.* xl 16f. and xli 7f. See von Arnim *Dio v. Prusa* p. 358f.
[r] Dio xxxiv 48. See von Arnim p. 463.   [s] Dio xxxiv 7, 10-14, 27 and 43-48.

An even greater evil was the discord existing within the cities themselves, arising from the ancient and wide-spread source of class-hatred.[14] The policy adopted by the Romans of so arranging the constitutions of the cities as to give the wealthier citizens a preponderance of power aroused the envy and hostility of those who had not participated in the influence and prosperity of this class and were ready to follow agitators promising to better their social and economic condition. The attack made by the mob on Dio's house, already mentioned,[t] although directly motivated by resentment at his building-activity, was primarily due to hostility against a man of wealth. There was evidently the same class-enmity at Nicaea, where Dio, in the course of a speech, uttered a prayer that the gods might grant the citizens love for one another with unanimity of thought and wish, casting out strife and envy.[u] In fact, the disorder at Prusa arising from this bitterness became so great that the Roman governor found it necessary to issue an edict depriving the citizens of the right to hold public assemblies.[v] Dio also mentions an "evil governor" who tyrannized over the province, going so far in his repressive measures as to banish or put to death those found guilty of sedition.[w]

In the province of Asia there was factional strife, even among kinsmen, at Sardis, and at Smyrna a feud had for a long time existed between the men of the "upper city" and the "men of the seashore," evidently the wealthy and the working-classes.[15] In Pamphylia there were bread-riots at Aspendus, where the rich were hoarding grain in the expectation of selling it at a large profit. At Tarsus opposing factions were formed, respectively, by the members of the Council with their adherents and by those who claimed to represent the people, and with both of these the associations of the Elders and the Young Men were at variance. One source of this strife was the status of the linen-workers, free-born but apparently without the right of franchise, who aspired to become full citizens. So bad, in fact, was the disorder that Dio warned the Tarsians against "the destructive tumult and strife, engendered by envy, greed and jealousy, in which everyone, without regard to the fatherland and the common good, is concerned only with his own advancement."

The troubled state of Bithynia was not improved by the senatorial governors, two of whom, after their return to Rome at the opening of

[t] See above p. 581.   [u] Dio xxxix 8.
[v] Dio xlviii 2f. and 6f. See also von Arnim *ibid*. pp. 373f. and 377 and *Herm*. xxxiv p. 377f.
[w] Dio xliii 11.

the second century, were brought to trial by the provincials. The first of these, Gaius Julius Bassus, perhaps the "evil governor" censured by Dio Chrysostom, was accused, according to one of his advocates, because he had "given offence to the most factious" in the province, but the actual charge was extortion.[16] The suppression of the "factious," far from seeming to the Senators reprehensible, was regarded as meritorious, and the leading part played in the accusation by a personal enemy of Bassus actually aided the latter's cause. It could not be denied, however, that the Proconsul had accepted what he was pleased to regard as "gifts," an action prohibited by law but none the less sanctioned by custom. After the rejection of a proposal to declare him guilty of extortion, a motion was passed, which, while permitting him to retain his membership in the Senate, ordered him to make restitution to the province, the amount to be determined by a special commission.[17] An attempt to right any wrong he might have committed in Bithynia was made by enacting that any of his decisions, should an appeal be made to the proconsul of the province within two years, might be pronounced invalid.

The second of the two governors of Bithynia to be accused at the expiration of his term of office was Varenus Rufus, the close, if not the immediate, successor of Bassus.[18] Whatever his faults as governor, he won favour at Prusa, at least, by restoring to the citizens the right to hold their public Assembly, and he was characterized by Dio—who, to be sure, may have been merely using the governor's official title—as "excellent." He was even invited by the Bithynians to act as one of Bassus's accusers. Nevertheless, after his return to Rome, a group of the provincials, appearing before the Senate, demanded that Varenus be brought to trial. The case for the prosecution was presented by one of the group, a certain Fonteius Magnus, who in his speech, according to Pliny (one of Varenus's advocates), like many Greeks, failed to distinguish between fluency and content. Despite the protests of his accusers, Varenus persuaded the Senate to grant him the special privilege—not allowed to the defendant by the law concerning extortion—of summoning witnesses to testify in his behalf.[19] But before the actual trial began, an envoy from the provincial Council appeared in Rome, requesting that the action be dropped. When Magnus none the less persisted in the prosecution, the envoy demanded that the case be transferred to the Emperor's jurisdiction, and to this the Consuls assented. Trajan, after hearing both sides, ruled that no decision could be rendered until the actual wishes of the province had been fully ascer-

tained. The outcome of this inquiry, however, and its effect on Varenus's prosecution have not been recorded.

It may be assumed that the continuance of the disordered condition
of Bithynia under senatorial governors finally impelled Trajan to take
direct control of the province by sending Pliny to govern it as his own
representative. Besides the task, already described, of curtailing the
extravagant expenditure of public funds, the new governor had to
cope with the strife of the factions in the cities. One of the great dangers
to harmony lay in the formation of political clubs, which might resort
to open violence or, at best, organize the voters against the rule of the
wealthy and more conservative element favoured by Rome. Pliny, accordingly, acting on instructions from the Emperor, issued an edict
prohibiting the formation of so-called "brotherhoods," a name which
might easily be used as a cover for an association of a political character.[20] So far, in fact, was this precaution carried that Trajan refused to
permit the formation of a much-needed fire-brigade at Nicomedeia
on the ground that, in a province where factions were rife, there was
great danger that such an organization might become a brotherhood.[x]
As a special concession to the free city of Amisus, however, the Emperor
consented to permit the formation of a society for aiding the poor, but
only on the understanding that the money raised for this purpose
would not be used for promoting disorder or for unlawful gatherings.[y]
At the same time he ordered that in the subject cities even organizations
of this kind should be prohibited.

The factional strife at Prusa in which Dio Chrysostom had been
involved reappeared in a charge brought against the Orator by two
of his enemies, one of whom, a self-styled philosopher, had some years
previously been convicted of forgery and condemned to work in the
mines but had escaped and succeeded in reinstating himself in his
native city.[z] These men, appealing to Pliny, accused Dio of the misuse
of funds appropriated for a public building erected under his supervision and demanded an accounting; hoping to strengthen their case,
they brought an additional charge of lese-majesty, alleging that Dio
had shown disrespect toward Trajan by burying his wife and son in
the court of a building which contained the Emperor's statue. When
Pliny, after a protracted hearing, ordered both sides to present their
pleas in writing for examination by Trajan and only the defendant
complied, the Emperor ruled that the accounting must indeed be
furnished but that the charge of lese-majesty should be quashed, since

[x] Pliny 34.   [y] Pliny 92-93.   [z] Pliny 81-82; see also 58-60.

respect for his name must not be sought by inspiring fear or by trumped-up accusations of treason.

For the suppression of actual violence Pliny had only a small force of soldiers, the command of which had been given him by the Emperor.[21] It included a mounted cohort and a garrison stationed at Nicomedeia. In addition, the fleet which patrolled the Black Sea was at the disposal of the governor, should the need arise; the prefect, however, who welcomed Pliny "with the greatest respect and courtesy," needed soldiers and was not satisfied with the number assigned to him. The troops, to be sure, were of little use for maintaining order in the cities, for Trajan, although he endorsed Pliny's action in detailing a few men for attendance on the imperial procurators, gave orders that in general the soldiers should not be assigned for police-duty in the various communities but kept together under the colours.[a] He even rejected a suggestion that a detachment be quartered at Juliopolis, an important road-station near the border of Galatia.[b]

Some of the problems in regard to which Pliny asked Trajan for a decision concerned the application of the old law of Pompey on which was based the organization of the Bithynian communities.[c] The particular clause of the law which fixed thirty years as the minimum age for holding a local magistracy or for membership in a city-council had been modified by an edict of Augustus making it possible for a man to hold office at the age of twenty-two.[d] Since, however, Pompey's law provided that a council should be made up of ex-magistrates, the question had arisen whether these younger men, at the expiration of their terms of office, were eligible for membership in the councils; and, if so, whether other men under thirty years of age, who had not held magistracies, might be enrolled by the local censors as members. The ordinary practice, it appeared, was to regard these as eligible, on the ground that it was better for a community that the sons of the well-born should be chosen members of its council rather than men of the lower classes. Another problem arose from the fact that whereas the law contained no provision for the payment of an entrance-fee by a newly-elected member of a local council, a governor had recently issued a ruling which authorized certain of the smaller cities to demand that each new councillor should pay a fee, varying with the community concerned.[e] It was now a question whether a uniform fixed amount should not be paid in all communities alike. There had been, moreover,

[a] Pliny 19-20 and 27-28.
[b] Pliny 77-78. See Chap. XIII note 14.
[c] See above p. 369.
[d] Pliny 79-80.
[e] Pliny 112-113.

a general neglect of the clause in the law which forbad a city to enroll among its citizens the members of another Bithynian community,
with the result that in many places men from other cities had even
become members of the council.[f] The censors who were responsible for
the enrolling of councillors were now in doubt as to whether these
should be ejected. In each of these cases Trajan's decision showed his
usual excellent judgement: Pliny's action in admitting to the councils
young men who had held magistracies—but only these—was confirmed; the determination of the councillors' fees was to be left to
the individual communities; and as to the admission of strangers, past
violations of the law were to be disregarded, lest some local councils
might be too greatly disrupted, but in future its provisions were to be
strictly enforced.

Various previous decisions were likewise involved, such as one of
Augustus on the basis of which the Nicaeans asserted that the property
of those who died intestate should accrue to the community,[g] and a
ruling of certain proconsuls that in the collection of debts the community should have a preferential claim over other creditors.[h] In
regard to these questions Trajan refused to render a decision, in the
one case, bidding Pliny examine all available testimony and act in
accordance with the findings, in the other, referring him to the laws
of the individual cities concerned. Still another problem arose out of
Trajan's own order prohibiting grants of communal funds to private
individuals; this was used as the basis of a claim by the public prosecutor
of Amisus against a citizen of the place, who, twenty years previously,
had received a large sum of money by vote of the Council and People.[22]
In reply, the Emperor ruled that his order should not be applied to
a grant of such long standing.

It was necessary also for Pliny, in his capacity as governor of the
province, to render certain judicial decisions, but some cases he referred
to Trajan, reminding the Emperor of his permission to lay before him
any matters concerning which there might be doubt. One of these
was the question whether men who had been condemned to hard
labour or to service as gladiators might be used for menial (and easier)
tasks in the cities, ordinarily performed by the public slaves.[i] Another,
based on the Emperor's instructions that no person banished either by
Pliny or by any other governor might be restored, concerned the validity of an alleged restoration by a previous proconsul.[j] This involved

[f] Pliny 114-115.　　　　[g] Pliny 83-84.　　　　[h] Pliny 108-109.
[i] Pliny 31-32.　　　　　[j] Pliny 56-57.

also the action to be taken in the cases of those banished in perpetuity, as, for example, a man punished by Julius Bassus, whose decisions, if an appeal were made within two years, might be formally revoked. In his replies Trajan ruled that criminals condemned within ten years should serve their original sentences, only the older men being permitted to perform such services as road-construction and the cleaning of sewers or public baths. With regard to the banished, the Emperor promised to consult the governors who had taken the actions in question; at the same time he ruled that the man who had been sentenced by Bassus had lost his chance for a revocation because he had failed to appeal within the specified time.

Other questions concerned the right of free-born children who had been exposed and reared in slavery to assert a claim to freedom, as well as a request made by some of the provincials that Pliny would render decisions regarding the acknowledgement of children and the recognition of their civic rights.[k] In the former case, Trajan, in the lack of any general precedent, gave a reply in the children's favour; in the latter, he reserved judgement until a decree of the Senate which dealt with cases of this kind in senatorial provinces could be consulted.

Pliny's mission in Bithynia lasted, probably, less than two years.[23] Its success evidently seemed to Trajan sufficient justification for retaining Bithynia under his own control; for he sent another imperial legate, Gaius Julius Cornutus Tertullus, to govern the province, apparently as Pliny's successor.

Another administrative change effected by Trajan was the division, sometime between 107 and 113, of the united provinces of Galatia and Cappadocia.[24] In the new arrangement the Galatian province comprised, as before the union, the districts of Galatia proper, inland Paphlagonia and northern Pisidia; Cappadocia was combined with Lesser Armenia and part of interior Pontus, including Amaseia and Sebastopolis, attached to Galatia by Augustus,[l] as well as with the kingdom of Polemo, annexed under Nero.[m] It formed a frontier province extending along the Euphrates from the Pontic coast-range to the border of Commagene.

This change may have been due merely to the difficulty of administering so large and unwieldy a province, a task too great for a single governor.[25] On the other hand, it may have seemed more advantageous to make Cappadocia a compact military province which might serve as

[k] Pliny 65-66 and 72-73.   [l] See above p. 466.   [m] See above p. 561f.

the base of operations for the war soon to be waged on the eastern side of the Euphrates.

Trajan, having annexed Dacia, north of the lower Danube, and the land of the Nabataeans in northern Arabia as provinces of Rome, desired, like Alexander the Great, whose achievements he openly envied,[n] to find new regions to conquer. Grounds for invading first Armenia and then the kingdom of the Parthians were found by the ambitious Emperor in the resurgence of the Armenian question, which after a lapse of nearly a half-century—since the time when a Parthian prince had received the crown of the country as a vassal of Rome[o]— arose again to bring war to the East.

An account of the events which led to this war can be obtained only from scattered, fragmentary sources, and, in consequence, it is both meagre and uncertain.[26] A Parthian prince named Axidares (or Exedares), who was made king of Armenia either by his father, the Parthian monarch, Pacorus II, or by his uncle, Osroes I, had been deposed by the latter. It is not wholly clear, however, whether Trajan's ground for complaint lay in the Parthian King's failure to secure Roman recognition for the original investiture of Axidares or (more probably) in the deposition of this prince by Osroes and the appointment in his place of his brother, Parthamasiris. In any case, the Emperor, on the ground that a king of Armenia had received his crown from the Parthians without the endorsement of Rome, opened hostilities. With the purpose of taking the field in person, he left Italy for the East in the autumn of 113.[27] On arriving in Athens, he was met by envoys from Osroes, who offered gifts and asked for peace: the King, so their plea ran, had deposed Axidares as satisfactory neither to the Parthians nor to Rome and he now requested Trajan to recognize Parthamasiris as ruler of Armenia and present him with the royal diadem. By this request, an acceptance of all that the Romans since Nero's time had claimed in regard to Armenia, the point at issue might seem to have been conceded. Trajan, however, whose primary motive in undertaking the war, according to an ancient historian, was a desire for glory, rejected this attempt at conciliation. Refusing Osroes's gifts, he avoided a definite answer to the King's request, replying merely that on his arrival in Syria he would do all that was proper. Continuing his journey across the Aegean, he proceeded "through Asia and Lycia," more accurately, probably, along the Southern Highway to

[n] Cassius Dio LXVIII 29, 1.   [o] See above p. 561.

Laodiceia and thence through Pisidia to Attaleia on the Pamphylian coast, where he took ship for Seleuceia in Syria, arriving early in the year 114 at Antioch.[28]

It seems apparent that Trajan's purpose in going to Antioch was to take command in person of the legions stationed in the eastern provinces.[29] Of these, at least five furnished detachments for the war.[30] In addition, there were auxiliary cohorts, recruited in Galatia and Paphlagonia, and contingents may also have been brought from the region of the lower Danube. At the head of the troops stationed in Syria, Trajan advanced northward into Commagene, his plan being evidently to take possession of Armenia before encountering the Parthians. Proceeding, it may be supposed, along the road which led from the south, he halted at Samosata, whence he continued northward along the western bank of the Euphrates to Melitene in eastern Cappadocia.[31] This place, the headquarters of at least one of the legions stationed in the province, was now raised to the status of a city with the title of Metropolis. Increasing his army, probably, by the addition of troops quartered in Cappadocia, Trajan advanced to Satala in Lesser Armenia. Here he seems to have been joined by the Galatian and Paphlagonian recruits, who, after wintering in Ancyra, had marched eastward through Pontus, as well as by the troops summoned from the Danube region. There arrived also the King of the Heniochi from the mountainous region between Armenia and the Black Sea, who, in recognition of this act of allegiance, was rewarded by the Emperor with gifts.[32] Either here or subsequently at Elegeia, Trajan was met also by the rulers of other nations of the Euxine coast and even of the Trans-Caucasian Iberi and Albani. All these he confirmed in their kingdoms as vassals of Rome.

On beginning his march northward, Trajan received two communications from Parthamasiris, who was now ready to open negotiations. By refraining, in his second letter, from using the title of King, he even showed himself willing to admit the Emperor's right to invest him with the royal power. He merely asked that Marcus Junius, the governor of Cappadocia, might be sent to act as intermediary, a request which was granted to the extent of sending Junius's son. The young man, it may be presumed, brought him a command to meet the Emperor in person. In any case, when Trajan with his army had advanced from Satala to Elegeia on the high plateau of Greater Armenia, Parthamasiris appeared before him, ready for the ceremony.[33] In the presence of the Roman soldiery, the prince, removing his diadem, laid it at the Emperor's feet, expecting that it would be returned to him in a formal act of investiture. To his surprise and alarm, however, the only response was a shout from the soldiers, hailing Trajan as *Imperator*. When the prince, after a private interview, was ordered to make his plea in public, he reminded the Emperor that he had not been defeated or made captive but had appeared of his own volition to receive his kingdom, as Tiridates had once received it from Nero. In reply, he was brusquely told that Armenia would not be surrendered to him or to anyone else; for it now belonged to the Romans and would receive a Roman governor.

Thus the plan, initiated by Augustus and continued by his successors, of controlling Armenia through a client-king, was abandoned in favour of outright annexation; and, in accordance with Trajan's desire for expansion, the country, which had been at least nominally independent since the time of Antiochus III, was made Roman territory.[34] It was incorporated, together with Cappadocia, in a province which lay on both sides of the upper Euphrates, a violation of the principle of Augustus that this river should form the eastern boundary of the Empire. The first—and, as events proved, the last—governor of this enlarged province was Lucius Catilius Severus, who had been a friend of Pliny's and later, as prefect of Rome under Hadrian, cherished in vain the hope of succeeding to the imperial power.[35]

This supposed solution of the Armenian question, followed by the murder of Parthamasiris by his guard on the ground that he was attempting to regain his kingdom by violence,[36] left Trajan free to carry out his plan for further conquest by an invasion of the Parthian kingdom, a project rendered less difficult by the fact that Osroes's rule was contested and his position, accordingly, insecure. The story of this invasion, which falls outside the scope of this narrative, may be summarized briefly.[37] During the latter part of the year 114, Trajan, marching southward through Armenia, invaded Mesopotamia, which, after taking the city of Nisibis, he occupied almost without a struggle and "brought under the power of the Roman People." In the course of the next two years, in a victorious march the Emperor, having crossed the Tigris and seized the district of Adiabene—which was thereupon annexed as a third province with the name Assyria—captured the Parthian capital, Ctesiphon, which he entered in triumph. Thence he advanced to the head of the Persian Gulf, expressing regret that he was not young enough to go on, like Alexander, to India.

The conquest of the Parthian Empire, however, was but short-lived.

In the early summer, probably, of 116, after Trajan's return from the Persian Gulf to Babylon, a general revolt, stimulated by a Parthian prince, Sanatruces, broke out in the new provinces of Mesopotamia and Assyria, with the result that the Roman garrisons were driven out or massacred. Three armies were sent against the rebels, one of which was defeated and its commander, Maximus, slain in battle. Hoping to satisfy the national aspirations thus aroused and at the same time to preserve the prestige of Rome, Trajan had recourse to the expedient of creating a vassal-monarch for the Parthians.[38] He bestowed the crown on Parthamaspates, a son of Osroes, who had been sent to aid Sanatruces but was easily persuaded to abandon him in favour of Rome. The ceremony performed, Trajan withdrew northward, following the main route through the fortified city of Hatra on the eastern edge of the desert of central Mesopotamia. Meeting with resistance, he laid siege to the place, but so great were the sufferings of the Roman army that it became necessary to abandon the attempt, and the Emperor and his forces continued their long march to Antioch.

It was hoped to renew the campaign with greater success in the spring of 117. The fatigue and hardships, however, of the ill-judged expedition of the last two years had had their effect on the physique of the sixty-three-year-old Emperor. On departing from Hatra he showed signs of weakening health, and, his condition growing worse during the winter, he was subsequently stricken with paralysis. Accordingly, abandoning all his plans for a campaign in 117, and having appointed the son of his cousin (and husband of his great-niece), Publius Aelius Hadrianus, governor of Syria, Trajan set out for Italy, travelling by sea along the Cilician coast.[39] In the course of his voyage he put in at Selinus—afterward called, in his honour, Trajanopolis and raised to the rank of a Roman colony—and here, early in August, 117, he was suddenly overtaken by death. Dying after an expedition across the Euphrates, as had Gaius, Augustus's grandson, and after him Germanicus, also after crowning a vassal-king of Armenia, Trajan was the third Roman imperial victim to be claimed by the East.

The eastern conquests of Trajan were achieved at great cost of both money and men, and the military glory won for Rome was even more ephemeral than is the wont of such glory. The Emperor lived, in fact, to see the beginning of the disappearance of what he had gained. In consequence of the revolt in Mesopotamia in 116, Sanatruces's son, Vologases, had invaded Armenia, and since the governor, Catilius

Severus, was unwilling or unable to oppose him in battle, a portion of the country was surrendered to him as the price of peace.[40] In the course of the year 116/17, moreover, Europus on the right bank of the Euphrates, and with it, presumably, the adjacent territory, had been evacuated by the Roman garrison, perhaps as a concession to Partha-maspates. Even so, however, this new client-king of the Parthians soon began to lose his hold on his none-too-willing subjects, who, turning once more to Osroes and without hindrance from Trajan's successor, Hadrian, rejected their Roman-made ruler. In fact, it was but a short time after the old Emperor's death that all his conquests east of the Euphrates were abandoned; for Hadrian relinquished Meso-potamia and Assyria to the Parthian monarch and made Armenia once more a client-kingdom.[41] Thus the principle laid down by Augustus was re-established, and the Euphrates again became the eastern bound-ary of the Roman Empire.

CHAPTER XXVI

PEACE AND UNIFICATION UNDER HADRIAN

THE new Emperor, Hadrian, who had been appointed governor of Syria by Trajan and was proclaimed *Imperator* by the armies in that province on the announcement of the latter's death, was a worthy successor of Augustus. Talented and versatile, a man of great energy as well as of refined tastes, Hadrian possessed a greater measure of sagacity than any of those who had held the principate since the time of its founder. He came into power at a time when a combination of courage and sound judgement was greatly needed to bring peace to an empire on whose borders there was either the threat or the fact of war. Indeed, his accession at this juncture might well have appeared due to a peculiar favour on the part of the Good Fortune of the Roman Empire.

The heritage of power to which Hadrian succeeded was a troubled one.[1] The rebellion in Mesopotamia, which had done much to nullify Trajan's successes east of the Euphrates, had been accompanied by a general uprising of the Jews, not merely in Palestine but also in Cyprus, Egypt and Cyrenaica, and its suppression, begun by Trajan's order, was not yet complete. At the western end of north Africa, Mauretania was in revolt, in Britain there were signs of unrest, and in the Danube region there was open warfare. Both the Jewish rebellion and, subsequently, the disorders in Mauretania were suppressed by the able general, Quintus Marcius Turbo, but the situation on the Danube was more serious. It was evident that the costly conquests of Trajan both in the lands east of the Euphrates and on the northern frontier could not be maintained without great effort.

In the East, as has been already related, the problem was solved by placing Armenia under a client-king and restoring the basins of the Euphrates and the Tigris to their former owners. On the Danube, Hadrian himself, having marched to this region directly from Syria without even visiting Rome, made an agreement with the vassal-prince of the Roxolani near the mouth of the river; and the tribes farther west in the great plain of the Theiss were subdued by Turbo, who received an extraordinary command for the purpose. When order was thus restored, the general watchword of the new régime could be proclaimed on coins issued before the end of Hadrian's first year as Peace.[2]

In the course of his march from Antioch to the Danube in the autumn of 117, the Emperor, attended by the troops returning to Europe, travelled across Asia Minor. His route lay through Cilicia and western Cappadocia to Ancyra, where the chief priest of the imperial cult celebrated his visit by a distribution of money to the citizens.[3] Advancing farther on his way, he was met by the representatives of the Young Men's Association of Pergamum, who offered congratulations on his accession to power—merely one, doubtless, of many organizations which sought his favour. Another deputation came from the free island-city of Astypalaea, bringing a decree which told of the pleasure of the citizens at the fact that Hadrian was "succeeding to his father's office."[4] As an expression of their pleasure they promised to present him with a sum of money, perhaps the "crown-gold" which, on the analogy of the golden wreaths once sent by the Greek cities, nominally as a voluntary offering to the Hellenistic monarchs and later to Rome for Jupiter Capitolinus, was regularly presented, as practically a compulsory gift, to the emperors on their accession to power or after some notable achievement. Subsequently, however, unable to make this promise good, the Astypalaeans were compelled to ask for a reduction of the promised amount.

This initial journey across Asia Minor was but a prelude to further travelling, not merely in the East but over the whole Empire as well. In fact, Hadrian was the first ruling emperor after Augustus to cross the Aegean on a peaceful errand and, if Nero's tour in Greece be excepted, the first to leave Italy at all save for the purpose of war or conquest. It has been estimated that of the twenty-one years of his rule, twelve were spent by this "travel-Emperor" in journeys through the provinces,[5] an activity which has sometimes been ascribed to a restlessness approaching morbidity but seems in fact to have been due to a genuine desire to acquaint himself both with present conditions and with needs for the future. It was said of him by an ancient author that he "aided the cities, both allied and subject, with the greatest generosity; for he visited many of them, more, in fact, than any other emperor, and he assisted practically all of them, giving to some supplies of water and to others harbours or grain or public works or money or various honours."[a] As a modern writer has expressed it, he wished through his presence and his interest in the affairs of the provincials to win their hearts and their enthusiasm.[b] By adopting this policy of appearing in person in the provinces he did more than any of his predecessors to bring about the unification of the Empire.

As was natural in a man whose devotion to Hellenism in his youth

---

[a] Cassius Dio LXIX 5, 2f.   [b] Weber in *C.A.H.* XI p. 319.

had won him the nickname of "Greekling,"[c] Hadrian spent a large part of his travelling years in the Greek-speaking East. Not only did he devote much time to Greece itself but on two separate occasions, the first in the years 123 and 124, the second in 129-131, he made extensive journeys through Asia Minor.[6]

Even before the first of these journeys Hadrian's interest in the Asianic cities is shown by favours which led his predecessor's city of Trajanopolis in 119 to give him the title of Benefactor and Founder and within the next two years caused the Council and People both at Pergamum and at Magnesia to erect statues in his honour.[d] Meanwhile he received an appeal from the Elders' Association of Ephesus, presented by a special envoy sent to Rome for the purpose.[7] Certain Ephesians, it was asserted, who had borrowed money from the Association, had died, and those who had taken over their property were withholding payment on the technical ground that since the deceased persons had been in debt they themselves were actually creditors and so not heirs to any assets. In response to the plea, Hadrian, after signifying approval of the measures already taken by a former proconsul, wrote to the petitioners that he would send a copy of their resolution to the governor then in office, who, after consideration of the facts, would "render judgement in the matter under dispute and exact all that was owed to the Association." The case is of interest as showing that, while in a senatorial province a question of comparatively trivial importance might be brought directly to the notice of the emperor, the principle was still observed that the final decision in such cases was properly the function of the proconsul.

A general improvement of the roads in the Galatian province, carried out in 122 by the governor, Aulus Larcius Macedo, who rebuilt not only the great route from Ancyra to the Cilician Gates but also the roads radiating from Ancyra northward into Paphlagonia, eastward toward Pontus, westward toward Bithynia and southwestward toward Dorylaeum in Phrygia, suggests that it was Hadrian's intention to include this province in his visit to Asia Minor in the following year.[8] There is no evidence, however, to show that Galatia formed part of his itinerary. As far as can be determined, the Emperor's first journey was confined to the provinces of Bithynia and Asia, where his presence is amply attested by the record of the benefits conferred on the cities and the honours paid to him in return. Unfortunately, the order in

---

[c] *Vit. Hadr.* 1, 5. [d] *I.G.R.* iv 623 and 339: *Ins. Magn.* 174 and 175.

which the several places were visited cannot be satisfactorily determined.

In Bithynia, Hadrian evidently visited Nicomedeia and Nicaea, both of which had recently been damaged by an earthquake.[9] By appropriations of money from the imperial treasury he made it possible for them to rebuild many public places, as well as the city-walls, and in gratitude Nicomedeia assumed the appellation Hadrianē and honoured the Emperor as Saviour and Benefactor. The neighbouring Cius, which added the name of the Hadrian to its own and created a priest for his worship, was doubtless also included in his visit.

In eastern Bithynia, the naming of two of the city-tribes at Prusias-on-Hypius after Hadrian and his wife, Sabina, suggests that the Emperor visited the place in person.[10] Claudiopolis, which about this time resumed its ancient name Bithynium, received special attention as the home of the Emperor's favourite, the handsome youth, Antinous, and not only took Hadrian's name but also founded a festival called after both him and Antinous.

In the province of Asia, Cyzicus, which also had suffered from an earthquake, was evidently included in Hadrian's journey; for it may be assumed that this was the occasion on which he paved the market-place with slabs of marble and contributed money for the erection of a temple dedicated to himself.[11] This was presumably the building described as "the largest and most beautiful of all" and even regarded by certain late writers as one of the Seven Wonders of the World; the extant remains, indeed, show that it was a building of great size. The temple evidently served as a seat of worship for the whole province, for Cyzicus assumed the title of Temple-Warden, probably indicating that it possessed a provincial sanctuary dedicated to the imperial cult. The city also adopted the appellation Hadrianē and founded a festival called by the Emperor's name.

It was presumably during this journey also that Hadrian conferred some favour on the Roman colony of Parium, originally founded by Julius Caesar or Augustus, which gave him the title of Founder.[12] At Apollonia in northern Mysia he seems to have built or repaired a public building, and he was called Saviour and Founder both here and probably also at the neighbouring Miletopolis. It may be assumed that he visited Ilium, where it is said that he rebuilt the tomb of the hero Ajax.[e] In fact, the repair of the great coast road near the city in 124 may have been carried out in connexion with his arrival.[f] The "many

---

[e] Philostratus *Heroic.* 2, 3.   [f] *C.I.L.* III 466; see Chap. II note 19.

benefactions which Hadrian gave both to individuals and to the community" at the colony of Alexandria Troas and which the citizens acknowledged some years later by erecting a statue of him in Athens may possibly have been made at this time.[13]

In Pergamum a handsome hall, lined with marble slabs, which contained a statue of heroic size of the "God Hadrian" was perhaps connected with a visit during this journey.[14] In Smyrna the Emperor's interest in the city was quickened by Antonius Polemo, one of the "sophists" attached to the *Mouseion*, of whom it was said that "he conversed with cities as a superior, with rulers as not inferior and with the gods as an equal."[15] It is related that he succeeded in obtaining from Hadrian the surprisingly large sum of 10,000,000 drachmae, to be expended on a grain-market, a gymnasium, the most magnificent in Asia, and the great temple of Zeus which stood on a height overlooking the gulf. In another statement of favours obtained from the Emperor by the good offices of Polemo, the amount of money appears as one and a half million drachmae in addition to a number of columns of marble and porphyry, to be used for the anointing-room of the gymnasium. The same statement includes the foundation of a "sacred contest" and appropriations for sacred bards and choristers, similar, presumably, to those attached to the temple of Roma and Augustus at Pergamum. It also mentions a senatorial decree granting to Smyrna the title of "Twice Temple-Warden," suggesting, as in the case of Pergamum some years previously, that the city may now have had a second temple built by the province for the imperial cult. The "sacred contest" was evidently the festival afterward called Hadriancia Olympia. The gratitude of the city was expressed by the assumption of the appellation Hadrianē, and, in fact, the favour shown to it by the Emperor seems to have justified the allusion in a letter of a Roman official to the "most happy times" under Hadrian "when the world sacrifices and prays for his welfare."[g]

From Smyrna Hadrian seems to have visited Erythrae, apparently travelling by ship, for the city founded a festival called Hadrianeia Epibateria in celebration of his disembarkation.[h] He also visited Ephesus, said to have been his favourite among the cities of Asia, as well as Miletus, where monuments were dedicated to him by the chief magistrates.[16] At Ephesus the priests of Artemis erected a statue of the Emperor, and a year or two later "the Augustus-loving Council and the Temple-Warden People of Ephesus" dedicated a statue of his

[g] *I.G.R.* IV 1398 (A.D. 124).   [h] *I.G.R.* IV 1542.

wife, Sabina.[17] As in other cities, a festival called Hadrianeia was established in his honour. Either now or on the occasion of his second visit, Hadrian, by appointing a *curator* to supervise the finances of the Elders' Association, which had previously appealed to him in collecting its debts, attempted to introduce order into its affairs.

A visit of Hadrian to the interior of Lydia is suggested by a decree subsequently passed by the citizens of Thyateira recording gifts received from the Emperor, as well as by the existence in the city of both a public building and a festival named after him, and by the erection of a statue by the Council and People of Nacrasa.[18] His interest in Lydia and Mysia was shown especially in the creation of several cities which subsequently bore his name. These, in the conviction that civilization could best be promoted by urbanization, were founded in various places, not only in the plain of the upper Caïcus, where the old community of Stratoniceia was revived, but especially in the sparsely inhabited regions of central and eastern Mysia, as well as in the Bithynian-Paphlagonian borderland.

The situation of Stratoniceia, at the entrance to a valley through which led the main route northward to Cyzicus, made it a desirable place for development.[19] Even in the time of the Pergamene kings it had effected a combination with the neighbouring community of Indipedium in the plain of the Caïcus, but after the late second or early first century before Christ it is unknown to history. In the time of Trajan, however, the two communities formed a sympolity which issued coins under their joint names. Having received the rights of a *polis* from Hadrian, Stratoniceia assumed the additional name of Hadrianopolis and honoured the Emperor as its founder. Hadrian also, in response to a request brought by an envoy in 127, wrote to the magistrates, Council and People, granting to the new city the revenues which the neighbouring territory had hitherto paid to Rome, with the assurance that the proconsul and the imperial procurator had been officially informed of this grant. Even the request that the house of a certain Tiberius Claudius Socrates, apparently an absentee landlord, should be prevented from falling into ruin and so becoming a detriment to the place met with a response from the Emperor in an order that Socrates must either keep the house in repair or dispose of it to some native of the city.

In the interior of Mysia, the foundation of three cities, Hadrianotherae, Hadrianeia and Hadriani, was undoubtedly intended to further the development of this region, but little affected by the influence of

Hellenism. The first of these, according to tradition, owed its situation and origin to Hadrian's success in hunting bear in the neighbourhood.[20] In fact, coins were issued showing not only a bear's head but also the representation of the Emperor on horseback about to cast his spear at a bear in flight. There can be little doubt, however, that the site was chosen because of its natural advantages. Lying in a mountain-girt plain of great fertility, traversed by several streams which unite to flow into the Macestus, the place was a natural road-centre, through which ran not only the main route from Cyzicus to the plain of the Caïcus but also a road leading westward to the Aegean at Adramyttium.

Somewhat over forty miles toward the east, Hadrianeia lay in the mountainous region of Abrettene in a remote situation with difficult communications on every side.[21] Hadriani, with the descriptive epithet of "near Olympus," had a more favourable site, about thirty miles to the northeast, on the left bank of the Rhyndacus in the region of Olympene south of the great mountain from which the city took its distinguishing appellation.[22] The place was connected with the Propontis by a road over a pass southeast of Lake Apolloniatis, and on the west an easy route led to the valley of the Macestus. Both cities, evidently formed from the rural tribes inhabiting the two regions, established the usual government of a Greek *polis* and as late as the middle of the third century had their own councils and magistrates.

Near the border between Bithynia and Paphlagonia, the community of the Caesareis Proseilemmenitae or "the Annexed," already a *polis* with Council and People, was reorganized and added Hadrianopolis to its name.[23] Its situation, east of Vespasian's city of Flaviopolis, was likewise favourable, for it was on the line of the great route connecting Bithynia with the Amnias valley and Pontus.

As the beneficent traveller whose generosity caused happiness to the places he visited, Hadrian may well have seemed the incarnation of the god Dionysus, who, as he went through the world, brought joy and prosperity to the human race. It was not unnatural, therefore, that after he had confirmed the privileges granted by some of his predecessors to the musical and dramatic society of the Artists of Dionysus, he was adopted, as had been also (with less appropriateness) Trajan, as joint patron with the God himself.[24] Including in the name of the Society both the new deity and the old, this organization now assumed the official designation of "Artists from the inhabited world, winners of prizes in sacred games and of crowns, who gather about Dionysus and the Emperor Hadrian, the New Dionysus." Under the joint auspices of the two deities, the "Sacred Hadrianic Stage Guild," as it was less formally called, held contests during Hadrian's principate both at Ancyra and at Sardis. The festival in the former was celebrated in 128; although the contest, which was "mystical" in form as being connected with the mysteries of Dionysus, was officially given by the Emperor, the actual cost was borne by a "Helladarch," who, at the request of the city-council, acted as presiding-officer.

Hadrian, however, became a deity greater, even, than Dionysus. After spending the winter of 124-125 in Athens, he returned four years later for another winter before his departure for Ephesus, where he began his second visit to Asia Minor.[25] During this stay in Athens, the Emperor resumed the construction of the magnificent temple of Zeus Olympius, begun in the early second century before Christ but never completed.[26] Thereby he not only established anew the worship of Zeus but, by appropriating to himself a share both in the title and the temple of the God, became identified with him as Zeus Olympius. In the course of time, statutes honouring the Emperor as Olympius were erected in the Temple by several communities of Greece and by at least thirteen in Asia Minor.[27]

It was as the "Olympian," therefore, that Hadrian set out early in 129 on his second journey through the provinces east of the Aegean. This title, often combined with that of Saviour and Founder, appears in inscriptions on statues and altars, as well as on coins, from at least thirty-seven of the cities of Asia Minor, while the Empress Sabina was occasionally honoured as the New Hera.[28] Although it may not be assumed that the Emperor actually visited every city in which he appears as Olympius, it is possible, in contrast to his earlier travels in the East, to reconstruct at least the first part of this journey. There is enough evidence to show that from Ephesus, after an excursion to the neighbouring places as far as the coast of Caria, he travelled along the Southern Highway to Laodiceia, whence he turned through southwestern Phrygia to Lycia and from here proceeded, presumably by sea, to Cilicia and Syria.

At Ephesus a decree of the Council and People, passed in A.D. 129, expressed the city's gratitude to Hadrian for having presented Artemis with "unsurpassable gifts," including, apparently, certain rights to inheritances as well as to property to which there was no heir.[29] At this time also he provided for the importation of grain from Egypt and, by diverting the course of the river Caÿster which was silting up the harbours of the city, made these once more accessible from the sea.

Even the master of the ship in which Hadrian had crossed the Aegean was not forgotten; for the Emperor offered, should the city-council deem the man worthy of membership, to pay the fee which was expected from a newly-made councillor. A few years later, a citizen honoured him not merely as Olympius, but also with his later title of Panhellenius and even (with reference to the city's origin) as Panionius.

During this visit to Ephesus, apparently, the plan was made for the construction of an Olympieium, built on the outskirts of the city for the worship of the new Zeus Olympius.[30] On its completion, a few years later, Ephesus, now possessing a second temple dedicated to an emperor, obtained the title of "Twice Temple-Warden." The festival of the Hadrianeia, moreover, founded on the occasion of the Emperor's earlier visit, received the additional name Olympia.

At Miletus Hadrian's stay was commemorated in an inscription mentioning the "holy day" of his visit.[31] Small house-altars, moreover, of which so many have been found that it has been suggested that a large number of the citizens must have possessed one, were erected to him (sometimes in conjunction with Apollo or Artemis) not merely as Zeus Olympius but also as Saviour, Benefactor or Founder. His journey along the coast of Caria is attested by a letter subsequently written to the magistrates and councillors of Astypalaea—who had previously congratulated him on his accession—expressing his appreciation of an embassy sent to the mainland to convey greetings and gifts.[32]

At Tralles, in the course of his journey along the Southern Highway, Hadrian authorized the distribution of a large quantity of grain, amounting to 60,000 modii (nearly 15,000 bushels), which had been imported from Egypt.[33] The fact that the actual cost of the grain was borne by a patriotic official seems not to have detracted from the gratitude rendered to the Emperor, for both coins of the city and monuments erected by the citizens designate Hadrian as "Saviour" and "Founder." It may be assumed that the Emperor's interest in Tralles was due, at least in part, to the fact that one of his favourite freedmen, Phlegon, was a native of the place.[34] Another freedman, Publius Aelius Alcibiades, his chamberlain, whose original home was the neighbouring Nysa, erected statues of Hadrian in his own native city.

Farther along the Southern Highway, at Laodiceia-on-Lycus, whence Hadrian wrote to the Astypalaeans in 129,[1] a building dedicated to him

[1] See note 32.

and to Sabina may have been erected at this time.[35] From Laodiceia the Emperor evidently went southward by the route leading to the Mediterranean, and at Cibyra he conferred "honours"—which were probably gifts—on the community and was in turn hailed as Benefactor and Saviour of the Universe.[36] From here he seems to have travelled through Lycia to the southern coast, perhaps through the cities of Acalissus, in the mountains east of the Arycandus, and Corydalla, on the edge of the littoral plain. A visit of the Emperor was commemorated by the Council and People of each city; but since the inscriptions recording the event have been found at Phaselis on the eastern coast of the Lycian Peninsula, far away from both, it is possible that during his visit to this place the two communities sent delegations across the mountains to pay their respects.

In the course of his stay on the Lycian coast the Emperor ordered the erection of great granaries both at Andriace, the port of the city of Myra, and at Patara, farther to the west; but whether these were for the storage of the produce of the region or to serve as magazines for grain imported for distribution is unknown.[37] At Patara—which seems to have been the westernmost place reached in his journey through Lycia—gratitude was expressed by inscriptions on altars, in which he was called Saviour and Founder, while Sabina, as the consort of Zeus Olympius, was honoured as the New Hera.

On the eastern coast of Lycia Hadrian received the usual title of Saviour of the Universe from the Council and People both at Olympus and at Phaselis.[38] His visit to the latter city was commemorated by the erection of a large building, probably a temple, which, however, as the dedicatory inscription shows, was not completed until two years later. Farther to the east, Attaleia, the chief city of Pamphylia, was also visited, and it was presumably on this occasion that a city-gate was built, on which a dedication to the Emperor was inscribed in letters of gilded bronze. In the interior, various honours, such as the establishment of his worship and the erection of statues at Termessus, the dedication of a basilica, a forum and an exedra at the Roman colony of Cremna and statues at Pogla and Sagalassus, suggest that these places also were included in his itinerary.[39]

In Cilicia the wide-spread desire to honour Hadrian seems to show that he granted favours to the communities in person. No fewer than seven places in the province—Germanicopolis, Diocaesareia and Olba in Cilicia Aspera and Adana, Aegaeae, Mopsuestia and Tarsus in the Level District—assumed the name Hadrianē, and Zephyrium, also in this district, became Hadrianopolis.[40] At Tarsus the festival Hadrianeia was perhaps instituted in commemoration of the Emperor's visit, and statues were erected in his honour not only at Tarsus but also in the temple-city of Diocaesareia and at Corycus and Soli-Pompeiopolis on the coast.

From Cilicia Hadrian went onward to Antioch and thence travelled through Syria and Palestine to Egypt, from which, after a journey up the Nile as far as Thebes and a visit to Alexandria, he seems to have returned by ship to Syria.[41] It is possible that indications of his presence in various places in eastern Asia Minor which it is difficult to connect with his earlier visits may be dated after this return.

According to his biographer, Hadrian "took slaves from the Cappadocians for service in the camps,"[42] a statement which suggests that during a visit to Cappadocia he levied a force for the purpose of increasing the provincial militia and thereby strengthening the legion stationed at Melitene. There was perhaps already reason to fear an invasion of the Alans, who a few years later overran both the territory of the Albani and Media Atropatene and even endangered the kingdom of Armenia and the province of Cappadocia.[43] Nevertheless, every effort was made to preserve peace along the Euphrates frontier. Friendly relations with the Parthian monarch, Osroes, were established by the return of his daughter, whom Trajan had captured, and by a promise to give back the royal throne which had been taken at the same time.[j] The princes of the mountain-regions north and northeast of Armenia, who had assembled in 114 at the behest of Trajan, were invited to do homage to the Emperor. Pharasmanes, ruler of the Caucasian Iberians, however, as well as certain others, apparently, refused to attend.[44] Those who came are said to have been treated in such a way that those who did not regretted their refusal.

It may be assumed that from Cappadocia Hadrian went on to Satala in Lesser Armenia and that from here he crossed the coast-range to the Euxine. His journey over the mountains was compared by his friend Arrian, afterward governor of Cappadocia, to that of Xenophon, like whom he rejoiced at the sight of the sea.[45] On this coast, the port of Trapezus, although it served as a station for the Pontic fleet, had remained only a roadstead. Hadrian, however, ordered the construction of a harbour. He also founded a temple of Hermes, worshipped here

j *Vit. Hadr.* 13, 8. See *Vit. Pii* 9, 7.

in conjunction with Apollo, and in commemoration of his visit altars and a statue of him were erected.

While it is impossible definitely to determine the course of Hadrian's journey through Pontus, it seems probable that from Trapezus he returned to Satala and thence travelled by the road leading through Lesser Armenia to the valley of the Lycus; for the repairs on this road in 129 suggest that preparations had been made for his coming.[46] In any case, Nicopolis, Neocaesareia in the Lycus valley and Amaseia assumed the Emperor's name, and at Sebastopolis a priest of Hadrian was created and a portico erected in his honour.

There are likewise indications of a visit of Hadrian to Lycaonia, where, at Sidamaria in the southern part of the district, a public bath was dedicated to him by the Council and People.[47] Adopting the policy of Augustus and Claudius, who established Roman colonies in this part of the Empire, the Emperor conferred this status on the city of Iconium, now officially called Colonia Aelia Hadriana Augusta Iconensium. Like other colonies, it was administered by duumvirs, and its citizens had the status of complete liberty enjoyed by Romans. Farther to the northwest, apparently on the slope of the range of Sultan Dağ, another Hadrianopolis was founded, presumably in order to further the urbanization of this region. In the course of his return-journey, the Emperor appears again to have visited Bithynium-Claudiopolis, the home of Antinous—who had died while travelling with him in Egypt—where a statue was erected in 131 by the Council and People.[48] It was perhaps on this occasion that the Commonalty of the Bithynians issued coins bearing the portraits both of Hadrian and of Sabina and the representation of an octastyle temple, presumably erected for the imperial cult.

From Asia Minor Hadrian returned to Athens toward the end of 131 for his third visit to the city. During his stay there he took an important step in the development of his divine position by founding a temple of Zeus Panhellenius, with whom—although perhaps not until after his death—he himself became identified as the God Hadrian Panhellenius.[49] In connexion with this sanctuary, the Panhellenium, he established the festival of the Panhellenia. More important, however, was the creation of an organization, with an archon as presiding-officer, which was composed of Panhellenes, the representatives of all the Hellenic cities of the Empire. By forming a new league which brought together delegates from these communities for common counsel at Athens, the Emperor did much to promote the unification of the

Greek-speaking world and to revive the strength and influence of Hellenism.

In a decree of the Elders' Association of Magnesia the statement is made, somewhat verbosely, that "in the blessed time of the Emperor Hadrian it is fitting to increase more abundantly all that is serviceable to men."[k] In this concept of the period emphasis seems to be laid on the practical side of Hadrian's rule. It would be a mistake, indeed, to regard this extraordinary man as a mere visionary, who endeavoured to unify the Hellenic world by identifying himself with the gods of Greece. He was able also, when the need arose, to take measures of a practical nature, in which he showed himself as realistic an administrator as his efficient predecessor.

One of these measures had its origin in the need of a coinage which would pass current in the Asianic provinces as a general medium of exchange. The old cistophorus, minted by the Pergamene kings, had satisfied this need, and an attempt to fulfil the same purpose by a coin of corresponding value had been made by Augustus and some of his successors.[1] More recently, under Nerva and Trajan, these coins had also been issued, but those of Nerva, because of the brevity of his rule, were necessarily few in number, while the cistophori of Trajan were limited to the first three years of his principate.[50] Under Hadrian, on the other hand, these coins were minted in greater numbers and in more places than ever before in the history of Asia Minor. For whereas under Augustus they had been issued, apparently, only in Ephesus and Pergamum, and under Nerva and Trajan one new type, showing a representation of the Temple of Artemis at Perge, was evidently issued in Pamphylia, the cistophori of Hadrian were minted in at least ten different cities of the province of Asia. The abundance of these coins, some of which were issued before 128 and so perhaps in connexion with the Emperor's first journey to the East, and their wide distribution indicate that early in his principate Hadrian perceived the need for an increased currency for the eastern provinces.

The great variety in the types of these cistophori, moreover, is highly significant. The traditional temple-front, showing a figure of the emperor with an inscription recording a dedication by the commonalty of the province, which is found together with only a few other standard types on the cistophori of the earlier emperors, appears only on those coins of Hadrian which were issued in the name of the Commonalty

[k] *Ins. Magn.* 116.   [1] See Chap. XVIII note 40.

623

of Bithynia. His cistophori which were minted in the province of Asia bear among a vast number of new types the representations of deities worshipped in the several cities, as, for example, Asclepius of Pergamum, Artemis of Ephesus, the two "Nemeses" of Smyrna, Persephone of Sardis, Zeus of Laodiceia and Mylasa and Apollo of Miletus, Hierapolis and Alabanda. The appearance of these ancient deities on the coins, while in keeping with Hadrian's antiquarian interests, had also a practical purpose. The emphasis thus laid on the part which the cities played in issuing this coinage caused them to regard themselves as members of the greater unit for whose benefit the currency was introduced and so furthered the Emperor's general policy of unification.

Another measure for the improvement of economic conditions in Asia was the correction, generally attributed to Hadrian, of abuses practiced in connexion with the administration of the public bank of Pergamum, charges concerning which were laid before the Emperor by a delegate sent to Rome by the merchants of the city.[51] The bank, a municipal institution, had been leased to a group of private persons on a contract which called for a division of the profits between the city and the lessees. One of the chief sources of these profits was a monopoly of exchange whereby the bank was authorized to charge a commission for the changing of money under an agreement permitting the bankers to demand eighteen of the local bronze token-pieces (*assaria*) for a silver denarius but to give only seventeen in exchange for the silver coin. Not satisfied with this profit, however, the bankers— presumably with the connivance of the city-officials, who were not averse to increasing the profits of the bank and therewith the public revenues—had succeeded in effecting an arrangement enabling them to demand that even when several purchases made at the same time were paid for in silver they should receive (whether from the purchaser or the dealer is unfortunately not clear) the commission to which they would have been entitled had the silver been changed into bronze. This practice, burdensome to the merchants and apparently the chief subject of their complaint, was now prohibited in a rescript issued by the Emperor in response to their plea. Two concessions, however, were made to the bankers: one of these ordered that in the case of food sold by weight at a price fixed by the supervisors of the market the purchasers should pay in bronze (to be obtained, of course, from the bankers); the other forbad purchasers to combine and, with a view to depriving the bankers of their commission, make payment in silver.

Other abuses also were brought to the Emperor's notice, among them the bankers' refusal to accept worn coins except at a discount and the levying of a kind of hush-money extorted from dealers unable to take the oath customarily sworn at the end of each year that they had done nothing in violation of the city-ordinance dealing with exchange. Another ground for complaint was the practice of assigning to the bank as security a control over the entire stock in trade of a merchant who had borrowed money from the bankers but was unable to repay the loan. All of these abuses were likewise prohibited in the rescript, which also ordered that debtor-merchants should be tried by a special tribunal. This action, taken on the appeal of the Pergamenes themselves in a case in which they apparently had no other means of redress, seems to have involved a more minute investigation and consequent correction of the internal affairs of a city than any instance of imperial intervention heretofore presented.

Another case involving an investigation with a resultant action on the part of the Emperor appears in the decision rendered by Hadrian in 125/6 concerning the lands belonging to the Temple of Zeus at Aezani.[52] These lands, which had been assigned to the Temple by rulers of Pergamum and Bithynia, had at some unknown time been allotted to individuals but had nevertheless remained the property of the God. Not only had the size of the allotments been a matter of dispute among the holders, but these had for a long time paid no rentals to the Temple, even though a few years previously a proconsul had ordered that the payments should be made. The questions at issue were referred by the proconsul of Asia to Hadrian, who, "combining justice with kindness in conformity with his carefulness in judgements" put an end to the holders' "strife and jealousy toward one another" by ruling that the size of their allotments should be determined by the average size of those in the neighbouring communities. He also ordered that rentals should be paid from the day on which his decision was rendered, the payments to be made, apparently, to the temple-treasurer. At the request of the proconsul, the task of determining the size of the holdings was assumed by the procurator, but presumably for the sake of obtaining an impartial decision rather than because the interests of the imperial treasury were involved.

The control of the finances of cities and organizations by special curators was continued by Hadrian, who, as has been previously mentioned, appointed an official of this kind for the Elders' Association at Ephesus.[53] Following the precedent of Trajan in the case of Greece, he also named, about A.D. 135, a *corrector* to supervise the affairs of the free cities of Asia, choosing for this post the rich and distinguished orator, Tiberius Claudius Atticus Herodes, who during his incumbency built a bath costing 7,000,000 drachmae at Alexandria Troas.

About the same time, Hadrian, reviving Trajan's policy of replacing the senatorial proconsul of Bithynia by a legate responsible to the emperor, appointed a special commissioner as governor of the province. He chose for this post Gaius Julius Severus, a noble and wealthy Galatian from Ancyra, who claimed descent both from King Deiotarus and from one of the rulers of Pergamum.[54] Having earned the gratitude of the Roman government by caring for the troops quartered in Ancyra during the winter of 113-114 in preparation for Trajan's Parthian war, Severus had been made tribune of the Plebs by Hadrian and subsequently held various important posts, including the proconsulship of Achaea, on the expiration of which he was sent to Bithynia as "*corrector* and auditor" of the province with the right to use the five *fasces* regularly borne by an imperial legate.

It is said that the Bithynians needed a governor who was "just and prudent and a man of rank, and all these qualities Severus possessed," and that during his term he "managed and administered both their private and their public affairs" in such a way that he was long remembered.[m] Of his activities in the province, however, nothing is known except that, perhaps while holding this post, he determined "by order of Hadrian" the boundary between the territories belonging to Dorylaeum in the province of Asia and an adjacent, presumably Bithynian, community.[55] Whether, after the expiration of Severus's term of office, it was found necessary to name another imperial legate of Bithynia is uncertain; but during the principate of Hadrian's successor the province was once more governed by a proconsul appointed by the Senate.[n]

In this appointment of Severus, a native of Galatia, to high office under the Roman government Hadrian continued the policy begun, although sparingly, by the Flavian emperors and Trajan, under whom the Pergamenes, Julius Quadratus and Quadratus Bassus, the Ephesian Celsus Polemaeanus, and Caristanius Fronto from Antioch-near-Pisidia, becoming members of the Senatorial Order, were chosen Consuls and held important administrative and military posts in the provinces.[56] Another conspicuous example of this readiness to promote Orientals to important offices was the career of the historian Arrian, a native

[m] Cassius Dio LXIX 14, 4.   [n] See Chap. XXVIII note 7.

of Nicomedeia, who, after holding the consulship, became imperial governor of Cappadocia. As a general rule, however, members of rich and influential provincial families were admitted to the Equestrian Order and their sons, in turn, were advanced to Senatorial rank. In the course of the second century this process became increasingly frequent, and not only in Lycia, as has already been observed, but in the other provinces also it was regarded as claim to distinction to be called grandfather or grandmother, father, uncle, brother or cousin of members of the Senatorial Order.

The increased opportunity offered to natives of the provinces, not only of the East but also of the West, of entering into governmental service was the result of an important step taken by Hadrian in establishing a career for members of the Equestrian Order corresponding to that open to men of Senatorial rank. Augustus, it will be remembered, had usually chosen men of free birth to serve as his procurators in the provinces.[o] Claudius, on the other hand, on the theory that positions directly concerned with the emperor's interests should be held by members of the imperial household, employed freedmen in many of these offices as well as in those connected with his court and his treasury.[p] Even he, however, filled certain military posts with men of Equestrian rank, who were advanced from minor commands, sometimes through provincial procuratorships, to the higher posts of prefect of one of the fleets or of the Watch in Rome or of the Praetorian Guard. The increase in the number and importance of the procuratorships under the Flavians,[q] with the growing practice of appointing men of Equestrian rank to these posts, which were in fact essentially civilian, had led to the beginning of what amounted to an Equestrian career of office. These emperors, nevertheless, followed the precedent of requiring the holding of military commands (usually three) as a necessary preliminary for such a career. The change brought about by Hadrian, accordingly, was twofold.[57] Abandoning the custom of employing freedmen in higher positions in the imperial service, he reserved these for members of the Equestrian Order, whom he advanced from one office to another. Moreover, by permitting the substitution of such posts as advocate of the treasury or assistant in the emperor's council or secretary to the praetorian prefect for minor commands in the army, he separated the civilian from the military career. Thus men of Equestrian rank became eligible for purely civil posts, being promoted through procuratorships of various grades (and salaries) to the

o See above p. 489f. p See above p. 540. q See above p. 567f.

great court-bureaux, originally filled by freedmen, such as the super-vision of petitions or of the emperor's correspondence or of the im-perial treasury, surpassed in importance only by the prefectures of the grain-supply, of Egypt and of the Guard. The changes introduced by Hadrian which brought about the transformation of these formerly private bureaux into official governmental positions gave fresh strength to the administration by creating a highly-trained body of officials in a well-developed civil service. But they tightened the hold of the bureaucracy, "that greatest of curses," which ultimately strangled what was left of the Empire.

Another, although minor, administrative change was the reorgani-zation of the imperial post.[58] Since its creation by Augustus the com-munities themselves had been forced to assume the responsibility for maintaining the service. Under Hadrian, however, although the cost—often a burdensome one—was still borne by the communities, the post became a governmental institution with stations in charge of imperial officials and under the general supervision of a prefect of Equestrian rank.

In marked contrast to Trajan's attempt to achieve fame by military victories and the extension of the frontiers, the great glory of Hadrian was his policy of welding the Empire together by the care which he devoted to the far-flung dominions of Rome. This unification, "the crowning of his life-task," was expressed in four series of coins issued in the closing years of his rule, celebrating his world-wide visits and his interest in the provinces and in the armies which protected the Empire.[59] Of these coins, one series shows the names of eleven different provinces, represented as female figures, each with some characteristic attribute, as, for example, Asia on a ship's prow with a hook and rudder symbolizing the maritime importance of the province and Cappadocia wearing a tasselled cloak and holding a military standard and a model of its great mountain, Argaeus. Another series depicts the "Arrival" (*Adventus*) of the Emperor in at least seventeen prov-inces, while a third shows him as "Restorer," extending his hand to the figure which kneels before him. In these coins, also, the province is appropriately characterized—Asia, towered and holding a rudder and sceptre; Bithynia (and Nicomedeia) with a ship's stern-ornament or a rudder; Cilicia with a helmet and a military standard; Phrygia with a Phrygian cap and a sickle (or shepherd's crook). The distinctive attributes suggest, as has been recently observed, that the provinces were now regarded as no mere administrative districts but as national units possessing characteristics of their own, or, according to another view, that the Empire was "not the lordship of one mistress over many slaves but a willing partnership of many helpers in one great work." Still another series, on which Hadrian is represented as delivering an address, either from horseback or from a platform, to the assembled troops, is devoted to the armies—British, Cappadocian, Dacian, Dalmatian, German, Spanish, Mauretanian, Moesian, Norican, Rhaetian and Syrian. Now called by distinctive local names and no longer merely armies of Rome, they show the rise in importance of the provinces as contrasted with that of the ruling city. A corresponding decline in the supremacy of Italy is illustrated by the fact that the various series which commemorate the provinces, with the "arrivals" and "restorations" of the Emperor, include *Italia*, now on the same footing as the portions of the Empire.

Not unnaturally, this exaltation of the ruled at the expense of the prestige of the ruler was viewed with disfavour in Rome. It may well have been one of the reasons why the governing classes were so resentful at Hadrian that after his death, in July, 138, it was only by great effort on the part of his successor that the Senate was brought to accord him the usual deification. The hostility of these classes was based only on selfishness and prejudice, for they could not foresee that the equalization of the governed with the governing city and the consequent claim of the provincials to a greater share in the rule of the whole would result in the opposite of the Emperor's intention and finally lead to the dissolution of the Empire into these equalized portions with the ultimate disintegration of the Roman world. For over a century, however, unity was preserved by the general conviction that the several communities were members all of one body. This wide-spread sentiment was expressed by an orator from Asia who reminded his hearers in Rome that "no longer are the cities at variance, hearkening, some to one man and others to another, while to one city guards are sent and by another are expelled, but . . . the whole inhabited world, in more complete accord than any chorus of singers, prays that this Empire, welded together under its single leader, may endure for all time."[60]

CHAPTER XXVII

THE ANTONINES AND THE CITIES

LIKE Trajan, Hadrian, without heirs of his body, postponed until his later years the adoption of a son to become his successor. His first choice, however, Lucius Ceionius Commodus, adopted in 136 under the name Lucius Aelius Caesar, lived but little more than a year after his adoption. His death was probably to the advantage of the Empire; for he seems to have possessed few qualities either of mind or of character to fit him for the post of ruler.

Less than two months later, the aging Emperor, now stricken with a mortal illness, suddenly proclaimed as his son and heir Titus Aurelius Fulvus Boionius Arrius Antoninus, a mature man of fifty-one years, "handsome in appearance, distinguished in natural talents and kindly in temperament" and respected by all.[1] In order to provide for the succession, the stipulation was made that Antoninus, having no male issue, should in turn adopt two sons. One of these, the young son of Aelius Caesar, was subsequently known as Lucius Verus; the other, Antoninus's own nephew by marriage, afterward ruled as Marcus Aurelius Antoninus.

On Hadrian's death, on 10 July, 138,[a] Antoninus, surnamed Pius perhaps not so much because of his filial regard for his adoptive father's memory as for the purpose of signalizing his devotion to the best traditions of Rome, succeeded without opposition to the imperial power. In marked contrast to the travels of Hadrian, he had apparently spent his life in Italy except for the year in which he served as proconsul of Asia.[2] This year, according to a decree of Ephesus, passed on the occasion of his accession to power, had been the "cause of many great blessings" to the city; and in memory of these the Ephesians celebrated the new Emperor's birthday by a spectacle lasting for five days and the distribution to the citizens of money, to be provided from the public funds appropriated for furnishing sacrifices. The only known measure, however, taken by him during his proconsulship was an edict—presumably issued to ensure accuracy in the preferring of charges—which ordered the police-officials of the cities to question captured bandits about their associates and their hiding-places and to send the information under seal to the higher magistrates.

The principles according to which the new Emperor proposed to

---

[a] *Vit. Hadr.* 25, 6.

rule appear on the coins, issued soon after his accession, which are inscribed Equity and Clemency as well as Piety,[a] emphasizing, presumably, Antoninus's loyalty to tradition. Such was his concern for his subjects' welfare that in the judgement of a contemporary writer the title of Father of Mankind, which had been borne by the Persian King Cyrus, might well have been given to him, and, according to a later author, he fulfilled his public duties "with an incredible diligence in the manner of an excellent paterfamilias."[b]

It was said of Antoninus that he took no measures concerning the provinces without consulting his privy council and that under his rule they flourished.[c] By retaining good governors in office for protracted terms he was able to use the services of experienced men to promote a more capable provincial administration.[4]

Following the example of Hadrian on his accession to power, Antoninus refused to accept all the crown-gold offered to him on his adoption, returning in full what had been contributed by the towns of Italy and half the amount sent by the provinces.[5] His accession was celebrated also by a series of coins, issued by the Senate, on which the provinces and client-kingdoms are represented as female figures bringing wreaths of various shapes and, as in the similar series issued under Hadrian, provided with distinguishing attributes.

The policy of lightening the financial burdens of the provincials seems to have been consistently maintained.[d] In general, it is related, Antoninus disapproved of those exactions which caused hardship, and with a view to ensuring justice in taxation he acquainted himself with the budget of each province and the various sources of revenue. In order to prevent extortion, moreover, instructions were given to the procurators to use moderation in collecting what was owed to the imperial treasury. Accusations against these agents might be presented to the Emperor himself; when any seemed to have exceeded the proper limit, an accounting was demanded, and if he was shown to have been guilty of extortion and, in consequence, punished by the seizure of his property, the amount due for reparation was taken from his estate before this was handed over to the heirs.

Soon after Antoninus's accession to power there was need in Asia Minor of financial assistance when a severe earthquake caused much damage to various places in Caria and Lycia, as well as to the islands of Rhodes and Cos.[6] In Caria, Stratoniceia, evidently severely injured,

---

[b] Pausanias VIII 43, 6: *Epit. de Caess.* 15, 5. See also M. Aurelius *Medit.* I 16 and VI 30.
[c] *Vit. Pii* 6, 11; 7, 1.   [d] *Vit. Pii* 6, 1f.; 7, 8; 10, 7.

sent a special envoy to the Emperor to ask for aid, with the result that Antoninus gave the city 250,000 drachmae as a contribution to the work of rebuilding; and at Iasus the erection of a statue of the Emperor was perhaps an expression of gratitude for a benefaction of a similar kind. In Lycia, the wealthy Opramoas of Rhodiapolis aided many cities with generous gifts of money, but the fact that in at least six Lycian communities monuments were erected to Antoninus, often as "Saviour" or "Benefactor," suggests that the Emperor also contributed to the funds which these cities needed for repairing the effects of the disaster.

A few years afterward a similar calamity befell the region farther to the north, where a series of shocks inflicted great damage on the island of Lesbos and the coast of Ionia.[7] The flourishing and beautiful city of Mitylene was almost destroyed, and Smyrna and Ephesus were badly shaken and their inhabitants thrown into a state of panic. A statue of Antoninus as "Founder" erected by the Council and People of Mitylene and an altar dedicted to the Emperor at Smyrna suggest that these cities received aid from him in the work of rebuilding, and monuments in his honour at Magnesia-on-Maeander and Samos, both perhaps in the stricken area, may indicate that these places also had reason for gratitude on this occasion. Either at this time or somewhat later, Bithynia and the region of the Hellespont were similarly injured.[8] Among the places which suffered especially was Cyzicus, where the great temple of Hadrian seems to have been at least partially demolished.

At Ephesus there is also evidence of Antoninus's generosity. The statues erected to him as Founder were perhaps in recognition of his help at the time of the earthquake.[9] Even before this emergency, however, he had contributed to the beautification of the place. A certain Ephesian, who was also a Roman citizen, Publius Vedius Antoninus, had promised to erect certain public buildings for the city; but, unable to fulfil his promise and obtaining no assistance from his fellow-townsmen, he applied to the Emperor for financial aid. His request was granted, and in a letter informing the Ephesians of his contribution the Emperor took occasion to rebuke them for their failure to give support to Vedius, pointing out his superiority over the common run of citizens, who were accustomed to seek a reputation for generosity by giving money for distributions of cash or for spectacles and contests, whereas he, looking to the future, preferred to give dignity and beauty to his native place. Vedius, carrying out his original purpose, used the imperial gift—or so Antoninus reminded the Ephesians in a second letter—for the embellishment of the city, one of his achievements being the rebuilding of the gymnasium "from the foundation with all its ornamentation."

Many other cities also honoured the Emperor, in many cases, to be sure, because of an established custom.[10] At the Roman colony of Alexandria Troas a special *flamen*, or priest, was created for his worship; at Hyllarima in Caria a temple was dedicated to him jointly with Zeus Hyllus; and at Sardis (probably after his death) he was honoured "on account of his benevolence." At Pergamum, in addition to the usual honours conferred by the community, an ornamental gateway was dedicated by Claudius Charax, the author of an "Hellenic History" and a "Chronicle," with an inscription in which Antoninus was called Benefactor of the city, of the world and of the dedicator. In many other places also the name of the Emperor, often with the conventional titles, appears on the bases of statues or in dedications, sometimes in conjunction with the deified Augusti or the ancestral gods.[11]

As under Hadrian, the imperial government continued to exercise supervision over the finances of the cities with a view to preventing extravagance. At Ephesus even the appropriation of funds for the celebration of Antoninus's birthday, constituting a recurring charge on the public revenues, had to be officially confirmed.[12] Since Asia was a senatorial province, the city's action was ratified by the proconsul. In most cases, however, the supervision of a community's finances devolved upon the *curator*, an official apparently created by Trajan, who seems to have been appointed with increasing frequency and to have been vested with more and more extensive powers. Even the favoured city of Ilium, repeatedly declared exempt from all payments of money to Rome and expressly absolved by Antoninus himself from the obligation of assuming the guardianship of any who were not natives of the city, was placed under the charge of a curator, a citizen of Cyzicus, who was praised for "having by his curatorship and his advocacy corrected and accomplished many things of great importance, a man worthy of every honour because of his excellent character and his benevolence toward the city."

The extent of the control exercised by an official of this kind over the affairs of a city appears in an imperial rescript, probably issued under Antoninus, in which the duties of a curator appointed to supervise the finances of Ephesus are set forth in detail.[e] The accounts of

e *Ephesos* II no. 24 and *J.O.A.I.* XXVII (1932), *Beibl.* 21f. = *Ann. Ép.* 1932, 50. (two copies) the city-officials, both living and dead, for the past twenty years, so the rescript ordered, must be audited by the curator except in the cases of those who had died more than ten years previously, when the heirs were exempted from such an accounting. If the examination revealed that they owed money to the city, the amount in question was to be demanded by the curator as a debt, appeals being disallowed lest delay ensue. The curator had thereupon to make a report to the Emperor concerning the money recovered. By this measure the imperial government, taking direct action in Asia, although a province governed by a senatorial proconsul, sought to remedy the harm resulting from the sequestration of public funds by city-officials, an evil which Pliny, many years earlier, had found in the senatorial province of Bithynia.[f]

It proved necessary also to control the grant of special privileges. The bestowal on Antoninus of the title New Dionysus by the Artists of the God and the insertion of his name in their official title suggest that, like Hadrian, he confirmed the rights which the Society had long enjoyed.[g] The grant, however, of exemption from the ordinary burdens expected from the members of communities, which teachers and physicians in the public health service had received from Antoninus's predecessors,[h] had evidently been greatly abused. Many, hoping in this way to avoid their civic duties, had crowded into these favoured professions. It was, accordingly, considered necessary by the Emperor to check the growing numbers of those exempted, and in a letter addressed to the Commonalty of Asia but intended to have general validity, he imposed a strict limitation on the numbers of men thus privileged.[18] Henceforth, exemption was to be limited in the smallest cities to five physicians, three teachers of grammar and three of rhetoric; in those of greater size to seven physicians and four teachers of each of the two subjects; the largest might grant exemption to ten physicians and five teachers of each subject. It was specifically ordered that "none was to enjoy this exemption unless he had been enrolled by a decree of the Council in the number thus authorized and was performing his duties with all diligence."

On the other hand, Antoninus and his successor were liberal in granting exemption to those whose occupations seemed in themselves an essential service. On this ground it was granted to the members both of the corporation of grain-merchants and ship-owners, who supplied

[f] See above pp. 590 and 597.   [g] *I.G.* II² 1350 (see Chap. XXVI note 24).
[h] See Chap. XXIV note 15.

Italy with food, and of the associations of artisans who served as fire-fighters in their communities. It was also granted to those contractors who farmed the imperial estates.

The restriction imposed on the formation of societies, however, on which Trajan had insisted,[i] was still carefully observed. At Cyzicus it was deemed expedient—perhaps even necessary—to request the Senate to confirm by a special decree the existence of the association of the Young Men.[14] The city, to be sure, had had such an organization in the early third century before Christ and there were similar groups in most of the cities of Asia Minor. An official confirmation, however, may have been desirable for the reason that in many places the young men had come into disrepute by taking part in riots and causing serious disorder, which rendered it necessary to forbid their attendance at the public spectacles or even to have them beaten, and, in cases of a repetition of the offence, to order severer punishment. Even the formation of an Elders' Association, although these organizations were long recognized and wide-spread, was subject to a confirmation; for when, under Antoninus's grandson, Commodus, the city of Sidyma in Lycia wished to form an association of this kind, the Council and People requested the proconsul to give his formal approval.[15]

The need for governmental control of organizations, in fact, is shown by labour disputes in the cities.[16] At Pergamum the refusal of the artisans to continue the construction of a building called forth an edict of the proconsul, who, apparently after a personal inspection, promised leniency to those who were ready to work but imposed a fine on those who refused. At Miletus the artisans engaged in repairing the theatre were minded to leave the work and seek other employment, but the plan was abandoned on the advice of the oracle of Apollo to obtain the services of an expert. A more serious situation occurred at Ephesus, where a strike of the "brotherhood" of the bakers was attended with so much "disorder and tumult" that action was taken by an official, probably the proconsul, who, in order to prevent further violence, issued an edict forbidding the organization to hold unauthorized meetings or cause further disturbance and also commanding the bakers "to obey the regulations made for the general welfare and to supply the city unfailingly with the labour necessary for bread-making."

Another source of trouble, in which the imperial government found it necessary to intervene, was the discord caused by the vanity and rivalry of the cities in the matter of rank and titles.[17] At the beginning

---

[i] See above p. 602.

of the second century, it will be remembered, Nicomedeia and Nicaea were at enmity on account of their respective claims to the title of First City of Bithynia and there was also ill-feeling between Ephesus and Smyrna. Under Antoninus the bone of contention between these two great cities was also the right to use certain titles, especially, as it would appear, that of First and Greatest Metropolis of Asia, assumed by Ephesus and desired by the people of Smyrna. In order to allay the strife between the cities, the Emperor found it necessary to intervene by specifying the title which the Ephesians might adopt and urging them in a letter addressed to the Council and People of the city to overlook the Smyrniots' failure to refer to Ephesus in the proper manner. He also admonished them, when addressing their rival, to use the titles which Smyrna had the right to bear; for if they did so, it was hoped, the latter "would in the future be willing to adopt a conciliatory attitude."

Under Antoninus's successor, however, the dispute seems to have broken out afresh, with Pergamum as a third contestant.[18] On this occasion Smyrna was successful, for the city obtained a share in the position of primacy hitherto held by Ephesus; in fact, it appears in inscriptions and coins of the early third century not merely as the First of Asia but with the additional specification of "in beauty and greatness" and as the "Glory of Ionia." Pergamum, on the other hand, was forced to be content with the title of "Metropolis of Asia and the first city to be Twice Temple-Warden." Eventually some definite order of rank was established, for in the third century Magnesia-on-Maeander had the official rating of Seventh in Asia.

Other titles were no less grandiose, such as that assumed by Miletus as "First settled city of Ionia, Metropolis of many great cities in Pontus and Egypt and in many places in the inhabited world," and that of Heracleia on the Euxine, called "Mother of the cities founded by herself and the First of Pontus."[19] A claim to antiquity also was sought by Sardis and by Stratoniceia in Caria, each of which called itself "Autochthonous and Metropolis."

The most frequently used title was that of Metropolis, often found with the qualifying adjective "illustrious" and with the name of the province or the district attached. Thus Sardis was "Metropolis of Asia and all Lydia," and Stratoniceia "Metropolis of Caria." Cyzicus also was a "most illustrious Metropolis," and both Laodiceia and Tralles called themselves Metropolis of Asia.[20] So far was this absurd practice carried that even the former tribal centres Temenothyrae and

Silandus assumed the title of Metropolis of Moccadene. In the other provinces also, most places of importance were likewise called Metropolis either of the province or of a district, sometimes combining with this title that of First City.

Another favourite title was that of Temple-Warden. It has already been observed that during the first century by special permission of the Roman government those cities which were seats of the worship of the emperors, namely Pergamum, Ephesus and Smyrna, became officially "Temple-Warden of the Augusti"; and under Hadrian the title appears to have been assumed also by Cyzicus and Sardis and probably by Nicomedeia and Tarsus.[21] But whereas this title was perhaps originally held only by those places in which there was a provincial cult of the emperors, in the course of the second century this restriction seems to have disappeared; for cities such as Tralles and Philadelpheia, where the Commonalty of Asia may sometimes have held meetings but maintained no temples, also became Temple-Wardens. In the case of Philadelpheia, the title was assumed by special authorization from the Emperor Caracalla, and during the third century it was borne, frequently without the distinguishing addition of "the Augusti," by a number of places on which it was presumably bestowed by a similar imperial grant as an honorary appellation intended to gratify the cities' vanity. So eagerly, in fact, was it desired, that many cities, in consequence of further grants, called themselves "Twice Temple-Warden" and a few of the more important even assumed the title "Thrice Temple-Warden." On the other hand, Magnesia and Aezani, which received no imperial sanction for a cult of the emperors, satisfied their desire for a sacred title by calling themselves Temple-Wardens of their chief deities, Artemis and Zeus.

Certain cities, moreover, including Nicomedeia, Nicaea, Sardis and Aphrodisias as well as several in southern Asia Minor, sought to enhance their prestige by emphasizing a connexion with the Romans and taking the title of Ally or Friend and Ally of Rome.[22] Since there was no longer even a pretence of an alliance with the ruling city, these titles, based solely on a relationship—sometimes imaginary—in the remote past, were wholly meaningless.

Another fiction of an antiquarian character appears in the desire to establish an Hellenic tradition by claiming a connexion with the gods and heroes of Greece. Thus Nicaea honoured Dionysus, Heracles and Asclepius as Founders; Dionysus was claimed by Tieium, Heracles by both Cius and Nacoleia, and Hermes by Amaseia.[23] Others ascribed their foundation to heroes of the ancient epic poems. Some of these claims, to be sure, date from as early as the fifth and fourth centuries before Christ, when the Homeric seers Amphilochus and Calchas, as well as Mopsus, were regarded as the founders of various cities in Pamphylia and Cilicia. Other claims, however, such as those of the Phrygian cities Synnada, Dorylaeum and Metropolis to Acamas (either a son of Theseus or a Trojan leader of this name) and of the Abbaïtae to the Mysian Chromius, were evidently of late origin. Ancient eponymous heroes also were claimed. Pergamum, in addition to Telephus, had a Pergamus who was still regarded as founder in the imperial period; there were similar heroes in the Greek cities Erythrae and Iasus, and even Parium, although a Roman colony, had a mythical Parius. Similar heroes were fabricated by places which had no connexion with Greece. Dorylaeum, not content with Acamas, had a founder, Dorylaus, declared to be a descendant of Heracles; and Tralles, Cyzicus, Miletopolis, Poemanenum and Temenothyrae, boasting founders whose names were evidently derived from their own, endeavoured to create a similar claim to an ancient origin.

In spite of the feuds between cities and the disputes over rank and titles, there is evidence that in many cases a policy of entering into friendly relations was adopted. The decree of Smyrna, which, by failing to give Ephesus its full title—inadvertently, according to Antoninus's letter previously cited—offended the Ephesians,[j] dealt with a joint sacrifice in which both cities were to participate. At Aphrodisias statues of six different cities in the neighbouring parts of Caria and southwestern Phrygia, described as "participants in sacrifice," were erected by the *demos* "in consideration of the gift of the sacred contest."[23a] At Ephesus the city erected statues of Cnidus, its "sister," Cos, its "brother," and Nicaea, the principal town of the Cilbiani. In the colony of Antioch-near-Pisidia, the "sister" cities, Lystra and Tavium, erected statues of "Concord," and an inscription commemorating the "concord" between Mopsuestia and Anazarbus in Cilicia has been found in the former. The most striking example, however, of an attempt to establish relations appears in the bronze coins bearing the names of two or, sometimes, three cities and, usually, the legend "Concord." Of this joint coinage, issued in increasingly large numbers from the late first century onward, there are at least ninety-six reasonably well-attested examples. The purpose of these coins, to be sure, is not wholly clear. The presence on most of them of the legend "Con-

j See above p. 636.

cord" has suggested that they were intended to signify a reconciliation which terminated a feud. The large number of combinations, however, as well as the distance between some of the jointly issuing cities—as in the cases of an Asianic community and Alexandria in Egypt or a city in Greece—renders this explanation improbable, and the fact that some of the earlier issues, dating from the first century, lack this legend does not suggest a reconciliation. The distances in many cases, moreover, tell against the suggestion that these coins were intended to mark the establishment of a common cult or festival. It seems more probable, as has also been proposed, that their purpose was to create a commercial bond which would promote trade and, with it, "concord" between the cities which jointly issued these coins.

The increasing self-consciousness on the part of the cities may be regarded as the result of the policy of the imperial government shown both in promoting the growth of the number of urban centres and in encouraging the greatest degree of local autonomy that was compatible with Roman rule. This policy, instituted by Augustus, by which the Empire became a congeries of self-governing communities, was carried on most conspicuously by Vespasian and Hadrian, who either founded new cities in predominantly rural districts or transformed old tribal centres into *poleis*.[24] At the same time, the extent to which the central government controlled the process of urbanization appears in the grant of city-status to the community of Tymandus in northern Pisidia, which was conferred in a letter of an unknown emperor, addressed to a Roman official, authorizing the formation of a city-council composed of fifty members, the election of officials and "all else that was necessary." As the result of this process, the cities which during the second century and the first half of the third issued their own coins were at least 312 in number, and as many as 272 places (including the Roman colonies) had a council or civic officials or are otherwise known to have had the status of a *polis*.[25] The administration of these communities, now all subject alike—since free cities, except for the colonies and a few favoured places, had ceased to exist—was carried on by the *polis*, which had the right of local self-government with the management of its revenues, including those derived from public lands, from taxes and fines, from franchises and fees, and, especially after the end of the first century, from bequests by patriotic citizens.

In spite of these rights, however, the power of Rome had brought about a marked change in the form of government of the Asiatic cities; for, in contrast to the traditional Greek democracy, the preponderance of power, as has been previously observed, had passed from the citizens as a whole to the wealthier and presumably more responsible class.[k] The *demos*, to be sure, continued to meet in its Assembly and action was still taken in the name of the Council and People.[26] In certain cities, however, a distinction between "ecclesiasts" and "citizens" seems to show that not all who possessed the status of citizen had the right to vote in the Assembly. It has been suggested that this right was held only by those who possessed a certain amount of property and that consequently there was a disfranchised class, composed of members of the city proletariat as well as most of the peasants; at Prusias-on-Hypius, in fact, a distinction was made between "the registered" and "those who inhabit the rural territory."

The body of citizens included also men from other places, on whom the rights of the city had been bestowed. In Bithynia such grants to members of other communities in the province had been forbidden by Pompey's law providing for the organization of Bithynia, but in the early second century this clause of the law had fallen into abeyance.[l] Whether a similar prohibition had ever existed in the other provinces is unknown, but if so, it was likewise disregarded, for in the late second and the third centuries instances of multiple citizenship were frequent.[27] These outsiders were often distinguished athletes, musicians and actors, on whom communities both in Greece and in Asia Minor conferred this honour in recognition of their achievements.

As the result of the Roman policy of restricting power in the cities to the conservative few, the Assembly, although theoretically possessing supreme power, had become little more than a confirmatory body. While it appears to have been possible for others, presumably members of the Council, to introduce proposals or "ask for a vote," it had become customary for only the magistrates to bring resolutions before the *demos* for acceptance or, at least in theory, rejection.[28] Since these magistrates were members of the Council, it may be assumed that the resolutions which they offered had been approved by that body. Even the election of these magistrates was controlled by the Council; for while the Assembly seems to have gone through the form of voting, the actual choice was limited to a list which the Council submitted to the voters. Most of the known instances of action taken in the name of the Council and People deal with the bestowal of honours, but in

---

[k] See above p. 600.   [l] See above p. 604.

some cases matters of real importance were involved. The enactments had to be approved by the Roman governor, who might even, as a penalty for disorder, deprive the citizens of the right of public meeting.[29] Restricted, as it was, in these various ways, the power of the popular Assembly became largely nominal.

The actual administration of a city, consequently, was vested in the Council and the magistrates. The Council, according to the law of Pompey dealing with Bithynia, was composed of those who had served as civic officials,[m] and it may probably be supposed that this was the case in the other Asiatic provinces as well.[n] Since, as will be shown, only the wealthy could afford to hold public office,[o] the councils were definitely timocratic in character. In fact, in Bithynia, as an argument for enrolling as councillors a number of younger men who had not held office, it was maintained that it was to the advantage of the community that the sons of the better families rather than those of plebeian status should have seats in the city-councils.[p] Since the magisterial posts were filled by nominees of the councils, the latter became self-perpetuating permanent bodies, in which membership was practically hereditary.[30] The result was the formation of a wealthy ruling-class, composed of councillors and their families, which, like the Senatorial Order in Rome, held the reins of government and enjoyed both political and social privileges. Many, receiving Roman citizenship, had a career of office under the imperial administration.

The lists of the councillors, at least in cities of Bithynia and Galatia and at Pergamum and Aphrodisias, were controlled by censors, appointed from time to time for the purpose.[31] They had also power to expel members on certain specified grounds. While ordinarily there was a definite number of seats—which varied from city to city—it was possible for the censors to enroll additional councillors. These paid an admission-fee, determined by the city-authorities, and this, in Bithynia at least, was subquently made compulsory for all members alike. In the case of the ship-master Erastus, for whom Hadrian requested admission to the Council at Ephesus, it was paid by the Emperor himself. These additional councillors often included men from other places, who, since they obviously could not take an active part in deliberations, were merely honorary members. Frequently— as also in the cases of the honorary citizens already mentioned—they were prominent athletes or actors, some of whom became councillors

---

m See above p. 603.   n Cassius Dio xxxvii 20, 2.   o See below p. 650f.
p Pliny *Epist. ad Trajan.* 79, 3. See above p. 603.

in several cities. In the course of time, as private fortunes shrank, the office of councillor, on account of the expense involved, was often regarded as a burden rather than an honour and it was frequently evaded under various pretexts.

In several cities of the province of Asia the Council had as presiding-officer a "Bularch," who in general held the post for a limited time but in one instance at least was Bularch for life.[32] Decrees, to be valid, had to be passed at a session attended by not less than two thirds of the members. After enactment, they were in some cities drafted by a committee of councillors who guaranteed the authenticity of the version. A decree which favoured an individual, as, for example, the bestowal of land or money at the city's expense, was forbidden by the imperial government, and in general an enactment of the Council —like measures passed by the *demos*—must receive the sanction of the governor. In order, presumably, to prevent whimsical or ill-considered legislation, Hadrian in a rescript addressed to Nicomedeia prohibited the rescinding of a decree unless such action conduced to the public advantage.

The administrative functions belonging to the Council were many and various. It might assume the responsibility for the construction of public works and for the proper use of gifts presented to the city.[33] It might also authorize the erection of monuments and tombs. Having funds of its own and—at Pergamum at least—its own treasurer, it could make appropriations for honorific statues. In numerous instances the owners of a tomb ordered that the fine prescribed for violation of the monument should be paid into the Council's treasury. Gifts and bequests were likewise received, frequently to constitute endowments for periodic distributions to the councillors. The Council had also the power to name those teachers and physicians who, as has been already related, were granted exemption from civic duties. The general maintenance of law and order, moreover, devolved upon the Council. In some of the cities in the province of Asia it seems to have compiled a list of names from which the proconsul chose a "ruler of the peace," and at Ephesus it co-operated with the governor in suppressing the violence resulting from the strike, already mentioned, of the bakers. Measures of minor, and indeed trivial, importance were the provision for the singing of a hymn in honour of Zeus and Hecate at Stratoniceia and the assignment of seats in the theatre at Ephesus to the "gold-wearing" priests and athletic victors and of places to the market-porters at Smyrna who had put themselves under the protection of Asclepius.

The officials of the cities, as compared with those of the Hellenistic period,[q] were fewer in number, and their titles show a general tendency toward uniformity. Some of the older places, to be sure, retained their ancient officials with their traditional designations. Thus at Cyzicus the eponymous magistrate was still the hipparch and, at least in the first century, the old governing committees (*prytaneis*) of the Council performed their functions for a month at a time.[34] At Ephesus, Pergamum and Colophon (Notium) the eponymous *prytanis* was likewise retained and at Miletus there was still a stephanephorus. The eponymous stephanephorus—now, more than ever, merely a title of honour, since the duties of the office were confined to giving banquets and entertainments—was retained also in many of the older cities, such as Magnesia-on-Maeander and Smyrna, and adopted by many of later origin, like Nysa, Tralles, Hierapolis, Aphrodisias and Stratoniceia, as well as by other places of less importance. At Samos and Cnidus the eponymous magistrate was still the demiurge, and he was retained as a single official in the cities of Pamphylia and Cilicia as well as in a few places in Pisidia.

The administration of civic affairs was, as previously, carried on by executive boards. Certain cities, such as Miletus and Priene, retained their ancient *prytaneis*, headed by an arch-prytanis.[35] There were boards of *prytaneis* also at Smyrna and at Stratoniceia in Caria, but in other places in the province of Asia the mere mention of the title *prytanis* does not make it possible to determine whether this term was applied to a member of a board or to a single official. In the Lycian city of Myra the *prytaneis* constituted a board, but in the other cities of the district the exact meaning of the title is likewise uncertain. They formed a board also in the Hellenistic city of Seleuceia in Cilicia and in the Hellenized Castabala-Hieropolis and in Cappadocia in the temple-city of Comana; in Seleuceia they presented a resolution to the Council and People, in Castabala they arranged for the erection of a statue of a Roman governor.

The most wide-spread of these magisterial boards was that of the *strategoi*.[36] Found during the Hellenistic period in many of the Greek cities, under the Romans they became very frequent, especially in the province of Asia. In the new *poleis*, particularly, including those founded by the emperors, they were ordinarily the governing officials.

---

[q] See above p. 58f.

The board seems usually to have consisted of five members, although in some places it had only three or four; it was frequently headed by a "First *Strategos*," who often appears to have acted for his colleagues.

In many cities the magisterial board appears as archons. This, in fact, was the general term regularly applied to city-magistrates in the letters addressed to communities by emperors or Roman officials. Since in a large number of places both archons and *strategoi* are mentioned and it seems unlikely that two magisterial boards existed side by side with the same functions, it may probably be assumed that the former term was merely used as a general designation for the governing board, whether *prytaneis* or *strategoi*.[37]

One of the duties of the magisterial board, as has already been noted, was to bring resolutions to the popular Assembly for acceptance.[r] In general, however, its functions involved the administration of the community.[38] It was responsible for the management of the public finances, as at Ceramus in Caria, where a *strategos* leased out land bequeathed to the city, and at Cibyra and Orcistus in Phrygia, where the archons administered an oath to the *demos* to carry out the terms of a bequest and were responsible for the investment of an endowment. The board had also the duty of enforcing the enactments of the Council and People; at Mitylene the fine imposed for disobedience of a decree was to be collected by the *strategoi*, and at Mylasa the archons were ordered to co-operate with the Council in trying those accused of violating the law forbidding illicit exchange and, if these were found guilty, to impose fines or, in the case of a slave, sentence to corporal punishment and imprisonment. In Antoninus's edict, issued while he was proconsul of Asia, the magistrates were ordered to try those arrested on a charge of banditry. In a great number of cases, the name and title of a *strategos* or an archon, frequently the foreman of the board, appear on the bronze coins issued by a city, presumably with the authorization of the Roman government, indicating that it was during his term of office or at his expense that the issue took place.

In certain cities there was an individual *strategos*, whose title suggests the original military character of the office.[39] Thus Smyrna had a "*strategos* in charge of arms," whose duty may have been to supply the weapons needed to suppress riots. Other places had a *strategos* of the night-watch, presumably charged with policing the city after dark. The general maintenance of order outside the city was entrusted at Aphrodisias to two "*strategoi* in charge of the territory," whose

---

[r] See above p. 640.

office probably dated from the period of Rhodian rule but continued to be necessary for the reason that the city possessed a large rural district, exposed, on account of the neighbouring mountains, to raids by brigands.

By far the most important of the individual officials, however, was the clerk, who was no longer, as in the Hellenistic period, the mere secretary of the Council or the *demos*.[40] It was evidently in this capacity, to be sure, that he often acted in conjunction with the magisterial board in presenting to the popular Assembly resolutions which he had presumably formulated and that he bore the responsibility for the erection of statues decreed by the Council and People in honour of emperors and various notables. In general, however, the clerk was charged with many of the details of the administration of the city. At Ephesus he distributed to the councillors the money presented by Vibius Salutaris and had the charge of the endowment for doles to be given to the citizens; he also, in accordance with a measure passed by the Council and People, distributed money from the public treasury annually on Antoninus's birthday; and, it will be remembered, he dispersed the mob which assembled to attack St. Paul. At Cibyra he joined the *strategoi* in administering the oath taken by the *demos* to preserve intact the endowment for a gymnasiarchate, at Orcistus he was responsible for the management of the income from an endowment and at Stratoniceia he even chose the hymn to be sung by a chorus of boys in honour of Zeus and Hecate. The clerk's name and title, furthermore, appear on the coins of many cities, and inscriptions were frequently dated by his year of office.

As also during the Hellenistic period, the sale of merchandise was under the supervision of a special official, the controller of the market, or *agoranomos*.[41] The office was usually held by one man, but in some cities there was a board consisting of two or three members. The duties of the *agoranomos* included the maintenance and even the construction of the buildings of the market as well as of other public works, among them his office, the *agoranomion*. He was responsible also for establishing prices and determining the accuracy of the weights that were used. His chief concern, however, was with the articles exposed for sale, especially food and oil, for the supply and even the price of which he was responsible; at Magnesia, on one occasion, the *agoranomos* placed oil on sale at less than the regular price at a time when it was in great demand. In several cases, it was said in praise of an *agoranomos* that he held office during a famine or at a time of distress or pressure, and the frequent statements that a man performed the duties of the office "magnificently," "lavishly," "steadfastly" or "with distinction" suggest that these entailed considerable expense. This may well have been the reason why frequently the office was held for only a few months and why it was said in praise of a citizen of Tralles that he was the first and only *agoranomos* to serve for a whole year.

In addition to an *agoranomos*, many cities had a special commissioner for the purchase of grain (*sitones*), whose duty it was to supply the citizens at a reasonable price.[42] While sometimes there were public funds from which the requisite amount could be drawn—and repaid after the grain was sold—the commissioner had often to meet the difference between the buying and the selling price at his own expense. When, as not infrequently happened, the home-grown supply proved insufficient, it was necessary for him as well as for private benefactors to import grain from abroad, sometimes even from Egypt. A *sitones* at Thyateira was commended for having served at a time when food was hard to obtain, and it is recorded of a citizen of Teos that on several occasions he accepted the office during a time of great need when no one else would take it.

In a few places the general care of the fabric of the city, as also at Pergamum under the kings, was assigned to a particular official, the city-guardian, or *astynomos*.[43] It was his duty to see that the house-walls were kept in repair, in order that they might not become dangerous, and that they did not encroach on public highways. He was also responsible for the drains and the fountains and for maintaining the streets in good condition and keeping them free from encumbrances. In order that he might be able to enforce his commands he was authorized to impose fines on offenders. Sometimes the task of providing the city with a water-supply was entrusted to a special commissioner, who in one case, although public funds were appropriated for the purpose, nevertheless opened up a source at his own expense, and at Magnesia there seems to have been an official "in charge of the springs."

Sometimes the task of providing a city with oil—next to grain the most important commodity—was performed by a special official, the purchaser of oil, or *elaiones*.[44] Both at Aphrodisias and at Prusias in Bithynia there was a particular fund for the purpose.

As a rule, the public funds, as also during the Hellenistic period, were under the care of a treasurer.[45] His functions seem ordinarily to have been performed by a single official, but in some of the larger places, such as Smyrna, Pergamum and Miletus, by a board. Sometimes there were treasurers of special funds, as the grain-fund and the oil-fund at Prusias. In general, the treasurer was a subordinate official, whose duty it was to pay out the money appropriated by the Council. Sometimes, however, he might receive the fines imposed for the violation of a tomb, and at Pergamum the treasurers had charge of the slaves belonging to the city. At Smyrna, moreover, a treasurer's name and title appear on coins, and inscriptions were frequently dated by the year of office of one of the board.

The maintenance of order in a city was entrusted to a ruler of the peace, or *eirenarch*, who was "responsible for public discipline and reforming public morals."[46] The office, which is found in many of the cities of Asia Minor, is not known before the Roman period. The holder, chosen by the governor from a list of ten leading citizens submitted by the Council, had evidently a high rank, for the title usually appears among those of important officials. In one case, however, the office was held by an imperial slave. The duties of the *eirenarch* included, according to the edict of Antoninus Pius, already mentioned, which was adopted by later emperors, the arrest and interrogation of bandits; these, together with the evidence against them, were thereupon to be sent to the magistrates for a trial, at which the *eirenarch* must appear and give his testimony. Under his command was a body of troopers called *diogmitae*, who made the actual arrests. They appear in connexion with the persecution of the Christians; it is related that *diogmitae*, acting on orders from the *eirenarch*, arrested St. Polycarp in A.D. 155 and that a similar band seized St. Nestor in 251, also at the command of the *eirenarch*, who then took Nestor to the governor for trial.

Another police-official was the guardian, or *paraphylax*.[47] His post also was evidently an important one, for the title appears among those of officials of high rank. At Aphrodisias he and the clerk proposed a decree to the Assembly and a list of *paraphylakes* at Notium records that each provided the city with wine. The duties of the office were presumably somewhat similar to those of the *eirenarch*, but there was evidently some difference between them, for in several instances both existed in the same city at the same time. It is probable that the *paraphylax* was in charge of a city's rural territory; for a decree of Hierapolis forbad *paraphylakes* to receive perquisites from villagers, and an edict, perhaps of a proconsul, ordered that graziers who trespassed on vineyards should, if slaves, be reported to them for flogging. The *paraphylax* seems to have been in command of a body of gendarmes or "frontier-guards," for at Apollonia in Caria eleven of these joined him in building a sanctuary of the Great Mother. Their duty was presumably to protect the frontiers of a city's territory against incursions. That this might be attended by danger appears in the monument of one who was slain by brigands, especially frequent in the mountainous and more remote regions.

The collection of the taxes paid to Rome, for which the civic authorities were now responsible, was in charge of a board of ten men, composed of the "first" citizens.[48] They are not heard of before the early second century, and in some cities, almost all in Lycia, their number was soon increased to twenty. While possibly originally a sort of finance-committee of the Council, these *dekaprotoi* were hardly, as has sometimes been supposed, a commission composed of the first ten men on the list of councillors; for the appearance of the office among those held by important citizens and the fact that on the island of Amorgos the *dekaprotoi* acted with the *strategoi* in bringing resolutions before the Assembly indicate that they were regular officials of the *demos*. They may ordinarily have served for one year, but there are instances of tenures for three and ten years and even for the remainder of the holder's life. The board, as responsible for the payment of the tax levied on a city by the Roman government, appears to have been under obligation to make up any deficit at the members' expense. Other duties of a financial nature might be assigned to them; at Iasus the administrator of an endowment was chosen from their number, and in another case the foundress of a contest, who retained the capital sum in her own hands, was obliged to furnish security to the *dekaprotoi* that the interest thereon would be paid when due.

While the local courts probably continued to have jurisdiction in cases of minor importance, lawsuits between citizens, as also in the Hellenistic period, were frequently conducted by judges imported from other places.[49] The city itself, however, as in Hellenistic times, had a legal representative of its own, the *ekdikos*, who acted in questions needing adjustment with the Roman government as well as in matters affecting internal affairs. He differed from the *syndikos*, who also appears to have represented the city in a legal capacity, in that he was a regular official, whereas the *syndikos* seems to have been appointed only for special cases. It has sometimes been supposed that the *ekdikos* was the official representative of the governor and an intermediary between the Roman administration and the city. But, while it is true that he often pleaded a case for the city before the governor or even the emperor, he was elected by the *demos* and his title appears regularly among those of city-officials. In his capacity of counsel for the community, presumably, he is mentioned both at Aphrodisias and at Attaleia in Lydia in connexion with the civic finances. At Amisus the *ekdikos* acted in the interest of the city by bringing suit before the governor, Pliny, for the recovery of a sum of money granted to a citizen some years previously by the Council and Assembly, his plea being based on a ruling of the Emperor forbidding such grants. At Cibyra he conducted several suits for the city, including one in which he obtained for it an estate and a large number of slaves. Participation in internal matters appears also in the action of an *ekdikos* who was praised at Thyateira by the inhabitants of two villages for having effected the restoration of property belonging to their communities, as well as in a decree of Ephesus concerning the legacy left to the city by Vibius Salutaris, which specifically forbad the *ekdikos*, as well as any magistrate or private citizen, to make any alteration in the disposition of the bequest. At Ephesus, moreover, there was a special *ekdikos* for the Council, and at Alabanda a former Roman military tribune, apparently a native of the place, acted as *ekdikos* in restoring the boundaries of the city's territory.

In numerous instances the nominal character of many of these offices appears in the choice of incumbents whose chief qualifications were the possession of wealth and a readiness to spend. In certain cities, as has already been observed, during both the Hellenistic and the Roman periods the eponymous magistracy was held by a deity, from whose treasury the expenses of the office were paid.[8] Much more frequently, this and, occasionally, other offices were held by a woman.[50] This practice seems to have existed in a few instances in the second and first centuries before Christ, when women acted as stephanephorus at Sardis and Priene. It became much more general, however, during the imperial period, when women held the offices of hipparch (at Cyzicus), stephanephorus, prytanis and demiurge. Their duties were presumably purely honorary, and in those cases in which the title was borne also by the husband it was evidently given to the wife merely as a compliment. In what was probably a more active capacity, a woman served as *dekaprotos* at Sillyum in Pamphylia and perhaps as clerk at Tralles. None, however, seems to have held such an office as that of councillor, *strategos, agoranomos* or treasurer, the duties of which were presumably regarded as requiring the services of men.

[8] See Chap. III note 24 and above note 34.

Offices were also held nominally by minors.[51] It is usually stated that a father took the post in behalf of his son, but in one instance it is recorded that a youth was treasurer before the legal age. The office, if specified, was usually that of *agoranomos*, but more frequently the general statement of "offices and liturgies" was used. Even more surprising is the titular holding of an office by a dead person, described as a "hero," or departed spirit. The offices thus bestowed on the dead were, indeed, only the eponymous magistracies of hipparch at Cyzicus and of stephanephorus at Aphrodisias, Magnesia-near-Sipylus and Hierapolis, the duties of which were, of course, purely nominal.

The bestowal of these offices on those who were obviously unable to perform the functions attached to them had its origin in the custom of paying a sum of money in return for the post in question. In the case of the deities, as has already been observed, the payment from the sacred treasury seems to have been made when no citizen could be found who was able to bear the expense. The women, on the other hand—or perhaps their husbands—were willing to purchase the distinction thus obtained, fathers were ready to pay for their sons' early advancement to public office, and relatives or those who administered the estates of the deceased wished to confer on them this posthumous mark of honour.

The custom of making these payments seems to have arisen from the obligation assumed by the holders of eponymous magistracies, the stephanephorus and the prytanis, to meet the expenses which these offices entailed.[52] Originally, perhaps, the amount was commensurate with the wealth of the holder, but in the course of time it seems to have been commuted to a definite sum. The duties of the *agoranomos* also, as has already been observed, were frequently performed at considerable cost. Payments in return for public office, however, were not restricted to these posts, for it became the general custom that, like city-councillors,[t] other office-holders also, such as the *strategos* and the treasurer, should make a gift to the community in return for the honour which it conferred. This gift—consisting, probably, of a minimum fixed amount, which might be increased by the generosity of the donor—might be a sum of money or a public building or some other ornament to the city. It is recorded of a citizen of Sebastopolis in Caria that in return for two financial posts he paid respectively 4,000 and 11,200 denarii, for an honorary eirenarchate he paved the space in front of the gymnasium and for the post of *strategos* of the night-watch he erected a statue of

---

t See above p. 641.

Victory. Sometimes, as in the case of Aelius Alcibiades of Nysa, who presented the city with an "everlasting stephanephorate," to be available "whenever none of the citizens under obligation to hold the office was found able to do so," the gift was used for a perpetual endowment. The local priests of the emperors also paid for their priesthoods, and even the humble officials of a village-community in the valley of the Lydian Caÿster, the curators and the village-chiefs, gave modest sums for their posts.

It is evident that these gifts made in return for public office increased the income of the cities and so lightened the burden of taxation for the poorer citizens. At the same time, the city-budgets were not wholly relieved of the cost of these offices, for in some places, at least, the holders obtained a financial return from the emoluments attached to their posts. At Ephesus a former clerk contributed to the city a large sum of money from the income of his office, and at Apollonia-on-Rhyndacus a statue of Domitian was erected from surplus funds paid back by a magistrate.[53] Nevertheless, as the standard of payments rose as the result both of increased expenses and local pride, it was often difficult to find those who were willing to assume the financial burden which the holding of office involved. A comparative paucity of those who accepted the responsibility, especially in the smaller cities, is suggested by the large number of offices held successively by one man as well as by the fact that frequently the same post was held several times. It was occasionally said, moreover, in praise of a citizen that he held a public office voluntarily.

As a result of the practice of making payments for offices, the distinction, not always well determined in the Hellenistic period,[u] between a magistracy and a liturgy, or public service, which was expected and even required from all citizens and residents able to bear the necessary cost, became even less clear, for both involved the expenditure of money.[54] In fact, the ruling of Hadrian, previously mentioned, which granted exemption to certain professions included the posts of *agoranomos, sitones* and *elaiones* among those covered by the grant, thus placing them among the liturgies; and according to a jurist of the early fourth century, the classification of the treasurership varied in the different cities. There seems also to have been an uncertainty concerning other offices; for at Nysa under Antoninus Pius the stephanephorate endowed by Aelius Alcibiades was referred to as

[u] See above p. 61.

a liturgy, and at Smyrna in the early third century emphasis was laid on the fact that a "sophist," who on account of his profession was exempt from liturgies, had voluntarily accepted the office of *strategos*. Nevertheless, a distinction was made, for in countless instances it was said of a patriotic citizen that he had fulfilled every magistracy and every liturgy; and the jurists differentiated between the former as an honour conferring dignity and the latter as a service. The tenure of a magistracy, moreover, as has already been noted, brought membership in the Council and disqualification was considered a disgrace, whereas exemption from a liturgy was regarded as a privilege by those who enjoyed the right and was sought by those who wished to evade their duty to the community. Sometimes, indeed, the right was waived, as in the case of Sempronius Clemens of Stratoniceia, a Roman citizen, who, although he had an inherited claim to exemption, granted by decree of the Senate, nevertheless not only performed the liturgies of gymnasiarch and agonothete but also held the offices of *dekaprotos*, prytanis, stephanephorus and clerk. It was possible also to render these public services in the name of minors, who thus obtained a preliminary credit for their obligations to the community. At Erythrae a distinguished citizen was described as a "liturgist from the age of boyhood," at Stratoniceia it is recorded that a youth was gymnasiarch at the age of eleven, and at Xanthus in Lycia the holder of many offices performed liturgies not only for himself but even for his grandchildren.

The liturgies seem to have varied from city to city and probably also from time to time according to a community's needs. In practically every place, however, as also during the Hellenistic period, they included, as the most important, those performed by the gymnasiarch and the agonothete. The gymnasium was now, more than ever, the chief centre of the social life of the community, and there was at least one in every city of any importance.[55] Some places, in fact, had several. There were six or seven in Pergamum, four at Iasus, and three at Miletus, at Tralles and at Thyateira; at Dorylaeum there was even a gymnasium for women. The gymnasiarch was not only charged with the direction of the establishment, but, although in some cases the city made an appropriation for the purpose, he was responsible for the maintenance of the building and the current expenses, which at Apameia during the time of the governor's assizes (when on account of the crowded condition of the city the expense was unusually large) amounted to over 3,000 denarii per month. Among these expenses was the oil which the gymnasiarch was expected to furnish for varying lengths of time without cost to the users of the building. At Lagina and Panamara it was apparently customary for the priests to serve as gymnasiarch for this purpose. In some places an unusually generous citizen endowed a "perpetual" gymnasiarchate, and occasionally, as also in certain of the civic offices, a woman assumed the burden of expense and with it the title. In some cases, to be sure, in which her husband also appears as gymnasiarch, it is a question whether this title was not merely honorary.

Occasionally the holder of the office acted as gymnasiarch of all the gymnasia in the city.[56] Ordinarily, however, he administered only one, such as that of the association of the Young Men or of the Elders. The latter organization, the *gerousia*, although wholly distinct from the Council, as appears from the separate mention of councillors and "gerousiasts" in distributions of money as well as in the composition of the Association at Sidyma in Lycia, which consisted of forty-nine councillors and forty-seven "commoners," had an important position in civic affairs and frequently joined the Council and People in conferring honours. It may perhaps be supposed that the *gerousia* included councillors who had retired because of old age. The appearance of this organization in most cities during the Roman period suggests that its formation was encouraged by the imperial government as a means of increasing the influence of the older and more responsible citizens. When the *gerousia* was established at Sidyma by the Council and People the action was praised by the proconsul of the province.

While in some cities the festivals seem to have been under the general supervision of a panegyriarch, who was expected to supplement the amount appropriated by the city for the sacrifices and the customary banquets, the responsibility for the contests—probably, in the eyes of the public, the most important feature of the occasion—devolved upon the agonothete.[57] It was his duty to enroll the various contestants, to organize and conduct the events and to award the prizes. When, as was doubtless often the case, the funds appropriated by the city or obtained from an endowment proved insufficient to maintain the splendor of the occasion, he had to provide the necessary amount at his own expense. Sometimes he furnished oil and perhaps even refreshments for the populace, and at Ilium a series of agonothetes made contributions for some public purpose, probably a building. The expenses involved were great and hardly less costly than those borne by the gymnasiarch, and this was doubtless the reason why the post of agonothete was sometimes held by the local priest of the emperors, who naturally was chosen from among the wealthier and more important citizens. Frequently the title was borne by a woman, who, except in those cases in which she shared it with her husband, presumably paid the expenses of the contest. Ordinarily the service was performed for a single festival, but repetitions were not infrequent. There were instances in which the post was held for as many as four or five or perhaps even ten times, and in numerous cases a man was agonothete for life. In several cities there was a "perpetual" *agonothesia*, provided by an endowment, and in these cases the founder himself or a relative seems to have had a prior claim to the title.

The question inevitably arises as to the reason why the members of a community were willing to spend these large amounts of money for the benefit of their fellow-citizens. Often, to be sure, their generosity was not wholly voluntary; for, as the specific exemption of those who practiced certain professions or engaged in certain occupations[v] indicates, they were under practical, if not actual, compulsion to render these services. Even if this compulsion did not exist, the fulfilment of these public duties tended to become obligatory for a man who sought the good will of the members of his community. At the same time, there were doubtless many cases in which the expenditure was inspired by local pride or by the ambition to play the part of benefactor or even by a devotion to the community and a genuine spirit of generosity.

Such voluntary services—some of them not, strictly speaking, liturgies —for which a generous donor was often praised, included banquets and distributions of money to the public, characterized, somewhat cynically, by an ancient writer as among the devices used merely for the purpose of gaining popularity.[58] They also included gifts of grain, especially in time of famine, and of oil, often doled out in small vessels from a large container, both of which are frequently mentioned among benefits conferred, as well as official missions to Rome—a costly errand—at the envoy's own expense.

Sometimes a donor's generosity took the form of founding a festival, an action different, apparently, from the endowment of an *agonothesia*. For while as a rule the public festivals, accompanied by "musical" (including dramatic) and athletic contests, which existed in practically every city bore the name either of a deity or of a Roman emperor—frequently of both—there were also many named for private citizens.[59] These consisted of contests in which the prizes were furnished from the income from funds given or bequeathed by the per-

---

[v] See Chap. XXIV note 15 and above note 13.

sons whose names they bore. Contests of this kind were the Balbilleia at Ephesus, which was founded by Balbillus, a procurator of Claudius, and the "musical" Lysimacheia at Aphrodisias. The latter, held every four years, was established by a bequest amounting, perhaps with accrued interest, to 120,000 denarii, the income from which provided thirty-one prizes, ranging from 150 denarii, the second prize for an actor of the "Old Comedy," to 2,500 denarii, the first prize for a tragedian. In addition to the Lysimacheia, Aphrodisias, in the late second and the third centuries, had at least five contests named after a founder; Termessus in the third century had the surprisingly large number of fifteen; and there were similar endowments elsewhere, as, for example, at Antiocheia-on-Maeander, Aezani, Antioch-near-Pisidia and Sagalassus as well as in various cities in Lycia. In several places, chiefly in Pisidia, Cilicia and Lycia, there were individual gifts or bequests of money for prizes, sometimes repeated, which also bore the names of the donors.

A form of entertainment presented to the public which differed greatly from these characteristically Hellenic contests consisted of gladiatorial combats and fights in which wild beasts were pitted against each other or against huntsmen.[60] A spectacle of this brutal and demoralizing kind was first given in Asia, as far as is known, by Lucullus in 71/70 B.C. at Ephesus, and about the middle of this century gladiators fought at Laodiceia and at Mylasa. Under Augustus or Tiberius a succession of priests of the emperor at Ancyra presented spectacles in which gladiators fought and wild beasts were hunted. In the course of time, amphitheatres for such performances were built—a temporary wooden one at the colony of Antioch about the close of the first century after Christ and stone buildings at Laodiceia in A.D. 79 and during the next century at Pergamum and Cyzicus. So popular, in fact, were these combats in the Asianic provinces in the course of the second and third centuries and so widely prevalent under the influence of Rome that, according to the evidence of inscriptions and sculptured monuments, gladiatorial fights were exhibited in at least fifty-six cities, of which thirty-two were in the province of Asia, including such thoroughly Hellenic communities as Ephesus, Miletus and Pergamum.

The favourite types of gladiators seem to have been the heavy-armed "Thracian" and *myrmillo*, but the light-armed "net-man" (*retiarius*) also frequently participated in combats, and even horsemen and drivers of war-chariots are mentioned. Among animal-combats, bull-fights, including pursuits by men on horseback who grappled the animal's horns, were the most frequent, but there is mention also of "African beasts" (probably leopards or panthers) as well as of bears and lions. Spectacles were sometimes very elaborate; at Antioch twenty-six pairs of gladiators fought in the course of eight days; there were combats for twelve days at Miletus and for three at Magnesia; at Ephesus on different occasions thirty-one and thirty-nine pairs took part, the latter in the course of thirteen days; at Sagalassus twenty in four days, and at Ancyra thirty pairs. Similarly, there were bull-grapplings at Smyrna and Pergamum for two days and hunts at Ilium, Sardis and Smyrna for three days and at Ephesus for five days, during which twenty-five "African beasts" were killed. At Ancyra a series of gladiatorial combats, hunts and other entertainments lasted for fifty-one days.

The mention of such spectacles in honorific inscriptions indicates that they were regarded as meritorious on the part of the donors, who rivalled one another in their attempts thus to gain popular favour. Most of these donors were priests of the emperors, those who served both the provincial and the local cults. For this reason it has been suggested that spectacles of this kind were connected with the worship of the Augusti. At Antioch, however, the donor was a magistrate of the colony, and in other cases also there is no mention of a priesthood; and since priests sometimes acted also as agonothetes for local festivals, it is perhaps more probable that the apparent connexion was due to the fact that the priests were ordinarily men of wealth who were able to entertain the public in this lavish manner.

An effort to curb the expenditure of money on spectacles was made by the Roman government when, under Hadrian or Antoninus Pius, the Senate forbad the communities to use for entertainments of this kind even the income from bequests specifically designated for the purpose and authorized its diversion to any other object which might seem to the citizens to be necessary.[w] Some time afterward, in the later years of Marcus Aurelius, when the Emperor issued a proclamation intended to reduce the cost of spectacles, a senator was represented as delivering a speech in which he attributed to them the weakened condition of the provincial communities and the ruin of the fortunes of their leading citizens.[61] The description of conditions, however, implied in this argument was apparently exaggerated, for in the Asianic cities, at least, there is little evidence in the late second century of any

[w] Aburnius Valens in *Digesta* L 8, 6.

marked economic decline. The very lavishness of many of the spectacles of which there is record and the large sums of money donated for festivals and contests, as well as the amounts paid in return for public offices and spent on liturgies of various kinds, on banquets for the populace and on gifts of money, grain and oil by citizens are all indications of the possession of wealth.

This prosperity appears also in the construction by the wealthy of buildings which greatly beautified the principal cities. Antoninus Pius did, indeed, attempt to check undue extravagance by ordering that, if a city had a sufficient number of public buildings, any money bequeathed for erecting new ones should be used for maintaining those already in existence; and his successor issued a rescript to the effect that the provincial governor, if consulted about the erection of walls or city-gates or public works in general, must refer the matter to the emperor.[62] Nevertheless, the activity in building, carried on widely and lavishly, as has already been noted, under the Flavian Emperors and Trajan, was continued under Antoninus and Marcus Aurelius. In their time were constructed the round temple of Asclepius at Pergamum, built by Lucius Cuspius Pactumeius Rufinus, Consul in 142; the gymnasium and odeum of Vedius Antoninus and the colonnade and banqueting-hall of the sophist Flavius Damianus at Ephesus; the gymnasium and bath named for the Empress Faustina at Miletus; a public square and additions to the Gymnasium of Diogenes by Carminius Claudianus at Aphrodisias; a temple of Antoninus at Sagalassus; a colonnade and workrooms at Isaura; and the many buildings erected or repaired by Opramoas in the cities of Lycia. To these may be added the gifts of Publius Aelius Alcibiades and Sextus Julius Maior Antoninus Pythodorus, both of Nysa, of whom the former gave public buildings and large amounts of money to his native city as well as an endowment to the Artists of Dionysus, and the latter not only erected a house for the Elders' Association at Nysa but also built a public bath, a temple and a hospital at Epidaurus in Greece.

This activity, moreover, did not cease in the late second and early third centuries. From this period date, among others, the following public works: at Pergamum the rebuilding of an old temple for the worship of the Emperor Caracalla, which enabled the city to assume the title of Thrice Temple-Warden; at Ephesus an ornamental gate from a bequest, improvements for the theatre, pavements in public places and a gift of 20,000 denarii for dredging the harbour; at Philadelpheia an ornamental entrance to the basilica and a building containing shops; at Aphrodisias a record-office with colonnades on three sides, one containing a library; at Stratoniceia a sanctuary of the Egyptian god, Serapis, as well as a temple in the court of the council-house, and statues and an aqueduct erected by Sempronius Clemens at Panamara and Lagina; at Prusias money for paving a public square; near Amastris in Paphlagonia a temple of Zeus Bonitenus; at Sagalassus a market and a gift of 30,500 denarii for repairs to the Temple of Apollo and for festivals; at Termessus a gymnasium, a new public hall (*lesche*), temples of Artemis and the Earth-goddess and a large endowment for the distribution of money, all showing the great prosperity of the city.

Despite this extravagance, little was done to improve the economic condition of the humbler citizens; in distributions of money the amounts paid to them were smaller than those which the councillors received.[63] The only known instance, moreover, of what is now thought of as a charitable foundation was the gift of 300,000 denarii by a wealthy woman of Sillyum for the support of destitute children.[x] It is doubtless true that in comparison with the great mass of the poor, of whom no mention is made in existing documents, the number of wealthy families whose members served as officials and acted as donors was limited, and that a great gulf existed between the rich and their less fortunate fellow-citizens. But there is ample evidence to show that, even amid the wars and pestilence which, in the late second and early third centuries, brought disaster to Asia Minor, there was a continuance of the prosperity fostered by the rule of Hadrian and Antoninus Pius and by their efforts to establish the *Pax Romana* as a compensation to the Greek cities for the loss of independence.[y]

[x] *I.G.R.* III 800-802.   [y] See Aristides *Orat.* XXVI Keil *pass.*

CHAPTER XXVIII

'FROM GOLD TO IRON

AMID the general peace that prevailed under the rule of Antoninus Pius there was, nevertheless, occasional fighting along the frontiers of the Empire. In northern Britain the Brigantes rose up against the conquerors of the island; along the middle and lower Danube the Germans and Dacians invaded Roman territory; and in northwestern Africa the tribesmen attacked the province of Mauretania.[1] There was also a serious threat, soon after Antoninus's accession to power, of another war in the East. While the extant brief and fragmentary allusions to this threat to peace do not permit any definite account of its development, it seems to have originated in the incursions of the Alans, already mentioned, into Media Atropatene and Armenia.[2] The invaders were aided and abetted by Pharasmanes II, ruler of Iberia and a Roman vassal, who evidently permitted them to pass through his kingdom. This was regarded as a hostile act by Vologases II, the Parthian monarch who, long a rival of Osroes, the king recognized by Hadrian, had finally, about 129, established himself in power. Vologases, accordingly, sent envoys to Rome to protest. Pharasmanes, summoned to answer for his conduct, in turn sent envoys to the Emperor and even came to the Capital in person. He appears to have made his plea good, for it is recorded that he received an addition to his territory.

The favour thus shown to the Iberian ruler, together with Antoninus's refusal to recognize the sovereignty of Vologases by returning to him the golden throne which Trajan had carried away and Hadrian had promised Osroes to restore, seems to have aroused the anger of the Parthian monarch. He made preparations, accordingly, to invade Armenia, an attack on which, since the country was regarded as a client-state by the Romans, would inevitably have resulted in a war with Rome. Actual hostilities, however, were averted by the diplomacy of Antoninus, who by no more forceful means than a letter, it is related, induced Vologases to refrain from his projected invasion. It may perhaps be assumed that the Emperor's preparations, which included the despatching of additional troops to Syria "on account of the Parthian War" and the requisitioning of clothing from Egypt for the army in Cappadocia, may also have had a deterring effect. In any case, the two rulers seem to have agreed on a compromise by which a candidate for the throne of Armenia, perhaps a Parthian by birth,

659

was appointed by Antoninus as king of the country. This arrangement, a definite continuation of the policy of retaining Armenia as a vassal of Rome, appears to have satisfied Vologases, for during the lifetime of Antoninus he, as well as his successor, refrained from any hostile move.

It was perhaps in connexion with the threat of war just described that a change was made in the size of the province of Cilicia.[3] The districts of Lycaonia and Isauria, which, it will be remembered, were attached to Galatia by Augustus and had long formed a part of this province, were severed from it, apparently under Antoninus, and combined with Cilicia. As a result, the latter, no longer confined to the coast districts, henceforth extended far inland north of the Taurus and was greatly increased in both extent and importance.

On 9 March, 161 Antoninus Pius was succeeded by his two adopted sons, Marcus Aurelius and Lucius Verus, as joint rulers of the Empire. Almost at once Vologases III, who had ascended the Parthian throne thirteen years previously, evidently regarding the change of ruler as a favourable opportunity, launched an attack, probably long planned, on Armenia.[4] A Parthian army under the command of a leader named Osroes, crossing the Taurus, marched northward to Elegeia, where Trajan had dethroned King Parthamasiris and declared Armenia a Roman province. Here Osroes met Marcus Sedatius Severianus, the governor of Cappadocia, who, with one legion, had crossed the Euphrates to oppose the invasion. The Parthian commander, however, surrounding Severianus and his small army, destroyed the whole force. The leader himself committed suicide and Osroes, taking possession of Armenia in the name of his master, enthroned Pacorus, a Parthian, as king.

Meanwhile another army of Vologases, crossing the Euphrates, fell upon the province of Syria. Here also the Romans suffered a crushing defeat; the governor of the province, Lucius Attidius Cornelianus, who advanced to meet the invader, was put to flight and his army scattered.

The report of this double disaster roused the Emperors to vigorous action, and it was decided that Verus should go to the East as supreme commander. Leaving Italy early in 162, he went to Athens and thence travelled by sea along the coast of Asia Minor, where, according to later, and apparently hostile, critics, he lingered too long in the cities of Pamphylia and Cilicia. Nevertheless, he seems to have arrived in Syria before the end of the year. Taking up his quarters in Antioch,

Verus entrusted the campaign entirely to his generals. His enemies accused him of spending his time in amusements and dissipation; but this lack of participation in active service may have been due to a realization of the fact that he had no knowledge of warfare as well as to the need of a general administrator at headquarters. In the face of the emergency great efforts were made to mobilize a force able to cope with the enemy; the legions permanently garrisoned in Syria were ordered to repel the invaders of the province, and three legions from the Rhine and the Danube were hurried to Cappadocia to defend that portion of the frontier. As Severianus's successor the Emperors appointed the experienced Marcus Statius Priscus, imperial legate of Britain and previously governor of the province of Upper Moesia. With at least two of the legions brought from Europe and doubtless other troops as well, Priscus entered Armenia. In this offensive he drove the Parthians out of the country and, advancing as far as Artaxata, captured the city. Some of his soldiers even penetrated to the shore of the Caspian, north of the Caucasus, perhaps in order to punish the Alans for their raids. His victory re-established Rome's supremacy over Armenia and in 164 a Roman candidate, Sohaemus, was made king of the country in place of the Parthian appointee. In consequence of this successful campaign, the two Emperors assumed the surname Armeniacus, and the Roman hold on Armenia was strengthened by a garrison of legionaries, established by Priscus some twenty miles from Artaxata in the "New City" (Caenopolis), which was later regarded as the capital of the kingdom.

The repulse of the Parthians' invasion of Syria was equally successful. The command of the forces was entrusted to Avidius Cassius, of Syrian origin, who had recently held the consulship.[5] Finding the legions stationed in Syria enervated by a long-lasting peace and demoralized by their recent defeat, he subjected them to rigorous discipline and drove the Parthians out of the province. Then in the face of strong opposition he led his troops across the Euphrates into northern Mesopotamia, apparently by means of a pontoon-bridge. Farther north, the region of Osroene, whose ruler had been appointed by Vologases, was occupied by a part of the army which had reconquered Armenia. The main force, having captured Nicephorium, on the left bank of the Euphrates, and Europus, farther downstream, where a great battle was fought, seems to have marched down the river to Babylonia. Here the important city of Seleuceia on the Tigris, an Hellenic *polis* long antedating the foundation of the Parthian kingdom, surrendered to the Roman army. Nevertheless, perhaps later, on the ground that some agreement had been violated, the legions sacked the city and destroyed part of it by fire. The Romans also advanced on Ctesiphon, and the Parthian capital was captured and the royal palace destroyed.

The complete success of this campaign forced Vologases to sue for peace and brought an end to the war. In the summer or autumn of 165 Verus—and early in the following year Marcus Aurelius also—took the surname Parthicus Maximus and a little later both Emperors received that of Medicus, presumably on account of the penetration of Media Atropatene by some expeditionary force. Avidius Cassius was rewarded by an appointment as governor of the province of Syria.

In the spring of 166, probably, Verus set out on his return-journey to Rome. On the way he stopped at Ephesus, where a monument was erected to celebrate his victory and he himself was officially received by the clerk of the city.[6] The legions returning from the war were likewise entertained by Damianus the sophist, who also presented the city with a large amount of grain. On his arrival in Rome in the summer, Verus, together with Marcus, held a triumph in celebration of the victory.

The peace with the Parthians was concluded, in general, on the basis of the *status quo ante*. Measures were taken, to be sure, to protect the province of Syria on the east by constituting Osroene a Roman vassal-state under a king who took the title of "Friend of Rome." No further attempt was made, however, to resume Trajan's policy of expansion toward the east or to abandon the principle, laid down by Augustus and reaffirmed by Hadrian, that the eastern boundary of the Empire should be the Euphrates.

The necessity at the beginning of the war for moving troops from eastern Europe to the Euphrates frontier brought about an important administrative change in the provinces of Asia Minor. Since the western termini of the great roads which led through Paphlagonia and Galatia toward Armenia were in Bithynia,[a] it evidently seemed advisable to take this province directly under imperial control. Bithynia-Pontus, accordingly, which in the original division of the provinces under Augustus had been assigned to the Senate and under Trajan and Hadrian had temporarily been governed by imperial appointees, was transferred, perhaps in 164, to the emperor, who henceforth named his legates to the post of governor.[7] Some years later, presumably in

a See Chap. XIII notes 11 and 14.

return for this cession of Bithynia, the Senate was given the province of Lycia-Pamphylia, whose situation was much less strategic than that of Bithynia.

The victory over the Parthians was a costly one, for in addition to the ordinary casualties of war, many soldiers died in Mesopotamia from hunger.[8] Much more disastrous, however, was the pestilence which broke out about this time and which, it was generally believed, was brought back by the troops. They were supposed to have contracted this disease—sometimes regarded, on account of the reported symptoms, as the smallpox—at Seleuceia, and it is said to have caused the death of a great number during the return-march. Spreading westward, the pestilence reached Italy and created great havoc not only in Rome, where it attacked rich and poor alike, causing the death of thousands, but also throughout the country-side, where towns and farms were left deserted. It even extended to Gaul and to the frontier on the upper Danube, where, it is reported, large numbers of soldiers perished. After a partial subsidence, there seems to have been another outbreak following the death of Marcus, also of great virulence.

In western Asia Minor the ravages of the pestilence were described by the orator Aelius Aristides, and there is evidence of its presence at Smyrna, where the river Meles was praised for deliverance from "pestilence and evil."[b] In addition, many places also suffered about this time on account of the failure of the harvests, which wrought famine and suffering and caused men to leave their homes in search of better circumstances.[9] Although the combined pestilence and famine do not appear to have damaged permanently the general prosperity of the Asiatic cities, which, as has already been shown, continued into the third century,[c] these evils could not fail to have an adverse effect on economic conditions. Both the high mortality of the epidemic and the lack of food must inevitably have caused a shortage of labour and a rise in the cost of living. It is known, in fact, that in some places in Asia Minor the price of grain doubled during the second century. The war against the tribes on the Danube, moreover, involved the imperial government in enormous expense, which was met by a depreciation of the imperial silver currency, a measure which presumably increased the tendency toward inflation.

Nevertheless, the high-minded and conscientious Marcus did his best for the welfare of the provincials, and he is said to have shown them great consideration.[d] An example of his attention to the details

[b] *C.I.G.* 3165.   [c] See above p. 657f.   [d] *Vit. Marc.* 17, 1.

of administration may be found in a letter written, both in his name and that of Verus, to the *curator* of the Elders' Association at Ephesus.[10] In this letter the curator, in reply to his questions, was instructed to refrain from melting down the silver statues of former emperors owned by the Association in order to make new ones of Marcus and Verus and also to attach the property of those who without authority had collected debts owed to the Association and had withheld the money. The monuments, moreover, which were erected to Marcus, sometimes in conjunction with Verus, in many Asianic cities, although in some cases doubtless merely conventional marks of respect, may frequently have been expressions of gratitude.[11]

There was, however, little opportunity for Marcus to devote his attention to the eastern provinces. During the greater part of the time during which he held the imperial power he was occupied in defending the northern frontier of the Empire. The long-continued war against the tribes on this frontier began, probably in 166, when the Marcomanni from the region north of the upper Danube, crossing the Julian Alps, attacked northeastern Italy and forced both Emperors to take the field.[12] Although the invaders were repelled, the campaign was carried on at first by Marcus and Verus together, then, after Verus's death in 169, by Marcus and his generals. In the course of time the tribes bordering on the province of Pannonia along the middle course of the Danube and even those lower down the river became engaged in the struggle, which ultimately resolved itself into an effort to create a sort of safety-zone along the northern frontier of the Empire. Greatly hampered by a shortage both of men and of money, the Emperor resorted to every expedient, enrolling two new legions as well as adding gladiators, local gendarmes and bandits to the army and disposing of the palace-treasures at a public sale. Even some of the Asianic cities seem to have furnished contingents of troops. Although the Romans were often victorious, so that Marcus was several times acclaimed *Imperator* and received the surname Germanicus, the barbarians also were frequently successful, and the war dragged on, with one brief interval of two years (175-177), until 180, the year of the Emperor's death.

This general commotion among the tribes of central Europe affected also the Hellenic world. The Costoboci, from the eastern end of the Carpathians northeast of the province of Dacia, made an attack on Greece about 170, advancing as far as Eleusis in Attica, to which they seem to have done great harm.[13] Since the places mentioned in connexion with their raid were on or near the coast, it has been suggested that, in the manner of pirates, they attacked from ships, on which they embarked at the mouth of the Danube. It is possible that Asia Minor also was affected by this or a similar raid, for the apparent imposition of a "Bastarnian tax" at Thyateira about this time suggests that it was necessary for the Roman government to raise money for the defence of the province of Asia against the Bastarnians, another Carpathian tribe.

In 175, however, the Emperor at last achieved success on the northern frontier by a decisive victory over the Sarmatians along the lower Danube.[e] But about this time, perhaps because of the concentration of troops on this frontier, the northern Germans threatened the supremacy of Rome on the lower Rhine and an army of Moors invaded Spain. There was, in addition, serious trouble in Asia.

In Armenia the installation of a Roman-made king had not brought peace to that distraught country. In spite of the presence of the Roman garrison stationed at Caenopolis, a faction opposed to Sohaemus seems to have driven him from his throne. It had become necessary, accordingly, for Martius Verus, one of the generals in the Parthian war and now governor of Cappadocia, to send a subordinate to restore the Roman protégé to his kingdom.[14] A more dangerous situation, however, soon followed. Marcus, fully occupied with the war on the Danube and feeling the need, after the death of Lucius Verus, of a colleague to supervise the East, had vested Avidius Cassius, the governor of Syria, with an extraordinary command, similar to that granted to Vitellius by Tiberius and to Corbulo by Nero, over the imperial provinces in Asia.[15] This position of power fired Cassius's ambition to seek for a higher place and in the spring of 175 he proclaimed himself emperor. It was said in his behalf that he took this step only after receiving a false report that Marcus had died and even—what is less credible—that the Empress Faustina, fearing that an illness from which her husband was suffering might prove fatal and that her son, Commodus, was too young to succeed his father, urged Cassius, in the event of Marcus's death, to seize the imperial power. Giving out that he had been elected by the army on the Danube, Cassius was recognized as emperor by the Syrians, who welcomed this elevation of a fellow-countryman, and it is said that all the region south of the Taurus accepted his rule. He was accepted also in Egypt, where he

---

[e] See Mattingly-Sydenham III p. 238f., no. 325f. and p. 304, no. 1154f. (Sarmaticus).

had recently defeated the attempt of a group of desperadoes, composed of herdsmen and bandits, to terrorize the Delta of the Nile, and even the imperial prefect of the country supported him. At Rome many feared that he might seize the city, and the Senate, although some of its members had sided with him, declared him a public enemy.

On receiving the news of Cassius's revolt, sent by Martius Verus, Marcus decided that his presence in the East was urgently needed. Accordingly, taking advantage of his victory over the Sarmatians to come to terms with them and leaving western Europe to his generals, he set out for the eastern provinces. Accompanied by his wife, Faustina, and his only surviving son, Commodus, he travelled, apparently by sea, to Syria and thence went to Egypt, where he seems to have spent part of the winter of 175-176 in Alexandria. From here, probably in the early spring, he returned to Antioch. Before his first arrival in Syria, however, and in fact even before his departure for the East, the danger was past; for Cassius, after a rule of three months and six days, was assassinated by two of his soldiers, who, having cut off his head, set out with it to meet the Emperor. It is said that the kindly Marcus showed only distress and ordered the head to be decently buried; he also refused to punish the rebel's adherents. But as a precaution for the future it was enacted no man should serve as governor of a province of which he was a native.[f]

Leaving Antioch in the spring of 176, Marcus set out on his return-journey through Asia Minor. After crossing the Taurus on his way northward from Tarsus, he lost his wife, Faustina, who died suddenly in the town of Halala on the northern side of the range.[16] In her honour the Emperor renamed the place Faustinopolis and gave it the status of a colony.

Continuing his journey, presumably along the Southern Highway, the Emperor finally reached the Aegean. At Ephesus the city-council dedicated a monument to him and the Deified Faustina and their daughters.[17] He also visited Smyrna, where the society of the initiates in the mysteries of Dionysus had many years previously, under the rule of Antoninus, congratulated him on the birth of a son, an act of courtesy for which he expressed his thanks at the time and later, after his accession, perhaps requited by granting the society certain privileges. While in the city, he listened to a declamation by the gifted orator, Aristides. Two years afterward, when Smyrna had been badly damaged by an earthquake, a letter from Aristides describing the de-

[f] Cassius Dio LXXI 31, 1.

struction so moved Marcus that he promised aid for rebuilding the city and a ten years' remission of the tax paid to Rome was granted.

From Smyrna the Emperor crossed the Aegean to Athens and from here, in the autumn of 176, he returned to Rome, where on the arch erected to commemorate his successes on the Danube frontier he boasted that, "having destroyed or subdued the most warlike of nations, he had surpassed the glory of all the greatest emperors before him."[18] His victories over the Germans and Sarmatians were celebrated also by a triumphal procession of great magnificence. This triumph, however, was premature; before the end of the following year the northern tribes attacked once more, and in the summer of 178 Marcus, together with Commodus, was forced to set out for the front, from which he was destined never to return. Less than two years later, on 17 March, 180, while still in his fifty-ninth year but exhausted by long-continued exertions, the Emperor, the most righteous of all who had wielded the imperial power and undeserving of the many calamities which Fate allotted him, breathed his last in the camp in Pannonia.[g] The final entry in his *Meditations* is the exhortation, "Depart then satisfied, for he also who releases thee is satisfied."

The death of Marcus, with the transition from his mild and kindly rule to the cruelty and oppression of those who succeeded him, which affected the whole Empire, was characterized by an ancient writer as the end of a reign of gold and the beginning of one of iron and rust.[h] For the disastrous period that followed the Emperor himself was, indeed, partly to blame.[i] Abandoning the method employed by his four predecessors—who, to be sure, had no sons of their own—of adopting an heir to the imperial power, Marcus reverted to the dynastic principle by associating his son, Commodus, as co-ruler with himself, and on his death this youth, at the age of nineteen, became sole emperor. Giving up his father's plans for the protection of the frontier and coming to terms with the northern tribes, Commodus returned to Rome, where he devoted himself to pleasure and to developing his prowess as charioteer, gladiator and wild-beast fighter. So great, indeed, was his pride in his feats of strength that he finally called himself the Roman Hercules. Most of his father's counsellors and associates were dismissed and his own favourites appointed to positions of influence and power, in particular, those of court chamberlain and prefect

[g] Cassius Dio LXXI 33, 4[2]. [h] Cassius Dio LXXI 36, 4.
[i] But see J. Keil in *Klio* XXXI (1938), p. 293f.

of the Praetorian Guard, only to be soon deposed on the ground of treasonable designs or on account of a popular clamour against them.

In fact, the narrative of Commodus's rule of over twelve years, as it appears in the accounts given by the ancient authors, consists largely of a series of intrigues and conspiracies, real or alleged.[19] For supposed participation in these—often merely because the Emperor wished to confiscate the victim's wealth—many men of high rank, among them a proconsul of Asia, were put to death. Finally, on New Year's Eve of 192, Commodus's chamberlain and the prefect of the Guard, with the assistance of the Emperor's mistress, caused him to be strangled. The Senate officially condemned his memory and ordered his name to be erased from public monuments and his statues to be overthrown.

In his administration of the Empire Commodus has been represented as lax and careless and leaving all matters in the hands of his favourites, who sold appointments to posts in the provinces. In fact, it was even said that men were named governors who were his companions in crime or were recommended to him by persons of criminal character. Unfortunately, too little is known about the imperial governors of the eastern provinces under Commodus's rule to establish the truth or falsity of this statement; but of one at least, Lucius Fabius Cilo, who was imperial legate of Galatia during this period and probably of Bithynia also and afterward became governor of Upper Pannonia and then prefect of the city of Rome and Consul for the second time, it may be said that he had a distinguished career. A certain interest, moreover, in the welfare of the Asianic cities appears in the cases of Ephesus and Nicomedeia, which were badly damaged by earthquakes. In the former, the addition of the Emperor's name to the old festivals established in honour of Artemis and of Hadrian suggests that the city received imperial assistance; in the latter, Commodus is said to have aided in the restoration of the city. Nicomedeia also, through the influence of his chamberlain, so it is reported, obtained permission to found a contest named for the Emperor and to erect a temple for his worship, which made it possible for the city to assume the title of Twice Temple-Warden. This privilege seems to have been granted also to Tarsus, which founded a similar contest and took the same title and, in addition, called itself Commodianē. The contests which bore Commodus's name, added to an older festival of some deity, as at Pergamum, Miletus and Laodiceia, were perhaps similarly authorized. While the statues and the dedications for his welfare which were erected in various cities may possibly indicate a grant of some favour, it is perhaps more probable that they were only conventional expressions of loyalty; and the reference to the "most happy time" of his rule found in the decree of Sidyma, previously mentioned, by which an Elders' Association was formed, can hardly be regarded as more than mere flattery.

The return to the dynastic principle adopted by Marcus in appointing his son as his successor brought in its train a period of turmoil and strife reminiscent of the struggle after the death of Nero, when various claimants contended with one another for the imperial power. In the confusion that followed the death of Commodus, there rose and fell, first, Publius Helvius Pertinax, an appointee of the Senate, and, after him, Marcus Didius Julianus, who purchased the rule from the Praetorian Guard. Their combined terms of office lasted only five months. A more powerful claimant then appeared, Lucius Septimius Severus, governor of the province of Upper Pannonia, the candidate of the conspirators who had killed Commodus. Recognized as Emperor by the armies on the Danube and the Rhine, he marched on Italy with a body of soldiers. After receiving the support of the fleet stationed at Ravenna, he occupied Rome with an armed force, with which he compelled the Senate to accept him as ruler. His seizure by violence of the imperial power is generally regarded as the establishment of a military monarchy based on the power of the army.[j]

Severus's seizure of the power, however, was not accomplished without a protracted struggle. He was opposed in both the East and the West; in the former by Gaius Pescennius Niger, the governor of Syria, in the latter by Decimus Clodius Albinus, the governor of Britain, who in the beginning had agreed to support Severus and had received the title of Caesar and the promise of a share in the imperial power. It was not until nearly four years had passed that Severus, by defeating both his rivals, established himself as unopposed ruler. Meanwhile, the opposition of Niger brought war to the Asianic provinces, which, save for the recurring campaigns on the Euphrates frontier, had for more than two centuries enjoyed an unbroken peace.

This opposition took active form in the spring of 193, when Niger, after his adherents in Rome had aroused a popular demonstration in his favour during the brief rule of Julianus, was proclaimed Emperor at Antioch in Syria.[20] He was supported by the legions stationed in the province as well as by those in Palestine, and he was accepted also

[j] See Rostovtzeff *S.E.H.R.E.* pp. 352f. and 597.

in Egypt. In Asia Minor the proconsul of Asia, Asellius Aemilianus, his predecessor in the governorship of Syria and a man of outstanding ability, became one of his generals. Niger was also recognized as Emperor in Bithynia, where the cities of Nicomedeia and Caesareia-Germanice issued coins bearing his portrait and name. Once more, as in A.D. 69, the East was pitted against the West in a civil war.

The first move seems to have been made by Aemilianus, who, by crossing the Bosporus and occupying Byzantium, obtained a foothold in Europe. He appears to have invaded also the adjacent portion of the province of Thrace and to have been successful enough to make it possible for Niger to issue coins bearing the legends "Victory" and "Invincible." The troops of Severus, however, commanded by Fabius Cilo, prevented Aemilianus from seizing Perinthus, an important road-junction on the northern shore of the Propontis.

Meanwhile Severus, learning of the invasion, sent orders to the legions stationed in the Danube provinces to proceed against his rival. The armies of Pannonia and Moesia, accordingly, commanded, respectively, by Tiberius Claudius Candidus and Lucius Marius Maximus, advanced to Thrace. Unable to oppose their superior strength, Aemilianus was compelled to fall back on Byzantium. Soon, however, it became impossible for him to retain his position in the city, for Severus's generals, taking the offensive, crossed the Hellespont, and he was forced to leave Byzantium to its fate and return to Asia Minor. The city, after an heroic resistance against a siege lasting two and a half years, was finally compelled by famine to surrender.

Marching southward from the Bosporus, Aemilianus met the army of Severus in the neighbourhood of Cyzicus. In the battle which ensued he was badly defeated, his troops were scattered and he himself fled the field, only to be captured during his flight and put to death by the victors.

After this success the troops of Severus advanced northward into Bithynia. Nicomedeia, despite its previous support of Niger, abandoned his cause and, perhaps under pressure from the fleet, now in the Propontis, declared for Severus. Its rival, Nicaea, however, remained faithful to Niger, who by this time, after taking measures to protect Syria by barricading the Taurus, had come to western Asia Minor with an additional force. Severus also, who had left Rome in midsummer after recruiting soldiers and fitting out a fleet, conveyed his troops across the Adriatic and, marching through Macedonia, arrived in Thrace. He seems, however, to have taken no active part in the campaign which followed and to have left the command of his forces to Candidus.

The two armies met, probably in the late autumn or early winter of 193, between Nicaea and Cius, presumably on the southern side of Lake Ascania, where ran the road connecting the two cities. After an initial success on the part of the troops of Severus, an advance, led by Niger himself, forced his opponents to retreat. This would perhaps have won the day had it not been for the courage of Candidus, who, rallying his men, turned the tide of battle. Only the approach of night saved Niger's army from total destruction. Unable, after this crushing disaster, to offer further resistance, the defeated leader with the remnants of his force withdrew across the whole of Asia Minor to make a stand in the Taurus. All the Asianic provinces were thereby lost to him. Egypt also and even some of the Syrian cities, forsaking his cause, declared for the victor.

On reaching the Taurus, Niger ordered his men to defend the pass, perhaps the Cilician Gates, where the barricade had been erected. He himself went on to Syria to obtain reinforcements and to punish the faithless cities. Meanwhile the army of Severus, under the command of Publius Cornelius Anullinus, who had been proconsul of Africa, advanced in pursuit of the enemy, marching through Galatia, presumably either by the road leading by way of Dorylaeum and Pessinus or through Juliopolis and Ancyra, to western Cappadocia. As long as the winter rendered the Taurus impassable, Niger's men were able to defend their position. But when the spring rains and the melting snow had weakened the barricade, their pursuers succeeded in breaking through, and, crossing the mountains, they drove the defenders down the southern side of the range and across the Cilician plain to the border of Syria. Here, on the little plain of Issus between the mountains and the sea, the scene of Alexander's defeat of Darius, Severus's army met Niger with a large force collected at Antioch. Protected by the hills on one side and the Mediterranean on the other, Niger was in a strong position, and his superior numbers seemed about to give him the victory. But a sudden storm beating in the faces of his men and, simultaneously, an unforeseen attack by the enemy's cavalry, which, outflanking him through the hills, fell upon his rear, threw his army into the utmost confusion. The result was a total defeat which ended the war. A large number of Niger's soldiers—twenty thousand, it is reported—died on the field, the rest were completely routed and he himself, while in flight toward the Euphrates, hoping, it was said, to find a refuge with the Parthians, was overtaken by his pursuers and at once beheaded.

After the battle, apparently, Severus himself arrived in Syria and proceeded to reward those cities which had abandoned Niger and to punish those which had supported him.[k] Foremost among the latter was Antioch, which, on offering resistance, was captured and deprived of many of its privileges. In need of money for the donatives he had promised his soldiers, Severus demanded both from communities and from individuals four times the amount which they had given to Niger, whether voluntarily or under compulsion. To what extent the cities of Asia Minor were included in the punishment thus administered cannot be determined, but in any case they accepted Severus's rule and many courted his favour by erecting statues.[21] Nicomedeia and certain cities in Cilicia, either at this time or later, assumed the name Severianē, and several founded festivals in his honour, among them Tarsus, which instituted a "Severian Olympian" contest, apparently held at a triumphal arch erected near the battle-field of Issus. Cius and Nicomedeia, moreover, issued coins which declared that under the rule of Severus the universe enjoyed prosperity, and the citizens of Aezani, probably in 195, sent a delegation to express their pleasure at his success and at his designation of his young son as heir to the imperial power.

The war, however, did not end with the victory at Issus. The princes east of the Euphrates had offered Niger aid, and, although this was at first refused, a later request to the Parthian monarch, Vologases IV, brought assistance in the form of a force of archers, furnished by the ruler of Hatra in eastern Mesopotamia.[l] Niger seems also to have received support from the client-king of Osroene and from the ruler of Adiabene, east of the Tigris, a Parthian vassal. Severus's expedition into Mesopotamia, begun in the early spring of 195, therefore, although it was attributed by an ancient historian to a desire for glory, may in fact have been partly punitive and partly intended to restore peace in this region.[22] It would appear that the rulers of Osroene and Adiabene had combined to lay siege to the important city of Nisibis, but, after the defeat of Niger, fearing punishment for the support they had given him, they sent envoys to Severus, asserting that they had acted in his interest by destroying the partisans of his rival. They offered to return the booty and the captives they had taken but refused to evacuate the captured strongholds and to receive Roman garrisons.

[k] Cassius Dio LXXIV 8, 3f.: Herodian III 4, 7 and 6, 9: *Vit. Sev.* 9, 5f.
[l] Herodian II 8, 8; III 1, 2f.

Nevertheless, Severus, advancing into Mesopotamia in a march during which his army suffered greatly from a lack of water, occupied Nisibis. The King of Osroene seems to have submitted and to have been allowed to retain his throne. The rest of northern Mesopotamia was reduced to subjection by Severus's generals, among whom were Claudius Candidus and Cornelius Anullinus. They appear to have defeated the "Arabs" of the region and even to have crossed the Tigris into Adiabene. In all, three distinct victories were won, after each of which Severus was acclaimed *Imperator*, and before the end of the year he received the honorary surnames Arabicus and Adiabenicus.

At the close of this campaign Severus, postponing any attack against the Parthians, set out on his return to Europe, leading his soldiers across Asia Minor to the Bosporus. After halting at Byzantium, which meanwhile had been compelled to surrender, to punish the city for its opposition, he hurried on by forced marches during the early months of 196 to Moesia.[23] About this time he gave the title of Caesar to his elder son, Bassianus, now renamed Marcus Aurelius Antoninus but usually known by the nickname Caracalla (or Caracallus), taken from the Celtic or Germanic long, close-fitting tunic which he subsequently adopted. By the grant of this title Severus announced his intention of founding a dynasty, which he sought to legitimize not only by conferring this name on his son but also by fabricating a kinship with the Antonines and assuming officially the designation of brother of Commodus and son of Marcus Aurelius.

The cause of Severus's hurried departure for the West as well as of his attempt to legitimize the position of both himself and his son was the desire, now that Niger was no longer a menace, to put an end to the pretensions of his other rival, Clodius Albinus, whom, it will be remembered, he had prevented from any hostile move by the grant of the title of Caesar and with it a claim to a share in the imperial power. Albinus's claim, indeed, had been recognized not only in the West but in the East as well, where coins bearing his name as Caesar were issued at Smyrna, Sardis, Saittae in Lydia, Side in Pamphylia and Elaeussa-Sebaste in Cilicia.[24] But on learning that Severus, before leaving the East, had declared him a public enemy, he assumed also the name Augustus and, crossing over with an army from Britain into Gaul, prepared to make good his claim by force. Severus also, after a brief visit to Rome, hurried to Gaul, whither his troops had preceded him and had suffered a defeat from Albinus's forces. After his arrival the two armies met near Lyons on 19 February, 197,[m] and after desperate fighting Albinus's men were routed and he himself, to avoid capture, committed suicide.

With this victory all opposition to Severus came to an end, and now complete master of the Roman world, he returned to Rome with a body of soldiers and took vengeance on those who had supported his rivals by a reign of terror, in which many, including several of Senatorial rank, were slain and their property confiscated. He had not forgotten, however, that Vologases had sent aid to Niger and after the latter's defeat had given many of his partisans a refuge in the Parthian kingdom. As soon, therefore, as his position was secure, Severus resumed his interrupted campaign in Mesopotamia.[25] Sending his army, probably, across Europe to the Bosporus, whence it proceeded through Asia Minor, perhaps by the road leading through Prusias-on-Hypius and Crateia to Ancyra, Severus himself, after a short stay in Rome, set sail, in the summer of 197, from Brundisium for the East.

Meanwhile the Parthians had taken the offensive and attacked Nisibis. The Roman garrison in the city, however, under the command of Laetus, who had served as one of Severus's generals in the former Mesopotamian campaign, held out gallantly, and on the approach of Severus and his troops the besiegers withdrew. The Emperor's presence seems also to have impelled the Kings of Armenia and Osroene to appear before him and, in the case of the latter (Abgarus VIII), to offer him a company of archers. Returning to the Euphrates, the Emperor constructed a fleet of boats and on these he conveyed a part of his army down the river to the neighbourhood of its junction with the Tigris. From here he captured Babylon and Seleuceia and, probably at the end of 197, also Ctesiphon, which Vologases had left to its fate. The city was given over to the Roman soldiers to plunder, and a great number of the inhabitants perished and many were carried off as captives. This success Severus celebrated by taking the surname of Parthicus Maximus, thus proclaiming himself conqueror of the ancient enemy of Rome. He also chose this occasion for completing his plans for a dynasty by giving the boy Caracalla a share in the tribunician power as well as the name Augustus, thereby declaring him co-ruler with himself.

In the following spring Severus marched northward along the western bank of the Tigris. On the way he stopped to attack the city of Hatra, whose "satrap" had sent troops to aid Niger. The city, it

[m] *Vit. Sev.* 11, 7.

will be remembered, had successfully resisted Trajan in 116, and at this time also the inhabitants defended themselves bravely, using burning naphtha to destroy the Roman siege-engines. Partly for this reason and partly because Severus's soldiers were suffering from dysentery as well as tormented, so it is reported, by swarms of venomous insects, the attack was a total failure. A second attempt, probably in 199, after a winter presumably spent in northern Mesopotamia, was equally unsuccessful, not only on account of the damage wrought by the defenders' catapults and naphtha but also because the Roman soldiers mutinied. Thereupon the Emperor, despairing of capturing the city and forced to be satisfied with his victory over the Parthians, abandoned the campaign and returned to Syria.

The aggressive policy of Severus, nevertheless, resulted in an extension of the Roman Empire. Two new provinces, called respectively, Osroene and Mesopotamia, were formed in the territory conquered in the Emperor's two campaigns, and an attempt was made to Romanize this new border-land by settling veterans in at least four places and giving these the status of a colony.[26] Thus, somewhat over eighty years after Trajan's short-lived annexation of this region, the rule of Rome was carried far beyond the Euphrates.

The administration of the provinces, in general, was improved under Severus by various measures. The acceptance of gifts by governors was carefully restricted, and an attempt was made to ensure honesty in the courts by inflicting severe punishment on those imperial judicial officers whom the provincials had shown to have been guilty of corrupt practices.[n] Official recognition was given to endowments for the support of destitute children by making the governors of provinces responsible for their administration.[o] The cost of the imperial post, hitherto a heavy burden to the communities, was transferred—at least partially or temporarily—to the imperial treasury.[p] In order to prevent excessive or ill-considered taxation, the provincial cities were forbidden to levy new taxes unless these were approved by the governor,[q] and consideration was shown for the humbler citizens by permitting them to organize, as hitherto in Italy, societies for the purpose of burial and perhaps for mutual aid.[r]

There can be little doubt, however, that during the earlier years

[n] *Digesta* i 16, 6, 3: *Vit. Sev.* 8, 4.
[p] *Vit. Sev.* 14, 2 (see Chap. XXVI note 58).
[r] *Digesta* XLVII 22, 1 (see *R.E.* IV 387).
[o] *Digesta* XXXV 2, 89.
[q] *Cod. Iust.* IV 62, 1f.

of Severus's rule the eastern provinces fared badly. The fines which were imposed on the cities for their support of Niger and the confiscation of the property of his adherents have already been mentioned. In addition, the communities of Asia Minor, during the passage of the armies to and from the East, must have suffered not only from the inevitable depredations of the soldiers but also from the more legitimate requisitions of food with which the citizens were called on to provide the troops in lieu of part of their pay.[27] Nevertheless, as has been noted, many cities hastened to do homage to Severus by erecting monuments in his honour, and during the last sixteen years of his reign they continued this practice, showing a desire either to court his favour or to express gratitude for some benefit received.[28] The latter seems to have been the case at Eumeneia, where, in 196, Severus rebuilt the barracks destroyed by an earthquake, and at Ephesus, where, toward the end of his life, he was honoured as Founder.

The friendly relations between Severus and the cities appear also in the letters which he wrote to them. The congratulations on his success in the East and the announcement that the city planned to celebrate the bestowal of the title of Caesar on Caracalla, which were brought to him by a delegation sent by Aezani in 195, were acknowledged with great courtesy, as coming from a "city honoured and long of service to the Roman Empire." His letters to the Council and People of Prymnessus, also in 195, and to the city of Ephesus are, unfortunately, only fragments, but the former seems also to have been a courteous reply to an embassy sent by the city. In writing to Smyrna at the request of two citizens in behalf of the sophist Claudius Rufinus, who, out of patriotism, had waived the right of exemption from public office enjoyed by men of his profession and had served as *strategos* of the city, Severus issued an order that in the future Rufinus should not be required to forego this right.

The Asianic provinces benefited also from a general improvement of the roads, especially of those leading to the East, now more needed than ever for the passage of troops to the Euphrates frontier.[29] The numerous milestones dated in 198—the year spent by Severus in Mesopotamia—which have been found on the important route leading through the centre of Cappadocia to the Euphrates indicate that this road was entirely rebuilt. In Pontus, milestones, also of 198, show that the section of the northern highway between the Halys and Neoclaudiopolis and the road from Amaseia to Tavium were likewise repaired. In this year also improvements were made on the road leading westward from Prusa in Bithynia and near Amastris on the Euxine coast route, and the Lycaonian section of the road from Ancyra to Iconium was repaired under the governor of the Galatian province, Atticius Strabo. During his term of office the road from Apameia through northern Pisidia toward Antioch was likewise restored and in 202 the milestones along the southern section (along Lake Suğla) were renewed. In 197 the road leading from Corycus on the Cilician coast inland to the temple-city of Olba was repaired, and in 199, probably, a bridge over the river Chabina in northern Commagene was rebuilt, possibly in connexion with a restoration of the road running from Melitene west of the Euphrates to Syria. Toward the close of Severus's reign a section of the important route from Ancyra to Archelais in Cappadocia was also restored.

The province of Asia, moreover, was not neglected. Under the proconsul Lollianus Gentianus in 201/2 repairs were carried out on the westernmost section of the Southern Highway and on the roads from Smyrna to Sardis, from Stratoniceia in Caria to Lagina and from Cyzicus southward. The milestones on various roads in central Phrygia show that they were likewise repaired under Severus, as was also the route which ran from Laodiceia southward to Cibyra with an extension leading through the centre of Lycia to the Mediterranean.

It is noteworthy that whereas during the first two centuries, as has been previously observed, the task of maintaining the roads was assumed by the imperial government,[8] a responsibility which was expressed in the inscriptions on the milestones by the statement that the emperor built or restored the road in question, from the time of Severus onward many of these inscriptions take the form of a dedication to the ruler. This change seems to indicate that in many cases the expense of erecting the milestones—and presumably of maintaining the roads—was provided by some source other than the imperial treasury.[30] The record that in the second century the city of Amyzon, under the supervision of the imperial procurator, restored the road "allotted to it" and that under Severus the milestones on the road to Sardis were erected by the city of Smyrna shows that at least part of the cost was borne by the cities, among which, perhaps, the total expense was apportioned. Similar dedications were made by other cities during the third century, and the inclusion of road-construction among the regular civic duties required of citizens suggests, if the highways are meant thereby, that the cities were prepared to assume the burden.

[8] See above p. 547.

Despite the general submission of the provinces, there was, never-theless, disaffection. Former partisans of Niger still survived, and it may be assumed that the many murders committed by Severus after the defeat of Albinus aroused great bitterness. Niger's supporters, especially, were tracked down, and to such an extent, it is said, did the Emperor give vent to his suspicions that he even accused some of his own friends of plotting against his life.[t] Among the victims was Gaius Fulvius Plautianus, who early in his career had been Severus's chief instrument in carrying on the search for adherents of Niger and subsequently became prefect of the Praetorian Guard.[31] In this capacity he exercised great influence over the Emperor, who raised him to the consulship and, after marrying Caracalla to his daughter, even recognized him as a kinsman of the imperial family. His dominant position, however, aroused the jealousy of his son-in-law, who accused him of conspiring to kill Severus and make himself ruler. The charge seems to have been unfounded, but the Emperor, nevertheless, took no steps to protect Plautianus and permitted Caracalla to have him put to death. His property was confiscated and many who were sup-posed to be his adherents shared his fate.

Another victim of Severus's suspicions was the proconsul of Asia, Pedo Apronianus, who was condemned to death while absent in his province.[32] The charge against him, according to the historian Cassius Dio, who heard the evidence, was merely the statement that his nurse had once dreamed that he would become emperor and that he himself had used magic for this purpose. The Emperor's suspicious cruelty was perhaps increased by a plot against himself, his wife and his sons, which, according to a dedication at Ephesus by an imperial freedman, he escaped thanks to his foresight;[u] but whether this plot was con-nected with the alleged treason of Apronianus cannot be determined nor can the time of its occurrence be established.

Although Severus's cruelty seems to have been directed solely against the upper class and he appears to have adopted a general policy of humanitarianism toward the humbler folk, there was, nevertheless, a wide-spread condition of unrest and violence, accompanied by brigand-age, both in Italy and in the provinces.[33] In Asia—if the documents, as seems probable, may be dated in Severus's time—the villagers suffered greatly from the oppression and corruption practised by the military police agents, a force strengthened, if not actually organized, under Commodus, who were active both in lodging information and in carry-

---

[t] *Vit. Sev.* 15, 4.   [u] *C.I.L.* III 427 (not earlier than A.D. 198).

ing out arrests.[34] Believing that the outrages perpetrated by these officials
could be corrected only by the Emperor himself, three different communities in Lydia addressed petitions to him, asking for redress. In one
case the police agents had descended upon the village and oppressed
it with "unendurable burdens and exactions," so that the inhabitants,
exhausted by the expense attendant on the presence of so large a number of these agents, were not only unable to maintain the public bath
but were even deprived of the necessities of life. In another, the "great
and celestial and sacred majesty" of the Emperors was besought to restrain the agents, who, apparently on the ground that they were in
search of lawbreakers, but without any legally qualified accuser or a
definite charge, had entered the village and oppressed it cruelly. In
still another—that of the inhabitants of a village on an imperial estate
—the agents had arrested nine of the villagers, saying that they were
taking them to the imperial procurators for trial; one had been released on the payment of over a thousand drachmae, but the others
were still in prison and no one knew what would be their fate. Meanwhile the petitioners, threatened by the agents and in fear of their
lives, were prevented from tilling their fields and furnishing their
quota of produce and the other services expected from them. Consequently, so they declared, unless measures were taken to restrain
the police agents as well as those who were extorting money from them
on other grounds, they would be compelled to abandon their homes
and move to some privately-owned estate, where there was less danger
of oppression than on an imperial domain.

The third of these petitions is of especial interest in casting some
light on the status of the peasants who were tenants of an imperial
estate. The view has previously been expressed that, although there is
evidence for the existence of such estates in eastern Pisidia and perhaps
in Galatia and Lycaonia, these were not as numerous as has sometimes
been believed. Nevertheless, the fact that from the time of Augustus
onward there was an imperial procurator in the senatorial province of
Asia indicates that the emperor owned properties in this province.[35]
The actual evidence for the existence of these estates, however, dates
from the late second or the third century, and it may perhaps be assumed that by this time, either through confiscation, perhaps on the
part of Severus, or through a more legitimate means of acquisition,
such as a bequest, they had increased considerably in number. In addition to the Lydian estate, there are known to have been imperial properties in Phrygia, as those between Nacoleia and Prymnessus and in

the valley of the upper Tembris. The tenants of the latter, under the name of Aragueni, also addressed a petition (a second one) to the Emperor in 244-247, asking for protection against the oppression of governmental officials, who, it was alleged, took them away from their work and seized their cattle.

In these petitions both the Lydian and the Phrygian tenants, in addressing the Emperors, described themselves as "your farmers," evidently because they regarded their leases as held directly from them. These leases were presumably hereditary, for the Lydian tenants reminded the Emperor not only that they themselves had been born and reared on the estate but that their ancestors also had lived on it for generations and had been buried there. Nevertheless, they were not legally bound to the soil as serfs, for they asserted that, if no relief from oppression were forthcoming, they would move elsewhere. The rights and duties of these tenants were set forth in a charter, which specified the amount of produce which they were under obligation to deliver to the imperial treasury as well as the demands for other services which might be made upon them. According to the terms of this charter, their possessions served as security for the performance of their obligations to the treasury and hence were not subject to seizure from any other source. It was, therefore, in violation of the charter that the police agents were exacting a ransom from the tenants whom they had arrested. There was, moreover, a connexion between the Lydian tenants and a city or some kind of civic organization; for one of the petitioners' complaints concerned the demand for money which had been made "under the pretext of offices and liturgies." The nature of this connexion and the exact ground for this demand are, unfortunately, not made clear, but it may perhaps be assumed either that, although imperial tenants, these peasants were none the less regarded as having obligations to the city whose territory was adjacent to the estate or that certain of them, in the hope of escaping these obligations, had moved to the estate from some city. The Phrygian tenants, on the other hand, had a loose form of organization—called a commonalty—of their own, which belonged to a larger group, evidently formed by neighbouring communities. In their case there is no mention of any demand for money on the ground of civic duty. They were, nevertheless, molested by "the leaders of the prominent men of the city," who, like the soldiers and the imperial officers (the *Caesariani*), entered the estate and "exacted what was not owed to them."

It has been assumed that, as in the province of Africa, these estates were under the charge of special procurators, who were imperial freedmen. There is no specific mention in either petition, however, of any such official. The Phrygian tenants sent their plea by a member of the military police force directly to the Emperor, and he, both on this occasion and on a previous one (when nothing was done to grant the relief for which they asked), referred the matter to the proconsul of the province. The Lydian petitioners likewise requested the Emperor to command the acting-governor and the "most eminent procurators" to protect them. Unfortunately, it does not appear whether these were the same as the "most eminent procurators" to whom the police agents were professedly about to bring their prisoners for trial and to whom, as also to the procurator apparently in charge of the police force, the petitioners had already sent information concerning their wrongs. Nor is it clear what connexion these officials had with the estate. They were evidently subordinates of the imperial procurator of Asia, who, although the present incumbent of the office was temporarily acting as proconsul, was in general charge of the imperial property in the province.

The administration of the emperor's property in the provinces as well as in Italy underwent an important change during the reign of Severus, when a distinction was made between the imperial "patrimony" and the emperor's private fortune and, in keeping with the constant growth of the bureaucracy, each was placed under a separate procurator.[36] The "patrimony" consisted of the crown-property, as, for example, estates and mines, which passed to an emperor on his accession to power, whereas the private fortune included the land and money which he had previously owned or subsequently personally acquired. In the case of Severus, this had been greatly increased by the seizure of the possessions of Niger and Albinus and their partisans as well as by the confiscation of the property of those whom his general ruthless cruelty had stripped of their wealth or condemned to death. It has been suggested that, in the absorption of all power by the emperor, even the land in the senatorial provinces, which had been regarded as the property of the Roman People and had paid taxes into the Senate's treasury, was now included in the "patrimony" and that the taxes from these provinces accrued to the treasury of the emperor.

It was perhaps the acquisition of wealth from the partisans of Niger that enabled Severus to issue—for the first time since Hadrian—a new series of silver coins of the cistophoric standard.[37] The place of issue is unknown, but they were evidently intended for circulation in the

Asianic provinces, perhaps to be used for payment of the cost of leading the armies through Asia Minor to the East. Their appearance is
the more remarkable in view of the fact that Severus, presumably on
account of his lavish spending of money on the Roman populace and
on the army, lowered the silver content of the imperial denarius from
71 per cent, as it had been under Commodus, to about 57 per cent,[v] a
long step forward in the depreciation of this coin, which sixty years
after Severus's death had only a nominal value.

There was presumably a connexion between this depreciation and
an effort made at Mylasa, toward the end of Severus's reign, to prevent
a speculation in currency on the part of those who bought up the better
coins either for hoarding or for trade outside the Empire, especially
with the Orient.[38] In consequence of such transactions, there was a
scarcity of ready money, "which prevented the city from having the
necessities of life, many being in need and the community in want."
To meet this emergency, the Council and People enacted a measure
forbidding all persons save the lessee and the manager of the city-bank
to buy or sell silver coins. Should the person accused of so doing be
found guilty by the Council, he was to be punished, if he had made no
profit by the transaction, by forfeiting to the bank the amount in question; but if at a profit, by the payment, in addition to the forfeiture,
of a fine of 850 denarii, to be divided among the imperial treasury, the
city-council and the accuser. In the case of a slave, the penalty was
beating and six months' imprisonment in the debtors' prison. In spite
of this action, however, the city-authorities, despairing of being able to
deal with the difficulty by legislation, appealed to the Emperor on the
ground that only through his grace could a remedy be found. As an
argument for some sort of imperial action, they pointed out that in the
present predicament of the city it was hard to collect the taxes payable
to Rome.

In some places an effort seems to have been made to remedy the
financial situation by an increase in the number of local bronze coins.
A study of the coinage of six of the principal cities of Asia Minor has
shown that in the first half of the third century the issues of these coins
exceeded those of the previous century. With the depreciation of the
denarius to little more than a token currency, the worth of these coins,
which did not undergo a like depreciation, increased proportionately
and they acquired an actual value of their own.

[v] See note 9.

The end of the Parthian war was followed by an interval of peace. Leaving Syria before the end of 199, Severus visited Egypt,[w] whence he returned to Antioch about the close of the next year, and here, on 1 January, 202, he assumed his third consulship with Caracalla as his colleague. He then returned, by way of Asia Minor, Thrace, Moesia and Pannonia to Rome,[39] where, in the spring, he celebrated with great magnificence and lavish gifts to the populace the tenth anniversary of his accession to power.

This interval of peace, broken only by the unrest, previously mentioned, in various parts of the Empire, lasted for eight years. It came to an end in 208, when, after previous outbreaks, the tribes of northern Britain attacked Roman territory. Severus, deeming it necessary to conduct the campaign in person, set out for the island, accompanied by Caracalla and his younger son, Geta—Consuls, respectively, for the third and the second time. In spite of failing health, the Emperor took an active part in the war that followed, but, overcome by his exertions, he died at York on 4 February, 211, in his sixty-sixth year. On his death-bed he is reported to have urged all his sons to live in harmony, to enrich the soldiers and to disregard all others[x]—an injunction befitting the founder of a military monarchy.

It had been Severus's plan that Caracalla and Geta should succeed him as joint rulers. His injunction to them to live in harmony, however, was wholly disregarded by the two young men, who, returning to Rome after patching up a peace with the Britons, continued their former hostility toward each other and, in fact, became deadly enemies. Finally, less than a year after the old Emperor's death, the ruthless Caracalla caused his brother to be stabbed in the presence of their mother. The murder was followed by a general massacre of all, both civilians and soldiers, who were regarded as Geta's adherents, including the famous jurist Papinian, whom Severus had appointed prefect of the Praetorian Guard.

For the next five years the brutal and tyrannical Caracalla—evidently a psychopath—ruled the Empire under the once honoured name of Marcus Aurelius Antoninus.[40] Obsessed by an overwhelming desire for military glory, which found expression in his professed wish to imitate Alexander the Great, he courted the favour of the army in every possible way, even to the extent, it is said, of living, while on his campaigns, the life of a common soldier. While he devoted himself

---

[w] See note 25. [x] Cassius Dio LXXVI 15, 2.

to his favourite pursuits of chariot-driving and war, many of the practical details of administering the Empire were left to his council and his mother, Julia Domna, a daughter of the prince-priest of Emesa in Syria and a woman of unusual intelligence and ability, who for a time performed the duties of secretary for petitions and for the imperial correspondence.

After a campaign against the German tribes in the region of the upper Rhine and the upper Danube, in which he was successful enough to add to his various surnames that of Germanicus Maximus, Caracalla, in the spring of 214, set out for the East, which, as a would-be Alexander, he hoped to conquer. It was evidently his ambition also to surpass his father's achievements against the Parthians. Travelling by way of the lower Danube, he arrived in Thrace in the autumn. The time was well chosen, for the Parthians, broken by Severus's invasion, were still further weakened by dissension between Vologases V, who had succeeded his father a few years previously, and his brother, Artabanus, who was trying to gain possession of Mesopotamia.[y]

From Thrace, the Emperor, having added to his army a body of 16,000 Macedonians organized, in imitation of Alexander's army, as a phalanx, crossed the Hellespont into Asia.[41] At Ilium he offered sacrifices and held contests in memory of Achilles, and he even caused the body of a favourite freedman, who died at this time, to be burned on a great pyre in imitation of the funeral rites of Patroclus. During a visit to Pergamum a temple was rebuilt for his worship, and in consequence, the city obtained the title of Thrice Temple-Warden. Some further privileges also were granted to the Pergamenes, and the Emperor visited the Temple of Asclepius in the hope of being cured of a malady contracted in Germany. He went also to Thyateira, where he was received by a local dignitary, and made the city the centre of a new judiciary district, increasing its importance by thus designating it as one of the places in which trials were conducted by the proconsul of the province. In consequence, perhaps, of this privilege, he was honoured as Founder and Benefactor. The bestowal of the titles of Founder and Saviour at Hyrcanis suggests that some favour was granted to this community as well. He may also have visited Philadelpheia, to which, in the autumn of 214, he gave the title of Temple-Warden.

The winter of 214-215 Caracalla spent in Nicomedeia, training his Macedonian "phalanx" and making preparations for his eastern cam-

---

[y] Cassius Dio LXXVII 12, 2a; 13, 3.

paign as well as indulging in his favourite pastimes of chariot-driving and fighting with wild beasts.[42] He rewarded the city by building a great public bath, which afterward bore his name. It was presumably in the course of this winter that Smyrna became Thrice Temple-Warden and that permission was given to other cities also to assume the coveted title. Various statues and dedications erected in Caracalla's honour in many places may likewise be connected with this visit to Asia Minor.

Finally, in the spring of 215, the Emperor set out on his journey to the seat of his long-planned war, apparently travelling, like his father, by way of Prusias and Ancyra.[43] After crossing the Taurus he stopped at Tarsus, which now added his name to those of Hadrian and Severus, and he presented the city with a quantity of grain. He then went on to Antioch, where he arrived in the early summer.

As a prelude to the invasion of the Parthian kingdom, Caracalla invited the rulers of Osroene and Armenia to meet him for a friendly conference. The former, Abgarus IX, who, having succeeded his father, Abgarus VIII, was said to have made himself master of the neighbouring tribes and to have treated their leading men with great cruelty, was deposed from his throne and placed under guard. His kingdom was annexed to the existing province of Osroene, and his capital, Edessa, was either now or somewhat later made a Roman colony. The Armenian monarch, who had been at variance with his sons, was similarly treated, and his wife also seems to have been imprisoned. His subjects, nevertheless, refused to submit to Caracalla and even offered armed resistance. It was perhaps to meet this opposition that Roman troops were sent into Armenia under the command of Theocritus, formerly an imperial slave and a dancer on the stage, who had risen to a position of great power. The expedition, however, was a total failure, for the incompetent commander was badly defeated.

Caracalla had expected to find a pretext for his projected war with the Parthians in a demand for the return of two fugitives (one perhaps a son of the Armenian king) whom Vologases had taken under his protection.[44] This plan, however, failed of its purpose when the Parthian monarch consented to surrender the men in question. Accordingly, postponing his plan for the present, the Emperor went on to Egypt. During a visit to Alexandria, angered, it is reported, by the ridicule of the populace, he took his revenge by a general massacre in which great numbers perished. He then returned to Antioch, where he spent the winter of 215-216. In the following spring, finding a new pretext for a war, namely, that Artabanus—who by this time had succeeded Vologases—had refused to give him his daughter in marriage, he set out on his long-postponed campaign.

Meeting with little or no opposition from the Parthians, the Roman army advanced through Mesopotamia and crossed the Tigris into Adiabene.[45] The district was ravaged, many strongholds sacked, and the city of Arbela captured and the royal tombs destroyed. The invaded area was evidently limited in extent, but his success, trivial though it was, Caracalla magnified into a great achievement and coins were issued in Rome in celebration of a "Parthian Victory."

At the end of this campaign the Emperor withdrew to spend the winter of 216-217 at Edessa and to make preparations for the continuance of the war. The Parthians also spent the winter in raising a large army. Caracalla, however, was not destined further to prosecute this futile struggle. In April, 217, while on an expedition to Carrhae in the province of Osroene, he was assassinated by a group of conspirators headed by Marcus Opellius Macrinus, prefect of the Praetorian Guard, who, believing that he had aroused the Emperor's suspicions, took this means of saving his own life.

The war soon came to an inglorious end. Macrinus, almost immediately declared Emperor by the soldiers in Mesopotamia, was soon accepted, out of hatred for Caracalla, by the Senate as well. He had no desire to prolong the struggle, and when Artabanus advanced with a large army, he offered terms to the Parthian King in which he expressed himself as ready to restore the captives taken in the previous year.[46] The negotiations, however, came to nothing when Artabanus demanded the return of the captured strongholds, the restoration of the demolished cities, the evacuation of Mesopotamia and reparation for the desecration of the royal tombs at Arbela. After an unsuccessful engagement near Nisibis the Roman army withdrew, but Artabanus, advancing in pursuit, overtook it west of the city and in a great battle, lasting three days, gained an overwhelming victory. Terms were finally agreed upon, probably in the spring of 218, in which the Parthian King, also apparently unwilling to continue the war, gave up his former demands but obtained a large sum of money—said to have amounted to 50,000,000 denarii—as an indemnity for himself and his associated princes. Nevertheless, Macrinus, writing to the Senate, reported success, and again coins were issued in commemoration of a "Parthian Victory."

The extravagance of Caracalla, his gifts to the Roman populace and to the army, the cost of his wars and especially his addition of 50 per cent to the soldiers' pay,[z] did much to diminish the surplus left by Severus and to deplete the imperial treasury. The reduction in weight of the gold pieces known as *aurei* was evidently intended to give the government a greater supply of cheaper money with which to meet its obligations.[47] The issue of a new coin, the so-called *Antoninianus* (on which the emperor wears a radiate crown), with a weight, apparently, of one and one-half times that of the denarius and, like the denarius, of low silver content, may perhaps have been intended to serve the same purpose, but the reason for this issue is obscure. Attempts were also made to increase the imperial revenues by repeated demands, under all possible pretexts, for the requisition known as crown-gold, by the imposition of new taxes and by doubling the existing 5 per cent taxes on inheritances and on the manumission of slaves.

The desire to increase the number of those who paid these two taxes, imposed on Roman citizens only, was regarded by the historian Cassius Dio as the reason for the most important measure taken during Caracalla's reign—a measure probably to be attributed to the imperial council rather than to the Emperor himself—namely, the issuing, about 212, of the edict by which Roman citizenship was conferred on all free men throughout the Empire with the possible exception of the so-called *Dediticii*, or the "Surrendered," a term whose exact meaning is obscure.[48] It is true that this edict did impose taxes on those who, as non-citizens, had previously not been liable for them. But the mere need of raising money can hardly have been the sole cause of the grant. Nor could its effect be measured only in terms of the economic consequences which the historian envisaged. For, however little advantage, from the practical standpoint, the provincials may have gained from a grant of rights hitherto possessed by what seemed a privileged class, this creation of a universal citizenship, by which all free men were placed on the same footing, was the culmination of a long-continued process, the unification of the Empire and the equalization of the ruled with those who had been their rulers. Nevertheless, it marked the beginning of a general disintegration of the Roman world and it was the precursor of a period of rust and decay.

[z] Cassius Dio LXXVII 24, 1; LXXVIII 36, 3: Herodian IV 4, 7.

CHAPTER XXIX

DECAY AND CHAOS

THE rule of Macrinus, Caracalla's murderer, lasted but little more than a year. His overthrow was brought about by the intrigues of Julia Maesa, daughter of the prince-priest of the Sun God (Bel) at Emesa in Syria and a sister of Julia Domna, the wife of Severus.[1] This ambitious and astute woman, appearing in the camp of the soldiers stationed near Emesa, persuaded them by a liberal expenditure of money to accept as emperor her fourteen-year-old grandson, the son of her daughter by Sextus Varius Marcellus, a Syrian by birth, who had been advanced from Equestrian to Senatorial rank. This boy, who had been made priest of the Temple at Emesa, was presented to the soldiers as the natural son of Caracalla, and they, dissatisfied with the stern measures of Macrinus, hailed him as the heir of their friend and benefactor. Accompanied by Maesa and her grandson, they marched toward Antioch, the headquarters of Macrinus, who, with the few troops at his disposal, was in no position to withstand their attack. In the battle which ensued he suffered a decisive defeat and, deserting the remnants of his army, fled in disguise to Aegaeae in Cilicia and thence across the whole of Asia Minor to the Bosporus, where he was captured at Chalcedon. His captor proceeded to take him back to Syria, but on the way, at Archelais in Cappadocia, he received instructions to put his prisoner to death and at once obeyed the order.

As the result of Maesa's successful manoeuvre, two young rulers who alleged kinship with Severus held the imperial power for the next seventeen years.[2] Her grandson, the depraved youth who was now officially called, from his supposititious father, Marcus Aurelius Antoninus but was ordinarily known as Elagabalus, a name taken from that of the Sun God, aroused such contempt by his vices and follies that, in 222, less than four years after his accession, he met a well-deserved death at the hands of the soldiers in Rome. He was succeeded by his first cousin, the son of Maesa's second daughter, Julia Mamaea, by Gessius Marcianus, another Syrian, who, after holding several procuratorships, had been made a Senator. This youth, declared emperor at the age of thirteen, asserted a claim to kinship with the dynasty which he professed to represent by assuming the name Marcus Aurelius Severus Alexander. Although virtuous and kindly and in every way a great contrast to his cousin, he was indolent and weak-willed and under the control of his ambitious and masterful mother, who, after Maesa's death in 226, exercised a dominant influence. In the actual administration of the Empire these two women were aided by a commission of sixteen senators, who acted as co-regents, as well as by the imperial council, which included the eminent jurists, Domitius Ulpianus and Julius Paulus, the former of whom was prefect of the Praetorian Guard. A shrewd observance of constitutional forms, especially in dealing with the Senate, presented a welcome contrast to the cruelty and tyranny of Severus and Caracalla and caused Alexander's reign to be highly praised by the ancient writers. But he could not control the troops or command their loyalty, and in 235, during a campaign in Germany, the mutinous soldiers, under the leadership of Gaius Julius Verus Maximinus, a Thracian peasant who had risen from the ranks to the position of commander of recruits, seized Alexander and his mother and put them both to death.

The power of the armies both to advance and to overthrow claimants to the imperial power had been demonstrated in the rise of Severus. He, however, by his severity and cruelty had been able to hold them in check, and Caracalla by courting their favour had during his short reign succeeded in retaining their support. Under the rule, however, of two youths, despised as subject to the control of women, there was no longer a restraining hand, and the soldiers soon learned their power. This period, accordingly, was a turning-point, marking the beginning of a steady decay in the imperial power due to the increasing insubordination of the armies with a resultant disintegration of the Empire and the chaos which this produced.

The Asianic provinces, like the rest of the Empire, accepted Macrinus. During his reign of fourteen months, at least fifty-six cities issued coins bearing his portrait or that of his son, and in Cilicia Aegaeae called itself Macrinoupolis and Tarsus substituted his name for that of Caracalla in its complicated nomenclature.[3] On the other hand, Pergamum was deprived of certain rights granted by Caracalla, and when the angry citizens heaped insults on Macrinus they were punished by a diminution in the city's rank. In Armenia an attempt was made to quell a revolt resulting from Caracalla's deposition of the king by appointing the monarch's son as ruler of the country. The booty captured during the recent invasion was returned to the new ruler, and hope was held out to him of a renewal of the annual subsidy formerly granted by the imperial government as well as of the restoration of all the territory held by his father. This measure, while actually a concession to the rebels, could be represented as a resumption of the traditional policy of retaining Armenia as a client-state under a ruler appointed by Rome.

After the overthrow of Macrinus, the new Emperor, Elagabalus, travelled in state in the autumn of 218 through Asia Minor on his way to Italy. Passing through Cappadocia, where he was said to have gloated over the body of Macrinus,[a] he went on to Bithynia, where, at Prusias-on-Hypius, he was officially welcomed by the same citizen who had received both Severus and Caracalla.[b] During the winter, following his alleged father's example, he remained at Nicomedeia, where his fantastic costume as priest of his god as well as his manner of life aroused general disapproval, so that it was even possible for an adventurer to attempt to cause a mutiny in the fleet stationed at Cyzicus.[c] It may be assumed that this long stay in Nicomedeia, following so closely the visit of Caracalla, was a serious burden to the citizens. In an attempt to win the favour of the more important cities, Elagabalus authorized Nicomedeia as well as Ephesus and Sardis to add another Temple-Wardenship to their titles[d]—a privilege revoked after his death—and Thyateira, in response to a request brought by a special envoy, received permission to hold a "sacred contest."[4] But save for the repair of some roads, principally the restoration of the milestones on the great route through central Cappadocia to the Euphrates, the short reign of this degenerate youth seems to have left no traces in these provinces, and no inscription in his honour has been found in any of the Asianic cities.

Alexander, on the other hand, was honoured in several places, among them Tarsus, which added his name to its already long list.[5] In fact, the reduction of the taxes which is attributed to him may, if it actually occurred, have won general gratitude; and if an edict remitting the crown-gold, customarily contributed on important occasions and under Elagabalus apparently collected regularly in Egypt, was issued, as seems probable, by Alexander on his accession, this act of grace doubtless impelled the cities to do him honour. His care for the interests of the provincials appears also in a letter written to the Commonalty of Bithynia, guaranteeing the right of appeal to the emperor and ordering that forceful means must not be used against

[a] Cassius Dio LXXVIII 40, 2.
[b] *I.G.R.* III 62 (see Chap. XXVIII notes 20 and 43).
[c] Cassius Dio LXXIX 3, 2; 6, 1; 7, 3; 8, 3: Herodian v 5, 3f.: *Vit. Elag.* 5, 1.
[d] See Chap. XXVII note 21.

appellants by procurators or governors, "who will obey this command when they learn that my subjects' liberty is as much of a concern to me as their loyalty and obedience."[e]

Moreover, if a letter written under Alexander by a proconsul of Asia to the people of Aphrodisias may be regarded as an example of the Emperor's general policy, the rights of those cities which were nominally free were scrupulously preserved.[6] In this letter the writer professed in general a high regard for the cities devoted to Alexander, particularly those whose freedom, granted by former rulers, had been confirmed, with increased privileges, by the Emperor himself. He then announced his intention of visiting Aphrodisias, provided such a visit was not forbidden by the city's laws or a senatorial decree or an imperial order. It is significant, however, of the prevalent conception of the cities' status that in the proconsul's letter their freedom was regarded as an imperial grant. The proposed visit was evidently permitted, for the proconsul Sulpicius Priscus, whose statue was erected by the *demos* of Aphrodisias, was presumably the writer of the letter.

In general, the rulers of the dynasty of Severus abandoned, as far as the eastern provinces were concerned, the policy of founding new urban centres bearing the emperor's name. This policy, it will be remembered, had been widely adopted by the Flavians, Trajan and Hadrian, and it had been continued to a limited extent by Marcus, who gave his name to an Aureliopolis, to replace the defunct city of Tmolus in Lydia,[f] and created the colony of Faustinopolis in memory of his wife.[g] Caracalla, to be sure, seems to have founded an Antoninopolis in Mesopotamia.[h] But otherwise, as far as is known, neither he nor his father did more to promote the urbanization of the Asianic provinces than give the rank of colony to several cities already in existence. This rank had been conferred by Hadrian on Iconium[i] and during the second century on Selinus in Cilicia and Attaleia in Pamphylia.[7] Now, however, it was granted more widely—to Tyana by Caracalla, to Mallus in Cilicia by Elagabalus or Alexander and to Trebenna in Lycia by an unknown third-century emperor. In these cases it may be assumed that, in contrast to the colonies east of the Euphrates, where groups of veterans were probably established,[j] there were no settlements of soldiers and that the title of colony was purely honorary. After Caracalla's grant of universal citizenship, the political status of the in-

[e] *Digesta* XLIX I, 25 = *Pap. Oxy.* 2104.
[g] See Chap. XXVIII note 16.
[i] See Chap. XXVI note 47.

[f] See J. Keil in *R.E.* VI A 1628.
[h] See Fraenkel in *R.E.* I 2571.
[j] See Chap. XXVIII note 26.

habitants did not differ from that of the citizens of other cities, but, as colonies, these places may not have been subject to the taxes levied by Rome on the various provincial communities.

Nevertheless, attempts were made to promote trade, if not by urbanization, at least by establishing market-centres which did not have the status of a *polis*.[8] The details of Severus's foundation of such an *emporium* at Pizus in Thrace in 202 are known from an edict of the governor of the province. According to this document, the new community was formed by 181 settlers from nine neighbouring villages, who were induced to move to Pizus by the promise of exemption from certain liturgies, such as providing grain for the community, supplying frontier-guards and garrisons and the furnishing of animals and labour for the imperial post. It was to be administered, not by an ordinary resident serving as emporiarch, but by a "toparch" chosen by the governor from the councillors of a neighbouring city, who was authorized to dispense justice and "govern the inhabitants not with insolence or violence but with righteousness and equity." Similar centres seem to have been established in Asia Minor, particularly in Bithynia, where the city-territories were especially large and, consequently, the distances between the several *poleis* very long. There is record of an emporium near Dia on the Euxine, the revenues of which were increased and the buildings improved by a *curator* of the city, and the mention of an emporium or an emporiarch in two places in southeastern Bithynia indicates the existence of similar trading-centres in this region. Besides these places for permanent trade, occasional fairs might also be held, such as that conducted monthly in the later third century in a village in eastern Lydia by express permission of the proconsul of the province on the condition that it would not interfere with any other held in the same neighbourhood.

In spite of Alexander's consideration for the cities, the known number of monuments in his honour is smaller by far than those erected for Caracalla, a diminution which may perhaps be attributed to a general economic decline. In some places, however, there are indications, during this period, of considerable wealth.[9] At Ephesus, for example, the income from a bequest by a lady enabled the city to make improvements in the theatre, to build a porch for the temple of the goddess Nemesis and to pave the square in front of an auditorium and the Library of Celsus; members of the family of the Aurelii Metrodori, in return for various public offices, gave money for paving, for dredging the harbour and for other purposes, including a reduction in the price of oil; and a triumphal festival was celebrated, perhaps after Alexander's war against the Persians. At Miletus money was presented for a porch for the Temple of Serapis. At Philadelpheia, which seems to have been especially prosperous during the third century, a wealthy citizen, in addition to paying for a spectacle in which gladiators fought to the death, gave 10,000 denarii for the awning of the theatre and 550,000 for the purchase of grain, besides presents to the city-council and the Elders' Association. At Thyateira a triumphal festival was held in honour of Alexander. The priests of the temples at Panamara and Lagina, moreover, continued the practice of lavish hospitality to the worshippers.

In the other provinces evidence may be found for the prosperity of Nicomedeia and Nicaea both in the great number of coins which they issued and the festivals which they maintained. The wealthy city of Termessus continued to hold a large number of contests, and a gymnasium with colonnades was built in the new quarter of the city about the time of Alexander. At Oenoanda in Lycia a contest bore his name as well as that of the donor. While, as has already been observed, it grew increasingly difficult to find men who were willing to hold public office, the number of those who appear in the inscriptions of this period as civic officials indicates that several were still able to assume the necessary expense.

Nevertheless, it can hardly be doubted that the general prosperity of the second and early third centuries no longer existed. The increasing number of those who, because they had become members of the Senatorial or the Equestrian Order or occupied high official posts or had served as soldiers or practised the favoured professions or occupations,[k] were exempt from civic offices and liturgies, made the burden all the greater for those who enjoyed no such exemption. It was inevitable, moreover, that the extension of the inheritance-tax which accompanied Caracalla's grant of universal citizenship, although it had been reduced by Macrinus to the previous amount of 5 per cent[l] and was smaller by far than that which prevails in modern times, should cause a diminution in individual fortunes. In fact, evidence of a decline in wealth may be found in the marked decrease in the number of endowments established during the third century as contrasted with those of the period of Hadrian and the Antonines.[m]

---

[k] *Digesta* L 5-6 (see also Chap. XXIV note 15 and Chap. XXVII note 13).
[l] See Chap. XXVIII note 47.   [m] See Laum *Stiftungen* 1 p. 9f.

This decline may be attributed also to the series of wars waged by Severus and Caracalla and, as will presently be related, by Alexander. These necessitated not only the requisitioning of supplies, already mentioned,[n] which the soldiers received partly in lieu of pay, but also the expenditure of great amounts of money both for the transportation of the troops and for the presents given to keep them content. The constant drain on the supply of the precious metals forced the imperial government to continue the process of depreciating the currency. The expedient adopted by Caracalla of issuing 50 gold pieces to the pound instead of 45, as under Severus, was retained by Elagabalus and Alexander, and under the latter the silver content of the denarius, while by no means constant, sank to about 40 per cent.[10] In Asia Minor this depreciation was accompanied by a marked decrease under Alexander, as compared with the shorter reign of Caracalla, in the number of cities known to have issued a local coinage, to be explained, perhaps, by the inability of the smaller and less wealthy communities to provide themselves, at the higher prices caused by the currency-inflation, with the necessary amount of metal.

In spite of its impaired financial position, the imperial government under Alexander, as previously under Elagabalus, maintained the roads in the Asianic provinces, especially those in the East.[11] The road-bed and the bridges were restored both on the Cappadocian route and, in 230, on the road which led from the Cilician Gates southward to Syria. Early in Alexander's reign the road from Tyana to the Gates and in the Galatian province the important route from the Halys eastward to the Lycus valley and the roads from Ancyra through Tavium to Amaseia and from Ancyra southward were also repaired. In southern Pontus, now part of the province of Cappadocia, the road between Zela and Sebastopolis, a section of the route from Amaseia to Sebasteia and Melitene, was rebuilt in A.D. 231, apparently in great haste.

The maintenance of these roads was of importance for the protection of the eastern frontier, for a new enemy had appeared beyond the Euphrates. Soon after Alexander's accession, the Parthian Empire received its death-blow and another, stronger, power appeared in its place. Ardashir (whom the Greeks and Romans called Artaxerxes), the son of a Parthian vassal-ruler in southwestern Iran and himself perhaps an official at the court of the Parthian monarch, Artabanus, after strengthening his position by bringing part of Persia under his power, revolted against his suzerain.[12] Artabanus, weakened by strife

---

[n] See Chap. XXVIII note 27.

within his kingdom and perhaps—in spite of his success against Macrinus—by the invasions of Severus and Caracalla, was unable to offer effective resistance. After a series of battles with the invaders he was killed about 224 and Ardashir established himself as King in Ctesiphon, where his dynasty—called, from his grandfather, Sassanian —ruled for four centuries.

This vigorous and intensely nationalistic monarch promptly announced an ambitious programme, nothing less, it is said, than the restoration of the old Persian Empire as it had been under its last king, Darius. Although an attempt to capture Hatra in central Mesopotamia was a failure, he succeeded in extending his power northward along the Tigris until a further advance was checked by the Armenians. He then proceeded, in 230, to invade Rome's newly-acquired possessions in northern Mesopotamia. Undeterred by an embassy sent by Alexander, bidding him remain within his own boundaries, he even threatened the province of Syria.

The danger to the eastern provinces was soon realized in Rome. It seemed all the greater for the reason that the troops stationed in the East were ill-disciplined and inclined to desert to the enemy; some soldiers in Mesopotamia had recently mutinied and even killed their commander. It was decided that the Emperor should proceed to the front in person and that the army in the East should be strengthened by additional troops from the Rhine and the Danube. Alexander, accordingly, in 231 set out for Syria, accompanied by his mother, and soldiers from the northern frontier were hurried to the Euphrates, presumably by way of Pontus on the road hastily constructed anew in this same year.

While the only source which records the details of the campaign is often inaccurate and unreliable, it would appear that early in 232, after a winter spent at Antioch and another vain attempt to negotiate with Ardashir, the Romans crossed the Euphrates with their forces divided into three armies. Of these, one advanced into Armenia for the purpose of invading Media; another, formed of the troops from the Danube, the best part of the whole force, and commanded by Alexander himself, entered Mesopotamia; the third was ordered to proceed southeastward down the Euphrates toward Ctesiphon, which, it was hoped, would be the final objective of all three divisions.

The plan was not ill conceived, but, according to the same source, its execution was a failure. It is related that the force sent to the southeast was surprised by Ardashir and completely destroyed; that on the announcement of this disaster the soldiers of Alexander's army, already suffering from the effects of the climate, became demoralized, so that the Emperor, who also had fallen ill, felt compelled to abandon the campaign and withdraw his men to Antioch; and that the troops sent to Media, after meeting with some success, also received orders to return. It seems apparent, however, that the failure of this expedition was not altogether complete. Ardashir, although afterward under Alexander's successor he took possession of Nisibis in Mesopotamia and Carrhae in Osroene, made no move at this time to attack the Roman territory bordering on the Euphrates. It may be supposed that his losses were greater than the historian's account suggests and that he was unable to continue further his policy of aggression.

In 233 Alexander with Mamaea returned to Rome, where he spent a year before setting out on his ill-fated expedition to Germany. During this year he celebrated a triumph, in connexion with which he distributed largesse to the populace and assumed the surnames Parthicus Maximus and Persicus Maximus in commemoration of what he claimed to have achieved in the East.

For a half-century after the death of Alexander the Roman Empire was ruled by a bewildering succession of emperors, most of whom rose and fell through assassination and none save the able but much-hated Gallienus remained in power for longer than seven years. In consequence, this was a period of anarchy and increasing chaos.

The reign of Maximinus, the murderer of Alexander, was marked in eastern Asia Minor by an earthquake of great severity, which is said to have caused much damage to cities in Pontus and Cappadocia.[o] This upstart emperor, indeed, held his power for only a brief time; for after a rule of a little over three years he in turn was slain by mutinous soldiers near Aquileia in northeastern Italy. His death was preceded by a revolt in Africa, where a group of nobles, resenting the excessive taxes demanded by the imperial procurator, proclaimed as Emperors the highly respected proconsul of the province, Marcus Antonius Gordianus, and his son of the same name.[13] They were soon accepted by the Senators, who, hating Maximinus as a barbarian, declared him a public enemy and appointed a commission of twenty of their number to defend Italy for the two Gordians. Both, however, while still in Africa, perished within a month, the son in a battle against the partisans of Maximinus, the father, in despair caused by his son's death, by suicide.

[o] Cyprian *Epist.* 75, 10.

Then the Senate, taking the initiative, appointed as Augusti two members of its commission, Marcus Clodius Pupienus Maximus, who had at some time previously been proconsul of Asia and perhaps governor of Bithynia-Pontus, and Decimus Caelius Calvinus Balbinus, who also is said to have governed Bithynia-Pontus and Galatia. With them, at the demand of a riotous mob composed of the Roman populace and the soldiers, was associated a third Gordian, the youthful son of the Proconsul's daughter, to whom was given the title of Caesar. The two Augusti, however, after a rule of about three months and probably not more than a month after Maximinus's death, were slain by the soldiers of the Praetorian Guard, and Gordian, at the age of thirteen, became sole ruler. During the latter half of his reign a dominant influence was exercised by the able Gaius Furius Sabinius Aquila Timesitheus, who in 241 was appointed prefect of the Praetorian Guard and by the marriage of his daughter to Gordian became the Emperor's father-in-law.[14] He was well qualified for high office on account of a distinguished career, in the course of which he had been responsible for the grain-supply during a war in the East conducted by one of the emperors; he had likewise served as procurator in several provinces, including both Bithynia-Pontus, where he had been in charge of the imperial "patrimony" and of the Emperor's personal property, and Asia, where he had also been acting proconsul.

It was evidently Timesitheus who was responsible for the chief military success of Gordian's brief reign.[15] About the time of his appointment as prefect, Ardashir, the Persian monarch, died and was succeeded by his son Shapur (Sapor), who at once resumed his father's aggressive policy by advancing toward the Euphrates and threatening Syria, so that even Antioch seemed to be in danger.

This advance called for vigorous measures. In 242 the gates of the Temple of Janus were opened, signifying that Rome was at war, and Timesitheus and the young Emperor set out for the front. Proceeding by way of the lower Danube, where they collected some detachments of the legions, and advancing through Thrace, they crossed the Bosporus and traversed Asia Minor, which again had to endure the passage of an army. While details of the campaign are lacking, it seems clear that the enemy's advance was successfully repelled. Crossing the Euphrates into Osroene, part of which appears to have been previously restored to its former status as a client-kingdom under Abgarus X as ruler, the Romans recaptured Carrhae and, after a victory at Rhesaena, Nisibis as well. Continuing their advance into eastern Mesopotamia, they occupied Singara, which had been the headquarters of a legion under Severus and now became a Roman colony. From here they turned to the southwest, intending, apparently, to proceed down the Euphrates, as Caracalla had done, to Ctesiphon.

This advance was presumably made possible by the efficiency of Timesitheus, who is said to have provided stores of supplies and exercised a constant supervision over the army.[p] In the midst of the campaign, however, this capable leader contracted an illness which proved fatal, and operations came to a sudden end with the halt of the army on the eastern bank of the Euphrates near its junction with the Khabur. Here Timesitheus's successor as prefect, the ambitious and ruthless Marcus Julius Philippus, a native of the district of Trachonitis on the border of the Syrian Desert, having aroused disaffection in the army against Gordian on the ground that he was too young and incompetent to conduct the war, obtained the support of some of the higher officers in a plan to depose the Emperor and seize the imperial power. Refusing even to accept Gordian as co-ruler, Philip, early in 244, caused him to be murdered. He was at once proclaimed Emperor by the soldiers. After coming to some kind of agreement with Shapur, he left the East and returned to Rome, where, like Alexander, he assumed the surnames Parthicus Maximus and Persicus Maximus.

During Gordian's brief reign, presumably by action of his advisers, various decisions were rendered confirming the rights of the provincials, especially on the administration of justice.[16] Thus an imperial procurator, unless he was acting as governor, was not permitted to appoint judges in civil lawsuits, and his verdicts in cases which properly came under the governor's cognizance were declared invalid. The power of a *curator* of a community was likewise lessened by forbidding him to impose fines. The right of appeal was reaffirmed by the decision that in a case in which the defendant, during his absence and hence illegally, had been condemned to capital punishment by the provincial governor, might appeal to the prefect of the Guard as the highest judicial authority. In order, moreover, to help the cities by lightening the burden of holding civic office, an interval of three years was permitted between one office and another; and in order to safeguard the position of members of a city-council, it was ordered that a councillor condemned to exile might on the completion of his sentence resume his seat, although he might not become eligible for

[p] *Vit. Gord.* 28, 2f.

a civic office until after an interval equal in length to the period of his exile.

An attempt was also made to prevent extortion by reviving a previous regulation which prohibited the lending of money by an official, either in his own name or that of another, during his term in a province.[q] Indeed, the same need for checking oppressive demands on the part of governmental officials which is known from the petitions already mentioned, addressed, probably, to Severus,[r] is illustrated by a petition which was presented to Gordian, a few months after his accession, by the inhabitants of the village of Scaptopare in Thrace through a former soldier of the Praetorian Guard, now a property-owner in the community.[17] The villagers, both because there were hot springs, much frequented as a health-resort, in the neighbourhood and because a popular festival was celebrated regularly only two miles away, had been forced to receive visits, evidently under Gordian's predecessors, from provincial governors and imperial procurators, who demanded entertainment at the community's expense. An evil still harder to bear was the presence of others who came to the festival, especially soldiers, who exacted "presents" and requisitioned supplies without payment. The petitioners had frequently presented their case to governors of the province, who, in obedience to imperial injunctions, had commanded that they should not be molested. These orders, however, had had no permanent effect; in consequence, many of the inhabitants had left the village and those who remained were ready also, unless relief could be obtained, to abandon their homes and move elsewhere, to the detriment, as the petitioners pointed out, of the imperial revenues. The only reply, however, which they received from Rome was that their complaints should have been submitted to the governor of the province before they were referred to the Emperor. It may probably be assumed from the fact that the petition was inscribed in the village that at least a promise of protection was received.

The inability of the imperial government to restrain the exactions of its officials and soldiers appears also in the petition to which reference has already been made, addressed by the Aragueni, the tenants of an imperial estate in Phrygia, to the Emperor Philip, which evidently reflects conditions existing under Gordian. In this case also, the petitioners, harassed by those who demanded their cattle and their services, had appealed to Rome and had been likewise referred to the governor,

q *Cod. Iust.* IV 2, 3: *Digesta* XII 1, 33.   r See above p. 678f.

699

from whom, however, they had received no relief, with the result that "their farms were desolated and laid waste."

At this time or soon afterward the proconsulship of Asia was held by Lucius Egnatius Victor Lollianus, probably a native of Prusa, who, since he had previously been imperial legate both of Bithynia-Pontus and of Galatia as well as of Arabia, was an experienced and presumably capable governor.[18] He was proconsul late in Gordian's reign or in the first or second year of Philip and remained in office for the unusually long period of three years. During his term he repaired the Southern Highway near Magnesia-on-Maeander and the coast road in the Troad. His administration of the province seems to have been excellent; he was praised at Ephesus for his justice, and his generosity to the cities is shown by the title of Benefactor given to him at Ephesus, Miletus and Tralles, as well as by his assumption of the office of agonothete of the contest of the Commonalty of Asia held at Smyrna. A certain proficiency in oratory also appears in the fact that at Smyrna he was called the foremost of rhetoricians.

It is said that Gordian was greatly beloved not only in Rome but in the provinces as well,[s] and this statement seems to be borne out by the honours paid to him and his wife in the cities of Asia Minor. In Ephesus three statues were erected, describing him not only by the frequently found appellations of Lord of Land and Sea and of the Human Race and a New Sun but also as "an excellent and righteous ruler, who by his own well-ordered ways restored and enhanced the ancient peacefulness of life."[19] There were also statues in his honour in other places in the province of Asia as well as in Lycia-Pamphylia and perhaps Galatia, often with the usual title of Saviour of the World.

The roads in the Asianic provinces, moreover, were not neglected. Repairs were carried out on the road from Pergamum *via* Thyateira to Sardis and on the coast road near Elaea; in Bithynia, on the roads from Prusa to Cius and from Chalcedon to Nicomedeia; in Galatia, near Sebastopolis and between Ancyra and Parnassus; in Pontus, between Comana and Neocaesareia; and (with Maximus and Balbinus) in many places on the great highway through central Cappadocia, carefully maintained also before Gordian's reign by Maximinus and, after his death, by Philip.[20]

The financial position of the imperial government, however, grew steadily worse. The four donations given to the army during Gordian's short reign of six years—the chief means, since the time of Severus, of

[s] *Vit. Gord.* 30, 8.

retaining the soldiers' loyalty—were a great drain on the treasury.[21] This is apparent not only from the reduction in the weight of the gold coins (*aurei*) which were presumably issued for these donations but also from the lack of a definite standard; for, as contrasted with the ratio of 50 *aurei* to a pound of gold which prevailed under Severus Alexander, those of Gordian vary from 64 to 72. An effort was made also to conserve silver. The minting of the Antoninianus, first issued under Caracalla but given up by his successors, was resumed by Maximus and Balbinus and continued in large quantities under Gordian. But, although actually about 10 per cent lighter than its former weight of $1\frac{1}{2}$ denarii, it was now tariffed at 2, and the denarius seems henceforth to have been practically discontinued. The average silver content of these new coins, as in the case of Alexander's denarii, was slightly over 40 per cent.

In Asia Minor, seventeen cities in Lycia issued their own coins for the first and only time under Gordian, a fact which suggests that they had previously depended on the bronze coinage of the Lycian Federation and that this was no longer issued, perhaps on account of the relatively higher value of the metal. On the other hand, this increase in value seems as yet to have had no effect on the number of the Asianic cities which issued their own coins. Whereas under Alexander the available lists contain 155 of these cities, in the decade comprising the reigns of Gordian and Philip they show (exclusive of Lycia) as many as 168 names, an increase which may have resulted from a preference for their own coins over the new, depreciated Antoninianus.

During the reign of Philip various decisions were rendered by the Emperor protecting the rights of the provincials. The privilege of an appeal to the governor was granted in the case of a man appointed guardian of those whose claim to an inheritance he disputed, and against a guardian who, by withholding documents, had failed to support his ward in a lawsuit.[t] A governor was forbidden to free from all liability in the future a guardian who had administered property belonging to his ward, but in order to protect the guardian from injustice, he was permitted to appeal to the procurator in the event that during the performance of his duties his own property had been unjustly declared forfeit to the imperial treasury.[u] A decision of a governor, moreover, if rendered by some underhand means in a place other than that appointed for the hearing and consequently in the

---

[t] *Cod. Iust.* v 62, 16 and 48, 1.   [u] *Cod. Iust.* v 48, 1; ix 49, 5.

absence of one of the parties concerned, was declared invalid, and a mere proclamation on his part was not permitted to have the validity of a legal decision.[v] In order to prevent the avoidance of civic obligations, the principle was reaffirmed that a man, unless domiciled in his mother's native place, must hold office and perform liturgies in the city of his father.[w]

Nevertheless, the calm and peaceful life which the tenants of the imperial estate in Phrygia,[x] in contrast to their own sufferings, attributed to the Empire in general, did not exist under Philip's rule. Apart from the repeated invasions of the tribes beyond the Danube, which compelled the Emperor himself to take the field, his power was disputed in both the North and the East. On the Danube frontier, the soldiers acclaimed Tiberius Claudius Marinus Pacatianus, an officer in one of the legions, as Emperor.[22] In the East, the exactions of Philip's brother, Priscus, who had been given extraordinary powers with the title of *Rector Orientis*, caused such discontent that a certain Iotapianus declared himself Emperor and, claiming descent from Alexander, found a following in Syria and Cappadocia. Pacatianus, to be sure, was soon slain by the soldiers who had acclaimed him, and Iotapianus met a like fate at the hands of the troops in the East.

Another claimant, however, was more successful. Gaius Messius Quintus Decius, who later added Trajanus to his name, vested with a supreme command by Philip and sent, much against his will, to the Danube to punish the supporters of Pacatianus, was in turn proclaimed Emperor by the soldiers. His professed intention of resigning his newly-acquired power was refused credence by Philip, who set out with an army to repel his advance into Italy. In a battle near Verona, probably in September, 249, the Emperor met his death.

In spite of the programme of peace announced on the coins inscribed *Pax*,[y] the reign of Decius, lasting somewhat less than two years, was largely spent in a war against the Gothic tribes, who in the course of the second century had established themselves in southern Russia. After several raids into Roman territory, they had been persuaded to cease their attacks by the promise, under Gordian, of an annual subsidy from Rome.[23] But angered by Philip's failure to make the expected payments, they crossed the Danube, probably late in 249, and invaded the province of Lower Moesia. One detachment even advanced over the great Balkan Range and fell upon Thrace. Decius, having pro-

[v] *Cod. Iust.* VII 43, 5 and 57, 6.   [w] *Cod. Iust.* X 39, 3.
[x] See above p. 699.   [y] Cohen *Descr. hist.*[2] v p. 194f., no. 50f.

ceeded to the front, together with his son, in the summer of 250, with the aid of Gaius Vibius Trebonianus Gallus, the governor of Lower Moesia, won a great victory over the invaders of this province. Those who survived joined their comrades in Thrace, and here their combined forces surprised and defeated the Roman army, which had advanced southward under Decius himself. In a second battle, in the Dobrudja, where the Emperor attempted to intercept the invaders during their homeward march, he suffered another defeat, and both he and his son were killed. Trebonianus Gallus, who, perhaps with treasonable intent, failed to come to Decius's support, was declared Emperor by the remnants of the army. He bought off the Goths by permitting them to keep their booty and prisoners and promising to renew their annual subsidy. Their next attack, as will presently be related, was directed against the coast of Asia Minor.

Meanwhile the Asianic provinces could not fail to be seriously affected by an edict of Decius which resulted in a general persecution of the Christians, for by this time many in these provinces had been converted to the new religion.[24] In an effort to bind the Empire together by exacting an expression of loyalty in entreaties to the gods for his own welfare, the Emperor, late in 249, ordered that all the inhabitants of the Roman world should offer sacrifice to the deities officially recognized by Rome. The act was performed before one or more official commissioners, and those who complied received certificates testifying that they had thus shown their loyalty. Those who refused were punished with imprisonment, exile or fine or even with death. In Asia Minor, it is reported, the commissioners at Smyrna even employed agents to find those suspected of Christianity and force them to appear for the ceremony. Many, including Euctemon, the head of the Christian community in the city, apostatized, but a priest, Pionius, who with some others refused to offer the required sacrifice, was burned alive. In Pontus the Bishop of Neocaesareia, Gregory "the Wonderworker," with some of his flock avoided the ceremony by taking refuge in the mountains, but many who remained behind were put to death. According to the Acts of the Martyrs, trials were held and punishments inflicted in various cities, including Lampsacus, Nicaea, Side and Antioch-near-Pisidia, but as these Acts were compiled at a much later time, little credence can be given to their narratives.

Christian writers, not unnaturally, reviled Decius, calling him a cruel tyrant and even an accursed beast.[z] Less prejudiced authors, on

[z] Cyprian *Epist.* 55, 9: Lactantius *De Mort. Persec.* 4.

the other hand, praised his good qualities and commented on his reign with approval.[a] The provinces presumably benefited from his decisions that a governor should not allow an action to be brought against a man for an amount greater than the sum of his possessions and that a procurator might not try cases in which the status of a citizen was involved.[b] In Asia Minor, an imperial letter, probably to be ascribed to Decius, addressed to the magistrates, Council and People of Aphrodisias in response to an embassy sent to the emperor, promised to preserve the city's "freedom and all other existing rights as obtained from former emperors."[25] The promise seems to indicate, as previously under Alexander, that, however nominal the position of a free city may have been, it still had some semblance of rights. In the Asianic provinces, moreover, the care of the more important routes shown by Decius appears in the inscriptions which record the repair of the road in southwestern Phrygia between Eumeneia and Peltae and of those in Pontus leading from the Halys to Amaseia and from Neapolis to Neocaesareia, as well as the maintenance of the Cappadocian highway and the construction of a bridge in Lesser Armenia, in most of these cases obviously ensuring the main means of communication with the East.

Nevertheless, there were rebellions on the part of pretenders to the imperial power, such as Julius Valens Licinianus in Rome during Decius's absence in Moesia and Lucius Priscus, the governor of Macedonia, who was supported by the Gothic invaders.[26] Both, however, were soon overthrown. In the East, an adventurer named Lucius Julius Aurelius Sulpicius Uranius Antoninus proclaimed himself Emperor at Emesa in Syria. His name and portrait appear on both gold and bronze coins, on the latter of which, issued at Emesa, he is called Augustus. The actual time of his revolt is uncertain, but the bronze coins show that his pretensions were still asserted under Trebonianus Gallus.

The new ruler, Gallus, was accepted by the Senate in Rome as well as in the provinces.[27] His reign, however, like that of his predecessor, lasted not more than two years; for he was overthrown by his successor in the governorship of Lower Moesia, Marcus Aemilius Aemilianus, who had successfully conducted an expedition against the Goths and after this victory was acclaimed as Emperor. Having marched on Italy with his army, he was opposed by the forces of Gallus, but before the issue was settled the Emperor, together with his son, was killed

[a] *Epit. de Caess.* 29, 2: Zosimus I 23, 3 and 25, 2.　　[b] *Cod. Iust.* x 16, 3: III 22, 2.

by his own soldiers in despair of success. The victor ruled for not more than three months, during which, however, he received recognition in a few cities of Asia Minor. His brief reign came to an end after Publius Licinius Valerianus, a highly respected senator in command of troops in the North, probably on the upper Rhine, received orders to hasten to Gallus's aid against Aemilian. Learning, however, that the Emperor was dead, Valerian himself assumed the imperial power and in the early autumn of 253 led an army into Italy. The fate of Gallus befell Aemilian also, for he likewise met his death at the hands of his soldiers. Valerian, now master of the situation, caused the Senate to name his son, Publius Gallienus, as co-ruler.

The reign of Valerian and his son constituted the most calamitous period that the Roman world had known since the civil wars of the first century before Christ. The series of disasters, indeed, began under Gallus, when a great plague once more swept over the Empire, sparing neither Italy nor the provinces.[c] The Goths and their allies, moreover, taking advantage of the strife between the claimants for the imperial power, again began their attacks. These, however, were no longer confined to Europe, for the barbarians proceeded also to make raids on Asia Minor.[28] It was the first time that the country had been invaded by an enemy from outside since the Parthian army had overrun it in 40 B.C. and the first time that it had suffered from northern barbarians since the raids of the Galatians in the third century before Christ.

Unfortunately, both the chronology and the extent of these raids are far from certain. According to one account, they began under Gallus with an invasion by sea, in which the territory of Ephesus was ravaged, and an expedition to Cappadocia, by which perhaps Pontus was meant. Whatever be the truth of this statement, it seems clear that, about the beginning of Valerian's reign, the Borani, allies and neighbours of the Goths from the eastern shore of the Sea of Azov, having forced the city of Chersonesus to furnish the necessary ships, descended on the coast at the eastern end of the Euxine. Here the stronghold of Pityus, at the western end of the Caucasus, was bravely defended by its Roman commandant, Successianus, and the invaders, after suffering great loss, were forced to withdraw. In a second expedition a year or two later, however, they were more successful; for in the meantime Successianus had been made prefect of the Guard and

[c] Eutropius IX 5: Orosius VII 21, 5: Aurelius Victor de Caess. 30: Vit. Gall. 5, 5f.: Zosimus I 26, 2: Zonaras XII 21: Eusebius Hist. Eccl. VII 22.

summoned to Syria by Valerian, and Pityus, no longer skilfully defended, fell into their hands. Sailing southward, the barbarians then attacked the rich city of Trapezus (Trebizond) on the coast of Pontus. The place was well protected by its walls and provided with a garrison, but the raiders, taking advantage of the carelessness of the defenders, were able to scale the fortifications and a general slaughter and rapine ensued. After taking much booty and many captives from the city and the surrounding country, the invaders returned to their home.

The next invasion of the northern barbarians had even more serious consequences. Encouraged, probably, by the successful raid of the Borani, the Goths, perhaps in 256 or 257, with an army, which advanced around the western end of the Black Sea, and a fleet, which sailed directly to the Bosporus, fell upon Bithynia. The garrison stationed at Chalcedon deserted in terror and allowed the city with much booty to be captured. Nicomedeia, also abandoned by its terrorized inhabitants, was seized and burned, and Nicaea, Cius, Apameia Myrleia and Prusa were likewise plundered by the raiders. Cyzicus was saved from attack only by the swollen waters of the Rhyndacus, which the invaders were unable to cross. Satisfied with their plunder, however, they left Asia Minor for a time unmolested.

A few years later, another, more disastrous, invasion took place. After again attacking—and this time demolishing—Chalcedon, the Goths sailed onward through the Hellespont and ravaged the coast of the Aegean, where they plundered the cities of Ionia. At Ephesus, in particular, the damage was very great, for the Temple of Artemis was sacked and burned. At Miletus a wall was hastily built to meet the emergency; the enemy was repulsed under the leadership of Macarius, an Asiarch, and the Temple at Didyma, to which the invaders laid siege, seems to have been successfully defended. Even in the interior, cities feared for their safety. At Stratoniceia the citizens inquired of Zeus of Panamara whether "the sinful barbarians" would attack the city and its territory and were assured by the God that, although they might indeed suffer harm, he would not allow them to be destroyed or enslaved. On their return-voyage the Goths plundered the much-revered city of Ilium, but they appear to have suffered some loss from an attack by Roman troops at Byzantium.

Either at this time or soon afterward another band of Goths, presumably by way of Pontus, seems to have raided Cappadocia and northern Galatia. At Ancyra a patriotic citizen strengthened the walls "against the inroads of the barbarians," but it is related that they succeeded in plundering many cities. They then went on to Bithynia, where they rejoined their ships. A plan to intercept either this or a later band of raiders at Heracleia Pontica was made by Septimius Odenathus, prince of Palmyra and a Roman vassal, but he was murdered before his purpose was accomplished.

The lack of any effective effort on the part of the Roman government to protect Asia Minor from these barbarian invaders may reasonably be attributed to a preoccupation with another war on the Euphrates frontier. The aggressor was once more Shapur the Persian.[29] During the troubled reign of Trebonianus Gallus he had sent an army into Armenia after King Chosroes, a vassal of Rome, had been assassinated, apparently by a Persian agent, and by this advance he had gained possession of the country. Chosroes's young son, Tiridates, was forced to take refuge in Roman territory. Having thus secured himself against any attack from the North, Shapur, probably shortly before Valerian's accession, resumed his invasion of the provinces east of the Euphrates, which Rome was now unable to defend. Nisibis fell into his hands, but Edessa seems to have held out valiantly. His troops then proceeded to cross the river and ravage Syria. Even Antioch was endangered if not actually plundered. This, like the King's subsequent invasions of Syria, seems to have amounted to little more than a raid, from which the Persians returned with prisoners and booty; for Shapur appears to have made no effort to occupy the province permanently. The situation, however, was serious enough to rouse Valerian to action. Soon after the beginning of his reign, the old Emperor, entrusting the European portion of the Empire to Gallienus, set out for the East.

Owing to the inadequacy of the historical sources, the events of the war that followed, as well as the chronology, are highly uncertain. The pretender Uranius Antoninus, who had set himself up as Emperor at Emesa, was somehow eliminated, and Successianus, the courageous defender of Pityus against the Borani, was appointed prefect of the Guard and summoned to Syria. Valerian himself, after arriving at Antioch, is said to have moved northward into Cappadocia, whence he sent a general named Felix to Byzantium. He seems at one time to have established headquarters at Samosata, where he could defend the crossing of the Euphrates and the road which led to Edessa. But in spite of his claims to success on coins inscribed "Restorer of the Orient" and "Parthian Victory," a lack of energy, combined with the weakness of his army resulting from the ravages of the plague, appears to have prevented him from taking vigorous measures against the enemy.

Antioch was in Roman hands in May, 258, but either before this time or in 259, Shapur, under the guidance of a traitor, Mariades, a native of the place, advanced on the city and captured it by a surprise-attack. Antioch was set on fire and many of its inhabitants perished.

In 260 Shapur, who had retired from Antioch with much booty, attempted again to take Edessa. This attack impelled Valerian at last to go to meet the enemy. But by the time the Roman army reached the city, the illness among the troops and his own lack of resolution led the Emperor to propose negotiations. These, however, were unsuccessful, and, whether as a result of a defeat in the field or through treachery during an interview with Shapur—the sources are wholly at variance—Valerian was taken prisoner and carried away to Persia, where he was kept in captivity for the remainder of his life. This great achievement the Persians commemorated by rock-cut reliefs depicting the Emperor kneeling before his captor, but to the Romans it was an unparalleled humiliation. The Christian writers, mindful of Valerian's resumption of the persecution of their coreligionists, represented it as the vengeance of God.[d]

This terrible disaster was fraught with dire consequences to southeastern Asia Minor. Shapur, apparently with little or no resistance from the disheartened and disorganized remnants of the Roman army and perhaps accompanied by Mariades, drove through Syria, where Antioch again fell into his hands, to the Mediterranean.[30] Then turning northward, he invaded Cilicia, capturing Alexandria on the Gulf of Issus, Aegaeae, Nicopolis, Anazarbus and Tarsus, and apparently some of the coast cities of Cilicia Aspera. He then crossed the Taurus and fell upon Cappadocia and the adjacent part of Lycaonia. Mazaca-Caesareia, after a valiant defence led by a certain Demosthenes, was finally betrayed by a captive, who showed the Persians a way into the city. Much booty and many prisoners are said to have been taken.

Gallienus, meanwhile, could do nothing to defend either western Asia Minor against the Goths or the eastern provinces against the Persian invaders, for he was fully occupied in Europe.[31] After some years of warfare against the Germans, who finally penetrated to northern Italy only to be defeated at Milan, he had to cope with a series of pretenders, Ingenuus and Regalianus in Pannonia and later, more formidable than the others, Postumus, who succeeded in setting up what amounted to an independent empire in Gaul and passed on his power to a successor. The East, however, was saved from the Persian

[d] See *e.g.* Lactantius *de Mort. Persec.* 5, 1.

invaders by two of Valerian's officers, Callistus (or Ballista) and Titus
Fulvius Macrianus, who had been stationed at Samosata in charge
of the supplies for the troops. After rallying the demoralized remnants
of Valerian's army, Callistus advanced to the coast of Cilicia. Having
collected some ships, he came to the relief of Pompeiopolis, besieged
by Shapur's forces, and apparently of Sebaste and Corycus as well. He
also inflicted a serious defeat on the Persians who were scattered
through the country, engaged in plundering. Shapur, withdrawing
with what he could save of his booty, retired across the Euphrates at
Samosata into Osroene. By surrendering part of his treasure to the
people of Edessa, he purchased permission to lead his weakened army
past the city and so was able to return through Mesopotamia to Ctesiphon. Any further invasion by him of Roman-held territory was prevented by Odenathus of Palmyra, who once, and perhaps twice, made
a successful campaign against the Persians. This able and vigorous
man had, before Valerian's capture, received the rank of consular, and
he was now appointed to an extraordinary command in the East.[32]
Although he remained a Roman vassal, he nevertheless assumed the
titles Imperator, Corrector of the entire Orient and even, in imitation
of the Persian monarch, King of Kings. On the strength of his victories Gallienus celebrated a triumph and took the surnames Parthicus
Maximus and Persicus Maximus.

Meanwhile Callistus, after his success against the Persians, had joined
forces with Macrian in the autumn of 260 in Syria. Renouncing their
allegiance to Gallienus, the two leaders proclaimed as Augusti Macrian's
two sons, Titus Fulvius Junius Macrianus and Titus Fulvius Junius
Quietus, doubtless intending themselves to be the power behind the
throne. Recognized as Emperors in Syria, where they issued coins at
Antioch, the two young men were accepted also in Egypt.[33] In Asia
Minor, some of the cities during Valerian's reign had honoured him
and Gallienus and the latter's sons. Now, however, the remoteness of
Gallienus, on the one hand, and the predicament in which he was
placed by the various pretenders, and, on the other, the proximity and
prestige of Callistus and Macrian impelled the Asianic provinces to
welcome the new Emperors as Lords of Land and Sea. The Bithynian
cities especially, both Heracleia Pontica and Nicaea, as well as Byzantium issued coins bearing their names and portraits.

The rule of these two claimants, however, was short-lived. In the
spring of 261, Macrian, not content with an eastern empire, crossed
the Bosporus into Europe with an army said to have numbered 30,000,

taking with him the older of the two Emperors. Somewhere in Thrace or Pannonia he met Aureolus, Gallienus's general, who had previously defeated and killed the rebellious Ingenuus and was now sent by the Emperor to repel this invasion. In the battle which followed, Macrian's eastern troops, enveloped by the enemy, surrendered. The two leaders, at their own request, were put to death by some soldiers who had remained loyal.

Quietus, left behind in Syria with Callistus, although at first successful in establishing his power, finally fared no better. On receiving the news of the defeat and death of the two Macrians, the cities became disaffected and refused their support; and in the autumn of 261, Odenathus, advancing against the rebels on orders from Gallienus, defeated them at Emesa in Syria. Callistus, perhaps after attempting treachery, was killed by Odenathus and Quietus was slain by the townsfolk.

These successes won by Gallienus's generals did not, however, bring a respite from war to the sorely harassed Emperor. In the years that followed, there was a long-continued struggle with the ambitious Postumus, who had set himself up as ruler in western Europe with a capital at Treves and a Senate and a mint of his own. On the lower Danube the barbarians north of the river could be held in check only by the expedient of establishing settlements of them on Roman soil. In 268 a new invasion of the Balkan Peninsula by the Goths and their neighbours, the Heruli, forced the Emperor to take the field against them.[34] In the course of the campaign, however, he was called away by the news that his trusted general, Aureolus, had rebelled at Milan and declared himself Emperor. Hastening back to Italy, Gallienus defeated the rebel and shut him up in the city; but during the siege that followed, the Emperor was killed, in the summer of 268, as the result of a plot formed by some of his higher officers. Thereupon, Marcus Aurelius Claudius, said to have been one of the conspirators, was proclaimed as his successor.

The character of Gallienus has been undeservedly blackened by the ancient historical writers, who represented him as effeminate and dissolute. Only in recent years has he been cleared of these charges and shown to have been a vigorous and—except for his misfortunes—a generally competent ruler. The calumnies evidently had their origin in the hatred felt for him in Senatorial circles in return for the blow that he dealt at what remained of the Senate's power and prestige. Wishing, in view of the continual invasions from the outside and the

frequent rebellions within the Empire, to have in his own hands the complete control of all the armed forces, he extended the process of militarization begun by Severus by completing the increase of power acquired by the bureaucracy of the Equestrian Order. Whereas members of this order had previously been appointed regularly as governors of certain provinces, such as Egypt and Mesopotamia, and had even, from the time of Severus onward, been placed temporarily in charge of others,[e] Gallienus took the step of excluding men of Senatorial rank from all military commands and conferring these on *Equites* appointed by himself.[35] The consequent separation between the civil and military powers deprived a governor of the command of any troops stationed in his province. The senatorial provinces, which had no legions, but at most only small companies of soldiers, were but little affected by this measure, but even in them proconsuls were occasionally replaced by Equestrian governors under the subterfuge that these were acting as substitutes. In the case of Asia, a certain Julius Proculus, a procurator, served in 276, "in place of the proconsul." In many of the imperial provinces also the senatorial legate was gradually replaced by one of Equestrian rank, although without recourse to any such subterfuge. Thus in Bithynia-Pontus, which in 269 was governed by an "illustrious consular," ten years later an *Eques* served as imperial legate, and Cilicia under Gallienus was also governed by a member of this order. In Galatia and especially in Cappadocia, where troops were stationed, it may be assumed that the command of these, if not the governorship of the province, was likewise assigned to men of Equestrian rank.

Like many of their predecessors, Valerian and Gallienus rendered decisions of importance to the provincials, such as the reaffirmation of the principle that no new local taxes might be imposed without an imperial endorsement; the order that in a compromised settlement of a debt to a community the governor of the province should not permit the community's interests to suffer through any favouritism shown by its officials to the debtor; and the decision in the case of a citizen who had become a city-councillor at his father's request, that the latter's estate should be held responsible for the expenses entailed by the office.[f] The privileged position of the Senatorial Order in the provinces, moreover, was strengthened by a letter to a resident of Smyrna—probably of Senatorial rank—which, if the fragmentary inscription has been interpreted correctly, contained a ruling exempting

e See note 14.
f *Cod. Iust.* IV 62, 3 (see above p. 675); II 4, 12; X 32, 1.

the property of a member of the Order from the imposition of a fine by a local magistrate.[g]

The provinces in general, however, as has already been noted, suffered greatly from the disasters of this reign, and none more than those of Asia Minor. The raids of the northern barbarians were continued during the great invasion of 268, when one division attacked Cyzicus.[h] Although the city itself was able to resist, its territory doubtless suffered greatly. The depredations of Shapur in Cappadocia and Cilicia caused terrific loss and misery in these provinces. The requisitions of Macrian's large army, moreover, on its way from Syria to the Bosporus, could not fail to be a burden to the region through which it passed, adding to the impoverishment of the country. It is not improbable that the brigandage of the half-wild mountaineers in the Taurus, never really Hellenized or wholly conquered by Rome, against whom it was necessary, a few years later, to conduct a regular war, had already begun. A certain commander of detachments of soldiers—perhaps local militia—who, designated by the proud title of "Ally of the Augusti," was praised at Termessus Minor in Lycia under Valerian for "having provided for peace on sea and land," may have been engaged in repelling the raids of these brigands as well as in suppressing piracy.[36] A milestone erected under Valerian and Gallienus, moreover, on the route leading from Iconium to Isauria suggests that the road may have been repaired for the purpose of bringing troops into this region. In addition to all these evils, the ravages of the plague continued,[i] and, in 262, one of the earthquakes frequent in Asia Minor greatly damaged some of the cities.[j]

Nevertheless, there are indications that the cities still enjoyed some degree of prosperity. At Pergamum an agonothete was able to celebrate the festival of Asclepius at his own expense.[37] At Nicaea it was possible, about the time of Macrian's campaign, to begin the repair of the walls, damaged by the Gothic invasion, and in 269 the work seems to have been completed. The importance and with it, presumably, the economic prosperity of Cyzicus was increased, perhaps under Gallienus but certainly under his successor, Claudius, by the establishment of an imperial mint in the city. Ephesus, on the other hand, never fully recovered from the barbarians' attack, for the Temple of Artemis seems never to have been completely restored.

The evidence afforded by the coinage, however, shows that during

[g] *C.I.L.* III 412 = *I.G.R.* IV 1404 (see *R.E.* x 166).
[h] See note 34.   [i] Zosimus I 37, 3.   [j] *Vit. Gall.* 5, 2f.

this disastrous period the economy of the cities was seriously affected. Whereas, in the decade of Gordian and Philip, 168 cities (exclusive of Lycia) are known to have issued their own bronze coins, under Gallienus the number decreased to 122,[k] and with his reign local currency came almost entirely to an abrupt end. Under his successors coins were issued only in Cyzicus, in the colonies of Antioch and Cremna and in some half-dozen other places in Pisidia and Pamphylia, all of which for some reason were able to maintain their local mints.[38]

During the reign of Gallienus also, especially after the capture of Valerian, a marked depreciation took place in the imperial currency. This was the inevitable result partly of a decline in the supply of precious metals but largely of a generally reckless financial policy and the continuous warfare, necessitating the expenditure of vast amounts of money for donations to the soldiers in order to retain their support. Not only did the weight of the *aureus* fluctuate greatly, sometimes decreasing to the point of 80 or even 90 to the pound, but the silver content of the Antoninianus sank to a new low, in some cases only 5 per cent, and appearances were preserved by merely giving a light wash of silver to the base metal. It is difficult to regard this depreciation and the almost complete cessation of local coinage in Asia Minor as a pure coincidence; but it must remain a question whether this cessation was due to the decreased purchasing power of the imperial coins to a point where there was no longer any need for the fractional local currency or whether the bullion value of the metal in these coins had become so much higher than their nominal value that the cities could issue them only at a loss.

Although large transactions involving the use of gold were not necessarily affected by this debasing of the silver coins, since payments appear to have been made by weight rather than by tale, the depreciation of this currency could hardly fail to have an effect on ordinary fortunes and the purchasing power of incomes. In the larger cities, those who lived on the proceeds of industry and trade were presumably able to demand higher prices for their wares, as did the bread-makers of Ephesus, where the price of a loaf doubled during the second century. The commercial class, therefore, probably suffered less than those whose livelihood depended on salaries and fees: the physicians, the architects, the rhetoricians and other teachers.[1] The class most affected was that which lived on the income from investments, especially if

[k] See Chap. XXVIII note 38.
[1] See Broughton in *Econ. Surv.* IV p. 849f. and A. H. M. Jones *Greek City*, p. 264f.

during the third century, as has been supposed, the rate of interest fell far below the earlier legal maximum of 12 per cent.[39] Endowments, in particular, must have suffered. Even in the time of Maximinus, in a bequest establishing a foundation at Orcistus in Phrygia the testator specified that the fund should consist of Attic drachmae of "silver of account," presumably meaning the value in undepreciated currency, and other instances in this century ordering payment to be made in Attic drachmae seem also to have ensured against depreciation.

On the other hand, when private fortunes and endowments were invested in land, the loss of income was less great, for the produce could be sold at current prices. Since many of the wealthier urban dwellers owned estates in their city's rural territory, it may be supposed that the monetary yield from these, whether derived directly from the sale of the produce or from the rentals paid by tenants to the absentee landlords, was less impaired. Nevertheless, these payments drained the wealth of the rural districts; and if the wide-spread abandonment of land, which caused the imperial government to take preventive measures, occurred in Asia Minor also, it may be assumed that during the third century there was in these provinces a general decrease in productivity and, consequently, in value. Even early in this century the principle was laid down that a provincial governor must compel those members of city-councils who had left their native cities, apparently in order to avoid civic burdens, and moved to other places to return to their homes and fulfil their obligations.[m] Soon after Gallienus's death the amount of land thus abandoned was so great that the Emperor Aurelian gave orders that the councils should be held responsible for the payment of taxes levied on deserted properties,[n] a source of income which the imperial government was, naturally, unwilling to forego. This measure was presumably intended to ensure the improvement of exhausted land, since, if taxed, this would not be permitted to remain untilled and so would help to produce the supply of food-stuffs of which the Empire was always in need and never more so than in this period of turmoil.[o] The abandonment of land, however, continued, and a half-century after Aurelian's order it had become necessary for the Emperor Constantine to relieve the councils of part of the burden by transferring the payments of the tax to the landholders as a body.[p]

Nevertheless, there is no reason to suppose that the peasants ceased

[m] Ulpian in *Digesta* L 2, 1. [n] *Cod. Iust.* XI 59, 1.
[o] For waste land in Egypt see Rostovtzeff *S.E.H.R.E.* p. 428f.
[p] *Cod. Iust. ibid.*

to cultivate the property of land-owners. A large estate in the basin of the upper Lysis in northwestern Pisidia, which in the early third century belonged to a noble Roman family and was tilled by the people of the villages forming the *demos* of the Ormeleis, was evidently still cultivated in the latter part of this century.[40] A list, which may be dated in this period, contains the names of many who seem to have been tenants, and dates corresponding to A.D. 261 and 262 appear on a marble chair, presumably the official throne of the priests of a local cult. In the hill-country of northeastern Pisidia, moreover, lists of contributions, which, as late as the time of Gallienus, were made by the members of a society composed partly of city-folk but mostly of villagers, contain amounts large enough, even with allowance for the depreciation of the coinage, to suggest a very considerable degree of prosperity. However much many of the cities may have declined economically,[41] the villages, composed of peasants' houses with a local sanctuary, which, usually independent of the cities, were scattered through the rural districts, continued to prosper. As a result, the Asianic provinces do not seem to have fallen into the state of economic decay which befell other portions of the Empire; and the author of a "Description of the Entire World," writing about the middle of the fourth century, could praise the wines of Cilicia, the hides of Cappadocia, the clothing of Galatia, the oil of Pamphylia, and the crops, the wine and the oil, as well as the textiles, of the province of Asia.[q]

The general chaos did not, indeed, end with the death of Gallienus, for the brief reign of his successor, Claudius, was almost entirely spent in fighting.[42] He succeeded, to be sure, in overthrowing the claimant Aureolus and defeating the German invaders of northern Italy in a great battle near Lake Garda. He also completed the success of Gallienus against the Goths by driving the invading forces out of the Balkan Peninsula—his most famous achievement, which won him his usual surname, Gothicus. Nevertheless, he was unable to make any serious move against the successor of Postumus in Gaul or prevent a piratical expedition of the northern barbarians from attacking the Aegean islands and the southern coast of Asia Minor, where they plundered Pamphylia and besieged Side, only to be repulsed by a valiant defence on the part of the townsfolk. Any further attempt to restore order, moreover, was cut short by his death, early in 270, apparently as the result of the plague. His brother, Quintillus, who was

q *Expositio totius Mundi* 39f. (Riese *Geogr. Lat. Min.* p. 115f.)

appointed by the Senate to succeed him, was soon superseded by the choice of the army, Lucius Domitius Aurelianus. Like Claudius, he had been a general of Gallienus and was said to have been implicated in the conspiracy which brought about the latter's death. He was a military leader of great skill and a man of outstanding strength and courage—the qualities needed to cope with the increasing disintegration of the Empire.

In the East, a new power had arisen which seriously threatened the supremacy of Rome not only in Syria and Egypt but in the Asiatic provinces as well. Zenobia, widow of Odenathus, the prince of Palmyra who had received from Gallienus an extraordinary command in the East with the title of King of Kings,[r] was no longer content to remain a mere vassal of Rome but aspired to become the independent ruler of a kingdom of which Palmyra was to be the capital. On the basis, perhaps, of her husband's title, she called herself Queen and conferred the kingship on her young son, Vaballathus Athenodorus, whom she associated with herself in the rule.[48] To further her ambitious plans, she built up a great army, composed not only of Palmyrenes—especially archers and heavy cavalry—but also of troops from across the Euphrates. Against a force of this size the Roman garrisons in the East, depleted by the revolt of Macrian and his sons and perhaps by the transfer of soldiers to Europe, could offer but little opposition. Accordingly, the able and ambitious Queen, with the aid of her general, Zabdas, succeeded in making herself mistress of the provinces of Syria and Arabia as well as of a large part of Egypt. Not satisfied with these conquests, she seems to have planned to bring Asia Minor also under her rule, for it is recorded that she sent troops to invade Cappadocia and Galatia as far as Ancyra and even to have threatened Bithynia. While this reported invasion may have been little more than a raid, there seemed to be reason to fear that unless her ambitious designs were checked she might include the Asiatic provinces also in her empire.

Although an army which Gallienus, after the death of Odenathus, seems to have sent to the East, professedly against the Persians but perhaps actually to combat the increasing power of Zenobia, was badly defeated by a Palmyrene force, there had been no further hostilities between Rome and her vassal either during the remainder of Gallienus's reign or under Claudius.[44] The latter, indeed, fully occupied with the wars against the Germans and the Goths, was unable to

[r] See above p. 709.

restore Rome's power east of the Aegean. Some sort of *modus vivendi*, in fact, seems to have been established, for the imperial mint at Antioch continued to issue coins bearing Claudius's name, and even during the first year of Aurelian gold *aurei* were struck showing the Emperor's portrait. A certain pretension to equality, however, appears in coins minted in both Antioch and Alexandria, which bore on one side the portrait and titles of Aurelian and on the other those of Vaballathus as King and Imperator; and soon all pretence of vassalage was thrown off when Zenobia assumed the name of Augusta and her son that of Augustus as well as other imperial titles. By this action they declared themselves the equals of Rome.

It was necessary, therefore, for Aurelian to take active measures to check the growing power of this rival and to prevent the severance of the eastern provinces from the Empire.[45] After driving back the tribes from across the lower Danube, who had invaded Roman territory, and defeating a large army of Germans which had even invaded northern Italy, the Emperor, in the summer or autumn of 271, crossed the Bosporus to restore Rome's supremacy in the East. Once more Asia Minor was traversed by a Roman army. Whatever Palmyrene troops had occupied Galatia had evidently been withdrawn, for there seems to have been no opposition until Aurelian, on his way to the Taurus, reached Cappadocia. Here, at Tyana, there was some resistance, but after a brief siege a native betrayed the city to the Roman army. Wisely refraining from inflicting any punishment, the Emperor gave orders that the place should be spared.

After two great battles in Syria in the summer of 272, in both of which the Romans were victorious, Zenobia, with Zabdas and the remnants of her army, retired to Palmyra, prepared to withstand a siege. But when supplies grew low, the Queen, hoping to obtain assistance from the Persians, made her way with an escort out of the city. On reaching the Euphrates, however, she was captured by a body of Roman cavalry sent in pursuit and was at once taken to Aurelian. Thereupon Palmyra surrendered. It also was spared but became once more a subject of Rome. To ensure—or so it was hoped—the submission of the East, an officer named Marcellinus was made prefect of Mesopotamia with a general supervision over the Orient.

Palmyra, nevertheless, was destined to receive punishment. An anti-Roman faction, under the leadership of a citizen named Apsaeus, gained the upper hand and, after massacring the Roman garrison, chose as ruler a certain Antiochus, perhaps a relative of Zenobia. It was necessary, therefore, for Aurelian, who learned of the revolt after crossing the Bosporus on his return-journey, to reverse his march and hasten once more to Syria to repress the rebellion. This time, no mercy was shown. Palmyra, probably early in 273, was given over to the Roman soldiers to plunder. Its treasures were seized, its walls demolished, and the proud and wealthy city was reduced to an ordinary provincial town.

It now remained for Aurelian to complete the unification of the Empire by putting an end to the power of the separatist rulers of Gaul. This was soon accomplished by a battle fought near Châlons, in the course of which Tetricus, a former Roman senator who had followed Victorinus, the successor of Postumus, surrendered and his troops ceased all further resistance. The victories of Aurelian were then celebrated by a splendid triumphal procession, held early in 274, in which both Zenobia and Tetricus marched as captives. In commemoration of his successes, the Emperor issued coins with the legends Restorer of the Orient and Restorer of the World as well as others declaring his victories both in the East and in the West.

Now at the height of his prestige, Aurelian made plans for another war against the Persians.[46] Whether the purpose of this campaign was to protect or regain Rome's possessions in Mesopotamia or whether it was due merely to the lure of eastern conquest cannot be determined. In any case, the time was favourable; for Shapur was dead and the son who had succeeded him in 272 had lived little more than a year, leaving his throne to his brother. Taking advantage of the change of ruler, Aurelian set out, in the summer of 275, on his way to the East. He was destined, however, not to accomplish his purpose. While marching through Thrace, he was assassinated by a group of officers who had been falsely told by his confidential secretary that he had sentenced them to execution. For once, the troops had no candidate for the imperial power. The choice of an emperor, therefore, was left to the Senators, who, after an interval lasting perhaps several weeks, finally persuaded Marcus Claudius Tacitus, a member of their body now in his seventy-fifth year, to accept the dangerous office.

Meanwhile, the deterioration of the imperial currency, already noticed in connexion with Gallienus's reign, had gone from bad to worse. The increasing poverty of the government, due, on the one hand, to the expense of unceasing warfare and, on the other, to the loss of the revenues from the Gallic provinces under the rule of Postumus and his successors as well as from the East during Zenobia's conquests, had brought the coinage to its lowest ebb. In addition, early in Aurelian's reign, it was discovered that the mint-workers in Rome were stealing the metal intended for the coins, and so numerous were the offenders and their sympathizers that an attempt to check their dishonesty led to disorders amounting almost to a civil war, in which many persons lost their lives.[47] As the result of these various causes, in Aurelian's early years not only were gold *aurei* issued, in some cases, on the low scale of 70 to the pound, but the silver-washed Antoniniani, of especially poor workmanship, had an average silver content of but little over 3 per cent, so that the coins were in themselves almost worthless.

To meet these wretched financial conditions some kind of reform was urgently needed if bankruptcy was not to ensue, and this Aurelian attempted. While his reform was in no way drastic, it may have helped to improve the credit of the government in the provinces as well as in Italy. The workmanship of the coins was in general greatly improved and the weight of the *aurei* slightly increased. To replace the discredited Antoninianus, the usual medium of exchange in ordinary transactions, a new coin was issued, still showing the emperor's head with a radiate crown but a little heavier and with an increase of about ½ of 1 per cent in its silver content. In an attempt to stabilize the value of this coin, many pieces bore a legend recording a ratio of 20 to 1, indicating, presumably, that it was worth 20 of some smaller unit, but what this unit was has, unfortunately, not been definitely determined. In addition, the subsidiary currency was increased by the issue of some bronze coins—omitted under Aurelian's immediate predecessors. These, however, were no longer inscribed, as had previously been the custom, with the letters indicating that they were issued by virtue of a senatorial decree.

The impoverishment of the central government as well as of the cities during this period appears also in the neglect of the roads in the Asianic provinces. Under Valerian and Gallienus improvements seem to have been made only on the Southern Highway and the route to Isauria already mentioned, and during the twenty-five years that followed the Emperor's capture little was done to keep the roads in repair.[48] Single milestones erected by Aurelian or dedicated to him show that some effort was made to maintain the routes from Phrygia to Ancyra and from Ancyra southward to Parnassus—the road to the Cilician Gates usually followed by armies on their way to the East —and under Aurelian, as well as under Tacitus and the latter's successor, Probus, some attention was given to roads in Lydia, in particular to those which led from Smyrna to Sardis and from the valley of the Caïcus to Thyateira and Sardis, maintained in part by the city of Thyateira. Both Probus and his successor, Carus, rebuilt the roads around Sinope, and under one or the other—it is uncertain which—the city of Hieropolis erected a milestone on the route leading through southwestern Phrygia. But except for a single milestone erected under Probus, there is no indication of any repair of the important highway from the Halys through Pontus to Armenia, and there is no record whatever during this entire period of any rebuilding of the great roads leading through the Cilician Gates and through Cappadocia to the Euphrates.

In Asia Minor, Tacitus's brief reign was marked by a new invasion by the barbarian Heruli.[49] Setting out, presumably in ships, from their home on the Sea of Azov, they fell upon Pontus by way of Colchis and seem to have ravaged all eastern Asia Minor as far as Cilicia. Despite his advanced age, Tacitus bravely took the field against them. He appears to have won enough success to assume the surname of Gothicus Maximus and to issue coins bearing the legend "Gothic Victory." But while at Tyana in the course of his campaign against the invaders, he met his death, either through illness or at the hands of some soldiers. His half-brother, Florianus, who claimed the imperial power and found general recognition in the West, carried on the war against the Heruli with success. He was opposed, however, by the able general, Marcus Aurelius Probus, the choice of the soldiers in Syria and Egypt. Forced by Probus's advance to return to Cilicia, he met his opponent near Tarsus, where he was defeated and placed under guard and presently slain by his own soldiers, apparently at Probus's instigation.

The first task of Probus was to complete the expulsion of the barbarian invaders of Asia Minor. This seems to have been accomplished, if the Emperor's coin commemorating a "Gothic Victory" and his assumption of the surname of Gothicus Maximus may be connected with this undertaking.[50] Another task also awaited him in Asia Minor, namely, the subjection of the "Isaurian" tribesmen of the Taurus. These turbulent mountaineers, never wholly brought under Roman rule, had for some years past plundered the lowland country. It is reported, although in a source of no great trustworthiness, that Claudius planned to solve the problem of preventing their depredations by moving them out of their mountain-fastnesses into Cilicia and bestowing their region on those who were friendly. This plan, however, was never carried out, and so bold had these brigands become that one of their chieftains, it is said, even raided Lycia and Pamphylia. It was necessary, therefore, to take vigorous measures to protect these provinces from the marauders. Accordingly, after repelling the Germans who had invaded Gaul and those who had crossed the Danube into Thrace, Probus set out for the East, in 279 or 280, to wage a regular war against them. One of their leaders, unable to contend with a Roman army, seized the stronghold of Cremna, from which, in order to save his store of provisions, he drove out the townsfolk. During the siege that followed, however, he was slain by one of his own men, whom, in his cruelty, he had wounded, and the rest of the band surrendered. This seems to have been followed by a general surrender of the mountain-strongholds, and the Emperor, on the principle that it was easier to keep out brigands than to drive them out, settled groups of veterans in these inaccessible places, giving them the land as their own property on the condition that their sons, on arriving at the age of manhood, should enter the Roman army.

So far, Aurelian's plan for an aggressive war against the Persians had never been carried out, and Probus, occupied with the war on the northern frontier as well as by the necessity of contending with a series of pretenders, was willing enough, for the time, to remain at peace with them. It is reported that he received the envoys sent by King Vahram II, the grandson of Shapur who had succeeded his father in 276, at the same time refusing haughtily to accept the gifts they had brought.[s] In 282, however, after a triumph held during the preceding year to celebrate his successes,[51] the Emperor made preparations for the war which, he expected, would add to his fame. Meanwhile, his troops were ordered to clear some lands belonging to his native city, Sirmium in Pannonia. This order was deeply resented, and when the soldiers heard that their comrades whom Probus had sent against Marcus Aurelius Carus, declared Emperor by the army in Rhaetia, had deserted to the claimant, they mutinied in a body and murdered their emperor.

Nevertheless, the plan for an expedition against the Persians was resumed by Carus. After driving back the tribes from across the Danube who had again invaded Roman territory, he left his elder son, Carinus, to govern the western part of the Empire and hastened to the East, accompanied by his second son, Numerian. While no details are given

---

[s] *Vit. Probi* 17, 4f. (where the King is incorrectly called Narseus).

in the very inadequate sources for the history of this campaign, it is recorded that the enemy, evidently much weaker than in the time of Shapur, was soon driven out of Mesopotamia.[52] Not content with this success, the Emperor advanced to Babylonia, where he captured Ctesiphon and the neighbouring Coche. Vahram, faced by a rebellion of his brother, the governor of a part of Persia, was eager to make peace, even to the point of surrendering Mesopotamia to the Romans. In celebration of his victory Carus took the surname Persicus Maximus, and on coins issued after his death he appears also, evidently to commemorate his capture of the old Parthian capital, as Parthicus. From this expedition, however, the Emperor never returned; after a reign lasting, at the most, a little more than a year, he met his death on the bank of the Tigris, by a stroke of lightning, according to the official version, but perhaps by the hand of Aper, the prefect of the Guard, who in the course of the army's return-march through Asia Minor caused Numerian to be killed.

During his short reign Carus rendered several decisions of importance to the provincials.[53] The administration of justice was furthered by rulings which declared invalid the imposition by a governor of any fine greater than the lawful amount; which forbad a referee named by a governor to procrastinate in his hearing of a suit submitted for his verdict; which declared that an opinion expressed privately by a governor should not be regarded as a decision prejudicial to the outcome of the case; and which ordered a governor to relieve any man of the duty of supplying animals and labour for the imperial post if imposed by the *curator* of a community in which he was not regularly domiciled. Measures were taken also to prevent the evasion of civic duties by the decision that neither old age nor the number of a man's children should serve as a ground for exemption from those duties attached to the holding of property, and that even an imperial procurator should be liable for those which were consistent with his official rank.

After Carus's death, his son, Carinus, ruled as sole emperor for a little more than a year and a half. Represented generally as cruel and dissolute, he incurred the hatred of his soldiers and was assassinated by them early in 285 during a campaign in Moesia against the candidate for the imperial power acclaimed by Carus's army, Gaius Aurelius Valerius Diocletianus, an Illyrian of humble birth who had risen from the ranks to become commander of the imperial body-guard. He was destined to bring order out of the prevailing chaos and to found a new Roman Empire on the ruins of the old principate.

The power of the army to make and in turn murder emperors, the disintegration of the Empire due to the rebellion of these many claimants, the inroads of the northern barbarians, the high cost of continuous warfare accompanied by the loss of revenue from lost provinces and the consequent depreciation of the currency with a ruinous effect on the economic life of the provinces, the heavy hand of an ever-increasing centralized bureaucracy oppressing the rural districts and crushing out what remained of the Augustan conception of the Empire as a commonwealth of self-governing cities—all these factors contributed to the decay, during the third century, of the power of Rome and to the resultant chaos.

With this dark picture this narrative comes to an end. The advent to power of Diocletian and his associate, Maximian, with the substitution of a complete absolutism for the little that was left of the Augustan principate and with the introduction of a state-controlled economy; the division—permanent except for short intervals—of the Empire into eastern and western portions; the new organization of the provinces, divided by Diocletian into small units; the subsequent establishment by Constantine of the capital at Byzantium, whereby Rome, once the ruler, was reduced to a mere provincial city; and the Emperor's substitution of Christianity for the worship of the ancient deities—all marked the beginning of a new era, the period of transition to Mediaevalism in the West, and in the East to the Byzantine Empire, which, with increasing feebleness and gradually relaxing hold, continued the rule of Rome over the provinces of Asia Minor.

AN INDEX FOR BOTH VOLUMES
APPEARS AT THE END OF VOL. II